LAW AND THE HUMANITIES

Law and the Humanities: An Introduction brings together a distinguished group of scholars from law schools and from an array of the disciplines in the humanities. Contributors come from the United States and abroad in recognition of the global reach of this field. This book is, at one and the same time, a stock-taking of different national traditions and of the various modes and subjects of law and humanities scholarship. It is also an effort to chart future directions for the field. By reviewing and analyzing existing scholarship and providing thematic content and distinctive arguments, it offers to its readers both a resource and a provocation. Thus, *Law and the Humanities* marks the maturation of this "law and" enterprise and will spur its further development.

Austin Sarat is the William Nelson Cromwell Professor of Jurisprudence and Political Science at Amherst College. He is author or editor of more than seventy books, including *Mercy on Trial: What It Means to Stop an Execution; When the State Kills: Capital Punishment and the American Condition; The Cultural Lives of Cause Lawyers* (with Stuart Scheingold); and *The Blackwell Companion to Law and Society*, among many others. Sarat is editor of the journal *Law, Culture and the Humanities* and of *Studies in Law, Politics, and Society*. In 1997, Sarat received the Harry Kalven Award given by the Law & Society Association for distinguished research on law and society. In 2004, he received the Reginald Heber Smith Award, given biennially to honor the best scholarship on the subject of equal access to justice. It was given in recognition of his work on cause lawyering and the three books he had produced on the subject. In 2006, the Association for the Study of Law, Culture and the Humanities awarded him the James Boyd White Prize for distinguished scholarly achievement in recognition of his "innovative and outstanding" work in the humanistic study of law. In 2009, he received the Stan Wheeler Award from the Law & Society Association for distinguished teaching and mentoring.

Matthew Anderson is Associate Professor and Chair of the Department of English and Language Studies at the University of New England. His teaching and scholarship combine an interest in law and in literature, particularly the ways in which issues of trauma and justice are registered in legal and literary texts. In 2005, he edited a special issue of *Studies in Law, Politics, and Society*, "Towards a Critique of Guilt: Perspectives from Law and the Humanities." In 2009, he and Cathrine O. Frank received a grant from the National Endowment for the Humanities (USA) to direct a summer institute for college and university faculty on "The Rule of Law," with an emphasis on the place of legal studies in the liberal arts.

Cathrine O. Frank is an Assistant Professor in the Department of English and Language Studies at the University of New England. Frank teaches and publishes in the areas of Victorian studies and law and literature. She has written on testamentary law and the realist novel as legal and literary modes of creating individual and cultural identity in such journals as *Law and Literature, College Literature,* and *English Literature in Transition.* Her book *Law, Literature, and the Transmission of Culture in England,* 1827-1025 is forthcoming in 2010.

Law and the Humanities

AN INTRODUCTION

Edited by

Austin Sarat
Amherst College

Matthew Anderson
University of New England

Cathrine O. Frank
University of New England

CAMBRIDGE
UNIVERSITY PRESS

32 Avenue of the Americas, New York NY 10013-2473, USA

Cambridge University Press is part of the University of Cambridge.

It furthers the University's mission by disseminating knowledge in the pursuit of education, learning and research at the highest international levels of excellence.

www.cambridge.org
Information on this title: www.cambridge.org/9780521899055

© Austin Sarat, Matthew Anderson, and Cathrine O. Frank 2010

This publication is in copyright. Subject to statutory exception and to the provisions of relevant collective licensing agreements, no reproduction of any part may take place without the written permission of Cambridge University Press.

First published 2010
First paperback edition 2014

A catalogue record for this publication is available from the British Library

Library of Congress Cataloguing in Publication data

Law and the humanities : an introduction / edited by Austin Sarat, Matthew Anderson, Cathrine O. Frank.
   p.   cm.
Includes bibliographical references and index.
ISBN 978-0-521-89905-5 (hardback)
1. Law and the humanities.   I. Sarat, Austin.   II. Anderson, Matthew,
III. Frank, Cathrine O.
K487.H86L39   2009
344´.097 – dc22   2009019749

ISBN 978-0-521-89905-5 Hardback
ISBN 978-1-107-41536-2 Paperback

Cambridge University Press has no responsibility for the persistence or accuracy of URLs for external or third-party internet websites referred to in this publication, and does not guarantee that any content on such websites is, or will remain, accurate or appropriate.

To my son Ben with the hope that he will grow up in a more humane world. – AS

Contents

Contributors		*page* ix
Acknowledgments		xi
Introduction: On the Origins and Prospects of the Humanistic Study of Law		1
Austin Sarat, Matthew Anderson, and Cathrine O. Frank		
I	**PERSPECTIVES ON THE HISTORY AND SIGNIFICANCE OF SCHOLARSHIP IN LAW AND THE HUMANITIES: THREE VIEWS**	**47**
1	A Humanities of Resistance: Fragments for a Legal History of Humanity	49
	Costas Douzinas	
2	Three Tales of Two Texts: An Introduction to Law and the Humanities	73
	Kathryn Abrams	
3	Law, Culture, and Humility	98
	Steven L. Winter	
II	**IDEAS OF JUSTICE**	**123**
4	Biblical Justice: The Passion of the God of Justice	125
	Chaya Halberstam	
5	Ideas of Justice: Natural and Human	141
	Catherine Kellogg	
6	Ideas of Justice: Positive	161
	Matthew Noah Smith	

vii

viii Contents

7	Postmodern Justice *Peter Goodrich*	188
III	**IMAGINING THE LAW**	211
8	Imagining the Law: The Novel *Susan Sage Heinzelman*	213
9	Imagining Law as Film (Representation without Reference?) *Richard K. Sherwin*	241
10	Law and Television: Screen Phenomena and Captive Audiences *Susanna Lee*	269
11	Imagining the Law: Art *Christine Haight Farley*	292
IV	**LINGUISTIC, LITERARY, AND CULTURAL PROCESSES IN LAW**	313
12	Language *Penelope Pether*	315
13	Interpretation *Francis J. Mootz III*	339
14	Narrative and Rhetoric *Ravit Reichman*	377
15	Justice as Translation *Harriet Murav*	398
16	The Constitution of History and Memory *Ariela Gross*	416
V	**INSTITUTIONAL PROCESSES**	453
17	Trials *Lindsay Farmer*	455
18	Testimony, Witnessing *Jan-Melissa Schramm*	478
19	Judgment in Law and the Humanities *Desmond Manderson*	496
20	Punishment *Karl Shoemaker*	517
	Index	531

Contributors

Kathryn Abrams is Herma Hill Kay Distinguished Professor of Law, University of California, Berkeley

Matthew Anderson is Associate Professor of English, University of New England

Costas Douzinas is Professor of Law and Director of the Institute for the Humanities, Birkbeck College

Christine Haight Farley is Professor of Law, Washington College of Law, American University

Lindsay Farmer is Professor of Law, University of Glasgow

Cathrine O. Frank is Assistant Professor of English, University of New England

Peter Goodrich is Professor of Law and Director, Law and Humanities, Cardozo Law School

Ariela Gross is John B. and Alice R. Sharp Professor of Law and History, School of Law, University of Southern California

Chaya Halberstam is Assistant Professor, Department of Religious Studies, Indiana University

Susan Sage Heinzelman is Associate Professor, Department of English, University of Texas

Catherine Kellogg is Associate Professor, Department of Political Science, University of Alberta

Susanna Lee is Associate Professor, Department of French, Georgetown University

Desmond Manderson is Canada Research Chair in Law and Discourse, McGill University

Francis J. Mootz III is William S. Boyd Professor of Law, School of Law, University of Nevada, Las Vegas

Harriet Murav is Professor of Slavic Languages and Literatures, University of Illinois

Penelope Pether is Professor of Law, Villanova University School of Law

Ravit Reichman is Associate Professor of English, Brown University

Austin Sarat is William Nelson Cromwell Professor of Jurisprudence & Political Science, Amherst College

Jan-Melissa Schramm is a Fellow at Trinity Hill and Newton Trust Lecturer in English, University of Cambridge.

Richard K. Sherwin is Professor of Law and Director, Visual Persuasion Project, New York Law School

Karl Shoemaker is Associate Professor, Department of History and Law School, University of Wisconsin

Matthew Noah Smith is Assistant Professor, Department of Philosophy, Yale University

Steven L. Winter is Walter S. Gibbs Professor of Constitutional Law, Wayne State University School of Law

Acknowledgments

We are grateful for the enthusiastic response and commitment of our distinguished contributors.

We are grateful for the skilled research assistance of Tovah Ackerman and Luke O'Brien.

Together we have enjoyed a very fruitful collaboration as we have looked for ways of advancing a field of inquiry to which we are very committed.

Introduction

On the Origins and Prospects of the Humanistic Study of Law

Austin Sarat, Matthew Anderson, and Cathrine O. Frank

> [It is] a fact too often forgotten – that law touches at some point every conceivable human interest, and that its study is, perhaps above all others, precisely the one which leads straight to the humanities.
>
> – Ernest W. Huffcutt "The Literature of Law" (1892)

At the start of the twenty-first century, interdisciplinary is the watchword in legal education and legal scholarship. In law schools and within the liberal arts, practitioners of various "law and" movements find themselves much in demand. Law and economics, law and social science, law and history, empirical legal studies: These labels are by now quite familiar. One of the most recent of these "law ands" is the burgeoning field of Law and the Humanities.

Today, scholars in that field are supported by a well-developed infrastructure of professional associations and scholarly journals,[1] but the precise contours of this field are anything but clear. What is its relationship to law and literature? What, if any, relationship does it have to the qualitative social sciences, for example, anthropology? In addition, there are open questions about the significance of Law and Humanities work. What payoff does work in the humanities promise for legal scholarship and legal understanding? How does the examination of law enrich the humanities?

Law and the Humanities: An Introduction brings together a distinguished group of scholars from law schools and an array of the disciplines in the humanities to address those questions. Our contributors come from the United States and abroad in recognition of the global reach of this field. This book is, at one and the same time,

---

[1] Professional associations include: the Association for the Study of Law, Culture, and the Humanities; the Law and Society Association; the American Society for Legal History; the Society for the Study of Political and Legal Philosophy; and, since 2003, the Consortium of Undergraduate Law and Justice Programs, whose stated purpose is "to support and promote programs in law and justice broadly conceived." There are now three academic journals devoted solely to the study of law and the humanities: the *Yale Journal of Law and the Humanities*; *Law, Culture, and the Humanities*; and *Law and Humanities*.

a stock taking of different national traditions and of the various modes and subjects of Law and Humanities scholarship. It is also an effort to chart future directions for the field. By reviewing and analyzing existing scholarship and providing thematic content and distinctive arguments, it offers to its readers both a resource and a provocation. Thus, *Law and the Humanities: An Introduction* marks the maturation of this "law and" enterprise and will, we hope, spur its further development.

The Genesis of the Field-I: From Law and Literature to Law and the Humanities

Efforts to bring humanistic perspectives to bear on legal questions are by no means new.[2] As the statement by E. W. Huffcutt in the epigraph attests, a sense of the interrelatedness of law and the humanities was self-consciously articulated in the Anglo-American tradition during the Victorian era, alongside a pronounced interest – notably among lawyers – in the interrelations between law and literature. (Huffcutt defined the humanities as literature, and literature as poetry and fiction.) Reaching back to the classical period, one hears distinct echoes of this idea in Cicero's admonition that rhetoric without poetics is a dead letter.[3]

The first blush of the humanistic study of law in the modern era occurred with the exploration of the conjunction of law and literature, an exploration sparked in turn by the publication of James Boyd White's seminal textbook, *The Legal Imagination* (1973).[4] As is now well known, since that book's publication scholars have devoted themselves to the examination of law in literature, ferreting out legal themes and images from canonical as well as less well-known works of fiction.[5]

---

[2] There have been significant moments of institutional interest in the idea of law as one of the liberal arts, for example, the Harvard conference in 1954 on the teaching of law in the liberal arts, and the 1975 report by the Law Center Consultative Committee at the University of Massachusetts, which noted the following: "[there is a] coherent body of knowledge about the social functions and consequences of legal institutions and processes . . . [that amounts] to more than the extraprofessional study of law; it is itself a new scholarly enterprise . . . The perspectives of law, on the one hand, and of social science or humanities on the other, cannot merely be placed side by side. Only an uneasy accommodation, perhaps spliced by occasional moments of communication, can result from that approach. What is needed is an effort toward a real synthesis of the intellectual heritage and analytic capabilities of law, social science, and the humanities – one that aims at the creation of a distinctively new and broader scholarly discipline with law and legal systems at its core." These efforts are discussed in *LJST and Interdisciplinary Legal Scholarship*, http://www.amherst.edu/~ljst/aboutus.htm#program, quoted in Austin Sarat, ed., *Law in the Liberal Arts* (Ithaca and London: Cornell University Press, 2004) 2–3.

[3] Peter Goodrich, "Rhetoric and Somatics: Training the Body to Do the Work of Law," *Law/Text/Culture* 5 (2002): 241, 253, quoted in Susan Sage Heinzelman, "'Termes Queinte of Law' and Quaint Fantasies of Literature," *Law in the Liberal Arts*, 166–92, Austin Sarat, ed. (Ithaca and London: Cornell University Press, 2004): 16.

[4] James Boyd White, *The Legal Imagination* (Chicago and London: University of Chicago Press, 1973).

[5] Law and Literature as a movement is typically divided into two related but distinct approaches to the convergence of the legal and the literary: law in literature and law as literature. On the one hand, these designations are historical terms, that is, ones that mark out phases – here the two earliest – in a movement that has been succeeded by increasingly complex and expansive notions of what constitutes

Introduction 3

Still others have been more concerned with the literary dimensions of legal life, identifying features of narrative, rhetoric, and genre in lawyers' arguments or judicial opinions.[6] In the formation of the community of Law and Humanities scholars, this last emphasis has been most influential and most controversial, and White has been

> either the legal or the literary text. On the other hand, the phrases are definitional and denote two broad and persistent categories or rubrics with their respective evolutions. Law in literature, for example, arguably begins with John H. Wigmore's various classifications of the "legal novel" in "A List of Legal Novels," *The Brief* 2 (1900): 124–7. For representations of the lawyer-as-figure of resentment, see Richard H. Weisberg's *The Failure of the Word: The Protagonist as Lawyer in Modern Fiction* (New Haven: Yale University Press, 1984) as well as *Poethics, and Other Strategies of Law and Literature* (New York: Columbia University Press, 1992).
>
> For studies that contextualize literary representation in legal history, see for example, Theodore Ziolkowski, *The Mirror of Justice: Literary Reflections of Legal Crises* (Princeton: Princeton University Press, 2003); Brook Thomas, *Cross-Examinations of Law and Literature: Cooper, Hawthorne, Stowe, and Melville* (Cambridge: Cambridge University Press, 1991); Jon-Christian Suggs, *Whispered Consolations: Law and Narrative in African-American Life* (Ann Arbor: University of Michigan Press, 2000); Deak Nabers, *Victory of Law: The Fourteenth Amendment, the Civil War, and American Literature, 1852–1867* (Baltimore: Johns Hopkins University Press, 2006).
>
> New historicist considerations of the relationship among literary narrative practices, genre, and specific legal forms and concepts have no Ur-text per se. Rather, they participate in the general new historicist impulse to specify an "anecdote" and read it for its instantiation of the various discourses circulating at its specific cultural moment. In the case of law and literature, those discourses are legal and literary, and the anecdote may be any legal form, for example, the construction of chains of circumstantial evidence, as in Alexander Welsh's *Strong Representations: Narrative and Circumstantial Evidence in England* (Baltimore: Johns Hopkins University Press, 1991). Welsh's study has influenced numerous similar investigations (notably of English law and literature) including Lisa Rodensky's study of criminal intention and narrative omniscience, *The Crime in Mind: Criminal Responsibility and the Victorian Novel* (Oxford: Oxford University Press, 2003); Jonathan Grossman's paralleling of the sites of justice with specific literary forms in *The Art of Alibi: English Law Courts and the Novel* (Baltimore: Johns Hopkins University Press, 2002); Jan-Melissa Schramm's analysis of testimony in *Testimony and Advocacy in Victorian Law, Literature, and Theology* (Cambridge: Cambridge University Press, 2000), and Kieran Dolin's study of the normative functions of both law and literature in *Fiction and the Law: Legal Discourse in Victorian and Modern Literature* (Cambridge: Cambridge University Press, 1999). For objections to the practical irrelevance of the law and literature enterprise generally, see Richard Posner, *Law and Literature: A Misunderstood Relation* (Cambridge: Harvard University Press, 1988).
>
> 6 Where studies of law in literature focus on literary (typically narrative, novelistic) representations of legal professionals, the use of legal forms and documents, legal settings or, more fundamentally, the pervasiveness of legal culture that literature both helps to constitute and critique, law as literature reads the law for its own narrative procedures and rhetorical functions. For Benjamin N. Cardozo's classic argument for reading law as literature, see "Law and Literature," *The Yale Review* 14 (1925): 699–718. For a general assessment of the place of storytelling in law, see Peter Brooks and Paul Gewirtz's collection of essays *Law's Stories: Narrative and Rhetoric in the Law* (New Haven: Yale University Press, 1996). Martha Nussbaum discusses the empathic potential of the narrative imagination in *Cultivating Humanity: A Classical Defense of Reform in Liberal Education* (Cambridge, MA: Harvard University Press, 1997). For studies of law indebted to the use of literary critical methods of interpretation – the hermeneutic approach to law – see Peter Goodrich, *Reading the Law: A Critical Introduction to Legal Method and Techniques* (London: Blackwell, 1986) and *Legal Discourse: Studies in Linguistics, Rhetoric, and Legal Analysis* (New York: St. Martin's, 1987); Sanford Levinson and Steven Mailloux, eds., *Interpreting Law and Literature: A Hermeneutic Reader* (Evanston: Northwestern University Press, 1988). For rhetorical and cultural analysis of specific legal processes, the act of confession, for example, see Peter Brooks, *Troubling Confessions: Speaking Guilt in Law and Literature* (Chicago: University of Chicago Press, 2000).

among the most prominent of its advocates. For more than three decades he has argued that legal education can and should be a liberal education, in the Arnoldian sense of a formation that develops a sense of culture. Lawyers, he said, should be given "a training in the ways one can learn from one's own experience and acquire experience of a new and better kind; in the ways one can learn from one's culture and contribute to it; in the ways one can live with an increased awareness of the limits of one's knowledge and mind, accepting ambiguity and uncertainty as the condition of life."[7]

White's concern lies with how lawyers are trained to think, write, and speak. He calls for legal education to cultivate in students a self-reflexive sense of how they use legal forms as they acculturate to law's language and processes.[8] If this point of view could be reduced to a maxim, it might be this: Law is a language and language matters. Another way to put it would be to say that the education of lawyers should include the cultivation of a meaningful appreciation of law as a rhetorical practice – not just in the sense of an art of persuasion, but of a disciplined, textured, self-directed habit of reading, speaking and, above all, writing, that has at its root a critical understanding of the links among language, consciousness, and power. The idea is that what we say matters and is indissociably bound up with the forms in which we say it. These forms may not be of our devising, but this does not mean that we cannot make them our own; and in the case of law, where the consequences of our rhetorical acts of interpretation are not merely symbolic – law takes place on a "field of pain and death"[9] – we owe it both to ourselves and to each other to assume responsibility for our use of the linguistic forms and processes of law and to speak and write in a voice that is our own. "The central task for the lawyer from this point of view," White observes, "is to give herself a voice of her own, a voice that at once expresses her own mind at work in its best way and speaks as a lawyer, a voice at once individual and professional."[10]

In short, White calls us to a vision of the lawyer as artist. It is a vision of art in which beauty and sublimity of thought and expression are not ends in themselves, but rather one of the best defenses we have against what White, in his most recent book,

---

[7] White, *The Legal Imagination*, xv.

[8] Ibid., xxi: Consider, for instance, the following passage from his "Introduction to the Student." "To ask how to read and write well is to ask practically everything, one might say, and indeed a legal education could be defined by saying that one learns to read and write the professional language of the law, to master a set of special ways of thinking and talking. Your central question in the course could then be put this way: what does it mean to give yourself such an education, to learn to think and speak like a lawyer? You will see that the question so stated has two obvious branches: how do you do it, in what does the lawyer's art consist? And what does it signify to have mastered that art – what have you gained, what lost?"

[9] Robert Cover offers this formulation in his celebrated essay, "Violence and the Word," *Yale Law Journal* 95 (1986): 1601.

[10] White, *The Legal Imagination*, xv.

Introduction

Living Speech (2006), calls "the empire of force."[11] We need to make sure that our speech is alive – that we mean what we say, say what we mean, and have something to say – so that our language, especially our legal language, does not become an empty instrument for the unrestrained exercise of power.

Indeed, if there is a concern that runs throughout and drives White's work, it is one born of a keen sense of what happens to legal language–and thus to the human beings whose lives are subject to it – when legal actors have to come to terms with law's fragmentariness, inconsistencies, incommensurabilities, and attendant uncertainties. When confronted with these and with the moral pressures of adjudication, the temptation is great to shirk the burden of judgment and displace the locus of responsibility onto the language of law itself, to empty law of its meaning and conceive of legal judgment as the impersonal, methodological enactment of a linguistic form, a mere procedure.[12]

Here it seems that White's version of law and literature is at bottom a critique of liberalism.[13] In this connection, the following description of Lionel Trilling's

---

[11] James Boyd White, *Living Speech: Resisting the Empire of Force* (Princeton: Princeton University Press, 2006).

[12] See ibid., 72–5: "It is common for people to try to learn law, at the beginning of the process, as if it were a set of rules to be applied more or less routinely to the facts of cases as they arise. This is to think of the law as a simple system of commands. But as almost every law student learns, often to his or her profound discomfort, this image of the law will not work, either in law school or in practice. The lawyer and judge are constantly presented with real difficulties of interpretation and harmonization of the law, in relation to facts that are themselves uncertain, all presenting a set of problems about which much can be said on each side and through which they must think their ways as independent minds. . . . In the law, as elsewhere, the task of the legal mind is to find a way to be present as a mind, a person, a voice, in a context that seems to invite the replication of standard forms. The lawyer who simply moves phrases around in his head and on the page, never really meaning anything he says – and there are plenty of lawyers like that – is never actually thinking about the case, or the law, and is certainly incapable of saying something fresh or transformative. As for judges, the need to be present in one's speech and writing is even more crucial, for there are serious public consequences. The judge who simply articulates phrases, concepts or ideas in an unmeaning way can likewise not be attended to, for he is not present as a mind or person. This means that his opinion cannot be read with the care and attention lawyers are trained to give authoritative texts in the law; it means, too, that he in a real way cannot be responsible for what he is doing. This kind of writing, to use the distinction made prominent by my colleague Joseph Vining, is authoritarian, not authoritative. It is part of what Simone Weil would call the empire of force."

[13] This suggests a point of contact with Paul Kahn's perspective. As Kahn elaborates in a recent book, the problem with liberalism is that it is often unmindful of its internal contradictions. These contradictions owe not just to the limits of reason, but also to an insufficiently critical sense of the extent to which the Enlightenment faith that the problems of experience and of political life will yield to the proper application of the faculty of reason and will find expression in the popular will – a faith that lies at the heart of classical liberalism – is just that, a faith. This means that we tend to underestimate the degree to which, to borrow Karl Schmitt's insight, the forms and conceptions of the religious Judeo-Christian imaginary migrate to and haunt the secular liberal imagination that ostensibly displaces it. It also means, however, that we are insufficiently aware of what Kahn calls the "genealogy of liberalism" and the "architecture of the liberal world" – that is, the way that the classical liberalism of the Enlightenment builds upon two other traditions and structures of thought, namely those of

landmark work of literary criticism *The Liberal Imagination* (1950),[14] in a recent retrospective essay by the American literary scholar Louis Menand, merits lengthy citation, as it provides a context for understanding the inspiration behind White's work:

> In Trilling's view, the faith that liberals share, whether they are Soviet apologists, Hayekian free marketers, or subscribers to *Partisan Review*, is that human betterment is possible, that there is a straight road to health and happiness. A liberal is a person who believes that the right economic system, the right political reforms, the right undergraduate curriculum, and the right psychotherapy will do away with unfairness, snobbery, resentment, prejudice, neurosis, and tragedy. The argument of "The Liberal Imagination" is that literature teaches that life is not so simple – for unfairness, snobbery, resentment, prejudice, neurosis, and tragedy happen to be literature's particular subject matter. In Trilling's celebrated statement: "To the carrying out of the job of criticizing the liberal imagination, literature has unique relevance . . . because literature is the human activity that takes the fullest and most precise account of variousness, possibility, complexity, and difficulty." This is why literary criticism has something to say about politics.[15]

There is, here, a clearly discernible line of influence and inspiration that runs from Arnold's *Culture and Anarchy* (1869),[16] through Trilling, to White's seminal book, *The Legal Imagination*. Menand's account of Trilling's text enables us to read White against the contextual backdrop of a critique of liberalism and to further our understanding of White's vision of the value of literature for legal education. If we follow Trilling's lead, literature can help cultivate a capacity for and tolerance of nuance, ambiguity, and uncertainty – what White calls the limits of knowledge and mind and Keats would term "Negative Capability"[17] – which in turn makes it possible to imagine integrating literature with the best uses of legal language. In other words, a literary sensibility helps legal education develop into a form of liberal learning.

For White, however, this is neither the only claim that literature has on law, nor the only foundation of a new interdisciplinarity. For White, the study of literature can

---

classical Greece and Christianity. See *Putting Liberalism in its Place* (Princeton: Princeton University Press, 2006) 144.

[14] Lionel Trilling, *The Liberal Imagination* (New York: New York Review of Books, 2008).

[15] Louis Menand, "Regrets Only: Lionel Trilling and His Discontents," *The New Yorker* 29 Sept. 2008: 82.

[16] Matthew Arnold, *Culture and Anarchy* (Cambridge: Cambridge University Press, 1990).

[17] "Keats to George and Thomas Keats," London, 21 December 1817, *Letters of John Keats*, Robert Gittings, ed. (Oxford: Oxford University Press, 1970) 43: "I had not a dispute but a disquisition with Dilke, on various subjects; several things dovetailed in my mind, & at once it struck me, what quality went to form a Man of Achievement especially in literature & which Shakespeare possessed so enormously – I mean *Negative Capability*, that is when man is capable of being in uncertainties, Mysteries, doubts, without any irritable reaching after fact & reason."

Introduction

lend integrity to legal language not only because it can help us cultivate a sensibility and a voice as writers, but also because the psychological intimacy it affords makes possible moments of sympathetic identification with people whose experiences and contexts may be quite different from our own. This capacity to cultivate sympathy opens the possibility for literature to have a salutary counter-hegemonic effect; it can raise consciousness about the effects of power and historical patterns of oppression, exploitation, and marginalization. In White's view, we must not only make the forms of legal language our own, but also develop and integrate a sensitive understanding of the ways in which language can shape our perception of others and, thus, the way we treat each other. In short, literature can help us see, understand, and identify with those whose lives and experiences are often illegible before the law.

White's emphasis on the discursive and rhetorical foundation of communities provided and still provides an important impetus for humanists to study law and to bring their insights to it. Yet for some it seems too bounded, too self-contained. For them it describes one important dimension of the way communities are formed and transformed, but, as Robin West argues in "Communities, Texts, and Law: Reflections on the Law and Literature Movement," it leaves out much that is nontextual in our interaction with actual people.[18] The textual and the nontextual often overlap, to be sure, but insofar as many people simply cannot participate in the reading, writing, and critical activity White describes, West observes, "Our community, defined by the interactive effects we have on others, is considerably larger than the community as defined by our texts."[19]

Putting her "interactive community" against White's "textual" one, she freely allows that texts, whether legal or literary, have the capacity to "reflect," "constitute," and "convey" "moral and cultural traditions,"[20] but their reach is not as extensive as, for example, that of a particular law, which actually shapes how we as people interact with one another. Understood as a real effect instead of a textual production, law impacts the subjectivity even of those who will never be part of the textual community.[21] She also points out, one text will function differently in the two registers. *Dred Scott*, for example, embodied a moral respect for property within the textual community, but its impact on the interactive community was to make property of slaves.

Although West does not abandon literature, her perspective pushes beyond the literary and poses a new question for humanists interested in law: How would a

---

[18] Robin West, "Communities, Texts, and Law: Reflections on the Law and Literature Movement," *Yale Journal of Law and the Humanities* 1 (1988): 154. West writes: "A law can affect the subjectivity of the lives of many creatures – human and otherwise – who will never produce, participate in, or criticize its textual meaning." Robin West, "Communities, Texts, and Law: Reflections on the Law and Literature Movement." *Yale Journal of Law and the Humanities* 1 (1988): 154.

[19] Ibid.

[20] Ibid.

[21] Ibid.

study of the way law constitutes persons proceed? Shifting our attention from the relative merits of academic versus practical approaches to law and legal texts, West encourages an appreciation of those points at which the theoretical merits of law run up against the real, potential travesties of its impact in human experience. Hers is an argument, therefore, about the relationship between legality and justice. West sees that our judgment will depend on whether we position ourselves within the textual or interactive community and concludes that "justice" might better be gauged by law's effects on people, even where that seems to contradict the central texts of law.[22]

Turning to the "narrative voice and law-and-literature movement," West declares that these have become the best, if not the only, means for lawyers to hear the stories of the "textually excluded" (inclusive of the natural world).[23] Seeing only a partial solution in White's efforts to improve community by creating "better readers," West looks for a way to create "better people."[24] The best way of changing how we treat others in the interactive community, how lawyers understand the human consequences of their legal texts, she argues, was to heed the stories of the oppressed.

To claim that an understanding of law needs the humanities hardly seems polemical to us these days, so far have the arguments of White and West (and many others) spread. The only clear difference between then and now is that other humanities disciplines have energetically joined the fray in seeking to cultivate the kind of sensibility and potential for critique for which West calls. In so doing, as the work collected in this book demonstrates, they have altered the terms of engagement with law as well as the terms on which humanistic understanding and criticism can be offered.

The Genesis of the Field-II: The *Yale Journal of Law and the Humanities* and the Rearticulation of the Humanistic Ideal

Fifteen years after White's book, in 1988, the first scholarly journal devoted exclusively to the field, the *Yale Journal of Law and the Humanities*, was launched. Born at the Yale Law School, the journal bore a prestigious pedigree, but more than that it embodied an aspiration to be something other than a traditional law review.[25]

Explaining that the "humanist's vision of the law" had grown "more complex" by virtue of its engagement with the "coercive and the constitutive" bases of law, the editors of the *Yale Journal of Law and the Humanities* set this vision – examples from Kafka, Dickens, and Dostoevsky show it was a distinctly literary one – alongside a legal point of view, which was beginning to see engagement with the humanities, not as a

---

[22] Ibid., 155.
[23] Ibid., 156.
[24] Ibid.
[25] Thus, its editorial staff was drawn from the graduate school at Yale as well as the law school.

Introduction

preliminary to "real work" but as an adjunct to it.[26] Sensitive to the material as well as symbolic effects of legal culture, the editors urged cultural analysis that would look at the way legal culture, in concert with "other cultural forms," organizes and informs perception in the first place.[27] As they put it: "The study of law must be informed by an examination of the socio-cultural narratives that shape legal meaning and empower legal norms; conversely, the study of culture requires an understanding of the law as a normative edifice and coercive system."[28] In other words, the layperson's conception of law and, more importantly, the average person's affective attachment to and support of the idea of law is generated through culturally specific narratives that can become more apparent and be better understood when approached from the perspective of the humanities.

Conversely, it is only when we appreciate that even aspects of our subjective selves as fundamental as personal desire have been informed by the complementary legal processes of reward and punishment that we can begin to comprehend why we tell the particular stories we do.[29] These two projects, the editors suggested, would encourage readers to become more self-conscious and reflective cultural critics, not for the sake of an idle, academic interest but specifically to "develop a critical stance that allows us to imagine a more tolerant, plural community."[30]

In light of such a far-reaching remit, Owen M. Fiss predicted that the journal's greatest challenge would be to provide a "definition of its field of inquiry,"[31] or to answer "the question of domain and definition"[32] – and he was not wrong. The task was made especially challenging, as he saw it, because the allied field of the humanities was (and remains) itself so capacious: neither institutional attempts to define it (merely as a group of disciplines not found in the social and natural sciences), nor efforts to identify a common methodological foundation (for example, in interpretation) could succeed because they were either too restrictive or too broad, respectively. If resistant to categorical definition, however, the field could still be described, and in no way better than by considering the actual motive forces and cultural conditions that informed the journal's creation.[33]

Law and humanities were, as Fiss saw it, a reaction specifically to law and economics and the dominance of "the economic model" – "individuals trying to maximize their welfare under conditions of scarcity" – of social organization.[34] As the

---

[26] "Note from the Editors," *Yale Journal of Law and the Humanities* 1 (1988): v.

[27] Ibid., vi.

[28] Ibid.

[29] See Austin Sarat and Thomas R. Kearns, "Beyond the Great Divide: Forms of Legal Scholarship and Everyday Life," *Law in Everyday Life*, Austin Sarat and Thomas R. Kearns, eds. (Ann Arbor: University of Michigan Press, 1993) 27–32.

[30] "Note from the Editors," vi.

[31] Owen M. Fiss, "The Challenge Ahead," *Yale Journal of Law and the Humanities* 1 (1988): viii.

[32] Ibid., ix.

[33] Ibid.

[34] Ibid.

articles in the inaugural issue show, law and humanities scholarship then was identified with new historicism, cultural studies, and, most strongly, with law and literature all of which shared a desire, according to Fiss, to escape the individualistic, conservative politics of an economic movement that assumed market forces were the best regulator of social – and human – relations.[35] He is quite clear that at its inception Law and Humanities had a politics ("left-leaning," "progressive and liberal"), but he suggested that theoretical foundations were even more important than political orientations.

In contrast to the "instrumental" view of law's function and the "scientism" of its study,[36] law and humanities – and the journal specifically – aimed "to restore to legal studies a proper place for the question of values."[37] Having offered this view, however, Fiss is careful to point out the potentially negative side effects of the assumption that law itself cannot raise questions about value without being wedded to another value-oriented discipline.[38] (In fact, where interdisciplinary work makes law look less like law, he suggested, it diminishes the professional relevance of academic inquiry.) Ever attuned to the present cultural conditions, however, Fiss's sense of the "barren" state of legal studies and legal practice made humanistic inquiry into law an "imaginative response to urgent practical needs."[39]

The editors and Fiss remind us that they, like White, see in the union of law and the humanities a corrective to certain tendencies in law schools and in professional legal education, among them most importantly the rise of value neutral, technocratic approaches which allegedly undermine the vision of lawyer as "statesman."[40] In addition, Guido Calabresi, then dean of Yale Law School, suggested that turning to the humanities was important to the degree that it "feeds" law.[41] For him the test of law and humanities scholarship would be its impact on the character and conception of lawyers. Thus he recounted how former Supreme Court Justice Hugo Black told him, on the second day of his clerkship, that if he had "never read Tacitus . . . then, you are not a lawyer."[42]

The admonitions of Fiss and Calabresi, as well as White's, depend on a trope of rescue or recuperation, a trope that remains quite powerful in certain genres of law and humanities scholarship. Turning to the humanities helps to rescue law or, depending on one's historical perspective, helps to recuperate parts of law that might otherwise be lost. As White put it, "[t]o imagine the law as a rhetorical and

[35] Ibid., x.
[36] Ibid., ix.
[37] Ibid., x.
[38] Ibid.
[39] Ibid., x–xi.
[40] Ibid.
[41] Guido Calabresi, "Introductory Letter," *Yale Journal of Law and the Humanities* 1 (1988): vii.
[42] Ibid.

Introduction

literary process may help us to see each moment in the law differently . . . It leads to a different conception of the teaching of law and may help the practitioner conceive of its practice differently too . . . the poems by Frost, Dickinson, and Keats do much to suggest standards by which we might learn to do . . . [law] better."[43] Reading "great" literature expands the imagination, and, as a result, it enables lawyers and judges to make more impartial, yet empathetic, judgments.

Closely related to the trope of recuperation is a "high culture" conception of the humanities. The humanities, correctly understood, provide uplift and inspiration; they raise the deepest questions about our lives and the values we pursue. It is not, we suspect, coincidental that Calabresi names Kant, Bentham, and Captain Vere, in addition to Tacitus, as examples of humanities texts,[44] or that Fiss warns that a definitional equation of the humanities with "interpretation" would exclude the work of John Rawls.[45] By pointing out the "high-culture" preferences among some who turn to the humanities to help rescue law, we do not mean to denigrate the authors, works, or characters cited. Surely there is nothing to be gained from reigniting the canon wars. In measuring the progress of law and humanities scholarship we might ask how far we have come from a high-culture conception.

We look back to the first issue of the *Yale Journal of Law and the Humanities*, as a valuable point of reference for the work that *Law and the Humanities: An Introduction* attempts to do. Today, as the work collected here suggests, critical impulses abound, not looking to save or humanize law or lawyers, but to expose the hidden assumptions that structure their work, the values that privilege some views and silence others, the identities that law privileges and those it pushes to the margins and, in so doing, to call law and lawyers to account.

Looking at the field as it is today, one might ask: Does the current, self-consciously programmatic constellation of interest in law and humanities as a field really represent something new? How has the field benefited from the inclusion and incorporation of global perspectives and voices outside the American frame? To what extent is law and humanities scholarship still linked to the effort to rescue professional legal education and to the artifacts of high culture? What is the field's genealogy and institutional history? What, if any, are its politics? We invite readers of this book to contemplate these questions as they examine its contents.

Resistances to Law and Humanities

From the beginning, the development of the humanistic study of law has met resistance on both sides of the disciplinary divide. In American law schools, law and

---

[43] James Boyd White, "Imagining the Law," *The Rhetoric of Law*, Austin Sarat and Thomas R. Kearns, eds. (Ann Arbor: University of Michigan Press, 1996) 55.
[44] Calabresi, "Introductory Letter," vii.
[45] Fiss, "The Challenge Ahead," viii.

humanities is sometimes perceived as "useless"; despite the efforts of White and others, a common view is that the field does not offer anything useful for a practical understanding of law or the purposes of legal reform.[46] On the other hand, from the perspective of the humanities, the study of law is frequently viewed with suspicion and resisted because it feels treacherously close to a preprofessional orientation and thus seems at odds with a humanist's commitment to more putatively "disinterested" modes of enquiry and learning.

Moreover, many now feel that there is something not only elitist but, more to the point, counterfactual in the idea that the humanities are a propaedeutic to humane action, that to think of the humanities as offering a kind of moral supplement to law is to misunderstand the ambit of humanistic learning. The objection is as familiar as it is well grounded; one need not look far, after all, to find examples of atrocities committed in the shade of a refined humanistic sensibility. This questioning of the relationship between liberal learning and ethical conduct – especially with respect to the conduct of our civic life – is one of the central, productive tensions surrounding the humanities. Indeed, it is still the case that with varying degrees of self-reflexivity the stated mission of the humanities today is more or less a version of Matthew Arnold's argument for "culture" as a bulwark against "anarchy"[47] – and by the latter we are meant to understand, pace Raymond Williams, the depredations of industrialization and the even more terrifying prospect of liberal democracy, the Scylla and Charybdis of the modern age.

Continuing doubts about the usefulness of the humanities to and for law require that we either expand our notion of what is useful, meaningful, and important in legal studies to encompass the good that can come from humanistic learning – a revalorization not just of the humanities as they pertain to law but of the human-ities tout court – or that we at least suspend the notion of usefulness with some

---

[46] Resistance to the idea of law and humanities in American law schools has its roots in the intellectual and institutional history of legal studies. Put differently, law already is a discipline, and introducing the humanities into legal studies means coming to terms with the history of law's early efforts to establish itself institutionally – more specifically, as a form of systematic knowledge that would have the status and methodological rigor of a science. This is not the place to rehearse in detail the history of Legal Formalism, or of the rise of Legal Realism as a response to its felt shortcomings. We note only that although Legal Realism, in its concern with the real-world effects of law and its concomitant turn toward the social sciences – sociology, psychology, and, above all, economics – marks a sharp departure from the hermeticism and doctrinal scholasticism of Legal Formalism. Both schools of thought favor a way of knowing and of thinking about knowledge that orients itself in terms of the paradigms of the sciences.

[47] Arnold, *Culture*, 82: "Now, if culture, which simply means trying to perfect oneself, and one's mind as part of oneself, brings us light, and if light shows us that there is nothing so very blessed in merely doing as one likes, that the worship of the mere freedom to do as one likes is worship of machinery, that the really blessed thing is to like what right reason ordains, and to follow her authority, then we have got a practical benefit out of culture. We have got a much wanted principle, a principle of authority, to counteract the tendency to anarchy which seems to be threatening us."

Introduction

semblance of good faith. Given the genealogy and institutional history of legal study, asking about the field's use-value from within the established perspectives of legal studies approaches the tautological. Humanistic perspectives on questions of value, meaning, and interpretation are, in some sense, defined out of law's framework of normative concerns, treated as trifles, when law moves to establish itself as a discipline in the Anglo-American tradition, in the nineteenth century.[48]

This skepticism does not mean that we should abandon any concern with the question of the usefulness of such investigations. Quite the contrary, if many scholars are animated by an interest in this field it is precisely because they see it not only as useful but also important, for a range of reasons. One reason, as we have seen in Fiss's introduction to the inaugural issue of the *Yale Journal of Law and the Humanities*, has to do with the politics of knowledge in legal studies. We agree with Fiss that law and humanities gets much of its institutional momentum as a self-consciously programmatic response to the pervasive influence of law and economics. (Today we would add empirical legal studies.)

The idea is that the humanities can provide a much-needed counterweight and help ground the law in a standard of value that is qualitative, not merely quantitative. Moreover, scholarship in law and the humanities can unearth the privileged identity categories that comprise law's taken-for-granted world, help to give voice to the marginalized while reminding us that voice does not guarantee power, help to expose the constraints that legality seeks to impose on national sovereignty while pointing out the ways sovereignty exceeds and/or manipulates the law for its own purposes.

In addition, the emergence of law and humanities as a field can be read against the backdrop of a philosophical crisis of value that goes well beyond legal studies, one that still encompasses much of Western thought – what Jean-François Lyotard calls "The Post-Modern Condition."[49] Lyotard claims that in the vacuum created by the loss of faith in both the traditional and modern meta-narratives that organized and gave meaning to experience (i.e., the Judeo-Christian religious imagination, secular ideas of the inevitability of historical progress), efficiency – the standard of economic logic – has emerged as the sole criterion of legitimation.[50] His account provides a

---

[48] For an insightful reading of law's relationship with "trifles," see Ravit Reichman, "Making a Mess of Things: The Trifles of Legal Pleasure," *Law, Culture, and the Humanities* 1:1 (2005): 14–34.

[49] Jean-François Lyotard, *The Postmodern Condition* (Minneapolis: University of Minnesota Press, 1984) xxiv: "[s]implifying to the extreme, I define *postmodern* as incredulity toward meta-narratives."

[50] Lyotard, *The Postmodern Condition*, 50–1: "[i]t is only in the context of the grand narratives of legitimation – the life of the spirit and/or the emancipation of humanity – that the partial replacement of teachers by machines may seem inadequate or even intolerable. But is probable that these narratives are already no longer the principal driving force behind interest in acquiring knowledge. If the motivation is power, then this aspect of classical didactics ceases to be relevant. The question (overt or implied) now asked by the professionalist student, the State, or institutions of higher education is no longer "Is it true?" but "What use is it?" In the context of the mercantilization of knowledge,

useful philosophical context for understanding the stance of law and humanities because many would see it as aptly describing the condition of legal studies: The doctrinal thought of Legal Formalism opens to the world of experience, through Legal Realism, only to see legal studies then brought under the influence of a similarly self-enclosed and limited system of meaning, the science of economics.

The idea that drives humanistic resistance to law and economics is not that the values of efficiency, productivity, and supply and demand should not obtain, but that they should not be the only ones; that the logic of the marketplace cannot be left to stand alone as the sole standard of value, in legal studies no less than in the world. A well-functioning, well-regulated economy can lead to prosperity, which in turn can provide, when equitably distributed, the material well-being without which the idea of freedom and human flourishing is empty. That said, notwithstanding the mantra that "a rising tide lifts all boats," many feel that there is not any rational, historical basis for crediting the belief that the market is the necessary and sufficient answer to questions of social justice. It is hard to tell whether that position still counts as a politics, in the wake of the recent collapse of global credit markets, but if it does, then it is a partial answer to the question of whether law and humanities has a politics; it does. (A partial, not complete answer, because it does not speak to structural inequalities and histories of oppression that many would argue are not reducible to economic forces even though they have a strong basis in them, for example, traditions of racism or patriarchy.)

Yet some favor a more disinterested understanding of the aims of law and humanities scholarship. That is, one might argue that research in the humanities, at least in the United States, has never aimed for anything more than the production of knowledge. This claim is unconvincing for two reasons. The first is not hard to find. In the wake of Foucault, the notion that the project of knowledge could ever be decoupled from the interests of power has been subjected to a withering critique;[51] in the contemporary humanities, one would be hard pressed to find claims made for the autonomy and disinterestedness of any of the disciplines.[52] We have grown accustomed to the idea that the modern disciplinary configurations of knowledge – the social sciences, in particular – emerge in tandem with the rise of the liberal

---

more often than not this question is equivalent to: "Is it saleable?" In the context of power-growth: "Is it efficient?" Having competence in performance-oriented skill does indeed seem saleable in the conditions described here, and it is efficient by definition. What no longer makes the grade is competence as defined by other criteria true/false, just/unjust, etc. – and, of course, low performativity in general." See also, ibid., xxiii–xxv.

[51] The question of the relationship between truth and "Power" radiates throughout Foucault's work even when, as is the case in his early works, "Power" (see above "Power") is not explicitly named. For a useful, brief introduction in English to his conceptualization of this relationship, see Michel Foucault, "Truth and Power," in *The Foucault Reader*, Paul Rabinow, ed. (New York: Pantheon, 1984) 51–75.

[52] For an exception, see Stanley Fish, *Save the World on Your Own Time* (New York: Oxford University Press, 2008).

Introduction

bureaucratic state and cannot be conceived of apart from the role they play as technologies of governance; it is understood that they are ways to exercise and maintain power by shaping and defining the domains of subjectivity and, thus, an entire matrix of material, social, and political reality. In this account, with the turn to the so-called "sciences of man," knowledge is not merely descriptive but normative and constitutive of subjectivity: the disciplines make each person knowable as an individual subject and thus bring her within the domain of régimes of truth and normalization. A discipline is never a mere body of knowledge and an intellectual practice; it is part of an institutional structure that produces docile, useful bodies to serve the interests of the state and, behind it, of power.[53] In short, there can be no such thing as "mere" research.

The second reason why the idea of the autonomy and disinterestedness of the humanities disciplines has a hollow ring to Western ears, and tends to be muted even when it is proffered, is less appreciated but equally telling. It is because the idea of academic research has been unmoored from the philosophical understanding that provides its rationale in its original context. Indeed, although it is frequently noted that the University of Berlin and its conception of the academic disciplines as being research intensive serves as the model for Johns Hopkins University – a model that is then replicated widely throughout the United States in the development of programs of graduate study – it is often forgotten that the underlying vision that shapes and motivates the founding of the University of Berlin owes to Alexander von Humboldt and German Idealist philosophy, notably the philosophy of Fichte, who held the first chair of philosophy at Berlin, and of Hegel, who succeeded him.[54]

In this model, the disciplines are overseen by philosophy, the "queen of the faculties," which does not direct their discrete practices but articulates the regulative idea that orients and discloses the meaning of the project of knowledge and makes it intelligible as belonging to a single, shared universe of ideas – that is, makes the disciplines visible as constitutive of a university. From a Fichtean viewpoint, the significance of research, or Wissenschaft, lies not so much in its content as in its form; the critical distance, or disinterestedness, that the disciplines deepen and

---

[53] Michel Foucault, *The Foucault Reader*, 180–2: "The classical age discovered the body as object and target of power. A body is docile that may be subjected, used, transformed, and improved. These methods, which made possible the meticulous control of the operations of the body, which assured the constant subjection of its forces and imposed on them a relation of docility-utility, might be called 'disciplines.' Many disciplinary methods had long been in existence in monasteries, armies, workshops. In the course of the seventeenth and eighteenth centuries, the disciplines became general formulas of domination. The historical moment of the disciplines was the moment when an art of the human body was born, which was directed not only at the growth of its skills, or at the intensification of its subjection, but at the formation of a relation that in the mechanism itself makes it more obedient as it becomes more useful, and conversely. Thus discipline produces subjected and practiced bodies, 'docile' bodies."

[54] Lyotard provides a succinct account of this history. See Lyotard, *The Postmodern Condition*, 31–5.

depend upon is a manifestation of our capacity for self-consciousness, that is, our ability to stand apart from our own consciousness and thus be aware of it.[55]

Today, in the arts and the interpretive humanities the hermeneutics of suspicion – typically of Freudian, Nietzschean, or Marxist inspiration (e.g., critiques of globalization or elaborations of Frankfurt school approaches to culture and ideology) – still figure as the most common horizon of expectation. It is, as Auden observes, an "age of anxiety,"[56] of self-doubt and pessimism, in which many are deeply skeptical, indeed apprehensive, of even the barest suggestion of a meliorist narrative about the project of knowledge or the trajectory of Western civilization; an age in which, to borrow from Yeats, "the best lack all conviction, while the worst are full of passionate intensity."[57]

If law and humanities scholars do not quite recognize themselves in this portrait of cultural exhaustion, it is not just because we may be wary of such high-minded despair, but also because for many the gods are not yet dead or even dying. Indeed a reverence for law can be a form of faith, in the fullest sense. Indeed, in the case of the United States in particular, the religious imaginary is more than vestigial; it is arguably at the core of the American cultural experience of the idea of the rule of law.[58] After Bush, reverence for the rule of law and anything that sustains it is very attractive to many who not so long ago were some of its severest critics.

[55] If we typically forget this philosophical inheritance in our thinking about the rationale of the academic research disciplines, it is no doubt, in part, because of our visceral unease with its history. The unease is understandable: Fichte is sometimes considered the father of German nationalism – his late work, *Rede an die Deutsche Nation*, is often considered its foundational text – and it is not hard to trace a line of thought that runs from German Idealist philosophy, through German Romanticism, up to National Socialism. The rhetoric of self-consciousness and freedom can lend itself to a kind of triumphalism, much as a dialectical vision of history as the progressive manifestation of an idea can become messianic, if not apocalyptic. It is a short step, from there, to the idea that the people – the Volk – through whom this understanding of freedom and history has been made manifest have a special destiny; the consequences of the German experience of this idea are still fresh in the collective memory of Western civilization and haunt its conceptual imagination.

In other words, if we resist the framework of German Idealist thought it is not simply because the idea of philosophy as the "queen of the faculties" strikes us as quaint. Rather, this resistance is the symptomatic expression of a far-reaching and widely felt cultural moment. According to Lyotard, as we have seen, a profound distrust of totalizing meta-narratives is the salient characteristic of this moment, a loss of faith both in the Judeo-Christian imaginary and the secular gospels of millennial progress through boundless scientific and technological innovation, the triumph of political and economic liberalism, or communism. All of the gods failed.

[56] Wbyn H. Auden, "The Age of Anxiety," *Collected Poems*, Edward Mendelson, ed. (New York: Vintage, 1991) 449: "When the historical process breaks down and armies organize with their embossed debates the ensuing void which they can never consecrate, when necessity is associated with horror and freedom with boredom, then it looks good to the bar business."

[57] William Butler Yeats, "The Second Coming," *Selected Poems*, W. B. Yeats and M. L. Rosenthal, eds. (New York: Collier, 1966) 91.

[58] Paul Kahn, "Freedom, Autonomy, and the Cultural Study of Law," *Cultural Analysis, Cultural Studies, and the Law*, Austin Sarat and Jonathan Simon, eds. (Durham: Duke University Press, 2003) 176.

Introduction

One can go further and suggest that in the United States more than ever the rule of law has the trappings of a civic religion. It is a point that Paul Kahn returns to repeatedly in his writings, notably *The Cultural Study of Law: Reconstructing Legal Scholarship*.[59] As the title of the book suggests, Kahn proposes a cultural study of law, by which he means a critique of law – more specifically, of the rule of law in the United States – in the Kantian sense of an investigation of the conditions necessary for the possibility of experience. Drawing inspiration from Ernst Cassirer's "inquiries into the varieties of symbolic forms,"[60] Kahn views the rule of law as a culturally specific way of structuring experience – of imagining self, world, and the sacred – that both rests upon and cultivates a distinctive form of sensibility and consciousness: "This is just the spirit with which I approach the study of the culture of law's rule, as a distinct symbolic form that constructs one possible world of meaning."[61] The assumption, here, is that life under the rule of law is more than an implied social contract; it is a structure of feeling, a way of being in the world, which reflects a rich, complex, and deeply embedded set of traditions and cultural practices, a way of being that law and humanities scholars seek to understand.

As Kahn observes, there are two reasons why it is difficult to open up legal studies to philosophical critique and to a conceptualization of the study of law as a humanistic discipline. The first is that it means clearing a space in legal studies for research that is not directed toward legal reform, that is, toward "having an impact" on legal practice.[62] The second, related reason is that the traditional, reform-minded conception of legal studies collapses the distinction between its subject (the legal scholar) and its object (the rule of law).[63] That is, it is difficult for legal scholars to step outside of the structures that shape their own legal consciousness and establish the necessary, self-conscious, critical distance. "To achieve such a disciplinary stance with respect to law's rule is particularly difficult... because the study of law is itself a part of the practice of law.... Law professors, for the most part, are not studying law, they are doing law."[64] To be engaged in a practical project of reform is to be part of that which one would study. Again, for Kahn the problem is not that legal scholarship has been too theoretical and disconnected from the practice of law, but rather that legal scholarship has not been theoretical enough – that it has not established enough critical distance between theory and practice.

We are not as free as we may think we are, yet for Kahn the exercise of our critical faculty, which creates the distance necessary for those forms to become objects of

---

[59] Paul Kahn, *The Cultural Study of Law: Reconstructing Legal Scholarship* (Chicago: University of Chicago Press, 2000).

[60] Kahn, "Freedom," 171.

[61] Ibid., 171–2.

[62] Ibid., 154.

[63] Kahn, *The Cultural Study of Law*, 7.

[64] Kahn, "Freedom," 154.

study, is precisely what establishes the ground of a meaningful sense of freedom. In Kahn's view, the exercise of this critical faculty represents a significant risk for us, because it means a willingness to put our identity at stake – to see it as bound to cultural forms and thus deeply contingent and variable. "[I]f the cultural study of law is to be a project of transcendental freedom, rather than another angle on the project of reform, then the beliefs exposed must be our own, and the distance created must be within ourselves.... Without putting the self at risk, there can be no experience of freedom. Philosophy, even in the form of a cultural study of law, need not justify itself at the bar of politics."[65]

It would be understandable to read the claim Kahn makes in this last sentence, about the relationship between a cultural study of law and "the bar of politics," as polemical, that is, as an argument against connecting legal studies to political questions of social justice and legal reform. That is not his intent, however, and he is careful to recognize the overlap between philosophical and political understandings of the significance of legal scholarship, although insisting at the same time that it is vital to create and maintain a disciplinary space for an approach whose azimuth is defined by a capacity for critical distance, not political engagement. Kahn's argument is not that we should not have politically minded or reform-oriented legal scholarship, but that it should not be all that we have – that there should be space enough both for such scholarship and for a disciplinary approach of the kind he explores.

Lest we be misunderstood, we share with Kahn the desire to decenter a narrow instrumentalism as the reason for being of law and humanities work. At the same time, we recognize the worry that his approach might both deify the rule of law and canonize the humanities. We think that it is possible to do work that might march under the banner of law and humanities although thinking of oneself as a critic of the rule of law as well as a neohumanist, a posthumanist, or even an antihumanist scholar. Indeed the contributors to *Law and the Humanities: An Introduction* represent such a diverse array of perspectives, many of which do not comfortably fall within the ambit of Kahn's idealism. They remind us that one can worry as much about the ways in which some humanities scholarship has inscribed particular patterns of advantage/disadvantage, or hidden contingency under a veil of false universalism, and still effectively participate in a scholarly enterprise that examines the ways law is "implicated in the creation of symbols and structures which provide meaning in everyday life."[66]

Overview of the Book

Twenty years after Fiss's contribution to the inaugural issue of the *Yale Journal of Law and the Humanities*, it is appropriate to reconsider the cultural conditions that frame

---

[65] Ibid., 182–3.
[66] "Note from the Editors," vi.

Introduction

the work of law and humanities scholars. Here again we point to the phenomena of globalization, the flowering and current crisis in neoliberalism, the proliferation and consolidation of identity politics, and the reaction to and against terrorism as some of the most important of those cultural conditions. These conditions are explicitly addressed by some of the contributors to *Law and the Humanities: An Introduction*, but they are in the background of all of the work collected here.

Today the breadth of work in the field is such that we can fruitfully identify key areas of inquiry for law and humanities scholars: Where do ideas of justice come from? How is law imagined? What are its linguistic, literary, and culture processes? What are the relevant histories and values embedded in and exemplified by its critical institutional processes? As a result, after a brief examination of several perspectives on the state of the field, *Law and the Humanities: An Introduction* devotes a separate section to chapters that address each of those questions.

Part I: Perspectives on the History and Significance of Scholarship in Law and the Humanities: Three Views

This book begins by taking stock of the major theoretical statements on the origins and cultural implications of law (e.g., Derrida, Benjamin, Bourdieu) as well as the disciplinary histories of scholarship in law and humanities.

The first section begins with Costas Douzinas's overview of the nature of humanist scholarship. Douzinas offers a reading of Roscoe Pound's article "The Humanities in an Absolutist World." Pound believed that the "Humanities is a last stand defence against the imposed ignorance and philistinism which must 'cancel' the past to usher in the new era of consumerism, absolutism, and apathy." Only by studying the humanities can we approach the social sciences with any wisdom. Thus the justification of humanities is deeply political, for in the humanities (the Classics in particular) Pound finds strategies of resistance against catastrophic political turns such as hypercapitalism.

Douzinas then examines two essays, written 65 years after Pound's, which give opposing answers to the question of what is the proper relationship of law and the humanities: Nussbaum's "Cultivating Humanity in Legal Education" and Balkin and Levinson's "Law and the Humanities: An Uneasy Relationship." Douzinas argues that "the birth of the disciplines out of the womb of legal study led to a cognitive and moral impoverishment of legal scholarship and education which have become an entomology of rules, a guidebook to technocratic legalism, a science of the existent and an apology of current policies. Nussbaum has accepted however this poverty of legal education and, against Pound's injunction, sees Humanities as just palliative." Thus, "Nussbaum's defence of the (limited) role of the Humanities in legal education takes . . . a methodological and hermeneutical form. It is not so much the traditional humanities that can improve the moral compass of lawyers but the values they promote. Law should be taught humanistically helping to develop a reflective approach, moral values, and critical reasoning to young lawyers."

Balkin and Levinson abandon Pound's values altogether, Douzinas argues, by rejecting any substantial connection between law and the humanities: They "proclaim the realist, pragmatist, and brutal nature of American legal education and welcome its 'dehumanizing tendency.' Their attack on Pound's and Nussbaum's *bien pensant* humanism is twofold. The belief that great works of art 'convey moral notions' is wrong. In any case, 'law's business is to promote tough mindness rather than moral values."

Despite this disagreement about the contribution of the humanities to law, Douzinas sees similarities in "the ground concept that unites them. This is "humanity," the "human," "human nature:" a family of concepts and institutions that have brought together the exploration of man's civilization, tradition, culture, and values with the age-old attempt to regulate the social bond." But this idea of "humanity" "has been consistently used to separate, distribute, and classify people into rulers, ruled, and excluded."

It is in this common frame of reference between humanism and legal humanism that Douzinas sees the link between humanities and the law: "Modern law re-defined human beings as creatures of will and desire by making rights its building blocks. There can be no positive law with the humanist legal subject, the bearer of rights and duties; there can be no conception of rights without a positive set of laws and institutions that bring the subject into existence and endow it with the patrimony of rights." Recently, the humanist promise of autonomy has receded, and rules and regulations have turned human relations into legal rights. Douzinas concludes, "The pressing moral and political task is [not] the development of delicacy of discernment, the sharpening of hermeneutical aptitude or even moral edification. Adopting from the classics and Roscoe Pound the idea of education as critique of dominant practices which divide, dominate, and oppress, the new Humanities must commit themselves to the re-assertion of principles of truth as unconditional resistance to the bio-political turn of post-political and culture."

This picture of law and humanities as a resistant practice in the legal academy animates Steven Winter's account of some of the important developments in twentieth-century legal thought. During the late eighteenth century, Winter argues, the study of law was transformed from apprenticeship and practical knowledge to a greater focus on conceptual knowledge. Law schools (starting at Harvard) became part of universities, and some legal scholars believed that law could be taught as a science. In the early twentieth century, Legal Realists argued that "to be properly understood, concepts had to be de-hypostatized and resolved into their constitutive activities and processes . . . (and) that the *meaning* of an idea lay in its use; a concept, they maintained, is but a tool for accomplishing a particular end."

Introduction

By the middle of the twentieth century this critique, Winter contends, had been domesticated and incorporated into mainstream legal thought. Nonetheless, the old "legal science" largely lived on. During the 1970s "prominent scholars were using the tools of moral and analytic philosophy to argue against instrumentalism in law and to claim that there is a principled "right answer" to all legal questions. On the left, critical legal studies reinvigorated the realists' argument that legal rules are insufficient to determine outcomes." Twenty years later, critical legal studies had generally run their course although economic and rational approaches had become entrenched in the legal academy. Winter writes, "All of these approaches are essentially technocratic visions that focus on social actors and legal tools – that is, on the linear connection between knowing subjects and the objects of which they are master – as the crucial objects of analysis and study."

Echoing Fiss's contribution to the first issue of the *Yale Journal of Law and the Humanities*, Winter argues that economics is the most reductive, powerful, and self-confident methodology today in legal studies. Although this model is useful for analyzing many areas of social life, it hardly explains everything: "The greater the complexity of the psychological and social phenomena, the more the economic model falls victim to its own reductivism and becomes prone to errors of pre-commitment and misrecognition." The problem, Winter contends, with analytic work, then is not logical but methodological, because this method of reasoning is much too abstracted from social and historical context. As a result, Winter writes, "Although in the contemporary legal academy the lines between analytic philosophy and instrumentalist approaches such as law and economics are sharply drawn," both are reductivist in the same way and both end in authoritarian prescriptions.

Winter contends that law and humanities scholarship emerges as a corrective to these tendencies in legal thought. Winter believes the most important aspect of this field is its insight into the constitutive and contingent character of our communicative practices. Winter says that the specter of contingency seems threatening because it undermines the foundations of our current "fundamentalist" worldview. By fundamentalism he means an assumption of transparency, hierarchy, linearity, and universality concerning human reason and its relation to the world.

The humanist stance, Winter writes, requires the acceptance and revaluation of contingency. It also requires confidence and humility, affirmation and suspicion. Winter concludes, "The promise of law, culture, and humanities scholarship . . . is a disposition both to do away with idols and to listen attentively to our symbols. That is, the distinctive stance of law, culture, and the humanities work is a hermeneutics of suspicion and hope – a critical openness – that simultaneously critiques and affirms the human nature of truth."

The next chapter moves from Winter's sweeping overview of legal thought to a reading of Herman Melville's *Billy Budd* and the film *Death and the Maiden*.

Through this reading Kathryn Abrams develops three narratives of the field of law and the humanities. The first is a narrative of movement, the second of heterogeneity, and the third of continuity.

Of movement, Abrams writes, "The first story accepts at face value the frank disparity of these works. It argues that the movement from *Billy Budd* to *Death and the Maiden* as a paradigmatic text for Law and the Humanities reflects a field in transition. The first phases of this work aimed at humanizing legal decision making through exposure to its depiction in great works of literature; later versions sought to elaborate legal decisions as texts through the theories or analytic strategies that had been applied to literature; more recent work has sought to explore the more diffuse and encompassing world of "legality" by examining diverse cultural products with a range of disciplinary tools."

The agonizing, high-stakes, and difficult decision depicted in *Billy Budd* and the story's equivocal ending served as perfect fodder for analysts seeking to "humanize" the law. Although the story was used to highlight tensions in the application of law, it was not used to unsettle conventional understandings of what law is. Soon, though, these understandings began to change within law and humanities scholarship. Scholars began to treat law *as* literature. Scholarship began to turn away from law's decisional aspects toward its discursive elements. Much scholarship has also moved toward focusing on the cultural as a basis of regulation and analysis, and the subjectivity both of lawmakers and those affected or formed by law.

All of these changes, Abrams writes, explain the legal interest in cultural texts like *Death and the Maiden*: The film's focus on norms of sexuality, vengeance, and violence reflects an interest in the broader scope of legality, as opposed to the creation or imposition of legal decisions or rules. Currently, Abrams writes, "Law and Humanities scholars come to this film not to understand or humanize the operation of the law, but to understand the larger sociocultural environment in which law operates, and how that environment can change."

Of heterogeneity, Abrams suggests that while certain kinds of textual foci or analytic frames or objects emerged earlier in time, "the pattern has been more accretive than successive. In individual works, in specific subgenres, and in the body of scholarship as a whole, one finds many kinds of pluralism or heterogeneity: in the understandings of what constitutes 'law,' in the envisaged relations between law and other social or cultural phenomena, and in disciplinary materials that structure explorations in the field . . . This body of work is distinguished by scholarship which draws on plural analytic frames with plural understandings of its projects." *Billy Budd* for example, has been subject to numerous scholarly interpretations including psychoanalytic and narrative analyses. Film, as well, has invited a number of types of analyses such as comparative analysis between law and film and even film's, constitutive effect on law.

Introduction

Of continuity Abrams writes, "One could also argue that these works, and the scholarship that has addressed them, reveal important continuities within Law and Humanities work, features that distinguish such work from other genres of legal scholarship." Scholarship on *Billy Budd* and *Death and the Maiden*, Abrams argues, reflects a shared assumption about the kinds of texts that have bearing on and can help illuminate law. They also demonstrate a belief that law exists as merely "one kind of influence, discourse, system of power, within a larger field of social and cultural relations."

These efforts in law and humanities may seem unsettling to some, as they do not offer the kind of "practical direction to legal decision-makers that comprises the normative in the minds of mainstream legal scholars." This non conventionality seems today to restrict the appeal of this type of work. But, "This uneasy standoff may prove temporary," Abrams suggests. In her view "descriptions of the embeddedness of the law, and its continuity with other social and cultural practices, do not simply modify our view of the legal domain, they invite us to revise our conventional conceptions of legal normativity."

Part II: Ideas of Justice

The chapters in this section focus on a particular vision of the normative associated with the idea of justice. They examine the meaning of justice as an idea in scholarship on law and the Bible, natural law, positive law, and law and the post modern condition. Law is a moral and ethical achievement, but the values and practices that define justice or shape its pursuit are culturally contingent. Similarly, law depends on traditions of interpretation that determine our expectations of what is possible – and desirable – to say and do. The chapters in this section address, among others, the following questions: How do ideas of justice change over time and under what conditions? What are the principal ideas of justice and what is their genealogy? How does law come into being and what is its impulse or purpose?

Chaya Halberstam helps us understand the different views of the idea of justice that emerge in the Hebrew Bible/Old Testament (HB/OT) and offers an insightful new reading that sees the passionate, often violently vindictive justice enacted by God as rooted in a powerful, reflexive feeling of disgust. She begins by squarely examining the "tired cliché" about the contrast between the ideas of justice manifested in the HB/OT and the vision of justice articulated in the Gospels – the claim that the New Testament marks a paradigm shift, a move away from the HB/OT principle of *lex talionis* (an eye for an eye) and the wrathful, retributive justice of an intemperate God toward a sense of justice founded upon love, mercy, and forgiveness. As she describes, over the ages many Jewish and Christian scholars and commentators have been uneasy with the image of a vengeful God and have tried to attenuate it or reconcile with it the register of the Gospels through various interpretive strategies. One approach develops the metaphor of the marriage between God and Israel and reads the violence of the deity as the abusive behavior of a betrayed husband, enraged by acts of infidelity; his behavior may not be excusable, but it is at least comprehensible in the context of a certain patriarchal tradition and conception of masculinity.

Another approach, by contrast, involves radically depersonalizing the relationship between God and Israel and reading the deity as simply the medium through which justice is dispensed and the universal moral order is maintained. In this account, God's response to Israel's trespasses is automatic, not personal; the retributive justice he enacts is a kind of reflex, not a summary judgment. This view entails a significant adjustment of traditional conceptions of the foundation of morality and justice in the HB/OT, as it moves away from a doctrine of divine retribution and toward something akin to a concept of karma. Halberstam observes that although it is hard to bridge the gap between this depersonalized idea of justice and the personal, covenantal relationship between God and Israel established in the HB/OT, the idea that God's response to perceived violations of that relationship has the automatic quality of a reflex is a significant insight. Halberstam develops this insight and combines it with both scholarly and theoretical accounts of disgust as a response to defilement, physical or moral. She proposes that God experiences the ethical or religious failings of the people of Israel as acts of defilement that provoke a feeling of disgust and a concomitant, violent reflexive response intended to expurgate the moral contaminant. She demonstrates how this view of the etiology of YHWH's retributive violence allows us to make sense of it as at once intensely personal and yet also intelligible as the expression of the cultural logic of defilement and disgust.

Catherine Kellogg helps us turn from the HB/OT to questions of natural and human justice, by examining two readings of Sophocles' *Antigone*: Hegel's nineteenth-century interpretation and Lacan's twentieth-century treatment: "The distinctive difference," Kellogg writes, "between the nineteenth- and twentieth-century readings is the discovery of the unconscious, and I make use of this difference to point to the ways that this 'discovery' does not limit itself to how we read *Antigone*, but also bears directly on the 'tradition' of debate about natural justice."

Kellogg notes, "For Hegel, the 'truth of both the law of the state and the law of the gods rests in their 'recognition' of each other. . . . The peril inherent in this process is made clear in the Greek myth: both Antigone and Creon remain faithful to only one of these laws." Alternately, for Lacan, "Antigone's desire – and her place within the symbolic order of her community – does not uphold the natural law of duty to family, but rather marks the *limit* of 'natural' insofar as she violates the limit of the symbolic order of the city, and indeed, of the human." Hegel reads in *Antigone* the conflict between human and natural laws, but Lacan reads in *Antigone* the limits of the 'natural' in terms of pleasure.

Introduction

Unlike Oedipus who resists or denies the guilt that fate has doled out to him, Antigone "takes it on directly through a death driven desire," the most unnatural desire of all. Kellogg points out that Antigone's invocation of natural justice makes her appear unnaturally *excessive* in her desire for death. Kellogg notes, "This brings us back to the question at stake here: if the so-called new natural law theory is characterized by an argument that emphasizes the objective *naturalness* of morality, such that it seems possible to argue about objectively determinable 'crimes' against the human, what might psychoanalysis be able to tell us about the *inhumanity* that characterizes that human, which can also (maybe) be seen as 'natural'?"

Kellogg then turns to the history of natural law theory, summarizing its development from the seventeenth century to today. Most importantly, Kellogg focuses on Kant and Freud. Although she admits Kant is not a natural law theorist, he discussed the "meaning and classification of natural law from a phenomenological point of view." Kant's categorical imperative (the so-called moral law) is what Freud calls the superego: "Thus, if, as Freud asserted, the concept of ethics suffers a 'blow of disillusionment' at the hands of psychoanalysis, the path for this blow was first prepared by Kant...The crucial step between Kant's ethical theory and psychoanalysis involved taking desire – the very thing excluded from the traditional field of ethics – and turning it into the *only* legitimate territory for ethics."

Lacan proposes another formulation: "On his account, with the introduction of desire into the moral field, the idea of a natural connection between law and the good reaches an impasse. This is what his reading of the *Antigone* sought to highlight." Antigone's unnatural desire is human and yet not. She represents a denaturalization of desire that mirrors our contemporary moral predicament.

Kellogg turns back to *Oedipus Rex* arguing, "In crudely psychoanalytic terms, Oedipus had no Oedipus complex, but he created it for subsequent generations. Thus, Oedipus sets in motion the 'unwritten law' that Antigone will later represent. Oedipus then, is in fact, the *founder* of a new order, but is not part of it himself. The source of the *natural* law to which the natural law tradition turns, then, is in the first place the most *un*natural of crimes for which no one strictly speaking can be held to account." This explains why psychoanalysis has posed such a problem for modern Western philosophy because "The ability to answer for oneself, the ability to know what one means, the ability to be master of oneself, freely and autonomously, means something entirely different in the face of 'discovery' of the unconscious. This is the challenge that ideas of natural law and justice pose today; how to account for what appears inhuman and unnatural in the human. This is a challenge that has not yet been met by contemporary natural law theory, which refuses this principle."

Matthew Noah Smith's chapter examines Anglo-American theories of justice that, he says, consist of nonutilitarian allocative principles: "that is, principles governing, to put it as broadly as possible, who gets how much of what." Within this broad framework Smith provides an overview of four different forms of justice, and attempts to explicate different ideas of justice in terms of narrative form: "I shall argue that, on the one hand, two forms of justice – retributive and corrective – embody the character-driven story (CDS) form, whereas another form of justice – distributive justice – embodies a different narrative form, namely what we might call the utopian form."

A CDS, he says, has a beginning, a middle, and an end, as well as characters who are generally distinct from the narrator. The utopian form does not require characters, only a narrator, and usually "articulate[s] distinct spaces that are geographically related" rather than being chronologically, logically, or characterologically related. Smith uses stories as allegories for different forms of justice, as Plato does in *The Republic*.

The first form of justice Smith discusses is retributive justice. The aim of retributive justice is to bring an end to the "course of events instigated by the commission of a crime." Thus, retributive justice is a character driven story (involving the wrongdoer and the wronged) with a beginning (commission of a crime), middle (determination of guilt), and an end (punishment). Also, the progression of events involved in retributive justice is critical because the punishment must always occur *after* the transgression. Retributive justice, Smith writes, is not surprisingly the most commonly played out storyline in police and courtroom dramas.

The second form of justice that Smith examines is corrective justice, which is as follows: "As a matter of corrective justice, if A is *outcome responsible* for a harm suffered by B, then A owes a duty of repair to B." This notion of responsibility for the end result is meant to "cast a wider net than the [retributive] notion of moral blameworthiness." The backward-looking format of corrective justice (as well as its character-driven chronology) also makes it amenable to the CDS. Smith notes that in corrective justice we also find another "hallmark of CDS, namely the presumption of certain conditions that constitute the space within which the drama of the harm, the claim for repair, and then the repair unfolds. In the case of corrective justice, the presumed and unchangeable condition is the initial allocation of goods. That is, corrective justice operates over entitlements under the presupposition that they are as they ought to be, and does not offer prescriptions on how entitlements ought to be distributed from the get-go."

Smith next turns to distributive justice, which governs the distribution of goods across a unified population. Smith writes, "There is . . . a kind of anonymity in distributive justice: It immediately shapes the lives of all who are members of a society and not simply those who have particular histories." This type of justice embodies a system of principles for a whole community and is not a framework for virtuous individuals: "Thus, there is both a distinctively un-Manichean character to principles of distributive justice – in the sense that there is no Evil threatening the Good, but instead regular humans living morally nuanced lives – and a very 'scientific' character to distributive justice – in the sense that institutional technology is what we rely upon in order to create the just order."

Introduction 27

Next, Smith discusses transitional justice, the problem of responding to totalitarian regimes and genocide. In the wake of great atrocity, the individualized retributive or corrective justice are not systematic enough to bring about reconciliation. The problem with a system of transitional justice is that, "repairing wrongs and compensating losses can, when the background allocation is deeply unjust, involve wronging others in deeply profound ways, thereby perpetuating the cycle of injustice. Thus, although it is natural to associate transitional justice with the various trials and purges that have erupted in response to totalitarian and murderous upheavals, it is hard to see how such practices, however legalistic, amount to forms of *justice*."

In many ways transitional justice, though it cries out for personalized CDS form, follows the utopian narrative form because "the narrative required is not a temporal one that has a closure as its aim, but instead the god's-eye, static narrative characteristic of distributive justice." Thus, "on the one hand we understand the warranted response [to atrocity] in terms of a traditional CDS, although on the other hand we understand the warranted response as a utopian project." To Smith, this newest form of justice is – as Kellogg writes – paradoxical in its logic/form and also, although in a different way, represents the struggle to deal with that which appears unnatural and inhuman in the human condition.

In the final chapter in this section, Peter Goodrich examines the limited yet critical impact of postmodernism on law. Using an architectural metaphor, Goodrich argues that the postmodern is a "new form of bricolage or building technique; it expresses a visceral sense of no longer feeling at 'home'; it questions 'foundations'; challenges the 'monumental' character of the modern tradition; lays bare the myth of 'foundations'; and obliterates all sense of preordained system and structure."

Goodrich focuses the first section of his chapter on postmodern architecture, writing, "If modernism privileged the building over its inhabitants, the postmodern resistance aimed to take the building back, to take responsibility for the inhabitants and to pay attention to the plethora and plenitude of what and who is there." Goodrich continues, "the postmodern signals a turn to interpretation – to rhetoric and semiotics – and to difference understood as an ethics of responsibility." This invocation of ethics brings Goodrich to the question of postmodern justice.

Goodrich proceeds by comparing George Wither's frontispiece to his *Collection of Emblemes* (1635) and Hobbes, frontispiece to *Leviathan* (1651). The former is an example of premodern justice and the latter as an example of modern justice. In Wither's frontispiece, "There is ... one obvious and intriguing feature to the emblem. It shows a realm that is vastly populous, teeming with people, a veritable theatre of social scenes and human endeavors." Of Hobbes' frontispiece he writes, "The image is both striking and somewhat opaque. The sovereign rises up and dominates the landscape, his body populous and vast, whereas the kingdom, the realm surveyed, consists only of neatly placed villages, prominent churches and then at the front and perspective point the well-ordered, indeed thoroughly regimented, geometrically proportioned city ... In this interpretation, the physical body is of itself nothing, a mere and mortal carapace, a ghostly form encrypting an even more ghostly soul. Be that as it may, the polity is physically empty of people because the physicality of the body is not only unimportant but in fact it is an impediment to reason and to faith alike." Only the linear and geometrically precise rows of buildings remain.

Goodrich writes that it is against this structural, symmetrical, and linear concept of modern law that postmodernists rebelled. Crucial to the articulation of postmodern justice, Goodrich notes, was Derrida's 1989 lecture on deconstruction and the possibility of justice. The 1970s and 1980s had seen early postmodern legal scholars challenge the law but Derrida "reformulated this generically negative passion into the positive question and questioning of justice." In his lecture, Derrida called for "an ethics of responsibility, for a political accounting of legal scholarship and he spelled out, in his slow and tentative style, the desideratum of not simply observing from 'the monadic or monastic ivory tower that in any case never was' but intervening in the contemporary institutions of the 'cité, the polis . . . the world.'" This meant a call for pluralism, expansion, and attention to difference (sexual, racial, political, etc.). What distinguished Derrida's lecture, Goodrich writes, is that he took justice seriously, in a strongly premodern sense of justice "as particularity, as indulgence, meaning the giving of time and attention to those who come before the law."

In much the same way that Venturi looked at the surface of buildings to read what was there, postmodern justice demands that attention be turned away from edifice and structure to the diverse inhabitants of a built space. Postmodern justice thus seeks to give a social presence and voice "to those whom the modern building or here modern law has turned aside."[67] Goodrich writes, "Postmodern justice rendered law differently, it added a plaster, a new surface, as well as a new attention to surfaces, to the dogmatic tradition, to the theory of law as it was when postmodernism arrived." Postmodern justice, Goodrich concludes, was never meant as a revolutionary attempt to get rid of law. Instead, "postmodern justice refers to an ethical turn, a demand for responsibility in the form initially of a politics of scholarship."

Part III: Imagining the Law

Part III poses the question of how culture imagines law, and it explores the ways that a cultural vision of law compares with the historical and ethical self-image promoted in and by the legal profession. "Culture" here means two things: first, the full range of phenomena that informs but is nevertheless distinguishable from the legal profession itself (for example, the different geographical, historical, political,

---

[67] In a sense, postmodern justice also goes beyond Smith's utopian justice because it is no longer anonymous but is character driven. Postmodern justice does not fit Smith's CDS story form either because there is no distinct beginning, middle, and end. It, like transitional justice, is somewhere in between these two narrative structures.

Introduction

and aesthetic conditions that at any given time provide a context for the law, or the set of overarching questions and values that preponderate at any given moment so as to define its character in a general way). A cultural vision of law is therefore one that can contextualize, explain, and comment upon the image of law that emerges when law is divorced from culture and reconstituted as an independent profession. Second, "culture" refers specifically to the imaginative renderings – both popular and "aesthetic" – of legal themes, practices, and professionals that are the foundation of most people's understanding and expectations of their legal system.

"Imagining the Law: The Novel" begins with Susan Sage Heinzelman's reflection on the way the generic development of the novel – that mainstay of the law and literature movement that, as our discussion of White and West has shown, has provided the most continuous expression of a humanistic study of law – has historically called forth assumptions about and associations with law. Organizing her chapter around four distinct phases in the history of the novel and the history of novel criticism (from the disinterested rationalism of the eighteenth century to the skepticism and playfulness of twentieth-century postmodernism), Heinzelman tracks formal and aesthetic tensions within the genre itself alongside literary critical accounts of its material, ideological, and aesthetic standing in relation to the structures and processes of law.

Heinzelman is careful to situate her critical history as much as she does her discussion of representative works by Defoe, Austen, Dickens, and Nabokov and suggests, "The literary critical account of the relationship between the novel and the law has helped to shape a particular version of what constitutes the legal order and the legal subject." In other words, literary criticism of the novel, ranging from Ian Watt's classic analogy of the middle-class reader and a jury member at trial to Foucaultian treatments of the surveilled private reader, has developed a version of law fully as much as it has analyzed the novel. As a result, reading literature and literary history together can produce an understanding of what it means to conceive of oneself as a legal subject as well as contribute to our perception of the contours of legal order.

More particularly, Heinzelman draws our attention to the sometimes explicit and frequently implicit effects of sex and class on received accounts of the novel and the law. There can be no doubt that sex and class have influenced the specific forms the novel has taken at specific points in time, nor that their influence is equally prevalent in jurisprudence and legal procedure, yet it is worth reiterating that sex and class necessarily influence how the novel has depicted the law. Where literary and legal forms emerge within the same cultural configurations of power, their parallel histories can nevertheless reveal asymmetries in their depiction and ordering of that world. For example, to conceive of the novel as Ian Watt does – that is, as a specifically masculine, realist, English, bourgeois commodity directed toward a similarly defined, "judicious" readership – is to forget, she reminds us, the parallel history of the equally popular romance and the sentimental literature associated with women. By restoring this history, Heinzelman allows us to see two origins of the novel, or the novel as it would have appeared to nineteenth-century writers and readers. Against Watt's privileging of a manly English realism that, like law, depicted marriage as contract, Heinzelman's history of the romance and the marriage plot shows that where nineteenth-century law adhered to this contractual view of marriage, the novel sentimentalized it, firmly linking "moral obligations and expectations" to legal ones. By looking at theory and practice in both domains – the genre and literary criticism, legal practice and jurisprudence – and focusing on *Moll Flanders, Pride and Prejudice, Bleak House,* and *Lolita,* Heinzelman traces the continuities and disjunctions between the literary and legal, between the way configurations of power based on sex and class influenced the role the novel could play in supporting or challenging the legal status quo.

With Richard K. Sherwin's chapter, "Imagining Law as Film," we move from the literary and the linguistic to the visual. Sherwin offers an overview of the burgeoning "law and film" movement and, in particular, of the way it is being combined with attention to new media (e.g., the Internet, multiperson gaming, computer simulations, television programming) and pointing toward a broader rubric, "visual legal studies."

As he notes, the dominant approaches in law and film studies can usefully be understood as falling into one of two categories (which parallel a similar pattern in law and literature studies): law in film and law as film. The latter is undoubtedly the more epistemologically daring of the two, and yet, as Sherwin's account makes plain, a considerable amount of law and film scholarship focuses on the former, and for good reason. Filmic representations of law, legal procedure, and scenes of justice or injustice can be a useful resource for taking the measure of law's justice, notably (but not only) with respect to the experiences of people who are marginalized or disenfranchised by the dominant culture and the legal system. The heuristic value works in both directions. That is, film is valuable not only because it can hold up a mirror to justice, but also, no less saliently, because in our age film and other visual media are such an ineluctable, constitutive dimension of the sensibility that informs popular conceptions of how law works or does not work, and of the kind of justice that is available. If as scholars, teachers, and legal actors we care about law, we need to be conversant in the language, conventions, and popular forms of film and visual media, because these often go a long way toward determining how the rule of law is imagined and experienced.

As a practical matter, a compelling case can be made that the training of lawyers should equip them with the rhetorical skills both to use visual media effectively and, equally important, to challenge or contest their presence in the courtroom. As Sherwin writes, "[u]nderstanding how visual representations are made and construed, how they generate meaning and move the will of the viewer – whether on the basis of explicit or implicit reasons, or on the strength of largely unconscious mental

Introduction 31

associations, moods, memories, and feelings – has now become an inescapable part of what it means to practice, teach, and theorize law in the digital age of audiovisual representation."

Broader epistemological, ontological, and ethical issues arise from a concern that even as the visual displaces the linguistic and offers the feeling of unmediated contact with reality, this feeling of immediacy may be coming at the price of a fraying of our sense of the real and, with it, the possibility of meaningful justice. On one level, as the domains of law and popular culture merge in the cultural imagination through the influence of film and television programs, there is reason to be mindful of what Sherwin, echoing the political scientist Douglas Reed, describes as "the (con-)fusion of law, politics, and the entertainment industry" – what Reed dubs "the juridico-entertainment complex" – for it "poses a significant risk of skewing the policymaking and governing process." On another level, the concern is that if it is true that in our time "the world itself has become a picture," as law migrates to the screen it "exposes itself to new ethical and ontological possibilities as well as uncertainties."

Relatedly, "[i]f there is nothing to constrain the monadic will to command and control the flow of digital information on the screen, in whatever form it may take, how does the self-absorbed subject decenter itself sufficiently to identify with the plight of others? Without the capacity for such self-transcending responsiveness to (and responsibility for) others, what then becomes of justice?" These are some of the concerns that Sherwin raises that speak to the need for a multi-leveled approach to the relationship between law and visual media, and to the contribution that the interpretive humanities can make to that project.

In her chapter on "Law and Television," Susanna Lee builds upon Sherwin's call for a field of visual legal studies by offering, through a reading of two long-running, law-oriented American television programs – *Law and Order* and *Cops* – an exploration of the so-called "*CSI* effect." (*CSI* is a more recent television program in the same genre.) She cites Max Houck's definition: "The *CSI* effect is basically the perception of the near-infallibility of forensic science in response to the TV show." Lee notes, "[w]hat is interesting about the *CSI* effect is not so much that television shows like *CSI* have altered public perception of the way the law does (or should) work, but that the step from the role of television spectator into the role of juror should seem so natural in the first place." She suggests that the explanation for this intriguing phenomenon lies "with the ways in which law on television interpolates the viewer: at once as singular witness, and also as a potential stand-in for a crucial enforcer."

As she explains, this phenomenon owes much to features that are peculiar to television alone and that distinguish it, notably, from film:

> For one, television literally comes into the home, which film does not do, or at least, does not do in its original form. This entry into the home breeds familiarity, or rather the illusion of familiarity. Furthermore, television shows

banality, mundane daily life, and the domestic sphere. It is possible for a program to run for years, for instance, with no other set than the characters' living room and kitchen. Along with the domestic scenes, we have the fact that television operates on a much smaller scale than movies.

She adds that there are two further features of television "that bring television viewership in line with legal subjectivity." The first is the fact that television programming can be recorded by the viewer, through devices such as a TiVo – a technology that has the effect of stripping any sense of the special significance of the time or place when one might view a show: that is, we now have "spectatorship on demand." For Lee, these features account not simply for why "television conventions (domestic forum, viewer participation, short form, repetition) have paved the way for juries/viewers to expect the same combination of drama and resolution in actual legal proceedings," but also for the perhaps more intriguing question of why television conventions take root in the first place? As she puts it, "[w]hy do viewers care, not just enough to watch the program, but to absorb its conventions and (in the case of the *CSI* effect) take them on the road?" It is because the relationship between television and law is "symbiotic."

Understood in this light, the *CSI* effect is the name for a pattern whereby viewers, when they become legal actors, interpret the procedural performance of law in terms of the conventions of television programming not so much because they have been passively influenced by television but rather, more actively (if still unselfconsciously), because the form-giving conventions of television satisfy a number of yearnings, chief among them a yearning for reality, such as it is, to *have* a reassuringly familiar, orderly narrative form – a form in which we, as legal actors, figure as effective characters.

Lee contends, "[b]y analyzing television representations of law, we can understand what viewers believe the law to be, want the law to be, and what the law in fact *is*." Put differently, it may well be that the plot of "reality TV" television programming marks a loss of fidelity to the actual legal story in question, but to insist on the gap between the law and the cultural life of the law (e.g., its narratological representation on television) is to miss or underestimate the degree to which the law itself already encodes a yearning to create a reality that would reflect certain socially agreed upon conventions – in this case, the conventions of realist fiction.

Law's relationship to art – to its creation, its production, and dissemination, its restriction, as well as to commercial and contractual agreements about art works – is as multiform and complex as the category of art itself. Acknowledging that there is no discrete body of law that governs art (and, consequently, that "as a field of study" art law appears "haphazard and incoherent"), Christine Haight Farley defines art law instead as "the survey of legal issues raised by art, artists, and the art world." In her chapter, the last in our section, "Imagining the Law: Art" she organizes and surveys

Introduction

33

the central themes that have occupied scholars over the last thirty years: the law as art, the law of art, the law of creativity, and the collision of art and law. Noting, however, that much of this work is descriptive (i.e., "not theoretically based"), Farley seeks to place specific instances of "what happens to art in various areas of law" in relation to "larger phenomena in law." As she observes, "we imbue art works and cultural objects with our values and aspirations . . . [and] reflect onto art objects fundamental attitudes about culture and society." In light of art's fetishistic potential and the symbolic, cultural capital it conveys, any legal dispute about art usually evokes a plea for "special legal rules" or "special approaches" that makes visible the ubiquitous and theretofore immanent conviction that "art occupies a different and unique space in our society." Opening with the recent case *Nussenzweig v diCorcia* (2006) – in which a photographer's secretly captured images were held not to be an invasion of their subjects' privacy, to be art – Farley's chapter points the way toward a study of law in its relationship to creative, cultural practices, particularly to the notion of aesthetic judgment in the domains of art and law.

Law typically works to promote and protect, rather than to impede, artistic creation on the logic that art is a social good; the more of it there is, the better. As previously suggested, questions about art's role in the creation of culture, as well as the rights of the artist, frequently enter the legal domain for their answers, even though art education is no requirement of a law degree. In cases of the illegal trade of art treasures, for example, the courts have had to decide whether art constitutes a specific cultural heritage or a broader, human achievement. Assumptions that art is a crucial component of a particular culture and hence of its heritage (the "cultural nationalist" position) run afoul both of opposing internationalist claims that art is a shared human achievement and should be available to as many people as possible, as well as the economic interests of private individuals who view art as a tradeable commodity that should be subject to the free market just as any other good would be. Like the debates over cultural property, controversies in intellectual property, although they focus on the individual artist, are similarly bound up with creative and economic interests that reveal fundamental inconsistencies between law's stated mission to incent the production of art, thereby improving the common weal, and its outmoded "creativity threshold," which works to restrict innovation, for instance, in its response to conceptual or appropriation art. Here, the legal understanding of creativity, disengaged as it is from changing aesthetic theories, undermines the court's laudable willingness to promote it.

In these specific skirmishes between artists and judges over definitions of creativity, Farley sees a potential and much broader "collision" between art and law based on their (ostensibly) fundamentally different cultural functions. Problematizing the sometimes overly crude perception of art as radically transformative and law as obdurately resistant to change, she explains that both positions nonetheless follow from a definitional question that in law is rarely explicitly addressed: What is art? In spite of the court's assurances of objectivity, Farley contends that judges "intuitively" apply private ideas about aesthetics when they should "take up the debate about what constitutes art consciously and openly and abandon their nominal adherence to neutrality and nonsubjectivism." If legal scholars should "better use art historical interpretive theories," Farley concludes that art historians should also engage more critically with law, but opportunities exist for both groups of scholars to become more attentive to the relationship between law and culture, to the changes in law wrought by art's critique and to the changes in artistic practice handed down in law's aesthetic judgments.

Part IV: Linguistic, Literary, and Cultural Processes in Law

Theorists of law and literature have established the fundamentally linguistic nature both of law and literature and their shared ability to reflect and create reality through language. This section therefore considers forms of language and their various functions (e.g., constitutive, persuasive, expository, narrative, interpretive, etc.), as well as the disjunctions between the uses to which language is put – its goals – and the ability of the linguistic medium to achieve them. Here, for example, the ability of the black letter to convey one meaning only and forever – to achieve both transparency and permanence through language – can conflict with the spirit of the law, with the intentions of the writer, as well as with the interpretive frameworks governing its reception for the present and for posterity. Although the instability of language can create the problem of preserving meaning over time, the gaps created by history have their analogue in those created by the attempt to translate meaning from one language to another (a problem for international law), from one discourse to another (from law to other disciplines), and from one constituency to another (interpretive communities). The problem of language notwithstanding, language is our chief – albeit not exclusive – means of communication. The power of rhetoric and the appeal of narrative are integral parts of the way we conceptualize, organize, historicize, and communicate ideas about the world and our place in it.

Penelope Pether opens her chapter on "Language" with the story of her participation in a live-client clinical education project leading up to and following the asylum hearing of a family of detainees. Her account of the experience or, as she calls it, her "war story," introduces a host of "culturally resonant and significant signifiers, tropes, and narratives" – among them "family," "shelter," "aliens," "undocumented," "Middle Eastern," "suspect" – in play in the various legal, academic, and cultural venues that were its setting. Acknowledging that her story – and indeed the very telling of it – may raise skepticism about the place of stories in legal scholarship, she concedes that the application of linguistics methodologies (e.g., those of "linguistic humanities and/or critical linguistic human sciences") to any discipline of study or professional practice will produce valuable insights into how language shapes personhood; in

Introduction

this respect, law is no more available to or significantly marked out for this kind of inquiry than any other "practices of subject formation." Even allowing for a unique relationship between law and language, for the widely held view that legal "institutions, discourses, and texts" do in fact call more strongly for linguistic analysis and do yield more significant insights than may be garnered from other "language ands," Pether nonetheless argues that existing law and language scholarship would benefit from closer engagement with language and discourse theory, including semiotics and linguistic philosophy. As she puts it, the main opportunity for further work lies in the "interrelationships between theories of language, of subject formation, and of law."

Pether's history of law and language scholarship begins with the liberal humanist project of James Boyd White, which, for her, adumbrates but one kind of subjectivity (or, at least, that assumes an achievable commonality among all subjects) that remains to be fleshed out by phenomenological and discourse-oriented theories. Although taking a radically different approach, instrumentalist accounts of legal language rendered by linguists and social scientists – those informing jury instruction reform projects, for example, which mistakenly assume that clearer instructions will mitigate the power of the competing "cultural stories" that every juror brings with her and every set of instructions encodes – would benefit from a similarly revised approach. Outlining the methodological, "superficial split between applied and theoretical work" in this area of law and language scholarship, Pether mindfully directs us away from taxonomical, formal approaches toward more inquisitive, philosophical critiques both of jurisprudence and language such as those exemplified in the work of Marianne Constable, Drucilla Cornell, and the late Robert Cover.

Pether's advocacy of the merits of theory is predicated, however, on a commitment to politics and practice, not their division. Her chapter advocates a self-aware, theoretically informed scholarship and legal practice that examines not only what law's subjects say but also how they become communicative subjects. Pether concludes with a reminder that whether reform-oriented or invested in critical-theoretical readings of law, "both critique and change require subjects"; thus, law and language scholarship must turn its eye inward, examine the "gap" in its own make up, and more fully "account for subjects, and thus for agency and cultural reproduction and change."

Francis J. Mootz's chapter focuses on what is arguably the core common denominator across the domains of the humanities and legal studies, the question of interpretation – a subject that has had a predictably complex and multifaceted history in the Anglo-American legal tradition and that is of enduring interest and concern. He outlines four theoretical currents within this tradition and considers their respective advantages and disadvantages for the practical work of interpretation and legal judgment: the Natural Law tradition, analytical legal positivism, the view of legal texts as communicative events, and the "hermeneutic turn."

With respect to the first of these, Mootz suggests that natural law, "[i]n its most dogmatic form," is not primarily concerned with interpretive practice as much as with establishing some manner of ontological claim." This concern with a "preinterpretive reality" is out of step with the interests of the majority of today's legal theorists, who "have rejected natural law foundations and adopted some version of legal positivism, in which law is a textual communication that must be interpreted." Nonetheless, as Mootz makes plain, natural law theories "cast a long shadow," especially with respect to questions regarding the moral and ethical underpinning of constitutional law.

Next, Mootz turns to analytical legal positivism, which, as he indicates, secured its standing, in the 1950s, through the work of H. L. A. Hart. "Stated succinctly, Hart assumed that language has core meanings that can be applied to situations without difficulty or need for active efforts of interpretation, but in difficult cases on the fringe the meaning of a governing phrase must be interpreted and, after a point, simply would be exhausted." Mootz observes, "[l]egal positivists following Hart generally remain agnostic about theoretical debates concerning the genuine goal of interpretation, focusing instead on how the law works in practice."

Whereas analytical legal positivists "caution against the urge to theorize interpretive practices in law rather than tending to those practices," many legal scholars and theorists have worked against the grain of this "agnosticism" and "debated the proper manner of interpreting legal texts in the shadow of a single proposition: that legal texts are communicative events that should be interpreted in light of this function by uncovering a meaning that exists prior to interpretation." This approach – sometimes called "originalism" – is arguably the most well-established and dynamic one in American legal studies.

As Mooz indicates, "originalism" has two primary variations: "intentionalism" – which proceeds from the assumption that "the text means precisely what its drafters intended to communicate" and "claims the virtue of identifying a univocal meaning for all legal rules, even if that meaning is not always easy to determine" – and "textualism" or "new originalism," which shifts attention away from the genesis of legal texts and toward their reception – and which, according to Mootz, "has spread across the legal academy like a prairie fire."

As Mootz indicates, analytical legal positivism and the various forms of "originalism" share "the idea that legal interpretation is founded on communication in a text that precedes interpretation"; this premise, which reflects the Anglo-American philosophical tradition, "has been challenged by contemporary European philosophers working in philosophical hermeneutics, semiotics, and deconstruction." With the work of hermeneutical thinkers such as Heidegger and Gadamer as their touchstone, legal scholars who embrace this perspective call for us to view legal practice as "an argumentative and creative activity in which invention plays the primary role rather than discovery." At bottom, the hermeneutical perspective is not only an

Introduction

epistemological claim about the phenomenological relationship between subject and object – that is, a rejection of the idea "that a reader confronts a text like a free standing object that has an objective meaning prior to the interpretive event" – but a philosophical account of the "judicial virtues" that the act of interpreting legal texts demands of us.

Throughout the chapter, Mootz balances his overview of these principal approaches to interpretation with a keen sense of the limitations of theory. He is mindful to return to and provide substantive accounts of the nexus between theory and practice – in contract law, statutory law, and constitutional law – that is, of what the work of interpretation actually looks like in practice and, more specifically, of how the particular contours of actual legal cases tend to undo, if not embarrass, even the most principled commitment to a single interpretive framework. As Mootz makes clear, interpretation will remain an ineluctable concern, especially in constitutional democracies, not only because of the challenge inherent in applying general rules or principles to particular cases, but, more vexingly, because of a tension at the heart of the idea of the rule of law: on the one hand, to parse James Madison, the rule of law means government by laws, not people; on the other hand, those laws, to be effectuated, call for interpretation and judgment *by* people – judges. In one form or another, all of the approaches to the interpretation of legal texts that Mootz reviews are mindful that "every construction has the potential to undermine the rule of law."

In her chapter, "Narrative and Rhetoric," Ravit Reichman considers the emergence and recent development of literary approaches to legal scholarship, which draw upon the classical roots of law as a rhetorical practice but reinvest that practice with a distinctly modern set of concerns. To reach back to the Ancient Greeks, for instance, means more than simply rehearsing the belief in law as the art of persuasion. Rather, as scholars like James Boyd White propose, it demands that we think critically about the sorts of communities that we are being persuaded to imagine, join, or reject. It means, too, to accept (and encourage) the mutability of such communities, founded as they are on dialogue and revision rather than unassailable dogma or static texts.

Reichman explains that the work that has been built on this renewed commitment to rhetoric in law has issued from at least two divergent positions: Although some critics maintain that rhetorical (that is, literary) parsing of law does not (or should not) alter our legal world, others hold that attention to rhetoric can and should give way to legal change by exposing and revising our latent assumptions. For the proponents of legal change through literary strategies – Critical Legal Studies and Critical Race Theory present vivid examples of this stance – what needs to be laid bare is how juridical language obscures its own agency, presenting itself as neutral and inevitable rather than forceful and world creating. Critics turn to the rhetoric of legal and literary texts (and more broadly, to any narrative that figures in the wider canvas of culture) to discover contingencies and exigencies of jurisprudence;

to imagine possibilities for justice beyond the law; and to understand the desires that enter into the experiences of legal subjects. More recently, this nonreformist approach has turned to silence in law as a powerful rhetorical instance of justice, a potent moment that can be construed neither as wholly act or omission, but as a site where we can refigure – or in some cases, refuse – our relationship to law.

To illustrate one key instance of the tightly knit relationship among rhetoric, narrative, and the law, Reichman offers a reading of a particularly painful moment of American legal history: the 1896 Supreme Court opinion *Plessy v. Ferguson*, which upheld the separate-but-equal doctrine that formalized racism until it was overturned almost sixty years later by *Brown v. Board of Education*. She reads *Plessy* alongside a contemporaneous work of fiction, Robert Louis Stevenson's *Dr. Jekyll and Mr. Hyde*, to suggest what rhetorical analysis might offer to the larger cultural study of law. In her view, on its best day such study dwells less on thematic content (like the fact that Stevenson's story begins with a lawyer's perspective) and emphasizes instead those formal properties that shed light on underlying expectations, anxieties and frustrations involved in "doing justice." As she suggests, the pairing of these two narratives also implies that our recognition of these expectations and anxieties, begins in seeing them differently: What the literary text delivers, in other words, is precisely what the Supreme Court seems to lack (and what it demands of its plaintiff) in *Plessy*.

With Harriet Murav's chapter, we turn our attention from narrative and rhetoric to the idea of "Justice as Translation," both as a practical concern in the life of law and, on a more conceptual and metaphorical level, as a way of describing some of the possibilities and challenges of law as a language of justice. Drawing inspiration from post-colonial studies and from French poststructuralist philosophy – specifically, the work of Derrida and of Lyotard – she organizes her chapter around a critique of James Boyd White's *Justice as Translation*. For White, translation *is* the work of law, at every procedural and institutional level: "White argues there is no legal action without translation: 'at the center of the law is the activity of translation'... The lawyer and her client, the lawyer explicating expert testimony before the jury, the officer and a suspect, the judge interpreting a legal opinion, and the heads of state negotiating a treaty – all are engaged in transferring meaning from one type of language to another."

In White's view, "Appreciating justice as translation offers enhanced possibilities for open-endedness and intersubjectivity among individuals and peoples." As Murav observes, the process of resolving disputes through litigation is in many respects the crux and paradigmatic example of this view of the potentialities for justice that open up through translation into the language of law. "To have their day in court," she writes, "both parties in a legal dispute are compelled to speak this language" – the language of law – a language that is "not their own." She calls our attention to the fact that "[White] finds much to praise in this compulsion, specifically, "that the

Introduction

compulsion imposed on both parties in a dispute to speak in a language not their own advances the possibility of justice."

Murav is skeptical of this optimistic view of law as a forum for translating grievances into a language that is more abstract, universal, and dispassionate and of thus making possible a movement toward resolution, if not indeed mutual understanding and reconciliation. Her skepticism has several dimensions. First, she feels that White's conception of the self and its language – for instance, his implied sense of the structure and implications of both the first person singular and plural – is too stable, univocal, and "monolithic." If for White the subject who speaks the language of the law "creates a character, a version of the self," for Murav, a close reader of Derrida, that view of the self is still too unitary, too confident in the self's transparency to itself and its motives.

Second, White recognizes but undervalues the loss of fidelity that accompanies the attempt to apply a general, abstract legal rule or system to the contours of a singular case and a particular body. In her account of Derrida's reading of *The Merchant of Venice*, Murav asserts that "[j]ustice and translation demand an impossible fidelity." White and Derrida may agree that law is fundamentally an act of translation, but their views of the consequences of translation in law are diametrically opposed.

White's view of the potential for justice through translation into the language of law does not, Murav suggests, make visible what Lyotard calls "the differend" – "the unstable state and instance of language wherein something must be able to be put into phrases yet cannot be." Put differently, it is the gap that opens up when the language of one of the parties in a legal dispute – typically that of a party seeking redress for unjust suffering – is not legible or recognized *as* a language by the law. For an example of this, Murav turns to Alisoun Neville's analysis of an Australian case, *Cubillo v. Commonwealth*, in which two aboriginal plaintiffs "claimed damages for loss of cultural and other aspects of Aboriginal life and loss of rights under the *Aboriginal Land Rights (Northern Territory) Act 1976*" that resulted from their forcible removal when they were children. In this case, as in many other similar child-removal cases in Australia, the plaintiffs "could not show that they suffered a wrong."

The Australian court, however well intentioned, would never be able to bridge the gap between its language – the dominant language, the language of the colonizer – and that of the colonized; but the point is that the question is moot, because the playing field on which the two groups meet, so to speak, is not a level one: the dominant group determines the boundaries of acceptable speech: who can speak, what can be said, and "what counts as proof of a wrong." Under such conditions, the idea of justice as translation starts to look less like a dialogical act of communication and more like a coercive act of silencing, in the guise of putatively disinterested legal procedure.

As a counter to the cautionary tale of the *Cubillo* case and a way of offering a sense of the kind of justice that is achievable through an openness to translation, properly conceived, Murav closes her chapter by turning to an example drawn from Mark Sanders' reading of the South African Truth and Reconciliation Commission hearings. On the one hand, in Sanders' words, "[w]itness and questioner alike are heard in a language not their own. Response, responsiveness, responsibility – all appear paradoxically to require the apparatus of removal or displacement of self." In other words, it appears that compelling the hearing's participants to have their speech translated into a language that is not their own runs the risk of producing a form of justice that is neither anodyne nor especially human. On the other hand, if we shift our attention to the interpreters themselves, we learn something striking. As Murav writes, "[t[he interpreters reported that describing an episode of torture and saying "I" in the place of the victim was an extraordinarily powerful experience."

For Murav, this takes us to the heart of the potential for justice in translation. It is not so much a matter of a "self" developing a respect for the "other" – of connecting with and developing sympathy for another human being across the divide of language – but rather of opening oneself up to the possibility of allowing the language of the other to reconstitute the parameters of one's subjectivity and structures of feeling. As Murav says, "[i]t is not mere respect for the other that is implied here but rather the risk of the loss of self in the face of other human beings on whom my humanity depends." Murav's critique of White's "Justice as Translation" exemplifies the thoughtfulness and conceptual richness of the conversations taking place between law and humanities scholars who see translation as central to the work of law.

Where Ravit Reichman writes on narrative as both a literary and legal process, in "The Constitution of History and Memory" Ariela Gross considers the role historical narratives and memory play in constituting both individual and national identities, particularly in the context of the need to integrate collective traumatic experience for the purpose of remedying harms and "repair[ing] the social fabric." Much of this repair and integration has taken place in what Gross (borrowing from Pierre Nora) calls "the quintessential 'lieu de mémoire' today,' the courtroom or truth commission hearing room." That is, most public efforts to confront and assimilate the trauma of mass atrocities, especially the Holocaust and apartheid, have situated the project of remembering in terms of legal justice. The pragmatics of using law to reform the past has become accordingly a central concern among historians and scholars of memory, but, as Gross explains, no less important theoretical inquiries into the origins and consequences of a postmodern obsession with memory itself are as yet still peripheral.

Despite the considerable scholarship produced over the last twenty years on the workings of collective memory, and notwithstanding a "new surge of scholarship on the memory of slavery" in particular, critical analyses of the role played by legal

Introduction

processes in shaping and integrating the memory of slavery and the international slave trade are scant. Because most work on slavery, whether in the United Kingdom and France or in the United States, has remained within the realm of creating memory rather than in theorized critiques of what "memory" is or of its efficacy in promoting public healing, too little attention has been given to the various historical narratives that inform legal and political debate about how to achieve justice in relation to slavery. Because "slavery is a crime with no perpetrators to try" – hence its exclusion from the courtroom and, where the court is the dominant site of justice, from the possibility of justice – other modes for achieving justice have emerged. Reparations for slavery has assumed greater prominence in French and American public discourse, for example, yet, Gross argues, more study is needed of the potential hazards, as well as the merits of this approach in each country's particular racial past. Using scholarship on mass atrocities as a point of departure, then, Gross's chapter calls for a similar intervention in our understanding of the international slave trade, of slavery's legacy in configurations of American identity and law, and, more specifically, of the therapeutic adequacy of legal reparations for slavery.

Part V: Institutional Processes

The linguistic structures and practices of law are matched by institutional structures and processes that situate or embody them, for example, trial narratives that emerge out of the courts where they take place or sentences that inflict punishment through imprisonment. The final section of this book turns from language to the institutional ways that law establishes a presence, does its work, and makes itself felt in the community. This section also considers the way that processes of law, such as testifying or witnessing, the use of precedent or judgment by peers, become institutions. That is, legal modes of knowing and effectiveness can exceed the boundaries of law, ramifying throughout a culture and becoming a general way of knowing and acting in the world. A humanistic perspective on the ways such institutions work can consider how procedures change when ideas of justice do, and how law happens when texts do not speak for themselves. What are the institutional processes at work in the law? How do they appear to legal professionals and culture at large?

In his chapter on the trial, Lindsay Farmer explains that every trial is as much a cultural as a legal production. Focusing on the modern adversarial criminal trial (the "reconstructive" trial), Farmer argues that its form, even more than the particular legal matter being adjudicated, "encourages us to think that it is appropriate that certain social conflicts be played out through law." That is, the dramatic form of the trial, in particular the elaborate "staging" of historical trials – "from the language used to the legal rituals to the symbols of justice and the architecture of the courtroom" – have afforded scholars of law and humanities ample material for understanding political, social, and cultural realities of past times, including the "image of the law" projected via these productions. For Farmer, however, our contemporary propensity to dub so many trials "the trial of the century" implies a certain intensity of need (he calls it a "distinctively modern sensibility," and "a belief that *this* trial is capable of revealing a truth about *our* society and *our* time") that the form or, more aptly, the performance of the legal trial will produce insights into cultural character and stabilize social norms (to the extent that stability is necessarily consequent on genuine insight). As the crucial mechanism for acquiring cultural self-knowledge, this preponderance of "trials of the century" has made the twentieth century, in Farmer's view, "the century of the trial."

Beginning with the development of the reconstructive trial, he explains that when the locus of justice shifted from the public scaffold to the courtroom in the nineteenth century, justice itself was divested of her potentially volatile "severity and mercy" and assumed qualities of "distance, uniformity, and impartiality" instead. To match this model of justice, the trial literally had to be reformed. By the end of the nineteenth century, the reconstructive trial (with its introduction and examination of testimony) had become the dominant mode of criminal investigation and the means by which "the actuality of the past" could be made present to the court. Farmer carefully notes that the reproduction of the event for the "identification and punishment of wrongdoers" is not the reconstructive trial's only purpose or domain. Rather, "it [is] always also about other things" . . . "It is a communicative process, which might either conflict with or reinforce the image of a universal and impartial legal order. It is a form of public ritual of shaming or degradation. It is also an imaginative space in which complex stories were told and new forms of subjectivity and responsibility are constructed and contested."

Following on this history, Farmer discusses three themes or aspects of this staging that have preoccupied humanistic studies of the trial: the narrative reconstruction of events as a form of "imaginative understanding," changing conceptions of subjectivity – and hence liability – that reflected new research into mental states, and the new physical spaces of the courtroom that "structured communication within the trial," emphasizing the authority of key figures (judges and lawyers) and of law itself. It is this dramatic, reconstructive model of the trial that has become the basis for both actual and fictional trials, whose effectiveness is evaluated, Farmer argues, by reference to its staging, to the truths thereby revealed, and finally to the particular trial's social function. So, for example, the theatricality of the trial is linked to the public performance of justice, which publicity is linked, in turn, to the "wider conception of a (frequently idealized) political community" and the perceived legitimacy of its legal institutions. Where such publicity may in one sense encourage belief in the transparency of the rule of law, the trial's very staginess in contrast also runs the risk of undermining the pursuit of justice, turning it from drama to "morality play" (in which the outcome is known in advance) or, worse, into farce, as evidenced

Introduction 43

by the many high-profile, media trials that convert civic, public participation into passive consumption. In light of the risks and opportunities that attend the trial's dramatization, Farmer's chapter concludes with an examination of our apparent and peculiar need for the trial itself – that crucible of character, value, and justice – as a function of its form.

As Susan Sage Heinzelman's chapter on the novel explained, sex and class exerted tremendous force both on the rise of the novel and its particular audiences in the eighteenth and nineteenth centuries, as well as on the structures and processes of law that the novel implicitly copied or blatantly depicted. Jan-Melissa Schramm's chapter takes us into the history of one of those processes, testimony. Schramm situates testimony, arguably "the sole medium of judicial evidence," within histories of the jury and the professionalization or "lawyerization" of the criminal trial in the late eighteenth and nineteenth centuries. For modern-day jurists, concerned largely with the competency of witness testimony, these histories enrich our understanding of the "essential ambiguity" of testimony. They also encourage us to examine more closely the distinctions between stories deemed admissible and those that are excluded, as well as the way these stories may be "compelled." Although it is clear that we continue to value and seek out stories, it is less obvious that their telling is always voluntary or that the experiences revealed can be put into the legal record, and hence that their power to corroborate the truth of any evidence is either uniform, predictable, or ultimately reliable.

Like Peter Brooks and Peter Goodrich, Schramm explains that as empirical epistemologies prevailed following the Enlightenment, testimony's Aristotelian, rhetorical traces, as well as its association with confessional modes (themselves increasingly linked to continental, i.e., French radicalism), came to be viewed with suspicion. The legislative and judicial response was therefore to develop rules to test and confirm the validity of all testimony, which worked "simultaneously to suppress its similarities to narrative fiction and story," even as they continued to rely on the swearing of the "Christian oath of truthfulness." For Schramm, these maneuvers place testimony at the center of a triangulated relationship among literature, theology, and law in which all three discourses vied for access to truth.

Each of these remains an important vector for consideration of testimony today. Citing the work of Richard H. Weisberg and Shoshana Felman, Schramm highlights the "great ethical weight" testimony carries in fiction and other forms of narrative art that privilege the immediacy and intimacy of the witness's account and, most especially, in historiographic accounts of persecution where its dual nature "as both a story of personal experience and a type of evidence" supplements and potentially counters official stories. Yet it is precisely this immediacy – the lack of an objective mediator – that the legal profession and legal procedure has sought to overcome and that the profession continues to wrestle with in contemporary debates, not only about how to instruct a jury, but also how to evaluate eyewitness testimony. As

Schramm concludes, through "their attention to such issues as agency, audience, duress, voluntariness, mistake, and misapprehension," these studies remind us of the complex literary and theological histories informing contemporary legal approaches to testimony even as they map new directions of study.

With Desmond Manderson's chapter we shift our attention to the question of "Judgment," an important thematic focus of humanistic studies of law. In recent years this work, like scholarship on interpretation, has drawn heavily upon continental philosophy, in particular the writings of Heidegger and Derrida. As Manderson reveals, interest in these philosophers has yielded two principal streams or strands of thought, which share the view "that positivism is incapable of either adequately describing the nature of legal reasoning or seriously justifying its core claim that law is a system of determinate rules capable of neutral application." The Heideggerian- and Derridian-inspired approaches are similar, however Manderson argues that they "part company on the crucial question of judgment in law." (He acknowledges that his view of the difference between them is contestable on the basis, notably, of Derrida's "flirtation with the mysticism of the 'madness of decision.'") For Manderson, in respect of the philosophical question of judgment, Derrida's work points the way out of the impasse both of positivism and of approaches that issue from Heidegger.

In his view, the Heideggerian stream draws inspiration from and is contiguous with the New Romanticism movement in German thought of the late nineteenth century; as such, it aims for transcendence as an answer to the "intellectual poverty of positivism." The way to resolve or overcome the unsettling uncertainties and incommensurabilities that attend questions of judgment is not to ask that the faculty of Reason reveal and apply a single, fixed rule, but rather to transcend them, that is, to achieve a transcendent insight – a kind of moment of the sublime – that reveals the "natural," authoritative, foundational, prelinguistic truth of justice at the heart of every instance of judgment. By contrast, the Derridian stream directs its energies toward exposing the nostalgia and melancholy at the heart of such a yearning for transcendence and argues that no such foundational, transcendent ground ever has existed or ever will: The yearning for transcendence is just that, a yearning, and it is forever defeated or disappointed by the inherent hermeticism and referential instability of language and thus of consciousness and experience.

For Manderson, the Derridian perspective is not merely deconstructive; it does more than unsettle fixed ideas. The work of revealing the ineluctable instability of all acts of judgment – precisely *because* it loosens or undermines our faith in the possibility of certainty – is a propaedeutic to establishing the only form of judgment and justice available to us and worthy of the name. In this view, legal judgment embraces uncertainty and the tension produced by the incommensurability, present in every act of judgment, between "the prior rule, general and certain, and the question of its application in *this case*." Thusly conceived, legal judgment is "exactly

Introduction 45

opposite to the closure and finality – the death wish or *Thanatos* of discourse – to which both Romanticism and positivism, in their very different ways, are drawn." In the best sense, it emulates the example of much narrative fiction and its polyvocal and dialogical discourse. Like the novel, "[i]t multiplies voices; it sets characters' perspectives *against* each other; it does not shy away from but embraces the resulting uncertainty." The insights that it produces are provisional, contestable, and subject to revision. As Manderson writes, "correction is the soul of justice." Above all, acts of legal judgment must remain public and answerable: Because justice is unattainable, because there is a necessary imperfection to this process, the obligation to render a judgment is not severable from the obligation to *expose* one's judgment, to explain, to justify, and be subjected to critique for it In sum, the humanities are vital to our thinking about justice – the judgment of law – because their influence "makes the process of judgment more contentious and continuous, but at the same time more democratic than ever before."

Punishment, understood as the infliction of pain in response to a wrong and hence a mode of justice, ranks with ideas of sovereignty and the power to make war as one of the key characteristics of the "modern state," and, as Karl Shoemaker points out, in the West the conceptualization, justification, and administration of punishment have been matters chiefly for the law and lawyers to decide. Yet, citing the absence of "juridical reflection" in Roman attitudes toward punishment as well its presence in medieval poetry (*Beowulf*, for example), Shoemaker asks how it is that the discipline of law has nevertheless come to "claim priority in discussions of punishment" and what exactly the humanities might contribute to them.

The force of historical habit is one explanation of law's priority. Twelfth-century jurists were the first to systematize punishment and establish themselves as authorities and advisors on penal law. Noting those moments when law's dominion over punishment was most strongly challenged, however – for example, Beccaria's Enlightenment critique in *On Crimes and Punishments* or the "'open warring'" between jurists and social scientists in the mid-twentieth century – Shoemaker points out that even the eventual "truce" between law and the empirical social sciences, although it loosened the former's centuries-old control, did so without reference to the humanities. Indeed, for Shoemaker, the success of the social sciences essentially eclipsed law's other centuries-old, albeit erratic, relationship with the humanities.

Following consideration of the highs and lows of this relationship, of what historically has been meant by the term "humanities," as well as how it is defined in the contemporary academy, Shoemaker makes the following claim: "The humanities provide a realm for thinking about man as a being who punishes, and to think about this essential quality of man in a manner that is not bound by any necessary result." He suggests, in other words, that the absence of such practical constraints on our thinking creates the possibility of reaching "deeper (if utterly impracticable) understandings of ourselves, insofar as we are historical beings who punish." Readings of Nietzsche and Foucault follow, along with historicist critiques of Foucault's argument, studies of the impact of art and literature on creating penal discipline, critiques of particular forms of punishment (especially the death penalty in the United States), as well as studies of "clemency and pardons" as ways of avoiding it. Turning to Hegel's discussion of the dangers of abstraction, particularly in response to the spectacle of punishment, Shoemaker concludes that the ability to think – "the ability not to abstract a being into some one-sided caricature," for example, "murderer" or "object of pity" – is not a measurable "occurrence," or a formal "doctrine," or even an historical "event." As such, it does not belong exclusively to law, the social sciences, or history, and its practice does not even require special academic training. Rather, for Shoemaker, it is the very uselessness of the humanities that constitutes its humble claim: "to provide a realm in which such thinking is not impossible."

In their respective ways, each of the contributions in this book attests to the vitality and fruitfulness of efforts – past, present, and future – to bring humanistic perspectives to bear in understanding law and to make such perspectives more self-reflexively internal to law's self-conception. At the same time, they vividly demonstrate what law offers as an object of study to the humanities. We join our contributors in a vision of law as a moral achievement that emerges from rich traditions of rhetoric, textual interpretation, and ethical and philosophical argument, and institutional practice – traditions that are at the heart of humanistic inquiry. We also see in humanistic scholarship on law a reminder of the costs of that achievement, of the violence that law does, the silences it imposes, the travesties to which it has been, and can be, put. This reminder points to the radical partiality and incompleteness of law's achievement as well as to the urgency of repair. The vibrancy of the field of humanistic inquiry about law promises, we think, to keep us poised between celebration and humility, between the awareness of what law is and the unfulfillable promise of what law can be.

PART I

PERSPECTIVES ON THE HISTORY AND SIGNIFICANCE OF SCHOLARSHIP IN LAW AND THE HUMANITIES: THREE VIEWS

1

A Humanities of Resistance

Fragments for a Legal History of Humanity

Costas Douzinas*

I first realized that there was something strange about the term "Humanities" when, as the director of my university's Humanities Institute, I participated in a meeting to set up a European Consortium of Humanities Centers. Except for the host center in Utrecht and mine, no other participating European university had a Humanities Institute. The aspiring founding fathers and mothers came from single disciplines: Archeology, English, Dutch, Media, and Philosophy. Then it struck me: No proper or widely used term translates the term Humanities in Greek or Italian, their supposed mother tongues. The Humanities, despite their desperate look eastward and backward, are a consummately modern and decidedly American invention. No faculties, courses, or centers for the Humanities existed in European universities until recently. The few British exceptions – of which my own institution is a shining example – do not follow a long tradition of Humanities education. They are, rather, the result of our "special relationship" with our transatlantic cousins and of the managerial culture that has replaced the older genteel governance of universities, and is perennially trying – and on the whole failing – to create economies of scale, grant-producing interdisciplinary initiatives, and a teaching, scholarship, and evaluation culture that rather pathetically imitates the marketplace.

What are the Humanities? According to the flourishing American debate, the Humanities have been defined in two related ways. They are either a set of academic subjects that typically consists of Classics, Philosophy, History, and Literature (the disciplinary approach) or an attitude toward teaching and learning that could be extended to all types of subjects (the humanistic approach). Humanities subjects are linked through a common origin, through their shared object of concern, or through the use of common strategies.

The Classics had initially pride of place in the enumeration of Humanities disciplines. "As late as 1918 . . . the word *humanities* and the phrase *Greek and Latin* [were

---

* Professor of Law and Director, Birkbeck Institute for the Humanities

used] as synonyms." Ullman reported in 1946 that in Scotland, "a professor of Latin is called a professor of humanity."[1] The 1934 edition of Webster's dictionary defined the Humanities as "the branches of polite learning regarded as primarily conducive to culture; esp., the ancient classics and belles-lettres." As the sciences gradually became dominant in universities and wider society and the emphasis on the classics started waning, the definition became negative and parasitical on the Humanities' competitors. A number of reviews conclude that the Humanities "are whatever science is not."[2] The once mighty humanities have now a reduced kingdom, "a musty place filled with tombs, monuments, libraries, and talkative old guides who stroll around with their hands in their pockets, wearing glasses and out of touch with reality, conducting you for a small fee to the graves of Beethoven, Shakespeare, and Sophocles."[3]

At the other end, the attempt to defend the Humanities against the onslaught of the "soulless" scientific mentality emphasizes the humanistic tradition and extends it "to embrace whatever influences conduce to freedom,"[4] or, even more grandiosely, to the study of "the sum total of man's activities." The Humanities chart "greatness, monumental scale, fineness of artistic sensibility, and deep insight" as they examine "the nature of human experience as an object of awareness, and the nature of human acts as both content of awareness and events observed."[5] In this second sense, every scientific endeavor and object of study can be approached humanistically. These claims are grand on the surface. Yet the Humanities seem to be in perennial crisis, which has generated a huge literature defining its contours and principles, defending its standing in relation to other fields, in particular the sciences, and even discussing the role of the Humanities in wartime. The repetitive and occasionally embarrassed tone of the debate indicates, however, that the stakes are lower. They are a last-stance defense of the modest kingdom of university Humanities and a shield to protect their "small fee" in the form of fast-diminishing research funds.

It is not unreasonable to conclude that the Humanities as an academic institution are closely associated with American education. The long debate about their scope and value, indeed about the meaning of the term Humanities is linked with the survey course in Literature and History degrees. Such courses were first introduced at Stripps College and Stephens College in 1928 and at Chicago in 1931. The Chicago Humanities course was widely publicized and "probably has done most to

---

[1] B. L. Ullman, "What are the Humanities" 17/6 *Journal of Higher Education* 301, at 302 (1946).

[2] James Schroeder, "The Enemy Within" in 25/8 *College English* 561(1964); cf. "If 'the humanities' indicates a set of nonrelated subjects, then it would include those areas that could not be classified under the sciences," Walter Feinberg, "To Defend the Humanities" 3/2 *The Journal of Aesthetic Education* 91 (1969).

[3] Shroeder, ibid.

[4] Ralph Barton Perry, "A Definition of the Humanities" in *The Meaning of the Humanities* (Princeton: Princeton University Press, 1938), 4.

[5] Richard Kuhns, 1/2 *The Journal of Aesthetic Education* 7 (1966), 12, 15.

A Humanities of Resistance

associate the term *humanities* with a survey course."[6] The pedagogical value and organization of the different disciplines into a single subject in which "everything was dumped in" is a mainstay of the debate.[7] The Great Books or the dead-white-men tradition in Humanities survey courses has been criticized from many directions. The relationship between these bucket courses and their constituent disciplines is uneasy; the compilation course dumps down the disciplinary expertise and undermines the independence and integrity of the disciplines. Still the term Humanities seems to refer either to federal administrative and financial arrangements (Humanities Faculties or Schools) or to "from Plato to NATO" survey courses that form the backbone of liberal arts education.

In genealogical terms, the Humanities are as much the product of pedagogical and disciplinary concerns of American educationalists as of the Classic and Renaissance humanistic tradition. Against this background, interest in law and literature and, recently, law and the humanities takes additional importance. What is the link between these two disciplines that, on first look, are miles apart?

Law with Humanities

In 1943, while World War II was raging, Roscoe Pound, perhaps the greatest American legal theorist, penned a remarkable article entitled "The Humanities in an Absolutist World."[8] Pound wrote at a point when the rift between the Western powers and the Soviet Union, which would dominate the postwar period, had become all too evident, and he finds many shared pitfalls between what he calls autocracies and Western autocratic democracies. Pound is scathing about the emerging new era of materialism and consumerism; of "unmanageable bigness" in government; of obsession with power, security, and "grandiose schemes of world organization" the West promotes. One would be hard pressed to improve on this list of evils for our world today.

Pound draws a sharp line between the sciences and the Humanities. Unlike the standard humanist position, however, he argues that the Humanities are dispensable and are dismissed for political and ideological reasons. "Men are to be trained in the physical and natural sciences so as to promote material production. They are to be trained in the natural sciences so as to promote passive obedience" (pp 12–13). For that to happen, however, Pound avers sarcastically, "the past is to be cancelled. We are to begin with a clean slate. Our accumulated control over external nature has gone so far that there remains only the task making it available for universal human contentment . . . The causes of envy and strife are to go with want and fear. Mankind

---

[6] Ullman, op. cit., 304.

[7] Ibid., 303.

[8] Roscoe Pound, "The Humanities in an Absolutist World" in XXXIX/1 *The Classical Journal* (October 1943), 1. Page numbers in the next part of the text refer to this article.

will settle down to a passive enjoyment of the material goods and will neither require nor desire anything more" (pp 2–3).

Humanities is a last-stance defense against the imposed ignorance and philistinism that must cancel the past to usher in the new era of consumerism, absolutism, and apathy. A generation cut off from its past cannot fully understand and criticize the present. The Humanities help develop a historical and critical approach; they can be used to resist the all-out attack of utilitarian materialism. This is precisely why they must be downgraded, why a clean slate is necessary. Choosing to base his defense on the importance of learning the classical languages rather than literature, Pound castigates those who find the study of the classics a waste when "time is needed for the natural and physical sciences which teach us how to harness more of external nature to producing the material goods of human existence and to the social sciences which are to teach us how these goods are to be made to satisfy desires" (p 9).

Pound dispels any suspicion of prejudice against the social sciences and a facile recapitulation of the "two cultures" argument. He proudly declares that he taught jurisprudence from a sociological perspective for forty years but adds curtly that the social sciences "do not impart wisdom; they need to be approached with acquired wisdom," which only the Humanities offer. Throughout the essay, the argument remains deeply political. "If we are content to seek nothing more than a general condition of undisturbed passivity under the benevolent care of an omnicompetent government, we can well leave education to the sciences which have to do with providing the material goods of existence and those [social sciences] which teach us how the government secures or will secure them for us" (p 14).

For Pound it is a question of resisting a certain type of autocratic government that bases its power on the biopolitical manipulation of desire (his preferred pejorative term is "contentment") through the production and consumption of material goods, in the hope that this would end strife. Pound correctly anticipates the move toward a disciplined hypercapitalism in which material success becomes the sole aim in life. Citizen contentment can be achieved only after the blind satisfaction of material wants has been raised into the goal of individual and state and has been accompanied by a governmentally promoted political apathy. The role of science is central: The natural sciences develop new ways of using material resources for the production of goods while the social sciences manipulate the psyche and install political and cultural passivity.

This is a scathing attack not so much on science as on the politics and ideologies that Pound rightly feared would dominate the postwar period. Coming from a patrician culture steeped in the Greats, Pound finds in the Humanities and the Classics, in particular, strategies of resistance against this catastrophic turn. Law is not discussed explicitly but the essay is full of references to legal learning and scholarship. Without a good understanding of the Greek and Latin languages and culture, law could fall into the same predicament as the wider culture. Pound

A Humanities of Resistance

castigates the uneducated, almost illiterate students who cannot read the Bible or the *Magna Carta* in the original, do not understand the meaning of proceedings *in rem* or mistake *son assault demense* for Anglo-Saxon and *non compos mentis* for French (pp 10, 11). We are all used to tales of student ignorance and examination script gems. If I were to argue today that law students should have a passable knowledge of Latin (I am often tempted to do so), I would be laughed out of court and my radical credentials would suffer irretrievably. Pound must have been the last American to do so.

Palpable elitism and an antidemocratic whiff color these examples. The Humanities make the human but their work must be done before university in families, schools, and on Main Street. One either has humanity or not; it is a matter of birth, early education, and class. Pound's defense of classical education sounds occasionally anachronistic and even reactionary, but there is also a melancholy *finis Austriae* tone throughout the essay. Pound's classical education will not survive. The cultural barbarians are at the gates; resistance is both necessary and impossible. Yet its tenor differs from later defenses of the Humanities. The Classics are a bastion of resistance, a last-ditch defense against rising political apathy and oppressive state omnipotence. Their gradual displacement accompanied by the idiotic assertion that only the sciences are necessary for democracy will make intelligent Americans "bow the knee to Baal" and "sink into materialistic apathy" (p 14). This is a lament and obituary for a dying patrician world but also a battle cry against the looming biopolitical turn of postwar culture.

Some sixty-five years after Roscoe Pound's wartime cry of despair and pessimism, the question of the role of the Humanities has returned to the cultural and educational agenda as the present volume attests. Have his Cassandra-like predictions come true? Can the Humanities play the role he assigned to them in 1943? What can a humanistic education offer the young student and aspiring lawyer at a time when humanism and the values of liberalism and democracy have allegedly triumphed? Is it possible today to remain loyal to Pound's injunction and develop a new Humanities of resistance?

Two recent essays address these issues, giving almost opposing answers to the question of the relationship between the Humanities and Law. Martha Nussbaum's "Cultivating Humanity in Legal Education" and Jack Balkin and Sanford Levinson's "Law and the Humanities: An Uneasy Relationship"[9] share much in their diagnosis of the state of legal education. Although Nussbaum gives a rather timid defense of the Humanities, Balkin and Levinson dismiss any substantial link.

Nussbaum, a classicist and historian of ideas turned law professor, has consistently promoted the role of the Humanities in education and legal education in

---

[9] Jack Balkin and Sanford Levinson, "Law and the Humanities: An Uneasy Relationship", 18 *Yale Journal of Law and the Humanities* 155 (2006).

54   Costas Douzinas

particular.[10] For Nussbaum, the Humanities mission is extremely broad. They address the problems of "how to live with dignity as a rational animal, in a world of events that we do not fully control. Issues... of vulnerability and need, of terror and cruelty, also of pleasure and vision."[11] Such a huge agenda is delivered through three core values: Socratic self-examination, world citizenship, and the narrative imagination. The first refers to a reflective approach to self and tradition closer to Habermasian liberal orthodoxy than to classical Greece. Students should be taught to defend sound values and criticize those that do not stand the test of deliberation. They should learn to "reason logically, and to test what one reads or says for consistency of reading, correctness of fact, and accuracy of judgment." Second, the Humanities should prepare for world citizenship, a rather fashionable oxymoron in the post-1989 world. Nussbaum, a key promoter of neo-Kantian cosmopolitanism, wants to cultivate the humanity of citizens and their ability to see themselves as not simply citizens of some local region or group but also, and above all, as human beings bound to all other human beings by ties of recognition and concern. Bonds of recognition and concern should be built not just with our immediate group but also with minority cultures and people and with humanity at large. Finally, the literature and the arts help develop something called "narrative imagination." This is the "ability to think what it might be like to be in the shoes of a person different from oneself, to be an intelligent reader of that person's story, and to understand the emotions, desires, and wishes that someone so placed might have" (pp 269, 270).

Turning to legal education, Nussbaum concedes that is a form of specialized professional training. In a rather amazing admission for a staunch defender of the Humanities, she accepts that the "values and goals of [humanity] are not germane to legal education" (p 272). In a further twist of old-style positivism, Nussbaum claims that students "need to learn the law as is." Lawyers are out to win, not to fight for truth, and in this sense they are closer to the Sophists rather than to Socrates.

Yet historically the relationship between Law and the Humanities has been intense and intimate. All great philosophers, from Plato to Hobbes, Kant, Hegel, and Weber, either studied the law or had a deep understanding of legal operations. Legal issues have been central to philosophical and political concerns throughout history. Well before the creation of the various disciplines, when thinkers wanted to contemplate the organization of their society or the relationship between authority and the citizen they turned to law. Plato's *Republic* and Aristotle's *Ethics*, as much as Hegel's *Philosophy of Right*, are attempts to examine the legal aspects of the

---

[10] Martha Nussbaum, "Cultivating Humanity in Legal Education," 70/1 *University of Chicago Law Review* 265 (2003). Page numbers in the next part of the text refer to this article. See also "Humanities and Human Development" 36/3 *Journal of Aesthetic Education* 39 (2002). Both essays are applications of Nussbaum's wider thesis in *Cultivating Humanity: A Classical Defense of Reform in Liberal Education* (Cambridge: Harvard University Press, 1997).

[11] Nussbaum, "Humanities and Human Development," 39.

A Humanities of Resistance

social bond, to discover and promote a type of legality that attaches the body to the soul, keeps them together, and links them to the demands of living. Seen from the perspective of the *longue durée*, the law represents the principle of social reproduction. Whenever classical philosophy occupied itself with the persistence of the social bond, it turned to law and became legal philosophy, the great source from which political philosophy and then the disciplines, sociology, psychology, and anthropology, emerged in the seventeenth and nineteenth centuries, respectively. All major early modern philosophers were jurists. Thomas Hobbes was preoccupied with the common law; *Leviathan* is a clear exercise in jurisprudence. Immanuel Kant, the philosopher of modernity par excellence, wrote extensively on legal issues and at the end of his life came up with a blueprint for a future world state based on international law and respect for freedom and rights. Hegel and Marx wrote superb jurisprudential texts but were also well versed in the positive law of their time. Emile Durkheim and Max Weber, the founders of sociology, wrote extensively on law and used types of legality as markers for the classification of different social systems. The birth of the disciplines out of the womb of legal study led to a cognitive and moral impoverishment of legal scholarship and education, which have become an entomology of rules, a guidebook to technocratic legalism, and a science of the existent.

In an essay written in 1993, Nussbaum argued that philosophy should be incorporated into legal education because it is necessary for the understanding of key concepts.[12] Free will, the emotions, sexuality, the quest for a good life are germane to legal questions and only philosophy can clarify them. Following Plato's *Theaetetus*, Nussbaum accepts that philosophy begins in "wonder" and criticizes the use of "science as normative for legal reasoning," which places emphasis on the "right answer." "[L]et the law students learn to wonder, and then perhaps, wherever they are, they will feel the pressure of a Socratic question rising up to annoy them as they are trying to be simple."[13]

Yet, by 2003, Nussbaum has accepted the poverty of legal education, and, against Pound's injunction, sees the Humanities as just a palliative. Marx classically described the bourgeois as a split person who goes about his business using and exploiting people during the working week but who, reverse-Cinderella-like, turns into a citizen concerned with the common good on the Sabbath. A similar inner split of the lawyer allows a small role for the Humanities: Lawyers, in addition to being aggressive litigators unconcerned with truth and justice, are influential citizens. They should be trained, therefore, into "normative ethical reasoning by examining alternative accounts of decisionmaking, social justice, and related topics" (p 274).

---

[12] Martha Nussbaum, "The Use and Abuse of Philosophy in Legal Education," 45 *Stanford Law Review* 1627 (1993).

[13] Ibid., 1640.

Nussbaum admits that these are diversions, adornments, and peripheral-only problems. In 1993, she had advocated the appointment of philosophers in law schools. In 2003, the solutions proposed are anodyne. The need to teach ethical reasoning is partly met by the standard course in legal ethics. Essay writing should replace the obsession with written examinations; courses in international and comparative law would encourage a more global and a la mode understanding of the world, and innovative courses such as the "decisionmaking" one Nussbaum has been teaching at Chicago would expose students to good normative reasoning and an empathetic *education sentimentale juridique*. Nussbaum admits, on the other hand, that her law and literature course failed in this quest. Students expected a "lighter more entertaining" kind of course about the literary representations of legal situations. Law and the Humanities courses end up entertaining and lightening the heavy load of law students as well as giving them a useful cultural gloss. A few references to Sophocles, Shakespeare, Melville, and Kafka can impress the professional cocktail party circuit.

This is humanism of the lightest kind. It has been repeatedly and incisively criticized, and there is no need to add much here.[14] The cosmopolitan self and the ethical community Nussbaum envisages are too closely modeled on the values and norms of American liberal elites suitably finessed to extend humanitarian empathy to the unfortunates of the world. Rational deliberation, ethical reasoning, and a fictive changing of places do not go far in addressing social inequality, oppression, and domination. As Rosi Braidotti put it, Nussbaum has claimed "monopoly over basic values of human decency by allocating them exclusively to . . . American liberal individualism."[15] As we know, this kind of individualism is often accompanied by high-altitude bombers and ethically aware torturers.

Martha Nussbaum's loss of nerve is intriguing. Lawyers are sophists, rhetoricians, and litigators, people driven, like society, by profit. They try to persuade audiences at any cost rather than search for the truth. There is not much that can be done to improve their ethical sense. Nussbaum's defense of the (limited) role of the Humanities in legal education takes therefore a methodological and hermeneutical form. It is not so much the traditional Humanities that can improve the moral compass of lawyers but the values they promote. Law should be taught humanistically, helping to develop a reflective approach, moral values, and critical reasoning.

Roscoe Pound's prediction has come true: Even the professor of Humanities concedes that she has little to offer to the cultivation of culture in law. Nussbaum openly admits it at the end of the essay. Legal education makes "ambitious idealistic

---

[14] Homi Bhabha, "Unpacking my Library . . . Again" in Iain Chamber and Lidia Curti, eds. *The Postcolonial Question* (New York: Routledge, 1996); Rosi Braidotti, *Transposition* (Cambridge: Polity Press 2006).

[15] Braidotti, 15.

A Humanities of Resistance

young people become narrower, more fixed on narrowly instrumental goals... Soon [the law students] will be out working for firms. Meanwhile, while they are here, while they have time to deliberate and imagine, let us cultivate their humanity" (p 279). The role of humanistic legal education is to instill a sense of liberal morality and openness to the students who come to law school without the elite cultivation that Pound could still rely on in 1943. The Humanities have retreated from Roscoe Pound's agenda: They can offer no resistance to the firm. Could it be, however, as Roscoe Pound insinuates, that it is precisely the kind of "humanism light" Nussbaum advocates that leads to the neglect of deliberation and imagination and facilitates rather than resists the efficient integration of the young lawyer in the mentality of the firm? Could it be that liberal legal pedagogy has contributed to the predicament Nussbaum both accepts and regrets? In Roscoe Pound's terms, the barbarians are not just amassing at the gates. They have entered the citadel and the guards have abandoned the fight.

Law without Humanities

If Nussbaum offers a tepid and unconvincing defense of the Humanities, Balkin and Levinson's article marks the near abandonment of the ideas and values for which Pound stood.[16] These authors proclaim the realist, pragmatic, and brutal nature of American legal education. Their attack on Pound's and Nussbaum's *bien pensant* humanism is twofold. The belief that great works of art convey moral notions is wrong. In any case, law's business is to promote tough-mindedness rather than moral values. "[L]aw seems almost to relish the extirpation of [tender-heartedness] as if tender-heartedness were a mental disease that only the discipline of law can cure" (p 184).

Our authors disagree with Pound in most particulars. The establishment of the advanced administrative and administered state (Pound's great fear) has been a great success. It released the courts from being "insulated oracles of eternal legal verities" (p 169). Judges, like legislatures and administrators, are now involved in complicated issues of governance, in the definition of the public interest for all aspects of social life, and in the implementation of public policy. As a result, economic efficiency has become the aim of the legal system; economics the most relevant discipline for legal scholars; law and economics the dominant jurisprudential tradition; the rational actor approach its methodology and technical internalist legal argument, enriched by interdisciplinary social scientific expertise, the form of legal education. If they are right, Pound's prediction has come true but it is not as bleak as he thought. Against his fears, these developments are a great achievement of American law, scholarship, and pedagogy.

---

[16] Balkin and Levinson op. cit., fn. 10. Page numbers in the next part of the text refer to this article.

The downgrading of the role of the Humanities in legal education is programmatic, global, and somewhat ironic if not cynical. Lawyers and legal academics are gladiators (rhetors) out to win battles (arguments) with different audiences. They are motivated by a strong prescriptive urge. Other disciplines are useful to lawyers only as aids to victory. This premise determines their cognitive and political function: legal philosophy's role is to help legitimate the legal system and clarify its main concepts; legal history provides useful data for making normative legal and political arguments (pp 175–6). Interdisciplinary studies are admitted to the extent required by the prescriptive nature of legal scholarship and a professional, results-oriented pedagogy. Knowledge of economics helps the lawyer's quest for scientific authority and rhetorical persuasion. As Justice Holmes apparently would have put it, "reading literature or engaging in the humanities [does] not have edificatory effect" (p 186). Only the study of rhetoric is useful because it improves the forensic skills of litigators.

I have neither the expertise nor the brief to defend American legal education against this portrayal. I would be surprised if American legal theorists would recognize (or approve) the image of law and education presented here as an amoral, gladiatorial, results-driven enterprise that colonizes other disciplines. The authors could claim that this is a realistic depiction and not their own preference. After all, they aver in passing that they carry out research in law and poststructuralism, that they promote law and the humanities, and that they have launched a new field called law and the performing arts. Yet their own claim is that legal academics see themselves as legislators or judges. Lawyers describe in order to prescribe; our authors are lawmakers because they are legal academics; because they are interdisciplinary (one has a Ph.D. and the other is a poststructuralist and reads Derrida, 'a literary theorist,' and Deleuze and Guattari); and because, finally, they teach in prestigious universities.

Balkin and Levinson's law is crystal clear: A "good lawyer" is a rigorous thinker who does not waste time denouncing injustice at the expense of legal analysis. The job of the lawyer is, following the *bon mots* of O. W. Holmes, to become a supple tool of power and to help his fellow citizens to go to Hell if that is what they want. Their job is not "to do justice," but "to play the game according to the rules..." (p 185). Pragmatism is identified with dominant ideology and a moral *grundnorm* that reads "succeed at all costs" – let us call it the "xeroxing" principle.

One of the authors describes an exchange with our editor, who invited him to help set up a PhD program in law and the humanities. Professor Balkin's refusal was monosyllabic: "xeroxing." He worked in a richly endowed law school and all his xeroxing was free, whereas our editor had to buy copy cards. "A law department that cut itself off from the goal of professional education would soon find itself as well supported financially as the average art history or music department, which is to say, it would not be very well supported at all" (p 177). This simple morality tale confirms the prescience of Roscoe Pound. In the sixty-five years since he wrote his article,

A Humanities of Resistance

material "contentment" has become the motivation for scholarship, "free xeroxing" the drive of intellectual life. To be sure, if free xeroxing is the aim of academic life, it would have been much better for many of us to go into the legal profession and own the xerox machine itself.

"A favourite phrase of the realist is 'the brute facts'; a phrase used not in sadness that there should be such facts, but with a certain relish, as if brutality were the test of reality . . . the significant things in the world are force and the satisfaction of material wants"[17] wrote Pound in 1943. Balkin and Levinson offer an interesting twenty-first-century example. Commenting on the infamous torture memoranda drafted by Justice Department lawyers from the "highest reaches of the elite legal academy" to legitimize the practices of the American military and give President Bush absolute power to conduct war, they find little surprising or worrying in this capitulation. Against Roscoe Pound's protests, they believe that a Humanities education would have made no difference. "Acquaintance with Homer and Shakespeare would not have changed what ambitious young lawyers in the Office of Legal Counsel wrote to please those in power. Even a torturer can love a sonnet . . ." (p 186). To support their claim they mobilize the humanist judge Learned Hand and the realist O. W. Holmes who, the authors speculate, would have perhaps agreed with the interpretations of the elite lawyers. Whether these legendary judges would have concurred with these counterintuitive interpretations is a moot point. No evidence is given in support, something that stands at odds with the essay's proclamations of cool reason and hard realism. This is the lesser problem nevertheless.

The post-WWII Western consensus was that certain acts – torture is prime among them – are not tolerable in liberal democratic societies. In the West, torture was declared unacceptable and was discussed as part of a barbaric and long-gone history. Torture, we were told, takes place elsewhere only, in exotic and evil places, in dictatorships and under totalitarian regimes. This consensus, however, has now broken down. Torture has become a respectable topic for conferences on practical ethics, and the "ticking bomb" hypothetical offers entertainment at dinner parties. What is particularly disturbing is the way in which lawyers are prepared to enter into debate about the morality and legitimacy of torture and to develop detailed plans about ways of legalizing it through torture warrants, sunset clauses, and judicial supervisory regimes.[18] As Lord Hoffman put it in a case examining the legality of detention without trial in the United Kingdom, "the real threat to the life of the nation comes not from terrorism but from laws such as these."[19] The problem is not

---

[17] Pound, op. cit., 3.
[18] Michael Ignatieff, *The Lesser Evil* (Edinburgh: Edinburgh University Press, 2004); Alan Dershowitz, *Why Terrorism Works* (New Haven: Yale University Press, 2002); For a hilarious retort see: John Gray, *Torture – A Modest Proposal in Heresies* (London: Granta, 2004), 132.
[19] A & Ors v Secretary of State for the Home Department [2004] UKHL 56, Para 97.

the torturers who love sonnets,[20] but the lawyers and philosophers who are prepared to dress in legal and moral verbiage the dictates of brutalizing power and the legal academics who offer scholarly support.

In this world of brute facts, law is technical reason assisted by appropriate scientific expertise at the service of power. References to justice, on the other hand, are a waste of time indulged by the feeble-minded and the emotional. "It is only the insufficiently rigorous and well trained, whom legal training has inadequately 'disciplined' who think that the solutions to a legal problem is resolved by asking which result is more just" state our authors ambiguously located between constantive affirmation and performative irony (p 185). To assert that a legal system is unjust, says Alf Ross, is an "emotional expression. To invoke justice is the same thing as banging on the table: an emotional expression that turns one's demand into an absolute postulate."[21] Nonformal conceptions of justice are "illusions which excite the emotions by stimulating the suprarenal glands."[22] When "someone says "that thing is unjust" what he means is that the thing is offensive to his sentiments."[23] This radical separation of law from justice is, however, both cognitively wrong (deciding what is lawful is impossible without an evaluation of the moral, just, or desirable outcome) and morally impoverished (it reduces morality to private subjective choices and/or to a predication of legality). It became the legitimation and rationalization of the atrocities of the last seventy years.

Allow me here a little detour that briefly sketches a different approach to the nexus of law and justice. The eternal return of (new versions of) naturalism despite its repeatedly proclaimed fallacy indicates that law and morality are not opposed. They are linked in inner and paradoxical ways. For the Greeks and Romans, justice was the prime, albeit missing, virtue of the polity and the spirit and reason of law. A just constitution was a legitimate constitution and a just legal system has a valid claim to the obedience of its citizens. We find similar ideas in the writings of the common lawyers. Justice is cumulatively the foundation, the spirit, and the end of the law. As law's immemorial and unwritten foundation, justice links the common law with divine will and its expressions in nature and reason. After the Reformation, justice as equity is explicitly associated with the divine order and becomes law's spirit. When law and justice, in the form of equity, are in conflict, the law must give way to higher reason. In all these formulations, justice is seen as the "primitive reason"[24] of law, its virtue and ethical substance, an ideal or principle that gives rules

---

[20] As we know of a number of people who tortured prisoners in Guatanamo Bay and Abu Ghraib, an interesting social scientific research project would examine their artistic and cultural preferences and determine whether certain cultural "memes" lead to torture practices.

[21] Alf Ross, *On Law and Justice* (London: Stevens & Sons, 1958), 274.

[22] Ibid., 275.

[23] Friedrich von Hayek, *Law, Legislation, and Liberty* (London: Routledge and Kegan Paul, 1972), 168, fn 30.

[24] Sir H. Finch, *Law, or, A Discourse Thereof in Four Books* (London: Society of Stationers), 1627, at fol. 57.

A Humanities of Resistance

their aim and limit, and remedies their defects. Justice is also something outside or before the law, a higher tribunal or reason to which the law and its judgments are called to account. In this sense, a law without justice is a law without spirit, a dead letter; it can neither rule nor inspire.

Legal justice is only one limited facet of justice. It misfires and decays if it stays on its own, unaccompanied by the wider conception that has inspired European critical legal theory.[25] This is a justice that operates in relationship to the other as a singular, unique, finite being with concrete personality traits, character attributes, and physical characteristics. This finite person puts me in touch with infinite otherness. Both inside and outside, justice is the horizon against which the law is judged for its routine successes and failings and for its broader neglect and forgetting of oppression and domination. Whether we see the law as an historical institution or as a formal system of rules and decisions, the deconstruction of its operations discovers the violence of origins in its daily operations and unravels the ordered bipolarities (fact-value, public-private, objective-subjective, lawful-unlawful), showing that they cannot stabilize the legal system.[26]

The axiom of justice "respect the singularity of the other" is radically different from our authors' injunction "be a winner," "success succeeds," and get free photocopying. This principle emerges in theological, philosophical, and literary texts as well as in the legal archive. It indicates what a Humanities of resistance might look like today against both liberal beautification and realist simplification of Law and the Humanities. Unless this or some other defensible principle of justice informs legal teaching and scholarship, academics become functionaries of power and technicians of skills accepting our exclusion not just from the Humanities but from all intellectual endeavor and political aspiration.

Fragments for a (Legal) History of Humanity

Three ways of linking law and the Humanities have emerged from the discussion thus far. The Humanities can help resist the onslaught of materialism, consumerism, and an all-powerful state (Pound); they have a limited role in cultivating the moral and rational abilities of law students (Nussbaum); finally, they have no major role to play because they can neither help lawyers win arguments nor prepare law students for the battles ahead (Balkin and Levinson).

Now this seems to me a rather restricted way of pursuing the link. It is associated more, as argued previously, with the perceived needs of American education rather

---

25 Costas Douzinas and Adam Gearey, *Critical Jurisprudence* (Oxford: Hart, 2006) Ch. 1–4.
26 Balkin's earliest writings were not inimical to these ideas; see Jack Balkin, "Deconstructive Practice and Legal Theory," 96 *Yale Law Journal* 743 (1987). The 1990s made both Nussbaum and Balkin move toward a more "brutal" pragmatism. The undergraduate character of the Law degree, the relaxed connection with the legal profession and the enduring influence of the Critical Legal Conference have somewhat shielded British academics from this trajectory.

than with the history of the two fields. Indeed even if we were to restrict our search to the academic aspects of the relationship, the itinerary would be different. It would first explore philosophy, literature, and law as the oldest forms of Western education. The Greeks, lacking a clerical caste and holy books, learned about their past, their world, and their Gods from a poet. Homer became the tradition, textbook, and source of learning for young Greeks, from the sixth century BC – a matter that greatly annoyed Plato and set up the ongoing ancient quarrel between philosophy and literature. Poetry – a central case of the Humanities – and the law were from the beginning the main ways of learning and ruling.

After the Christianization of Europe, the role of philosophy was assumed by theology. Theology and law were taught to students versed in the *artes liberales*, mainly the *trivium* (grammar, dialectic, and rhetoric), which formed the backbone of the medieval university. This expertise brought together patristic and secular study and cross-fertilized them. Bologna, the first European university, was established in the twelfth century as a law school but it developed out of the liberal arts that flourished there early in the eleventh century. By the thirteenth century, up to 10,000 students from all over Europe studied in Bologna. After graduating, they went to work for Church and the nascent state, using their legal expertise to protect secular leaders from ecclesiastical incursions. The task of these jurists was to extrapolate from principles of canon law the axioms of a secular legal science, helping develop on the way the theory of royal sovereignty and legitimacy against papal claims. The various types of knowledge placed today in the basket called Humanities had an intrinsic link with law and were the mainstay of education from Classical Greece to the late pre-Modern period.

Once this *longue durée* approach is taken to the Law–Humanities nexus, the focus of interest changes. If the two areas are closely linked, the zone of intersection should be sought in the target of their intervention, the ground concept that unites them. This is humanity, the human, human nature: a family of concepts and institutions that have brought together the exploration of man's civilization, tradition, culture, and values with the age-old attempt to discipline the subject and regulate the social bond.

"In the large sense the humanities mean the sum total of man's activities – nothing that touches man is alien to the humanities," wrote John Dodds in 1943 alluding to Terence's dictum that "*Homo sum; humani nil a me alienum puto.*"[27] If we accept this expansive definition, the Humanities and human rights, modern law's noblest claim, share their concern to address every aspect of humanity. Human rights are the acme of modern law; they have been created for the sake of humanity. As a combined term, they draw both from the moral and political tradition of (legal)

---

[27] John Dodds, "Place of the Humanities in a World of War," Vital Speeches of the Day (March 1943) 311.

A Humanities of Resistance

humanism (with its obvious links with the Humanities) and from the institutional and conceptual empire of law. If according to a standard approach, human rights are a category of rights given to people on account of their humanity and not because of any other attributes or belongings, the history, the (contested) concept, and meaning of humanity are important normative sources for contemporary law that escape the parochial nature of jurisdiction.

Liberal philosophy adopts a normative definition of humanity according to which, in one version, "our species is one, and each of the individuals who compose it is entitled to equal moral consideration."[28] Yet throughout Western history, the meaning, extension, and scope of humanity has varied wildly. Slaves have been excluded from humanity and are typically defined as things (*res*) among others by Aristotle, the philosopher of philosophers. Pigs, rats, leeches, and insects, on the other hand, were regularly and formally indicted and tried in law courts in the Middle Ages. In early modernity, companies became recognized as legal persons. A strong movement argues today that animals as well as trees, parks, and other natural objects should be given the protection of rights. The question of human nature has continued to "haunt modern thought and has become more complicated as a result of the contradictions engendered by positive science and historicism."[29] My argument is that humanity has not been a normative attribute shared by all humans, as liberal jurisprudence asserts, or a universal standard of civilization and distinction, as argued by the academic Humanities. Despite these important normative claims, humanity has acted as a strategy for ontological separation, distribution, and classification. Law and the Humanities share this strategic use. Let us start with a brief history of humanity.

Pre-Modern societies did not develop a comprehensive idea of the human species. Free men were Athenians or Spartans, Romans or Carthaginians but not members of humanity; they were Greeks or barbarians but not humans. The word *humanitas* appeared for the first time in the Roman Republic as a translation of the Greek word *paideia*. It was defined as *eruditio et institutio in bonas artes* (the closest modern equivalent is the German word *Bildung*). The Romans inherited the concept from Stoicism and used it to distinguish between the *homo humanus*, the educated Roman who was conversant with Greek culture and philosophy and was subjected to the *jus civile*, and the *homines barbari*, who included the majority of the uneducated non-Roman inhabitants of the Empire. Humanity enters the Western lexicon as an attribute and predicate of *homo*, a term of separation and distinction. For Cicero as well as the younger Scipio, *humanitas* implies generosity, politeness, civilization, and culture and is opposed to barbarism and animality.[30] "Only those who conform

---

[28] Michael Ignatieff, *Human Rights as Politics and Ideology* (Princeton: Princeton University Press, 2000).

[29] Claude Lefort, *The Political Forms of Modern Society*, John Thompson, ed. (Cambridge: Polity Press, 1986), 240.

[30] Ullman, op. cit., 302.

to certain standards are really men in the full sense, and fully merit the adjective 'human' or the attribute 'humanity.'"[31]

The job of philosophy, literature, and learning is to instill *humanitas* in the deserving. Humanity is an acquired taste, a construct, the outcome of education, edification, and discipline. It marks the distinction between the cultivated man of letters, the exemplar of real humanity, and the uneducated, uncivilized beings who, because they lack the subtlety of aesthetic discrimination and judgment, are lesser humans. These two aspects, the artificial nature of humanity and its use for separating people have been a mainstay of Western history. The modern quarrel between the sciences and the humanities, exemplified in the two cultures debate between C. P. Snow and Leavis,[32] in attacks on the culture industry and the society of the spectacle and the juxtaposition between high and low culture, constantly reconstructs humanity's cutting edge. Richard Kuhns argued in 1966 that to be well educated is to be conversant with a set of great books. Kuhns claims unconvincingly that "executive cadres trained for our great industries, workers on assembly lines, businessmen who want to become 'humanized'... right now as I write are given training in the humanities which raises in the student beliefs about greatness, about goodness, about the quality of his contemporary cultural environment,"[33] Only the learned are fully human with the rest falling on a point between barbarism and animality.

The political and legal uses of *humanitas* follow a similar history. The concept of humanity has been consistently used to separate, distribute, and classify people into rulers, ruled, and excluded. This strategy of separation curiously entered the historical stage at the precise point when the first proper universalist conception of *humanitas* emerged in Christian theology; it was captured in the St. Paul's statement that there is no Greek or Jew, man or woman, free man or slave (epistle to the Galatians 3:28). All people are equally part of humanity because they can be saved in God's plan of salvation and because they share the attributes of humanity now sharply differentiated from a transcended divinity and a subhuman animality. For classical humanism, reason determines the human: man is a *zoon logon echon* or *animale rationale*. For Christian metaphysics, on the other hand, the immortal soul, both carried and imprisoned by the body, is the mark of humanity. The new idea of universal equality, unknown to the Greeks, entered the Western world as a combination of classical and Christian metaphysics.

The divisive action of humanity survived the invention of its spiritual equality. Pope, Emperor, Prince, King, these representatives and disciples of God on earth,

---

[31] H. C. Baldry, *The Unity of Mankind in Greek Thought* (Cambridge: Cambridge University Press, 1965), 201.

[32] See Shroeder, op. cit.

[33] Kuhns op. cit., 12. Similarly, Nussbaum reports that the defense of some Classics scholars against criticisms of irrelevancy is that they prepare good managers.

A Humanities of Resistance

were absolute rulers. Their subjects, the *sub-jecti* or *sub-diti*, take the law and their commands from their political superiors. More importantly, people will be saved in Christ only if they accept the faith because non-Christians have no place in the providential plan. This radical divide and exclusion founded the ecumenical mission and proselytizing drive of Church and Empire. Christ's spiritual law of love turned into a battle cry: let us bring the pagans to the grace of God, let us make the singular event of Christ universal, let us impose the message of truth and love upon the whole world. The classical separation between Greek and barbarian was based on clearly demarcated territorial frontiers. In the Christian empire, the frontier was internalized and split the known globe diagonally between the faithful and the heathen. The barbarians were no longer beyond the city as the city expanded to include the known world. They became enemies within to be appropriately corrected or eliminated if they stubbornly refused spiritual or secular salvation.

The meaning of humanity after the conquest of the New World was vigorously contested in one of the most important public debates in history. In April 1550, Charles V of Spain called a council of state in Valladolid to discuss the Spanish attitude toward the vanquished Indians of Mexico. The philosopher Ginés de Sepulveda and the Bishop Bartholomé de las Casas, two major figures of the Spanish Enlightenment, debated on opposite sides. Sepulveda, who had just translated into Spanish Aristotle's *Politics*, argued, "the Spaniards rule with perfect right over the barbarians who, in prudence, talent, virtue, humanity are as inferior to the Spaniards as children to adults, women to men, the savage and cruel to the mild and gentle, I might say as monkey to men."[34] The Spanish Crown should feel no qualms in dealing with Indian evil. The Indians could be enslaved and treated as barbarians and savages to be civilized and proselytized.

Las Casas disagreed. The Indians have well-established customs and settled ways of life, he argued, they value prudence and have the ability to govern and organize families and cities. They have the Christian virtues of gentleness, peacefulness, simplicity, humility, generosity, and patience and are waiting to be converted. They look like our father Adam before the Fall, wrote las Casas in his *Apologia*; they are unwitting Christians. In an early definition of humanism, las Casas argued that, "all the people of the world are humans and the only one definition of all humans and of each one, that is that they are rational. Thus all races of humankind are one."[35] His arguments combined Christian theology and political utility. Respecting local customs is good morality but also good politics: the Indians would convert to Christianity (las Casas' main concern) and also accept the authority of the Crown and replenish its coffers, if they were made to feel that their traditions, laws, and

---

[34] Gines de Sepulveda, *Democrates Segundo of De las Justas Causa de la Guerra contra los Indios* (Madrid: Institute Fransisco de Vitoria, 1951) 33 quoted in Tzvetan Todorov, *The Conquest of America*, Richard Howard, transl. (Norman: University of Oklahoma Press, 1999) 153.

[35] Bartholomé de las Casas, *Obras Completas*, Vol. 7 (Madrid: Alianza Editorial, 1922) 536–7.

cultures were respected. Las Casas' Christian universalism was, like all universalisms, exclusive. He repeatedly condemned "Turks and Moors, the veritable barbarian outcasts of the nations" because they cannot be seen as "unwitting" Christians. An empirical universalism of superiority and hierarchy (Sepulveda) and a normative one of truth and love (las Casas) end up being not very different. As Tzvetan Todorov pithily remarks, there is "violence in the conviction that one possesses the truth oneself, whereas this is not the case for others, and that one must furthermore impose that truth on those others."[36]

The conflicting interpretations of humanity by Sepulveda and las Casas capture the dominant ideologies of Western empires, imperialisms, and colonialisms. At one end, the (racial) other is inhuman or subhuman. This justifies enslavement, atrocities, and even annihilation as strategies of the civilizing mission. At the other end, conquest, occupation, and forceful conversion are strategies of spiritual or material development, of progress and integration of the innocent, naïve, undeveloped others into the main body of humanity.

These two definitions of otherness and strategies toward it are linked with our own needs and desire: They act as supports of Western subjectivity. The helplessness, passivity, and inferiority of the undeveloped others turns them into our narcissistic mirror image and potential double. These unfortunates are the infants of humanity – ourselves in a state of nascency. They are victimized and sacrificed by their own radical evil; they are rescued by us who help them grow, develop, and become our likeness. Because the victim is our mirror image, we know what his interest is and impose it for his own good. At the other end, the irrational, cruel, victimizing others are projections of the Other of our unconscious. As Slavoj Zizek puts it, "there is a kind of passive exposure to an overwhelming Otherness, which is the very basis of being human . . . [the inhuman] is marked by a terrifying excess which, although it negates what we understand as humanity is inherent to being human."[37] We have called this abysmal Other lurking in the psyche and unsettling the ego various names: God or Satan, barbarian or foreigner, in psychoanalysis death drive or the Real. Today they have become the axis of evil, the rogue state, the butcher of Baghdad, the beast of Belgrade, and the bogus refugee. They are contemporary heirs to Sepulveda's monkeys, epochal representatives of inhumanity.

Becoming human is possible only against this impenetrable inhuman background. Split into two, according to a simple moral calculus, the Other has a tormented and a tormenting part, both radical evil and radical passivity. He represents our narcissistic self in its infancy (civilization as *potentia*, possibility, or risk) and what is most frightening and horrific in us: the death drive, the evil persona who lurks in the midst of psyche and society. Empirical and normative humanity (humanity as

---

[36] Todorov op cit., 166, 168.
[37] Slavoj Zizek, "Against Human Rights," 34 *New Left Review* 56 (July–August 2005).

A Humanities of Resistance

quality shared or as a project to be achieved) will eventually coincide through the West's surgical intervention. Either the deceased, unworthy, inferior members will be cut off or they will be humanized and integrated once they accept the wrong of their ways and agree to be civilized; severing or prosthesis are the ways of making human.

The religious grounding of humanity was undermined by the liberal political philosophies of early modernity. The foundation of humanity was transferred from God to (human) nature. Human nature as the common denominator has been interpreted as an empirical fact or as a normative value or both (Habermas). Science has driven the first approach. The mark of humanity has been variously sought in language, reason, evolution, or its upright posture (the etymological meaning of *anthropos*). It was legal and political innovations, however, that turned humanity, man as species existence, into the common and absolute value around which the whole world revolves. The great eighteenth-century revolutions and their declarations paradigmatically expressed the modern universalistic conception of humanity. Yet at the heart of this new universalism, humanity remained a strategy of division and classification.

We can follow briefly this contradictory process that both proclaims the universal and excludes the local in the text of the French Declaration of the Rights of Man and Citizen, the manifesto modernity. Article 1, the progenitor of legal universalism, states, "men are born and remain free and equal of right," a claim repeated in the inaugural article of the 1948 Universal Declaration of Human Rights. Equality and liberty are declared natural entitlements, independent of governments, epochal, and local factors. Yet the Declaration is categorically clear about the real source of universal rights. Article 2 states, "the aim of any political association is to preserve the natural and inalienable rights of man." Article 3 proceeds to define this association: "The principle of all Sovereignty lies essentially with the nation."

Natural and eternal rights are declared on behalf of the universal man; however, these rights did not preexist but were created by the Declaration. A new type of political association, the sovereign nation and its state and a new type of man, the national citizen, came into existence and became the beneficiaries of rights. In a paradoxical fashion, the Declaration of universal principle established local sovereignty. From that point, statehood and territory follow a national principle and belong to a dual time. If the Declaration inaugurated modernity, it also started nationalism and all its consequences: genocides, ethnic and civil wars, ethnic cleansing, minorities, refugees, and the stateless. The spatial principle is clear: Every state should have one nation and every nation should have its own state – a catastrophic development for peace as its extreme application after 1989 has shown.

The new temporal principle replaced religious eschatology with a historical teleology, which promised the future suturing of humanity and nation. This teleology has two possible variants: Either the nation imposes its rule on humanity or universalism undermines parochial divides and identities. Both variants were evident when the Romans turned Stoic cosmopolitanism into the imperial legal regulation of *jus gentium*. In France, the first alternative appeared in the Napoleonic Wars, which allegedly spread the civilizing influence through conquest and occupation (according to Hegel, Napoleon was the world spirit on horseback); the second was the beginnings of a modern cosmopolitanism, in which slavery was abolished and colonial people were given political rights for a limited time after the Revolution. From the imperial deformation of Stoic cosmopolitanism to the current use of human rights to legitimize Western global hegemony, every normative universalism has decayed into imperial globalism. The split between normative and empirical humanity resists its healing.

A gap separates universal man, the ontological principle of modernity, and national citizen, its political instantiation and real beneficiary of rights. The nation-state came into existence through the exclusion of other people and nations. The modern subject reaches humanity by acquiring political rights of citizenship, which guarantee admission to the universal human nature by excluding others from that status. The alien as a noncitizen is the modern barbarian. She does not have rights because she is not part of the state and she is a lesser human being because she is not a citizen. One is human to greater or lesser degree because one is a citizen to a greater or lesser degree. The alien is the gap between man and citizen. In our globalized world, not to have citizenship, to be stateless or a refugee is the worst fate. Strictly speaking human rights do not exist: If rights are given to people on account of their humanity, then refugees, economic migrants, and prisoners in Guantánamo Bay and similar detention centers who have little if any legal protection should be their main beneficiaries. As we know, however, they have very few if any rights. They are legally abandoned, bare life, the *homines sacri* of the new world order.

The epochal move to the subject as the metaphysical principle of modernity is driven and exemplified by legal personality. As species existence, the "man" of the rights of man appears without sex, color, history, or tradition. He has no needs or desires, an empty vessel united with all others through three abstract traits: free will, reason, and soul – the universal elements of human essence. This minimum of humanity allows man to claim autonomy, moral responsibility, and legal subjectivity. At the same time, the empirical man who actually enjoys the rights of man is a man all too man: a well-off, heterosexual, white, urban male who condenses in his person the abstract dignity of humanity and the real prerogatives of belonging to the community of the powerful. Indeed, one could write the history of human rights as the ongoing and always failing struggle to close the gap between the abstract man and the concrete citizen: to add flesh, blood, and sex to the pale outline of the human and extend the dignities and privileges of the powerful (the characteristics of normative humanity) to empirical humanity. This has not happened, however, and is unlikely to do so through the action of rights.

A Humanities of Resistance   69

Here finally, in the common frame of reference between "humanism" and "legal humanism" we find the link between the Humanities and law. Humanism claims that there is a universal essence of man and this essence is the attribute of each individual who is the real subject. Linking empirical and normative humanity, humanism marks the concern of modernity to escape cosmological or theological determinations, to discover humanity's worth exclusively in itself. "The *humanitas* of *homo humanus* is determined with regard to an already established interpretation of nature, history, world, and the ground of the world, that is, of beings as a whole."[38] By dealing with beings as a whole, however, and accepting a dominant interpretation as absolute, humanism mistakes the transient and historically determined turn to the subject as eternal and assigns to it absolute mastery over the natural, social, and psychic world. This metaphysical closure is accompanied by the exclusion of those who do not fully meet the requirements of the human essence. Classical humanism juxtaposed the *humanum* to the *barbarum*; contemporary versions are followed by a "double marking, of a return to half-understood Greek ideals and a gesture of setting oneself apart from some perceived barbarism."[39] Humanism, personified by the subject of human rights and exemplified by the academic Humanities, veers tantalizingly and dizzyingly between an empirical globality and a normative universalization, perennially excluding and subjugating those who do not meet its rigorous standards.

Legal humanism follows closely this metaphysics and shapes the institutions of humanism. It is the "tendency to posit man as the principle and end of everything . . . for nearly all modern thinkers about law, man is the author . . . of law."[40] For legal humanism, the subject is an isolated monad with solitary consciousness who faced with a disenchanted, threatening but also malleable world, turns to itself as the basis for self-legislation. Legal humanism posits man as the author and end of law. "The starting point of the science of law is Man, as soon as man is constituted into a legal subject. The point of arrival of modern legal science is man. This science does not move, it starts with man and ends up rediscovering the subject."[41] For the legal mentality, the essence of humanity is the free, willing, and solitary legal subject. The legal subject becomes the mark of humanity through the mediation and the restraints of the posited objective legal universe.

Modern law redefined human beings as creatures of will and desire by making rights its building blocks. There can be no positive law without the humanist legal subject, the bearer of rights and duties; there can be no conception of rights without

---

[38] Martin Heidegger, "Letter on Humanism" in *Basic Writings*, D. F. Krell, ed. (San Francisco: Harper, 1977), 201–2.

[39] Joanna Hodge, *Heidegger and Ethics* (London: Routledge, 1995), 90.

[40] Michel Villey, "L'Humanisme et le droit," in *Seize essais de philosophie du droit* (Paris: Dalloz, 1969) 60.

[41] Bernard Edelman, *Le Droit saisi par la photographie* (Paris, Maspero, 1973) 102.

a positive set of laws and institutions that bring the subject into existence and endow it with the patrimony of rights. The Sovereign too is presented in the guise of a superindividual entity with desires and powers. Sovereign and subject, positive rule and right emerge together and presuppose one another.

Law's subject exemplifies the dialectics of legal enlightenment: As the double genitive indicates, the subject both legislates the law and is subjected to it. According to the humanist paradox, an external constraint supports freedom. In late modernity, however, autonomy recedes. The proliferation of rules and the obsession with regulation and governance turns human relations into legal rights. Technologies of power overwhelm the self-legislation of autonomy and the universalism of (legal) humanism retreats.

Prolegomena for a Law and Humanities of Resistance

Human rights have expanded and are in the process of colonizing every part of daily life. Humanity is now defined in scientific terms, whereas the normative realm has been entrusted almost exclusively to law in the form of regulation. Law is no longer the form or the instrument, the tool or restraint of power; it has started turning into the very operation, the substance of power. Legal form is squeezed and undermined by the privatization of public areas of activity and the simultaneous publicization of domains of private action. Legal content, on the other hand, becomes coextensive with the operations of power. As a result, law is autopoetically reproduced in a loop of endless validity that becomes progressively devoid of sense or signification.

The global biopolitical turn has turned human rights, the moral high ground of modern law, into an integral part of the world dispensation. Rights precede, accompany, and legitimize the penetration of the world by neo liberal capitalism. The gap between normative principle and its realization, underlying structure and surface appearance, has been closing down. Immanent critique has little purchase and the utopian dream has atrophied, chased from the public domain by those who have the power to turn their interests and desires into normative common sense.[42] To put it another way, while the law in modernity expressed both the will of a community to live together from which it drew its normative strength and energies as well as the structure of domination and subjection or subjectivation, precarious as it always was, in the era of globalized capitalism this bifurcation is retreating.

Classical natural rights protected property and religion by turning them into apolitical institutions; the main effect of the ever-expanding reach of (human) rights is to depoliticize politics itself. Politics is fast morphing into a type of market economics legitimized by humanistic moralism. As an economic operation, politics has become the terrain where negotiations and compromises are worked out, accounted

---

[42] Russell Jacobi, *The End of Utopia* (New York: Routledge, 1996).

A Humanities of Resistance

and aggregated between groups and classes that have accepted the overall social balance, distribution, and inequality. In the moral mode, the assumed agreement around values and principles replaces conflict and argument, leaving large parts of humanity unrepresented and defenseless. Law is in the process of becoming coextensive with the natural life of society, mapping the social landscape by replicating within itself the facts of social life and helping reproduce the existing order. At this point, science becomes the dominant paradigm for legal pedagogy. Yet as the early Nussbaum put it, "science is rarely Socratic . . . it cannot be scrutinizing its own conceptions and foundations."[43] Justice becomes synonymous with the law (and therefore almost redundant) and the Humanities' civilizing mission a palliative for the inhumanity of willing subjugation.

History has taught us that there is nothing sacred about any definition of humanity and nothing eternal about its scope. Humanity cannot act as the a priori normative principle and is mute in the matter of legal and moral rules. Humanity has no foundation and no ends; it is the definition of groundlessness. Its metaphysical function lies not in a philosophical essence but in its nonessence, in the incessant surprising of the human condition and its exposure to an undecided open future. Humanity exists as an endless process of redefinition and the necessary but impossible attempt to escape external determination. This speculative humanity can, however, only come forth in conflict with a subjugating legal humanism and a civilizing Humanities that divide and discipline.

Humanity as a concept is a floating signifier without a necessary or motivated signified.[44] It is both the prerequisite of autonomy and the construct of power, discipline, and strategy. The pressing moral and political task is to develop a Humanities of resistance to accompany a pedagogy of justice. The stakes are no longer or exclusively the development of the delicacy of discernment, the sharpening of hermeneutical aptitude, or even moral edification. Adopting from the classics and Roscoe Pound the idea of education as critique of dominant practices that divide, dominate, and oppress, the new Humanities must commit themselves to the reassertion of the principle of truth as unconditional resistance to the biopolitical turn of post-political politics and culture. The duty to resist places the university (Law and the Humanities) in opposition to many and great powers, which include the nation, the state and its sovereignty, and those mediatic, ideological, religious, and cultural forces that stop and prevent the cosmopolitanism to come.[45] More generally, the law must revive and strengthen its intimate relationship with justice, which nowadays is explored mainly in philosophy and literature, history and art. Law does not need the Humanities for their civilizing influence. Law is a central contributor to the project

---

[43] Nussbaum, op. cit. fn. 12, 1640.
[44] Costas Douzinas, *The End of Human Rights* (Oxford: Hart, 2000) 253–61.
[45] Costas Douzinas, *Human Rights and Empire* (London: Routledge, 2007) Ch. 12.

of constructing the human. Against the dominant combination of Humanities, law, and education that separates the human from the inhuman and classifies into rulers and ruled, humanity achieves itself not as a future project of unification of the normative (civilization, culture, and liberalism) and the empirical but in overcoming finitude and facing the infinite within historical immanence (in the here and now).

2

Three Tales of Two Texts
An Introduction to Law and the Humanities

Kathryn Abrams

Scholars in "Law and the Humanities" create meaning by examining texts that lie outside the formal confines of the law. They then relate these texts, often through narrative conceptualizations, to the work of the law – be it the focused activity of adjudication or the broader field of legality and its social and cultural manifestations. In this chapter I introduce this body of work, by taking a similar methodological path. I begin by focusing on two nonlegal texts; I then offer a series of narratives that connect these texts, not with the work of the law per se, but with the trajectory of this shifting, flourishing field.

The first text is Herman Melville's novella, *Billy Budd, Sailor: An Inside Narrative*.[1] This canonical text concerns an act of judgment on the Bellipotent, a nineteenth-century vessel of Her Majesty's Navy. A false accusation of mutiny triggers an act of violence by a handsome and greatly beloved young sailor. The ship's captain must decide whether to impose the law's most stringent command on a man who is depicted as characterologically innocent and perhaps even circumstantially excused. Although its subtle elaboration of character and inconsistencies of narration bring to the tale the illuminations and provocations of literature, the novella unfolds in a vein of sober and painful realism. This realism is, transparently, about the command and the application of the law. *Billy Budd* traverses act, accusations, arguments to a drumhead court, and the issuance and execution of a sentence. Its stern yet uncomfortable resolution – in which Billy's acceptance of his fate is countered by a series of more ambivalent postscripts – confronts the reader with the tension between public responsibility and private morality, between legality and justice, and logical reasoning and intuitive, affective judgment.

---

[1] Herman Melville, *Billy Budd, Sailor: An Inside Narrative* (1924), in Frederick Busch, ed., *Billy Budd and Other Stories* 287 (New York and London: Penguin Books, 1986).

The second text is the Roman Polanski film, *Death and the Maiden*.[2] The film concerns the aftermath of a repressive dictatorship. A violent storm brings Paulina Escobar, a victim of state-sponsored torture, together with the doctor who was one of her assailants. Sparked by the new government's neglect of her injury,[3] Paulina resolves to "try" Dr. Miranda in her living room, appointing her husband Gerardo, a human rights lawyer, as his defense counsel. Deliberations in this trial, however, do not take the usual course: Paulina demands Miranda's confession, adding that if he acknowledges his acts of torture she will spare him, but if he refuses, she will kill him.[4] Miranda first protests his innocence, but facing imminent death, he offers a chilling confession that Paulina accepts as truthful. She releases him, sentencing them all to coexist in the world "after." The film explores the role and the limits of law, in affording due process to the accused, and in fostering repair after state-sponsored violence.

Even a brief synopsis reveals the many differences between these works. *Billy Budd* is an early-twentieth-century work, whose nineteenth-century action serves mainly as a setting for a paradigmatic conflict. *Death and the Maiden* is a late-twentieth-century work, whose dilemmas resonate urgently with contemporary viewers who have witnessed genocidal governments in transition. *Billy Budd* is a classic novella, by a great American man of letters, whose understated, eloquent narration invites readers to contemplate the competing claims of Billy and Captain Vere. *Death and the Maiden* is a mass-market film by a controversial director, whose dramatic setting, visual metaphors, and emotionally charged exchanges confront viewers with its substantive challenges. *Billy Budd* uses the context of a specific trial to explore the tensions between the rule of law and the particularized demands of substantive justice. *Death and the Maiden* uses a hybrid of due process and vigilante justice – conducted by a impassioned survivor on her former captor, at gunpoint in her living room – to raise questions about the relationship between law and transitional justice, among law, violence, and memory, and about law as a fact-finding method, epistemological stance, and characterological disposition. Finally, despite its status as "An Inside Narrative," *Billy Budd* focuses almost exclusively on public processes. The one encounter between Billy and Vere that reveals a more private dimension

---

[2] *Death and the Maiden* (Fine Line Features, 1994), directed by Roman Polanski, screenplay (based on his original play) by Ariel Dorfman.

[3] We learn at the beginning of the film that the government has appointed a Human Rights Commission to investigate state-sponsored violence during the prior regime, and Gerardo, Paulina's husband, has agreed to serve as the Commission's chair. To prevent divisiveness in the fledgling democracy, and direct the public's focus toward the future, the government has limited the Commission's jurisdiction to cases in which government violence ended the lives of its victims. Thus cases like Paulina's, which involve victims who survived, will not be pursued by the Commission. See id.

[4] To her husband's shocked response that this 'trial' is a travesty, Paulina retorts, "I'll give him all the guarantees he never gave me," but admits grimly that "if he is innocent, then he's really screwed." See id.

Three Tales of Two Texts

of each man is related as a matter of hypothetical speculation.[5] In *Death and the Maiden*, the characters' efforts to confront the legacy of public repression play out in a private setting, and they are also intertwined with Paulina and Gerardo's efforts to confront their complicated personal history: her refusal to implicate him under torture, and his betrayal of her with another woman while she was in captivity.

Notwithstanding these differences, *Death and the Maiden* and *Billy Budd* are typical of the kinds of texts that have stimulated and sustained scholarship in Law and the Humanities. How does a field accommodate, integrate, or coalesce around two such disparate works? In this chapter, I will offer three different answers. Reflecting the interest of many Law and Humanities scholars in narratives,[6] I will offer these answers in the form of thematized stories about how these works illuminate particular dimensions or directions of the field. I will offer first a narrative of movement, suggesting that these foci reflect the early and later dimensions of a field in transition. I will turn then to a narrative of heterogeneity, which finds examination of such disparate works typical of a field characterized by plural methodological and substantive pursuits. I will finish with a narrative of continuity, which suggests that, framed by the larger characteristics and commitments of this field, these two works may be less different than they first appear. As readers may suspect, these narratives are not necessarily mutually exclusive, but may also be read in conjunction with each other. My hope is that they will illuminate the intricate, expanding topography of this field.

Movement

The first story accepts at face value the frank disparity of these works. It argues that the movement from *Billy Budd* to *Death and the Maiden* as a paradigmatic text for Law and the Humanities reflects a field in transition. The first phases of this work aimed at humanizing legal decision making through exposure to its depiction in great works of literature; later versions sought to elaborate legal decisions as texts through the theories or analytic strategies that had been applied to literature; more recent work has sought to analyze a range of cultural products, particularly film, as creating revealing parallels to law and contributing to the more diffuse and encompassing

---

[5] In what Lawrence Douglas refers to as a "crisis of omniscience," see Lawrence Douglas, "Discursive Limits: Narrative and Judgment in Billy Budd," 27 *Mosaic* 141, [145] (1994), the narrator observes, "beyond the communication of the sentence, what took place at this interview was never known." Melville, *Billy Budd, Sailor*, supra note 1, at 366.

[6] There are actually incipient subgenres within the field, reflecting the diversity of this interest. See e.g., "Legal Storytelling," 87 *Michigan Law Review* 2073 et seq. (1989) (exploring the role of experiential storytelling, or "narrative," in the law); Robert Cover, "Nomos and Narrative" 87 *Harvard Law Review* 4 (1983) (examining law's creation and destruction of narratives). See also Peter Brooks and Paul Gewirtz, eds., *Law's Stories: Narrative and Rhetoric in the Law* (New Haven: Yale University Press, 1998) (edited volume exploring plural relations of narrative to law).

world of "legality." *Billy Budd* is an emblematic focus for the early phases of this effort; *Death and the Maiden* takes us to the outer reaches of what this effort has become.

Billy Budd served as a pivotal text in one of the earliest phases of Law and Humanities scholarship: the effort to illuminate legal decision making by studying its depiction in great works of literature.[7] The focus on *Billy Budd* itself reflects a conventional judgment about the domain of "literature." *Billy Budd* is a canonical text in Law and Humanities and in the academic world beyond its boundaries. The view of "law" that is reflected in its action is – at least at first glance – no less conventional. Although it is set on the high seas, rather than in a traditional court of law, *Billy Budd* offers an examination of the painful choices involved in applying, and indeed in maintaining, a system of laws. The actors are public actors: Captain Vere is an officer in Her Majesty's Navy, charged with responsibility for enforcing the Mutiny Act, or at least the 1749 Articles of War.[8] The story concerns an act that violates the legal, if not the moral, order under which the characters work and live. The disposition of Billy's case is tied to the maintenance of legal order, albeit in this circumscribed sphere.

The goal of bringing law and literature together through the analysis of *Billy Budd* is, for many commentators, edifying and ameliorative: It seeks to shed a "humanizing" light on the workings of the law.[9] Analysts aim to illuminate the workings of law for those who might come before it; through exposure to a nuanced, ambivalent, affectively infused exploration of law's most painful dilemmas, they seek to broaden the perspective of those who might one day be charged with its operation. The evocative depictions of Captain Vere and Billy Budd underscore the stakes, and the anguish, of the decision on the Bellipotent. The story's equivocal, successive

---

[7] For an illuminating discussion of this (and subsequent) phases in the scholarship on Law and Literature, see Gary Minda, *Postmodern Legal Movements: Law and Jurisprudence at Century's End* (New York: New York University Press, 1996) 149–66.

[8] According to some commentators, Captain Vere invoked the Mutiny Act to press on the drumhead court the stringency associated with martial law; but because that act applied only to land forces, Billy was not subject to that act and was, in fact, charged under the Articles of War. See e.g., Martha Merrill Umphrey, Law's Bonds: Eros and Identification in Billy Budd, 64 *American Imago* 413, 421 (2007); Robert Weisberg, *The Failure of the Word* 148–58 (New Haven: Yale University Press, 1984). Other commentators refer simply to the Articles of War. See e.g., Daniel Solove, Melville's Billy Budd and Security in Times of Crisis, 26 *Cardozo Studies in Law and Literature* 2443 (2005).

[9] For general statements of this humanizing mission, see Guido Calabresi, Introductory Letter, 1 *Yale Journal of Law and Humanities* vii (1988); Owen Fiss, The Challenge Ahead, 1 *Yale Journal of Law and Humanities* viii (1988). This vision was, of course, contested, even in the relatively early years of Law and Humanities scholarship. See e.g., Austin Sarat, Traditions and Trajectories in Law and Humanities Scholarship, 10 *Yale Journal of Law and Humanities* 401, 402 (1998) (challenging trope of "recuperation and rescue" of law by humanities); Peter Brooks, A Slightly Polemical Comment on Austin Sarat, 10 *Yale Journal of Law and Humanities* 409, 409 (1998) (rejecting view of humanities as providing "uplift and inspiration" to law).

Three Tales of Two Texts

endings trouble the stern resolution of the sentence and Billy's acceptance of his fate; they draw into question the power of law to achieve the closure that is widely ascribed to it. Although the story highlights tensions in the application of the law, the main thread of its action does not disturb conventional understandings of what law is or of the separateness of the sphere within which it operates.

Subsequent currents within Law and Humanities scholarship, however, began to unsettle these assumptions. First, the "humanizing" goal of depicting "law *in* literature" was succeeded by different ways of conceiving the relation between the legal and the literary. Some scholars, schooled by the critical theories that had come to shape the study of literature, began to focus less on representing the human drama than on investigating the textuality of legal decisions. The law was not simply an object to be portrayed or illuminated by literature; it was an activity with salient parallels to literature. Lawmakers struggled through language to produce meaning; their work engaged and mobilized interpretive communities.[10] Consequently, many Law and Humanities scholars began to treat "law *as* literature," addressing legal decisions as texts that could be analyzed by recourse to deconstruction psychoanalytic theory, Foucaultian analysis of the circulation of power, feminist, queer, and other forms of antifoundationalist theory that had increasingly been applied to literary texts.[11]

Recourse to these theoretical frames did more than simply revise scholars' view of the relation between law and literature, however. It gradually transformed the conceptions of "law" that informed scholarship in Law and the Humanities, and the contexts that elicited scholarly attention. Increasingly, scholarship turned away from law's formal, decisional aspects, toward informal systems of regulation, and toward the contending discursive currents, structures, and other relations of power that infused and shaped law more generally. Formal statutory law or legal doctrine came to be understood as a product of political and cultural assumptions, group-based identifications, histories, and hierarchies, and social and institutional practices – many of which became part of the analytic frames constructed by legal scholars.[12] Legal academics also traced with increasing interest the complex trajectory of power that moved outward from legal decisions. Case law, statutes, new forms of legal argumentation could shape the social or behavioral expectations of those who lived

---

[10] See e.g., James Boyd White, *Justice as Translation: An Essay in Cultural and Legal Criticism* (Chicago: University of Chicago Press, 1990). See also Stanley Fish, *The Law Wishes to Have a Formal Existence, in There's No Such Thing as Free Speech, and It's a Good Thing, Too* (Oxford and New York: Oxford University Press, 1994) (noting parallels between contract law and literature).

[11] For discussions of this development, see Minda, Postmodern Legal Movements, supra note 7; Naomi Mezey, Out of the Ordinary: Law, Power, Culture, and the Commonplace 26 *Law and Social Inquiry* 145, 145–50 (2001).

[12] Mezey, Out of the Ordinary, supra note at 145–50.

under them, as well as their notions of political or legal legitimacy, and their sense of themselves as subjects.[13] Foregrounding these intricate relations meant that legal scholars in Law and the Humanities[14] became increasingly preoccupied with a broader conception of "legality," which Naomi Mezey has described as "the more dispersed and less visible workings of power and discipline."[15]

In rendering these accounts, scholars sometimes described the workings of power as unpredictably variant and localized;[16] however they also, perhaps more frequently, analyzed them as enacting patterns of hegemony or domination.[17] This latter thread fueled an interest, within this literature, in group-based inequality, producing work that intersected with feminism or critical race theory.[18] Because power that strives for domination works through the production of particular kinds of subjects, scholars became more focused on subjectivity: not simply the subjectivity of legal decision makers such as Captain Vere, but the subjectivities of those affected and formed by law.[19] Even analyses that focused on the hegemonic character of power described dominance as necessarily incomplete, as inevitably inciting or coupled

[13] See e.g., Susan Silbey & Patricia Ewick, *The Common Place of Law: Stories from Everyday Life* (Chicago: University of Chicago Press, 1998) (describing varying forms of legal consciousness that emerge from individual subjects' engagement with legal rules and institutions); Kristin Bumiller, *The Civil Rights Society: The Social Construction of Victims* (Baltimore: Johns Hopkins University Press, 1992) (describing deauthorized or victimized subjectivity emerging from recourse to civil rights laws).

[14] This transition to a focus on "legality" has occurred in Law and Society scholarship as well. Law and Society work shares the constructivist emphasis of recent Law and Humanities work, and its view of the deep interpenetration of law with other social structures and practices. Traditionally, Law and Society work has focused on social institutions and has drawn more consistently on research in sociology and political science; but in more recent years Law and Society scholars have turned to the analysis of culture and cultural productions such as film. See e.g., Austin Sarat, Presidential Address: Imagining the Law of Father: Loss, Dread, and Mourning in The Sweet Hereafter, 34 *Law and Society Review* 3 (2000) (Presidential lecture of Law and Society Association, arguing that Law and Society scholarship should encompass analyses of film); see e.g., Austin Sarat & Jonathan Simon, Beyond Legal Realism? Cultural Analysis, Cultural Studies, and the Situation of Legal Scholarship, 13 *Yale Journal of Law and Humanities* 3 (2001) (past President and Program Chair of Law & Society Association describing turn from society to culture in contemporary law-related scholarship). In addition, a number of scholars, such as Austin Sarat, Jonathan Simon, Naomi Mezey, and Steven Winter, contribute to both bodies of scholarship.

[15] Mezey, Out of the Ordinary, supra note at 149.

[16] See e.g., Rosemary Coombe, Tactics of Appropriation and the Politics of Recognition in Late Modern Democracies, 21 *Political Theory* 411 (1993).

[17] Mezey, Out of the Ordinary, supra note 11, at 146–47.

[18] Katherine Franke, Becoming a Citizen: Post-Bellum Regulation of African American Marriage, 11 *Yale Journal of Law and Humanities* 251 (1999); Steven Winter, The Power Thing, 82 *Virginia Law Review* 735 (1996); Symposium, Intersections: Sexuality, Cultural Tradition, and the Law, 8 *Yale Journal of Law and Humanities* 93 et seq. (1996).

[19] Naomi Mezey, Out of the Ordinary, supra note 11, at 150–4. See also Susan Silbey & Patricia Ewick: *The Common Place of Law*, supra. These authors acknowledge, however, that these constructive effects can be reciprocal: the response of individual subjects and groups of subjects to legality can shape the way it is understood.

Three Tales of Two Texts

with resistance.[20] Consequently, Law and Humanities scholars also became interested in resistant discourses, practices, or acts.

These patterns have joined a more recent development: an interest in the affective dimensions of the law.[21] This shift was spurred partly by challenges to legal objectivity, which questioned the descriptive and normative commitment to law's dispassion and rationality.[22] It was also fueled by critical scholars' attention to the affective consequences of legal decisions.[23] Scholarship drawing on the humanities has become a vehicle for exploring these dimensions: Analysis of specific emotions germane to law has drawn on a strong base in philosophy and, occasionally, anthropology or literature. Cultural productions highlighting trials or other occasions of legal decision making have illuminated affective dimensions as well as more familiar facets of legal rationality.

These moves within Law and Humanities scholarship have been reinforced by a turn, within legal theory and theories of governance more generally, toward the "cultural" as a ground of regulation and analysis.[24] A focus on culture parallels the increasing focus on subjectivity – because cultural analysis frequently targets subjectivity as opposed to behavior;[25] it reflects an understanding that assertions of value, power, or resistance may take place far from the realm of law or even formal institutions. Legal scholars, conceiving culture as "a description of a particular way of life, which expresses certain meanings and values not only in art and learning, but also in institutions and ordinary behavior,"[26] have begun to deploy disciplinary knowledge from semiotics to anthropology to social theory to the emerging field of cultural studies[27] to frame their investigations. This view of culture – as formed and

---

[20] See [sources cited supra note 19]. This Foucaultian line of inquiry has provided a bridge of sorts between work within the field of Law and Society, and work in Law and the Humanities.

[21] See generally Susan Bandes, Introduction, *The Passions of Law* 3 (New York: New York University Press, 1999).

[22] See e.g., Martha Minow & Elizabeth V. Spelman, Passion for Justice, 10 *Cardozo Law Review* 37 (1988); Judith Resnik, On the Bias: Feminist Reconsiderations of Aspirations for Our Judges, 61 *Southern California Law Review* 1877 (1988); Martha Minow, The Supreme Court 1986 Term, Foreword: Justice Engendered, 101 *Harvard Law Review* 10 (1987).

[23] Lynne Henderson, Legality and Empathy, 85 *Michigan Law Review* 574 (1987); Patricia Williams, The Obliging Shell, 87 *Michigan Law Review* 2128 (1989).

[24] Sarat & Simon, Beyond Legal Realism? supra note 14; Naomi Mezey, Law as Culture, 13 *Yale Journal of Law and Humanities* 35 (2001). See generally, Austin Sarat & Thomas Kearns, *Law in the Domains of Culture* (1998). Sarat and Simon argue that this shift has been informed by a growing scholarly perception that governance effected through social institutions – and informed by social science – has lost momentum and has begun to be supplemented by attention to cultural practices, norms, and production. See Sarat & Simon, supra.

[25] Sarat & Simon, Beyond Legal Realism?, supra note 14.

[26] See Stuart Hall, Cultural Studies: Two Paradigms, in Nicholas Dirks, Geoff Eley & Sherry Ortner, eds., *Culture/Power/History: A Reader in Contemporary Social Theory* 520, 527 (Princeton: Princeton University Press, 1994) (quoting Raymond Williams).

[27] Mezey, Law as Culture, supra note 24.

Kathryn Abrams

contested through the distinct, contributing understandings of subgroups,[28] and as constantly in the making – has directed scholars toward more localized meanings and practices, toward the private as well as the public, toward the informal as well as the formal, toward the quotidian as well as the transformative or epic.[29] The legal consciousness of ordinary people,[30] the understandings produced and circulated through mass media or the Internet,[31] and the products of popular culture[32] have become the focus of legal analysis.

Within this more recent body of work, the analysis of film – be it popular cinema,[33] classic works,[34] or documentary filmmaking[35] – has garnered particular attention.[36] The growth of interest in this medium among legal scholars reflects the focus on popular culture as well as the informal, private, quotidian, and affective. Scholars also readily grasped the parallels between law and film, observing that many films reflect a structure similar to that of a trial: Viewers confront dramas of responsibility, which require them to confront conflicting evidence that unfolds slowly over the course of the work.[37]

Death and the Maiden reflects many of these developments. Like *Billy Budd*, it addresses the tension between law and justice; yet it does not ask us to consider simply what happens when law prevails. It projects the viewer into an alternative universe in which not law but a form of rough, private justice claims the upper hand. It asks what is gained and what is lost through a kind of self-help in which the goals

---

[28] Mezey, Law as Culture, supra note 24, Rosemary Coombe, Critical Cultural Studies, 10 *Yale Journal of Law and Humanities* 463 (1998).

[29] See generally, Austin Sarat & Thomas Kearns, *Law in Everyday Life* (1993).

[30] See Silbey & Ewick, The Common Place of Law, supra note 13.

[31] See Rosemary Coombe, Critical Cultural Studies, supra note 28; Rosemary Coombe, Tactics of Appropriation, supra note 16.

[32] See e.g., Katherine Franke, Cunning Stunts: From Hegemony to Desire a Review of Madonna's Sex, 20 *New York University Review of Law and Social Change* 549 (1992); Susan Keller, Review Essay: Justify My Love, 18 *Western State University Law Review* 463 (1990) (legal scholars analyze work by Madonna).

[33] Sarat, Imagining the Law of the Father, supra note 14 (arguing for the place of analysis of contemporary film in law and society scholarship).

[34] See e.g., Orit Kamir, *Framed: Women in Law and Film* (Durham: Duke University Press, 2005) (analysis of classic films relating to law featuring women, such as *Adam's Rib, Rashomon, Anatomy of a Murder, A Question of Silence*, and others).

[35] Regina Austin, Foreword: Engaging Documentaries Seriously, 16 *Fordham Intellectual Property, Media & Entertainment Law Journal* 707 (2006).

[36] During the same period, legal scholars have explored the meanings associated with the advent of photographic evidence in forensic settings. See e.g., Jennifer Mnookin, The Image of Truth: Photographic Evidence and the Power of Analogy, 10 *Yale Journal of Law and Humanities* 1 (1998).

[37] See e.g., Jennifer Mnookin, Reproducing a Trial: Evidence and Assessment in *Paradise Lost*, in Austin Sarat, Lawrence Douglas, & Martha Merrill Umphrey, *Law on the Screen* 153 (Palo Alto: Stanford University Press, 2005) (noting "structural affinity" between documentary films and trials). I would argue that this point can be extended beyond the factual dramas of responsibility depicted in documentaries, to fictional dramas of responsibility depicted in films such as *Death and the Maiden*.

Three Tales of Two Texts

of justice – and even some formal attributes of due process – are achieved under the constraint of coercion. Viewers are challenged to judge not simply Dr. Miranda, but also Paulina's method of seeking justice for the violations of the past.

If, however, the film functions as a trial and demands an interpretation of Paulina's extralegal means of achieving justice, it also points toward a more complex and encompassing notion of legality. In *Death and the Maiden*, "law" is not simply – as it was in *Billy Budd* – the resolution reflected in a particular decision. It also encompasses the rule of law: the forms of justice that prevent arbitrariness and secure respect for the humanity of all participants. These forms, in the context of the film, have significance beyond the individual case of Dr. Miranda. As the impending work of the Human Rights Commission makes clear, the film is also concerned with law as a means of restoring public confidence in the state after genocide or state-sponsored violence. Set, literally and figuratively,[38] in a hiatus between lawlessness and the restoration of a legitimate, democratic order, the film asks what role law can and should play in fostering reconciliation between neighbors who have become enemies. It questions the extent to which law can acknowledge and assuage memory – with all the pain, flaws, and susceptibilities that memory entails, and it asks how law, which inevitably perpetrates its own violence, can and should respond to violence.

Yet if *Death and the Maiden* is alert to law's distinctive potential in fostering reconciliation and reestablishing normalcy, it also displays a pointed awareness of law's limitations. In the constantly shifting dynamics among Paulina, Gerardo, and Miranda, the film highlights the varied and dispersed forms of power that come into play in this turbulent political moment. At one moment, the viewer may be struck by the claims of survivors' justice, at another by the appeal of a return to normalcy.[39] In this vexed context, the claims of legality appear modest at best. Gerardo – the human rights lawyer who is to chair the Commission, and Miranda's "defense counsel" – represents the attributes of the law, at their most ambivalent. He is palpably torn

---

[38] The setting and symbolism of the film underscore this position quite clearly: the isolation of the setting, the fall of night, and the temporary disruption of electricity and telephonic communication created by the storm all communicate this notion of a hiatus. The impending resumption of a democratic order is also symbolized by the impending arrival of the government agents who will provide protection to Gerardo during his role as chairman of the Commission, a development that cuts short Paulina's experiment with due process.

[39] In a related reflection of antifoundationalism, the film also highlights the complex, ambivalent subjectivity of each of the major characters. They are not simply archetypes of political positions within the old regime, but also instruments for the vindication of a particular view of law, and private, particularized individuals with their own scars, tics, and failings, making their way through a fateful moment in their own lives, as well as in the life of their society. Paulina, for example, is not simply the terrorized victim who withstood torture without implicating her partner; she is the originator of a daring, or abusive, plan for vindicating the forgotten interests of living victims of the regime, and a woman who wants to move beyond her torture and her husband's betrayal, so they can "live like suburban idiots." See *Death and the Maiden*, supra note 2.

between the claims of one mired in a nightmare past and one blinded by denial and the appeal of a stable, harmonious future. He is temperate, temporizing, and persistent in his efforts to navigate the maze of coercion and process thrown down by Paulina; yet he is always on the verge of impotence.[40] His interventions serve to slow, although never to change the course of the tumultuous ordeal; despite his constant attentiveness, his repeated sidebars, it is clear that he cannot decide whom to believe. His lawyerly commitments ultimately seem tepid and tactical in the face of the emotional ferocity of the survivor and the desperate indignation of the accused perpetrator.

The mobility and ambivalence that characterizes the film's view of power, and of its characters' subjectivities, is also present in its moral or political conclusion. The film's stance on the substantive questions raised by the drama is, itself, equivocal. Like the perspective of the viewer, it shifts vertiginously from one standpoint to another, throughout the long night's confrontation. Is Gerardo's vision of law's role preservative and forward looking or impotent and deeply unjust? Does Paulina's "trial" produce justice for a survivor or lawlessly impose the same forms of torture that she herself suffered? Is Dr. Miranda an innocent who has been unjustly accused in a vengeful travesty of a trial, a decent man who gave way in the midst of widespread, repressive chaos, or an amoral monster? Although the film – unlike the play on which it was based[41] – ultimately points to Miranda's culpability, it is more equivocal on the questions of the rule and role of law. It is not clear either whether Paulina's experiment in survivor's justice has given her what she needs to continue her life or whether her compensatory, or therapeutic, emphasis is to be preferred to a legal strategy privileging forward-looking harmony.

In the film's ambivalent ending, we see all three protagonists assembled at a concert featuring Schubert's *Death and the Maiden* quartet, the music once played by Miranda as he repeatedly raped Paulina. Paulina has returned, to some degree, to society: She is no longer hiding in her isolated cabin, but is seated in the midst of a crowded, public event. Her marriage to Gerardo, who sits attentively if warily beside her, appears to be intact.[42] Yet this is not a scene of pure transcendence; echoes of the past continue to shape the present. Paulina's extraction of a confession has not destroyed Dr. Miranda: He has survived to resume what appears to be a peaceful life with his family. He looks down (literally and perhaps figuratively)

---

[40] At one point in the film, Paulina drops her gun; when Gerardo fails to grab it, Miranda exclaims in exasperation, "he just stood there!" Paulina retorts, "of course he just stands there, he's the Law." *Death and the Maiden*, supra note 2.

[41] The play features a taped confession by Miranda during which a large mirror descends and permits members of the audience, literally and figuratively, to examine themselves regarding his culpability, the role of law in reconciliation, and other central questions. For a fuller discussion see David Luban, On Dorftman's *Death and the Maiden*, 10 *Yale Journal of Law and Humanities* 115, 133–4 (1998).

[42] Her white-knuckle grip on his arm suggests need and formality, more than a restoration of intimacy; his tense and somewhat pained expression throughout the scene reinforces this impression.

Three Tales of Two Texts

on Paulina, with an expression of gentleness and gratitude. Moreover, Paulina's distinctive brand of survivor's justice does not appear to have brought her everything she hoped. Although she may have been released from her self-enforced solitude, the almost-frozen anxiety with which she meets Miranda's gaze makes clear that his confession has not restored the two of them to the position of equals in her mind, and has not permitted her to live in anything approaching the easy mindlessness she craves.

Although the film's insights on subjectivity and law reflect the influence of prevalent humanistic theories, many of the ways in which it conveys these insights are distinct to this newer cultural medium. Polanski's use of actors familiar from other cinematic settings brings home the point of currency: This is a contemporary drama about a pressing political/legal dilemma. Polanski also uses the familiar attributes of his actors to fuel the moral dilemmas the film presents. Sigourney Weaver's signature ferocity reflects psychological damage and barely controlled vigilante urges but also survival and a will to justice. Ben Kingsley, whose aura of saintliness accompanies him from films like *Gandhi* and *Schindler's List*, projects a perfect image of the "good Samaritan" whose appearance of rectitude and normalcy viewers may be reluctant to dislodge. The bland, mannerly, almost generic appearance of Stuart Wilson as Gerardo evokes the model of the lawyer in its measured regularity. Moreover, if the development of the characters reflects an intense psychological realism, the physical setting of the film allows for potent symbolism. The physical constraint of the small cottage reflects the claustrophobic pressure of trauma, the ineluctable burden imposed by the violence of the past. The hiatus created by the storm – the interruption of phone service, electricity, and other connections to the familiar world – reproduces the distinctive hiatus of the political interregnum, the moment in which a society teeters between past and future. The film's forceful evocations of the storm, the darkness, and the seaside cliffs to which Miranda is ultimately forced also enhance the drama of the action.

The medium of film also permits *Death and the Maiden* to communicate a strong affective charge as it delivers its message. The forceful emotions of the film flow not only from the actors' powerful performances: cinematic elements such as the lighting[43] and camera angles[44] underscore the heated conflicts among the characters, which contrast with the formality and the controlled deliberation of *Billy*

---

[43] Because much of the action takes place during a storm that has cut electricity to the Escobar's cabin, the exchanges between the characters often occur in candlelight or framed by the glare of a flashlight. In one recurrent image, Miranda sits against a wall, framed by his much larger, and darker, shadow.

[44] As some commentators have noted, Sigourney Weaver has the vast majority of close-ups, middle-range and point-of-view shots; in addition hers is the gaze that most often frames the rest of the action, all of which contributes to making hers the subjectivity that most potently informs or structures the film. See e.g., Orit Kamir, Cinematic Judgment and Jurisprudence: A Woman's Memory, Recovery, and Justice in a Post-Traumatic Society (A Study of Polanski's *Death and the Maiden*), in Sarat, Douglas, & Umphrey, supra note 37, at 27, 51–2.

Budd.[45] Nowhere is this so clear as in the contrast between Billy Budd's cryptic and enigmatic "God bless Captain Vere" – which poses a question to our heads more than a challenge to our affective sensibilities[46] – and Miranda's (Kingsley's) final confession – which combines pity, guilt, the erosion of responsibility in face of desire, pleasure in the violent subjection of another, in an apparently seamless and baffling flow. Moreover Gerardo's even and deliberate manner, which seems pallid and ineffectual amidst the searing passions and bold stratagems of the other protagonists, raises potent questions about law's penchant for rationality.

Heterogeneity

This narrative of movement or progression is not the only way to connect the work of Law and Humanities to these two texts. Indeed, the postmodern analyses that entered the mainstream of this work counsel skepticism about meta-narratives of forward movement or progress.[47] Instead of describing Law and Humanities work as proceeding, stagewise, through different kinds of texts, analytic frames, or conceptions of "law," one can describe the field as heterogeneous. Although it may be true that some kinds of texts (e.g., classic works of literature), goals (e.g., edifying lawyers through exposure to humanistic accounts of legal proceedings), or analytic frames (e.g., understanding law as decisional and as distinct from sociocultural practices or phenomena) emerged earlier in time, the pattern has been more accretive than successive. In individual works, in specific subgenres, and in the body of scholarship as a whole, one finds many kinds of pluralism or heterogeneity: in the understandings of what constitutes "law," in the envisaged relations between law and other social or cultural phenomena, and in disciplinary materials that structure explorations in the field. Notably, specific texts, or kinds of texts, have no exclusive relation with any conception of law, or mode of analysis: This body of work is distinguished by scholarship that draws on plural analytic frames with plural understandings of its projects.

One can see this pattern even with respect to so "classic" a text as *Billy Budd*. Although the novella has frequently been thought to exemplify the ways that literature can illuminate the formal, decisional aspects of law, it has also been examined in other ways. Some scholars have seen in *Billy Budd* a vehicle for comparing law

[45] There are comparatively few moments of powerful emotion in *Billy Budd* – one would surely be the crew's echo of Billy's last words. Melville, *Billy Budd, Sailor*, supra note 1, at 375; another is the embrace between Vere and Billy following Vere's delivery of the verdict (which is only hypothesized by the narrator), id. at 367.

[46] But for a focus on the discrete moments of affectively charged drama in *Billy Budd*, see Umphrey, Law's Bonds: Eros and Identification in *Billy Budd*, 64 *American Imago* 413 (2007).

[47] See e.g., Seyla Benhabib, *Feminism and Postmodernism*, in Benhabib et al., *Feminist Contentions* (Oxford, London, and New York: Routledge, 1995) (describing "death of history" – including teleological accounts of progress through time – as paradigmatic feature of postmodernism).

Three Tales of Two Texts

with literature. In his essay on *Billy Budd*, Lawrence Douglas describes the law not simply as a decision-making process, but as a narrative, meaning-making activity with salient parallels to literature.[48] In this vein, for example, he explores the parallels between the inconsistent omniscience of Captain Vere and that of the novella's anonymous narrator.[49]

Still other commentators have treated the novella as a medium for exploring legality more broadly: law not simply as a set of decisions but as a force that mobilizes obedience and produces a range of social effects. Robin West sees *Billy Budd* as highlighting the deep patriarchal structure of the law.[50] Both Billy's peacemaking tendencies and his silence reflect what West regards as feminine attributes, and the law's inability to respond with compassion, or even contextualized judgment, mark it as a masculinized domain.[51] Martha Umphrey offers a psychoanalytic interpretation, which connects Vere's decision to a larger set of relationships on the Bellipotent and to the theoretical question of what animates obedience to law.[52] Her analysis also gestures toward law's participation in diffuse circuits of power that produce subjectivity and may provoke resistance.[53] Captain Vere's prosecution of Billy Budd shaped what it meant to be a sailor on the Bellipotent, and this view was projected to a wider audience, as the account of the act and its punishment were published in the naval circulars referenced at the end of the story. One might expect, for example, that sailors became more suspect and more anonymous, as they were subjected to more stringent surveillance for mutiny and to forms of justice that took little account of their specific characters. They were not without recourse, however, as the novella's final ending suggests, although it lay elsewhere than in the formal theaters of naval justice. Umphrey sees in Billy's parting benediction an embrace of the affective, or even erotic, bonds that Captain Vere refused, and in the sailors' repetition of that blessing a "erotic circuit"[54] that depicts love and attraction, rather than fear, as the motivation for obeying the law.[55] Umphrey describes the composition and

---

[48] Lawrence Douglas, Discursive Limits: Narrative and Judgment in Billy Budd, 27 *Mosaic* 141, 141 (1994). Douglas also accords credence to the opposing view, expressed by Robert Cover, that the violence of law distinguishes it from other species of interpretation. His point in the article is to illustrate the way that both of these views are prefigured in the text of *Billy Budd*. Id.

[49] Douglas, Discursive Limits, supra note 48, at 143–45.

[50] See Robin West, The Feminine Silence: A Reply to Professor Koffler, 1 *Cardozo Studies Law and Literature* 20 (1989).

[51] See West, The Feminine Silence, supra note 50.

[52] Umphrey, supra note 46.

[53] Umphrey, supra note 46, at 428–30.

[54] The term, as Umphrey notes, comes from Eve Kosofsky Sedgwick, *The Epistemology of the Closet* (Berkeley: University of California Press, 1990). Umphrey, offering a psychoanalytic interpretation, emphasizes the erotic connection to Billy. This response might also reflect a form of resistance to Captain Vere, whose speech to the drumhead court emphasized fear as the motivation for obedience to law.

[55] Umphrey, supra note 46, at 414.

circulation of the sea shanty "Billy in the Darbies" – with its elaborate identification with the executed man – as "the sailors' fantasy of a lost love object, a melancholic introjection of the Handsome Sailor."[56] The shanty also counters the "smugness" of the naval account that "falsified 'facts' to ratify a classic narrative about the efficacy and legitimacy of legal violence"[57] – suggesting that this expression of grief also serves as a form of resistance to the official account.

This heterogeneity also marks the analysis of more recent cultural products.[58] Film, as noted previously, has become the focus of a rapidly growing body of legal scholarship, which reflects a wide range of goals, assumptions, and methodologies. Some of this scholarship works in a "law in literature" vein, focusing in particular on the capacity of film to spotlight the adversarial, rhetorical, or deliberative dimensions of the trial.[59] Some examples of this work have an explicitly pedagogical emphasis, exploring the ways that film can be used to incite reflection on different aspects of advocacy.[60] The role – and indeed the character – of the lawyer is the focus of another subset of this work, aiming to explore what separates the Atticus Finches of the profession from their mercenary or morally compromised counterparts.[61]

Yet not all law and film scholarship works on this representational, and edifying, premise. Other work has treated law and film as texts with analogous features,[62] comparing the Court's decision in *City of Mobile v. Bolden* with *Casablanca*,[63]

---

[56] Umphrey, supra note 46, at 429.

[57] Umphrey, supra note 46, at 429.

[58] As Melville's novella combined a fictional narrative with naval circulars and sea shanties, some scholars have analyzed novels or short stories in conjunction with poetry or film to make an argument about legality or law. Not only are such works heterogeneous in the sources they mine; they are also diverse in the relations they conceive between law and cultural products. Philip Meyer's "Why a Jury Trial is More Like a Movie than a Novel," 28 *Journal of Law and Society* 133 (2001), offers a comparison of two kinds of cultural products to underscore particular dimensions of a formal legal proceeding. Peter Hutchings, Modern Forensics: Photography and Other Subjects, 9 *Cardozo Journal of Law Literature* 229 (1997), uses Edgar Allen Poe's short story *The Man of the Crowd* and the Antonioni film *Blow-Up* to make a critical point: that literary works grasp the "problem of the subject" in the way that law so far has not.

[59] A 2001 symposium in the *Journal of Law and Society* contains several examples of such work. See Stefan Machura & Peter Robson, Law and Film: An Introduction, 28 *Journal of Law and Society* 1 (2001).

[60] See e.g., Regina Austin, The Next "New Wave": Law-Genre Documentaries, Lawyering in Support of the Creative Process, and Visual Legal Advocacy, 16 *Fordham Intellectual Property, Media & Entertainment Law Journal* 809 (2006).

[61] See J. J. Osborn, Jr., Atticus Finch – The End of Honor: A Discussion of *To Kill a Mockingbird*, 30 *University of San Francisco Law Review* 1139 (1996); Sarat, Imagining The Law of the Father, supra note 14.

[62] Austin Sarat and his coauthors have described this focus as a comparatively new way to analyze of law-oriented films, which is aimed at "connecting law and film as narrative forms." See Austin Sarat, Lawrence Douglas, & Martha Merrill Umphrey, On Film and Law: Broadening the Focus, in Austin Sarat, Lawrence Douglas, & Martha Merrill Umphrey, *Law on the Screen* 1, 4–5 (2005).

[63] Avi Soifer, Complacency and Constitutional Law, 42 *Ohio State Law Journal* 383 (1981).

Three Tales of Two Texts

or explaining *Why A Trial Is More Like a Movie than a Novel.*[64] A still larger and burgeoning body of work focuses on film's constitutive effects in the legal as well as the cultural domain. Such work explores film's power to constitute paradigmatic legal subjects: stock characters – be they Erin Brockovich or Hannibal Lector – whose stories help us frame and assess actual legal controversies.[65] It also highlights the capacity of film to shape popular views of the law itself.[66] In the legal field, life can imitate art: Cultural performances we may see as *representations* of law may actually *shape* the way observers understand the operation of a legal rule,[67] think about law's potential to respond to injury,[68] or see their own relation to the legal system.[69] Cinematic characters, imagery, or aesthetics can even influence the outcome in particular cases. In *When Law Goes Pop*, Richard Sherwin describes a criminal case in which the defense attorney used the ironic aesthetic of *Pulp Fiction* and the split-screen technique of *Annie Hall* to transform a minor member of a mafia family from a cold-blooded murderer to a humorous, blundering braggart.[70] In all of this work, film becomes a vital part of the extended system of circulating discourses that constitute "legality."

Many of these distinct modes of analysis have been applied to *Death and the Maiden*. Much of the scholarship on the film analyzes its role in complex circuits of social construction. Some commentators see in the character of Paulina, for example, a challenge to rethink the relation between sex and justice. Paulina is a woman who has suffered the paradigmatic crime against women – sexual violation. She responds to a legal system that is poised to erase her injuries, by improvising a hearing that combines coercion with due process; she seeks not punishment or compensation but a face-to-face encounter and a confession. On the one hand, the

---

[64] Philip Meyer, *Why a Trial Is More Like a Movie Than a Novel*, supra note 58. See also Jennifer Mnookin & Nancy West, Theatres of Proof: Visual Evidence and the Law in *Call Northside 777*, 13 *Yale Journal of Law and Humanities* 329, 388–89 (2001) (suggesting parallels between trials and filmed reinactments).

[65] Sarat, Douglas, and Umphrey describe this as a more established focus in humanistic scholarship on law-oriented films. See Sarat, Douglas, Umphrey, On Film and Law, supra note 62, at 3.

[66] Sarat, Douglas, and Umphrey describe this focus – "reception... [or] the social life of images" as being a newer mode of analyzing films related to law. See Sarat, Douglas, & Umphrey, *On Film and Law*, supra note 62 , at 6–7.

[67] Naomi Mezey discusses the way that depictions of the Miranda warnings in television and film have changed the public's understanding not only of their relation to law enforcement, but of the constitutional character of the rights protected by the warnings. See Naomi Mezey, supra note 24, at 35. On a more arcane note, many a property professor has gloried in the description of *Body Heat* (1981) as a film about the rule against perpetuities.

[68] Sarat, Law of the Father, supra note 14 (describing the ways that *The Sweet Hereafter* inclines viewers to think about the capacity of law to respond to mass disasters and the resulting human loss).

[69] Cf. Sarat, Douglas, & Umphrey, *On Film and Law*, supra note 62, at 3 (recent film scholarship shows "how film speaks to particular desires and anxieties about law that exist in the wider culture").

[70] Richard Sherwin, *When Law Goes Pop* 30–33: *The Vanishing Line between Law and Popular Culture* 254 (2000).

film destabilizes dominant images of the wronged female subject. Paulina's rage and her violent strategy for securing justice show that she is not a saintly, suffering victim; however, the reality of her suffering, the keenness of her intuition, and the fulfillment of her promise to release Miranda on his confession also distinguish her from the stereotype of the crazed or vengeful harpy.[71] On the other hand, some critics see in the film the enduring questions of sex equity: Can women who have been victimized by rape, as paradigmatic sociopolitical "others," find in the law a level playing field or make their voices heard?[72]

The film also unsettles popular notions of due process. In proposing to hold a formal hearing at gunpoint, Paulina raises the question whether process secured through coercion offers any kind of protection that deserves the name legal,[73] or whether the protections to which one is entitled are consistent across the range of human subjects or depend on the subject's demonstrated respect for human dignity and volition.[74]

Not all scholarship relating to *Death and the Maiden* focuses on its constructivist effects on legality. Some analysts have highlighted the parallels it seems to establish between film and trials. Several commentators have observed, for example, that Polanski made a crucial decision not to "open up" the original play by offering viewers authoritative flashbacks of Paulina's captivity.[75] Thus, as the story unfolds, the viewer is in the same position as the juror in a trial (or as Gerardo, the embodiment of

[71] Cf. Kamir, Cinematic, Jurisprudence and Judgment, in Sarat, Douglas, & Umphrey, supra note 44, at 51–58, esp. 51–51 (describing Paulina as "confident, determined . . . completely secure in her moral position and admirable in her unyielding strength to resist the men's suspicion, distrust, and manipulations," but also "crude and aggressive," "fragile and hurt").

[72] Robert Barsky, Outsider Law in Literature: Construction and Representation in *Death and the Maiden*, 26 *SubStance* 66 (1997). Barsky is concerned primarily with women as victims of rape in the context of repression or genocide; he does not take the position characteristic of some feminist theorists that rape is paradigmatic of women's condition. Nonetheless, his analysis is also addressed more broadly to the barriers to autobiographical performance confronted by "outsiders" to the legal system.

[73] Lest one answer "no" too precipitously, it is interesting to note that one reviewer describes Paulina's coercive gambit as a process necessary to extract the truth from Miranda. Gordana Crnkovic, *Death and the Maiden* by Roman Polanski, 50 *Film Studies* 3943–45 (1997). One might also see a parallel to the Miranda warnings (one might wonder whether Dorfman's choice of this name was intentional), in which police offer suspects the process of certain warnings on pain of being deprived of any evidence that might come out of the encounter if they do not.

Some commentators also see the film as investigating the merits of a remedial strategy that is aimed less at punishment than at narration, validation, and healing, attributes sometimes associated with the feminine. See Kamir, *Cinematic Judgment and Jurisprudence*, supra note 44, at 35–44.

[74] Paulina evokes this dimension by her angry assertion that "he's going to get all the process he never gave me" (and of course he never gave her anything, so it is not clear what he's going to get), and her admissions that "if he's innocent, he's really screwed." Again, our legal system tends to think of due process as a kind of value that emanates from our own moral/procedural commitments rather than bearing a relation to the subject who receives its protections, but in fact there are contextual dimensions to due process – because the process due has depended on the nature of the right (though not, as a doctrinal matter, the person who bears it).

[75] See Kamir, *Cinematic Judgment and Jurisprudence*, supra note 44, at 50; Crnkovic, *Death and the Maiden*, supra note 73, at 40–41.

"the law" who is struggling to assess the evidence before him): trying to determine, as the facts emerge, whether Miranda is in fact the sadistic doctor who raped Paulina. Still other scholars treat the film in an edifying vein, as a dramatic parable that nonetheless challenges us to reflect on the role of law in social reconstruction following repression or genocide[76] or on the forms of process that might be deployed in hearings involving refugees from repressive or genocidal conflicts.[77]

This pluralization of modes of analysis has brought richness and variety to the humanistic study of law; however, the accretion of different forms and objects of analysis has also occasioned controversy. One example is a spirited debate about normative dimensions of legal scholarship.[78] Legal scholarship has tended to be distinguished by its normative demands, that is, its expectation that a legal scholar will move forward from her analysis or critique, to say something precise and prescriptive about how law should respond. Because conventional legal scholarship has tended to conceive of law as autonomous, exceptional or at least discontinuous with other social institutions, practices and relations of power, these recommendations are frequently expected to take a stylized, institutionally focused form: a proposal for judges, legislators, or other legal decision makers.[79]

Some early examples of Law and Humanities scholarship seemed to adapt this form of normativity to the emerging genre. Examples of "law in literature" work that espoused an edifying goal – reading *Billy Budd* or other works of literature so as to determine what did or did not constitute the best faces of the law – seemed to embrace some of the premises of traditional legal normativity. Legal scholarship was aimed toward the goal of improving actual legal decision making: if not through the recommendation of the next three-part doctrinal test, then by asking law students, and perhaps legal professionals, to consider how decisions should be made in the fictional "hypotheticals" framed by the classics of literature. Law and film work that examined depictions of lawyering sometimes reflected similar normative

[76] Luban, On Dorfman's *Death and the Maiden*, supra note 41.
[77] Barsky, Construction and Representation, supra note 72.
[78] See e.g., Margaret Jane Radin & Frank Michelman, Pragmatist and Post-Structuralist Critical Legal Practice, 139 *University of Pennsylvania Law Review* 1019 (1991); Pierre Schlag, Normativity and The Politics of Form, 139 *University of Pennsylvania Law Review* 801 (1991); Pierre Schlag, Stances 139 *University of Pennsylvania Law Review* 1059 (1991); Steven Winter, Contingency and Community in Normative Practice, 139 *University of Pennsylvania Law Review* 963 (1991); Steven Winter, Without Privilege, 139 *University of Pennsylvania Law Review* 1063 (1991); Pierre Schlag, Normative and Nowhere to Go, 43 *Stanford Law Review* 167 (1990).

Although this contention has not occurred primarily in works that focus on cultural products such as novels or films, many of the participants are scholars whose work is shaped by humanistic disciplines, and the postmodern critiques of the (liberal) subject that underlie much of this debate have migrated to law from the worlds of philosophy and literary studies. Moreover, it is clearly germane to such works, which only rarely feature conventional forms of legal normativity.
[79] See Edward Rubin, The Practice and Discourse of Legal Scholarship, 86 *Michigan Law Review* 1835 (1987) (legal scholarship aspires to "identity of discourse" with judicial decision making). For a trenchant, systematic critique of legal normativity, see Schlag, Normativity and the Politics of Form, supra note 78.

goals: Analysis of the different approaches to lawyering represented in film was aimed at producing legal professionals who resembled Atticus Finch more closely than Mitchell Stephens.[80]

Still other scholars took a more contextualized, yet still recognizable, approach to legal normativity: Daniel Solove's examination of *Billy Budd* argues that it may illuminate the role of law in the current "state of emergency," yet without specifically elaborating the lessons that legal actors should draw.[81] Similarly Robert Barsky uses *Death and the Maiden* to reflect on the procedures that should be applied in tribunals responding to genocide or governmental violence, again without offering specific proposals.

Yet not all Law and Humanities works operate in this specifically didactic or normative vein. Early emphasis on the edifying mission of "law in literature" scholarship prompted spirited disagreement, with some scholars decrying the focus on forming legal professionals as a limiting and elusive objective.[82] These participants argued that Law and Humanities work was better directed toward exposing law's peculiar "hermeticism" through literary practices of "close reading,"[83] understanding the functioning of law in relation to other structures of power or applying a critical lens to both law and the humanities.[84] Although this perspective did not end or even curtail scholarly efforts aimed more self-consciously at edification or instruction of legal professionals, they strengthened the bridge that the analysis of literary works had begun to create between legal scholars and those in the humanistic disciplines.

A final group of Law and Humanities scholars, influenced by postmodernism and other forms of antifoundational theory, took more explicit aim at legal scholarship's penchant for normativity. Stanley Fish argued bluntly that his critiques of such integral matters as law's autonomy had no normative implications.[85] Pierre Schlag argued that legal normativity – far from being effective or transformative – simply

---

[80] Mitchell Stephens, the central character in Atom Egoyan's *The Sweet Hereafter*, is depicted as an anguished and morally ambivalent – if not indeed morally disturbing – character. His tragic struggle to understand his failed relationship with his drug-addicted daughter is rendered as a poignant and perhaps influential counterpoint to the potentially exploitative approach he takes to the grieving parents he seeks to recruit as clients, following a bus accident that claimed the lives of many of their children. See Sarat, Imagining The Law of the Father, supra note 14.

[81] See Solove, Melville's *Billy Budd* and Security in Times of Crisis, supra note 8.

[82] Sarat, Traditions and Trajectories, supra note 9; Brooks, A Slightly Polemical Comment, supra note 9.

[83] See Brooks, A Slightly Polemical Comment, supra note 9, at 410–11.

[84] See Sarat, Traditions and Trajectories, supra note 9, at 404–05.

[85] See e.g., Fish, *There's No Such Thing as Free Speech*, supra note 10. This conclusion is stated, and restated, throughout the book. A particularly succinct example may be found on p. 307, where Fish concludes: "[T]he point is that there *is* no point, no yield of a positive programmatic kind to be carried away from these analyses.... [E]ither in the form of some finally successful identification of a foundational set of standards or some program by which we can move away from standards to ever-expanding liberation – it's the unavailability of such a yield that *is* my point.... People absolutely go bonkers when they hear that, but *that's the way it is*."

Three Tales of Two Texts

reflected "the operation, performance, reproduction, and proliferation of bureaucratic practices and institutions."[86] For Schlag, legal normativity positioned the legal scholar as a purposeful, originary intellect, when his normative utterances actually revealed him to be a well-scripted (although perhaps unwitting) participant in a self-reproducing system of bureaucratic rationality; it posited a powerful, even relatively autonomous set of actors to whom legal proposals could profitably be addressed, when both the diffusion of the "political"[87] and defects in the liberal conception of agency meant that there is "no one in charge at the other end of the line" to respond to such utterances.[88] Although the film version of *Death and the Maiden* suggested Miranda's guilt, Dorfman's original stage version eschewed normative resolution in a style not far from Schlag's own. By lowering a large mirror across the stage during the final moments of the play,[89] it challenged members of the audience to find their moral bearings in a world without clear authority to appeal to, or clear answers to their most pressing questions.

These critiques of legal normativity are sufficiently radical that mainstream legal scholarship has often had difficulty assimilating them; however, Law and Humanities scholars have engaged them in plural and creative ways. Some, such as Margaret Jane Radin and Frank Michelman, acknowledged the embeddedness of legal scholars in various forms of professional practice and the limits of conventional forms of legal normativity, yet argued that some impetus toward amelioration was inevitable in works grounded in critique and was manifest even in Schlag's more radical critique.[90] Others, such as Steve Winter, defended Schlag departing from conventional legal normativity, by making meaning on the "field of action."[91] Still others sought to devise more constructive visions of postmodern normativity. Richard Sherwin, for example, argued against a potentially nihilistic "skeptical postmodernism" in favor of a "tragic constructivism."[92] This approach recognizes the pluralization and diffusion of influences that render social life radically contingent, but it also embraces the

---

[86] Pierre Schlag, Normativity and the Politics of Form, supra note 78.

[87] For a thoughtful discussion of this conception of politics, see Kirstie McClure, On the Subject of Rights: Pluralism, Plurality, and Political Identity, in Chantal Mouffe, ed., *Dimensions of Radical Democracy* (London and New York: Verso, 1992).

[88] Schlag, Normative and Nowhere to Go, supra note 78, at 179.

[89] See Luban, On Dorfman's *Death and the Maiden*, supra note 41, at 124.

[90] See e.g., Radin & Michelman, supra note 78 (grounding this critique in a broad conception of normativity, which includes argument aiming at persuasion, and in the ubiquity of meliorative, agentic impulses among human actors). See also Kathryn Abrams, The Unbearable Lightness of Being Stanley Fish, 47 *Stanford Law Review* 595, 612–13 (1995) (arguing that Fish's engagements as a public intellectual suggest a commitment to normativity that seems to follow, analytically, from his critiques).

[91] Winter, Without Privilege, supra note 78, at 1065.

[92] See Richard Sherwin, *When Law Goes Pop: The Vanishing Line between Law and Popular Culture* 254 (2000). Sherwin also refers to this approach as "affirmative postmodernism," id. at 230, and, citing the terminology of Ernst Cassirer, "mature constructivism," id. at 221.

possibility of human empathy, connection, and "merciful justice"[93] that can emerge from this contingency and seeks out new legal narratives that harness law's powers of "enchantment" to this end.[94]

Continuity

As the preceding section demonstrates, one need not see *Billy Budd* and *Death and the Maiden* as two utterly distinct scholarly targets. Instead of focusing on the heterogeneity of the analysis that has encompassed these works, one could instead focus on its continuities. A close analysis permits us to glimpse several patterns that bring seemingly disparate bodies of work into alignment.

One can see first a set of shared substantive preoccupations, which inform scholarly responses to these works. The first is the relation of the forms of law to the achievement of substantive justice. This question is posed in *Billy Budd* in the conflict between the verdict of the drumhead court and Billy's characterological innocence. Does Captain Vere commit a grievous wrong by enforcing the letter of the law – in hastening to trial[95] and to judgment from a fear that mutinous men will find leniency "pusillanimous"[96] – rather than attending carefully to Billy's potentially exculpating circumstances? It is also a central question in *Death and the Maiden*, where the abdication of formal legal actors compels Paulina to improvise a strategy for addressing her state-sponsored injuries. This focus, on form versus substance in legal determinations, is not surprising, given the kinds of works that serve as objects of analysis in this genre. Cultural products, from literature to film, can reveal with vivid factual detail or evocative psychological realism the ways that law bears on the lives of specific subjects. They can illuminate the ways that a law that is plausible in the abstract, or fair in form, takes on a different aspect when it meets the lives of those before it.[97]

This point connects with a second, substantive theme in this literature: law's role in exigent circumstances. In many works within the Law and Humanities canon, law is asked to serve as a kind of bridge[98]: between land and sea (*Billy Budd*), between past

---

[93] Sherwin, *When Law Goes Pop*, supra note 91, at 262. In Sherwin's view, it may be precisely this sense of contingency – which embodies not simply complexity but irrationality (a sense of being, to a large degree, hostage to an uncontrollable fate) – that engenders in people a sense of compassion or fellow-feeling. Id. at 260–63.

[94] See Sherwin, *When Law Goes Pop*, supra note 91, at 205–33.

[95] Melville's narrator reveals that another option was available: Vere could have waited until the Bellipotent rejoined the larger fleet and then referred Billy's case to the admiral for decision. See Melville, *Billy Budd*, supra note 1, at 354–55.

[96] Melville, *Billy Budd*, supra note 1, at 364.

[97] It is a project analogous, in some respects, to Law and Society's empirical preoccupation with "law on the ground": yet it uses different media to highlight the ways in which law produces tangible effects on particular human lives.

[98] In Nomos and Narrative, Robert Cover described law as a bridge, "linking a concept of reality to an imagined alternative." See Robert Cover, The Supreme Court 1982 Term, Foreword: Nomos and

Three Tales of Two Texts

and future (*Death and the Maiden*), and between the generalities or hypothetical circumstances envisioned by the framers of a law and the urgent complications that can arise in its application (both). Whether law has the flexibility and creativity to respond to the exigent: Can it follow the nightmarish or surprising turns that human lives can take? Can it serve the functions of collective memory, using a painful past to instruct the future? These are central questions throughout this body of work. Texts from the Humanities often depict law in its most challenging moments: at collective turning points, or when a community confronts the unexpected. We learn from these moments, as we do in *Billy Budd* and *Death and the Maiden*, what resources law brings to these tasks and in what ways it may fall short.

A final substantive theme in this literature is the plural relations between law and violence. Robert Cover famously argued that legal decision making was distinct from other acts of interpretation – those performed by poets, artists, and storytellers – because of the violence that law perpetrates.[99] The patterns and paradoxes of law's relation to violence infuse these works. Law plays a crucial role in limiting violence: by forestalling the violence of those, like Paulina, who might seek to right unrecognized wrongs through their own agency, and by penalizing those outbreaks of violence that can threaten collectivities, such as the Bellipotent. Law also, almost inevitably, produces violence, as Cover also observed.[100] Because it reflects the culmination of an adversary process that can grant victory to only one of the contending parties, because it reflects an effort to embody in the institutions of a community a particular nomos selected from a field of plural nomoi, the action of the law is inevitably "jurispathic."[101] It fosters community by exiling nonconforming nomoi; it secures order by inflicting violence on those who would disturb it. The drumhead court, as *Billy Budd* makes clear, cannot give full recognition both to Billy and to the needs of the Bellipotent; the new regime Gerardo seeks to build cannot be grounded both in forward-looking reconciliation and backward-looking justice for survivors. In a final twist, law can be a vehicle for domesticating the violence done by the pursuit of shared norms. Paulina's "process," for all its failings, seems superior to the torture she suffered at the hands of the regime; although it provides a less effective set of safeguards than would the investigation of her injuries by the Human Rights Commission.

One can also glean from this body of work a set of insights that bear on methodology. The first, not surprisingly, concerns the resources that are capable of

---

Narrative, 97 *Harvard Law Review* 4, 33 (1983). It is interesting, in light of the more recent humanistic debate over legal normativity to note the frank (although certainly not narrow or conventional) normative character of this statement.

[99] See Robert Cover, Violence and the Word, in Minow, Ryan, & Sarat, Narrative, *Violence and the Law* 204 n.2 (Ann Arbor: University of Michigan Press, 1992) (noting that "the violent side of law and its connection to interpretation and rhetoric is systematically ignored or underplayed" in the work of J. B. White and Ronald Dworkin on legal interpretation).

[100] See Cover, Nomos and Narrative, supra note 97. See also Violence and the Word, supra note 98.

[101] See Cover, Nomos and Narrative, supra note 97.

illuminating the workings of the law. These resources are far broader than traditional legal scholars have assumed and include a range of cultural products. Whether the focus be a "great book" such as *Billy Budd*, a contemporary example of visual culture such as *Death and the Maiden*, or a group of monuments,[102] photographs,[103] or musical compositions,[104] Law and Humanities scholars have made clear that we can learn about law and legality by analyzing the ways it is represented. These cultural productions simultaneously depict law and help constitute the environment in which it operates. Moreover, these materials can be illuminated by fields beyond political science and economics,[105] which have, since the time of the realists, been deployed regularly in legal policy making. The literary, historical, and psychoanalytic analyses that have been applied to *Billy Budd* and the feminist theory and film studies that have been brought to *Death and the Maiden* are also proximate to the legal enterprise.

A second insight concerns law's continuity with other discourses, practices, or systems of power, within a larger field of dynamic, often hierarchical relations. To focus exclusively on formal legal decision making is to present an incomplete picture of the way law permeates and is shaped by its surrounding environment. Neither the focal works nor the scholarship that has emerged around them reflect the premise of legal autonomy or exceptionalism that has structured most of legal scholarship. They describe law as being in constant relation with other social and cultural practices and norms.

In *Billy Budd*, this premise is subtle or implicit. Although much of the novella explores the anguish surrounding the formal imposition of the law, its final sections reflect the ways that human will, desire, and connection – and the surrounding relations, technologies, and cultures they create – complicate the meaning derived from law's commands. Billy's final words, "God bless Captain Vere," are famously ambivalent in this regard. They may appeal to a higher authority to right the wrong reflected in the imposition of the law; they may illustrate a capacity for human connection and forgiveness that dwarfs the operation of formal legal rules; or – when coupled with the immediate echo of the stunned crew – they may exemplify an unpredictability in the human will that the law cannot grasp. The successive endings that follow the scene of execution demonstrate more directly both law's

---

[102] See e.g., Sanford Levinson, *Written in Stone: Public Monuments in Changing Societies* (Durham: Duke University Press, 1998); Norman W. Spaulding, Constitution as Counter-Monument: Federalism, Reconstruction, and the Problem of Collective Memory, 103 *Columbia Law Review* 1992 (2003).

[103] See Mnookin, The Image of Truth, supra note 36.

[104] See e.g., Sanford Levinson & J.M. Balkin, Law, Music, and Other Performing Arts, 139 *University of Pennsylvania Law Review* 1597 (1991).

[105] See Fiss, The Challenge, supra note 9 (describing the study of works within the humanities as a response to the arid character of legal analysis structured by economic thought). The move toward the humanities need not be an explicit or conscious response to economic analysis to broaden the (inter)disciplinary frame of legal scholarship.

Three Tales of Two Texts

ripples into the larger society and society's power to infuse new meanings into law's acts. Each reflects a social or cultural form that renders its own verdict on Billy and on Vere, through a distinctly nonlegal medium. The fact that the novella ends with Vere's deathbed cry, a military circular that flattens the ambivalent drama into a closed case, and a sea shanty that transforms Billy into a kind of cultural icon, demonstrates the almost seamless embeddedness of the law in a range of relations that can infuse and transform its message.

Death and the Maiden presents the porous boundaries of the law as a central theme. Virtually every turn of the plot demonstrates law's comparability to, and its interpenetration with, other means of fact finding, judgment, and social control. This film is riveted on the comparison between the work of the commission (procedurally regular but substantively limited) and Paulina's improvised form of fact finding (broad and penetrating in its reach but coercive in its means). In the background lurk comparisons between Paulina's treatment of Miranda and the treatment imposed on Paulina by her torturers, also aimed at the extraction of critical information. The film's conclusion also illustrates the psychic processes that mediate and mitigate the law's effects. The fact that Miranda remains free to enjoy the same cultural pleasures as his victims – neither Gerardo's legal reconstruction nor Paulina's rough justice has been sufficient to remove him from society nor transform him in the eyes of his fellows – highlights the factors, from individual denial to a potent collective desire to "move beyond" an episode of state-sponsored violence, with which law must contend. Paulina's grim and anxious mien illustrates the force of memory that may haunt the most forward-looking efforts at legal reconstruction.

Because of this deeply situated view of law, these works reflect commonality in an area that has sparked controversy among Law and the Humanities scholars: the question of legal normativity. Notwithstanding the distinctions between works that seek to edify or illuminate contemporary controversies and works whose postmodern frame calls into question the normative legal project, we can glimpse continuity in the ways that these efforts call the most conventional forms of legal normativity into question.

The cultural forms at the heart of this work are equivocal in their normative stance, crafted to raise as many normative questions as they answer. Although readers may cringe at the grim stringency of Captain Vere's view of legal obligation, this is not the only reaction *Billy Budd* evokes. Vere's apparent if unstated anguish,[106] Billy's calm acceptance of his fate, and the confusion of the successive endings induce a more equivocal response. Similarly, *Death and the Maiden* elicits mingled appreciation and horror at Paulina's desperate gambit.

---

[106] Melville's narrator notes: "The first to encounter Captain Vere in the act of leaving the compartment [after conveying the verdict to Billy Budd], was the senior lieutenant. The face he beheld, for the moment one expressive of the agony of the strong, was to that officer, though a man of fifty, a startling revelation." Melville, *Billy Budd*, supra note 1, at 367.

Moreover, commentators who analyze these works offer conclusions that are frequently normatively ambivalent or indeterminate. In some cases, the normative implications of the scholar's analytic observations are unclear: If erotic bonds, as Martha Umphries suggests, may animate our obedience to law, or if Paulina's quest for "healing," as Orit Kamir contends, reflects a therapeutic element that is often absent from the law, is this a good thing or a bad thing? In other cases, the normative impetus of the argument takes place at a higher level of abstraction than is characteristic for legal scholarship. *Billy Budd* has provided a vantage point on recurrent theoretical questions about the goals of law and literature. Might literature enhance legal thought or decision making by providing a "school for moral sentiment"[107] (a perspective advanced within "law in literature" scholarship) or by providing an illustrative example of "nuanced reading"[108] (a dimension of comparability mined by law as literature scholars)? Is law distinct (from the literary) in its inevitable reliance on violence[109] – physical force on the one hand and moral or political exclusion on the other – or can the law be justified by discourse?[110] *Death and the Maiden* asks viewers to reflect on the ways that legal process resembles and diverges from violence and challenges us to consider what, if anything, we secure through the forms of due process when these forms overlay radically unequal status or bargaining power. These are projects with clear normative implications for the Law and Humanities movement because they reflect on the kinds of insights to be derived from recourse to literature or film in thinking about law. Yet they provide a spur to reflection rather than a specific remedial proposal. Even where particular inquiries have implications for legal decision makers, Law and Humanities scholars frequently stop short of drawing out specific consequences. Understanding the dilemmas facing Captain Vere may help legal scholars to reflect on the role of Justice Lemuel Shaw in enforcing the Fugitive Slave Act,[111] or may provide part of the backdrop against which contemporary legal decision makers assess the exigencies implicit in the current state of war.[112] The fictional alternative spotlighted by *Death and the Maiden* might provide scholars with one lens through which to view the constraints imposed on tribunals established to respond to state-sponsored violence. These Law and Humanities efforts do not culminate in the kind of practical directions to legal

---

[107] See e.g., Martha Nussbaum, *Love's Knowledge* 101 (Oxford and New York: Oxford University Press, 1990); Calabresi, supra note 9.

[108] See Douglas, Discursive Limits, supra note 48, at 141.

[109] See Robert Cover, Violence and the Word, supra note 98, 203–13.

[110] See Douglas, Discursive Limits, supra note 48, at 141–2. Douglas does not take an explicit position on whether law is distinct from other acts of interpretation because characterized by violence, or whether it is capable of justification by discourse; his point is to demonstrate that both positions are illustrated within the text of *Billy Budd*.

[111] Robert Cover, *Justice Accused*; Steven Winter, The Failure of the Word: Melville, Slavery, and the Failure of Judicial Process, 26 *Cardozo Law Review* 2471 (2005).

[112] See Solove, *Melville's Billy Budd and Security in Times of Crisis*, supra note 8.

Three Tales of Two Texts

decision makers that comprise the normative in the minds of mainstream legal scholars.

This divergence may well have restricted the appeal of this genre of work among some legal scholarly audiences.[113] Those who may initially be nonplussed by the extralegal materials on which Law and Humanities scholarship draws may feel a particularly acute need to understand how such analysis "cashes out" in terms of legal decision making. The fact that the work aims primarily at illuminating the operations of law or at troubling the assumptions that underlie its conceptualization, or that even its most "normative" moments have a rather oblique relationship to concrete legal action, may lead some conventional readers to feel that it is a genre apart: that they are uncertain what it offers those who must think and work within the institutions of the legal system.

This uneasy standoff may prove temporary, however, if we continue to see the penetration of the genre's descriptive or analytic insights. The expectation of specific legal prescriptions rests, at base, on an assumption of legal autonomy or exceptionalism – a premise that the varied forms of Humanities-oriented scholarship have called into question. Descriptions of the embeddedness of the law, and its continuity with other social and cultural practices, do not simply modify our view of the legal domain, they invite us to revise our conventional conceptions of legal normativity. If one sees the law, not only in its formal, positivist guise, but also in the plural intersecting practices comprising "legality," then one can no longer see legal normativity as limited to the next proposed statute or three-part doctrinal test. Understanding how law becomes intertwined with proximate discourses and practices, grasping how it modifies and is modified by the self-understandings of those who live under it, permits legal scholars to comprehend not only how law achieves meaning in the world, but also how legal meaning can change and be changed.

---

[113] Cf. Kenji Yoshino, The City and the Poet, 114 *Yale Law Journal* 1835 (2005). This article asks why law and literature has remained such a "peaked" genre, less widely practiced and less fully accepted than law and economics, or legal history or jurisprudence. One of the key questions in Yoshino's examination (which he derives from Plato's implied defenses of the poet in the city, in the *Republic*), is whether this activity "has the capacity to serve, rather than merely to subvert, the proper ends of the state," id. at 1839. Yoshino answers this question – which roughly corresponds to whether law and literature scholarship has normative value in relation to the goals of the state – in the affirmative for some forms of this scholarship, such as the use of experiential narratives.

3

Law, Culture, and Humility

Steven L. Winter

> Hermeneutics seems to me to be animated by this double motivation: willingness to suspect, willingness to listen; vow of rigor, vow of obedience. In our time, we have not finished doing away with *idols* and we have barely begun to listen to *symbols*.
>
> – Paul Ricoeur[1]

If there was a moment when the study of Law and Humanities came of age, it was at the 1989 Annual Meeting of the Association of American Law Schools. In a packed Grand Ballroom B, Margaret Jane Radin talked about how she uses the poetry of Wallace Stevens in her first-year law, language, and ethics course. Martha Minow read a poem by Adrienne Rich. James Boyd White talked about the Cathedral of Chartres and the generations of workmen who toiled in its construction without, of course, any expectation of ever seeing the completion of their handiwork.[2] Law, I recall him saying, was a similar communal work of art that calls on us to engage with it in dialogue.

Or something like that . . . the synopsis in the meeting program was only marginally more helpful. It described the panel's subject as "that of personal and community wholeness, characterized by dialogue, the translation of disciplinary languages, and the grasping together of scattered realities."[3] In fact, I distinctly remember Martha Minow saying afterward that she had been on panels with White before and that still she had no idea what he was talking about. I could relate to her

---

[1] Paul Ricoeur, *Freud and Philosophy: An Essay on Interpretation*, Denis Savage, trans. (New Haven & London: Yale University Press, 1970), 27.

[2] According to the *New York Times*, he also talked about Shakespeare's sonnets, Burmese art, Dante, Picasso, and Gertrude Stein. David Margolick, "Conclave in Herringbone Ponders Lofty and Mundane in Legal Education's Muddled Mission," *The New York Times*, January 13, 1989, B6. I discuss Radin's reading of the Stevens poem, among others, in "Death Is the Mother of Metaphor," *Harvard Law Review* 105:3 (Jan. 1992), 745, 750–3, 769–72.

[3] Margolick, "Conclave in Herringbone" at B6.

Law, Culture, and Humility

bemused reaction, having taught from *The Legal Imagination*[4] in my criminal law class the previous year. I was nevertheless intrigued.

Later that year, White reviewed Judge Posner's book on law and literature.[5] In that review, he reprised the themes of his Association of American Law Schools address.[6] More importantly, White noted the emergence of a loose sort of Law and Humanities movement –

> not in the political sense of the term, for there are no leaders, no manifestoes, no agendas, and no common program, but in a larger sense, as one might think of movements of the earth. What has happened is that many minds . . . have turned from the language of social science that has so dominated legal thought for the last fifty years to the humanities, and in doing so have expressed a widespread sense of the inadequacy of our current languages (and texts) to our experience of law and legal criticism (p 2026).

It is a terrific essay, and reading it again almost twenty years later I am struck by the clarity of its exposition, the sophistication of its worldview, the incisiveness of its critique, and the gracefulness of its language. Its pivotal insight, familiar to anyone acquainted with White's work, is that legal texts (like all forms of expression) are *constitutive*: "The contribution of rhetoric here, from Aristotle onwards, is to help us see that in all our talk we define ourselves, our audience, and a relation between us; that our talk is constitutive of a social and ethical reality" (p 2037).

In the twenty years since, Law and Humanities scholars have produced some fine scholarship of this sort. Gene Garver's exploration of the interrelationships among reason, character, and friendship and Marianne Constable's marvelous book about the meaning and possibilities that reside in our silences are noteworthy examples.[7] In my view, however, the real promise of Law and Humanities scholarship lies

---

[4] James Boyd White, *The Legal Imagination* (Boston: Little Brown & Co., 1973).

[5] James Boyd White, "What Can a Lawyer Learn from Literature?" *Harvard Law Review* 102:8 (June 1989), 2014 (reviewing Richard A. Posner, *Law and Literature: A Misunderstood Relation* (Cambridge: Harvard University Press, 1988)). Subsequent page numbers are given in the text.

[6] The following passage captures the sense of that earlier talk:

> Think of the way one engages with a literary text, or other artifact to be read in a humanistic way: a poem or a painting, say, or a church, or perhaps a ritual, drawn from another culture, or from another moment in our own culture. The central question one asks is about its meaning, to the maker and to us. This is not reducible to a summary or other propositional statement but lies in the experience of the original: it is specific to its form, to its materials, to its language, to its cultural and even to its physical context. The makers of a Gothic cathedral, for example, could not say in words what their building meant – for that they needed stone and space, light and dark – and much the same is true of the musical composition, the drama, the poem. The meaning of such a text cannot be reproduced in other terms without loss (pp 2018–19).

[7] Eugene Garver, *For the Sake of Argument: Practical Reasoning, Character, and the Ethics of Belief* (Chicago: University of Chicago Press, 2004); Marianne Constable, *Just Silences* (Princeton & Oxford: Princeton University Press, 2005).

elsewhere. It can be observed in the Nietzschean and Heideggerian influences in Constable's work.[8] It is on display more generally among scholars who gather under the banner of the Association for the Study of Law, Culture, and the Humanities – many of whom are collected in this volume – as they work toward a post-Enlightenment, hermeneutically grounded understanding of the nature and efficacy of human knowledge.[9]

When I was first thinking about this chapter, I happened by a local church whose sign read: "When truth becomes relative, all things are doubtful." This is the fear that drives all fundamentalisms, secular as well as religious.[10] It is why even the most enlightened secularists adhere so steadfastly to an understanding of the world as amenable to human reason through ever more precise definition and description. It is a mainstay of postmodern or antifoundationalist thought that everything about humanity is socially contingent and, therefore, open to the work of interpretation. Taken radically, however, this way of apprehending the world risks atavism to the extent that it (wittingly or otherwise) implicates the Enlightenment schema of subject and object. It is precisely that way of thinking about the world which must be overcome if we are to achieve a genuine humanism.[11]

Consider, for example, White's fundamental (and highly conventional) opposition between the humanities, on one hand, and the language of social science, on the other. Rather than marking a new direction or "movement," this way of characterizing the issue remains firmly anchored in the Romantic past. Thus, as Charles Taylor observes, "the best and most sensitive minds" from J. S. Mill to Nietzsche

---

[8] Constable, *Just Silences* at 175 (invoking "the metaphysical problem of nihilism and the devaluation of values that Nietzsche and Heidegger identify with our particular age.").

[9] According to its website, http://www.law.syr.edu/academics/centers/lch/main.html, the Association is "an organization of scholars engaged in interdisciplinary, humanistically oriented legal scholarship" that "brings together a wide range of people engaged in scholarship on legal history, legal theory and jurisprudence, law and cultural studies, law and literature, law and the performing arts, and legal hermeneutics."

[10] *Cf.* Richard J. Bernstein, *Beyond Objectivism and Relativism: Science, Hermeneutics, and Praxis* (Philadelphia: University of Pennsylvania Press, 1983), 16–18 (describing as the "Cartesian Anxiety" the fear that: "*Either* there is some support for our being, a fixed foundation for our knowledge, *or* we cannot escape the forces of darkness that envelop us with madness, with intellectual and moral chaos.").

[11] What is, for me, the *Ur*-text is Merleau-Ponty's remark in *Signs* that:

> There were values and, on the other hand, realities; there was mind and, on the other hand, body; there was the interior and, on the other hand, the exterior. But what if it were precisely the case that the order of facts invaded that of values, if it were recognized that dichotomies are tenable only this side of a certain point of misery and danger? Even those among us today who are taking up the word "humanism" again no longer maintain the *shameless humanism* of our elders. What is perhaps proper to our time is to disassociate humanism from the idea of a humanity fully guaranteed by natural law, and not only reconcile consciousness of human values and consciousness of the infrastructures which keep them in existence, but to insist on their inseparability.

Maurice Merleau-Ponty, *Signs*, Richard C. McCleary, trans. (Evanston: Northwestern University Press, 1964), 226–7.

Law, Culture, and Humility

have since the end of the eighteenth century decried modernity's Philistine quality in just these terms:

> In different ways these critics castigate modern society as expressively dead, as stifling expressive fulfilment through the power of conformity, or through the all-pervasive demands of utility, of producing a world in which all acts, objects, institutions have a use, but none express what men are or could be. This stream of opposition has its source in the expressivist current of the late eighteenth century.[12]

Personal and community wholeness cannot come from an expressivist stance that merely attacks or supplements what is lacking in the relentlessly utilitarian modern identity because it is that very opposition which is the problem. Rather, what is needed at the current moment is a mode of understanding – more accurately, a mode of being – that could plausibly transcend the deeply etched oppositions that characterize modernity.

Contemporary Law and Humanities scholarship is one of the more promising venues for that project. This is, in part, because it is situated at the juncture of the practical and the interpretive. It is also, in part, because of the wealth and scope of its dispositions and methodological commitments. It has been a mainstay of the humanities at least since the Romantics that the object of understanding is to make the familiar strange and the strange familiar. Humanities scholarship, in other words, participates in a tradition of inquiry that is critical and iconoclastic. At the same time, its methodological commitment to an interpretive conception of "truth" as that which emerges from the complex of human meaning, purpose, and goals places it beyond the facile objectivity of the more technical discourses that dominate legal studies today.

The project I have in mind is a formidable one, too ambitious in scope to more than sketch in the space of a single chapter.[13] Here, I situate that project critically by exposing the hegemony and distortions that characterize the current social and intellectual landscape. In doing so, I am following Constable's critique of what she identifies as the positivist, sociolegal worldview that monopolizes legal studies today.[14] I begin by observing the primacy of the fundamentalist view of subject/object relations at this moment in history and explore its purest form in law and economics. I then take up work in philosophy, seen by some as congenial to Law and Humanities and show how it is afflicted by this same schema with all of its characteristic reductionism, essentialism, and abstractionism. In the final section, I explore the value

---

[12] Charles Taylor, *Hegel* (Cambridge: Cambridge University Press, 1975), 543–44.

[13] At the least, it would seem to me to require attention to our embodiment (*see* note 11 *supra*) and its pivotal role in cognition and imagination. *See* Steven L. Winter, A *Clearing in the Forest: Law, Life, & Mind* (Chicago: University of Chicago Press, 2001).

[14] Constable, *Just Silences* at 89 ("[I]s law other than a tool of social self-constitution, a social policy produced by social knowledges that gauge the social options in, and social preferences of, a society governed by social policy? What else could law be?").

and potential of Law and Humanities scholarship. I, first, review and, then, dismiss the debate over the emergence of law and literature scholarship on the ground that it merely recapitulates, rather than advances, the fundamentalist understanding of subject/object relations. In its place, I offer an alternative account of what defines an approach to inquiry as humanist. I conclude with a sketch of the parameters that would provide sense and shape to a genuinely humanist scholarship.

Rationality and Circularity

After the linguistic, hermeneutic, and cultural turns of the twentieth century, the idea of an unmediated reality to which we have direct and accurate access should seem like the kind of primitive belief that the West once reflexively imputed to "less civilized" societies. Yet everywhere one turns, this kind of fundamentalism seems to characterize the times in which we live.

By "fundamentalism," I refer to a set of presuppositions about human reason and its relation to the world that assumes transparency, hierarchy, linearity, and universality.[15] On this view, reason is propositional, rule-governed, and independent of language or culture; people everywhere have the same inherent capacities and values; and the world – both physical and social – is reducible to the laws or principles that determine its shape. Fundamentalism, of course, is a term conventionally applied to religious movements; for us, as children of the Enlightenment, science and rationality stand in opposition to religion and received dogma. But, as I have argued elsewhere, rationalism too can be a form of idolatry.[16] The point of bringing these otherwise disparate forms of thought together under a single rubric is to draw attention to the common conceptual schema at work in both cases. With or without a deity, both assume a "God's-eye" point of view with respect to a world that is straightforwardly open to understanding.

Already at the midpoint of the twentieth century, Merleau-Ponty warned "fear of contingency is everywhere " and that the "vertiginous idea" that the entire human undertaking rests upon nothing but itself spawns its own anxious rejection:

> It is understandable that our contemporaries, faced with this idea (which they glimpse as well as we do), retreat and turn aside toward some idol. It is the fear of the new which galvanizes and reaffirms precisely the very ideas that historical experience has worn out.[17]

---

[15] The characterization is from Mark Johnson, "Ain't No Fun in Fundamentalism" (ms. 2003). Johnson identifies fundamentalism in morality and law as resting on the assumptions that: 1) reason is universal; 2) there are universal principles or laws; 3) there are absolute values and laws; 4) concepts are literal; 5) categories are classical in structure (i.e., defined by necessary and sufficient criteria); 6) principles and values are arranged hierarchically; and 7) subjects are radically free.

[16] Winter, A Clearing in the Forest at xiv, 9–11 ("In academic circles, the rationalist model has something of the status of an ideology. As such, it is largely impervious to refutation on empirical grounds.").

[17] Merleau-Ponty, Signs at 241.

Law, Culture, and Humility

For most people, uncertainty gives rise to feelings of vulnerability and dread that make the appeal of certain truth seem all the more alluring. Indeed, there is much to be gained from the sense that one has a firm grasp on the truth. Not only is it a comfort, it can be quite enabling. When you are sure of your bona fides, all things seem possible. When one has confidence in one's methodology, every conclusion it produces will appear robust.

To a large extent, American foreign policy in the Bush years was driven by convictions of just this sort. However one understands the underlying notion – whether the assumption that the desire for freedom is an essential aspect of human personhood, that a rational actor would choose Western-style democracy and a market economy, or that democracy is God's gift to humanity – the premise of American engagement with the world has been that Western-style political and economic freedom is an objective, universal good. Indeed, some version of this idea has been the underlying assumption of our policy toward Russia, China, and the former Communist bloc for over two decades.[18] Despite the mixed results in those countries, it was also the refrain behind United States policy in Iraq where, we were assured, we would be "greeted as liberators." Former President Bush went so far as to claim that the events of September 11, 2001, require us to affirm that our commitment to freedom is not a mere "reflection of convention and culture," but a necessary response to "the universal demand of conscience and morality."[19]

It may be that the change of administrations will bring a change in these assumptions; the more general phenomenon of certainty about the truth and instrumental efficacy of our knowledge is, nevertheless, a characteristic of modernity that is widely entrenched. Despite the fact that we have barely more genes than a fruit fly, the cracking of the human genome has led to widespread expectations and enthusiastic claims about the ability to identify the genetic determinants of everything from breast cancer to capitalism.[20] Notwithstanding the developments in second-wave cognitive

---

[18] During both the first Bush and Clinton administrations, the basic idea behind American policy toward China was that the development of free markets should provide the ground for the emergence of democracy (and vice versa). David E. Sanger "Opening to China: New Realism Wins the Day," *The New York Times*, Sept. 20, 2000, A1.

[19] George W. Bush, "Securing Freedom's Triumph," *The New York Times*, Sept. 11, 2002, A33.

[20] *Cf.* Gregory Clark, *A Farewell to Alms: A Brief Economic History of the World* (Princeton: Princeton University Press, 2007), 186–88. Indeed, a highly publicized recent study has overturned the finding – previously widely celebrated – that a single gene determines the risk of depression. Benedict Carey, "Report on Gene for Depression, Widely Hailed in '03, Is Now Found to be Flawed," *The New York Times*, June 17, 2009, A17. This really shouldn't be surprising, however. As Eric Turkheimer notes, "the one-gene-one-disorder" model is now "universally recognized as inadequate for medical disorders as complex as diabetes or heart disease, to say nothing of schizophrenia or delinquency." Despite the obvious limitations of the linear, reductive model, it nevertheless "acquires a crisply technological, optimistically modern ring when exactly the same mistake is made in a genetic context." Eric Turkheimer, "Mobiles: A Gloomy View of the Prospects for Developmental Behavioral Genetics," in *Wrestling with Behavioral Genetics: Science, Ethics, and Public Conversation*, Erik Parens, Audrey R. Chapman, & Nancy Press, eds. (Baltimore: Johns Hopkins University Press, 2006), 107.

science, much of the field's mainstream remains mired in a rigidly mechanistic view of mind that notoriously has gone decades without being able to make much progress on artificial intelligence.[21]

Perhaps nowhere is this hubris more firm than in the legal academy, where decades of sophisticated, skeptical critique have yielded quickly and without much of a fight to the scientism and relentless instrumentalism of economics and rational choice theory.[22] More broadly, as Constable argues, modern sociolegal studies are dominated by a common form of legal and social positivism that tends to view law as an autonomous, ahistorical set of practices, which functions effectively and authoritatively "as instrument or strategy within a field of social power."[23]

There is, perhaps, no more reductive, powerful, and self-confident methodology in legal studies today than economics. The basic idea is simple. People are assumed to be rational actors who maximize their utility. Accordingly, they respond to incentives (or disincentives) in relation to the desirability of the preferred behaviors, goods, or ends. The more they value the end result, the higher the cost they are willing to incur. Correspondingly, as costs rise, those who value the ends less will desist. If markets are left unfettered, resources will gravitate through exchange toward those who value them most (as manifested by willingness to pay). It does not matter, moreover, that people may be psychologically more complex as long as the model in fact has predictive power.[24]

There is no denying the elegance and frequent usefulness of this model, but it can also fail quite spectacularly. The financial meltdown of 2008 was not only shocking in its magnitude, but also in its provenance. At the highest levels of government, it was assumed as an article of faith that rational market actors would not extend risky subprime loans or invest in exotic (later toxic) derivatives unless it were in their long-term interests. The determination, which followed ineluctably from the economic model, was that "the self-interest of lending institutions" would lead to decisions that "protect shareholders' equity." When it did not turn out that way, no less a figure than Alan Greenspan was forced to admit publicly that he had "found

---

[21] As Douglas Hofstadter observes: "I get a huge kick out of laughing at the hilariously unpredictable inflexibility of the computer models of mental processes that my doctoral students and I codesign. It helps remind me of the immense subtlety and elusiveness of the human mind." An Interview with Douglas R. Hofstadter, http://tal.forum2.org/hofstadter_interview?NewOnly=2&LastView=2008-06-19%2006:25:38, June 11, 2008, reprinted in *The New York Times*, June 15, 2008, WK4. See Hubert L. Dreyfus, *What Computers Still Can't Do: A Critique of Artificial Reason*, 2nd ed. (Cambridge: MIT Press, 1992).

[22] See Steven L. Winter, "When Things Went Terribly, Terribly Wrong," in *On Philosophy in American Law*, Francis J. Mootz, III, ed. (Cambridge: Cambridge University Press, 2009), 35–43. See also Steven L. Winter, "John Roberts's Formalist Nightmare," *University of Miami Law Review* 63:2 (Jan. 2009), 501.

[23] Constable, *Just Silences* at 10–11.

[24] Richard A. Posner, *Economic Analysis of Law*, 3rd ed. (Boston: Little, Brown and Co., 1986), 15–16.

Law, Culture, and Humility

a flaw" and was "in a state of shocked disbelief." As he conceded before Congress: "The whole intellectual edifice collapsed."[25]

There is no real mystery, however, about the source or nature of the flaw. It lies in the radical reductionism of the rational actor model and all that follows from it. The rational actor model takes a remarkably one-dimensional view of human behavior. It is not a claim that, in the financial sphere, people operate to maximize wealth; it is, rather, a claim that we can model all of human behavior on the basis of this single motive of maximizing preferences. As Posner puts it: "'Economic man' is not . . . a person driven by purely pecuniary incentives, but he is a person whose behavior is completely determined by incentives; his rationality is no different from that of a pigeon or a rat."[26] Moreover, the claim is not that this is true some of the time in some circumstances, but all of the time in all circumstances. Thus, Posner asserts that "people are rational maximizers of their satisfactions – *all* people (with the exception of small children and the profoundly retarded) in *all* their activities (except when under the influence of psychosis or similarly deranged through drug or alcohol abuse)" (p 353).

Posner (p 366) defends against the "reductionist" criticism by pointing out that: "All science involves abstraction. Newton's law of falling bodies abstracts from many of the particulars of such bodies (for example, was the apple red?)." This analogy, however, is both revealing and inapt. It is revealing because to compare human subjects to apples is a kind of parapraxis: It is only within the Enlightenment schema of subject and object that one would conceive of humans as transparent "objects" of study like bodies falling through space (or rats in a maze). It is also inapt because the color of the apple is irrelevant to the rate that a body falls through a gravitational field (as is the fact that the falling body happens to be an apple). Human beings, however, are not apples; they are remarkably complex psychosocial systems.

True, Posner's point about abstraction in science is correct. Scientific method (like any methodology) makes it easier to tackle a problem or organize data because it foregrounds those elements that are most relevant to the job at hand, relegating to the background the welter of other details. In simplifying a task to make it more manageable, however, one may also be *falsifying* it – that is, omitting factors which actually matter.[27] When we are talking about humans, we are talking

---

[25] Edmund L. Andrews, "Greenspan Concedes Flaws in Deregulatory Approach," *The New York Times*, Oct. 24, 2008, B1. Similarly, Posner observes, "The movement to deregulate the financial industry went too far by exaggerating the resilience – the self-healing powers – of laissez-faire capitalism." Richard A. Posner, A *Failure of Capitalism: The Crisis of '08 and the Descent into Depression* (Cambridge: Harvard University Press, 2009), xii. But *cf. ibid.* at 235 (declaring that "Bankers and consumers alike seem on the whole to have been acting in conformity with their rational self-interest.").

[26] Richard A. Posner, *The Problems of Jurisprudence* (Cambridge: Harvard University Press, 1990), 382. Subsequent page numbers are given in the text.

[27] This is the insight that underlies Kuhn's observation that science progresses not by achieving better and better descriptions of reality, but rather by shifts in scientific paradigms that better solve the problems

about complexities of behavior that traverse a terrain in which primitive drives interact with sophisticated systems of symbolic meaning. Reductionism in this context is almost certain to matter. Indeed, Posner concedes (as he must) that the basic assumption of economics is "seriously incomplete. People have difficulty in dealing with low-probability events, which are important in many areas of behavior studied by economists; and much human behavior appears to be impulsive, emotional, superstitious – in a word, irrational" (p 365). His more modest conclusion is that economics "seems to capture an important part, though possibly only a small part, of the phenomena it seeks to explain" (p 366).

The profound problem with the reductionism of the economic model is not that it is descriptively inaccurate, but rather that it leads to inaccurate descriptions. An economist is like the proverbial person with a hammer for whom everything looks like a nail. Because the model allows for only one dimension of human motivation, it can logically see only that single dimension. Consider the case of the substance abuser. It is always possible to reformulate such behavior in rational actor terms.[28] Thus, one could say that substance abusers value their high so much that they are willing to pay the cost in ruined lives and health.[29] But such reformulations beg the question in at least three ways. First, if the goal of the substance abuser is to maximize his or her pleasure, then the severity of the medium to long-term costs means that the enterprise (judged only from the perspective of maximizing pleasure) is ultimately self-defeating.[30] Second, the reformulation is both artificial and highly inappropriate. It is not just that the substance abuser is overvaluing current utility over long-term utility. Rather, as anyone with personal experience or professional familiarity knows, those afflicted with such pathologies often act out in counterproductive ways and engage in repeated cycles of self-destructive behavior. "Rational" action is neither an a priori nor a metaphysical faculty that individuals just "have," but a psychological and socially contingent capacity that depends

---

at hand. Thomas S. Kuhn, *The Structure of Scientific Revolutions,* 2nd ed. (Chicago: University of Chicago Press, 1970). Because scientific formalizations simplify in just this way, more than one method or theory may actually work (and, in that sense, be "true") – albeit depending on one's purposes.

[28] *Cf.* Posner, *Problems of Jurisprudence* at 363–4:

> [E]conomic theory has become so rich, so complex, that almost any hypothesis, even one that appeared to deny a fundamental implication of the theory such as the law of demand, could be made to conform to the theory. In fact, it is distressingly easy to explain away empirical findings that appear to conflict with the basic theoretical assumptions and propositions of economics.

[29] Posner's caveat would seem to exclude this example. In fact, however, this illustration is adapted from the observation of another well-known law and economics scholar (who for obvious reasons will go unnamed) who once explained to me that the homeless mentally ill who abuse alcohol are just rational actors choosing to "self-medicate."

[30] Which is to say that, even when people are maximizers, they are often quite irrationally so. Although the example of the substance abuser may seem extreme, it is in many ways more typical of human behavior than the economist's idealized rational actor.

Law, Culture, and Humility

on such factors as proper development, education, and mental and emotional health.[31]

Third, and most critical, the reductionism of the rational actor model sets up a circularity of the *post hoc ergo propter hoc* sort: Whatever the activity at whatever the price, the very fact that someone made the choice is itself evidence that that person valued the activity highly and, thus, acted rationally. In this way, economic theory becomes entirely self-confirming. Thus, in the context of the financial markets, the understanding was that because market actors continued to buy and sell derivatives it must be the case that the market had determined that they were sound investments. When it turned out that the market was actually engaged in a very human mix of fallible judgment, greed, and herd behavior,[32] true believers like Alan Greenspan were simply caught unawares. In cases such as that of the substance abuser, the self-confirming quality of the theory makes it all too easy to rationalize suffering.

The greater the complexity of the psychological and social phenomena, the more the economic model falls victim to its own reductivism and becomes prone to such errors of precommitment and misrecognition. Several recent economic studies of the death penalty, for example, claim to demonstrate that executions save lives by deterring other murderers. One goes so far as to claim that each execution prevents eighteen murders.[33] As Donohue and Wolfers explain: "The theoretical premise underlying the deterrence argument is simple: raise the price of murder for criminals, and you will get less of it."[34] However, after carefully reviewing these studies (including analyses of the underlying data sets), Donohue and Wolfers conclude that the data are quite equivocal:

> The U.S. data simply do not speak clearly about whether the death penalty has a deterrent or antideterrent effect. The only clear conclusion is that execution policy drives little of the year-to-year variation in homicide rates. As to

---

[31] Significantly, Damasio has found that subjects with injuries to their ventromedial prefrontal lobe who have lost the capacity for emotion are also unable to make rational plans or projections about the consequences of their actions. Antonio R. Damasio, *Descartes' Error: Emotion, Reason, and the Human Brain* (New York: Harcourt Brace & Co., 1994), 1–62.

[32] The same might be said of the postcrash phenomena of corporate and financial managers continuing their accustomed profligate behaviors – fancy new corporate jets, large year-end bonuses, extravagant junkets – after accepting huge taxpayer bailouts and long after the popular backlash had taken hold. *See, e.g.*, Joe Nocera, "It's Not the Bonus Money. It's the Principle," *The New York Times*, Jan. 31, 2009, B1; Stephen Labaton & Vikas Bajaj, "Executive Pay Limits Seek to Alter Corporate Culture," *The New York Times*, Feb. 5, 2009, A1; Alan Feuer & Karen Zraick, "It's Theirs and They're Not Apologizing," *The New York Times*, Jan. 31, 2009, B4.

[33] Hashem Dezhbakhsh, Paul H. Rubin, & Joanna M. Shepherd, "Does Capital Punishment Have a Deterrent Effect? New Evidence from Postmoratorium Panel Data," *American Law & Economics Review* 5:2 (2003), 344.

[34] John J. Donohue & Justin Wolfers, "The Ethics and Empirics of Capital Punishment: Uses and Abuses of Empirical Evidence in the Death Penalty Debate," *Stanford Law Review* 58:3 (Dec. 2005), 791, 795.

whether executions raise or lower the homicide rate, we remain profoundly uncertain.[35]

Part of the problem is that crime is a sociologically complex phenomenon; it is affected by many other factors (particularly demographics) besides the incentive structures of the criminal justice system. For example, despite the fact that Canada carried out its last executions in 1962 and completely abolished capital punishment in 1976, during this period homicide rates moved "in lockstep" with those in the United States; after abolition, homicide rates in the United States remained high but fell in Canada.[36] Part of the problem is the complexity of the data themselves. Thus, detailed examination of the methodology of the various studies of the U.S. data demonstrated that the results "change dramatically even with small changes in econometric specifications."[37] Nonetheless, Donohue and Wolfers note that the confident claims of proof are not really surprising: Because basic principles dictate that the amount of an activity drops as the cost of that activity rises, economic studies of capital punishment are predisposed toward finding a deterrent effect.[38] As one of the authors later noted: "To say anything else is to brand yourself an imbecile."[39]

The Prison-House of Reason

Law and economics is a perfect avatar of the modern age in which, as Constable observes, the "world threatens to become" nothing more than "an object or resource for the social human being who would master it through knowledge."[40] In the contemporary legal academy the lines between analytic philosophy, on one hand, and instrumentalist approaches such as law and economics, on the other,

---

[35] *Ibid.* at 841. As Donohue and Wolfers explain:

> Year-to-year movements in homicide rates are large, and the effects of even major changes in execution policy are barely detectable. Inferences of substantial deterrent effects made by authors examining specific samples appear not to be robust in larger samples; inferences based on specific functional forms appear not to be robust to alternative functional forms; inferences made without reference to a comparison group appear only to reflect broader societal trends and do not hold up when compared with appropriate control groups; inferences based on specific sets of controls turn out not to be robust to alternative sets of controls; and inferences of robust effects based on either faulty instruments or underestimated standard errors are also found wanting (*ibid*).

[36] *Ibid.* at 799–800.
[37] *Ibid.* at 843.
[38] "Alternatively, to frame the issue as a Bayesian would, one's posterior belief about the deterrent effect of the death penalty surely looks a lot like one's prior belief." *Ibid.* at 844.
[39] Adam Liptak, "Does Death Penalty Save Lives? A New Debate," *The New York Times*, Nov. 18, 2007, A1 (quoting Wolfers).
[40] Constable, *Just Silences* at 175.

Law, Culture, and Humility

are sharply drawn.[41] In the circumstance of modernity, however, even a discipline once so central to the humanities as philosophy takes the same distorted form as its instrumentalist rivals. Ronald Dworkin, for example, employs the tools of moral and analytic philosophy to argue against instrumentalism in law and to claim that there is a principled, "right answer" to all legal questions that a suitably intelligent judge endowed with unlimited time – Hercules – would be able to work out.[42] This is a vision of a transparent moral and social world, open to human mastery; more accurately, it is a *belief* in such a world. Famously, Dworkin makes no affirmative argument to justify his "right answer" claim, but mostly argues against the viability of skeptical views.[43]

A more detailed example, however, will provide us with a clearer view of the surprising isomorphism between these otherwise disparate disciplines.

In *Democracy and Equality*,[44] Robert Post examines the relationship between those two core values. He begins by "fixing" a definition of democracy in terms of autonomy understood in the Kantian sense of being governed only by those rules one gives oneself.[45] A democratic form of government is one committed to the value of collective self-determination. This definition is problematic, though, because in a diverse, heterogeneous society, people often disagree; under a system of majority rule, the losers will by definition be bound by a rule other than the one they would give to themselves. This gap can be bridged, however, if the dissenters can nonetheless identify with the decisions of the polity and view those decisions somehow "as their own." This identification can be achieved, according to Post, if people are treated equally as autonomous participants in public discourse. In that case, people can have "the warranted conviction that they are engaged in the process of governing themselves" (p 144) because the state is potentially responsive to their values and ideas. "This form of equality," he concludes, "is foundational because it follows from the very definition of democracy" (p 147).

This very narrow conception of equality creates a very large problem for democratic theory. Historically and conceptually, the democratic ideal carries with it

---

[41] *See* Richard A. Posner, *Problematics of Moral and Legal Theory* (Cambridge: Harvard University Press, 2002); Louis Kaplow & Steven Shavell, *Fairness Versus Welfare* (Cambridge: Harvard University Press, 2006).

[42] Ronald Dworkin, *Taking Rights Seriously* (Cambridge: Harvard University Press, 1977), 110–30, 279–90; Ronald Dworkin, *A Matter of Principle* (Cambridge: Harvard University Press, 1985), 119–45.

[43] *See* Michael S. Moore, *Educating Oneself in Public: Critical Essays in Jurisprudence* (Oxford: Oxford University Press, 2000), 268–9.

[44] Robert Post, "Democracy and Equality," *Law, Culture, and Humanities* 1:2 (2005), 142–53. Subsequent page numbers are given in the text.

[45] It is not enough, he argues, to identify democracy with popular sovereignty and majority rule because the former "is a normative idea" while the latter two "are descriptive terms that refer to particular decision-making procedures" (p 143).

strong notions of equality.[46] This is evident in the Declaration of Independence's pronouncement that "all men are created equal"; the French revolutionary's slogan *liberté, egalité, fraternité*; and the American revolutionary desire to live "by no man's leave." Conceptually, the democratic ideal implies strong egalitarianism because hierarchy is antithetical to self-rule: The subordinated *do* live by some other man's leave; they live under conditions of heteronomy. For Post, however, the only form of equality democracy permits is "an equality measured in terms of the autonomous agency required by democratic legitimacy" (p 151). This pits democracy and equality against each other because "many forms of equality can actually interfere with the individual liberty required by this project" (p 152).

One can see the conflict in the case of private property: The autonomy to acquire property entails both the right to accumulate it and, of course, to exclude others from using or otherwise appropriating it.[47] Much the same is true with respect to other aspects of individual autonomy. In the context of public discourse, "the relevant equality of agency inheres in the liberty to express oneself in the manner of one's choice" (p 148). Egalitarian claims of fairness and distributive justice such as prohibitions of hate speech, regulation of corporate speech, or limitations on campaign expenditures are in tension with democracy because they threaten that autonomy. Post concludes, "the logic of democratic legitimacy" (p 151) implies that strong egalitarian principles must yield whenever they "compromise the autonomous participation of persons within democratic self-governance" (pp 149, 150). Otherwise, citizens would no longer be able to sustain the necessary identification with the process of creating the social order in which they live.

Democratic theory resolves the conflict between autonomy and equality by recasting the latter as formal equality. Thus, Post notes that the "one person, one vote" principle "signifies that each person is to be regarded as formally equal to every other in the influence that their agency can contribute to public decisions" (p 148). Famously, however, formal equality both conduces to and underwrites substantive

[46] Post recognizes that "it is generally thought that implicit within the idea of democracy is a notion of strong substantive equality that flows from the moral equality of all citizens (pp 151–2)." He insists, however, that the concept of democracy "does not itself entail these principles (p 153)."

[47] The inevitable inequality that follows from protecting the right of property was forthrightly acknowledged by the Supreme Court during its infamous substantive due process era. *Coppage v. Kansas*, 236 U.S. 1, 17 (1915) ("since it is self-evident that, unless all things are held in common, some persons must have more property than others, it is from the nature of things impossible to uphold freedom of contract and the right of private property without at the same time recognizing as legitimate those inequalities of fortune that are the necessary result of the exercise of those rights"). It was a mainstay of Legal Realism that this inequality is in no way "private" or "natural," but rather a product of the background distribution of entitlements enforced by the legal system. *See* Robert Hale, "Coercion and Distribution in a Supposedly Non-Coercive State," *Political Science Quarterly* 38:3 (Sept. 1923), 470; Morris Cohen, "Property and Sovereignty," *Cornell Law Quarterly* 13:1 (Oct. 1927), 8.

Law, Culture, and Humility

inequality: The law, in all its majesty, prohibits the rich as well as the poor from sleeping under the bridges of Paris. Democratic equality, Post concedes, "can easily be experienced as thin and formal" (p 150).

A humanist might well shrink from this conclusion, and Post seems obviously uncomfortable with it. Accordingly, he suggests that there might yet be a role for strong egalitarian principles. Imagine, he says, a group of citizens with the autonomy to participate in public discourse but who are so destitute, marginalized, and stigmatized by the majority that they are alienated from the polity and can no longer view its decisions as their own. In that case, democracy requires rectification of those inequalities: not because it is fair and right to do so, but because it is necessary to restore the sense of identification needed for democratic legitimacy. "The distinction is significant," he warns, because it means that democracy "does not require the full rectification of these inequities, but only the rectification necessary to maintain democratic legitimacy" (pp 152, 153). Post recognizes that his argument is "unsettling" because it implies that "democracy is quite compatible with important forms of status subordination" (p 153).

Unsettling, indeed. And ahistorical too. The democratic revolutions of the modern era were all about the overthrow of ancient hierarchies. The successive democratization of American society – the abolitionist movement, the universal suffrage movement, the public school movement, the women's suffrage movement, the labor movement, the progressive movement, the New Deal, the civil rights movement, the women's movement, the gay and lesbian liberation movement – has been the result of egalitarian assaults on the various forms of social, political, and material subordination. Even the word "democratize" connotes the intimate conceptual connection between democracy and equality: To democratize a practice, resource, or capacity is to make it more fully available to everyone, without regard to status, on terms of equality. Any theoretical account of democracy that puts democracy in conflict with equality and comfortably in bed with subordination is an account that has somehow gone terribly, terribly awry.

The flaw in Post's argument is not logical, but methodological. The problem, as Heidegger teaches, is that "conceptual definitions of terms, while necessary for technical and scientific purposes, are by themselves unfit to assure, much less advance, the soundness of language." When adopted by "academic philosophy," it makes a total hash of things: "thought in the sense of logical-rational representations turns out to be a reduction and an impoverishment . . . that beggar the imagination."[48] To start with an analytic, one-dimensional definition of democracy, as Post does, and then systematically unpack its implications is inevitably to distort the concept

---

[48] Martin Heidegger, *What Is Called Thinking?* J. Glenn Gray, trans. (New York: Harper Row, 1968), 139–40.

precisely because it is abstracted from the social and historical contexts that give it meaning.[49]

There is, in sum, a striking isomorphism between analytic philosophy and its putative rival, economics. Both adopt an acontextual and ahistorical view of the social world as straightforwardly open to definition. Both assume that the process of definition should proceed by identifying the unique, *essential* quality of the "object" of study. Both are, thus, fundamentalist and reductive in exactly the same way. Although one takes a strongly normative stance toward that world and the other an instrumentalist one, both end in authoritative prescriptions to the field of social practice. Moreover, neither approach can "capture the practices, let alone serve to regulate them, because it must redescribe and simplify them in order to make them the subject of scientific investigation."[50]

This affinity between the normative and the instrumental becomes an identity the minute that one moves from analysis to prescription. To invoke the concept of democratic autonomy as a regulatory principle is to *instrumentalize* the idea of democracy as a strategic intervention in the field of ongoing social relations. It is, inevitably, to take sides in a power struggle – and not just any side, but the side of hierarchy and status subordination. Post chides egalitarians for not recognizing that in a democracy, we "decide the meaning of moral equality in the context of public discussion and debate" (p 152) and complains that they instead defend equality employing "the idea of rights... defined by reference to various forms of philosophical reason" (*ibid*). Post, however, is guilty of the very same error. There is, in his argument, no normative discussion of how best to mediate between conflicting values; no question of "who are we?" or "whom should we become?" There is, rather, the assertion of a particular principle as "definitional" and the insistence on submission to the power of a purely deductive, abstract argument.[51]

Post's argument, moreover, illustrates the way in which this devaluing of values becomes infectious. It is not just that his notion of democratic autonomy is expected to regulate the social field, but Post entirely instrumentalizes equality as a mere tool for maintaining the identification with the polity necessary for his conception of democratic legitimacy. In relegating equality to a mere means, his argument robs equality of any independent normative force: Equality becomes relevant – that is, tolerated – only to the extent that it operates as a tool of legitimation. By the same

---

[49] The ungroundedness of this kind of abstract argument from principle also assures its indeterminacy. Thus, one can easily imagine a parallel argument in which one starts with the equality of all citizens as foundational to democracy and then unpacks the implications of that principle to conclude that various forms of autonomy are inconsistent with democracy.

[50] Linda Ross Meyer, "Is Practical Reason Mindless?" *Georgetown Law Journal* 86:3 (Jan. 1998), 652.

[51] Thus, one could just as well argue that, in a democracy that takes the equality of all citizens as foundational, we decide the meaning and proper scope of autonomy "in the context of public discussion and debate" and not, as he proposes, "by reference to various forms of philosophical reason."

Law, Culture, and Humility

token, this instrumentalization of equality robs it of all substantive content because it makes legitimation rather than fairness the measure of its scope.

In the end, the method of analytic philosophy shares in the same fundamentalism, the same relentless abstractionism, the same desire for transparency and certainty, and the same distortions and dysfunctions as its more crassly instrumentalist rival. As White elsewhere observes, "The habit of mind that yearns for these methods and their certainties is bound to be delusive, and ultimately – despite its claims to superior rationality – to be irrational, because it will not be in accordance with the nature of our world and our experience."[52]

Culture, Contingency, Community

What is the alternative? What would a genuinely humanist approach look like?

From the earliest days of the law and literature movement, the most common claim on its behalf has been that the study of literature (or narrative or rhetoric) serves an edifying function. Variously stated, the basic argument is: first, that by reading literature (or attending to narrative or to our constitutive rhetoric) we are able to develop and hone a capacity for empathy,[53] to understand the plight of the excluded and oppressed,[54] or to understand what it really means to treat the Other as an end in himself; and second, that these capacities cannot be captured in the deracinated logic of law, science, or moral philosophy.[55] The responses to this claim have been varied and often inconsistent. Some question the dichotomy between

---

[52] James B. White, *Heracles' Bow: Essays on the Rhetoric and Poetics of the Law* (Madison: University of Wisconsin Press, 1985), 24.

[53] *See, e.g.,* White, "What Can a Lawyer Learn" at 2036 ("the heart of the teaching of literature lies in the stimulation of our capacity to imagine other people, not only as they suffer or enjoy what we do not, but more deeply as they inhabit different universes of meaning, different spheres of language"); Lynne Henderson, "Legality and Empathy," 85:7 *Michigan Law Review* (June 1987), 1574; Julius G. Getman, "Voices," 66:2 *Texas Law Review* (Feb. 1988), 577.

[54] *See, e.g.,* Richard Delgado, "Legal Storytelling for Oppositionists and Others: A Plea for Narrative," 87:8 *Michigan Law Review* (Aug. 1989), 2411; Mari J. Matsuda, "Public Sanction of Racist Speech: Considering the Victim's Story," 87:8 *Michigan Law Review* (Aug. 1989), 2320; *cf.* Richard Rorty, *Contingency, Irony, and Solidarity* (Cambridge: Cambridge University Press, 1989), 141–78 (discussing the sort of books that are "relevant to our relations with others, to helping us notice the effects of our actions on other people" and "relevant to the avoidance of either social or individual cruelty").

[55] *See, e.g.,* White, *Heracles' Bow* at 5 ("What does it actually mean . . . to treat another person as a 'means' to an end, or, by contrast, as an 'end in himself'? [T]hese questions can best be addressed in a language of art, and that a purely conceptual and logical language, like that of modern analytic philosophy, will always be incomplete or defective."); Martha C. Nussbaum, *Love's Knowledge: Essays on Philosophy and Literature* (Oxford: Oxford University Press, 1990). The strongest version of this claim, that there is a correlation between good writing and good decision making, appears in Richard H. Weisberg, *Poethics: and Other Strategies of Law and Literature* (New York: Columbia University Press, 1992), 251.

empathy and reason or between the literary and the legal.[56] Others insist that the literary and the legal are so distinct as to have nothing of importance to say to one another.[57]

Perhaps the principal criticisms of the law and literature project, however, have focused on its perceived unreliability. Critics of narrative scholarship have pointed to its subjectivity, questioned the accuracy and representativeness of its accounts, and argued that there is no way in which it can be subjected to the rigors of verification and disputation.[58] Similarly, skeptics of the law and literature movement have argued that there is no necessary connection between literature and the ethical edification extolled by the movement's advocates. Books may be virtuous or evil.[59] Stories may subvert hierarchy or legitimate it.[60] Worst of all, different people will each bring their own preconceptions and experience to reading and, therefore, will come away from reading literature or narrative with very different understandings and conclusions.[61]

Although I paint here with a broad brush, the reason should be obvious: The entire debate merely reenacts the fundamentalist view of subject/object relations. This is apparent in the initial claims of the movement, which juxtapose the ways of empathy with the cold reason of law, science, and philosophy. It is apparent, too, in the critique of storytelling as unreliable. Thus, as I have argued elsewhere,[62] this critique presupposes strong notions of objectivity and subjectivity. On one hand, it assumes that there is some unadorned "true" account of the brute facts against which the narrator's "subjective" rendition must be substantiated. On the other, it treats

---

[56] Toni M. Massaro, "Empathy, Legal Storytelling, and the Rule of Law: New Words, Old Wounds?" 87:8 *Michigan Law Review* (Aug. 1989), 2099, 2106–16; Guyora Binder & Robert Weisberg, *Literary Criticisms of Law* (Princeton: Princeton University Press, 2000), 261–83, 287–91. I take a radical version of that position in "Death Is the Mother of Metaphor" at 749 ("[W]e do not have separate minds for poetry and for law. Necessarily, we do each with the same mind – indeed, the whole mind").

[57] Posner, *A Misunderstood Relation*.

[58] Daniel A. Farber and Suzanna Sherry, "Telling Stories Out of School: An Essay on Legal Narratives," *Stanford Law Review* 45:6 (April 1993), 807; Anne M. Coughlin, "Regulating the Self: Autobiographical Performances in Outsider Scholarship," 81:5 *Virginia Law Review* (August 1995), 1229; Richard A. Posner, *Overcoming Law* (Cambridge: Harvard University Press, 1995), 369–80.

[59] *See, e.g.*, Geoffrey P. Miller, "A Rhetoric of Law," 52:4 *University Chicago Law Review* (Winter 1985), 247, 257–9 (reviewing James Boyd White, *When Words Lose Their Meaning: Constitutions and Reconstitutions of Language, Character, and Community* (Chicago: University of Chicago Press, 1984)) ("No one would seriously argue, I suppose, that the relationship between the author and reader of *Mein Kampf* somehow establishes values of friendship and respect for humanity").

[60] *See* Binder & Weisberg, *Literary Criticisms of Law* at 266–79. As Binder and Weisberg insightfully point out, the "covert authorial performance" of the standard clinical narrative reinforces the privileged position of the professional who narrates the encounter with her client. *Ibid.* at 254–7.

[61] *See generally* Norman N. Holland, 5 *Readers Reading* (New Haven: Yale University Press, 1975). As White observes: "This experience of reading is not coercive or uniform in character, and will naturally be different for different readers. Indeed there is nothing automatic in the process at all: it is perfectly possible for someone to misread a text, or to fail to respond to it, or to put even the greatest literature to base or trivial purposes." White, "What Can a Lawyer Learn" at 2020.

[62] Winter, *A Clearing in the Forest* at 132–8.

Law, Culture, and Humility

authorial voice reductively as a function of pure, unfettered agency abstracted from the social context and cultural constraints that give that voice meaning. Similarly, the skeptics' concern that reading literature does not necessarily entail the sought after edification is premised on a totalizing essentialism: Either the capacity for ethical betterment is an essential quality of the literary experience or it may be dismissed entirely. As if a practice could only be worthwhile if it succeeds 100% of the time. As if any human endeavor – law, science, or medicine – could meet that standard.[63]

We will need to start elsewhere if we are to understand the full value and potential of Law and Humanities scholarship. A better place might be Merleau-Ponty's 1951 declaration:

> Today a humanism does not oppose religion with an explanation of the world. It begins by becoming aware of contingency. It is the continued confirmation of an astonishing junction between fact and meaning, between my body and my self, my self and others, my thought and my speech, violence and truth. It is the methodical refusal of explanations, because they destroy the mixture we are made of and make us incomprehensible to ourselves.[64]

The form of scientific explanation that constitutes Enlightenment rationality is, on the view I have been elaborating in this chapter, antihumanist in that it radically separates the subject from the grounds of her own intelligibility.[65] It does so, as we have seen, through its reductionism, essentialism, abstraction from history and context, and pretension to an Olympian point of view. Actual human beings partake not of the absolute, but of the contingent. We are embodied creatures who exist in time, in culture, and in language. We are finite and fallible. We are socially situated and socially dependent. We are the products of particular forms of life and possessed of (and by) particular perspectives.

A humanist approach to inquiry, then, would be one that recognizes these as constitutive dimensions of the human condition. It would embrace at least the

---

[63] To be clear, there is little doubt that the study of literature has the *capacity* to edify. In literature (although not, certainly, in literature alone) we come into contact with the complexity of human understanding and can learn to appreciate the implications for our lives of the assumptions, postures, and institutional practices that characterize any particular society. A literary turn of mind, moreover, is vital to morality because it is through narrative enactment that we imagine how various situations might be carried forward and, thus, are able to assess their ethical implications. Mark Johnson, *Moral Imagination: Implications of Cognitive Science for Ethics* (Chicago: University of Chicago Press, 1994).

[64] Merleau-Ponty, *Signs* at 241.

[65] It was Nietzsche who pointed out that the traditional insistence on the absolute is nihilist and antihumanist because it devalues what we ourselves have wrought.

> Here precisely is what has become a fatality for Europe – together with the fear of man we have also lost our love of him, our reverence for him, our hopes for him, even the will to him. The sight of man now makes us weary – what is nihilism if it is not *that*? – We are weary of *man*.

Friedrich Nietzsche, *On the Genealogy of Morals and Ecce Homo*, Walter Kaufmann, trans. (New York: Vintage Books, 1969), Essay I, §12.

following five attitudes or positions: 1) hermeneutic suspicion and critical openness; 2) the affirmation of contingency; 3) reflexive subjectivity; 4) the indispensability of culture and community; and 5) humility.

First, to accept that what one understands as true may be a product of history and culture is to recognize that one's beliefs are corrigible not just to new information, but also to different perspectives, theories, values, assumptions, methods, and traditions of inquiry. This requires a hermeneutics of suspicion toward knowledge generally: one that probes beneath the surface, first, to disclose and, then, to question the underlying values and assumptions that enable it. It implies a critical attitude with respect to one's own beliefs and, at the same time, an openness toward those of others. The point of this critical posture is, simultaneously, to make the familiar strange and the strange accessible. In both cases, the goal is to unpack the conditions of intelligibility from which a perspective takes its shape to illuminate the ways in which it is distorting or revealing, attractive or problematic, challengeable or provocative.[66]

This attitude of critical suspicion stands in sharp contrast to the "hard" skepticism of the Enlightenment and modern science that submits truth claims to the insistent demands of reason and empirical proof. *That* approach introduces the epistemological problem of how as minds we can know the world: "For the enlightenment philosophers, thinking was only a reflection of the world in a consciousness, a consciousness that was alien to the world and hence could never understand the world 'in itself.'"[67] The Enlightenment schema that radically separates the subject from the objects of its inquiry enables science, but it simultaneously creates the philosophical problem of skepticism: It needs an absolute spectator – a God's-eye point of view – to assure the accuracy and reliability of its data. Merely human observation is always at risk of distortion by prejudice, particularism, and perspective.[68]

The hermeneutics of suspicion, in contrast, is a matter of deciphering.[69] In its paradigmatic form, the hermeneutics of suspicion unmasks surface meanings of a text – its false consciousness – as a concealment or mystification of the political, social, or psychological dynamics that it obscures. As Ricoeur explains, however,

---

[66] *Cf.* Stanley Fish, *Doing What Comes Naturally: Change, Rhetoric, and the Practice of Theory in Literary and Legal Studies* (Durham: Duke University Press, 1989), 297–305.

[67] Meyer, "Practical Reason" at 658.

[68] *Cf.* Taylor, *Hegel* at 564 ("[T]he scientific objectification of human nature presupposes a subject of science whose activities and judgments about truth and depth of explanation cannot be accounted for in the reductive theory. He remains the angelic observer outside the objectified stream of life").

[69] Ricoeur, *Freud and Philosophy* at 33. Writing of the "three masters of suspicion," Marx, Nietzsche, and Freud, Ricoeur says:

> Descartes triumphed over the doubt as to things by the evidence of consciousness; they triumph over the doubt as to consciousness by an exegesis of meaning. Beginning with them, understanding is hermeneutics: henceforward, to seek meaning is no longer to spell out the consciousness of meaning, but to decipher its expressions (*ibid*).

Law, Culture, and Humility

this is not a process of revealing a "true" meaning. Hermeneutics "consists not in the relation of meaning to thing but in an architecture of meaning."[70] The fundamental relation is not true-false, but hidden-shown. It is a question not about what the text says or the author intended, but rather about the meaning the text *simulates* and the hidden meaning it *manifests*. We have seen, for example, how a text ostensibly about democracy both defended and enacted hierarchy by insisting on the authority of an argument that was itself ungrounded in anything but an abstract definition. In sum, hermeneutic suspicion shares with Enlightenment skepticism a disposition to do away with idols but departs from it – both substantively and substantially – in its commitment to listen critically and attentively to symbols.

Second, a humanist approach recognizes that contingency and historicity are the prerequisites for knowledge of the only sort we as humans can have:

> Since we are all hemmed in by history, it is up to us to understand that whatever truth we may have is to be gotten not in spite of but through our historical inherence. Superficially considered, our inherence destroys all truth; considered radically, it founds a new idea of truth. As long as I cling to the ideal of an absolute spectator, of knowledge with no point of view, I can see my situation as nothing but a source of error. But if I have once recognized that . . . [history] contains everything which can *exist* for me, then my contact with the social in the finitude of my situation is revealed to me as the point of origin of all truth, including scientific truth.[71]

A humanist interested in the relationship between democracy and equality, for example, would begin with a critical examination of the social practices and historical struggles that ground our intuitions about those ideals. The resultant notions of democracy and egalitarianism are not, as the fundamentalist might have it, just some contingent historical facts that might have been otherwise. (Although they might have been.) They are, rather, precisely what constitute us as who we are. From our point of view, in other words, our historicity is not contingent at all; rather, it is necessary and *foundational*.[72] We may question, resent, challenge, resist, or modify our historical practices and beliefs. For us as situated humans, however, they are not optional. Our very ability to "have" a world is dependent on the preexisting social practices and conditions that form both the grounds of intelligibility for and the horizons of our world.

Third, it follows closely that subjectivity is a thoroughly social phenomenon: We are, as Merleau-Ponty says, "through and through compounded of relationships

---

[70] *Ibid.* at 18.
[71] Merleau-Ponty, *Signs* at 109.
[72] I elaborate this argument more fully in Steven L. Winter, "Human Values in a Postmodern World," *Yale Journal of Law & Humanities* 6:2 (Summer 1994), 233–48.

with the world."[73] For the fundamentalist, the claim that subjectivity is socially con-structed seems to entail a determinism in which the subject, deprived of its originary agency, could only statically reproduce that which constituted it.[74] This conclu-sion, however, is mistaken for it reflects both a reductivism and an essentialism: It simultaneously reduces the subject to its social determinants and essentializes the conditions of its formation. In contrast, to see subjectivity as constituted in *relation-ships* is rather to emphasize its dynamic qualities. Subjectivity, in a word, is *reflexive.* Although it necessarily reflects the social context and history through which it is constituted, subjectivity is simultaneously that which expresses, enacts, and thereby changes that context. To be a "human subject," is to be one "who, by means of a continual dialectic, thinks in terms of his situation, forms his categories in contact with his experience, and modifies this situation and this experience by the meaning he discovers in them."[75]

Indeed, we can unpack just this conclusion about reflexivity from a critical analysis of each of two opposing instantiations of the conventional view of subjectivity: White's expressivist claims for the value of rhetorical and literary studies, on one hand, and, on the other, the critique of narrative scholarship as unreliable and hopelessly subjective.

Consider White's claim that our communicative practices are constitutive. To say that how we communicate and interact with one another shapes who we are is to say that our values and identities are contingent on nothing more than our own practices. The danger of this rhetorical focus, however, is that it elides both our historicity and cultural contingency. To say with White (or Aristotle) that we define ourselves in our talk is to focus attention on activities and choices in the present. For example, White offers a subtle account of the "dialectic process" of reading in which

> we are constantly testing the person that the text is inviting us to become against the other things we are, or wish we were, and we must try to remain open simultaneously to the possibility that the shift is corrective of our own deficiencies and that it is not, that we are right to resist it.[76]

[73] Maurice Merleau-Ponty, *The Phenomenology of Perception*, Colin Smith, trans. (London: Routledge & Kegan Paul Press, 1962), xiii.

[74] Robert Post, "The Relatively Autonomous Discourse of Law," *Law and the Order of Culture*, Robert Post, ed. (Berkeley: University of California Press, 1991), xiv.

[75] Maurice Merleau-Ponty, *Sense and Non-Sense*, Hubert Dreyfus & Paula Dreyfus, trans. (Evanston: Northwestern University Press, 1964), 133–4. I elaborate this "double sense" of the situated subject as constituted and constituting, along with its relationship to law, in Steven L. Winter, "Indeterminacy and Incommensurability in Constitutional Law," *California Law Review* 78:6 (Dec. 1990), 1485–94. On the inevitably dynamic nature of social reproduction, see Steven L. Winter, "Contingency and Community in Normative Practice," 139:4 *University of Pennsylvania Law Review* (April 1991), 991–1001.

[76] White, "What Can a Lawyer Learn" at 2020.

Law, Culture, and Humility

This immediately raises the question of what motivates us either to assume or to resist the identity the text is inviting us to become. White offers only the platitude, "we are each responsible for what we make of these experiences."[77] At this point, however, the reading process is no longer dialectic but originary and subjectivist. It may be, as White says, "what is most ineradicably different about us [is] that we see and construct the world through different languages."[78] There can be, however, no such thing as a private language. Language "connects us to the past, not only our personal past but the past of our culture."[79] If our communicative practices are constitutive, then it must also be true that whenever we read or write a text we come to that task already constituted by the social and ethical relationships enacted by the communicative and other social practices that precede us. So, too, it must also be that the ways in which we constitute that text will influence (and be reflected in) the social and ethical interactions that we understand it to authorize or inspire.

Much the same can be said with respect to the critique of narrative scholarship as unreliably subjective. Anne Coughlin, for example, argues that autobiographical narrative is a realist discourse "devoted to the distinction between events that are 'in principle observable or perceivable' outside the narrative and those that reside solely inside the world constructed by a storyteller."[80] Yet, there is nothing that can be observed – "in principle" or otherwise – outside our frames of reference.[81] The converse, moreover, is also true: There can be no purely subjective perceptions free of the value-laden, culturally shared categories and understandings that constitute us and through which we experience our world. Indeed, anything that existed "solely" in the world constructed by a story would be incomprehensible to us.[82] True, the

---

[77] *Ibid.* In similar subjectivist terms, White notes that the process "will naturally be different for different readers (*ibid.*)" and that the value of a literary education for lawyers is "a question that can have no programmatic or automatic answer, but depends on the response of the individual mind." *Ibid.* at 2028.

[78] *Ibid.* at 2036. He concludes, "so that what seems wholly natural to me is unseen by you, what moves you leaves me cold, and vice versa."

[79] Meyer, "Practical Reason" at 661.

[80] Coughlin, "Regulating the Self" at 1271 (quoting Hayden White). Thus, she maintains that when the author of an outsider narrative "describes an event that she experienced, she is representing that the event in question had an existence independent of her textual reconstruction of the event." *Ibid.* at 1272.

[81] As Nelson Goodman famously observes,

> If I ask about the world, you can offer to tell me how it is under one or more frames of reference; but if I insist that you tell me how it is apart from all frames, what can you say? We are confined to ways of describing what is described. Our universe, so to speak, consists of these ways rather than of a world or worlds.

Nelson Goodman, *Ways of Worldmaking* (Indianapolis: Hackett Publishing, 1978), 2–3. *See also* Hilary Putnam, *Reason, Truth, and History* (Cambridge: Cambridge University Press, 1981), 54.

[82] *Cf.* Donald Davidson, "On the Very Idea of a Conceptual Scheme," in *Inquiries into Truth and Interpretation* (Oxford: Clarendon Press, 1984), 183.

narrator's account of her experience is an interpretation; but it cannot "in principle" be a purely subjective one. The narrator, no less than the reader, can only apprehend and communicate her experience in terms of the cultural understandings that give form to its events.[83] It is precisely because the subjectivities of both author and reader are constituted reflexively by shared perceptions and understandings that communication can take place at all.

Fourth, to affirm contingency and the reflexive nature of subjectivity is to resituate the human "in an order which is not that of knowledge but rather that of communication, exchange, and association."[84] Culture and community are indispensable aspects of being. This requires a different understanding of the relationship between the individual and the social, along with an entirely different conception of freedom.

The Enlightenment schema of subject and object not only isolates the subject from the objects of its inquiry, it also isolates the subject from other subjects. Its focus is on the individual consciousness and its relation to the world. (One can scarcely imagine Descartes proclaiming: "We think, therefore we are.") From the perspective of the Enlightenment schema, social context can only be understood as an external condition and, as such, it can only be seen as a source of constraint. Freedom, on this view, can only be conceptualized in terms of "a set of limits to be overcome, or a mere occasion to carry out some freely chosen project, which is all that a situation can be within the conception of freedom as self-dependence."[85]

On the humanist point of view I have here been elaborating, culture and community are indispensable and unavoidable aspects of being. They are not external constraints that the individual must overcome but the enabling conditions of possibility. "Society for man is not an accident he suffers but a dimension of his being. He is not in society as an object is in a box; rather, he assumes it by what is innermost in him."[86] It follows – paradoxical, though, it may seem – that freedom can only be a function of context, community, and constraint. Our freedom is constituted in the fact that we are situated beings who together both construct and transform the world in which we live. Which is not to say that culture and community are unalloyed goods. They can be restrictive or enabling, suffocating as well as liberating. The question with respect to any particular community or tradition is whether its social

---

[83] Thus, the value of such outsider narratives lies not in their facticity, but in their ability to convey in a powerful, affective way a social and psychological truth. Indeed, as I have argued elsewhere, the outsider narratives whose reliability the critics question would be no less true if they were unabashedly allegorical. Winter, *A Clearing in the Forest* at 134–5.

[84] Maurice Merleau-Ponty, *Adventures of the Dialectic*, Joseph J. Bien, trans. (Evanston: Northwestern University Press, 1973).

[85] Taylor, *Hegel* at 563. *See also ibid.* at 555 ("to make the transition comprehensible to mainstream science we have to think of it not as a step from blind law to meaningful situation, but as simple sloughing off of restraints. We leave the nature of the subject and his agency in the new social form as an unexplored point of complete spontaneity").

[86] Merleau-Ponty, *Sense and Non-Sense* at 128–9.

Law, Culture, and Humility

and cultural conditions stifle or promote human flourishing. That is a question not for categorical reason (e.g., which is better, communitarianism or individualism?), but for critical reflection.

Fifth, and finally, to reconceptualize freedom as an emergent condition of a cultural situation is profoundly to change our sense of self and place in the world. It is not just that our agency is dependent on the social practices and historical conditions through which we are constituted, but also that the hubris of the knowing subject who masters the world through reason cannot be sustained. Science and knowledge still have their value. But we need to approach those matters – as all else – with greater humility.

IDEAS OF JUSTICE

4

Biblical Justice
The Passion of the God of Justice

Chaya Halberstam

The diverse and multivocal books of the Hebrew Bible may share a preoccupation with one theme that incorporates notions of reward and punishment, blessing and curse, compassion and anger: justice. As James Crenshaw writes, "The qualit[y] of justice . . . runs through the Bible like a red thread. [It is] intricately woven into the various literary forms that enliven its pages from beginning to end."[1] As prominent as this theme is, however, the Hebrew Bible never offers us a definition, theory, or "idea" of justice. Nicholas Wolterstorff notes that the biblical authors

> speak a great deal about what is just and unjust; every now and then they step back a bit to speak about the role of justice in God's life and ours. What they do not do is step up to the meta-level and talk about how to think about justice. They do not articulate a conception of justice. We ourselves have to extract the underlying pattern of their thought from their testimony.[2]

One such underlying pattern may indeed be the demand for retribution. It is perhaps an old cliché that the Old Testament is consumed with judgment and retaliation whereas the New Testament transcends these baser concerns with a Christian emphasis on compassion and love.[3] Passages that align the Hebrew Bible with "primitive" notions of unthinking vengefulness include the famous "eye for an eye" law of *talion*, and the description of God (Yhwh) in Exodus as "a jealous God, punishing children for the iniquity of parents, to the third and the fourth generation" (Exod 34:6–7). Scholars and commentators have tried to nuance the retributive posture of the Hebrew Bible so that it need not bespeak a general vindictiveness in Israel's God.

---

[1] James Crenshaw, *Defending God: Biblical Responses to the Problem of Evil* (New York: Oxford University Press, 2005), 14.

[2] Nicholas Wolterstorff, *Justice: Rights and Wrongs* (Princeton: Princeton University Press, 2008), 67.

[3] This sentiment, perhaps shared by many, may be attributed to Schleiermacher. See John Gwyn Griffiths, *The Divine Verdict: A Study of Divine Judgment in the Ancient Religions* (Leiden: Brill, 1991), 14.

Elliot Dorff and Arthur Rosett posit that much like an abusive husband, the loving God of the New Testament can be glimpsed in the retribution of the Old: "the vision of the jealous God . . . suggests the underlying love that leads to the threats and promises."[4] Klaus Koch famously argued, alternatively, that even though sins are requited in the Hebrew Bible, it is not God who punishes; rather, sins automatically and reflexively bring about their own unwanted consequences.[5] God, therefore, is no lofty judge declaring retaliatory verdicts but a mere facilitator of the natural cosmic forces of reward and punishment.

I would like to suggest that as both interpretations attempt to distance the personality of God from the retributive and vengeful impulses evidenced in the Hebrew Bible's pages, they distance themselves from the essence of the Hebrew Bible's thinking about justice. When the Hebrew Bible depicts juridical situations, it never veers far from the emotions that drive the need to see justice done, emotions that include anger, jealousy, outrage, and even disgust. These strong feelings, portrayed most vividly in the realm of divine justice and imputed to God, are not considered distasteful or unholy but rather righteous, moral, and just. In this chapter, I will attempt to show that even as biblical prescriptions for human jurisprudence control and channel judges' and victims' emotions and relegate them to the background, the moral passions of anger and disgust are seen as integral to God's activity in the world and made primary in prophetic visions of divine justice.

Feelings for Recompense in Human Justice

The divine commandments regarding the fair practice of human justice requires some distance from the forces of private emotion. Leviticus 19 dictates, "you shall do no injustice in judgment; you shall not be partial to the poor or defer to the great, but in righteousness shall you judge your neighbor" (15). Thus compassion or pity for the poor, or fear of the powerful, should not influence a judge's decision, according to Leviticus. Deuteronomy explains this injunction further: "you shall not pervert justice; you shall not show partiality; and you shall not take a bribe, for a bribe blinds the eyes of the wise and subverts the cause of the righteous" (16:19). In this verse, Deuteronomy suggests that judges' emotions may be manipulated to subvert justice and warns the judge to remain impartial.

Nevertheless, a verse in Exodus similarly warns against perverting justice, but it also exhorts compassion: "And you shall take no bribe, for a bribe blinds the officials, and subverts the cause of those who are in the right. You shall not oppress a stranger;

---

[4] Elliot Dorff and Arthur Rosett, *A Living Tree: The Roots and Growth of Jewish Law* (Albany: SUNY Press, 1988), 96.

[5] Klaus Koch, "Is There a Doctrine of Retribution in the Old Testament?" in *Theodicy in the Old Testament*, James L. Crenshaw, ed. (Philadelphia: Fortress Press, 1983), 57–87.

Biblical Justice

you know the heart of a stranger, for you were strangers in the land of Egypt" (23:8–9). Rather than appealing to abstract concepts of impartial or dispassionate justice, Exodus insists that judges realize their capacity for empathy to refrain from treating the stranger unfairly – because you know *how it feels* to be a stranger, you should show him[6] no unkindness. Passages such as this one, which attempt to bridge Israel's first hand knowledge of slavery at the hands of the Egyptians with the ethical and legal standards Israel must live up to as rulers and judges, appear throughout the normative sections of the Pentateuch.[7]

It is, however, not only these benign emotions that biblical legal procedure fosters. The famous law of talion – expressed in the case of homicide as "a life for a life" – is not merely an indifferent procedural rule administered by the state. As Gerhard Von Rad has pointed out, "law in ancient Israel diverges from the Codex Hammurabi in giving a considerably greater place to private vengeance, especially to the blood-feud."[8] Indeed, although law codes throughout the ancient Near East reserved the right of punishment for the state, biblical law imbues the next of kin of the victim with the power of retaliatory punishment, as he becomes the *go'el ha-dam*, or "blood-avenger." Homicide is thus resolved through the institution of "blood feud," which, as Pamela Barmash reminds us, is "not a paroxysm of rage, careening out of control."

> This process [of] blood feud [is] avenging the killing of kin by the taking of the life of the slayer by the victim's kin. This label allows us to link this process to two essential characteristics of blood feud: it is local in nature, and it is rule-bound. These characteristics are interrelated because blood feud is a legal mechanism that both assures the redress of wrongs and controls the violence to a level tolerable in a community.[9]

Although ancient Israelite law sought to control the spilling of blood and the tit-for-tat murderous impulses of feuding families, it nonetheless gave vent to the vengeful outrage of the victim's family – it allowed the blood-avenger "the right to kill the slayer on sight with impunity."[10] Although the blood-avenger's emotional state is never discussed and the structure of blood feud may have been institutionally expedient or related to the structure of Israelite society,[11] there can be little doubt that such private vengeance carried with it deep emotional stakes. Robert Solomon

---

[6] Rather than obscure the patriarchal context of the biblical text, I use male-gendered pronouns when the Bible does rather than the gender-neutral "him or her."

[7] See Exod 22:21, Lev 19:34, Deut 10:19, 24:18.

[8] Gerhard Von Rad, *Old Testament Theology: The Theology of Israel's Traditions* (Louisville: Westminster John Knox Press, 2001), 31.

[9] Pamela Barmash, "Blood Feud and State Control: Differing Legal Institutions for the Remedy of Homicide During the Second and First Millennia B.C.E." *Journal of Near Eastern Studies* 63.3 (2004): 185.

[10] Barmash, 199.

[11] See Barmash's overall argument, 183–99.

contends that although vengeance certainly entails a "kernel of rationality" (the rule-bound nature of blood feud), it "does not mean that vengeance is dispassionate. Vengeance displays all of those traits of intensity, intractability, adamancy, and single-mindedness that are typical of powerful emotions. We might thus [identify] outrage as an underlying motivational structure."[12]

The institution of blood feud, then, begins to align justice not only with empathic and benevolent emotions but with hurt and murderous rage as well. At the same time, the law specifies that these emotions must be curtailed and constrained by socially acceptable limits on violence. As Solomon writes, "vengeance is a powerful and therefore dangerous passion, but it is also a socially constructed emotion that can be cultivated to contain . . . a full appreciation of the general good and the law."[13] Envisaged within a social setting, justice in the Hebrew Bible is driven by emotional torment but shaped by laws that aim to be fair and equitable – to protect those who did not cause harm intentionally and to prevent the "collateral damage" of unrestricted fury. It is only once we turn to the heavens that we can witness the unhampered exercise of divine justice free of human and social constraint.

Sinners in the Hands of an Angry God

Given the permissibility of vengeance within Israel's conception of justice, one might expect such talionic retribution to serve as the cornerstone of Israel's understanding of divine justice as well, and we can in fact see that biblical narratives endeavor to portray a sense of symmetrical divine justice, in which God rewards or punishes according to one's just deserts.[14] One need look no further than Genesis for numerous examples of this principle demonstrated in biblical narrative, from God's destruction of the whole earth with a flood after "all flesh had corrupted its ways upon the earth" (Gen 6:12) to his destruction of Sodom and Gomorrah after hearing "how great the outcry is against Sodom and Gomorrah and how very grave their sin!" (Gen 18:20).

Patrick Miller has shown that all of the prophets as well use rhetoric that attempts to forge a correspondence between the crimes of the people and the imminent divine punishment, which was to take the form of Israel's military defeat. According to Miller, the prophetic emphasis on this correlation between sin and punishment

---

[12] Robert P. Solomon, "Justice v. Vengeance: On Law and the Satisfaction of Emotion," in *The Passions of Law*, Susan A. Bandes, ed. (New York: New York University Press, 1999), 130.

[13] Solomon, 144.

[14] For a full discussion of this idea, see R. Adamiak, *Justice and History in the Old Testament: The Evolution of Divine Retribution in the Historiographies of the Wilderness Generation* (Cleveland: Zubal, 1982) and H. Boecker, *Law and the Administration of Justice in the Old Testament and Ancient Near East* (Minneapolis: Augsburg Publishing House, 1980).

Biblical Justice

"sets at the center of Yahweh's judgment the affirmation of *appropriate justice*. What Yahweh requires in all human beings – *mishpat*."[15] This justice, then, is inextricably linked not only to the notion of retribution but personal vengeance as well. An example of Miller's analysis of the prophets may be drawn from Hosea, an early prophet of divine judgment. Hosea pronounces:

> Ephraim has become like a dove, silly and without sense; they call upon Egypt, they go to Assyria. As they go, I will cast my net over them; I will bring them down like birds of the air; I will chastise them when I hear their bargaining. (Hos 7:11–12)

The correspondence between sin and punishment, as Miller points out – the sin of Israel (Ephraim) making treaties with other nations, instead of relying solely on God for its security, and the punishment of the imminent defeat of Israel by the Assyrian armies – here "depends entirely on figures of speech, metaphor, and simile. The key clause in this regard is the beginning of verse 12, [*ka'asher yeleku*], 'as they go' referring back to [*ashur halaku*] of verse 11, 'they go to Assyria.' So even as Israel plays the fowl, then Yahweh will play the fowler."[16] This wordplay underscores the idea that God's defeat of Israel (at the hands of Assyria) corresponds in kind to Israel's sin. An equivalence in degree may also be implied, as Israel's sin of abandoning God and placing its hope in foreign powers warrants God's abandonment of them to the hands of that same foreign power.

If this is justice, however, is it also unmistakably personal? That Israel has specifically sinned against God and did not just formally transgress the commandments or violate the covenant is demonstrated in the next verse: "Woe to them, for they have strayed from me! Destruction to them, for they have rebelled against me!" (Hosea 7:13). What lies behind divine retribution is revealed as a sense of betrayal rather than impartial judgment. Terrence Fretheim focuses on the rejected God's intense sadness, contending, "God . . . grieves because the people have rebelled."[17] Indeed, even in Genesis, right before God decides to destroy the world in a flood, as we saw previously, we are told, "Yhwh regretted that he had made humankind on the earth, and it grieved him to his heart" (Gen 6:6). The biblical authors thus connect God's retributive judgment with sadness, regret, and disappointment in the failings of his creatures.

A vast literature on the prophets focuses not on God's sadness but on his wrath, especially as it is expressed within the marriage metaphor between God/Yhwh (male) and Israel/Judah (female) in which God seeks to satisfy his anger by beating his

---

[15] Patrick D. Miller, *Sin and Judgment in the Prophets* (Chico, CA: Scholars Press, 1982), 111.

[16] Miller, 16–17.

[17] Terence E. Fretheim, *The Suffering of God: An Old Testament Perspective* (Philadelphia: Fortress Press, 1984), 111.

wayward lover. Gerlinde Baumann reviews the multifaceted images of God that emerge from the prophets' use of this metaphor, among which is a deity who "exercise[s] excessive forms of violence primarily against women."[18] The prophet Hosea makes use of this image as well to depict the punitive disasters God would wreak upon Israel:

> Plead with your mother, plead... that she put away her whoring from her face, and her adultery from between her breasts, or I will strip her naked and expose her as in the day she was born, and make her like a wilderness, and turn her into a parched land, and kill her with thirst. (Hos 2:2–3)

In this passage, Israel's worship of other gods is likened to an adulterous prostitute-wife's dalliances – for money – with men other than her husband. There can be no doubt that God, as described in this passage, is no impassive judge rendering a verdict upon an idolatrous nation. Instead, God is depicted as the betrayed husband who would shame, beat, and even kill his wife in retaliation for her infidelities. God's response to Israel's sin is "personal and... intensive,"[19] his red-hot anger barely concealed in Hosea's poetic language.

As God's punishments of Israel are thus clearly imagined as acts of personal vengeance and God is imbued with a potent emotional life, a parallel begins to emerge between human retributive justice, which allows for limited acts of vengeance, and divine justice, which is fashioned as a similar retaliation for the wounds of betrayal. Whereas some have argued that God's vengeance is as restrained as human legal vengeance,[20] Ellen van Wolde begs to differ. In a linguistic study of the terms for anger in the Hebrew Bible, she concludes:

> [o]ne may... challenge the view that YHWH (or Elohim) in the Hebrew Bible exemplifies control over his feelings, for more than 500 times he is represented as subjected to the explosive force of fury and aggression leading to violence. [I]n the Hebrew Bible, it appears that the sentiment of anger is seen as 'in charge': it exerts control over a person.[21]

Van Wolde's depiction of God's "explosive force of fury and aggression leading to violence" is displayed in the previous passage in Hosea and described in other passages such as this one in Nahum: "Yhwh is avenging and wrathful; Yhwh takes

---

[18] Gerlinde Baumann, *Love and Violence: Marriage as Metaphor for the Relationship between Yhwh and Israel in the Prophetic Books* (Collegeville, MN: Liturgical Press, 2003): 134.

[19] John Gammie, "The Theology of Retribution in the Book of Deuteronomy," *Catholic Biblical Quarterly* 32 (1970): 5.

[20] Fretheim, 111.

[21] Ellen J. van Wolde, "Sentiments as Culturally Constructed Emotions: Anger and Love in the Hebrew Bible," *Biblical Interpretation* 16.1 (2008): 14, 17.

Biblical Justice

vengeance on his adversaries and rages against his enemies" (Nah 1:2). Joel Kaminsky also observes that God's anger is largely unbounded:

> Divine wrath, within the Hebrew Bible in general, . . . is frequently portrayed as having the following qualities: (a) it can be set off accidentally or unintentionally; (b) it is sometimes stored up over a long period and then released in a disproportionate way upon the individual, or group, who happens to cause its release; (c) once it is set off either accidentally, or by the intentional error, it may spread indiscriminately to the larger surrounding population.

Seen in this light, the indiscriminate violence of God's anger seems hardly to align with justice, even in the Hebrew Bible's own terms. Yet the Hebrew Bible continues to offer mixed messages regarding God's stance toward humans, portraying him also as trustworthy judge, as in a typical verse from Psalms: "for you judge the people with equity and guide the nations upon earth" (Psa 67:4). Kaminsky contends that this tension between the divine unjust unleashing of anger and a more equitable, impartial justice may be explained historically; the uncontrolled nature of divine wrath represents "the more ancient ideas that are traditionally associated with this concept," whereas the "theological framework of Deuteronomy and the deuteronomistic historian has covenantalized the notion of divine wrath by linking it to both human sin and divine punishment."[22] In other words, early notions of an erratic and overwrought deity are contextualized by biblical authors within a juridical framework, allowing God's behavior to be viewed in light of a philosophy of retributive justice. Whether or not we accept this historical mapping and the relegation of divine emotional responses to a realm of "more ancient ideas," these authors or compilers who brought the concept of justice into dialogue with uninhibited, heartfelt emotion offer us an image of justice that is inextricable from the sadness, anger, betrayal, and outrage that accompany victimization and the normative response to it. As the Psalmist perceptively and unexpectedly puts it, "God is a just judge, who rebukes in anger every day" (Ps 7:12).

Reflexivity and Divine Emotion

Despite many apparent depictions of emotional, punitive retaliation against Israel on the part of God in the Hebrew Bible, the biblical scholar Klaus Koch disputed the entire notion of divine punishment in his famous monograph and essay titled, *Is There a Doctrine of Retribution in the Old Testament?* He posited that the divine violent, retributive acts witnessed throughout the Hebrew Bible are not at all akin to God's meting out punishment in the service of either justice or vengeance; instead,

---

[22] Kaminsky, Joel S., *Corporate Responsibility in the Hebrew Bible*, Journal for the Study of the Old Testament Supplement; 196. [S.l.] (Sheffield: Sheffield Academic Press, 1995): 56.

Koch argues that these violent, punishing acts are not authored by God at all. In the worldview manifest throughout the entirety of the Hebrew Bible, according to Koch, harm that comes upon the world or humanity is understood to be caused literally by sin itself. Koch reminds us that the ancient Israelites' understanding of the workings of the cosmos certainly differed from our own, and he claims that there is ample evidence in the Hebrew Bible to lead us to believe that they held a concept very similar to what we think of colloquially as "karma" – the belief that a sin mechanistically and automatically would return all of its evil back upon the sinner. Koch writes:

> The text presumes that an action and its consequences have to have an inherent relationship to one another, linked hand in hand as it were. An action which is performed in faithfulness to the community brings on blessed consequences. A wicked action brings with it disastrous consequences. The *action* could also be described as *having an immediate effect on the person's body and life*."[23] (60, 61)

The boldness of Koch's theory is striking: how can Koch argue that the Hebrew Bible "presumes" the idea of automatic retribution when the texts never fail to attribute either reward or punishment to the God of Israel? How is God's role as the judge of human affairs imagined if these effects are said to take place automatically? Koch responds to these crucial questions by envisioning a slightly different role for God than what is normally imagined:

> Yhwh is obviously described as a *higher authority* in relationship to humans, but this is not meant in the juridical sense of a higher authority who deals out reward and punishment on the basis of an established norm, but rather somewhat like a 'midwife who assists at a birth' by *facilitating the completion of something which previous human action has already set in motion.* One can understand [God's] activity . . . as *setting in motion and bringing to completion the [previously established] Sin-Disaster Connection on the one hand and the Good Action-Blessings Connection on the other.*[24]

Koch here explicitly opposes his idea of a mechanistic universe with a more juridical idea of God's role in the life of the Israelite community. He actually compares Yhwh to a "midwife," helping to make sure that the mechanism of automatic retribution is working correctly, much as we can imagine God ensuring that the laws of nature, such as the cycle of seasons, continues to progress on its own course. He points out that there is actually no word for "punish" in biblical Hebrew (an assertion that is arguable) and that the Bible instead opts for Hebrew words such as *heshib* or *shillem*, which mean to "return" or "repay"; he writes that these terms denote "turn[ing] (the

---

[23] Koch, 60–1.
[24] Koch, 60, 62.

Biblical Justice

effects of) an action back towards the person who did something"[25] rather than the idea of "punishing."

Koch bases his conclusions, for the most part, on texts in Proverbs and Psalms that are part of Israel's wisdom tradition, known to be more universalizing and overtly didactic than much of the Bible's other literature. In these wisdom texts, sin and punishment are likened primarily to natural laws such as gravity, for example, Proverbs 26:27 reads: "He who digs a pit falls into it; and a stone comes back upon him who rolls it." Koch also marshals passages in other, more "divinely retributive" books such as the prophets, to support his claim. For example, he notes this passage once again in Hosea, in which God declares:

> When I would heal Israel, the corruption of Ephraim is revealed, and the wicked deeds of Samaria; for they deal falsely, the thief breaks in, and the bandits raid outside. But they do not consider that I remember all their wickedness. Now their deeds surround them, they are before my face. (Hos 7:1–2)

In this passage, according to Koch, it appears that God would like to heal Israel, to help, to be merciful, but even God is prevented from doing these things because of the automatic, almost material quality of sins and their effects. It is almost as though in a physical, spatial sense, Israel's "deeds surround them," blocking all outside intervention, and insisting that their own automatic consequences be brought to completion.

Koch's idiosyncratic theory has not gone without criticism, especially when he has applied it to the entirety of the Hebrew Bible. For instance, John Gammie criticizes Koch's idea primarily from the standpoint of the book of Deuteronomy; he writes, "Koch's thesis that an evil deed creates of itself a sphere of misfortune is in the final analysis incorrect because it ignores how pervaded [biblical texts] are with the notion of the *intensity of God.*"[26] He asks, as we might, how God can be relegated to the role of midwife, or facilitator, when he seems so personally betrayed, saddened, and invested in seeing Israel suffer in kind. Just a few verses before the previous quotation from Hosea, we hear God uttering the following:

> What shall I do with you, O Ephraim? What shall I do with you, O Judah? Your love is like a morning cloud, like the dew that goes away early. Therefore I have hewn them by the prophets, I have killed them by the words of my mouth. [Israel] transgressed the covenant; there they dealt faithlessly with me. In the house of Israel I have seen a horrible thing; Ephraim's whoredom is there, Israel is defiled. (Hosea 6:4–5)

God's personal involvement in the fate of Israel seems undeniable in this passage, as through much of the rest of the Hebrew Bible: God expects "love," but instead

---

[25] Koch, 63.
[26] Gammie, 4.

he has been dealt with "faithlessly"; God sends divine rebuke to "kill" Israel; Israel's transgression is perceived by God as betrayal or "whoredom." Is it this level of intensity that for Gammie provides a counterargument to Koch's sidelining of God as no more invested than a midwife at another woman's childbirth? God is neither impartial nor indifferent: His words betray a fury and a woundedness that implicate him as an active participant in Israel's historical drama.

Why, then, is there still something compelling about Koch's thesis? Why does it remain an important counterpoint to all of the scholarly studies of God's wrath, his domestic battery, his retributive judgment? I would like to suggest that in the notion of punishment's automatic reflexivity, Koch has captured a crux of biblical retribution that is tied to emotion – a kind of *emotional* reflexivity that God, at times, seems hardly to be able to direct. Although sadness, indignation, and even rage seem to be less the result of the sin itself and more a product of the person who embodies these emotions, there is perhaps a more visceral emotion that appears as reflexive as Koch's notion of biblical retribution, and it is encapsulated by the final phrase in the previous passage. When the prophet declares, "Israel is defiled," we are immediately in the biblical sphere of disgust. Perhaps Koch's observation that transgressions appear to bring about their own punishment results from a primal divine disgust that is so automatic that we hardly notice it functioning. To unearth the effect of disgust on divine retribution, we must look more closely at its contours within biblical literature.

The previous passage demonstrates God's intensity toward Israel by invoking the highly charged and potent language of defilement. According to most scholars and commentators, this language of acts that "defile," "render impure," or "infect" is borrowed from the biblical corpus on ritual impurity, specifically as laid out in Leviticus. In this priestly system, much of the stuff of bodily life – dead and decaying flesh, skin diseases, genital discharges – is considered contagious, conveying a status of ritual impurity to those in its proximity. Similar to the procedures we have today for people stricken by infectious disease, the person or persons affected in ancient Israel would have to wash themselves and their clothes and be quarantined for a specified period of time before they would be allowed to rejoin fully the community.[27] Contagion and defilement thus become a particularly apt metaphor for the silent and invisible power of sin and corruption: Just as those who are close to a "diseased" person may be infected, sick, perhaps even doomed and all the while not even know it, so also are those who collaborate and consort with criminals. One can wallow in filth, but there will be palpable repercussions.

Recently, biblical scholar Jonathan Klawans has disrupted this simple idea of the metaphorical use of impurity language in priestly and prophetic biblical texts.[28]

---

[27] See Leviticus 11–15.

[28] Jonathan Klawans, *Impurity and Sin in Ancient Judaism* (New York: Oxford University Press, 2000).

Biblical Justice

He brings to light an underlying presumption that ought not be taken for granted, that ritual impurity is "real" whereas sin is only metaphorically or symbolically impure. He first probes our assumptions about the supposed "reality" of priestly ritual impurity. The sources of ritual impurity are real in a material sense: dead bodies, blood, scaly skin, and so forth. But in what way is the "impurity" they convey real? Even though these substances may make us revile, in most cases there is no actual contagion, like the kind one would experience with infectious disease; in other words, the sources of impurity are material, but the lasting effect of contact with them, even after the removal of the offensive object, is undoubtedly conceptual.

Next, Klawans examines the symbolic use of impurity language as a rhetorical device for emphasizing the real danger of sin. When one actually looks at the texts in which ritual impurity for material substances is delineated as opposed to those in which metaphorical impurity for moral depravity is invoked, the symbolic, moral impurity consistently appears in *earlier* texts than the literal, ritual impurity. From a strictly historical and chronological point of view, it is difficult to argue that the discourse of moral impurity is a metaphorical extension of literal impurity when all written record of literal impurity postdates its metaphorical use.

Klawans asks why we cannot simply take both discourses of impurity at face value: Perhaps ancient Israel believed that a status of defilement or impurity could result from either a material *or moral* lapse. In each case, an invisible, conceptual, yet nevertheless real stain attaches to the individual until some sort of ritual cleansing is performed. The kinds of cleansings that are required for each type of impurity are different but still analogous. Klawans thus develops a schema for the totality of ancient Israelite conceptions of impurity.[29]

Impurity Type	Source	Effect	Resolution
Ritual	Bodily flows, corpses, etc.	Temporary contagious impurity	Bathing, waiting
Moral	Sins: idolatry, incest, murder	Desecration of sinners, land, and sanctuary	Atonement or punishment, and ultimately, exile

The second system of moral impurity here is clearly a description of our issue of sin and retribution. Klawans thus implies, like Koch, that God's retributive, destructive acts, such as punishment and exile, are not a kind of juridical punishment. For Klawans, however, these acts are not reflexive, but cleansing – acts that are analogous to bathing and washing. Divine violence is necessary because of the defilement of Israel's transgression.

---

[29] Klawans, 27.

Thus, Klawans concludes that each type of impurity – ritual and moral – ought to be understood as a system of defilement and purging. He also suggests that the differences between them are considerable, and so they ought simply to be studied and analyzed as separate phenomena. Although the rituals entailed to redress each type of transgression substantially differ, the language of defilement used in the biblical texts to describe both kinds of impurity insists upon a relationship of some kind, even if not a simple or thoroughgoing one. Klawans himself remarks, "in the end, one cannot eliminate the possibility that the two impurity systems are connected on some deeper level."[30]

This deeper connection, I suggest, is the potent emotion of disgust. Julia Kristeva, in developing her theory of the abject in *Powers of Horror*, writes extensively about biblical ritual purity laws. She describes how in order for an individual to first separate and keep a distinct sense of self-identity, he or she must clearly define and delineate that which is not-self; those elements that come closest to blurring these boundaries – such as bodily fluids, skin diseases, decay – are those that are the object of the most vehement rejection, producing a feeling of horror, nausea, or disgust. The rejection of these elements Kristeva terms "abjection." She speaks of abjection as

> an extremely strong feeling which is at once somatic and symbolic, and which is above all a revolt of the person against an external menace from which one wants to keep oneself at a distance, but of which one has the impression that it is not only an external menace but that it may menace us from the inside.[31]

This "extremely strong feeling which is at once somatic and symbolic" most accurately describes the feeling of nausea or disgust – the need to expel, to vomit, to jettison one's insides out. Thus, elements eschewed by the levitical ritual purity laws are seen as *abject* and are thoroughly distanced from any association with the self. They comprise those elements that threaten to confuse self-identity and blend the self with that which surrounds it. Oozing bodily fluids, for example, are at once part of the body and yet flow away from it, threatening to extend or confound the well-defined contours of one's individuated body. By immediately rejecting these ambiguous parts of bodily and fleshy life, calling them impure and hence utterly "not me," the individual can become part of the symbolic, the realm of the father (psychoanalytically speaking) and of law. In biblical ritual impurity, one can be inscribed in the divine symbolic system only when the abject is kept at bay.

---

[30] Klawans, 38.
[31] Julia Kristeva, *Powers of Horror: An Essay on Abjection*, Leon S. Roudiez, trans. (New York: Columbia University Press, 1982), 135–6.

Biblical Justice

Even though Kristeva is loath to apply notions of the abject to the divine, symbolic system,[32] disgust undoubtedly plays a major role in moral, ethical, and legal – especially criminal – systems,[33] and in the Hebrew Bible, God is completely enmeshed in the murky moral world of criminal, transgressive behavior. Timothy Beal has shown that "Yhwh internalizes abjection"[34] in the realm of the nonjuridical by referring to passages in which God reappropriates the "mother" and the feminine by making such declarations as "I will cry out like a woman in labor, I will gasp and pant" (Isa 42:14). I would like to argue that God *consistently* internalizes abjection in the realm of the moral and juridical, and his reflexive, cleansing expulsion of the abject – the distancing from impurity necessary to remain part of the symbolic – aligns with moral, punitive retribution. Let us return once again to the book of Hosea to examine the full passage referenced previously, which testifies not only to God's juridical anger and retaliation, but also to his primal disgust:

3 I know Ephraim, and Israel is not hidden from me
For now, O Ephraim, you have played the whore
Israel is defiled.

4 Their deeds do not permit them to return to their God.
For the spirit of whoredom is within them, and they do not know Yhwh.

5 Israel's pride testifies against him
Ephraim stumbles in his guilt
Judah also stumbles with them.

6 With their flocks and herds they shall go to seek Yhwh, but they will not
find him;
He has withdrawn from them.

7 They have dealt faithlessly with Yhwh
For they have borne illegitimate children.
Now the new moon shall devour them along with their fields.

8 Blow the horn in Gibeah, the trumpet in Ramah.
Sound the alarm at Beth-aven, look behind you, Benjamin!

9 Ephraim shall become a desolation in the day of punishment
Among the tribes of Israel I declare what is sure.

---

[32] See Timothy K. Beal, "The System and the Speaking Subject in the Hebrew Bible," *Biblical Interpretation* 2.2 (1994): 174.

[33] Dan Kahan argues that "no other moral sentiment" – other than disgust – "is up to the task of condemning such singular abominations as 'rape, child abuse, torture, genocide, predatory murder, and maiming.'" Dan Kahan, "The Anatomy of Disgust in Criminal Law," *Michigan Law Review* 96, (1998): 1628.

[34] Beal, 184.

10 The princes of Judah have become like those who remove the landmark
On them I will pour out my wrath like water.

11 Ephraim is oppressed, crushed in judgment, because he was determined
to go after vanity.

12 Therefore I am like maggots to Ephraim,
And like rottenness to the house of Judah.

13 When Ephraim saw his sickness, and Judah his wound,
Then Ephraim went to Assyria, and sent to the great king.
But he is not able to cure you or heal your wound.

14 For I will be like a lion to Ephraim, and like a young lion to the house
of Judah.
I myself will tear and go away; I will carry off, and no one shall rescue.

15 I will return again to my place
Until they acknowledge their guilt and seek my face. (Hos 5:3–15)

This passage can almost be seen as the Rorschach test for notions of retribution, for each scholar can find in it his or her favored theory. For Klaus Koch, this passage demonstrates automatic, mechanistic retribution par excellence: "their deeds do not permit them..." (4) implies the spatial and material quality of sin in the world; in verse 5, Israel stumbles *in its own* guilt. Punishment is like the cycles of nature – as exemplified in the evocation of "the new moon" in verse 7; and in verse 11 such natural cycles of punishment are illustrated in the passive construction of the retribution that comes about because of Israel's sin: "Ephraim is oppressed, crushed in judgment." God is hardly mentioned as a contributing factor to Israel's suffering.

For Klawans, this passage spells out the source, symptoms, and cleansing of moral impurity. In verses 3 and 4, the prophet explicitly uses the terminology of "defilement" to refer to metaphorical "whoredom" and literal idolatry, transgressions that are both morally defiling in Klawans, understanding of the system. In verse 9, we are told that the punishment of Israel will result in "desolation" – the kind of purging of sin from the land that Klawans identifies with a method of cleansing moral impurity. This sentiment is furthered in verse 13, which refers to Israel's "sickness" and its desire for healing, only to find out the moral impurity they have contracted cannot be cured by conventional means.

Each of these authors picks up on different – and authentic – elements of this text. Indeed, Gammie's emphasis on the "intensity of God" is present as well: in verse 10 God "pours out [his] wrath;" and in verse 14 he "tears" at Israel like a lion. What picture of God and divine justice do we have in this passage? A thoroughly inconsistent one? A passive deity, relying upon the just processes of nature? An almost ajuridical notion of the washing away of sin through military defeat and exile? Or a jealous God, wreaking vengeance?

Biblical Justice   139

I would like to suggest that if we begin with God's intensity in this passage and look at it not as authoritarian and territorial but rather as an urgently self-defensive reaction grounded in disgust, all of Hosea's language becomes intelligible. God is not feeling jealous here, but rather threatened and betrayed. In verse 6, the prophet explains why Israel cannot find their God: because "he has withdrawn from them." Just as Kristeva explains regarding the abject, the element of separation from the threatening object is of paramount importance. Just as occurs with physical vomiting, so with the morally abject, the separation must be violent and thoroughgoing rather than quiet and passive. Thus in verses 14 and 15 we have the aggressive "tearing at Judah" followed by the withdrawal to "my place," the space where the (God)self can remain bounded and unthreatened. Further, in verses 7–13, we are presented with countless metaphors and similes that recall both sources of disgust and disgust reactions: "bearing illegitimate children" (7) recalls the intrusion upon the social self, the breaking of the boundary between a legitimate couple and illicit sex, and referring back to the "whoredom" of verse 4. Moreover, childbirth itself is prototypically part of the abject: a revolting image of that which has invaded the body only to later burst forth amid all sorts of oozing bodily fluids. The image of God's "pour[ing] out [his] wrath like water" in verse 10 invokes not only violent anger but the disgust reaction of vomiting, as the "wrath" is transformed into a material object, or *abject*, which is thoroughly expelled. Verse 12 contains perhaps the most obvious images of the *abject*: maggots, rottenness. There is also an inversion here, in which God declares himself to be the object of disgust instead of the sinning Israel. It is the precise threat of the abject, if not immediately expelled, to infect the subject, to decay not just that which is external to the self, but the self as well. Verse 13 continues the image of abjection in Israel's sickness, its wounds.

If we understand this system according to the contours of the emotion of disgust, Koch's theory is correct in the sense that the disgust response to violent expel *is* automatic: the idea of "reflexive retribution" is witnessed in the visceral and immediate, rather than controlled and reasoned, disgust reaction. Klawans is correct too, because there is a real, and not just symbolic impurity here. According to Paul Rozin, there is something universally human about this visceral feeling of disgust, which extends not just to our bodily selves but our social and moral selves as well.[35] We react identically – with disgust, horror, and separation – to that which repulses us, and that which repulses us covers the range from bodily fluids to personal betrayal. This reaction is intense, violent, and deeply felt, while at the same time we are little more than passive bystanders to ourselves when these feelings rise up, momentarily unable to control or suppress them.

I do not intend to justify the violence attributed to the God of Israel by locating it in the "reflexivity" of disgust, and I do not wish to imply that the motivation of self-protection, which disgust reactions serve, absolve a batterer, injurer, or murderer

---

[35] Paul Rozin, "A Perspective on Disgust," *Psychological Review* 94.1 (January 1987): 23–41.

from responsibility for his or her actions. What, then, do we do with a sacred text that imagines its god, its highest moral authority, as embodying what we may see as both weak and abusive traits? We have already seen that Israelite jurisprudence does not allow for uncontrolled violence or the unlimited satisfaction of emotion. Yet I would like to suggest that instead of lofty and high-minded rhetoric about the nobility or social value of punishment, Israel's depiction of its God provides a mirror of the most profound realms of human emotion, particularly the dark and dangerous emotions that provide the deep structure for retributive justice.

5

Ideas of Justice
Natural and Human

Catherine Kellogg

Although the distinction between natural and human justice – *phusis* and *nomos* – structures the foundations of Western political thought, the language and discourse of natural justice, law, right, and so forth have fallen into fairly profound disrepute. Indeed, that disrepute can be extended to the last two or three centuries if we can agree that the Western "discovery" of variation in religious and moral notions across time and place gave rise to a certain skepticism concerning the idea of "natural" or divine justice.[1] Nonetheless, over the last fifty years moral realism and natural law theory have made a comeback in the legal academy.[2] For instance, in the late 1950s,

---

[1] See Knud *Haakonessen's Natural Law and Moral Philosophy: From Grotius to the Scottish Enlightenment.* (Cambridge: Cambridge University Press, 1996).

[2] See, for example, John Finnis, *Natural Law and Natural Rights* (Oxford: Clarendon Press, 1980); "Moral Reality Revisited" *Michigan Law Review* 90 (1992): 242–533; Anthony J. Lisska, *Aquinas's Theory of Natural Law: An Analytic Reconstruction* (Oxford: Clarendon Press, 1996); Robert C. George, *In Defense of Natural Law* (Oxford: Oxford University Press, 1999); Robert C. Koons, *Realism Regained: An Exact Theory of Causation, Teleology, and the Mind* (Oxford: Oxford University Press, 2000); Sydney Hook, ed. *Law and Philosophy* (New York: New York University Press, 1964); Robert P. George, ed. *Natural Law Theory: Contemporary Essays* (Oxford: Clarendon Press, 1996) and Robert P. George, *Natural Law, Liberalism and Morality* (Oxford: Clarendon Press, 1996). According to the World Catalogue, 282 books on natural law were published during the 1950s, 486 during the 1960s, 493 during the 1970s, 557 during the 1980s, and 694 during the 1990s. The journal put out by the School of Law at Notre Dame, *Natural Law Forum,* was established in the 1950s, and it continued to publish under the title *American Journal of Jurisprudence* after 1968. The International Law Society, since 1980, has published wide-ranging articles from public and private, religious and secular, colleges, and from professionals outside of academic life. During the 1960s, an additional impetus in natural law arose from Pope Paul VI's encyclical letter *Humanae vitae*, in which the Pope supported his opposition to artificial contraception by appealing to Thomistic natural law theory as well as to religious considerations. There was a predictable reaction by proponents of birth control, but Catholic moralists such as Germain Grisez and John Finnis came to the Pope's defense, developing 'natural law' arguments against contraception, as well as against homosexuality, abortion, and other books on which the Church had taken a stand. Finnis' book *Natural Law and Natural Rights* offered a systematic and sympathetic defense of a theory that has become known as the "new natural law theory." It has been subsequently shored up by Robert George, Joseph Boyle, and others, but has

legal positivist H. L. A. Hart entered into a debate with Lon Fuller in the *Harvard Law Review*, a debate that was eventually joined by Ronald Dworkin concerning the extent to which there is necessarily some kind of "natural" moral content in law.[3] This debate in turn gave rise to an important Thomistic rejoinder – from the likes of Jacques Maritain, Yves Simon, Henry Veatch *inter alia* – concerning the nature of the relationship between so-called natural law and a lawgiver. Notably, debates about natural law have not been limited to academia. The Natural Law Party has branches in the United States, Canada, Great Britain, Israel, New Zealand, and Pakistan. Thus, although *nomos* seemed to have won out in a historical contest over *phusis*, the ideas of natural justice and natural law are far from finished. For this reason, a volume such as this one seems an auspicious occasion to both revisit this foundational idea as it has played itself out in political and legal theory and to look at how the ideas of natural justice and natural law make themselves felt in contemporary political discourse.

The question that is most clearly at stake in all discussions of "natural justice" is whether or not law always or by definition overlaps with morality; in other words, whether an ultimate separability of morality (or the "good") and law is possible. Although this question is as old as law itself, as Howard Kainz recently pointed out, the Nuremberg Trials after the Second World War provided a major impetus for the contemporary interest in natural justice and natural law.[4] The possibility of "crimes against humanity," which were nonetheless legally valid according to the positive law of the German state, raised the problem of the source of authority for judgment in these trials. By what standard was it possible to make a judgment that activities clearly sanctioned by sovereign authorities were nonetheless punishable? If Nazi crimes were not crimes in the conventional sense of being in violation of state law, what was the higher law against which they could be judged? Who was the "humanity" in whose name the judgments of crimes could be made? It is in answer to questions like these that natural law theory appeared as a response. The question, however, of what is meant by natural law in the modern context is unclear. Developments in biological sciences have transformed the meaning of the term "nature" itself and thus muddied the question further. If nature was once understood to *link* the human and the divine (as in the early modern notion that human nature *includes* the rational capacity to discover the eternal law), in contemporary scientific discourse, nature is no longer the subject of knowledge but rather entirely its *object*. In this sense, the meaning of "the natural" in contemporary natural law theory is quite laden. Does it stand for an innate rational capacity of humans, or does it

---

also been subjected to considerable criticism by natural law ethicists from the Thomistic tradition, including Ralph McInerny, Henry Veatch, and Russell Hittinger.

[3] See H. L. A. Hart, *The Concept of Law* (Oxford: Clarendon Press, 1961); Lon Fuller, *The Morality of Law* (New Haven: Yale University Press, 1969), and Ronald Dworkin "Morality and Law: Observations Prompted by Professor Fuller's 'Novel' Claim," *University of Pennsylvania Law Review*, 1965.

[4] Howard Kainz, *Natural Law: An Introduction and Reexamination* (Chicago: Open Court, 2004) xiii.

Ideas of Justice

designate something else, something divine? Finally, in the absence of a divine lawgiver can natural law be considered law in any meaningful way?

I frame my investigation into the controversies that animate the natural justice and natural law traditions through readings of Sophocles' famed rendition of the Greek myth of *Antigone*. The most consistent reading of Sophocles' play is that it presents a conflict between the claims of the law of the state to our obedience and the claims of individual conscience in the name of natural justice, especially as it relates to following the demands of heaven. Thus, like the central set of questions in Plato's *Crito*, or Thrasymachus' response to Socrates in Plato's *Republic*, *Antigone* presents us with the question of whether it is possible to argue that justice (or goodness or right) is naturally coexistent with law. In other words, *Antigone* presents us with the question of whether it is plausible to make the case that good and evil and right and wrong are real features of the so-called natural world and thus whether justice (or the good) and law are separable.[5]

To begin situating my comments, it is instructive to note that, as Judith Butler recently pointed out, *Antigone's* function as representative of natural justice has itself recently come into crisis.[6] My point of departure is that this crisis may turn out to be constitutive of any representation of natural justice insofar as the idea of the natural in natural law signals a limit for the work that *any* law can do, the degree, that is, to which it can be truly *sovereign*. It is in this regard that in a wide variety of political and legal readings Antigone has functioned as the marker of the limit between the divine/natural and the human/political, between the imaginary and the symbolic, between the laws of kinship and those of the state, between life and death, and so forth.

In this chapter, I first review the Greek myths of Oedipus – Antigone's father – and of Antigone herself, and then rehearse Hegel's nineteenth-century reading of Sophocles' play on the one hand and Lacan's twentieth-century reading of it on the other. The distinctive difference between the nineteenth- and twentieth-century readings is the discovery of the unconscious, and I make use of this difference to point to the ways that this discovery does not limit itself to how we read the *Antigone*, but also bears directly on the tradition of debate about natural justice. To begin to sketch out the peculiarities of the twentieth-century reading of *Antigone* – a play marked as it is by the so-called contest between conventional or human law versus divine or natural law – it bears noting that on the psychoanalytic account, the emergence of law is necessarily linked to the murder of the Father, which is why I will also discuss the myth of Oedipus.[7] Importantly for our more immediate purposes, which is assessing the question of the meaning of the natural in conceptions of natural justice and law,

---

[5] There is a vast literature on Sophocles' *Antigone*. The most authoritative literary/philosophical compendium of that literature is George Steiner's *Antigone* (Oxford: Clarendon Press, 1984).

[6] Judith Butler, *Antigone's Claim: Kinship Between Life and Death* (New York: Columbia University Press, 1998) 2.

[7] Sigmund Freud, *Civilization and its Discontents* (London: Penguin, 2002).

Lacan says, "The myth of the murder of the father is the myth of *a time for which God is dead.*"[8] I will elaborate the ways that the discovery of the unconscious and the "time for which God is dead" are related (and in fact, synonyms for each other) in my discussion of Lacan's reading of *Antigone*, but for now it is important to emphasize that the time for which God is dead does not exactly refer to the effective separation of church and state or to increasing atheism in an age of science (although these things are obviously related). Rather, as Lacan says, "the true formula of atheism is not *God is dead*... the true formula of atheism is *God is unconscious.*"[9] For Freud and Lacan alike, God does not simply function as a guarantor for the possibility of justice and law (as in, "if God does not exist, then anything is permitted"). More importantly, God is the figure for an idea of wholeness, totality, or oneness (ontotheology) that has been at the foundation of the Western tradition of law and its relation to justice since its Greek inception. If God is *unconscious*, then at first blush, perhaps the possibilities of wholeness, oneness, indivisibility, nature, or totality have immediately been foiled. Said differently, psychoanalysis is the science of subjectivity that has at its core a form of knowledge (the unconscious) that is and must remain unknown. Thus, insofar as the subject is necessarily divided, he is neither "one" nor is he master of himself.

Psychoanalysis, then, emerges as a symptom of what Eric Santner has recently described as "signifying stress" or the decreasing efficiency of the idea of wholeness.[10] It is a science that emerges in the same moment that the discourse of justice, law, and right that refer to a natural or a divine lawgiver is losing its efficacy. It is no accident that Nietzsche announced the death of God at the same moment that psychoanalysis emerged as the new science of subjectivity: for both Nietzsche and Freud, whereas premodern subjectivity was characterized by the *subject supposed to believe* (for instance, that God is in His heaven), modern subjectivity is a form of subjectivity that *knows too much* (for instance, that God is dead). For Lacan, the question of the death of God is to ask what a law not premised on an indivisible master or sovereign would look like. On the psychoanalytic account, the terms law and the natural (or the divine) are radically reformulated.

This perspective stands in sharp contrast to that of contemporary natural law theorists who attempt to argue that, for instance, natural law theory and secularism can be considered continuous with Thomism, insofar as Aquinas was himself the first strictly secular natural law theorist.[11] Notwithstanding whether Aquinas can be argued to have been a secular thinker – in terms of the Thomistic so-called

---

[8] Jacques Lacan, *The Ethics of Psychoanalysis*, Jacques Alain Miller, ed., Dennis Porter, trans. (New York: Norton, 1992) 177.

[9] Jacques Lacan, *The Four Fundamental Concepts of Psychoanalysis* (Harmondsworth: Penguin Books, 1979) 59, cited in Slavoj Zizek, *How to Read Lacan* (New York: Norton, 2006) 91.

[10] Eric Santer, "Miracles Happen: Benjamin, Rosenzweig, Freud, and the Matter of the Neighbour,' in *The Neighbour: Three Inquiries in Political Theology* (Chicago: University of Chicago Press, 2006).

[11] See Charles Covell, *The Defense of Natural Law* (New York: St. Martin's Press, 1992) 222–3.

Ideas of Justice

hierarchy of natural inclinations – suicide, homosexuality, and stem cell research all still turn out to be unnatural and thus in contravention of natural law. The Lacanian perspective also stands in contrast to the ways in which contemporary natural law theorists are working (necessarily) with a thesis about nature that links an unproblematic "unnatural" to a clear "immorality" (which would include such arguments as the Pope's against artificial contraception). Going beyond the question of natural inclinations, and toward the even more loaded moral language of perversion, John Finnis, also drawing on a Thomistic set of natural law arguments, argues that masturbation, homosexuality, and bestiality are serious sexual sins.[12]

To sort out these diverging perspectives on natural justice, this chapter surveys the Greek origins of the idea of so-called natural justice (and the three Theban plays that are often referenced to form this origin), and some of the history of natural law theory – from the scholastic renaissance in the seventeenth century to social contract theory, and into the developments in moral and political theories of the eighteenth century – showing the ways that this intellectual history is marked by the question of how European states struggled to ground an emerging practice of popular sovereignty by way of theological resources. I then review some of the ways that natural justice and natural law have been recently deployed in American jurisprudence. For the most part – although not exclusively – this has been the work of the American Christian right. Finally, the chapter turns its attention back to Oedipus and *Antigone* and specifically toward Lacan's reading of them to show the ways, that for Lacan, nature is no longer understood to be what is continuous *between* the divine and creation but rather the *limit* of the human and the conventional itself.

Antigone and Natural Justice

To really appreciate the significance of *Antigone*, it is useful to place it in the context of the three linked plays by Sophocles: *Oedipus at Colonus*, *Oedipus the King*, and *Antigone*.[13] In these plays, Sophocles made use of a set of myths that were important to Dionysian cults in the fifth century BCE. The myth of Oedipus is the story of the "swollen-foot" (the etymological meaning of Oedipus) who saved the city Thebes by solving the riddle of the Sphinx, and along the way, inadvertently killed his father and married his mother.[14] The back story of Oedipus's life is certainly revealed within *Oedipus the King*, but the action of the drama is acutely focused on one day in Oedipus's life: the day when he discovers what he has done. He responds to this

---

[12] John Finnis, "Natural Law and Unnatural Acts." *Heythrop Journal* 11 (1970).

[13] Sophocles, *The Three Theban Plays*, Robert Fagles, trans. (Harmondsworth: Penguin Classics, 1984). All subsequent references will be made to this edition and this translation, unless otherwise marked.

[14] The Sphinx's question to Oedipus is: "What is it that first goes on four feet, then on two, and finally on three?" Oedipus' response to this was a single word: *anthropos*. Man is the creature who, as a child crawls (on four feet), as an adult, walks on two feet, and when old, walks with a cane.

self-knowledge with the act of self-blinding, so that Oedipus the King turns out to be Oedipus the blind outcast. On this day, his fortunes instantly reversed from the hero of the day, the King of Thebes to the most defiled, ashamed, and beleaguered man alive, the sort of man you would least want to be.

As Sophocles renders the story, Oedipus has become King of Thebes after the murder of King Laius, and the kingdom is under a pall of plagues. The citizens are pleading for King Oedipus' help and so he has dispatched his brother-in-law Creon to Delphi. Creon returns with the message that the gods command that for the plagues to end, King Laius' murder must be avenged. The murderer must be identified and either exiled or put to death. Oedipus interviews, interrogates, and accuses several persons: the blind prophet Tiresias, his brother-in-law Creon, his wife Queen Jocasta, the Messenger from Corinth, and an old Shepherd. Although many of the characters plead with him to halt his investigations (most notably his wife Jocasta) he does not let up, and so while he solves the mystery, answers the riddle, and avenges the gods, he is destroyed by the knowledge of what he did unawares: unwittingly murdered his own father and married his own mother.

Is Oedipus guilty or innocent? Did he kill Laius (his father) and marry Jocasta (his mother)? Obviously the answer is yes. Did he do these horrible deeds knowingly? No. Indeed, Oedipus' insistences that he is not guilty are central to the development of the play. In fact, as I will elaborate later, it is Oedipus' great lament that he bears an unfair burden of responsibility for his actions. One of the great many peculiarities of this myth is that although Oedipus is born (as we shall see, like Antigone,) into a situation in which the course of his life is determined in advance, everything he does is marked by a lack of knowledge and attempts to try to *avoid* this cursed path. When it turns out that he has carried out the prophecy *precisely by trying to avoid it*, he blinds himself. (Interestingly, Oedipus does not die at the end of *Oedipus the King* – as would befit a tragedy – but emerges as the principal character in the sequel *Oedipus at Colonus*. It is only in that play that the nature of the tragedy – the tragedy of his fate – emerges).

As Sophocles renders the myth of the third play in the series, Oedipus' daughter Antigone is faced with the aftermath of her brother Polyneices' attempts to regain the throne of Thebes from his brother Eteocles.[15] Polyneices' attempt fails, and both he and his brother are killed. The new King Creon (who is also Antigone's uncle and prospective father-in-law, as she is engaged to his son Haemon) decrees Polyneices a traitor and forbids his burial, a decree that Antigone defies. As punishment for burying Polyneices, Creon condemns Antigone to be buried alive in a cave where she hangs herself. Subsequently, Haemon kills himself over Antigone's body, an

---

[15] Judith Butler makes quite a lot out of the order of the three plays. Whereas in "imaginary real time" the order is 'Oedipus Rex' followed by 'Oedipus at Colonus' followed by 'Antigone,' they were not written in this order. See *Antigone's Claim: Kinship Between Life and Death* (New York: Columbia University Press, 2000).

Ideas of Justice

act that precipitates the suicide of his mother. As is typical of the Greek tragic form, almost everyone dies and an entire order is brought down; both the houses of Oedipus and Creon are destroyed.

For our purposes, what is most interesting about the play is the basis of Antigone's claim as to why she violates Creon's edict. As typically understood, she makes her claim on the grounds that Creon's law was not issued by the gods and that it goes against their natural justice. The logic behind this defense is that overarching both the state and the individual are the unwritten ordinances that bind the individual and state against which no ordinance of the state can be valid. The idea that Antigone makes recourse to a natural (or divine) form of justice is most often illustrated by the following lines of the play:

> That order did not come from God. Justice, that dwells with the gods below, knows no such law. I did not think your edicts strong enough to overwrite the unwritten, unalterable laws of God and heaven, you only being a man. They are not of yesterday or of today but everlasting, though where they came from, none of us can tell. Guilty of their transgression before God, I cannot be, for any man on earth.[16]

This passage is often used as evidence to support the idea that natural law, as it came to be understood by Cicero and the Stoics – which is to say, as a higher justice, by means of which individuals might critically evaluate the positive laws of the society in which they find themselves – originates with the Classical world of the Athenian city state. Indeed, this is an argument that Aristotle famously makes use of in *The Rhetoric*. Aristotle classifies just and unjust actions with reference to two kinds of law. As he says:

> I call law on the one hand specific, on the other common, the latter being unwritten, the former written, specific being what has been defined by each people in reference to themselves, and common that which is based on nature; for there is in nature a common principle of the just and unjust that all people in some way divine, even if they have no association or commerce with each other, for example, what Antigone in Sophocles' play seems to speak of when she says that though forbidden, it is just to bury Polyneices since this is just by nature.[17]

Of course, for *his* part, Creon also defines justice in terms of one's behavior toward the city and claims that Zeus and justice are on his side. As far as Creon is concerned,

---

[16] Sophocles, *Antigone*, edited by Watling, 1970, 138.

[17] Aristotle, *On Rhetoric*, George A Kennedy, trans. (New York, Oxford University Press, 1991). Here, Aristotle is actually offering arguments to prosecutors faced with arguments that appeal to eternal laws. He is not actually making an argument in favor of such a law. In the *Nichomachean Ethics*, Aristotle does make observations about natural justice, but these should not be confused with natural law theory in any strict sense. *Nichomachean Ethics*, V, 7, 1134b18–1135a4.

Polyneices is an enemy of the state, and in order to return the city to a normal state after the civil war he decrees that Polyneices is not to be granted the symbolic rites that apply to citizens. As Creon sees it, then, Antigone's actions are also unjust, for by performing the burial rights for Polyneices, she challenges his power and the foundation of the laws of the city.

Given its organization around a tragic clash between two laws – the human law of the *polis* represented by Creon on one hand, and the divine law of the gods represented by Antigone, on the other – this tragedy has become exemplary of the contest between human versus natural understandings of justice. Although the play is referenced by Aristotle, and by a great many other legal and political philosophers – Pindar, Montaigne, among others – Sophocles' play finds perhaps its most eloquent modern reader in Hegel.[18] Indeed, Hegel regularly used Greek tragedy to illustrate his central ideas. Although the use of drama to convey philosophical insights is typical of nineteenth-century German philosophy, tragic drama is particularly suited to Hegel's specific philosophical position. For according to Hegel, the discovery of the truth is a necessarily painful and treacherous process. If human consciousness – like Spirit whose path it both emulates and guides – is to find self-realization, it must first pass through the risky and unavoidable ordeal of self-diremption. For Hegel, the greatness of the characters in Sophocles' plays issues from the fact that they have no choice in what they do. As he points out, for these characters, it is an honor to be guilty.[19]

For Hegel, the "truth" of both the law of the state and the law of the gods rests in their recognition of each other. On his view, the peril inherent in this process is made clear in the Greek myth: both Antigone and Creon remain faithful to only one of these laws. What most captivates Hegel's attention is Antigone's choice to defy the human law forbidding the burial of her brother. Antigone's decision to respond not to human law, but to a higher divine and natural law, makes her, as Hegel says in the *Aesthetics*, the "highest presence ever presented to literature or art."[20] Antigone is thus set above Jesus or even Socrates, in what George Steiner reminds us is "a formidable elevation," given "the talismanic status of Socrates as the wisest and purest of all mortals in both Idealist thought and Romantic iconography."[21] Hegel

---

[18] On this question, see Hegel's *Natural Law*, T. M. Knox trans., with an introduction by H. B. Acton (Pittsburgh: University of Pennsylvania Press, 1975).

[19] *Hegel's Aesthetics: Lectures on Fine Art*, T. M. Knox, trans. (New York: Oxford University Press, 1977) 215.

[20] *Hegel's Aesthetics: Lectures on Fine Art*, T. M. Knox, trans. (New York: Oxford University Press, 1977).

[21] George Steiner, *Antigones* (Oxford: Clarendon Press, 1984). Hegel has Antigone represent the laws of the family or those of kinship. It is particularly interesting to note Hegel's insistence on the impossibility of incestuous feelings between brother and sister given the particularities of the family that he investigates. When Hegel cites Antigone's claim that a 'brother is a branch that grows no more' praising the nonsexual nature of the relationship between brother and sister, he seems to have forgotten that Polyneices is Antigone's brother, but so, too, is Creon insofar as Jocasta is both Antigone's and Creon's mother. In his master work on Hegel, *Glas*, Jacques Derrida interrupts his discussion of

Ideas of Justice 149

uses *Antigone* to make his central argument about the tragedies of modern life, which concerns the split between universality and particularity. For Hegel, the truth of Sophocles' *Antigone* is the ultimate indivisibility of ethical substance; natural justice is connected to the unwritten laws of the gods, and duty to kin is continuous with what is human, rational, and conventional. The truth of each rests in the other.

For Jacques Lacan, on the other hand, Antigone's desire – and her place within the symbolic order of her community – does not uphold the natural law of duty to family, but rather marks the *limit* of the natural insofar as she violates the limit of the symbolic order of the city, and indeed, of the human. If Hegel uses Antigone to think about a contest between the human laws of the state and the natural (and for the Greeks, divine) law of family, Lacan deploys her desire to think about the limits of the natural in terms of pleasure: she literally desires what is "beyond the pleasure principle." In this sense, Lacan takes a radical distance from Hegel in his understanding of the role of the natural in law and justice, objecting to the contest Hegel finds between human and divine law and concentrating instead on a desire that can meet its limit – and its satisfaction – only in a seemingly unnatural goal: death. On Lacan's reading, Antigone is at the threshold of the symbolic, yet remains unthinkable within the symbolic terms of her community. If ethics, as he says, is the "science of happiness," and psychoanalysis the science of subjectivity, then a heroine who desires nothing other than her own death might have a great deal to tell us about the convergence between the two sets of knowledges.

It is instructive to note that Lacan's reading of the play focuses on the repeated statements made by the Chorus that Antigone has gone beyond *Ate*, a term that is normally translated as fate or doom. Here, it is also useful to remember Oedipus' downfall: he failed to know his fate. Unlike Oedipus, who does not know his fate, Antigone – whose family's terrible fortune has been foretold by the oracle – repeatedly says that she is condemned to take part in a game in which the outcome is already known in advance. If Antigone's fate is to issue from a cursed family in which she is always already guilty, her decision is not to resist or deny this guilt (like her father), but rather to take it on directly through a death-driven desire; she literally desires her own tragic death. This appears as the most unnatural desire of all, which puts it beyond the limit of human life. As Lacan says, "She has been telling us for a long time that she is in the kingdom of the dead, but . . . her punishment will consist in her being shut up in the zone between life and death. Although she is not yet dead,

---

Antigone's place in the Hegelian system, with a twelve-page set of excerpts of letters between Hegel and his sister Christiane. These letters suggest that Hegel's relationship with his sister – who died young and apparently at her own hand, after an unsuccessful therapeutic treatment by Hegel's friend Schelling – was itself infused with a kind of repudiated sexual desire. Jacques Derrida, *Glas*, John P. Leavey and Richard Rand, trans. (Nebraska: University of Nebraska Press, 1990) 151–62. This argument, of course, echoes Goethe's response to Hegel's reading of the play insofar as Goethe suggested that the incestuous relationship between Antigone and Polyneices hardly makes it representative of the ethical. (Cited in Judith Butler, *Antigone's Claim* [New York: Columbia University Press, 2002 86, ff. 14).

she is eliminated from the world of the living."[22] In so doing she literally places death *within* life. More specifically, on Lacan's reading, by taking refuge in the unwritten laws of the gods, an unassailable place of a law that is not in the chain of meaning or signification, Antigone is both inside and outside the symbolic order of her community.

It is thus perhaps not surprising that Lacan draws our attention to the chorus' repeated suggestion that Antigone is inhuman or somehow unnatural and beyond the human. She demonstrates the limits of naturalness insofar as she is not blinded like her father but rather blinding to her fellow characters in the play in her choice to take up, accept, and walk deliberately toward the fate of her cursed family. She is not "above" the human (in the sense of the gods) – although she has gone where only the gods go – rather she has opened up a third domain, the domain Lacan describes as "between two deaths."[23] She demonstrates that between the dead and the alive are those who are undead, neither alive nor dead. Her act is to coolly walk out of her social life, out of any legal or symbolic life, and toward death itself, and in so doing, she is literally acting "beyond the pleasure principle," beyond the principle that states that humans naturally seek what is good.[24]

In a specific (and contentious) long lament, after making the decision that she will accept the fate of her death, Antigone seems to change tacks, and bemoans to the chorus that she will never know a marriage bed and never have children. As Lacan points out, this abrupt dramatic move from a seemingly cold Antigone – one who, for example, remains unmoved by her sister's pleas to change her mind – to a character mourning what she will never have, has cast doubt on the authenticity of this part of the play in the minds of critics. Lacan also says:

> [This] is an absurd misinterpretation, for from Antigone's point of view, life can only be approached, can only be lived or thought about, from the place of the limit where her life is already lost, where she is already on the other side. But from that place she can see it and live it in the form of something already lost.[25]

In that she is living toward her death, living her life knowing it is already lost to her, what she laments is everything she will lose by virtue of her premature death. As Alenka Zupancic writes, "She begins to reel off what remains of her life, and this remainder is created and accomplished only through this gesture of sacrificing it;

---

[22] Jacques Lacan, *The Ethics of Psychoanalysis*, Jacques Alain Miller, ed., Dennis Porter, trans. (New York: Norton, 1992) 280.

[23] Ibid., 270–85.

[24] Indeed, Freud's theory is that the human being is driven by two opposing drives: one that seeks death, or a return to total rest, and one striving to maintain life. Freud himself concluded that there must be something beyond the pleasure principle, and that death itself is a final form of pleasure.

[25] Jacques Lacan, *The Ethics of Psychoanalysis*, Jacques Alain Miller, ed., Dennis Porter, trans. (New York: Norton, 1992) 280.

Ideas of Justice   151

she creates it by sacrificing it."[26] This time between two deaths – between the social and the final death – is reminiscent of what Giorgio Agamben calls "the time it takes for time to end."[27]

For my purposes, it is interesting to point out that in invoking a natural justice Antigone appears most unnaturally excessive in her desire for death. Indeed, Lacan is repeatedly drawn to the idea of the terrifying excess of humanity that is nonetheless constitutive of the human. As Adrian Johnston points out, Lacan says in his 1958 *ecrit* that the object of psychoanalysis is *antiphusis* (antinature), which is to say that analysis deals with something that seems unnatural in the human, something that is set against or commonly opposed to what is understood to be human nature.[28] As Zizek argues, "Lacan advocates an ethics that goes beyond the dimension of what Nietzsche called 'human, all too human' and [one that] confront[s instead] the inhuman core of humanity. This means an ethics that fearlessly stands up to the latent monstrosity of being human, the diabolical dimension that erupted in the phenomena broadly covered by the label 'Auschwitz.'"[29]

This brings us back to the question at stake here: if the so-called new natural law theory is characterized by an argument that emphasizes the objective naturalness of morality, such that it seems possible to argue about objectively determinable crimes against the human, what might psychoanalysis be able to tell us about the inhumanity that characterizes that human, which can also (maybe) be seen as natural? Conversely, what does it mean to base a legal theory – or a moral theory for that matter – on nature when there is something potentially unnatural about that nature? What does this term nature itself designate, and how is it used? Once these questions come into view, the terms natural law, natural justice, or the law of nature are revealed to be terms with no clear referent. Indeed, Erik Wolf came to the conclusion that there were 120 possible definitions of nature at work in debates about natural law.[30]

Nonetheless, natural law debates are not absent in American jurisprudence. According to Christopher Wolfe, currents of natural law have remained in American judicial thinking up to the present: in Lockean-inspired laissez-faire court developments that emphasize property rights; in Justice Felix Frankfurter's emphasis on the

---

[26] Alenka Zupancic, *Ethics of the Real* (London: Verso, 2000) 257.

[27] Giorgio Agamben, *The Time that Remains: A Commentary on the Letter to the Romans*, Patricia Dailey, trans. (Stanford: Stanford University Press, 2005).

On a more technical note, the time between two deaths is an important dimension of Lacan's approach to subjectivity. On the psychoanalytic account, death is something that has *already taken place* when the subject comes to be – through the cutting of castration or the entry into the symbolic. We are thrown into the world as wounded beings. The second death is the transgression of the original split.

[28] Adrian Johnston, "Ghosts of Substance Past: Schelling, Lacan, and the Denaturalization of Nature," in *Lacan: The Silent Partner*, Slavoj Zizek, ed. (London: Verso, 2006) 114.

[29] Slavoj Zizek, *How to Read Lacan* (New York: Norton, 2006) 46.

[30] Erik Wolf, *Das Problem der Naturreschtlehre: Versuch einer Oiientierung*. Ch. 1 Cited in Heinz, 55.

history and traditions of Anglo-American law; and in metaethical theories about law that supersede and offer criteria for positive law.[31] Perhaps most important to contemporary developments in natural law theories, however, are those thinkers who have tried assiduously to avoid the "naturalistic" fallacy. Among these, most important are likely Germain Grisez and John Finnis. Among the most controversial features of this new natural law theory is its understanding of the basic human goods to which practical reasons' underived principles are able to direct choice and action. Both of these thinkers start from a set of self-evident basic values from which logical inference rational people can arrive at the natural laws of individual and social conduct. Grisez lists eight "modes of responsibility" including working for intelligible goods, avoiding moral decision making on the basis of emotion, avoiding conflict among intelligible goods, and so forth.[32]

The new natural-law theory of Finnis and Grisez represents perhaps the most important recent contribution to the tradition of natural law and natural rights theorizing, bringing to a head a major ethical current in legal thought of the twentieth century.[33] As Kainz also points out, however, it is unclear whether this contribution can still be classified as natural law or in the tradition of natural justice. He says that for anything to be literally a law, one must presuppose a lawgiver and this has traditionally been God, although natural law theorists (such as we will see with Grotius later) sometimes try to soften or loosen that connection. For it to be natural, one seems to need to presume some connection with human nature, and neither God nor human nature is present in Finnis' formulation. To make sense of these debates – many of which recast old ones – it is useful to turn to a brief history of natural justice/natural law theories.

Natural Law Theory From the Seventeenth Century to the Present

According to Claude Lefort, it was really in the sixteenth century that we saw the beginnings of a modern reflection on the relationship among religion, morality, and law. The combination of the collapse of the authority of the Church (and the effects

---

[31] Christopher Wolfe, "Judicial Review" in *Natural Law and Contemporary Public Policy*, David Forte, ed. (Washington, DC: Georgetown University Press, 1998) 157 ff.

[32] Germain Grisez, *Christian Moral Principles*, Vol. 1 of Grisez's *The Way of the Lord Jesus* (Chicago: Fransiscan Herald Press, 1983) 225–6. This perspective might be dramatically contrasted to the ways that Lacan (and Zizek) read the Ten Commandments. On Zizek's view, the cherished ideals of liberal democracies turn out to be the right to break the Ten Commandments: " 'The right to privacy' – the right to adultery, committed in secret, when no one sees me or has the right to meddle with my life. 'The right to pursue happiness and to possess private property' – the right to steal (to exploit others). 'Freedom of the press and of the expression of opinion' – the right to lie. 'The rights of free citizens to possess weapons – the right to kill. And, ultimately, 'freedom of religious belief' – the right to worship false gods." Slavoj Zizek in *How To Read Lacan* (New York: Norton, 2006) 42.

[33] Howard P. Kaniz, *Natural Law: An Introduction and Re-examination* (Chicago: Open Court, 2004) 53.

Ideas of Justice

of the Reformation) meant that an emerging modern Europe saw the assertion of the absolute right of the prince, and of challenges to that right.[34] Although there are long-standing disputes about the status of Protestant natural law versus Thomism, they generally revolve around the question of the originality of Hugo Grotius, commonly understood as the father of modern natural law. Without entering into the disputes about Grotius' originality, it bears mentioning that sources reveal a remarkable continuity between scholastic natural law (not limited just to that of Aquinas) and the natural law doctrines that dominated Protestant Europe during the seventeenth and much of the eighteenth centuries.

Scholastic natural law theory was an obvious target for the kind of moral skepticism that had been revived during the European Renaissance, with such formulations as those of Montaigne. Scholastic natural law operated with an idea about God and the relationship between God and man that could hardly be considered natural unless it could be shown to be pervasive in the world outside Christendom. Indeed, one of the main points of modern skepticism was that this was not the case. Religious and moral notions were so relative to time and place that no theoretically coherent account could be given of them.

Protestant natural law's answer to skepticism started from its most fundamental objection to scholastic natural law: that it seemed to presuppose a moral continuity and interdependence between God and humanity.[35] For Protestant thinkers, the starting point was the complete discontinuity between God and man, a discontinuity that made it impossible to give a rational account of human morality by reference to God and his eternal law. Only faith could bridge the gap between humanity and its creator. If no amount of calculating human rationality could establish a link between people's moral behavior and God's rewards and/or punishments, then they had to live by faith alone or to find a purely human and temporal foundation for reward and punishment.

Hugo Grotius' point against skepticism is that if we claim moral knowledge and act accordingly, we can have society and thus the fundamentals of moral life.[36] At the beginning of his work, Grotius divides *jus* into three meanings:

> [First] Right signifies merely that which is just, and that too rather in a negative than a positive Sense. So that the Right of War is properly that which may be done without Injustice with Regard to an Enemy. No that is unjust which is repugnant to the Nature of a Society of reasonable Creatures. There is another signification of the word Right different from this, but yet arising from it, which relates directly to the Person: In Which Sense Right is a moral Quality annexed

[34] Claude Lefort, "The Permanence of the Theological-Political" in *Political Theologies* (New York: Fordham, 2006) 148.

[35] For a comprehensive survey of Reformation principles and their contexts, see Quentin Skinner, *The Foundations of Modern Political Thought*, 2 Vols. (Cambridge: Cambridge University Press, 1978).

[36] See Hugo Grotius, *Rights of War and Peace* (Indianapolis: Liberty Fund, 2005).

to the Person, enabling him to have, or do, something justly. There is also a third Sense of the Word Right, according to which it signifies the same Thing as law, when taken in its largest Extent, as being a Rule of Moral Actions, obliging us to that which is good and commendable.[37]

Jus is first a type of action. That is, *jus* characterizes any action that is not injurious to others in such a way that social relations break down. To determine what is injurious in this way is to turn *jus* as a feature of persons, which is the second point. Considered as a feature of the person, *jus* is the exercise of these two sides of human nature together. *Jus naturale* in the strict sense, then, is every action that does not injure any other person's personhood. Individuals with natural rights are the units of which all social organization is made. They are people who balance pure self-interest and social inclinations by entering into contractual relations with each other about property and about modes of living together. The emphasis, then, is on what can be used toward the individual's self-preservation compatibly with similar striving by others. The scholastic point was that human beings have the ability to understand what is good and bad even without invoking God, but they have no obligation to act accordingly without God's command, whereas Grotius is suggesting that people unaided by religion can use their rights to establish the contractual obligations upon which social life rests. God is simply an additional source perceived by Christians.

The legacy of Grotius' thought is rich and varied. For our purposes, however, it is the relationship between Grotius and Hobbes that is most germane. Like Grotius, Hobbes labors under a prima facie ambiguity. On the one hand, they both write from a theistic viewpoint, according to which life and morals are part of the divine dispensation. On the other hand, they both intend to account for the moral aspect of this dispensation in such a way that it explains how people who do not believe in God can have a moral life. According to Grotius, this dispensation consisted partly in the world provided for our use, and partly in a human nature equipped with a desire for and ability to limit such use to the socially sustainable. According to Hobbes, humanity is also given the world for use, but the extent and form of this use is not limited by either a tendency toward sociability or an ability to judge from the other person's point of view. On Hobbes' famous account, from the hand of nature we all have natural rights, including:

> [A] right to everything; even to one another's body. This *Jus* naturale is the Liberty each man hath, to use his own power, as he will himselfe, for the preservation of his own Nature; that is to say, of his own Life; and consequently, of doing anything, which in his own Judegment, and Reason, hee shall conceive to be the aptest means thereunto.[38]

---

[37] Ibid.
[38] Thomas Hobbes, *Leviathan*, R. Tuck, ed. (Cambridge: 1991), p. 91.

Ideas of Justice
155

This right is being exercised by individuals, who, according to Hobbes' elaborate anthropology, are inevitably concerned with self-preservation above all else. Human life consists in the satisfaction of a wide variety of desires, and the precondition for the satisfaction of any desire is to be first, alive. In view of our physical and intellectual equality, the exercise of everyone's right to everything would ultimately be defeated, creating a war of all against all. In the interests of self-preservation, people therefore tend to heed certain precepts that limit their natural liberty or rights. These precepts are the laws of nature: "A Law of Nature is a Precept, or generall Rule, found out by Reason, by which a man is forbidden to do, that, which is destructive of his life, or taketh away the means of preserving the same; and to omit, that by which he thinketh it may be best preserved."[39]

With this line of argument, Hobbes took to the limit the Grotian idea of subjective rights as the primary moral feature of human personality. To his contemporaries, it seemed a scandalous attempt to make our morals nothing but a human invention for self-serving purposes. To modern scholars, it has seemed odd that he chose to place such a program in the antiquated language of natural law – to some, so odd that they deny that this was in fact his program, and instead interpret him as a genuine natural lawyer. To others, Hobbes' traditional language is little more than a radical thinker's bow to conventional wisdom, probably with an eye to his own safety and quiet.

Of these, of most interest for our purposes is Richard Cumberland's criticism that Hobbes' dim view of human nature not only makes him morally dangerous but also epistemologically weak insofar as Hobbesian rights can only be understood in the context of some idea of a common good.[40] For these reasons (among others) Cumberland and other natural law theorists of the eighteenth century were motivated to find an ethical alternative to that proposed by Hobbes. Cumberland himself developed a set of arguments very close to what we now know as utilitarianism. As he says:

> The greatest benevolence of every rational agent towards all, forms the happiest state of every, and of all of the benevolent, as far as is in their power, and is necessarily requisite to the happiest state which they can attain, and therefore the common good is the supreme law.[41]

Cumberland argued for the existence of internal, private penalties resulting from infractions of the natural law, and in this regard he was in tune with German philosopher Samuel Pufendorf who also presupposed the inherent sociability of

---

[39] Ibid., 112.
[40] Richard Cumberland, *A Philosophical Inquiry into the Laws of Nature and A Confutation of the Elements of Mr. Hobbes' Philosophy* in *A Treatise of the Laws of Nature*, John Maxwell, trans. (New York: Garland, 1978).
[41] Ibid.

human beings. Combining this belief with a belief in God as a supreme lawgiver, he deduced duties that we must have to ourselves as well as to others:

> In natural liberty, if you do away with the fear of the Deity, as soon as anyone has confidence in his own strength, he will inflict whatever he wishes on those weaker than himself, and treat goodness, shame, and good faith as empty words.[42]

Pufendorf's insistence on duties to oneself – a problematic issue in natural law theory based on human sociability – leads us toward the least likely of natural law theorists, but one who developed a notion of obligation and moral law that was decisive for all subsequent developments in the field: Immanuel Kant. Although Kant was not a natural law theorist, he discussed the meaning and classification of natural law from a phenomenological point of view. That is to say, he looked to determine the proper subjective stance with regard to something that has a prima facie claim to objectivity and reality. As he said:

> Obligatory laws for which an external legislation is possible are called generally external laws. Those external laws, the obligatoriness of which can be recognized by reason *a priori* even without an external legislation, are called natural laws. Those laws again, which are not obligatory without actual external legislation, are called positive laws. An external legislation, containing pure natural laws, is therefore conceivable; but in that case a previous natural law must be presupposed to establish the authority of the lawgiver by the right to subject others to obligation through his own act of will. The principle which makes a certain action a duty is a practical law.[43]

As he puts it in the *Second Critique*, "Ask yourself whether, if the action which you propose should take place by a law of nature of which you yourself were a part, you could regard it as possible through your will."[44] This formulation corresponds exactly to what Kant elsewhere calls the categorical imperative.

Insofar as this categorical imperative (the so-called moral law) and the ethical subject meet at the level of a subjective "feeling" Kant calls "respect," Kant brought to the realm of moral theory something quite new: desire. On Kant's account, respect for the moral law does not mean respecting the law, nor does it mean having respect for the law. Rather, it is a subjective feeling that indicates the presence or nearness of the moral law. In his elaborate account of this feeling, he goes to great lengths to separate it out from other subjective feelings we might have: love, fear, admiration, wonder, and awe. According to Kant, respect is a "singular feeling, which cannot be

---

[42] Samuel Pufendorf, *On the Duty of Man and Citizen According to Natural Law* (New York: Cambridge University Press, 1991).

[43] Immanuel Kant, *Metaphysics of Morals* (Cambridge: Cambridge University Press, 1991).

[44] Immanuel Kant, *Critique of Practical Reason* (London and New York: MacMillan, 1993) 72.

Ideas of Justice

compared with any pathological feeling. It is of such a peculiar kind that it seems to be at the disposal only of reason, and indeed, only of practical reason."[45]

Notably, the Grisez–Finnis position – the so-called new natural law theory – begins from the proposition that practical reason can be demonstrated to be objectively determinable. The standard for *un*reasonableness they propose is somewhat obscure; indeed, even one of their most significant recent defenders, Robert George, suggests that although their modes of responsibility maybe appear "intuitively appealing to many readers ... [they] seem to pop out of nowhere."[46] He also says that these modes of responsibility are derived from the first principle of morality, which is full human fulfillment. John Finnis in particular has developed a theory of practical reasonableness based on seven basic forms of human good – life, knowledge, play, and so forth. These, he says, are known to be good simply by reflection – any reasonable person who reflects on these questions, will know them to be good – and they contain "the outline of everything one could reasonably want to do, to have and to be."[47] The proof of these goods, and the first moral principle that guides them, then, is our grasp of them as a kind of immediate intuition; this indicates their intelligibility. The first principle of morality directs all action toward intelligible ends and away from pointlessness.

If, however, we examine this immediate intelligibility from a psychoanalytic point of view, it emerges that what Kant loftily called the moral law is what Freud discovered as the superego.[48] Thus, if, as Freud asserted, the concept of ethics suffers a blow of disillusionment at the hands of psychoanalysis, the path for this blow was first prepared by Kant. The crucial step between Kant's ethical theory and psychoanalysis involved taking desire – the very thing excluded from the traditional field of ethics – and turning it into the only legitimate territory for ethics. As Alenka Zupancic puts it:

> Traditional ethics – from Aristotle to Bentham – remained on this side of desire. (The morality of power, of the service of goods is as follows: 'As far as desires are concerned, come back later. Make them wait.') Kant was the one who introduced the dimension of desire into ethics and brought it to its 'pure state.'[49]

To this formulation – that the ethical subject need not only discover the moral law, but actually is the point of its articulation through a subjective experience of

---

[45] Ibid., 75.

[46] Robert P. George, *In Defense of Natural Law* (Oxford: Clarendon Press, 1999) 50.

[47] John Finnis, *Natural Law and Natural Rights* (Oxford: Clarendon Press, 1992) 97.

[48] For instance, in *The Ego and the Id* Freud says, "As the child was once under a compulsion to obey its parents, so the ego submits to the categorical imperative of its superego" in *On Metapsychology* (Harmondsworth: Penguin, 1955) 389.

[49] Alenka Zupancic, *Ethics of the Real* (London: Verso, 2000) 4.

respect (a feeling that has much in common with what we might now call anxiety) – Lacan proposes another formulation. On his account, with the introduction of desire into the moral field, the idea of a natural connection between law and the good reaches an impasse. This is what his reading of *Antigone* sought to highlight. Antigone's unnatural desire is *human*, and yet cannot be reconciled with any human law. Although most of our fates will never reach the tragic dimensions of Antigone's, Lacan argues that the *denaturalization of desire* that her character represents, very aptly mirrors our contemporary moral predicament "whether we like it or not."[50] The natural connection between legal authority and morality (the so-called natural desire to obey the law, to seek what is good), which is the cornerstone of natural law theory, cannot be sustained. Indeed, the frailty or lack of sustainability of the maxim that there is a natural inclination to be good or just is precisely what makes those discourses that proclaim to return to "traditional values" so seductive. As Alenka Zupancic points out, it also accounts for the fascination evoked by those "extremists and fanatics" who seem to want nothing more than to die for a cause.[51]

This desire for lost causes brings us back to the curious question of Oedipus' guilt. In *Oedipus at Colonus*, Creon wants to persuade the Athenians that Oedipus is a criminal. Oedipus argues that he is not responsible because he did not know what he was doing when he killed an old man and later married a queen. In the play, the Chorus is asked to decide on Oedipus' culpability. After Creon uses many harsh terms to describe Oedipus – "father killer... the unholy husband of his own mother" – Oedipus addresses himself to the Athenians and makes the legal argument that although he did commit the acts, he did so without *mens rea*. He asks them to put themselves in his shoes. Were a stranger to appear before them who seemed to want to attack, would they ask if this stranger might be their father? Or, if they met a woman they loved, would they ask if she was their mother? Ultimately, the chorus is persuaded by this argument, declaring him to be not guilty and here is where the tragedy of the story becomes finally clear.

Oedipus' lament is this: "If **only** I were guilty." Indeed, from the point after which he successfully argues his innocence, he continuously seeks sympathy for all he has gone through: the wretched discovery that the stranger he killed was his father and that his beloved wife is actually his mother. Without even the penalty of guilt he cannot ever make restitution. Interestingly, although Oedipus declares that he would be better off dead and the chorus agrees, he does not kill himself, but rather blinds himself, curses his sons and spends the rest of his days in exile. Indeed, he spends the rest of his life wandering outside the city being cared for by his daughter Antigone, who will later be the one to *willingly* take up her father's guilt

---

[50] Jacques Lacan, *The Ethics of Psychoanalysis*, Jacques Alain Miller, ed., Dennis Porter, trans. (New York: Norton, 1992) 284.

[51] Alenka Zupancic, *Ethics of the Real* (London: Verso, 2000) 5.

Ideas of Justice

but which he could not bear. After Oedipus, nothing will be the same, for he could not bear the guilt of his crimes; his guilt is left to the next generation to negotiate. In crudely psychoanalytic terms, Oedipus had no Oedipus complex, but he created it for subsequent generations. Thus, Oedipus sets in motion the unwritten law that Antigone will later represent. Oedipus then, is in fact, the founder of a new order, but is not part of it himself. The source of the natural law to which the natural law tradition turns, then, is in the first place the most unnatural of crimes for which no one strictly speaking can be held to account. Oedipus' denial of guilt is the inauguration of the family *Ate* that Antigone will instantiate on the basis of the laws of the gods, but without recourse to a divine realm. What this reveals to modern readers is the unnatural and inhuman element at the heart of the human.

It is therefore no accident that psychoanalysis has been understood to pose such a dramatic challenge to modern Western philosophy. For the modern subject of politics is understood to be responsible insofar as he has rescued himself from his "self-incurred tutelage," as Kant put it, and has reached "the age of majority." Because the subject of modern politics is finally able to direct herself and the world, she is also able to answer in a sovereign manner (for herself) before the law. Freud's massive insight – and/or speculative thought, the "narcissistic wound" he imparts to that dream – is that human subjects are in fact always laboring imperfectly for autonomy against the inexhaustible and ultimately invincible conditions of heteronomy. The ability to answer for oneself, the ability to know what one means, the ability to be master of oneself, freely and autonomously, means something entirely different in the face of the discovery of the unconscious. This is the challenge that ideas of natural law and justice pose today: how to account for what appears inhuman and unnatural in the human. This is a challenge that has not yet been met by contemporary natural law theory, which refuses this principle.

By way of conclusion, I invoke Jacques Derrida's discussion of the "autoimmunity" function at the heart of law, which does not reconcile the issues this discussion has surfaced, but it does provide a set of terms for considering the implications of the death drive for the conceptualization of natural justice in legal theory.

Conclusion: Natural Justice to Come

Near the end of his 2005 text, *Rogues,* Derrida argues that if there is an Enlightenment still to come for humanity, it would mean an attempt to "reckon with the logic of the unconscious" and with "this poisoned medicine, this *pharmakon* of an inflexible and cruel auto immunity that is sometimes called the 'death drive' and that does not limit the living being to its conscious and representative form."[52] Derrida's characterization of the death drive in terms of an autoimmune response captures

---

[52] Jacques Derrida, *Rogues* (Stanford: Stanford University Press, 2005), 157.

the connection between natural and unnatural, human and inhuman, which I argued is the issue that psychoanalysis brings to natural law debates.

Specifically, Derrida argues that all legal orders have a natural capacity for the seemingly unnatural thing; self-annihilation. In *Rogues*, Derrida was considering law in the sense of modern legal orders based on the idea of nation-state sovereignty. He writes that if we see that even democratic forms of law contain the principle of their own destruction (notably in the form of provisions for declaring states of emergency, war measures, or marital law), "there are . . . *only* rogue states, and this is the always unapparent essence of sovereignty . . . A pure sovereignty is indivisible or not at all . . . This indivisibility excludes it in principle from being shared."[53] Autoimmunity is the process initiated by the legal system that destroys the integrity of the law in the course of trying to protect it. This is why Derrida's examples of autoimmune symptoms include strong states' tendencies to ignore established international and domestic law – whether in terms of endorsing a preemptive war as a principle of foreign policy or in the suspension of legal rights with respect to those imprisoned at Guantanamo – as an act of domestic policy. On Derrida's view, these developments actually undermine the authority and integrity of law.

Indeed, in his own updating of the Kantian moral law qua practical reason, Derrida says that human rights, reason, and law fall on the side of the determinable, the practical, the human as natural, whereas the possibility of a democracy to come as a new kind of law lies with what is indeterminable, nonnatural. As he says:

> I believe . . . that none of the conventionally accepted limits between the so-called human living being and the so-called animal one, none of the oppositions, none of the supposedly linear and indivisible boundaries resist a rational deconstruction – whether we're talking about language, culture, social symbolic networks, technicity or work, even the relationship to death, and to mourning, and even the prohibition or avoidance of incest – so many capacities of which the 'animal' . . . is said so dogmatically to be bereft, impoverished.[54]

In this way, Derrida points toward the ways that he hopes the destructive aspect of autoimmunity also opens up a space for something new in the future: a new form of the human, a new kind of politics, perhaps even a new form of law.

---

[53] Ibid., 101.
[54] Ibid., 151.

6

Ideas of Justice

Positive[1]

Matthew Noah Smith

We use the term "justice" in many different ways. In this chapter, I consider justice only as it used in Anglo-American political and legal theory. In this realm of discourse, all forms of justice consist of nonutilitarian *allocative principles*, that is, principles governing, to put it as broadly as possible, who gets how much of what. Some may wish to treat utilitarian principles as principles of justice. As a matter of nomenclatural pedantry, this is surely reasonable. Perhaps as a consequence of John Rawls' arguments in *Theory of Justice*,[2] or perhaps as a result of Aristotle's classifications of two forms of justice in the *Nicomachean Ethics*,[3] or perhaps as a result of John Stuart Mill's appreciation of the need for reconciling utilitarianism with justice,[4] we generally think of justice as consisting of principles that are sensitive to factors to which most forms of utilitarianism are blind. Furthermore, thanks to Rawls, we generally think of distributive justice in particular as being primarily applicable to political and social institutions and not to individual actors (this, however, has been challenged by those who would still recognize a sharp distinction between utilitarianism and justice[5]). Regardless of whether this distinction between justice and utilitarianism is sustainable in the long term, I shall presume it, if only to make clear what is at stake if we are to treat utilitarianism as just one form of justice.

There is much more to the moral and ethical universe than allocative principles of justice. What makes for a flourishing and good life (e.g., peace and the development of one's capacities), what makes an action or a character morally praiseworthy, and

---

[1] I thank Jenelle Troxell for her insights regarding literary theory. I thank Alex Galloway for comments on an early draft and Jules Coleman for his inestimable guidance.
[2] John Rawls, *A Theory of Justice*, 2nd ed (Cambridge, MA: Harvard University Press, 1999).
[3] Aristotle, *Nicomachean Ethics*, Terrence Irwin, trans. (Indianapolis, IN: Hackett, 1999), Book Five, esp. 1130b30 ff.
[4] John Stuart Mill, *Utilitarianism*, George Sher, ed. (Indianapolis, IN: Hackett, 1999) Ch 5.
[5] See, e.g., G. A. Cohen, "Where the Action Is: On the Site of Distributive Justice," *Philosophy and Public Affairs* 26 (1997) 3–30.

161

many ground floor moral principles (such as moral principles prohibiting intentional deception or torture) are not matters of justice even though they are deeply, morally, and ethically significant. For legal theorists, a focus on justice is particularly apt because there is a long tradition of seeing certain areas of both the civil and criminal law as realizing or promoting different forms of justice.

For example, many believe (*pace* the dominant law and economics theories) that criminal law realizes the requirements of retributive justice[6] or that tort law promotes conformity with principles of corrective justice.[7] According to these views, what criminal law is *for* and what tort law is *for* is to realize or promote certain forms of justice. If one wishes to eschew functionalist talk, one can say that the rationales that allow us to best make sense of these legal regimes is that they promote some form of justice. In both cases, though, if we are to understand some area of the law, we must grasp the relevant form of justice associated with that area of the law. On this view, then, prior to the question of evaluating the law's merits, we must understand what the law is for or the rationale that best allows us to make sense of the law. *This* requires understanding the character of some form of justice.[8]

There is, of course, much debate about whether norms of justice play this role in our law.[9] For a debate between those who defend what we might call a "justice-based" account and those who reject such an account of the law to be grasped, much less for such a debate to be fully engaged, all sides must have a shared understanding of the different concepts of justice that, according to the justice-based accounts of the law, define the functions of certain areas of the law. After all, how can one attempt to defend or attack the claim that what tort law is for is to realize corrective justice if one does not know what corrective justice is?

There is yet another reason why understanding different forms of justice is central to understanding the law: Considerations of justice can function as constraints on what form the law ought to take. For example, even if the aim of the law is to promote Pareto optimality in a range of human endeavors by shaping incentives, we may still justifiably criticize the law on grounds of justice, thereby making a case for changing or disobeying the law. This would be to view justice as what Robert Nozick called a "side constraint."[10] It is no insult to the majesty of justice to view it as the most significant side constraint governing the law, even if what the law is for is to maximize efficiency in a variety of different human endeavors.

---

[6] See, e.g., H. L. A. Hart, *Punishment and Responsibility* (New York: Oxford University Press, 1968).

[7] See, e.g., Jules Coleman, *The Practice of Principle* (New York: Oxford University Press, 2001) Ch 2–5, and also Ernest Weinrib, *The Idea of Private Law* (Cambridge, MA: Harvard University Press, 1995) Ch 3.

[8] See esp. Jules Coleman, *The Practice of Principle*, especially Ch 1.

[9] See, e.g., Richard Posner, "The Concept of Corrective Justice in Recent Theories of Tort Law," *Journal of Legal Studies* 10 (1981) 187.

[10] See Robert Nozick, *Anarchy State and Utopia* (New York: Basic Books, 1974), 33 ff.

Ideas of Justice 163

In short, sorting out the relationship between justice and the law is complex and tricky work. If we are to perform this task, we must have a fair grasp of at least some of the major forms of justice. Thus, in this chapter, I offer an overview of four forms of justice. To that end, I shall treat as posterior to this task complex questions about the relationship between the law and justice and instead focus exclusively on political morality itself. The following sections offer the reader an overview of three familiar forms of justice and a fourth emerging form of justice. These discussions are not meant to be an exhaustive overview of every possible form of justice. For example, I shall discuss neither procedural justice nor global justice (although global justice as it is debated today is more or less treated merely as a species of distributive justice). This lacuna is not accidental, as the four forms of justice I choose to discuss here are highly relevant to legal theory and have long histories of being at the centers of debates about the nature and justification of legal regimes.[11]

In the process of providing this overview, I offer a distinctive framework for understanding these forms of justice. This new method, which may appear merely suggestive to the analytic philosopher, is to understand justice in terms of different forms of *narrative*. That is, I shall try to make sense of forms of justice by showing how they embody different forms of narrative. I shall argue that, on the one hand, two forms of justice – retributive and corrective – embody the *character-driven story* (CDS) form, whereas another form of justice – distributive justice – embodies a different narrative form, namely what we might call the utopian form.[12]

Briefly, a CDS has a beginning, a middle, and an end. Additionally, a CDS has *characters* who, except in first-person narration, are usually distinct from the narrator.[13] The characters of a CDS experience or cause the events that make up the beginning, middle, and end of the story. The utopian form, on the other hand, does not require characters; it requires only a narrator. Additionally, the utopian form does not aim to relate chronologically, logically, or characterologically related events. Instead, stories in the utopian form articulate distinct spaces that are *geographically* related. The invention and exposition of these spaces is one of the aims of the utopian story form. We might say that the utopian form foregrounds the location of a story, whereas the CDS form backgrounds the location. A simple, although not failure-proof, test for distinguishing between the two is the following: would the narrative make sense in a different place? If the answer is "yes," then the narrative is

---

[11] For example, John Locke saw the question of retributive justice as so important to the justification of the state's legal order that he grappled with it in his *Second Treatise on Government* well before he dealt with the justification of private property. See John Locke, *Two Treatises of Government*, Peter Laslett, ed. (New York: Cambridge University Press, 1988) 271 ff. Aristotle, as mentioned previously, identified two forms of justice – corrective and distributive – and did so explicitly when discussing legal proceedings. See Aristotle, *Nicomachean Ethics* op. cit.

[12] The term "character-driven story" is invented. I owe it to Tanya Agathocleous.

[13] For more on first-person narrative see Dorit Cohn, *Transparent Minds* (Princeton, NJ: Princeton University Press, 1979).

a CDS; if "no" it is likely to be of the utopian form. For example, "Little Red Riding Hood" can take place in any forest or even outside of a forest in a city! The subject of Thomas More's *Utopia*,[14] on the other hand, is Utopia itself. So, the story cannot take place anywhere else.[15]

The primary theme of this chapter, then, is to show how we can gain insight into different forms of justice by understanding them in terms of certain narrative forms. In the next section I offer a framework for pursuing this project. The sections on Retributive Justice and Corrective Justice employ this framework to argue that we can best understand retributive and corrective justice most naturally in terms of the CDS form, and the section on Distributive Justice argues that distributive justice is best understood as manifesting the utopian form of narrative. The section on Transitional Justice uses this approach to show how this form of justice is a deeply complicated and perhaps theoretically unstable form of justice, because it manifests features of both the CDS and the utopian forms of narrative.

Justice and Narrative

When contemporary analytic philosophers write about justice, we write about norms, principles, reasons, and the like; stories do not play a central role. We nonetheless often do tell stories, although almost always as thought experiments intended to test particular principles against the intuitions elicited by the story.[16] That is, in the standard methodology of analytical political philosophy – insofar as there is a standard methodology – stories are instruments meant to elicit data (intuitions) that in turn play a role in theory construction.[17]

From a metatheoretical perspective, however, we might see another role for thinking in a literary manner when thinking about justice because our very concepts of justice answer to certain literary forms. In short, one deeply important way in which we can understand certain concepts of justice is *through* certain kinds of stories. In these cases, we do not treat the stories as thought experiments that elicit intuitions, but instead the stories serve as allegories for different forms of justice.

[14] Thomas More, *Utopia*, George M. Logan and Robert M. Adams, eds. (New York: Cambridge University Press, 1975).

[15] In fact, the narrators of *Utopia* are not in Utopia itself, but, the point here is that the subject of the story is a place and not a series of chronologically or characterologically related events. All of Shakespeare's plays – and pretty much all plays – are CDSs (some of Beckett's plays are not). Plato's *Republic* is a Utopian narrative as is, to some degree, Ridley Scott's famous film, *Blade Runner*. My arguments do not depend upon there being many pure forms of either CDSs or Utopian narratives, although there clearly are enough pure forms for my distinction to be sensical.

[16] The most striking example of this is found in Frances M. Kamm's work. See, e.g., Frances M. Kamm, *Intricate Ethics: Rights, Responsibilities, and Permissible Harm* (New York: Oxford University Press, 2007).

[17] See, e.g., Tamar Szabo Gendler, *Thought Experiment: On the Powers and Limits of Imaginary Cases* (New York: Routledge, 2000).

Ideas of Justice

The most well known instance of this is Plato's discussion of justice in the *Republic*. Plato does not identify norms or principles but instead makes an argument by analogy when asked to explain what justice in the soul is.[18] He asks us to see the city as a direct analogy to the soul and then, at what is surely the dramatic zenith of the *Republic*, describes in great detail five different *poleis*, moving from the ideal *kallipolis* (the beautiful city) to the tyranny. Plato does not offer to us and then defend what we would recognize as competing principles of justice. Rather, he tells us a story about a city, leaving the reader with the responsibility of *recovering* ethical–political norms or principles from the elaborate travelogue from the *kallipolis* to each of the other four increasingly degraded cities. Yet another famous (and already mentioned) instance of this methodology is found in More's *Utopia*, which is explicitly presented as a travelogue and whose message is not literary but is instead overtly political, as is the travelogue that is Dante's *Divine Comedy* (this has elements of a CDS, although it remains primarily a utopian – and dystopian – narrative).[19] On the other hand, CDSs transparently serve ethical and political masters all the time. The most obvious cases are, of course, found in the Bible, and especially the New Testament, which expresses ethical and political positions almost entirely through parables. The story of the Good Samaritan, for example, illustrates a moral principle, namely that we have a duty of care owed to those who are in need and whom we can also help.

In all these cases, we can see that moral and political principles of justice are represented, for whatever reason, through narratives and not through philosophical argument. This is not to say that philosophical argument can be replaced by narrative in moral and political theory. Rather, my point here is that we can access or appreciate concepts of justice by way of stories just as we can access and appreciate them by way of philosophical exposition. Thus, if we find that a certain narrative form is best suited for accessing, appreciating, or understanding a certain form of justice, then that will surely reveal something about that form of justice, namely a certain kind of deep structure of that form of justice. The deep structure would not vary across the different principles that might constitute principles constituting these forms of justice. Rather, this structure would be implicit in the way we think about that form of justice itself.

We can articulate this point more clearly if we borrow a distinction made famous by Rawls. Rawls distinguished between the concept of justice and different conceptions of justice.[20] Generically speaking, the concept of justice can be understood as posing a particular question about allocation. Thus, different concepts of justice simply pose questions about different problems of allocation: how to allocate

---

[18] Plato, *Republic*, C. D. C. Reeve, trans., 3rd ed (Indianapolis, IN: Hackett, 2004).

[19] Dante Aligheri, *The Divine Comedy*, John Ciardi, trans. (New York: New American Library, 2003).

[20] Rawls, A *Theory of Justice*, 4.

the benefits and burdens produced within a system of cooperation; how to allocate the costs associated with misfortune; how to allocate punishment when there is a crime, and so forth. Conceptions of justice can be understood as principles that *answer* these questions. For any one concept of justice, there can be many possible conceptions of justice, that is, many answers to the question posed by that concept of justice, and it is (part of) the work of political philosophy to determine which answer is best.

My thesis is that the narrative form that best suits the form of justice reveals something about the relevant *concept* of justice, which of course has an impact on the various conceptions of justice: By understanding the narrative form immanent in any concept of justice, we gain deep insight into the question posed by that concept of justice and the forms and limits of the principles that might answer those questions. In particular, we gain a sense of the perspective on human affairs that is presupposed by that concept of justice. As we shall see, talk of visual perspective is appropriate here because each concept of justice presupposes a kind of visual vantage point. In some cases, the story form is a CDS, and so always involves actors experiencing (or causing) a series of events that are linked together into a beginning, a middle, and an end. The CDS form draws us into the feverish grasp of the cascade of events. In other cases, the narrative form is the utopian form (which, as mentioned previously, is also found in travelogues but also often in science fiction), in which one has the perspective of a "solar eye" looking down on geographical space, holding its entirety in one's imagination instead of, we might say, our imagination being possessed by that space.

Let me summarize, now, the key point of this section. Concepts of justice can be articulated in many ways, and one way in which they can be articulated is through different story forms, in particular through the CDS and the utopian story forms.

Retributive Justice

We are perhaps most familiar with retributive justice, which consists of the principles governing required punishment of wrongs committed by others within one's community. The most famous principle of retributive justice is the Biblical requirement of *lex talionis*, which requires exacting equal retribution for each wrong (thus "an eye for an eye, a tooth for a tooth" is an iconic enthymatic formulation of *lex talionis*). Immanuel Kant advocated this very principle, famously remarking:

> Even if a civil society resolved to dissolve itself with the consent of all its members – as might be supposed in the case of a people inhabiting an island

Ideas of Justice

resolving to separate and scatter themselves throughout the whole world – the last murderer lying in prison ought to be executed before the resolution was carried out. This ought to be done in order that everyone may realize the desert of his deeds, and that bloodguiltiness may not remain upon the people; for otherwise they will all be regarded as participators in the murder as a public violation of justice.[21]

This strict form of retributive justice has seemed to some to enshrine as morally principled a deeply primitive and objectionable form of revenge. On these grounds, some have rejected all forms of retributive justice as sources of justification for *any* kind of punishment, much less state-sanctioned and state-imposed punishment. Surely this moves too quickly: Other more reasonable principles of retributive justice are available. For example, we might have a principle requiring that those guilty of committing wrongs must be punished in some humane fashion that embodies the very moral principles that were violated. Thus, we can imagine a call for humane imprisonment, or a stiff financial penalty, or some other form of punishment. Even if these responses to wrongs are understood as forms of revenge, they, because embodying the very moral principles that were violated by the individual who committed the wrong, are neither brutal nor dehumanizing. Thus, the question of whether this form of punishment as morally restrained revenge is morally objectionable is hardly settled.

Of course, we may worry that retributive justice expresses a commitment to *any* kind of revenge. The problem with revenge seems to be the way that it fails to be public in ways that do not meet an implicit demand of any principle of justice, namely that practices justified by those principles be accessible and assessable within the public sphere. This is typically accomplished in modern states through public trials presided over by (supposedly) neutral parties, the availability of appeals, and finally, punishment meted out in the name of all the citizens and not simply the person who suffered the wrong. Revenge, lacks these features. There is no publicly accessible method for accounting for the wrong done; the kind and extent of the punishment seems to be a matter of the private judgment of the individual seeking revenge, and the punishment itself is a private affair between the wronged agent (or his proxy, be it an authorized proxy or a vigilante) and the agent who committed the wrong.

Regardless, let us assume the viability of retributive justice as a form of justice governing the allocation of punishment in response to definite wrongs, what general form do the principles of retributive justice take? To answer this question, it is useful to contrast retributive justice with consequentialist theories of punishment (of which utilitarian theories of punishment are a species). Consequentialist theories of

---

[21] Immanuel Kant, *The Philosophy of Law*, W. Hastie, trans. (Edinburgh, 1887) 198.

punishment justify punishment by articulating a relationship between punishment and future goods. Retributive justice justifies punishment by articulating a relationship between punishment and past wrongs. Thus, it is natural to describe consequentialist justifications of punishment as *forward looking*, in the sense that the particularities of the commission of the original wrong drop out of view and punishment is understood as a means to promote some end, whereas it is natural to describe retributive justice as *backward looking*, in the sense that retributive justice requires that the particularities of the original wrong play the central role in determining both who is punished and how that person is punished, largely regardless of the connection any such punishment has to the promotion of unrealized goods. This contrast reveals the following formal constraint on all theories of retributive justice: It is contrary to retributive justice (however it is cashed out) to punish just *anyone* to promote some unrealized good, such as bringing people to view committing crimes as so risky that they no longer commit them.

We can now see how distinct retributive justice is from any consequentialist theory of punishment. Consequentialist theories of punishment do not operate according to the logic of retribution because retribution succeeds only when the one who has in fact committed the crime is punished. Standard consequentialist theories of punishment, on the other hand, succeed only when those who *would* commit a wrong are deterred by the present imposition of a punishment. The success of punishment according to a consequentialist theory of punishment is therefore dependent upon the truth of a counterfactual, namely: Had this punishment not been meted out, then such-and-such wrongs would have occurred. On the other hand, the success of punishment according to any theory of retributive justice depends upon the truth of a historical claim, roughly: So-and-so committed such-and-such a wrong.[22]

Does retributive justice have an aim, then? In an important sense it does, although this aim does not provide teleological justification for punishment. Rather, the aim is constitutive of retributive justice itself: The imposition of the punishment is meant to bring to an end the course of events instigated by the commission of the crime.[23] Within the context of retributive justice, punishment brings what is often colloquially called closure. Thus, unlike any consequentialist approach, retributive justice operates within the framework of a CDS, in that there is an actor, who engages in or experiences a series of events, which are in turn coherently ordered into a

---

[22] These propositions characterizing the success conditions of punishment as seen from two competing theories are schematic and therefore are meant to leave open the addition of many further conditions.

[23] This does not rule out principles of retributive justice being limited by some considerations associated with deterrence. But, the aim of deterrence must be understood as a kind of side constraint, e.g., punishments that reliably have the opposite effect of deterring crime might be ruled out from the menu of available punishments.

Ideas of Justice

beginning, a middle, and an end: the commission of the crime, the determination of guilt, and then the punishment.[24]

That is to say, the concept of retributive justice is best understood when we view the commission of a wrong as the beginning of a story, and in particular, a story that has a very specific kind of ending. Furthermore, there are not just any old actors in the story of retributive justice. Rather, there are the following central characters: the wrongdoer and the wronged. The omnidirectional temporality of this narrative is crucial because unlike any consequentialist narrative of the justification of punishment, according to any theory of retributive justice, the wrong must have been committed *prior* to the punishment, or else the punishment would be, as a formal matter, in violation of any possible principle of retributive justice. That is, the focus on a specific wrongdoing character is crucial. Even if A has committed a wrong just like the wrong committed by B it would be a violation of retributive justice (whatever specific form it takes) for A to be punished for B's wrong, or, for that matter, for B to be punished for A's wrong.[25]

There is a final and critical constraint on the CDS established by retributive justice. This constraint is that the broader narrative context must *take the world as it is*. That is, principles of retributive justice require that punishment is *contained* and not systematic. This last constraint on retributive justice requires that the punishment focus on the wrongdoer and not on any external (e.g., social, cultural, familial, etc.) conditions that may be connected, in some sense, to the wrong committed. These conditions may be admitted as mitigating factors in judging whether or how much to punish the wrongdoer, but taking action to change these conditions *in the name of retributive justice* is not permitted. For example, suppose that A murders B, and part of the explanation for A's violent behavior is that years before A's father had beaten A mercilessly (e.g., consider this factor as a matter of counterfactual dependence: had A's father not mercilessly beaten A all those years ago, A would not have murdered B). Retributive justice cannot require that A's father be punished as well as A, or that the state's child welfare system, which through its negligence allowed A to stay in a home where he was beaten mercilessly by his father, somehow be subjected to punishment because A committed some wrong. Conversely, such an extension is possible, but only if it is accompanied by a rereading of the past such that A's father or the state welfare system somehow becomes complicit in A's crime, thereby no

---

[24] For a general definition of a narrative, consider the following: a narrative consists of a story, which is a "fabula that is presented in a certain manner[; a] *fabula* is a series of logically and chronologically related events that are caused or experienced by actors[; an] event is the transition from one state to another state[;] *Actors* are agents that perform actions … *To act* is defined here as to cause or to experience an event." (From Mieke Bal, *Narratology*, 2nd ed. (Buffalo, NY: University of Toronto Press, 1997) 5.

[25] Although one might defend some principle of retributive justice allowing simultaneous symmetrical error – A being punished for B's wrong, and B being punished for A's wrong – such a principle would be a perverse form of retributive justice.

longer putting A at the center of the narrative about the commission of the wrong action, but instead putting A and his father, or A and the child welfare system at the center of the narrative of the commission of the wrong action.

We can therefore see that retributive justice is best understood as a CDS, where the central character is the *wrongdoer*, and in which there are, roughly, three acts. First, there is the commission of the crime by the wrongdoer. Then, there is the pursuit and trial of *that* wrongdoer for the commission of *that* crime. Finally, there is the punishment of the wrongdoer for *that* crime, but only as a consequence of the pursuit and/or the trial of the wrongdoer (sometimes the pursuit can lead to the wrongdoer suffering in some appropriate manner, which is "read" as the proportionate punishment for the wrongdoer given *that* crime). The victim of the crime plays a role in this CDS, but is a central character only at the initial stages. After that point, the wrongdoer is the narrative center-of-gravity around whom swirls all the events.[26] Of course, as represented in some text, the CDS of retributive justice may focus on the police or lawyers, but even then the wrongdoer (and the crime) looms silently in the foreground: It is the wrongdoer who is the target of the chase or the focus of the trial.

It is no accident, then, that the most common contemporary enactments of retributive justice are police and courtroom procedurals, dramas that begin with a crime, turn to drawn-out police investigations or lawyerly debates before a judge or jury, and then close with the wrongdoer being caught or, after having been caught, convicted. Importantly, in all these cases, the social, political, and economic context is presented as both given and immutable (i.e., as not constructed by the actors, and as not changeable by the actors); the story is woven within and according to the logic of this much broader tapestry without any meaningful querying of the constraints so imposed.

Perhaps one of the purest examples of this is an early police procedural, the great 1948 film, *The Naked City*, which begins with a dramatic aerial shot moving north over Manhattan, beginning at its southern tip. In a startling voiceover, the director announces to his audience that the story in this film is just one story within the great American metropolis of New York City and that this story, although fictional, is shot entirely on location in the city. Then, we almost immediately are shown the murder, the investigation of which is the focus of the film. The film ends with the murderer having been caught and a raw punishment meted out. *The Naked City* self-consciously takes New York City, and in particular its architectural, political, and social structures, as an immutable background against which the totally contained, and highly controlled and targeted police investigation unfolds. This is a near-perfect enactment of retributive justice: Against an utterly stable and given background, the

---

[26] Insofar as the wronged plays a role in later "acts," it is always within the context of the pursuit/trial or the punishment, and therefore becomes not only the wronged but also the pursuer or the punisher, which is a different kind of character.

Ideas of Justice

story follows *only* the wrong act, the wrongdoer, and the agents who mete out retribution. These components are then knit together within a simple temporal structure involving the linear passage of time.[27]

Retributive justice, then, can be understood formally in terms of a highly constrained and traditional CDS. Two of the most significant defining features of this structure are its temporality (there is a beginning, a middle, and an end) and its highly limited range of characters and actions. It is very important to recognize that who does the punishing is a matter *external* to the story. That is, as a matter of retributive justice, it does not matter *who* does the punishing; it only matters that the appropriate punishment is meted out to the correct party for the correct crime. That the state, for example, is the punishing agent only means that the state is responsible, in some sense, for realizing retributive justice, and *that* is a matter of the unquestioned background conditions.

In sum, the allocation of punishment required by retributive justice involves a small cast of characters operating against a stable, given background and once the allocation of punishment is completed (or rendered impossible due to bad luck), the book is closed.

Corrective Justice[28]

Corrective justice consists of principles regulating the reallocation in light of harms caused by one party and suffered by another. These harms need not require retribution and so the response to them need not be governed by norms of retributive justice. In particular, because the harms with which corrective justice is concerned are often due to "mischief," they are just as often due to misfortune and so are, on their face, beyond the bounds of retributive justice, which focuses on harms intentionally inflicted by one agent on another. Conversely, as in cases in which retributive justice is applicable, the harms must be, in some sense, "owned" by some agent or other, and not be due solely to some uncontrollable force of nature such as a tornado or a tsunami. Thus, even as we strive to preserve a distinction for the purposes of corrective justice between harms due to misfortune and harms due to mischief, both harms are of the sort that are owned by an agent.[29] Additionally, how

---

[27] Of course, Fyodor Dostoevsky's *Crime and Punishment* is perhaps the purest and most remarkable example of retributive justice portrayed as a CDS (and *The Brothers Karamazov* is a close second!). Another valuable film representing retributive justice as a CDS is Jean-Pierre Melville's great film, *Le Samouraï*. One text that mercilessly probes the immutability of the social structures within which the retributive narrative unfolds is Franz Kafka's "The Trial."

[28] This section draws on Jules Coleman, *Risks and Wrongs*, Jules Coleman, *The Practice of Principle*; Arthur Ripstein, "Equality, Luck, and Responsibility," *Philosophy and Public Affairs* 23 (1994) 3–23; Arthur Ripstein, "Torts," in *The Oxford Handbook of Jurisprudence and Legal Philosophy*, Jules Coleman and Scott Shapiro, eds. (New York: Oxford University Press, 2004).

[29] See Jules Coleman and Arthur Ripstein, "Mischief and Misfortune" *McGill Law Review* 41 (1995) 91 ff.

and where to draw the line between retributive and corrective justice is another quite difficult question to resolve. Are the harms associated with each different in kind? Or are they merely different in magnitude?[30] Although resolving these questions are central to any theory of corrective justice, I shall, due to space restrictions, address them only in passing here.

In the most general sense, corrective justice consists of principles governing how to *reverse* harms due to mischief or misfortune and so are *reallocative principles*. For example, if A steals B's car and then wrecks it, it may be a matter of retributive justice what punishment A must suffer, but it is an entirely different matter – a matter of corrective justice – whether and how A ought to reverse B's loss of her car (and as with retributive justice, there may be agent-neutral reasons to ensure that what is required by corrective justice is realized). A quick and dirty way to characterize corrective justice, then, is to say that, *as a matter of corrective justice*, if A harms B, then A owes a duty of repair to B. To capture the notion of A's ownership of the harm suffered by B, we can use Tony Honoré's turn of phrase and refine our quick and dirty characterization as follows: As a matter of corrective justice, if A is *outcome responsible* for a harm suffered by B, then A owes a duty of repair to B.[31]

This notion of outcome responsibility is meant to cast a wider net than the notion of moral blameworthiness. Thus Honoré writes, "People are responsible for their actions and the unintended outcomes of their actions even when not morally to blame."[32] So, while retributive justice squarely tracks moral blameworthiness, corrective justice tracks only outcome responsibility. As mentioned, some hold that the two may converge when it comes to some actions (although this is complicated: suppose A intentionally assaults B, and so it is the case that A is liable to be punished for assaulting B, but if A owes B a duty of repair for the harm B suffered as a result of the assault, it is not clear that this repairable harm is the same thing as the punishable assault). In most cases, however, the two do come apart (as in the familiar case in which A is blasting nearby B's domicile, and, although A takes precautions, as a result of the blasting A nonetheless unintentionally damages B's domicile, and so A is *not* liable to be punished for damaging B's domicile, although A does owe a duty of repair for the harm B suffered as a result of the damage to his domicile).

There are many complications associated with both the concepts of harm and outcome responsibility. Most importantly, we should note that not all harms are

---

[30] It should be noted that we can draw a bright line between retributive justice and corrective justice if we eliminate talk of harm and treat corrective justice as the form of justice that mandates certain responses to *wrongful transactions*. If we do this, we would need to appeal to some norm other than a norm of corrective justice to determine what counts as a wrongful transaction. For ease of exposition, however, I will talk only of harms. This is not meant to indicate that I am taking a stand on the question of whether we must understand corrective justice in terms of harms instead of wrongful transactions, though.

[31] Tony Honoré, *Responsibility and Fault* (Oxford: Hart Publishing, 1999).

[32] Tony Honoré, *Responsibility and Fault*, p 7.

Ideas of Justice

173

the same. Some harms are not wrongful, and it seems that corrective justice would require repair of only wrongful harms.[33] For example, when a surgeon performs surgery on a patient, there will be substantial postsurgery harmful side effects (swelling, bleeding, pain, etc.); however, these harms are not wrongful harms, even though the surgeon is outcome responsible for them. So, it seems that one necessary condition for A to owe B a duty of repair is for A to have *wrongfully* harmed B, and not just for A to have harmed B.

Turning now to outcome responsibility, we must ask whether being the "nearest" link in the causal chain is sufficient for being outcome responsible – or must one intentionally contribute to the occurrence of the harm? If we accept any form of strict liability, then merely being a nearby link in the causal chain may be sufficient. Even if we reject strict liability, we may accept that intentional harming is not a necessary condition for a duty of repair, but then we can ask what else must be present in addition to mere causal proximity. Perhaps foreseeability of the harm is a necessary condition for a duty of repair to be owed. If so, what is a standard of foreseeability? Any complete theory of corrective justice will answer this question.

Finally, we must keep in mind that this approach seems to give luck a central role in determining who bears a duty of repair. Consider two individuals who are both very careless in their driving and who both know that their carelessness may lead to a dreadful accident causing grave harm to others. One, as a matter of brute luck, manages to avoid ever causing an accident, whereas the other, as a matter of brute luck, causes a dreadful accident. Why should one be liable for the harm caused when the other is not when the only difference between the two is a matter of sheer, brute luck?[34] Again, any complete theory of corrective justice will have to resolve questions regarding the role of luck.

Turning now to broader reflections about corrective justice, we can see that it, like retributive justice, is backward-looking, in the sense that it requires allocations in response only to harmings that have already occurred and not preemptively to harmings that are merely likely to occur. To see the significance of this, consider an alternative to corrective justice: a norm requiring everyone to pay into an insurance scheme that would in turn pay out to those who have suffered a relevant kind of harm regardless of the circumstances of the harming. This alternative norm is rather more complicated than corrective justice because it involves both forward-looking and backward-looking components. It is forward looking in the sense that it requires payment into an insurance scheme that is meant to respond to events that have not yet occurred and may never occur. An apt analogy here is vaccination: one is vaccinated only because it is possible that at some point in the future one might be

---

[33] See Coleman, *Risks and Wrongs, passim.*
[34] See Jeremy Waldron, "Moments of Carelessness and Massive Loss" in *Philosophical Foundations of Tort Law*, D. Owens, ed. (New York: Oxford University Press) 387–408.

exposed to the relevant virus. The vaccination would have been reasonable even if, at the end of one's life, it turned out that one was never exposed to the virus. The analogy breaks down, though, if this alternative insurance scheme requires payout only in cases in which there have been wrongful harms, for in this case it would be backward-looking. If the insurance scheme was such that everyone received regular payments out of the scheme based upon actuarial calculations of the likelihood of his or her being harmed regardless of whether they had in fact suffered a harm, then it would be purely forward-looking. But both schemes – the janus-faced insurance scheme and the purely forward-looking scheme – are forward looking in ways that the norms of corrective justice are not, and so neither would embody (or meet the demands of) the norms of corrective justice.

As with retributive justice, the purely backward-looking character of corrective justice, along with its focus on determinate characters bonded together by a single event – the wrongful harming – invites us to understand corrective justice in terms of the CDS form of narrative. The narrative begins with a wrongful harm to B for which A is outcome responsible. Consequently, A owes a duty of repair to B until that duty is satisfied by some form of appropriate reallocation from A to B. A makes the reallocation and the duty of repair owed to B is discharged. At this (temporal) point, the story ends.

Importantly, the reallocation required by the duty of repair cannot be accomplished by just anyone. Rather, the reallocation must be performed by the party that is outcome responsible for the harm in the first place. Thus, even if a third party, out of a desire to help B out, fully makes up the losses suffered by B, A still owes B a duty of repair. In short, the story cannot end with just any reallocation; it ends only with the agent outcome responsible for the harm making up for the loss suffered by the harmed agent. As we can see, then, corrective justice requires well-defined characters linked together, with their actions driving a story that has a beginning, a middle, and an end: These features are hallmarks of the CDS form of narrative.

Turning now to the final feature of the CDS form of narrative, namely the presumption of a fairly broad set of background conditions, it turns out that corrective justice meets this criterion as well. To see this, note that a familiar objection to corrective justice is that it allows for the reallocation of X from A to B even when A never had a justified entitlement to X (e.g., suppose A is incredibly wealthy as a result of stealing from C and then after harming B must, as a matter of corrective justice, hand over most of his [stolen] fortune to B). This surely is a matter of concern. Corrective justice, however, is not the sovereign form of justice (if there even is a sovereign form of justice). Whether A has an entitlement to X is beyond question in matters of corrective justice. The implementation of norms of corrective justice requires the presumption that A has some initial entitlement to X and, insofar as A owes X to B as a matter of corrective justice, then B is entitled to X.

Ideas of Justice 175

As a result of cases such as the one just mentioned, one might go in for metanorms of corrective justice – norms governing corrective justice – that rule out reallocation when the original allocation is morally dubious. Such a norm, though, would not be a norm of corrective justice, but would instead be a norm determining when and how to apply norms of corrective justice, such as, where there are not morally suspect allocations, norms of corrective justice apply. Such a metanorm predicates the application of norms of corrective justice on both a standard theory of justified entitlement and a factual finding that the entitlement in question is sufficiently grounded by that theory. Resolving these matters has little to do with the matters at the heart of corrective justice because the issue with respect to these matters is not how to repair a wrongful transaction (or, if you think that duties of care are grounded by principles of corrective justice, what duties of care we owe to others with respect to their entitlements), but whether the prior allocation of X to A meets an independent justificatory standard. This latter question is *presumed settled* at the point at which arises any moral problem that principles of corrective justice are meant to address.[35]

Thus, we find the other hallmark of CDS, namely the presumption of certain conditions that constitute the space within which the drama of the harm, the claim for repair, and then the repair unfold. In the case of corrective justice, the presumed and unchangeable condition is the initial allocations of goods. That is, corrective justice operates over entitlements under the presupposition that they are as they ought to be (*modulo* the harm that triggers the duty of repair) and does not offer prescriptions on how entitlements ought to be distributed from the get-go. So, just like retributive justice, norms of corrective justice require taking the world as it is.

Consequently, the norms of corrective justice can neither require that agents who are not outcome responsible for the harm to repair the harm nor require those who do not suffer the harm to receive compensation for the harm. Only if *harmers* repair the wrong will the harmed no longer have against the harmer a claim-right grounded by a duty of repair.[36] For others' actions counting as discharging the duty of repair owed to the harmed, it would have to be shown that these others were, in fact, part of the story *all along*. That is, they were the harming parties from the get-go, and so were characters in the narrative from the start. We have seen this before in the case of retributive justice.

---

[35] Everyone in a community may be required to build legal-political institutions that realize corrective justice, although if this were the case, parties would have agent-neutral reasons for action and not the agent-relative reasons of corrective justice. Nor is it to deny that we all have reasons to be morally outraged at existing or past misfortune. These facts are, in important ways, external to facts over which corrective justice operates.

[36] For more on duties grounding claim-rights, see Joseph Raz, *The Morality of Freedom* (Oxford: Clarendon Press, 1996) Ch 7.

Unfortunately, there are no examples in literature or film of corrective justice that are quite as clear as *The Naked City* or *Crime and Punishment*. However, films such as *Philadelphia*, which is about a wrongful termination lawsuit, and *The Rainmaker*, which is about an insurance bad faith lawsuit, nonetheless demonstrate how corrective justice is best understood in terms of a CDS. Both films, insofar as they are about corrective justice, focus, usually via attorney proxies, on characters who have been wronged and the characters who have committed the wrongs. The films begin with the wrong, focus mostly on the process of seeking a reallocation from the wronging agent(s) so as to secure discharge of the duty of repair borne by the wronging agent(s), and conclude with the state ordering that those duties be discharged. Finally, the very logic of the films presupposes a static background allocation of rights and goods that allows viewers to make sense of the claim that a wrong has occurred. As a matter of the principles of justice governing this background allocation, the lawyer in *Philadelphia* was owed his job and the child in *The Rainmaker* was owed medical care and neither these principles nor their broader context could be questioned without kicking the feet out from under the moral logic of the films. So, in fairly straightforward ways, these films demonstrate how natural it is to treat corrective justice using the CDS form.

In sum, then, corrective justice is best understood on the model of the CDS. This model involves distinct characters bearing a special kind of causal–historical relationship to one another (one is outcome responsible for a harm borne by the other) – a relationship that corrective justice picks out as normatively significant – and that has a beginning (the harming), a middle (the claim for repair), and a conclusion (the repair being made). A background allocative "geography" is presumed and it is within this landscape that the narrative of corrective justice unfurls itself.

Distributive Justice

Distributive justice is most famously articulated by John Rawls as "a set of principles for assigning basic rights and duties and for determining . . . the proper distribution of the benefits and burdens."[37] More concretely, principles of distributive justice govern the distribution of state-backed rights, duties, liberties, liabilities, and immunities (all hereafter referred to as "rights") as well as goods – either a list of "primary goods," or some metrics of welfare, opportunity, or resources – across a population unified in some manner, for example, as in Rawls' theory's case a population unified by mutual cooperation (although there may be other considerations that determine the boundaries of the community over which the principles of distributive justice

---

[37] Rawls, *A Theory of Justice*, p. 5. Another central texts of contemporary philosophical reflections on distributive justice is Ronald Dworkin, "What is Equality? Part 1: Equality of Welfare," *Philosophy and Public Affairs* 10 (1981) 185–246; and Ronald Dworkin, "What is Equality? Part 2: Equality of Resources," *Philosophy and Public Affairs* 10 (1981) 283–345.

Ideas of Justice

operate[38]). Broadly speaking, then, distributive justice consists of a set of principles that determine the baseline allocation of rights and goods within a community. Importantly, distributive justice is not limited in scope with respect to over whom in the community it operates: Principles of distributive justice apply to the whole community and not to proper subsets of the community (although the principles can govern distribution at a coarse-grained level, as Rawls famously did when he presumed that the principles of distributive justice operated over individuals understood as heads of *families* and not understood simply as individuals). Every individual (or in Rawls' case, every head of a family) has claims by virtue of principles of distributive justice. This is why Rawls talks of principles of distributive justice determining the "basic structure" of a society, that is, those foundational institutions that govern every feature of the lives of those who live in that society.[39]

There is, therefore, a kind of anonymity in distributive justice: it immediately shapes the lives of all who are members of a society and not simply those who have particular histories. Each person is to be understood as a blank space in which a certain bundle of rights and goods is placed. There may be other principles of distributive justice governing the society, such as principles governing transactions between the members of the society, or principles governing interactions between social institutions and members of the society. Even in these cases, however, the principles of distributive justice shape the lives of *all* members of the society and therefore do not play any unique role in shaping the life of any particular member.

To get a clearer grasp on distributive justice, let us consider one unusual proposal for a principle of distributive justice: "finders-keepers." According to finders-keepers, the distribution of goods in society is fixed by the historical-causal relationships between individuals and the available goods, namely if A bears the historical-causal relationship to X of having found X, then A has claim to X. Even though this principle governs original allocation of goods, it fails as a principle of distributive justice because no basic structure (or even a less-than-basic structure) could be continuously ordered according to this principle. Consequently, such a principle of justice does not in fact determine the distribution of goods in general but only freezes in perpetuity whatever is given by chance at some arbitrary moment. Such a principle, therefore, cannot apply diachronically, that is, it cannot deal with the introduction into the society of new members, intestate goods, or the creation of new goods by the members of the society. But these are key functions that any principle of distributive justice must perform. Furthermore, insofar as distributive justice involves the distribution of rights and liberties and not just of concrete goods,

---

[38] See, e.g., Michael Blake, "Distributive Justice, State Coercion, and Autonomy" *Philosophy and Public Affairs* 30 (Summer 2001) 257–96.

[39] Rawls defines the basic structure as "the way in which major social institutions distribute fundamental rights and duties and determine the division of advantages from social cooperation." See Rawls, *Theory of Justice*, 3.

finders-keepers turns out to be a non-sequitur: How does one "find" a claim-right to political speech unfettered by government interference?

What does this reveal about the narrative form immanent in distributive justice? It renders clear that a causal-historical representation of a principle of distributive justice will not do. Principles of distributive justice govern geographical spaces time-lessly and so cannot be responsive to local changes in the causal-historical order. This is not to say that principles do not demand response to changes – it is to say that the principles cannot assist in determining how to respond to changes. However, the principles are fundamentally to be understood as descriptions of static states of affairs. So, we can clearly see that although conscientious members of the political community might be guided by principles of distributive justice in all their trans-actions with one another, distributive justice does not require such conscientious interaction. Regardless of whether we (rightly) abandon libertarian principles of dis-tributive justice in favor of some "patterned" form (e.g., some egalitarian principle like Rawls' Difference Principle or Dworkin's resource egalitarianism), the point of a theory of distributive justice is to provide principles that determine how society as a whole will be ordered *via some institutional "technology"* (e.g., via tax law, property law, civil rights law, takings jurisprudence, etc.) and not by virtue of the moral fiber of the individual members of that society.[40] Either way, principles of distributive justice will be *systematic*. That is, they provide a broad framework governing the overall order of a society.

Thus, distributive justice is best understood not in terms of histories of concrete individuals or even in terms of the relationships between concrete individuals, but instead in terms of standing rules governing relations between all members of a community. In short, nothing out of the ordinary needs to happen for the principles of distributive justice to apply, rather, they are meant to *define* the ordinary. Thus, deviations from the principles of distributive justice are what merit response, distributive justice is not itself responsive.

In many ways, principles of distributive justice give us the required normative background such that principles of retributive and corrective justice can apply. What counts as a theft, as a violation of liberty, and as a wrongful transaction requires a stable normative background. This has already been suggested in the discussions of retributive and corrective justice. For example, if we are to apply norms of corrective justice (and it is an open question whether we ought to do so), then we must assume that the allocation prior to the wrongful harming are grounded in some way. One

---

[40] For a challenge to this claim, see Cohen, "Where the Action Is" and Liam Murphy, "Institutions and the Demands of Justice," *Philosophy and Public Affairs* 27 (Fall 1999) 251–91. For objections to this challenge see David Estlund "Liberalism, Equality, and Fraternity in Cohen's Critique of Rawls," *Journal of Political Philosophy* 6 (1998) 99–112; and Andrew Williams, "Incentives, Inequality, and Publicity," *Philosophy and Public Affairs* 27 (Summer 1998) 225–47.

Ideas of Justice 179

way in which they may be grounded is by virtue of principles of distributive justice (although this is not the only way to ground these allocations – some nonjustice-based principle of utility may govern allocations).

Additionally, if one component of corrective justice is a duty of care owed by each to all others, then what it is each must care for will be determined by the principles of distributive justice. Most principles of distributive justice presume some *currency* of distributive justice, that is, some list of what is to be distributed (primary goods, welfare, opportunity, resources, etc.), even if this list is a product of overlapping consensus. This, in turn, determines the minimal domain of objects for which we all have a duty of care and, in turn, a corrective justice grounded duty of repair if we cause harm to those objects.[41]

Ultimately, even if a theory of distributive justice is minimalistic in the sense that it does not specify what is to be distributed, theories of distributive justice are, in a deep way, static: They do not contain principles stipulating how to respond to changes in allocation; they only contain principles stipulating how to allocate goods in a society, that is, how to organize society (and so contain principles stipulating how to respond to changes in the overall amount of goods available for distribution).

Because principles of distributive justice are realized via institutional technologies, they treat as given some account of human nature. For it is presumed that all that is needed are the appropriate institutional technologies that can generate and sustain a proper distribution of goods.[42] These technologies are presumed not to be impossible to construct and maintain. Thus, there is both a distinctively non-Manichean character to principles of distributive justice – in the sense that there is no Evil threatening the Good, but instead regular humans living morally nuanced lives – and a very "scientific" character to distributive justice – in the sense that institutional technology is what we rely on to create the just order.

So, when Rawls argues that his theory of distributive justice is an "ideal theory," he is not claiming that his theory presumes some societies are full of fantastical human-looking organisms capable of heretofore-unseen feats of altruism. Rather, as Rawls explains in *Law of Peoples*, an ideal theory is a theory of a "realistic utopia" in that, following Rousseau, the theory requires no more than "taking men as they are" (that is the realism) but "laws as they might be" (and that is the utopianism), where the latter – laws as they might be – is just another way of referring to institutional

---

[41] It would be very odd if we had a duty to care for that which is simply not valuable, and, it would be very odd if retributive justice required punishment for actions that had no effect on anyone's interests or that did not affect anything valuable. This does not rule out, by the way, some form of interaction between corrective and distributive justice such that the value of the distributive shares is partially shaped by the regime of corrective justice. Interaction does not signal sameness.

[42] For a powerfully put dissenting view, see G. A. Cohen, *Rescuing Justice and Equality* (Cambridge, MA: Harvard University Press, 2008).

technologies.[43] Thus, Rawls explicitly identifies the project of constructing ideal theories of justice with the utopian form, with Plato's *Republic*, or Thomas More's travelogue to Utopia, or with Dante's *Paradiso*, but also with science fiction, which takes "men as they are" but "technology as it might be."[44]

Three central features of the utopian literary form are the presumption of a reasonably stable human nature, the imagination of a complete and technologically possible sociopolitical space, and the anonymity of those who inhabit that space. An illustrative example of this is Frtiz Lang's great film *Metropolis*, and in particular the city that it imagines. Plot points aside (and we can do this because the plot of the film is not its only or even its primary narrative), the city of *Metropolis* is a filmic representation of a certain distributive scheme: the blessed few at the top of the city and the miserable thrown together at the bottom, with certain principles governing who gets the spoils of the labors of the many. There is no need to meet the main character, Freder Frederson, or to understand the Oedipal drama being played out between him and his father to appreciate the political significance of the city itself.[45] This is to be contrasted with aforementioned police procedural, *The Naked City*, which does not imagine an alternative space but instead explicitly locates itself in a space – New York City – whose characteristics, the director notes in his magisterial narration, are established by factors entirely external to the narrative itself. The imaginative project of *The Naked City* is, in short, profoundly limited. The imaginative project of *Metropolis*, on the other hand, is extraordinarily ambitious. The film aims to represent any entire society as an alternative to the existing one. The story of *Metropolis* can be understood as an imaginative snapshot of an entire (and entirely invented) city. We can, from the vantage point of the film, possess the eponymous Metropolis in our imagination. On the other hand, from the vantage point of *The Naked City*, New York City possesses our imagination, and the drama unfolds within those confines.

The upshot of this is that implicit in principles of distributive justice is the imagination of a complete space. It is a static and anonymous space – one with characters that lack what Frederic Jameson called "concrete existential density"[46] – but it is

[43] For Rawls, see John Rawls, *Law of Peoples* (Cambridge, MA: Harvard University Press, 1999), 11. For Rousseau, see Jean-Jacques Rousseau, *On The Social Contract*, Donald Cress, trans. (Indianapolis, IN: Hackett, 1988) 17.

[44] Contrast this with fantasy fiction such as the *Lord of the Rings* trilogy or the *Harry Potter* series, which both focus on the possible differences in the biological order (hobbits, dwarfs, dragons, and wizards all being different *biological* categories), while presuming a retrograde technological state of affairs. My comments here draw from Frederic Jameson, *Archaeologies of the Future: The Desire Called Utopia and Other Science Fictions* (New York: Verso, 2005).

[45] The ultimate aim of the film is primarily to articulate a vision of a community governed by a kind of Christianity-inflected socialism – one that bears a striking resemblance to Fascist ideology of the time. Thus, it fits quite squarely within the utopian form of narrative.

[46] Frederic Jameson, "The Politics of Utopia," *The New Left Review* 25 (January–February 2005) 35–54, 39.

Ideas of Justice

nonetheless complete and completely ordered. We can also see that distributive justice is atemporal. Distributive justice offers principles that fix allocation and the relationships between fixed allocations. Principles of distributive justice, however, cannot guide responses either to misallocations or to changes in the relationships between fixed allocations. Distributive justice points to where we must go – the city on the hill, the promised land, the utopian island – but it does not imagine where we were before, much less imagine a route that would take us from here to there, or even how to stay there if we ever arrived. In a slogan, principles of distributive justice tell us what the sunken treasure is, but do not provide the map to that treasure.

In light of this line of thinking, we must reject the attempts by some to unify distributive and corrective justice.[47] There is a distinct difference in the narrative forms most apt for each. Corrective justice gives us the bare bones of a CDS with a beginning, a middle, and an end, along with distinct characters playing canonical roles in the CDS. Distributive justice, on the other hand, makes no sense as a CDS but instead can be understood only in terms of the utopian narrative. Distributive justice is a theory of place, that is, a description of a settled allocation, and not a theory of transit, that is, an account of how to get from one allocation to another. Retributive justice and corrective justice, on the other hand, are theories of transit, that is, theories articulating the movement from one allocation to another. This is not to say that theories of retributive justice and corrective justice are insulated from distributional concerns – as already mentioned, they take as a given background *some* allocation, and perhaps a metaprinciple applying to each of these two forms of justice is that the background allocation must meet some minimum standard of justice; however, neither retributive justice nor corrective justice is *hived off* from distributive justice. These three forms of justice are qualitatively distinct, and we can see that quite naturally when we understand justice in terms of their narrative form.

Transitional Justice

In 1994, more than 800,000 Tutsis and moderate Hutus were murdered in an organized genocide led by a group called "Hutu Power." This genocide, like the Nazi genocide of Jews and the Khmer Rouge's genocide of the Cambodian community, was an organized massacre. It was not an accident. Philip Gourevitch, a journalist who has written extensively on the Rawandan genocide, writes,

> Genocide, after all, is an exercise in community building. A vigorous totalitarian order requires that the people be invested in the leaders' schemes, and while genocide may be the most perverse and ambitious means to this end, it is also the most comprehensive . . . the genocide [in Rwanda] was a product of order,

---

[47] For more, see Jules Coleman and Arthur Ripstein, "Mischief and Misfortune."

authoritarianism, decades of modern political theorizing and indoctrination, and one of the most meticulously administered states in history.[48]

The problem of responding to totalitarian regimes and genocide is the problem of *transitional justice*.

How do we respond to these atrocities? Do we follow the model of retributive and corrective justice and take as unchangeable givens the political, economic, and social structures as they happen to be postatrocity? Do we hunt down the perpetrators and put them on trial, thereby bringing the story to a close? Is this just *The Naked City* writ large? Or do we identify some reallocation that can repair the loss of the families of the murdered hundreds of thousands? Dragging political leaders to court might satisfy some norm of retributive justice, and paying out monetary reparations might give survivors a chance to cobble together a life after the genocide. However, as Gourevitch writes, genocide has profound effects that reveal these responses to be tragically incomplete:

> Hutu Power's crime was much greater than the murder of nearly a million people. Nobody in Rwanda escaped direct physical or psychic damage. The terror was designed to be total and enduring, a legacy to leave Rwandans spinning and disoriented in the slipstream of their memories for a very long time to come, and in that it was successful.[49]

Trials and corrective justice-based reparations reorient people one by one. They are, by design, not systematic. Therefore, there is no obvious reason to believe, as the legal scholar Ruti Teitel notes some believe, "[post-atrocity] trials operate not solely or even primarily for retribution but, rather, to effect change to end conflict and to bring about reconciliation."[50] Trials – at least the kinds of trials associated with retributive and corrective justice – are, by their very nature, technical, drawn-out, and better if less prone to spectacle. If trials are going to be the sorts of things that "effect change to end conflict and to bring about reconciliation," then they would have to be spectacular and systematic, that is, the sorts of things that can shape the perspectives and attitudes of everyone in the community and not just of those who happen to be directly involved in the trial. Trials of this sort always risk trending toward what Leon Trotsky dubbed a "Thermidorian degeneration" in which a reverse purge occurs and the streets once again end up flowing with blood, albeit not at the level of a genocide. Even if the trials do not degenerate into a White Terror, repairing wrongs and compensating losses can, when the background allocation is deeply unjust, involve wronging others in deeply profound ways, thereby perpetuating the cycle of

---

[48] Philip Gourevitch, *We Wish to Inform You That Tomorrow We Will Be Killed With Our Families* (New York: Picador, 1999) 95.

[49] Ibid., 224.

[50] Ruti Teitel, "The Law and Politics of Contemporary Transitional Justice," *Cornell International Law Journal* 38 (2005) 857.

Ideas of Justice
183

injustice. Thus, if we reflect on the previous discussion about revenge, we can conclude that, although it is natural to associate transitional justice with the various trials and purges that have erupted in response to totalitarian and murderous upheavals, it is hard to see how such practices, however legalistic, amount to forms of justice instead of forms of revenge.[51] Here Trotsky's worry about Thermidorian degeneration cuts deeply: we must have a theory of what it would be to have morally successful trials and purges, that is, trials and purges that were just and not simply cathartic for those who have managed to survive and to have come to power after the genocide.

The roots of transitional justice are firmly located in the Nuremberg Trials of 1945, and this strongly suggests that transitional justice has at its core a kernel of retributive justice, but for really, really awful crimes.[52] As just argued, however, this seems unlikely. The transition from Nazism to a post-Nazi Germany did not occur as a result of a (relatively) brief trial, a few hangings, and Herman Göring's suicide. That the story ends there, which is what we would expect given our reflections on the narrative form of retributive justice, turns out not to have been the case in any way. The moral sickness of the Nazi regime was not cured upon the deaths of those who infected German society. In particular, the conditions that allowed the Nazis to take power cannot be summarized in terms of particular wrongs committed at particular historical points prior to which there were *no* wrongs. Rather, the social order prior to the rise of the Nazis suffered from deep systematic ills. There was, consequently, no acceptable state of affairs that the Nazis disrupted or, concomitantly, that acts discharging the demands of retributive justice or corrective justice could have reestablished. It takes generations of reflection and struggle to achieve a complete restructuring of a society in which genocide and totalitarianism has reigned – reparations and memorializations dedicated to those who suffered are simply not enough for any genuine form of *societal transition* to occur. Transitional justice, it seems, requires something more than a trial and a sentencing or a repairing of harms: it requires the *reimagination of a society* that has been grotesquely transformed by genocide and totalitarianism.

So, is transitional justice more like distributive justice? According to many views, it is. On these views, what a theory of transitional justice describes is an ideal situation in which men are as they are and the law is as it might be. Thus, we are invited to imagine, for example, a Rwanda in which human rights are respected and the rule of law predominates. How we achieve this end depends upon the particular conditions of the wrongs that were committed: in South Africa, it is through Truth and Reconciliation commissions; in the Balkans, it is through international criminal courts; in Germany, it is through reparations, communal introspection, support for

---

[51] See Jon Elster, *Closing the Books: Transitional Justice in Historical Perspective* (New York: Cambridge University Press, 2004).

[52] See Teitel, "The Law and Politics of Contemporary Transitional Justice."

Israel, and strict rules governing hate speech. However, these routes are not specified by transitional justice; only the endpoint is (whatever that endpoint might be). What determines the routes is entirely a matter of the contingent historical conditions of the community in which the atrocities occurred and the atrocities themselves.

On this view, transitional justice is to be understood primarily as articulating what a just state of affairs following from a disastrous history would look like. The specific characters involved in the historical injustices are, in some sense, irrelevant to the project. We might imagine, for example, a norm of transitional justice requiring that those who were at one point at each other's throats achieve some form of reconciliation (which itself would have to be theorized!). The aim of truth and reconciliation commissions, for example, is not retributive justice (after all, most truth and reconciliation commissions grant some form of immunity to most of those who testify) but to reveal the truth of hidden crimes and then achieve reconciliation within the community.[53] Others might believe that the aim of transitional justice is for newly "liberated" states or communities to repossess the sources of economic power that lay in the hands of wrongdoers. We could imagine a norm requiring expropriation or nationalization to respond to past injustice, thereby making a norm requiring recognition of social and economic rights a central component of transitional justice. Two theorists of transitions from African colonialism to liberation describe this norm when they write, "[there] must be a new beginning toward the restructuring of African societies on the basis of economic equality and social justice."[54] The reason why is not to rectify some wrong, but to establish a kind of stable political order given the rather broad-gauge rage of the descendants of the colonized. Thus, the theorists write, "[it] would be unwise for Western students of Africa to underestimate the lingering sense of outrage at the heritage of exploitation and inequality."[55] That those in power in the West today instigated or supported and that many of the Africans alive today did not suffer under the colonial experience is unimportant here. What is important is that the vestiges of colonialism remain and the conditions produced by these vestiges fall afoul of the norms of transitional justice. Thus, what transitional justice requires is full transformation, by whatever contingently available means, into a state shaped by contemporary norms of sovereignty, democracy, the rule of law, and the international human rights regime and that no longer bears the horrid scars of European colonialism.[56]

---

[53] For more on the tension between reconciliation and justice, see the essays collected in Robert I. Rotberg and Dennis Thompson, *Truth V. Justice: The Morality of Truth Commissions* (Princeton, NJ: Princeton University Press, 2000).

[54] Prosser Gifford and William Roger Lewis, "Introduction," in Prosser Gifford and William Roger Lewis, eds. *Decolonization and African Independence: Transfers of Power, 1960–1980* (New Haven: Yale University Press, 1988).

[55] Ibid., xxv.

[56] See, e.g., A. James McAdams, ed., *Transitional Justice and the Rule of Law in New Democracies* (Notre Dame: University of Notre Dame Press, 1997).

Ideas of Justice 185

And yet this seems to miss something deeply significant about the kinds of histor-ical events that are governed by transitional justice. These are not merely objection-able politically and morally prescribed orders. They are profound *disruptions*. These disruptions are temporal and they involve discrete and fully formed characters. After all, particular individuals committed identifiable wrongs that were truly horrifying. Some form of targeted response is surely morally apt – would it not be a travesty of justice for those who committed these wrongs to escape punishment? Furthermore, there is also a definite need for closure – the kind of "closing of the book" that allows people not merely to be productive but to "have the lives back." At this point we might consider the words of Bruno Schulz, a Polish author and illustrator:

> Ordinary facts are arranged within time, strung along as on a thread. There they have their antecedents and their consequences, which crowd tightly together and press hard one upon another without any pause... Yet what is to be done with events that have no place of their own in time... events that have been left in the cold, unregistered, hanging in the air, errant and homeless?[57]

The atrocities – the mass public murdering, the rapes, the torturing – have left their deep impressions on the lives of those who experienced them. If the events are not incorporated both into the histories of the people who have committed and suffered these atrocities and into the collective understanding of the society in which the atrocities were committed, then the awful series of events is "left in the cold, unregistered, hanging in the air..." And what do people do with searing pains that they cannot integrate into the narratives of their lives? This is where Gourevitch's comment that genocide can leave people "spinning and disoriented in the slipstream of their memories" strongly suggests that prosecutions, purges, and truth commissions have their place in transitional justice. Justice that fits some kind of traditional "plotted" narrative form is appropriate here because it is how people can "replot" their lives, making sense of these atrocities without ceasing to make sense of themselves.[58]

We must also reckon with the systematicity of genocides and totalitarian regimes. For genocide and totalitarianism create society-wide disasters that rip any sense of control over one's community out of one's hand. Some systematic form of collective reclamation is necessary to overcome the consequences of this vast moral tumult. There is a poor fit between individual trials occurring here and there and the kind of ambitious reimagining of a society that is required to overcome the profound disorientation and dislocation associated with postgenocidal and posttotalitarian conditions. The required systematic reimagination itself requires the capacity to see

---

[57] Bruno Schulz, *Sanatorium Under the Sign of the Hourglass*, translated by Celina Wieniewska (New York City: Mariner Books, 1977), p 200.

[58] For more, see Mark Freeman, *Truth Commissions and Procedural Fairness* (Cambridge: Cambridge University Press, 2006).

oneself as part of a moral order again – to see oneself as motivated by moral ideals and not merely as trapped in another iteration of another epicycle of revenge and flight from revenge – and this new moral order is not something that existed prior to the atrocities. The kind of society-wide reimagination required here is actually hindered by individual, catch-as-catch-can trials, reallocations of stolen goods from one individual to another, and other individualized reparations. These procedures do not provide the opportunity to ascend above one's community – to achieve the aerial perspective – so that one may see oneself as a member of a community governed by systematic principles of justice. A series of trials and reparations alone would still allow the atrocities to possess the imaginations of those who suffered them, instead of facilitating the reappropriation of the moral and political sphere by the imaginations of the victims of genocide.

Given this fact, it seems that the principles of transitional justice would best be captured by the utopian story form. For those "spinning and disoriented in the slipstream of their memories for a very long time to come" to reorient themselves as members of just society, the citizens must repossess their political imaginations, that is, they must repossess their capacity to imagine their society as organized in a variety of different ways according to a variety of different moral and political ideals with which they can identify. What has been ruptured and scrambled is society itself, so the members of the society cannot take as *given* the existing background against which criminal trials aiming at retributive justice or civil trials that resolve tort claims proceed. In short, if there is ever a moment when the practical imagining a complete society is the appropriate thing to do, it is after systematic atrocities associated with totalitarianism and genocide. Those who suffered, those who committed the wrongs, and those who stood by and did nothing must realize their capacity to imagine a new political and social order in which they see themselves living lives that are not rent by systematic wrongdoing but are instead ordered by moral and political norms expressed by some principle of transitional justice. Thus, the narrative required is not a temporal one that has closure as its aim, but instead the god's-eye, static narrative characteristic of distributive justice.[59]

We can therefore see that there is a deep tension in transitional justice: on the one hand, it seems to cry out for the closed, temporal narratives of retributive justice; on the other hand, this seems too simplistic, too limited in scope, and the requirement for some more deeply systematic response to systematic atrocity suggests an approach more akin to the method used by theorists of distributive justice. This deep tension may explain why theorizing about transitional justice is so fraught:

---

[59] Thus, we should expect anyone to accept norms of transitional justice that overrode human rights norms (e.g., norms that allowed for vicious revenge) or norms that allowed for the construction of a regime that failed to be governed by the rule of law. What seems required by transitional justice is the imagination of something more like More's fantastic Utopia or Rousseau's impossible Social Contract.

Ideas of Justice 187

those who view themselves as working through these problems cannot agree upon a single way to understand the issue. In this section, I have diagnosed the philosophical underpinnings of this disagreement, namely (to put it far too simplistically) that on the one hand we understand the warranted response in terms of a traditional CDS, and on the other hand we understand the warranted response as a utopian project. A further and perhaps even more serious problem that emerges is that transitional justice begins to sound like some ugly hybrid of the three forms of justice already discussed. Is there really a distinctive norm of transitional justice?

Conversely, perhaps what this most clearly reveals is that a renewed imaginative effort on the part of political theorists is called for. The fantastical political stories that characterized Plato's reflections on justice, More's imagination of Utopia, Rousseau's Social Contract, Marx's inchoate theory of human emancipation, and Rawls' theory of justice all are characterized by their imaginative inventiveness. Although yoked to certain "scientific" conceptions of the human (in particular, to certain conceptions of human psychology), these theories provide us with systematic fantasies of justice that can serve as political ideals. The ideals can be achieved through institutional technologies operating on our stable human nature (e.g., constitutions that can create stable governments even from the materials of the crooked timber of humanity). The danger of Thermidorian excesses notwithstanding, our current efforts to face up to some of the darkest human practices – genocide and totalitarianism, for example – may require a radical form of political and narrative invention, namely an invention that synthesizes temporal and geographical narratives in a single form of justice.[60]

Conclusion

In this chapter, I have attempted to give the reader an overview of four forms of justice that play central roles in much of our legal theorizing. My aim has been to offer a new approach to thinking about justice, namely in terms of different narrative forms. Hopefully, this allows us to think more creatively when attempting to articulate principles of justice and resolve problems of justice even if it may not assist us in the analytic project of defending principles of justice. So, while I have not attempted to demonstrate that this is the sole or even the best way to understand different forms of justice, I do hope that it has allowed us to gain some insights into the deeper structure of these different concepts of justice.

---

[60] The following comment by Frederic Jameson is therefore quite apt: "It seems easier to imagine the thoroughgoing deterioration of the earth and of nature than the breakdown of late capitalism; perhaps that is due to some weakness in our imaginations." Frederic Jameson, *The Seeds of Time* (New York City: Columbia University Press, 1994), p xii.

7

Postmodern Justice

Peter Goodrich

Justice and the postmodern share the paradoxical quality of being unsusceptible to easy definition. Justice has the edge in terms of length of history and diffusion of uses and is second only to time as an intractably venerable object of conceptual elaboration. It is indeed often defined by reference to what it is not, its lack, the instance of injustice but then an ambiguous prefix has already complicated the plurality of definitions beyond any easy etymological or legislative redemption. The postmodern shares the problem of the prefix if not that of the stature and duration of the aporia of meaning.

The postmodern bears an amusingly ludic if not virtually unintelligible prefix. That is to say, on the one hand, that the prefix is post, the before is after, and on the other hand, and with equal obscurity the post here precedes the modern. As the modern is by most definitions that which is contemporary, here, now, and new, it is hard to make sense of a prefix that suggests a novelty that exceeds the modern. The quarrel between the ancients and the moderns, between the pre and the post, is thus here complicated not only through the contemporary context of culture wars but also by dint of the notion of an antiquity that comes after the modern.[1] To this it has to be added that the postmodern is used to qualify an already chimerical justice. It is evident that much of the following discussion of the neologism must be devoted to grounding this frequently polemical and sometimes playful conceptual cluster in the unlikely confines of legal philosophy.

Proceeding in lexical if not necessarily logical order, I will begin with the postmodern and address its seemingly viral progress through the disciplines, from architecture to law. Grounding a term such as the postmodern in its relevant discursive context

---

[1] See Joan DeJean, *Ancients Against Moderns: Culture Wars and the Making of the Fin de Siècle* (Chicago: Chicago University Press, 1997). For further, gloriously scholarly, admirably amusing, and ineffably timeless digressions on this theme, pointing out that the moderns are chronologically older than the ancients, see Robert Merton, *On the Shoulders of Giants: A Shandean Postscript* (New York: Harcourt, Brace, Jovanovich, 1985).

Postmodern Justice

already suggests an architectural trope in that to ground a discussion or proposition, category or term, is to lay foundations, and to address questions of structure and construction. To ground the postmodern thus connotes building a concept, constructing a trajectory, erecting a meaning brick by brick, room by room, or proposition by proposition. It also suggests that the word be used properly, that justice be done to the postmodern quite as much as the postmodern be allowed to render justice. The postmodern can here be made into the *mot juste*, meaning the appropriate word, the fitting term, the fair description for a justice that otherwise lacks definition or is bereft of any obvious relevance to law. The architectural thus grounds in the same sense that *nomos* or division grounds and appropriates, and it is in this sense that I will follow the disciplinary trajectory of the postmodern into its limited yet critical impact on law. Here it is very much a question of the interdisciplinary, of nonlegal texts, of literary and philosophical manifestations of the postmodern emerging and impacting law at that point where the legal institution has always been most vulnerable, namely in its image and practice of justice.

The Edifice Complex[2]

The roots of the postmodern, of the exhaustion, passage, or rupture of the modern have been canvassed and mapped by many.[3] The modern was from its beginning pregnant with its contrary. It has always contained within itself the seeds of its own disruption or fissure and thus from Marx onward it has been recognized, reluctantly or with alacrity, that modernity, understood here as industrial society, carries within it the seeds of its own destruction or at least supersession. The white heat of industrial production uprooted communities, disordered relations, and laid waste to the environment on an unimagined scale, leading Marx in the *Communist Manifesto* to foresee a future in which "All fixed, fast-frozen relations, with their train of ancient and venerable prejudices and opinions are swept away, all new formed ones become antiquated before they can ossify. All that is solid melts into air, all that is holy is profaned."[4] Written into modernity, expressed through political revolt

---

[2] This fine coinage is taken from the excellent Mark Wigley, *The Architecture of Deconstruction: Derrida's Haunt* (Boston: MIT Press, 1993).

[3] The most systematic history is Perry Anderson, *The Origins of Postmodernity* (London: Verso, 1998); to which should be added Frederic Jameson, *Postmodernism, or, the Cultural Logic of Late Capitalism* (London: Verso, 1991); and David Harvey, *The Condition of Postmodernity* (Oxford: Blackwell, 1990). Hal Foster, ed. *Postmodern Culture* (San Francisco: Bay Books, 1983), and Mike Featherstone, ed. *Postmodernism* (London: Sage, 1988) were two of the more influential collections of essays.

[4] In Robert Tucker, ed. *Marx and Engels Reader* (1978) at 475. This text and its implications are brilliantly dissected in Marshall Berman, *All That is Solid Melts into Air: The Experience of Modernity* (New York: Verso, 1982). A similar impetus can be discerned in David Graebar, *Fragments of an Anarchist Anthropology* (Chicago: Prickly Paradigm, 2003). In law, there was Zen Bankowski and Geoff Mungham, *Images of Law* (London: Routledge, 1976).

or artistic resistance, are multiple signs of its limits or lacuna. Thus for historians, the postmodern is simply a label that captures a sense of the destructive and so also creative power of the modern; it claims as its adherents *avant la lettre* not simply the Marxist avant garde, the Maoist cultural revolutionaries, but also Nietzsche, Rimbaud, Dada, situationism, the cinematic *nouvelle vague*, punk rock, relational aesthetics – make your own list – all the way to the contemporary antiglobalization movements ending, for example, with the clandestine insurgent rebel clown army.[5]

Modernity represented a seismic change, a material revolution that gained a fairly direct expression in artistic disorientation and reactive innovation, in an aesthetic radicalism, and a sense of homelessness or in Freud's terms the uncanny. The notion that "all that is solid melts into air" is both liberating and threatening but however viewed, it allows us an initial observation that the postmodern as it increasingly came to be labeled in the late 1970s represented a revolt within modernism, a radical or reactive political attempt to understand and reform the excesses of the modern mode of production. Put it like this: The roots of the postmodern are material and concrete. Exploitation, pollution, dislocation, loss of faith, inequality, and injustice are some of the more obvious themes of aesthetic postmodernism and these address the foundations or substantial ground upon which the modern tradition is built. The architectural metaphor is not accidental. The postmodern is a new form of bricolage or building technique; it expresses a visceral sense of no longer feeling at "home"; it questions "solidity"; challenges the "monumental" character of the modern tradition; lays bare the myth of "foundations"; and obliterates all sense of preordained system and structure.

Long before Kant's architectonic of thought, architecture provided the linguistic structure of the disciplines. Memory is a house, rhetoric a storehouse, history a building, or in Benjamin's depiction, a wreckage of things. By similar token, institutions are, in origin, things that stand, constructions, structures. All of which is to point to a linguistic and historical coincidence of architecture and truth, of edifice and law. Building is the materiality of the social, the most visible form of collective presence, its most evident or demonstrative meaning, its permanent and impermeable presence. It is no coincidence that the earliest laws were inscribed on tablets of stone, being literally and metaphorically building blocks, foundation stones. An early common law source depicts the law, the origin of honor, in a prefatory poem in the following image: "A court stāds twixt heavē and erth, al gorgeous to behold/of royal ftate, in fecond fphere, a hugie building olde."[6] Similarly, as Kafka's parable *Before the Law* famously illustrates, to get to law, at least in his literary and legal

---

[5] See David Graebar, 'The New Anarchists' 13 *New Left Review* 66 (2002). There is also brief discussion in Simon Critchley, *Infinitely Demanding: Ethics of Commitment and Politics of Resistance* (London: Verso, 2007).

[6] Richard Bosewell, *Workes of Armorie* (London: Totell, 1672) fol C iii r.

Postmodern Justice

interpretation, you have to pass through architecture, go through the gate, and enter the building.[7] The image is in fact premodern in its roots, in that the gate is a classical emblem of legality, and Janus, the deity of gates and transitions, was early on claimed, most explicitly by the Renaissance lawyer and antiquary John Selden, as the emblem and figure of common law.[8]

The premodern reemerged in the postmodern, and the postmodern emerged long before it gained any significant recognition as a radical token or political slogan. Although the term postmodernism had been used sporadically by literary critics and historians long before the advent of postmodernism as a cultural phenomenon in the late 1970s, it is to the latter era that the term now usually refers. The postmodern emerged first in the critique of modernist architecture and most immediately as a reaction against the functional brutalism of 1960s projects. The first glimpses of such a critique of the unity and conformism of modern monoliths came in Robert Venturi's early excoriation of Corbusier, of his "modernolatry" as Berman coins it, but gained its major statement in a later project and subsequent book, *Learning from Las Vegas*, a surprising paean of praise to the Las Vegas strip as the archetype of the architecture to come.[9]

Architectural modernism sought to break with history and the past in the name of unity, the beauty of function, and rational essence. Thus, for example, Le Corbusier dictated that the modern building should be "a unity [which] expresses the same law throughout."[10] An interior reason, the dictate of function, produces the exterior. The immanent principle of modernist buildings sharply separated interior and exterior, structure and ornament, and form and expression. Against this, and without repeating the myriad synoptic and argumentative histories, Venturi and his associates proposed an inversion of modernism, a celebration of diversity of form, contradiction in styles, the appreciation of ornament and symbol, hoarding and sign, the outside and visible over interior function or legal form. Thus, as Jencks puts it, "Modern architecture died in St. Louis, Missouri on June 15, 1972 at 3.15 pm."[11] This was the moment when an infamous housing project was dynamited after millions of dollars had been

---

[7] Jacques Derrida, 'Préjugés. Devant la loi,' in Jean-Francois Lyotard ed. *La Faculté de juger* (Paris: Minuit, 1985) analyzes Kafka's parable at length in terms of the meaning of the before of law: what does the peasant stand in front of? What does the peasant stand before?

[8] Thus John Selden, *Jani Anglorum facies altera* [1614], this history of English law is translated in 1683 under the title *The Reverse or Back-Face of the English Janus* by one Edmond Westcot (London: Basset, 1683).

[9] The first work was Robert Venturi, *Complexity and Contradiction in Architecture* (New York: MOMA, 1966). Robert Venturi, Denise Scott Brown, Steven Izenour, *Learning from Las Vegas* was published originally in 1972 and then in a popular, shortened and revised version in 1977. The other key text for the crossover of postmodern themes from architecture to the humanities was Charles Jencks, *The Language of Post-Modern Architecture* [1977] (4th ed., New York: Rizzoli, 1984).

[10] Henri le Corbusier, *Towards a New Architecture* [1920] (London: Rodker, 1927) at 79.

[11] Jenks, *Post-Modern Architecture*, op. cit. at 9. For discussion, see Steven Connor, *Postmodernist Culture: An Introduction to Theories of the Contemporary* (Oxford: Blackwell, 1989) ch 3.

192   **Peter Goodrich**

sunk unsuccessfully into "improvements" aimed at repairing the vandalism, erasing the graffiti and appeasing the complaints of its unhappy inhabitants.[12]

For the postmodernists, the significance of this architectural moment, the demolition of a purely functional housing monolith, lies precisely in the precedent signs of resistance to it, in the vandalism, the graffiti, the signs of inhabitation, and rebellion, ephemeral and superficial though they might at first seem. The postmodern concern, expressed first in architecture, was a desire to implode the unitary, the monolithic, the totalizing reason, the totalitarian truth, in whatever form it appeared. This radical and seemingly destructive project in fact had thoroughly constructive humanistic roots. Venturi, by contrast to his critics, began rather with the contradictory and plural nature of the extant strip: "Learning from the existing landscape is a way of being revolutionary for an architect."[13] So starts *Learning from Las Vegas*, with an almost deconstructive attention to detail, to what is there, to reading and through intensive scrutiny of surfaces – textual, mural, or monumental – learning to question how we see things and what they mean.

Learning from Las Vegas is a celebration of surfaces, of their complexity, their references, and their significations. What makes Las Vegas an archetype in Venturi's eyes is that it is so extreme, all hoarding, billboard, signs: "The little low buildings, gray-brown like the desert, separate and recede from the street that is now the highway, their false fronts disengaged and turned perpendicular to the highway as big, high signs. If you take the signs away, there is no place there."[14] For Venturi, the building is first and foremost a sign, an agglomeration of mixed media, "words, pictures, and sculpture [used] to persuade and inform."[15] The lesson then is to pay close attention, expend hermeneutic skill upon reading the built environment, the monumental city, the writing in stone, or brick, or plaster board, hoarding and now digital screen.

"Yale professor praises strip for $8,925," declaimed the local paper when Venturi's project first arrived in Las Vegas.[16] In fact he was never paid anything but he did praise the strip and drew postmodern pedagogy from it. His method was simple and can be gleaned from two basic principles. First, "We shall emphasize image – image over process or form – in asserting that architecture depends in its perception and creation on past experience and emotional association and that these symbolic and representational elements may often be contradictory to the form, structure,

---

[12] On the social semiotics of graffiti, see Alison Young, *Judging the Image: Art, Value, Law* (London: Routledge, 2005) who concludes her analysis with the suggestion that "when the question is raised, 'who wrote this graffiti?' we should answer, 'no-one; the city is writing itself.'"

[13] Venturi et al., *Learning*, at 3.

[14] Venturi et al., *Learning*, at 18.

[15] Venturi et al., *Learning*, at 52, and continuing to observe: "A sign is, contradictorily, for day and night. The same sign works as polychrome sculpture in the sun and as black silhouette against the sun; at night it is a source of light. It revolves by day and becomes a play of lights at night."

[16] Venturi et al., *Learning*, at xii.

Postmodern Justice

and program with which they combine in the same building."[17] Second, and as an elaboration of the first principle, the symbol takes priority, the sign comes to submerge, distort, and define the structure: "We shall argue for the symbolism of the ugly and ordinary in architecture and for the particular significance of the decorated shed with a rhetorical front."[18] The Long Island Duckling, a duck-shaped drive-in, became the exemplar of symbolism taking over structure, and elsewhere in the tour praise is lavished on the Leaning Tower of Pizza, Caesar's Palace, Aladin's Casino, the Golden Nugget, Stardust, and more. Their diversity of styles, eclecticism of borrowings, frivolous appliqué ornament and syncretism of reference, are compared with alacrity to a modern architecture that has become "a dry expressionism, empty and boring – and in the end irresponsible."

If modernism privileged the building over its inhabitants, the postmodern resistance aimed to take the building back, to take responsibility for the inhabitants and to pay attention to the plethora and plenitude of what and who are there. Alternately playful and rebellious, ethical and irreverent, the mood and sometimes shocking tone of postmodern explorations, its buildings, texts, and works of art, should not distract attention from a set of relatively simple principles of its critical stance, not least because, as Bauman has put it, the postmodern in the end "purports to capture and articulate the novel experience of just one, but crucial social category of contemporary society: the intellectuals."[19] Postmodernism as a movement, as the expression of a playfully serious architectural, aesthetic, and then academic rebellion, was a breaking free of institutional constraints, whether expressed in terms of the demands of structural form, Enlightenment reason, legal dogmatics, or vulgar, which is to say economist Marxism.

Returning to Venturi's classic text, the starting point is surface and not depth, the apparent rather than some unitary and tyrannical totality, reality, or truth. The philosopher Lyotard perhaps formulated this best in terms of the demise of grand narratives, terrorizing truths, and unitary reason: "Let us wage war on totality; let us be witnesses to the unrepresentable; let us activate the differences and save the honor of the name."[20] The consequences of this position are diverse and extensive. Staying with Venturi's version of the project, grounded in the materiality of architecture and the reality of the strip, the postmodern signals a turn to interpretation – to rhetoric

---

[17] Venturi et al., *Learning*, at 89.

[18] Venturi et al., *Learning*, at 90.

[19] Zygmunt Bauman, 'Is There a Postmodern Sociology?' 5 *Theory, Culture, and Society* (1988) at 217. This point is made at much greater length in his classic, Bauman, *Legislators and Interpreters: On Modernity, Post-Modernity, and the Intellectuals* (Oxford: Blackwell, 1987).

[20] Jean-Francois Lyotard, *The Postmodern Condition: A Report on Knowledge* (Manchester: University of Manchester Press, 1984) 82. This passage is cited, as a "clarion" for the postmodern, in the introduction to Peter Fitzpatrick and Alan Hunt, eds., *Critical Legal Studies* (Oxford: Blackwell, 1987) at 2, save that they omit the last clause, seemingly having no desire to save the honor of the name. It probably seemed a reactionary or at least antiquated exhortation although in its context the reference is not heraldic or chauvinistic but rather historical and plural. To honor the name is to take meaning seriously.

and semiotics – and to difference understood as an ethics of responsibility. Venturi's motives were, after all, humanistic in that his concern was for the boredom and despair of the inhabitants of modernist environments. His mission was to overcome the sensation of exclusion and to find a way back in to a modern architectural reality whose exemplary structures seemed rather to erase than support their occupants.

Moving from motive to method, the paramount concern with symbolism, with the symbolic, is a concern with history. Where modernism expelled history in favor of reason, enlightenment, and truth, the postmodern ethos is historicist, pluralist, and eclectic. This means attention must be paid to a wealth of styles and plenitude of symbols available through the careful scrutiny of the past in the present. Myriad little narratives gain expression in different styles, the past lives on in multiple figures, in complex ornaments, and in the wild variety of architectural tropes and emblems. To understand Las Vegas you have to have a head for the symbolic and by the same token the postmodern is defined as much as anything else by this mixing of temporal genres and historical styles, by classical figures on modernist towers, by syncretic and syncopated fronts to buildings, by juxtaposition of styles, and by *trompe l'oeil* and infinite regress. In other words, use the plenitude of forms and figures available – Greek, Latin, Medieval, or ultramodern – as occasion and use, inhabited form require.

Historicism, with its concern for forgotten classics, lost meanings, and submerged narratives, can also provide an impetus for the second defining feature of postmodern method. As Baudrillard in particular was fond of asserting, the postmodern has a fixation with surfaces and appearances.[21] In architectural terms this means a studious attention to the visible, to images, and to the façade. There is a dual drive to this concern. First, attention to the surface defies the siren call of the depths, which call has usually been a reference to a hidden god, an invisible yet universal truth, or some other ideal that cannot be seen or properly scrutinized. Second, the lure of the depths, of the unseen, is also a coded way of preferring the absent and invisible principle to the extant and present, the living. The appeal to the depths, to the real, to a unitary principle, to a universal structure and law, serves here to mask inequity and inequality, the despair and boredom, the poverty and unhappiness of the living. The image is the human, the surface is the face, or in Levinas' terms, the "call of the other," the infinite ethical demand.[22]

The irresponsibility of the modern, the call to an ethics of the surface, an attention to, reading of, and interpretative accounting for the demand posed by the face raises now the question of injustice and institutions. Before proceeding then to the

---

[21] See generally Jean Baudrillard, *Simulacra and Simulation* [1983] (Ann Arbor: University of Michigan Press, 1994), which offers a rather moralizing critique of the simulated character of the modern. This dimension of Baudrillard's work is most explicit, and questionable, in Baudrillard, *The Evil Demon of Images* (Sydney: Power Institute, 1987).

[22] The reference is initially to Emanuel Lévinas, *Totality and Infinity* (Pittsburgh: Duquesne University Press, 1969). For recent commentary on this text and its philosophical context, see Simon Critchley, *Infinitely Demanding*, op. cit., at 56–63 in particular.

Postmodern Justice

concept of postmodern justice, a final remark about architecture, institution, and law. The irony of Venturi's work was only superficially that of inversion. It is true of course that the postmodern concern with surfaces suggests intense attention to the superficial, to the inessential, or merely apparent but that is really too easy and dismissive a reading. The concern with symbols and signs is an expression of an ethical interest in the emotional and associative qualities of inhabiting buildings, institutions, and conurbations. The concern with the surface of buildings, with facades and ornaments, statues and figures, image and expression is a qualitative interest in a fleeting yet ethically essential existential presence, that of the building's inhabitants.

What transpires to be the most interesting feature of buildings, to the postmodern eye at least, is not their structure, their atemporal and monumental juridical presence but rather the interior life of the shadows that haunt them.[23] Buildings also look, or more precisely they overlook and it is the question of how, what, and whom they overlook, the subjects that they view, survey, house, and construct, that postmodern ethics invites us to examine. The edifice complex is the belief that the structure is invariant, stable, and self-defining, a crypt if you will that houses a secret, a truth. Against this, the postmodern position is that of a destabilizing of the edifice: It is what we make it to be, a ruin, a trope, a passage, a symbol, a screen, a circus, or whatever other haunting seems to fit both civic occasion and popular need. How then is justice housed? Who feels at home in the law?

Specters of Justice

Start with a comparison. Two images of commonwealth from two different books, published in 1635 and 1651, respectively. Only sixteen years between them but two different worlds. In visual and doctrinal terms the gulf between the lawyer and poet George Wither's frontispiece to his *Collection of Emblemes* and Hobbes' better known and ironically much more emblematic frontispiece to *Leviathan* is striking and fundamental. Wither was a member of the Inns of Court, a lawyer, and his collection is thoroughly legal in its themes.[24] The emblems he uses are taken from an earlier continental work, Rollenhagen's *Nucleus emblematum* of 1611. Wither appends his own verse explanations of the emblems, in the vernacular, but adds one image of his own invention, the frontispiece representation of the kingdom ecclesiastical and civil (Figure 1). The realm is divided by two complementary axes.

---

[23] I will simply note here that for the premodern legal tradition, a human being is a shadow that haunts. See Alciatus, *De notitia dignitatum* (1651), for example, borrowing from Ovid, defines man as "incarnate mind, the spectre of time, the eye of life" (*mens incarnata, fantasma temporis, speculator vitae*) and slightly earlier as the image of law (*legis imago*).

[24] George Wither, *A Collection of Emblems Ancient and Moderne* (1635). On justice and emblems, see the highly informative Valerie Hayaert, *Mens emblematica et humanisme juridique* (2007); and on the power of the emblem, see Peter Goodrich, 'The Visual Line: On the Prehistory of Law and Film,' 49 *Parallax* 55 (2008).

Postmodern Justice

On the right the Church, with a prelate at the door and a ceremonial procession below, signifies the ecclesiastical kingdom. On the left a castle with turret and flag, evidencing the temporal realm, nature, pleasure, and love. The second axis, top and bottom of the image, are heaven and hell, an underworld and the twin peaks of a mountain reaching toward the heavens. This is the *via dolorosa* of mortal existence and the many and various pitfalls and obstacles to salvation are graphically shown. As Wither himself points out this frontispiece emblem is "hidden in mysteries," an esoteric and erudite representation of earthly distractions and heavenly promises of good and evil as they impact and permeate the realm.

The occult or simply classically informed details of Wither's frontispiece belong firmly within the Renaissance humanistic tradition. Those details cannot be examined here. There is, however, one obvious and intriguing feature to the emblem. It shows a realm that is vastly populous, teeming with people, a veritable theatre of social scenes and human endeavors. Above this crowded landscape, holding a floating orb, an angel watches over the kingdom, with book and sword, laws and arms, in right and left hand, mirroring Church and State. Compare this emblem of government then to the familiar if abstruse image of Hobbes' *Leviathan* that formed the frontispiece of the first edition of the book and latterly became a common cover image for modern editions of the work (Figure 2). The title of the book, one of the most important of all early modern philosophical treatises on the constitution and law, is overlooked by an image of the social body, or more precisely by an emblematic representation of "that great Leviathan called a Common-Wealth, or State (in Latine *Civitas*)."[25] The image is that of the crowned sovereign, sword in one hand, staff of office in the other, looming over a landscape, in the foreground of which is a cathedral and city. There is no book in evidence, no ornament of laws, just force and the legitimacy of the sacral jurisdiction. The sovereign's torso, except for the hands, as is well known, is composed entirely of his subjects, all turned away from the viewer and obediently looking toward the sovereign's face. Many are kneeling. What does this signify? The jurisprudential tradition has not, of course, spent much time analyzing this frontispiece image. It is, after all, to modern eyes, merely an image, an incidental prelude to reason and text, now generally not reproduced except as a cover picture or dust jacket illustration.[26]

The image is both striking and somewhat opaque. The sovereign rises up and dominates the landscape, his body populous and vast, whereas the kingdom, the realm surveyed, consists only of neatly placed villages, prominent churches, and then at the front and perspective point the well-ordered, indeed thoroughly regimented, geometrically proportioned city. The significant and generally overlooked

---

[25] Thomas Hobbes, *Leviathan or the Matter, Forme and Power of a Commonwealth* mens. *Ecclesiastical and Civil* (1651) introduction (typography altered).

[26] On the significance of covers, see Peter Goodrich, 'The Anatomy of Covering' (on file with the author).

Postmodern Justice

fact, visually, is that there are only buildings: the landscape and walled and castellated city are strikingly empty of people, deserted, blank.[27] For the author of the image, humanity is definitively elsewhere. The people are not even on the ground but rather swept up, aloft, in the air, as the constituent parts or members of the sovereign body, Behemoth, Juggernaut, or here, Leviathan. It is a powerful and lasting image of sovereignty as governance that stands over us, watches, and threatens an absolute judgment. The sovereign is the embodiment of law, the *corpus iuris*, father and judge, and guide and arbiter of the social. That much conforms easily to the early modern view of positive law as the dictate of the legislator, as command or threat, but it does little to explain the disparity between the architecture and its apparent emptiness.

The solution to this enigma lies in the subtitle of the book. It is a commonwealth ecclesiastical (and civil) that is portrayed and this is a premodern concept, a theological spectacle. Such an interpretation allows us to incorporate the text into the emblem, which translates as "there is no power on earth comparable to him," meaning God, and by association, his delegate, the sovereign, Leviathan. This is, in other words, an image of an invisible polity in which the only humans discernible are specters, the shadows or souls of the population caught up in the spectral body of their supreme governor, the giant or Leviathan, God on earth. In this interpretation, the physical body is of itself nothing, a mere and mortal carapace, a ghostly form encrypting an even more ghostly soul. Be that as it may, the polity is physically empty of people because the physicality of the body is not only unimportant but in fact an impediment to reason and to faith alike. What remains are the buildings, the enduring edifices, the unitary law immanent in the perfectly ordered, geometrically precise, linear array of buildings. All of which can make usefully apparent the meaning of positive law within the modern tradition that follows from Hobbes.[28]

As an image of law, the frontispiece allows a number of salient observations. Civil law is first and most obviously a territory, a ground and series of buildings. It is an architecture and because it is empty, a site of uninhabited space, the order of law evidently attaches not to persons but to buildings, to architectural communities or structures, to the *civis* understood as the city. We can borrow here from the psychoanalytic jurist Pierre Legendre the well-worked Roman notion that law "institutes life" (*instituere vitam*).[29] It is first and foremost an architectural order, an institution,

---

[27] My thanks to Thanos Zartaloudis for originally pointing this out to me and for discussing its significance. In fact, for the sake of precision, it will here be noted that there are a few solitary figures in the city, a soldier guards the castle wall, some other soldiers are marching in the main square, but they are alone, the city is empty.

[28] A theme well discussed in Anthony Carty, 'English Constitutional Law from a Postmodernist Perspective' in Peter Fitzpatrick, ed. *Dangerous Supplements: Resistance and Renewal in Jurisprudence* (London: Pluto Press, 1991).

[29] Pierre Legendre, *Sur la question dogmatique en Occident* (Paris: Fayard, 1999) 106–8.

meaning a construction, a building, a tellurian and latterly civic *nomos* contained in the very structure or ordering of the city. Note that there are plenty of Churches, numerous spires and steeples, but no obvious law courts and this not because we are not concerned in *Leviathan* with law but rather because law, being the structure and rule of the *civis*, is incorporated into all of the buildings, it is their collectivity, their interrelation, their edifice, and the path or way between them. In other words, the city is the law, and the law does not die, it is immortal, like brick and stone, like God, and like Leviathan too.

The architectural character of Hobbes, image of governance is also thoroughly modern. Leviathan is literally a monolith, a singular and absolute symbol of rule, a towering presence that stands over the realm but is not in or of it. Leviathan absorbs humanity, carries it away rather as in the Christian narrative God is ever elsewhere, *deus absconditus*, a cryptic and opaque sovereign whose kingdom is in the clouds and has in any event yet to come. That said, modern justice, and here we can borrow from one of its finest representatives, John Rawls, author of *A Theory of Justice*, is portrayed philosophically in very much the same terms as is Hobbes' Leviathan.[30] Consider the opening chapter of Rawls' magnum opus: "For us the primary subject of justice is the basic structure of society," which he qualifies as the arrangement of its "major institutions." Borrowing from Hobbes, among others, the concept of a social contract, an "original agreement," Rawls then defines this in terms of a hypothetical "original position of equality," an original position in which "the principles of justice are chosen behind a veil of ignorance."[31] The veil already suggests a religious architecture, the temple protection of the holy of holies, as well as the veil that covers the face of the married woman as a sign of purity and modesty. There is equally a suggestion of the blindfold of justice in her modern representations. Be that as it may, the ignorance, or better, blindness of these first citizen legislators erases not simply the face of the other, but all of their attributes, their voice, their body, and their soul. All that is left is edifice, structure, buildings. An uninhabited city, an empty space, *tabula rasa*, blank (censored) form.

A little more detail from Rawls' various elaborations of the original position can help accentuate the homology between the image of Leviathan and that of modern justice. Again drawing on the initial statement of what should be expected behind the veil of ignorance, before the law, it is "the symmetry of everyone's relations to each other" that is first and foremost guaranteed.[32] This symmetry, this *more geometrico* of justice, is initially that of a common ignorance. As is well known, Rawls insists that those behind the veil of ignorance do not know their place in society, class position, or social status. They do not know their fortune in terms of natural assets or

---

[30] John Rawls, *A Theory of Justice* (Oxford: Oxford University, 1972).
[31] Rawls, *Justice*, at 11 and 12, respectively. The depiction of the original position is defended briefly in Rawls, *Justice as Fairness: A Restatement* (Cambridge, MA: Harvard University Press, 2001).
[32] Rawls, *Justice*, at 12.

Postmodern Justice

abilities, intelligence, strength, and the like. Then they are also ignorant of their own psychology, "aversion to risk, or liability to optimism or pessimism." Added to that is that they do not know anything about their own society: "That is, they do not know its economic or political situation, or the level of civilization and culture it has been able to achieve."[33] In sum, the denizens of the original position inhabit a limbo, removed from both society and their own bodies – the veil of ignorance precludes knowledge of race, sex, generation, gender orientation, and drive – the veil distances and obscures both individual attributes and collective identity. Compare this image of the origin of the social, of the institutions or building blocks of the collectivity, to Hobbes, frontispiece.

Rawls' city, the neo-Kantian architecture of the social, is empty. Deserted of all human forms, a pure but blank symmetry. The citizens are elsewhere or in the image of Leviathan, they have been swept up into another space, a spectral, floating body and with their backs turned, many on their knees; they face away from the city and look to the sovereign. The subjects of Leviathan or in Rawls' case of justice, are pictured – imagined – as faceless units, integral members of a foreign – extra- or superterrestrial – body. Knowing nothing of themselves, existing as spectral forms, as hypotheses, they have no relation to each other, no conversation, and no actual amity or justice, but rather exist in the empty and weightless exigency of holding up the aerial crown or "symmetry" of justice. If we then move down the frontispiece, below the image and the title to the smaller emblematic images at the bottom of the title page of *Leviathan* the subjects are shown returned and occupying now their proper – symmetrically assigned – emblematic social places.

Under the arm that holds the sword, in descending order, are pictures of a castle, a crown, a canon, arms of war, and then a battle scene. On the other side, the left hand, under the staff is a church, a mitre, a sign of lightning flashing, a symbol of knowledge, and then a courtroom scene. Law appears here under the aegis of the Church. It is in this representation an ecclesiastical polity, a spectral or spiritual realm, before it is a secular and diurnal order. Equally to the point, the subjects return from the top to the bottom of the title page image so as to fulfill institutional roles and functions. They exist as office bearers, generic types, conforming souls fitted to the architecture of the city and the choreography of the courtroom, to the dictates of castle and cathedral, canon and norm, rather than to any more immediate and tactile human cause.

Rawls and Hobbes share a perhaps inevitable acknowledgment and accession to things as they are, to what Blackstone and the English called the "establishment," the existing institutions, extant hierarchy, and common law. Both sought to legitimate the order of things and put in place a modernist theory of the city as an architectonic, as a unitary order, symmetry, and law. It is against this image, this edifice and

---

[33] Rawls, *Justice*, at 137.

structure that postmodern jurisprudence rebelled. Formulated variously in terms of postmodern resistance to enlightenment reason, deconstructive undermining of legal positivism, or as the subversion of the purportedly rational determinism of law, postmodern jurisprudence was a product of critical legal studies. It challenged the scientific orthodoxies of the Marxist theory of law just as much as it questioned the certainties of dogmatic legal thought. The sign of the rebellion was deconstruction, and the text that made the difference was Derrida's lecture on deconstruction and the possibility of justice, delivered in New York in 1989.[34]

The citadel did not fall, the edifice never crumbled, but Derrida did unsettle the legal establishment and his work in introducing a sense of the postmodern into the conception of justice was very much geared, as the term deconstruction suggests, to *arche* and trace, to the undoing of structures. The context of Derrida's intervention, coming on the back of his earlier work, was the linguistic turn throughout the social sciences. This meant a shift toward interpretation or more properly philosophical hermeneutics that pervaded the humanities in the 1970s and eventually law by the mid- to late-1980s.[35] Law lags behind, as a discipline and as a dogma and so the slow access is hardly surprising.

The initial impact of the interpretative turn, and specifically of the banner of deconstruction was in the domain of legal theory and was as a generic challenge to all modernist claims, on the left as well as the right, that asserted certainty and universality, absolute truth, or textual determinacy. The notion that texts, legal or other, were amenable to authoritative interpretation and, in the case of law application, by virtue of the univocal and certain uncovering of their meaning was anathema to the new radicals. This early version of postmodernism in legal studies traveled covertly, was fond of brandishing labels and catchwords – deconstruction, nihilism, indeterminacy, trashing, intertextuality – but was in the main an attempt to incorporate literary theory into legal philosophy.[36] Writing in the first British critical legal conference publication, Douzinas and Warrington, in the course of an emblematic deconstruction of a jurisprudential text, conclude that it is literary

---

[34] The text in question is Jacques Derrida, 'Force of Law: The Mystical Foundations of Authority' 11 *Cardozo Law Review* 919 (1990). On the influence of this text on jurisprudence, in the context of Derrida's work and the politics of U.S. legal studies, see Goodrich et al., 'A Philosophy of Legal Enigmas,' in Peter Goodrich et al., eds. *Derrida and Legal Philosophy* (London: Palgrave, 2008).

[35] The first substantial mentions of deconstruction are in a symposium on the Linguistic turn, published as 58 *Southern California Law Review* (1985) and in particular David Kennedy, 'The Turn to Interpretation' 58 *Southern California Law Review* (1985). Also of interest in that issue is David Couzens Hoy, 'Interpreting the Law: Hermeneutical and Poststructuralist Perspectives' 58 *Southern California Law Review* 53 (1985).

[36] See, for example, Peter Goodrich, 'Law and Modernity' 50 *Modern Law Review* 545 (1986), addressing the hermeneutic and rhetorical features of legal power. Anthony Carty, *The Decay of International Law? A Reappraisal of the Limits of Legal Imagination in International Affairs* (Manchester: University of Manchester Press, 1986) also makes an argument for literature, for "writings that are valued for their beauty of form," as the proper designation and inspiration of doctrine.

Postmodern Justice

language, the play of rhetoric that will "finish philosophy at the hands of literature." Deconstruction, for them, was "the task of legal philosophy."[37] Duncan Kennedy, writing or in fact talking at roughly the same time, had a different formulation: "I have a theory . . . which is a theory of the interstitial character, the implicit, caught up in the folds of freedom. That is, freedom exists in the interstices of these structures, and is a way of destroying them and transforming them but never being outside them. It looks like its trench warfare for decades."[38]

Critical legal scholars, the left legal scholars of the post-1960s generation, were keen to challenge law, to denounce its inequalities and injustices but it was Derrida who reformulated this generic passion into the question and questioning of justice. Returning to Derrida's text, the analysis of the force of law was explicitly placed in the context of the relation between literature and philosophy, law and politics as the critical points of an emerging critical legal scholarship. Derrida's call in that paper was precisely to an ethics of responsibility, to a political accounting of legal scholarship, and to the desideratum of not simply observing from "the monadic or monastic ivory tower that in any case never was" but intervening in the contemporary institutions of "the *cité*, the *polis* . . . the world."[39] This required the conjunction of philosophical and literary theory with "juridico-literary reflection and 'critical legal studies.'" All of which is to say that at a disciplinary level legal scholarship required expansion, pluralism, and attention to difference. This meant both a breakdown of the unitary edifice of dogmatic scholarship conceived as rational, scientific and certain, and an openness to contemporary trends in the humanities, to those other disciplines that address the questions of text and application, as well as justice and injustice.

The postmodern character of Derrida's analysis of justice was not simply a matter of pluralism, of an interdisciplinary intervention that challenged the "mystical authority," and the force and violence of law. What distinguished Derrida's intervention was that he took justice seriously, indeed he defined deconstruction *as* justice, and in doing so returned to a strongly premodern sense of justice as particularity, as indulgence, meaning the giving of time and attention to those who come before the law. His concern was postmodern in the sense of returning to the nascence of the modern, the moment of fissure or undecideability that founds the modern. His text was in this sense about as far as one could go from Rawls because it was the Jewish philosopher Lévinas who was to inspire this return to the question of justice. According to Lévinas, justice is the relation to others, and is defined in terms

---

[37] Costas Douzinas and Ronnie Warrington, 'On the Deconstruction of Jurisprudence: Fin(n)is Philosophiae' 33 *Journal of Law and Society* 37 (1987). This text, modified, became a chapter in Douzinas, Warrington, McVeigh, *Postmodern Jurisprudence: The Law of Text in the Texts of Law* (London: Routledge, 1990).

[38] Peter Gabel and Duncan Kennedy, 'Roll Over Beethoven' 36 *Stanford Law Review* at 53–4 (1984).

[39] Derrida, 'Force of Law,' reprinted in D. Cornell et al., eds. *Deconstruction and the Possibility of Justice* (New York: Routledge, 1992) at 9.

of the "equitable honoring of faces."[40] Contrary to Rawls, justice is thus defined not as equality or equivalence but as an absolute dissymmetry, attendant upon the uniqueness and the demand of the other's face. Veil removed, the bare, present, and insistent face emerges and persists.

Derrida went on in his article to spell out the entailments of a justice that attends to the call of the other, in terms of an ethics of responsibility that took into account the uncertain process of deciding as well as the impossibility of doing justice in the full in any given case: "there is never a moment that we can say *in the present* that a decision *is* just"[41] and this is because the uniqueness of the other, and of their circumstances, requires a novel decision, a "fresh judgment" in every case: "To be just, the decision of the judge... must not only follow a rule of law or a general law but must also assume it, approve it, confirm its value, by a reinstituting act of interpretation, as if ultimately nothing previously existed of the law, as if the judge himself invented the law in every case."[42] Justice requires, in other words, that in the process of deciding, the judge attend to the uniqueness of the other and in doing so suspend and reinvent the law.

Viewed from the perspective of the postmodern, justice is in Derrida's terms both undecideable and uncertain or yet to come. This acknowledgment of the heteronomy of disciplines and knowledge fits well with the chaos of surfaces, of rhetorical fronts, of facades that Venturi and others had invoked in architecture and that Lyotard had already formulated neatly in stating that "any attempt to state the law, for example, to place oneself in the position of enunciator of the universal prescription is obviously infatuation itself and absolute injustice."[43] Justice, and in this the postmodern accounts concur, is plurality. In this spirit, in holding back from judging, in determining, as Derrida had put it earlier, not to determine in advance, the postmodern rendering of justice was determined to remain open, undecided, uncertain, attentive to others for as long as is possible. Thus at the most general level, postmodern justice as a political intervention was one that demanded patience, attention, listening to the multiple subjects of justice and in contemporary terms that meant making law listen to the claims of women, minorities, immigrants, asylum seekers, gays and lesbians, transsexuals, minors, and more.

In very much the same spirit as Venturi and others forced architects to look to the surface of buildings, to read what was there, postmodern justice, the "momentary principle of justice"[44] demands that attention be turned from the edifice, from the

---

[40] Ibid., 22.

[41] Ibid., 23.

[42] Ibid., 23.

[43] Jean-François Lyotard & Jean-Loup Thébaud, *Just Gaming* (Manchester: Manchester University Press, 1985) at 99.

[44] This phrase is from Douzinas and Warrington, *Justice Miscarried: Ethics, Aesthetics, and the Law* (Hemel Hempstead: Harvester, 1994) at 240.

Postmodern Justice

structure and its hypothetical symmetries to the actual occupants, the living and breathing, diverse and numerous subjects who inhabit built space. It is a critique of Prometheus, of the absolute author, and an attempt, in Deleuze's formulation, "to be done with the judgment of Jupiter,"[45] in favor of a politicizing criticism that asks the question of justice, of responsibility for justice, in concrete sites, in the courtroom to be sure, but also in the Immigration and Naturalization Service detention center, the prison, the workplace, the hospital, the home, the Church, Guantanamo, Abu Ghraib, or wherever else the plurality of subjects shows the unique and demanding face of the other. This is the project that the critical legal studies movement invoked through the name of Derrida,[46] and which feminism,[47] critical race theory,[48] post-colonial jurisprudence,[49] and all the other skein of movements and identities thrust to the fore in the 1990s to the present day.

What the postmodern legal movements share is more than a negative response to the theological and inherently violent basis of legal claims to authority. There is also a positive commitment to using all available disciplinary and artistic tools to give space and hence both justice and jurisdiction – meaning a site of enunciation, a face, a voice, a visibility, and social presence – to the excluded, to those whom the modern building or here modern law had turned aside. Thus, to take some examples, the critical legal scholars turned to continental theory, and particularly to aesthetics, to art, literature, and film to broaden the scope of legal scholarship, to tell the story of the excluded and simultaneously to undermine the tacit laws of their exclusion.[50] Feminist jurisprudence emerged with the specific mandate of establishing a presence for the feminine in the public sphere and used all available

---

[45] Gilles Deleuze, *Essays: Critical and Clinical* (Minneapolis: University of Minnesota Press, 1998).

[46] The important works here were Douzinas, Warrington, McVeigh, *Postmodern Jurisprudence: The Law of Text in the Texts of Law* (London: Routledge, 1990); Duncan Kennedy, *A Critique of Adjudication: Fin de Siècle* (Cambridge, MA: Harvard University Press, 1997).

[47] Drucilla Cornell, *Beyond Accommodation: Ethical Feminism, Deconstruction, and the Law* (New York: Routledge, 1991) to Mary Joe Frug, *Postmodern Legal Feminism* (New York: Routledge, 1998). On the current state of the movement, see Janet Halley, *Split Decisions: How and Why to Take a Break from Feminism* (Cambridge, MA: Harvard University Press, 2006).

[48] Patricia Williams, *The Alchemy of Race and Rights* (Cambridge, MA: Harvard University Press, 1990); Richard Delgado, *The Rodrigo Chronicles* (New York: New York University Press, 1996).

[49] For a loose genealogy, see Peter Fitzpatrick, *The Mythology of Modern Law* (London: Routledge, 1992); Nasser Hussain, *The Jurisprudence of Emergency: Colonialism and the Rule of Law* (Ann Arbor: University of Michigan Press, 2004); Piyel Haldar, *Law, Orientalism, and Postcolonialism: The Jurisdiction of the Lotus Eaters* (London: Routledge, 2007); Douzinas and Gearey, *Critical Jurisprudence: The Political Philosophy of Law* (Oxford: Hart Publishing, 2005) Ch 11.

[50] See, for diverse examples, Anthony Carty, ed. *Postmodern Law* (Edinburgh: University of Edinburgh Press, 1990); Peter Goodrich, *Languages of Law: From Logics of Memory to Nomadic Masks* (London: Weidenfeld and Nicolson, 1992); Costas Douzinas and Lynda Nead, *Law and the Image: The Authority of Art and the Aesthetics of Law* (1999); Les Moran et al., eds. *Law's Moving Image* (London: Glasshouse Press, 2004); Carty, *The Philosophy of International Law* (Edinburgh: University of Edinburgh Press, 2007).

means, continental theory, literary criticism, poetry, James Joyce, and more. As Drucilla Cornell puts it, she was writing "an untitled mamafesta," a fable of a feminine reality sent as a letter in a feminine voice. It was necessarily "fici-fact," and fluid because, to borrow from the French philosopher Irigaray, *"The/a woman never closes up into a volume."*[51] For critical race theory, the project of theory was the politics of scholarly expression and from Patricia Williams' poetic storytelling, to the recounting of dreams of confronting white law professors with the rage of exclusion, to performances of jazz and law, it was the everyday that was the focus of analysis.[52] Here, in the intimate space of public institutions, what right did one have to be – to flaunt – a gay, Japanese, leftist, African-American, feminine, transsexual, or other identity and self-expression?[53]

More Than One, No More One

It is common usage in French and in English to speak of rendering justice – *rendre la justice* – and Derrida in fact comments on this locution as an instance of the active principle of judgment as a mode of construction, of doing or making justice.[54] This formulation can be followed further in the English. Rendering is a term drawn from the Latin *reddere*, meaning to give back but it has a secondary meaning and use, still current in plastering: To rend, is to cover a stone or brick surface with a render, to plaster. To render justice, in this connotation, means to plaster or cover over, to apply a molten or viscous mixture to a wall, a structure, an edifice, or building. Thus rendering justice, in its active form, fits well with the concept of postmodern justice as a process, as a suspension of law that both separates the moment of justice from calculability and rule and applies a novel mix, a render to the extant forms. It also allows for the formulation of a species of conclusion. The postmodern art of rendering justice, the application of the appliqué is architectural and the simile of plastering is a useful one. Postmodern justice rendered law differently; it added a plaster, a new surface, as well as a new attention to surfaces, to the dogmatic tradition, to the theory of law as it was when postmodernism arrived.

Adding a surface, taking note of difference, may seem superficial if surfaces are deemed unimportant. There are certainly many who view the postmodern as mere "throat clearing," and postmodern justice as weak thought or a confused and undisciplined attempt to circumvent the rigors of legal philosophy by means of a

---

[51] Cornell, *Beyond Accommodation*, at 8. For an excellent development of comparable themes, see Janice Richardson and Ralph Sandland, eds. *Feminist Perspectives on Law and Theory* (London: Cavendish, 2000).

[52] Patricia Williams, *The Alchemy of Race and Rights* (1976).

[53] Kenji Yoshino, *Covering The Hidden Assault on our Civil Rights* (New York: Random House, 2006) offers a compellingly personal account of the legal demand that identity be covered.

[54] Derrida, 'Force,' at 17.

Postmodern Justice

dilettantish and disordered set of borrowings from other disciplines.[55] There are certainly instances of such inelegance as also of overstatement and excess. By the same token, however, the detractors of postmodern thought have not always been either accurate or circumspect in their dismissals. Rather than parade or participate in such polemics, however, I will here simply make two positive points by way of conclusion.

First, it is without doubt the case that rendering walls, or rendering justice, is a play upon surfaces, a war over appearances and more specifically the sites of enunciation, the auditoria, and hence jurisdictions of law. It has to be admitted straight out that changing the plaster is not going to bring the building down. The edifice remains and so, if the project were to raze the building, destroy the institution, then postmodern legal thought was never going to get very far. The point, however, is a different one and concerns a more visceral question of the inhabitation of the building. Postmodern justice was not, and is not, a revolutionary attempt to get rid of law. It follows rather in the tradition of Foucault's questioning of discursive power. Those that speak the law and those spoken to deserve a name and description; they exist in an institutional relation predicated upon identity and authority: "Who is speaking? Who, among the totality of speaking individuals, is accorded the right to use this sort of language? Who is qualified to do so? What is the status of the individuals who – alone – have the right, sanctioned by law or tradition, juridically defined or spontaneously accepted, to proffer such a discourse?"[56]

In its primary meaning, and whether performed well or ill, postmodern justice refers to an ethical turn, a demand for responsibility in the form initially of a politics of scholarship. If the postmodern is primarily, as Bauman observes, a reflection of the experience of intellectuals, a scholarly designation and project, then postmodern justice represents the attempts of legal scholars to follow the lead of other intellectuals and professionals, architects and artists, who have insisted not only that what is there is "almost alright,"[57] the material with which one must work, but also that the task of the postmodern intellectual is at the very least that of paying attention to what is there, meaning the people, the temporary and contingent denizens of buildings, or courts, or prisons, or law offices. If existence is without foundation, epistemically uncertain, existentially multiple, and in all things a temporary contract, then ethical

---

[55] Gillian Rose, *Mourning Becomes the Law* (Cambridge: Cambridge University Press, 1996) at 9 defines postmodernism as "despairing rationalism without reason"; Alex Callinicos, *Against Postmodernism* (Cambridge: Polity Press, 1996) located the roots of postmodernism in over consumption and cynical hedonism. In law there were a few rather jejune dismissals of postmodernism but little substantive or informed debate. See Peter Goodrich and Linda Mills, 'The Law of White Spaces' *Journal of Legal Education* (2001) for dissection of the political and racial logic of such polemics in relation to critical race theory. The most substantial study was Douglas Litowitz, *Postmodern Philosophy and Law* (Lawrence, KS: University of Kansas Press, 1997).

[56] Michel Foucault, *The Archaeology of Knowledge* (New York: Pantheon, 1981 ed.) at 51.

[57] Venturi, *Learning*, at 6. (Billboards are Almost Alright).

responsibility takes the form of the suspension of prior judgment, calculus, and law – obsession with structures and symmetries – in favor of listening to the call and responding to the face of the other.

If architecture was the most durable site of the postmodern moment and movement, deconstruction was its banner and emblem. The struggle, as Derrida put it, had moved into the archive and the library. Cultural critique had become a war over writing and power, scribble and shibboleth, books and interpretations.[58] This might seem dismissive and a little unreal but it is simply necessary to recall that the public sphere is precisely the space of literacy, of art and writing, graffiti, and hoarding. Postmodern justice can then be formulated not simply as a humanistic and scholarly endeavor but also as the legal version of the architectural return to the premodern. Postmodern justice was at root an attempt to look behind and beyond law, formal calculus, and ossified rule, to the histories and in particular the deaths that law covered over. The call to justice was both a plural and in Lyotard's terms pagan enterprise, a demand to use all of the panoply of techniques and tools available to law, and also a more somber and long-term accounting of the injustices, of the exiles, the deaths, the expulsions, and other tragedies that litter the institutional history of law.

What then would it be for postmodern justice to be rendered, to be done? The answer to that question, of course, is that there is no answer. Justice is an aporia, a suspension of judgment, the bold acknowledgment of an instance of uncertainty. Justice is a capacity to look and to listen and that necessarily entails a resistance to predetermination: Until we know who it is that is in question, we cannot know what it is that justice requires. There are, however, indicators, trajectories, and possibilities that seem to conform to the postmodern project. If justice is plural and pagan, a play of texts and interpretations, an art or better rhetoric of dialogue and persuasion, then postmodern justice is an instance of law's entry into the multiplicity of language games, into the chaos of actually existing institutions. Here we return to the architectural roots of the postmodern. The institution is ultimately a crypt; it is founded upon forgetting, upon the hidden or secreted, and its history is that of the deaths that it houses.[59]

---

[58] Jacques Derrida, 'Scribble. Writing-Power' 58 *Yale French Studies* 24 (1979). This analysis of knowledge and power goes back, of course, to Nietzsche and Marx, but gains its most persuasive and dynamic accounting in the work of Foucault. See particularly the essays in M. Foucault, *Power/Knowledge* (New York: Pantheon, 1980).

[59] We return here, of course, to Derrida's analysis of Kafka's parable 'Before the law' as mentioned earlier. There are many commentaries but here, in terms of the architectural and postmodern connotations of the story, Wigley, *Deconstruction*, is again the best guide, remarking: "The essence of the law, which is to say, of the space, turns out to be its violation by spacing, a violation that is always hidden always cryptic." The door is therefore "an internal boundary opening on nothing. The space it marks is no more than the maintenance of this secret. The origin of the law is safeguarded by the space, not by being hidden within it but by being hidden by the space itself. It is the very idea that there is an interior that encloses the secret." at 152.

Postmodern Justice

The concern of postmodern justice is not with the law but with *nomos*, with the appropriations and exclusions, the divisions and deaths that have made up the space, the topology of the institution. If law – meaning structure, symmetry, the edifice before or separate from its contemporary and contingent inhabitants – is always secret and secreted, an encryption, then postmodern justice is the art of reading the signs of such encryption, the semiotic history of those who haunt the building. The postmodern accounting of institutional space is thus the enterprise of coming to know the ghosts who inhabit the building. It is a speculative enterprise in that its concern is with specters, yet this is not because of any belief in ghosts but rather out of a concern with justice. Ironically, the postmodern idea of justice is focused upon the "pre-," on the "before any present."[60] Listening to the past, to the history of injustice, means paying attention to what came before, to the beings who haunt the crypt. These specters are our inheritance and justice requires that we be hospitable to them, grant them space, audience, welcome, and life. Such being the case, and ending as I began, the task of postmodern justice is precisely to disencrypt premodern and modern injustices. This means daring to speculate, to look at specters, to imagine a post, which is to say a beyond of the modern, a beyond of law. The post is a justice yet to come.

---

[60] Jacques Derrida, *Specters of Marx: The State of the Debt, the Work of Mourning, and the New International* (New York: Routledge, 1994).

PART III

IMAGINING THE LAW

8

Imagining the Law

The Novel[1]

Susan Sage Heinzelman

The title of this chapter succinctly captures the terms that are in play when we talk about the relationship between the novel and the law. To represent law in the form of the novel is, in the most obvious sense, an act of the imagination, but "to imagine" the law also implies that the law does not exist *prior to* that act of the imagination, that it has no objective reality outside of the literary or cultural forms that invoke its presence. The implication that the law is not a "thing," that it endures only because of its discursive and material effects, has wide-reaching and potentially dangerous political and social consequences, not the least of which is the challenge those effects might pose to law's authority. Moreover, specifically representing law in literature might further undermine its authority given the ancient suspicion against *poesis* (or "making") as that which threatens the supposedly transcendent and nonhuman source of law's authority (identified either as divine or based on objective reason). At particular historical moments, of course, the social, moral, and aesthetic standing of specific literary genres can either promote or undermine law's authority – thus the high value placed on dramatic representations in antiquity would, when combined with the representation of legal events, reinforce law's privileged status in that culture.

This chapter focuses on the affiliation between the novel and the law, an affiliation that involves a delicate balancing act between the demands inherent in affirming the status of the rule of law and the generic demands of the novel, the most obvious of which is the commonly held assumption that law seeks the "truth," whereas the novel relies on "fiction." This apparent tension has a representational corollary: law engages with the real, fiction with the imaginary. Thus when the novel does engage with the law, it inevitably threatens to undermine law's legitimacy by providing representations that humanize the law or place its authority in question. This tension between popular appeal and law's legitimacy has shaped the novel's history and the

---

[1] My thanks to Michelle Ty whose penetrating questions and editorial pen have considerably strengthened this chapter.

development of common law as well as their historical affiliation. This chapter will trace a primarily English version of this connection, one in which gender and class interests have influenced both the specific form that the novel has assumed and its depiction of the law. These gender and class interests are, of course, reflected in the jurisprudential and practical interpretation of the law.

Before I begin what can be only a partial (in all senses of the word) account of this historically contingent affiliation between the novel and the law, a word or two about the terms I use and the assumptions that guide this chapter First, I assume that the novel is a form of social action, that it actively contributes to institutional formation, and that this ideological activity is produced not only by the novel's subject matter but also by the formal characteristics of the genre.[2] Moreover, the successive appraisal and reappraisal of those formal qualities – as apprehended and articulated by critics, novelists and readers – contributes to the emergence of new forms of subjectivity and new definitions of "experience." In turn, those newly emerging structures of social and individual consciousness promote further novelistic explorations of these forms of identity. There is, then, both a dialectical and, to use Mikhail Bakhtin's term, a dialogical relationship between the novel and quotidian reality through which the reader arrives at a temporary understanding both of her own identity and that of the world she inhabits. Just as the novel is engaged in cultural constructions (and yet is simultaneously the effect of those cultural constructions), so too is the law. I view the law in this chapter as having power comparable to that of the novel to shape both the institutional ideologies of a particular historical period, as well as the individual identities of those who see themselves as legal subjects. As with the novel, this cultural production is achieved not simply by the content of the law – its legislative actions, judgments, customs, and rituals – but also by the formal qualities through which this content is revealed. Changes in the scope of the law – its agency in prescribing and proscribing certain behaviors and social arrangements – as well as changes in the formal administration of the law, such as the introduction of the defense lawyer in English criminal trials in the 1730s, produce changes in the structures of feeling and the representational methods through which the ordinary citizen understands the law.[3] Moreover, as Bakhtin points out, "legal-criminal categories

---

[2] For elaboration on this position, see M. M. Bakhtin, *The Dialogic Imagination*. Michael Holquist, ed., Caryl Emerson and Michael Holquist, trans. (Austin: University of Texas Press, 1981), especially "Discourse in the Novel," 259–422; Dorothy J. Hale, *Social Formalism: The Novel in Theory from Henry James to the Present* (Stanford: Stanford University Press, 1998); Fredric Jameson, *The Political Unconscious: Narrative as a Socially Symbolic Act* (Ithaca, NY: Cornell University Press, 1981).

[3] Raymond Williams uses the term "structures of feeling" in a variety of his critical texts. I use the term here as he defines it in *Marxism and Literature* (Oxford: Oxford University Press, 1977) as the "affective elements of consciousness and relationships: not feeling against thought, but thought as felt and feeling as thought: practical consciousness of a present kind, in a living and interrelating continuity. We are then defining these elements as a 'structure': as a set, with specific internal relations, at once interlocking and in tension" (132).

Imagining the Law

in general have an enormous organizational significance" in the history of the novel.[4]

Given these assumptions about the way in which both the novel and the law engage with the world they claim to represent, we must conclude that the relationship between literary and legal discourse, between those cultural institutions we name as the novel and the law, will be both complex and historically contingent. At best, all we can hope to do is trace the effects of this relationship at historically specific moments. Generally speaking, there has been considerable critical attention paid to the way in which the law infuses the novel, most obviously in popular representations of judicial proceedings, criminal behavior, or trials – the law in fiction. Less critical attention has been paid to formal matters.[5] Almost no attention, however, has been paid to the reverse phenomenon – what John Bender calls the "novelizing" of the law.[6] Indeed, the law's dominant mode of representing itself has been as a discourse that is impervious to other discursive systems.

This apparent imperviousness to nonlegal systems has operated as one of law's primary "fictions," thereby both cementing its privilege and authority and producing a unitary conception of its nature. That law's boundedness is a fiction should be evident from the anxiety with which the professional guardians of the law confront any challenge to its established protocols and rituals and the absence, until recently, of sustained critical attention to the literariness, the figurative nature, of the law, although such recognition of law's inherent rhetoricity was commonplace before the eighteenth century. Moreover, legal discourse is riven with the fictional, understood as a mode of representing the relationship between quotidian reality and its legal version because, like the novel, legal discourse relies upon narrative and its interpretation as a form of knowledge.

In what follows, I will analyze representative novels to indicate the ways in which the two histories – of the novel and of the law – have both embraced and resisted the

---

[4] Bakhtin, 124, quoted in John Bender, *Imagining the Penitentiary: Fiction and the Architecture of Mind in Eighteenth-Century England* (Chicago: University of Chicago Press, 1987) 11.

[5] For a precise and elegant account of the relationship between novelistic representation and social institutions, such as the penitentiary, see Bender's *Imagining the Penitentiary*, in which he argues that novelists, such as Defoe and Fielding, introduced a new form of personal identity through innovative fictional techniques and that this personal identity helped to shape a new understanding of the function of the prison in social life. Thus "[n]ovelistic discourse becomes part of the culture's means of understanding" (3). See also Jonathan H. Grossman, *The Art of the Alibi: English Law Courts and the Novel* (Baltimore: Johns Hopkins University Press, 2002).

[6] "The appearance of defense counsel moved the struggle for control of narrative resources to the center of judicial consciousness by subjecting the prosecution's evidentiary constructs to articulated standards of reliability (realism) and by introducing expert voices competitive with the judge's legal authority. In light of Bakhtin's discussion of 'polyglossia' as the defining trait of novelistic discourse, which he considers as having increasingly penetrated the whole of culture during modern times, the 'lawyerization' of the eighteenth-century criminal trial could be called a form of 'novelization.'" Bender, 176.

implications of their affiliation. Specifically, I will pay attention to the way in which, at certain historical periods, the literary critical account of the relationship between the novel and the law has helped to shape a particular version of what constitutes the legal order and the legal subject, as well as privileging certain formal and thematic qualities in the novel. The chapter is divided into four sections: Fictional and Legal Realism; Fictional and Legal Romance; Fictional and Legal Reformation; and Fictional and Legal Misrepresentation.

Fictional and Jurisprudential Realism

In *The Rise of the Novel* (1957), the canonical account of the origins of the English novel, Ian Watt identifies the distinguishing generic characteristic of the novel as its "formal realism," which is conveyed through " a set of narrative procedures which are so commonly found together in the novel, and so rarely in other literary genres, that they may be regarded as typical of the form itself."[7] Most significant among these narrative procedures is the specificity of individual characters (as opposed to "types") and their physical environment, a specificity that requires particular names, recognizable cause-and-effect relationships, and their concomitant temporality.[8] To reinforce this mimetic relationship between everyday reality and the discourse of the novel, Watt compares the "novel's mode of imitating reality" to the

> procedures of another group of specialists in epistemology, the jury in a court of law. Their expectations, and those of the novel reader, coincide in many ways: both want to know 'all the particulars' of a given case – the time and place of the occurrence; both must be satisfied as to the identities of the parties concerned, and will refuse to accept evidence about anyone called Sir Toby Belch or Mr. Badman – and still less about a Chloe who has no surname and is 'common as the air'; and they also expect the witnesses to tell the story 'in his own words.'[9]

Quite clearly, this analogy between fictional and jurisprudential epistemology implies that only a reader of a certain class and gender can anticipate having his [sic] "expectations" fulfilled. No woman would sit on an English jury until 1920 and the formal and linguistic conventions of the legal system that grounded its epistemology could not be understood and interpreted by the laity with the same skill as those who practiced the law, a class of gentlemen that included professional lawyers, as

---

[7] Ian Watt, *The Rise of the Novel: Studies In Defoe, Richardson, and Fielding* (Berkeley: University of California Press, 1957) 32, 34.

[8] By character types, I mean those fictional characters whose name indicates their one-dimensional and predictable function in the text, such as Mr. Badman.

[9] Watt, 34.

Imagining the Law

well as privileged men of property acting in their capacity as justices of the peace, local magistrates, and landowners.

Furthermore, this turn to "realism," which Watt identifies as one of the foundational characteristics of the early novel, requires the erasure of those narratives that had preceded this peculiarly English type – both the scandalous memoirs and autobiographical fictions of writers like Delarivier Manley and Aphra Behn, as well as the idealized characters and heroic plots of the romance narrative, a form closely associated both with France and with women authors and made popular in England by authors such as Eliza Haywood.[10] Thus the English novel that Watt claims was "fathered" by Defoe, Richardson, and Fielding depends upon writing out of the history of those women novelists who were as popular in their day as their male counterparts: Eliza Haywood's novel, *Love in Excess*, for example, rivaled Defoe's *Robinson Crusoe* as the best seller of 1719.[11]

Watt's erasure of foreign influences and women authors for his critical history mimics precisely that of those eighteenth-century male authors who sought to make their own novel writing a respectable profession (in other words, to wrest its popularity from women writers) and to assert that their novels were exemplary moral texts. To advocate the respectability of their "new species of writing," Fielding and Richardson each claimed that their version of the novel could convincingly construct epistemologically and morally sound representations of a reality that was shared by author and reader alike.[12]

In much the same way as the English novel established its specific national identity, the legal profession insisted on the Englishness of the common law by noting its superiority to continental versions – the impartiality of the English jury system being, in particular, one of its finest accomplishments. In tandem with this

---

[10] Delarivier Manley (1670–1724), author of amatory fiction and scandalous political novels such as *Secret Memoirs and Manners of Several Persons of Quality, of both Sexes, From The New Atalantis* (1709), and the fictional autobiography, *Rivella* (1714). Aphra Behn (1640–1689), successful playwright and author of *Oroonoko; or The Royal Slave* (1688). Eliza Haywood (1693–1756), actress, playwright, novelist, and essayist, author of more than seventy works, including *Love in Excess* (1719).

[11] Daniel Defoe (1661–1731), author of poetry, political satire, pamphlets, and many novels, including *Robinson Crusoe* (1719), *Moll Flanders* (1722), and *Roxana* (1724). Henry Fielding (1702–1754), playwright, author, magistrate, and founder of a version of the London police force, the Bow Street Runners. Fielding is known best for the novel *Tom Jones* (1749), his ironic account of the master criminal Jonathan Wild, *The Life and Death of Jonathan Wild the Great* (1743), and *Shamela* (1741), his parody of Samuel Richardson's wildly successful epistolary novel, *Pamela*. Samuel Richardson (1689–1761) was also the author of two other epistolary novels, *Clarissa* (1748), and *Sir Charles Grandison* (1753). For an account of this erasure, see William B. Warner, *Licensing Entertainment: The Elevation of Novel Reading in Britain, 1684–1750. (Berkeley: University of California Press, 1998).

[12] "By reality Fielding means moral or factual truth apprehended by the reader, whereas he sees in Richardson a reality that means the true workings of a character's mind, without any concern for the truth or falseness of apprehension in relation to the external world." Ronald Paulson, *Satire and the Novel in Eighteenth-Century England* (New Haven: Yale University Press, 1967) 106, quoted in Bender, 145.

nationalistic elevation of English law came the gradual erasure of "the earlier, more relaxed and informal system of judge-made law," whose "sensitive and flexible methods . . . were being swept away by the growth of rather clumsier centralised legislation."[13] As one might expect, that centralized legislation promoted the well-being of an elite class, male and propertied, at the cost of those whose requests for justice might have stood a better chance of being answered in a less formal system: the poor, women, and children. It should be noted, however, that novels continued to represent justice "from beneath" – that is, the practice of settling disputes and criminal offenses outside the formal confines of the legal system.

In arguing for the commercial (and implicitly moral) triumph of the male-authored novel over its predecessors, Watt contends that success came from the similarity between fictional protagonists and the primary consumers of fiction: readers from the mercantile class, a class that united an English Protestant spirituality with a capitalist economy, supported by and embodied in legal and political ideologies and practices.[14] In other words, the literary conventions of realism produce a bourgeois ideology; in fact, realist fiction might be said, according to Watt, to bring the bourgeoisie into being, and the proof of their ongoing cultural power is the persistent popularity of the realist novel. Thus, argues Watt, both readers and fictional protagonists appeared to adhere to the same set of empirical beliefs, religious convictions, and moral values and expected those ideological systems to be represented in and secured through the law.[15] Readers learned how to judge evidence, how to distinguish reliable witnesses from unreliable ones and how to assess the moral choices made by fictional characters by following the advice of the narrator or the experiences of the protagonist; in other words, they learned how to become "judicious" readers and, by extension, to internalize what it meant to be "judicial" (or "juridical") subjects.[16] Thus the pervasive and growing professional force of the law was inculcated in the reader-subject through the novel, a form of narrative that *appeared* to reproduce the way ordinary citizens thought about their lives and told their stories.

Watt's reliance on the epistemology of realism for his account of the "rise" of the novel secures a particular version not only of the novel but also of mid- to

---

[13] Ian A. Bell, *Literature and Crime in Augustan England* (London: Routledge, 1991) 9.

[14] For a Feminist-Marxist reading women's role in changing the status of the novel from commodity to literature, see Terry Lovell, *Consuming Fiction* (London: Verso Press, 1987).

[15] For a Foucaultian analysis of the "news/novels" discourse that, arguably, produced the literary genre of the novel, see Lennard Davis, *Factual Fictions: The Origins of the English Novel* (New York: Columbia University Press, 1983), and for an analysis of the social function of "rogue" biographies, see Lincoln Faller, *Turned to Account: The Forms and Functions of Criminal Biography in Late Seventeenth- and Early Eighteenth-Century England* (Cambridge: Cambridge University Press, 1987).

[16] For the term "juridical subject" see John P. Zomchick, *Family and the Law in Eighteenth-Century Fiction: The Public Conscience in the Private Sphere* (Cambridge: Cambridge University Press, 1993). Based on Marxist analysis, Zomchick argues that eighteenth-century novels use "civil and familial grammars by which the juridical subject is doubly predicated" – as an individual member of civil society and as a member of a family (xii).

Imagining the Law

late-eighteenth-century law, a discourse that seems to speak, in Bakhtin's terminology, monologically.[17] Moreover, the retrospective narrative that Watt imposes on the affiliation between the novel and the law reproduces precisely those cultural and ideological values that the literary and legal authorities themselves promoted. Both the moral and aesthetic status of the novel and the apparent impartiality and intransigence of the law benefited from this alliance, which effectively disguised the class and gender bias embodied in both representational systems. Thus the fiction of mimesis generates the fiction of disinterested law, and both come to be seen as the particular property of the mercantile class.

Anxiety about property and its rightful possession produced two mutually enforcing social narratives. First, the unremitting representation of crime and criminality in print, from one-page broadsheets to full-length novels, from the confessions of highwaymen to the dying words of murderers, from trial records to criminal biographies, suggested that crime was pervasive, growing in intensity and primarily directed against the propertied classes. Second, partly in response to print culture's success in disseminating this version of a crime-ridden society, the number (and punitive severity) of laws passed to protect property grew rapidly through the eighteenth century, thus both confirming the impression that crime was out of control and producing more narrative examples of criminal behavior.[18] These narratives offered the reader a range of feelings from fear and disgust to approval and admiration, a heteroglossia that produced unexpected results and paradoxes over which the author had no control.[19] Furthermore, both the novel and the law constitute their representation

---

[17] In his essay on the reception of the novel in the eighteenth-century academy, Paul G. Bator argues that the novel was perceived as a hybrid genre, without the strict generic characteristics that Ian Watt, among other critics, has retrospectively associated with that genre. Thus, according to Bator, the early reception of the novel, at least among Scottish academicians, was closely akin to Bakhtin's understanding of the novel as a mixed genre that is a "different breed" from other literary genres because of its representation of the multiplicity of individual and social relationships. See Paul G. Bator, "Rhetoric and the Novel in the Eighteenth-Century British Curriculum," *Eighteenth-Century Studies* 30 (Winter 1996–97) 173–195. For a review of contemporary critical approaches to the novel from both eighteenth-century novelists and critics, see Joseph F. Bartolomeo, *A New Species of Criticism: Eighteenth-Century Discourse on the Novel* (Newark: University of Delaware Press, 1994).

[18] Bell, 13–28.

[19] In *Imagining the Penitentiary*, Bender argues that Fielding attempts "authoritative moral control" in his novels as part of his larger sociocultural efforts at reforming law enforcement. For Bender, Fielding's innovations as a novelist are consistent with his efforts to replace arbitrary and class-based forms of law with consistent evidentiary and procedural protocols. In particular, Bender argues that Fielding's use of the centralized moral consciousness of the narrator is an analogue to the emerging regulation and control of the state. On the other hand, John Richetti argues, "The social order as Fielding represents it is regulated by a variety of norms, some legal and statutory, some traditional and customary . . . and [that] their conflicting claims [are] part of his comic mechanism." "The Old Order and the New Novel of the Mid-Eighteenth Century: Narrative Authority in Fielding and Smollett, *Eighteenth-Century Fiction* 2 (April 1990) 184. For an analysis of the intersection of Fielding's practices as magistrate, businessman, and writer, see Lance Bertelsen's *Henry Fielding at Work: Magistrate, Businessman, Writer* (New York: Palgrave, 2000).

of social relations through language that is inescapably enmeshed in other linguistic and symbolic systems and thus never fully restricted by authorial or legislative intent. As Peter Goodrich argues, both the novel and the law are riven with "contingencies and heterogeneities of different jurisdictions and alternative forms of [representation] and law." Such fictional and legal jurisdictions challenge the illusion of a "sovereign and unitary law" of representation and interrupt the apparently seamless narrative of mimetic fictional discourse and the discourse of positive law.[20]

What this means to the specific relationship between the novel and the law is that both discourses are engaged not only in constituting social relations but are also always already constituted by them, in domains of representation that are constantly overlapping. Structures of feeling are socially organized through their formal repetition in the novel, just as the formal and repeated performances of the law in action are a way of organizing the subject's response to its authority and of thereby creating a legal subject. Both literary and legal performances, however, are constantly threatened by contradiction and disruption. To illustrate the tenuousness of fiction's social organization of feelings, I offer one example from many plausible narratives: Daniel Defoe's *The Fortunes and Misfortunes of the Famous Moll Flanders*, first published in 1722. Structured as a "confession" of both sin and criminality, the narrative proposes to instruct the reader in the necessity for remorse (a sensibility that is produced by the individual conscience) and reparation (a sociolegal formal act that restores society to its condition before the crime was perpetrated). It is precisely because the narrative participates in at least two different linguistic and symbolic systems that it represents the character of Moll as both "famous," that is, as a somebody, as an individual, and as a "type" – that is, as a nobody, as a representative set of social relations.[21] Such diversity is reflected throughout the narrative and undermines the claim that mimetic fiction (that is, realistic representation) produces a coherent narrative of the kind that is necessary to discipline the judicial subject.

One significant aspect of this diversity is reflected in the double-voiced narrative whereby Defoe uses the convention of presenting Moll's confessional autobiography through the voice of a male editor who frames both the criminal, Moll, and her legal and moral transgressions, thus locating both authenticity and "truth" in the male editor (and by implication, the male author) rather than the dubiously moral Moll. In *Licensing Entertainment*, William Warner argues that Defoe's development of

> the double-voiced memoir narrative enables him to make a particularly cogent
> intervention in the print market.... [The memoir narrative] allows him to

---

[20] Peter Goodrich, "Gynaetopia: Feminine Genealogies of Common Law," *Journal of Law and Society* 20, no. 3 (Autumn 1993) 2, 4.

[21] I use the term here to suggest to the "exchangeable tokens" of modern female subjectivity, modeling my argument on Catherine Gallagher's use in *Nobody's Story: The Vanishing Acts of Women Writers in the Marketplace 1670–1820* (Berkeley: University of California Press, 1994) where she uses the term to refer to the "exchangeable tokens of modern authorship" (xiii).

Imagining the Law

write other print genres, like criminal biographies and the erotic secret history, to which he has moral objections. At the same time, he can offer his own moral texts as a corrective and substitute for the pleasures of the narratives he would replace. Most crucially, the second admonitory voice in the text allows the reader to resist being absorbed by the fictional lures of a particular genre:... the liberating effect of criminal transgression, and the devious and furtive lubricity of sexual intrigue.

In addition to providing a way for the reader to resist being absorbed into the fiction, the double-voiced narrative technique intensifies the diversity of voices and personae represented in the text. Moreover, the tension between these two narrators – the male editor and the female narrator – parallels and inflects the relationship between two narrative strategies in the novel, the religious and the sociolegal. These tensions reflect particular historical anxieties about the connection between gender and truth, as well as the connection between secular law and God's law, given that the religious foundation for epistemological and ontological beliefs was under increasing pressure.[22]

The two narrative strategies are embodied in the explanations that Moll offers at different times of her life for her social status. At times she suggests a religious explanation: her social condition is a reflection of her moral condition and thus only her genuine remorse can alter her state. At other times, she argues for a sociolegal account: she is a victim of circumstances, trapped in a world of poverty amid a world of plenty. This narrative confusion also reflects the ideological move from a religious context of sin to a secular notion of crime, the latter being tied to a modern sense of individuality and the establishment of the right to private property as a legal and moral principle, twin concepts that are foundational to the bourgeoisie.[23]

In *Moll Flanders*, economic and legal concerns saturate the selfhood that the heroine narrates into being. Despite the confessional nature of her story, a form that relies on a religious sensibility and its narrative articulation, Moll Flanders returns again and again to a mercantile system of property and contract to value

---

[22] See Leopold Damrosch, Jr., *God's Plot & Man's Stories: Studies in the Fictional Imagination from Milton to Fielding* (Chicago: University of Chicago Press, 1985); and Barbara Shapiro, *Probability and Certainty in Seventeenth-Century England: A Study of the Relationships between Natural Science, Religion, History, Law, and Literature* (Princeton, NJ: Princeton University Press, 1983); and *"Beyond Reasonable Doubt" and "Probable Cause": Historical Perspectives on the Anglo-American Law of Evidence* (Berkeley: University of California Press, 1991).

[23] See Susan Staves, *Married Women's Separate Property in England, 1660–1833* (Cambridge, MA: Harvard University Press, 1990); John P. Zomchick, *Family and the Law in Eighteenth-Century Fiction;* Wolfram Schmidgen, *Eighteenth-Century Fiction and the Law of Property* (Cambridge: Cambridge University Press, 2002), and Susan Paterson Glover, *Engendering Legitimacy: Law, Property, and Early Eighteenth-Century Fiction* (Lewisville, PA: Bucknell University Press). For a wide-ranging analysis of the multitude of forms that "property" took in the seventeenth and eighteenth centuries, including literary property and ownership of the self, see John Brewer and Susan Staves, eds., *Early Modern Conceptions of Property* (London: Routledge, 1995).

herself and her activities in the world. A divine providential narrative still informs the individual conscience of the protagonist, but her social being is constructed through the language and activities of a mercantile economy. Readers learn that the social self must conform to laws that advance a commercial class, however much the individual conscience might seek alternative, less materialistic forms of satisfaction. Indeed, by the end of the novel, the sociolegal has overwhelmed (or absorbed) the providential: It is precisely her wealth and success as a plantation owner in the New World that signals her redemption in God's eyes, a redemption that is inextricably linked to property.

Moll's narrative is represented by her editor as a tale of reform and repentance, but to demonstrate the extent of her repentance, the narrative has to detail the extent of her crimes. Herein lies the problem with narratives about legal transgressions – they must be both educative and entertaining (*utile et dulce* as Horace suggested). The novel can assert a serious moral purpose but it frequently risks encouraging the very moral and social transgressions it wishes to condemn. From the moment it became a popular form of representing the middling classes to themselves, the novel was deeply implicated in simultaneously policing *and* promoting legal and moral transgressions.[24] The author inevitably relinquishes control over the effects of the narrative and the reader's interpretation of evidence of moral turpitude or reform. Readers encounter and resonate to the same set of conflicting representational strategies as the protagonist: On the one hand, we read about the "somebody," Moll, who wishes to be redeemed but must nevertheless conform to social laws that advance a mercantile economy. On the other, we read about the "nobody," the prostitute who has bartered herself in the marketplace, but who must voice genuine remorse even though her body and its pleasures have brought her wealth and success. *Moll Flanders* represents the paradoxical and conflicting narrative strategies that were played out every day in the courts of law, and the reader's response to that narrative models' ongoing and intense cultural struggle over what constituted a plausible narrative, what constituted sufficient evidence, who was entitled to present that evidence, and who was privileged to debate its value.[25]

Fictional and Legal Romance

The story of Moll Flanders, like the story of many other fictional heroines in the eighteenth and nineteenth centuries, locates bourgeois mentality and its concomitant

---

[24] D. A. Miller makes a similar point in his analysis of *Bleak House*. He suggests that what appears to be critique of the law can, in fact, be an alibi for maintaining the *status quo*. I explore this problem in more detail in the third section, "Fictional and Legal Reformation."

[25] See Shapiro, *Probability and Certainty*; and Alexander Welsh, *Strong Representations: Narrative and Circumstantial Evidence in England* (Baltimore: Johns Hopkins University Press, 1992).

Imagining the Law

range of sentimental and erotic emotions in the woman's body.[26] Indeed, the erotic and the financial are frequently interchangeable and reflect the growing legalization of both private and public relationships (especially laws governing marriage and the inheritance of property).[27] Despite the much-quoted observation by Sir Henry Maine in his *Ancient Laws* (1861) that the shift from status to contract was one of the marks of "modernity," the representation of marriage as a commercial transaction bound by laws of contract came under increasing attack during the eighteenth and nineteenth centuries.[28] Of course, Maine's assertion relied on the assumption that the parties to the contract were free, autonomous individuals, a condition that most women could only imagine, much less command, even in 1861.[29] The argument that marriage was nothing more than "legalized prostitution" was made directly or indirectly in many eighteenth-century novels and plays, as well as in satirical prints by Hogarth, among others, whose series, *Marriage á-la-mode* (1743–1746), follows a popular plot: the typically impoverished, upper-class father forces his daughter into a materially advantageous but emotionally sterile marriage with disastrous consequences to both parties.

Issues of property and gender, and the relationship of both to class, continue to dominate the English novel through the late eighteenth and early nineteenth century, embodied specifically in the erotic and economic relationship between men and women. By the end of the eighteenth century, however, the marriage plot had undergone a significant transformation. Although still inextricably tied to questions of property and socioeconomic status, novelists portrayed the relationship between husband and wife as a bond built on mutual affection rather than a financial contract, although the laws governing the inheritance of property and the rights of

---

[26] See Nancy Armstrong's *Desire and Domestic Fiction: A Political History of the Novel* (New York: Oxford University Press, 1987), in which she argues that the boundaries between public and private life (necessary to the construction of the middle-class family) were generated and enforced by methods of socialization that were represented most effectively in the novel, especially those written in toward the end of the eighteenth century by women.

[27] See Staves, *Married Women's Separate Property.*

[28] Sir Henry Maine, *Ancient Law*, Sir Frederick Pollock, ed., preface by Raymond Firth (Boston: Beacon Press, 1963) 165.

[29] It was not until the Matrimonial Act of 1857 that secular divorce was allowed for the first time in England. The act also achieved some significant victories for women: a court could order a husband to pay maintenance to a divorced or estranged wife; a divorced wife could inherit or bequeath property in her own right; and a divorced wife could protect her earnings from a husband who had deserted her. The act was weighted against women, however, in that a husband only had to prove that his wife had committed adultery to obtain a divorce but a woman had to prove adultery plus either incest, bigamy, cruelty, or desertion. Such inequities would provide the matter for many novelists in the nineteenth century, including Charles Dickens' *Oliver Twist* (1838), Emily Brontë's *Wuthering Heights* (1847), Ann Brontë's *Tenant of Wildfell Hall* (1848), and Wilkie Collins, *The Woman in White* (1859). See also, Marlene Tromp, *The Private Rod: Marital Violence, Sensation, and the Law in Victorian England* (Charlottesville: University of Virginia Press, 2000); and Lisa Surridge, *Bleak Houses: Marital Violence in Victorian Fiction* (Athens: Ohio University Press, 2005).

wives and widows did not necessarily reflect this change from the contractual to the sentimental. Moreover, this transformation was not achieved without considerable anxiety on the part of those who had always considered their status to be secure in terms of its superior moral, as well as material, wealth. In eighteenth- and nineteenth-century novels, to speak of estates is also to speak of other intimately connected systems of meaning, such as the family and society, as well as those less visible forms of signification, like morality and manners.

By 1800, approximately eighty percent of the land in England was owned by about three percent of the population (the peerage and the gentry), and even after the Second Reform Bill (1834), ownership of property remained the primary requirement for suffrage. One can see that possession of an estate – or the potential to inherit such a property – was the single most important determinant of one's social standing and was intimately related to a complex set of moral values – all of which were supported and protected by English law, which had, of course, been legislated by exactly those who would most benefit from its enforcement. Given the laws of inheritance that favored primogeniture and thus disadvantaged daughters, a romance between a woman with little prospect of inheriting property and a man already "in possession of a great fortune" was synonymous for the woman with a narrative of acquisition and status.[30] To secure a husband was also to proclaim one's paternity (one's legitimacy and virtue) and to acquire property. This narrative, one repeated endlessly in the novels of this period, describes a young woman who must reclaim her social status either denied her by her father's death, poverty, or negligence, or by a false charge of illegitimacy. Her success or failure is marked by her marriage to a man of property (or his economic and moral opposite), and thus readers understand that the laws that control property and those that regulate personal and social relationships are intimately and "naturally" connected. Such is the pattern of many of Jane Austen's novels, most particularly *Pride and Prejudice* (1813), the central legal and structural feature of which is the entailment that controls the disposition of the Bennet estate – or rather, entails the estate to the male line and thus enforces the disinheritance of the Bennet daughters, requiring them to seek the proper husband.[31]

As is appropriate in a novel whose premise is that owning property (that is, land) constitutes the foundation of both individual and social economic and moral value, the structure of *Pride and Prejudice* is determined by the various sites of that economic and moral value: Longbourne, Netherfield, Rosings, Pemberley, houses and seedy lodgings in London, cottages in the countryside, and regimental tents at the seaside. Characters walk, run, march, ride, drive, or are driven in private and public carriages

---

[30] The description of Darcy in the opening lines of Jane Austen's *Pride and Prejudice* (1813).

[31] Entail became very popular in the seventeenth century when it was frequently used by merchants and professionals who were rising into the gentry class and wished to protect their estates from being squandered after their death by reckless sons: They could threaten to or actually entail them away to a more reliable heir.

Imagining the Law

through this veritable catalogue of elegant and less-than-desirable real estate. As William MacNeil suggests, this landscape is, in effect, a "lawscape," each piece of property representing in its own way the legal constraints or freedoms of its owners or renters, its law-abiding subjects or illegal trespassers.[32] The property (house and land), then, literally and figuratively embodies the law that determines its value. As Sandra MacPherson argues, the distinctions between owners and renters are fundamental to the way in which we read these characters' moral stability – for example, Bingley's somewhat capricious behavior, is reflected in his inability to fix on an estate to buy, a move that would obligate a more permanent commitment to the local community.[33]

Although we find Mrs. Bennet amusingly resistant to reason on the topic of the entailment, as she is on so many other topics, her outraged response to the legal power assumed by a previous owner of the Bennet estate to dispossess her daughters is, in fact, shared by all her daughters, if not by the insouciant Mr. Bennet. The narrative of *Pride and Prejudice* depends entirely on this legal maneuver, but critics have been slow to acknowledge the significance to novelistic representation of securing a romance narrative upon a legal strategy. Not only does such a strategy indicate the deep reliance of one kind of social relationship upon another – romantic attachment upon property ownership – but it also suggests the way in which the law achieves its ends by relying on forms of individual and social desire. Austen uses the entail to open up a conversation about how moral obligations and expectations are inextricably tied to legal ones. Sandra MacPherson argues, for example, that "land law, rather than marriage or class, is the ground upon which Austen works out the way in which persons are, or ought to be, connected to others."[34] That the possession of land determines the manner in which one circulates through the social world is clear. Even though he will not pass on his estate to his children, Mr. Bennet nevertheless still owns it and thus can move freely through the world whereas his daughters are presumptively dispossessed by the entailment and are thus restricted, both literally and figuratively, in their movements.

One symbolic representation of Elizabeth Bennet's flouting of restrictive social conventions produced by property and inheritance laws occurs early in the novel when Elizabeth walks to Netherfield to visit Jane. She refuses her father's offer of the carriage, instead preferring to walk freely through the fields – fields that are at first owned by her father. Then she passes onto the Netherfield land rented by Bingley, who does not own the fields but whose inherited wealth (not class) gives him the right to claim them temporally as his own. However briefly and symbolically, Elizabeth does claim the same rights as a man to the land, even if she can never hope to

---

[32] *Novel Judgments* (forthcoming from Routledge). Ms. on file with author.

[33] Sandra MacPherson, "Rent to Own; or What's Entailed in *Pride and Prejudice*," 82 *Representations* (Spring, 2003) 1–23.

[34] MacPherson, 2.

lay permanent claim to her father's land. Upon her arrival at Netherfield, Bingley's sisters, one of whom, like the Bennet girls, must find a husband, attack Elizabeth's character, thus making the connection among property, gender, and propriety quite explicit. Mrs. Hurst exclaims:

> To walk three miles, or four miles, or five miles, or whatever it is, above her ankles in dirt, and alone, quite alone! What could she mean by it? It seems to me to show an abominable sort of conceited independence, a most country-town indifference to decorum.
>
> Miss Bingley: "I think I have heard you say that their uncle is an attorney in Meryton."
>
> "Yes; and they have another, who lives somewhere near Cheapside."
>
> "That is capital," added her sister, and they both laughed heartily.[35]

Assuming the privileges of a male landowner might seem "an abominable sort of conceited independence" for a woman, but Elizabeth's trespass is further compounded by her family's status (albeit on her mother's side): sister to two brothers who must work for their living, one as a lawyer, the other as a merchant. That is, indeed, as they remark "capital(ism)," but it is also, as we have been told, the source of their own wealth.

This exchange between two members of the *nouveau riche* occurs early in the novel but it is matched by another that takes place between Elizabeth and a member of the upper class just before Darcy proposes to Elizabeth the second time. I am referring to the conversation between Darcy's aunt, Lady Catherine de Burgh, and Elizabeth Bennet. Unlike their first meeting, when Elizabeth was the guest and Lady Catherine the autocratic hostess, this time, it is Lady Catherine who travels to meet Elizabeth on her own (albeit entailed) ground. Determined to prevent Elizabeth from engaging herself to Darcy, whom Lady Catherine has "contracted" from the cradle to marry her daughter and thus unite the two estates, Lady Catherine suggests to Elizabeth that Darcy may have forgotten "what he owes to himself and all *his family*" (emphasis added). To consider seriously

> "The upstart pretensions of a young woman without family, connections, or fortune. Is this to be endured! But it must not, shall not be. If you were sensible of your own good, you would not wish to quit the sphere in which you have been brought up."
>
> "In marrying your nephew," Elizabeth responds, "I should not consider myself as quitting that sphere. He is a gentleman; I am a gentleman's daughter; so far we are equal."

---

[35] Jane Austen, *Pride and Prejudice*, Donald Gray, ed. (New York: W. W. Norton & Co., 2001) 25.

Imagining the Law

True. You are a gentleman's daughter. But who was your mother? Who are your uncles and aunts? Do not imagine me ignorant of their condition. Are the shades of Pemberley to be thus polluted?"[36]

"He is a gentleman; I am a gentleman's daughter. So far we are equal." It's a very romantic sentiment but, despite its literal accuracy, everything we have witnessed in the novel tells us that they are not equal. Despite the scorn that Mr. Bennet casts on his wife for her failure to grasp the complexities of entail, Mrs. Bennet is actually the most insightful when it comes to assessing the value of her neighbors and the contribution they can make to ensuring that her daughters have some means of support once their father is dead – because as Mr. Bennet admits, he has done little to guarantee them any kind of financial security. When Mrs. Bennet first sees Darcy, she believes him to be the most handsome man in the room – 10,000 pounds handsome – but when he slights Lizzie, he falls rapidly in her estimation. She is superficial and constantly exposes the family to humiliation but she clearly understands that one's personal value is the direct result of one's property. Only a man who already owned Pemberley could afford to choose a wife who had such family connections as Elizabeth has – as Darcy makes clear in his first marriage proposal, and there is nothing in the rest of the novel to change this perception.

By the early nineteenth century, the boundaries between the middling classes and the gentry and aristocracy were dissolving and, as Nancy Armstrong has argued, part of what produced and consolidated that dissolution was the way the novel, especially that written by women, represented an "individual's value in terms of his, but more often in terms of *her*, essential qualities of mind" rather than her social status.[37] Women were thus separated from the political sphere, and their domestic virtues assumed the place formerly occupied by birth and the entitlements of title. Armstrong argues that the novel thus contributed to the organizing of gender relations in the eighteenth and nineteenth centuries, substituting male and female qualities of mind (their emotional and psychological acuity or its absence) for the more overt and traditional markers of power. Thus the cultivation of the mind as a moral instrument was advanced as the foremost task of educators, especially in the education of young women whose fortunes were limited. For the Evelinas, the Graces, the Fannys, the Elizabeths, the Janes, and the Dorotheas, marriage results from their discerning moral sensibility and not because of their birth or future wealth.[38] Moreover, such education not only brings individual good fortune, it also acts to reform society, producing families whose good moral standing ensures the

---

[36] Ibid., 232.

[37] Armstrong, 4.

[38] Evelina from Frances Burney's *Evelina* (1778); Grace from Maria Edgeworth's *The Absentee* (1812); Elizabeth from Jane Austen's *Pride and Prejudice* (1813); Fanny from Jane Austen's *Mansfield Park* (1814); Jane from Charlotte Bronte's *Jane Eyre* (1847); and Dorothea from George Eliot's *Middlemarch* (1874).

stability of society at large – acts of education and reformation that extend beyond the novel's fictional characters to those who read the novels. In the particular form that came to dominate the genre by the middle of the nineteenth century, then, the novel could be said to police the social through the sentimental.[39]

Fictional and Legal Reformation

The novel became the dominant literary genre during the nineteenth century, an ascendancy that both relied upon and reinvigorated the historical connection between the early eighteenth-century novel as a form of "news," originally disseminated as broadsheets and as criminal biographies, and the storytelling that took place in legal venues.[40] Victorian readers were exposed to multiple sources for their understanding of the law – as indeed we are today – from the quickly produced and published accounts of spectacular crimes to the more considered approaches of respectable newspapers to the even more sustained treatment afforded by the novel. Moreover, as Jonathan H. Grossman has argued, the gradual shift from the act of punishment (on the scaffold) to the imposition of punishment (in the courtroom), combined with the widespread readership of newspapers, created an audience eager for the details of court hearings and an analysis of the participants' motives.

> In the nineteenth century, newspapers brought the action of the law courts into ordinary lives. For the first time in British history a large number of people could be expected regularly to read a lengthy report of court proceeding. Whereas the broadsheet had once presented the scaffold as a socializing force, the newspapers began to inculcate a new forensic subjectivity. While foreign news helped establish a reader as English (in opposition to other nationalities) and coverage of the monarchy and parliament implied a reader who was a political subject, crime and trial reports constructed the newspaper reader as an answerable member of a lawbound state.[41]

[39] One can see a similar reliance on the sentimental to articulate legal and political relationships in the American novel; see in particular, Jane Tompkins, *Sensational Designs: The Cultural Work of American Fiction, 1790–1860* (New York: Oxford University Press, 1985); Cathy N. Davidson, *Revolution and the Word: The Rise of the Novel in America* (New York: Oxford University Press, 1986); and Wai Chee Dimock, *Residues of Justice: Literature, Law, Philosophy* (Berkeley: University of California Press, 1996).

[40] Theoretical analysis in law and literature has largely followed Alexander Welsh's model first articulated in *Strong Representations* (1993): The novel, as a form of discourse, is compared to legal discourse. Thus, judges' opinions, trial transcripts, and other legal narratives are juxtaposed with parallel legal language or rhetorical constructions in novels. Building on this approach, Jonathan H. Grossman's *The Art of the Alibi* addresses how the genre also defined itself against and through the cultural and material presence of the law court – both a symbolic and a real place where stories were reconstructed (6).

[41] Grossman, 32–3.

Imagining the Law

The literature of "moral outrage" and the concomitant appeal for social reform was widespread, appearing in the cheap popular press, in the more respectable newspapers, in literary weekly or monthly serials, and in novels. Fictional narratives of crime and criminality, of policing and punishment, represented a legal system that, in its most ideal version, partnered with society to reform the wicked and advance a progressive, reformist ideology. Moreover, in line with their expectations that crime would be punished and the offenders safely incarcerated behind bars, most novels also ended with society restored to proper order and the criminals properly identified and separated from the innocent.

Accounts of real and fictional legal events reflected changes that had occurred in evidential theory and practice over the last century. As Alexander Welsh has argued, the particular development of evidential narratives through the eighteenth and nineteenth centuries led to an increasing reliance in trials on circumstantial details and a forensic analysis of the character's motives and intent. Such traits were also evident in the work of those novelists whose fictional tales drew on both actual and imagined legal events for their subject matter. Thus, as Maximillian E. Novak suggests, "Just as the courts of law came to focus more and more on facts and evidence [as opposed to eye-witness accounts that could be falsified], so fiction came to function in a world of secondary causes and events."[42] The emplotment of facts and evidence within a circumstantial legal narrative that seemed, by virtue of its inevitable cause-and-effect logic, dispositive in a court of law, took on quite a different nature in a fictional narrative. The fictional world of "secondary causes and events" can make that which seems unfalsifiable open to question. Thus Welsh argues that at the moment when the "'probative force' of circumstantial evidence was most seriously sought after by theorists and practitioners of the law, the attitude of English novelists toward fictionality itself underwent a change."[43]

The nineteenth-century novel increasingly tested the limits of the apparently circumstantially true narrative through the characters' intervention, actual or speculatively, into the events. In this confrontation between the authority of the circumstantial narrative and the interventions of the individual characters, one can see the beginnings of a genre that would rise to enormous popularity by the end of the century: the detective novel, a genre that both identifies itself with, and yet inevitably critiques, the legal structures of society.

The result of this change in attitude by novelists is evidenced in the fiction of, among others, Dickens, Gaskell, and Eliot, where one finds both a reliance on circumstantial evidence to advance the plot as well as on the forensic analysis of character. One of the key formal innovations that enabled this authorial investigation into the characters' outward behavior through an analysis of their internal

---

[42] Maximillian E. Novak, *Realism, Myth, and History in Defoe's Fiction* (Lincoln: University of Nebraska Press, 1983) 125, quoted in Welsh, 41.

[43] Welsh, 42.

motives was the development of specific narrative techniques, such as free indirect discourse.[44] These techniques combined to create the effect of a transcendent and omnipotent authorial voice – one that, as critics such as D. A. Miller and John Bender have argued, seemed able to contain the world of criminality and illegality, producing, as Miller puts it, a *cordon sanitaire* between that illicit world and the orderly world of the novel's readers.[45] Miller asserts that the novel both separates the disciplined from the undisciplined and represents that disciplining in its very form; by so doing, it calls into question its subversive capabilities: "Whenever the novel censures policing power, it has already reinvented it, in the *very practice of novelistic representation*."[46]

Miller and Bender rely on Foucault, specifically his *Discipline and Punish* (*Surveiller et punir*), to advance their claims about the disciplinary force of the novel in the nineteenth century.[47] As Lisa Rodensky puts it in her analysis of the representation of criminal responsibility in the Victorian novel, *The Crime in the Mind*, Foucault "targets . . . changes in nineteenth-century jurisprudence that, in effect, shifted attention from an act to an intent, from external behavior to internal drives, from conduct to character."[48] Paraphrasing Foucault, Rodensky asserts:

> [u]nder cover of the relative stability of the law a mass of subtle and rapid changes has occurred. Certainly the "crimes" and "offences" on which judgement is passed are juridical objects defined by the code, but judgement is also passed on the passions, instincts, anomalies, infirmities, maladjustments, effects of environment or heredity.
>
> The criminal's soul is not referred to in the trial merely to explain his crime and as a factor in the juridical apportioning of responsibility; if it is brought before the court, with such pomp and circumstance, such concern to understand and such "scientific" application, it is because it too, as well as the crime itself, is to be judged and to share in the punishment.[49]

The extension of social and legal judgment from the crime to the criminal's intent and psychological condition and even, argues Foucault, to the criminal's soul, makes the task of reforming society both more difficult and more pressing: The belief in

---

[44] Free indirect discourse is a style of third-person narration, combining the voice of the narrator with a character's (indirect) first-person thoughts, views, and feelings. The use of free indirect discourse inevitably produces ambiguity as to whether the narrator or the character is voicing the sentiments expressed, and thus the technique can be used to produce an ironic contrast between external and internal points of view.

[45] D. A. Miller, *The Novel and the Police* (Berkeley: University of California Press, 1988) 5. See also, Bender, *Imagining the Penitentiary*; Grossman, *The Art of the Alibi*.

[46] Miller, 20. One might also argue that whenever the law insists upon objectivity and fact, it also acknowledges the "fictions" by which it operates.

[47] Michel Foucault, *Discipline and Punish*, Alan Sheridan, trans. (New York: Pantheon, 1977).

[48] Lisa Rodensky, *The Crime in the Mind: Criminal Responsibility and the Victorian Novel* (New York: Oxford University Press, 2003) 16.

[49] Rodensky, 16–17, quoting Foucault, *Discipline and Punish*, 17–18.

Imagining the Law   231

a providential narrative that would eventually bring criminality and corruption to judgment that had sustained Whig ideology in the eighteenth century was replaced by doubt as to the possibility of reforming the criminal. As the novel grew in influence and popularity, so too did its importance in promoting a law-abiding citizenry and reforming social corruption. The response to the so-called Newgate novels, fictionalized versions of true crimes popular in the 1840s and 1850s, reveals the ongoing tension between the admonitory and prurient intent in representing antisocial behavior: Praised and condemned by critics, the novels either demonstrated the inevitability of punishment or they encouraged the glorification and emulation of the criminal.[50] Unlike the apparently straightforward rehearsal of court narratives in newspapers or the overt fictionalizing of real crimes in the Newgate novels, Dickens' novels complicates this simple equation of the representation of crime with either admonition or promotion. Likewise, his novels complicate the reductive, antilegalistic position assumed by most critics of his works, despite Dickens' critique of certain unwholesome representatives of the law.

The novel most directly and obsessively concerned with the byzantine and often deliberately obscure methods of the law is *Bleak House,* at the center of which is the Court of Chancery and the case that epitomizes the workings of that court – *Jarndyce v. Jarndyce.*[51] England's Court of Chancery and its lawyers are the specific target of Dickens' criticism, but his novel addresses not only the flaws in the British legal system but uses that system as a metaphor for the corruption, inhumanity, and gridlock in the social system. Moreover, the interconnectedness of sociolegal and personal relationships is reflected in the interconnectedness of the characters' lives, bound together through the double-voiced narrative point of view: the first-person narrative of Esther Summerson, the revelation of whose mysterious parentage also unlocks the secrets of the lost Jarndyce will that resolves the lawsuit, and the omniscient narrator whose presence everywhere and nowhere epitomizes the pervasiveness of the law's effects, much like the fog that obscures the city of London.

Fog everywhere. Fog up the river, where it flows among green aits [islands] and meadows; fog down the river, where it flows defiled among the tiers of

---

[50] "Well beyond the Newgate novels of William Harrison Ainsworth and Edward Bulwer-Lytton (from both of whom Dickens distanced himself) and the Sensation novels of Wilkie Collins (which Dickens promoted), the novels of Trollope and Thackeray required (and require) of their readers serious thinking about responsibilities, both civil and criminal, legal, and moral. Yet beyond even Trollope and Thackeray are the deeply complicated representations of responsibility in the novels of George Eliot" (Rodensky, 7).

[51] The Court of Chancery, founded during the reign of Richard II (1377–1399), developed from the Lord Chancellor's jurisdiction and was a court of equity. That is, unlike the common law courts, based on precedent, the Lord Chancellor had jurisdiction to determine cases, on behalf of the monarch, according to equity or fairness, rather than according to the strict letter of the law. By Dickens' time the court was a model of inefficiency and was merged with the common law courts in 1873, with common law judges given the power to administer equity.

shipping, and the waterside pollutions of a great (and dirty) city. Fog on the Essex marshes. Fog on the Kentish heights.... And hard by Temple Bar, in Lincoln's Inn Hall, at the very heart of the fog, sits the Lord High Chancellor in his High Court of Chancery.[52]

We see the impossibility of pinning down the human face of the law and therefore the impossibility of locating justice: The Court resides at the heart of the fog and yet the fog is everywhere. Likewise, the effects of the court's action – or rather one should say inaction – are felt everywhere, reaching from the wealthy aristocrat to Jo, the poorest street sweeper. Moreover, there are no details offered about why the case is being litigated or what the proper (that is, just) outcome might be. The law is at once everywhere and nowhere and its subjects are simultaneously subject to the law and outside the law: Justice is obscure and obscured.

The alternative to the bleak house of the Court of Chancery is another Bleak House, located outside the city and whose owner, John Jarndyce, is a model of compassion. In this other Bleak House there is a type of justice unimaginable to the law courts and the metropolitan enforcers of that law, the police, who push Jo from one miserable sleeping place to another. Dickens seems to be arguing for a reliance on the individual and his or her small acts of compassion and affection rather than the official machinery of the social system. His view seems to argue for a conservative belief in the individual as the most significant producer of social change rather than a more radical belief in the possibility of social reform through the state and its official representatives in the law.

Dickens enforces the power of those bonds of personal and sentimental affection as refuge against a heartless world by weaving several romances (some tragic, some comic) throughout the narrative. Once again, the romance narrative, or the marriage plot, is linked inseparably to the questions of property, but unlike its earlier incarnations, the bureaucratic regime that manipulates and disseminates the rights to property actively assumes a role in the plot. Legal bureaucracy, no longer embodied in the singular person of the lawyer who enacts the contract to a marriage or settlement, now assumes a omnipresent and insidious presence in this modern version of romance. One version of this legalistic romance occurs in the relationship between Ada and Richard, the two wards of Chancery, who are the latest victims of the deadly *Jarndyce v. Jarndyce* virus. Richard's desperate and deadly pursuit of his inheritance through the labyrinthine legal system eventually causes his death, leaving Ada with their child. Even the evidence of others driven to madness and suicide by the unending delays and complexities of their cases cannot deter Richard. Moreover, Richard's suspicions of his guardian's motives in trying to keep him apart from Ada also generates a hostile relationship – another Jarndyce against Jarndyce. In these repetitions of the original lawsuit, we see not only the endless reach of

[52] Charles Dickens, *Bleak House* (New York: Bantam, 1992) 1.

Imagining the Law

the law but also the way in which the law's representation of individual and social disputes – as one party against another – pervades all other relationships, even those that seem to be entirely personal and intimate.[53]

Even though the law in its various manifestations – as court, as judge, as lawsuit, as lawyer, as legal scribe – seems omnipresent, the introduction of Inspector Bucket suggests that the law cannot produce closure or justice without the forensic skills of the individual whose flexibility and mobility undermines the fixity of the system. As Rodensky, paraphrasing Miller, argues:

> The great turn in D. A. Miller's essay on *Bleak House* . . . comes when Miller shows how the shift from the chancery/inheritance plot to the murder plot in Bleak House produces clarity of agency and of resolution, of action/reaction and cause and effect, which chancery thwarts but murder delivers. Miller suggests, then, that the shift from the civil to the criminal offers the fantastic and the longed-for simplicity of who did what to whom.[54]

Inspector Bucket solves the murder of the lawyer Tulkinghorn, tracks down Lady Dedlock, who turns out to be Esther's mother, and finds the will that finally ends the Chancery case. Inspector Bucket therefore does what the great Court of Chancery is unable to do – he makes something happen. In contrast to the story of the lawsuit *Jarndyce v. Jarndyce*, which is unreadable because there are so many tens of thousands of documents that have accumulated over the years, the murder mystery can be solved because there is a story with identifiable characters and events that have a cause-and-effect relationship rather than the arbitrary disposition of events that occurs in the Chancery Court. Unlike the ubiquitous presence of the court in which there is no evidence of a responsible agent or agents against whom one can protest, or to whom one can appeal for relief, the murder mystery is the result of individuals acting out of motives that can be apprehended and understood – although only retrospectively. In arguing that the murder mystery and the precise work of Inspector Bucket presents a contrast to the amorphous and elusive power of the court, Dickens suggests that the Court of Chancery makes an Inspector Bucket necessary – that one legal mechanism, in effect, produces the other, its necessary supplement. Such a way of reading the murder plot and the presence of Bucket in the narrative implies paradoxically that although the presence of Bucket gives a concrete form to the authority of the law, the figure of the detective is part of

---

[53] Another, more successful romance, is that between Esther, illegitimate daughter of Lady Dedlock, and Allan Woodstock. Their marriage reiterates the belief that domestic happiness is the antidote, not just for the court, but for the whole world that requires the police to manage events. In his vision of the city of London and its inhabitants caught in a bureaucratic, legalistic nightmare, Dickens prefigures the work of Franz Kafka; Dickens, however, can still rely on the myth of the domestic hearth in which the Esther Summersons of the world can offer comfort against a heartless society.

[54] Rodensky, 17.

a larger narrative that subsumes both him and the Court of Chancery. Indeed, if we follow Bucket as he makes his way through the passages and dark alleys that surround the court and its premises, or watch him as he tracks Lady Dedlock through a snowbound and dark winter's night, we must wonder if this landscape is not yet another version of the court – one that provides us with the comfort of believing in a story that makes sense but which may, in effect, be as endless and bizarre as *Jarndyce v. Jarndyce*. The satisfactions afforded by the detective story may be, in other words, a false consolation.

The introduction of the detective into the novel's repertoire of characters and mechanisms for controlling social and personal illegalities and deviance heralds the rapid rise of a narrative genre that has come to dominate our perception of law's representation in the novel: the detective novel (and its related, but not identical genre, the crime novel), the origins of which can be traced to mid-Victorian England's sensation novels.[55] Themselves a composite of gothic novels and the Newgate novel, sensational novels "revolve around the legal status of marriage and the conflicts created by inheritance and property laws. The crime most peculiar to the sensation novel is bigamy, in which a sexual relation or romance is directly under the jurisdiction of the law."[56] As novels both of romance and of property, they continue the tradition of narratives of novelists such as Frances Burney and Jane Austen but in their novels law's agency is not embodied in any specific character. In sensation novels, the law in either its formal or informal embodiment is pitted against the figure of the criminalized and sexualized woman who contrasts dramatically with the sentimentalized and idealized heroine of much Victorian fiction. In their focus on women's sexualized criminality, sensation novels both reflect the concerns of early-eighteenth-century novels and prefigure what will become a central obsession of twentieth-century narratives; moreover, in their implicit suggestion that there is something mysterious and potentially dangerous beneath the appearance of tranquility, these novels prepare the way for the modernist rejection of narrative verisimilitude.

---

[55] "The sensation novel is distinct as a genre from its precursors because its crimes and mysteries occur, not in foreign countries or wild landscapes, not among the lower classes or the inhabitants of monasteries and convents, but in the stately homes of the aristocracy, whose lives are depicted in realistic detail." Ann Cvetokovich, *Mixed Feelings: Feminism, Mass Culture, and Victorian Sensationalism* (New Brunswick, NJ: Rutgers University Press. 1992) 45. For a different trajectory of the detective genre, see Grossman:

> [A]lthough detective fiction and its relation to disciplinary systems has been well fathomed by critics . . . , this book [*The Art of the Alibi*] is the first to argue that in the era between gallows literature and the detective mystery, between Tyburn's scaffold and . . . Baker Street, the law courts crucially shaped the formal structures and political aims of the novel. In so doing, it aims broadly to present a new history of crime fiction and refigure our understanding of the link between storytelling and justice. (32)

[56] Cvetkovich, 46.

Imagining the Law

The sensation novels' first and best exemplar is Wilkie Collins' *The Woman in White* (1860), the "Preamble" to which claims the status of a quasilegal document made necessary, its author claims, because the legal system cares only for those with power and wealth. It falls upon the shoulders of Walter Hartright (whose name describes his character) to unravel the mysteries and illegalities surrounding the disinheritance of Laura Fairlie, who has been forced into marriage by her father with a wealthy but immoral suitor. (Note the resurgence of the plot so popular in the eighteenth century.) Hartright is not a lawyer but a poor art teacher and makes no claim to being instructed in the law but says that he will tell the story – by arranging a series of eyewitness accounts in epistolary form – so that the reader can follow the narrative just as the judge might hear it. Although disavowing the judicial procedures of English law, the narrator nevertheless relies on precisely that method to make his case. In fact, as Miller points out, it is no longer the policeman or detective who conducts the surveillance and inquiry necessary to solve the case, but the ordinary man, untrained in law and detective work, who takes it upon himself to make sense of factual and psychological mysteries, which are now perceived as part of the everyday world.[57]

Moreover, even though the eighteenth-century judicious reader seems to make a reappearance here as the one who will interpret the evidence, her nineteenth-century version gets more than the excitement of unraveling the mystery. As Ann Cvetkovich points out, the manner in which the mystery is untangled depends extensively on the shock of the unexpected.[58] "Nothing could be less judicial, or judicious, than the actual hermeneutic practice of the reader of this novel," insists Miller.[59] As one who participates (even enjoys) the sensational shocks that emplot the novel, the reader is now implicated in the fascination of witnessing sexualized and criminalized immorality; she is no longer permitted to withdraw to a safe distance and watch, an objective and rational observer. The reach of the law now extends beyond the pages of the book and into the very interior life of the reader: No longer are we simply exercising surveillance over the characters; we now "feel" the shock of being watched.

The intrusion of such disciplining strategies into the reader's psychological space prepares us, of course, for the manipulation of the reader's psychic and intellectual relationship to reality that accompanies modernist and postmodernist narratives. By the end of the nineteenth century, novelists will have been provided with a language (psychoanalysis) to account for what cannot be seen or felt, except in the innermost reaches of the unconscious. Authors will self-reflexively turn their gaze upon themselves, an overt scrutiny reserved previously only for their fictional

---

[57] Miller, 157.
[58] Cvetkovich, 72.
[59] Miller, 158.

characters. As the law becomes more reliant on scientific evidence and the logic of statistics, novelists will use narrative strategies and techniques that push more and more intensely against the traditional conventions of fictional representation, making anew the vexed relationship between the representation and its referent, the fictional and the real.

Fictional and Legal Misrepresentations

As a result, in part, of the privileging of empirical and technological criteria of value, contemporary society experiences radical doubt about language's capacity to capture either felt experience or historical event, an uncertainty that attends all efforts at representation. No cultural institution or discourse is exempt from this uncertainty, especially not the discourse of the law, despite (or because of) its claims to objectivity and authenticity. Indeed, it is precisely the conventions governing representation itself that have come under a frontal attack from the novel in the last 100 years, producing fictional texts that unsettle both the idea of what is "realistic" and of what is "representable." One consequence of this representational dubiety is an intensification of the perennial anxiety about the ethical effects of these unsettling fictions. In particular, the relationship between the aesthetic value of the text and its ethical implications has come under severe scrutiny. Nowhere is the tension between the aesthetics and ethics of a novel more pronounced than when the topic is sexuality, especially of the kind that lies outside of culturally normative boundaries. Indeed, aesthetics is central to legal judgments that determine whether the text under consideration is legally obscene. One novel that illustrates this explosive combination (or collision) of aesthetics, sexuality, and legality is Vladimir Nabokov's *Lolita* (1955).[60]

The novel continues to provoke debate about the connection between the representation of morally offensive behavior and the prohibition of such behavior in real life. When Nabokov first approached his publisher with the typescript of the novel, he was told that publishing the book would put both of them in jail. After several refusals from American publishers, Olympia Press, a Parisian publisher whose other authors included Samuel Beckett, Jean Genet, and William S. Burroughs, finally agreed to publish the novel. In addition to such avant-garde writers, however, Olympia Press also published down-market sex novels, with titles like *White Thighs* and *The Sexual Life of Robinson Crusoe*. The latter title is ironic considering that the full title of Nabokov's novel is *Lolita, or the Confession of a White Widowed Male* and that Humbert Humbert's confession is presented as a text that has passed through the hands of an editor before it reached the public – precisely the fictional

---

[60] Two other twentieth-century novels also immediately come to mind: *Ulysses* and *Lady Chatterley's Lover*, the latter representing class as well as sexual transgression.

Imagining the Law

conventions that govern the early eighteenth-century novel, one of the best-known exponents of which is Daniel Defoe, author of the confessions of *Moll Flanders* and *The Life and Strange Adventures of Robinson Crusoe*. Novelist Graham Greene first drew attention to the literary value of the novel in an article published in England in 1955 – but the British Home Office was unimpressed and ordered customs officials to seize all copies entering the United Kingdom. The British also pressured the French Minister to ban the book, which he did. It remained so for two years. *Lolita* was distributed in America, however, without any legal battle, surprisingly so because D. H. Lawrence's *Lady Chatterley's Lover* was still considered an obscene book until 1959. Together with the trial of Henry Miller's *Tropic of Cancer*, which was finally published in America in 1964, the trial of *Lady Chatterley's Lover* would mark the beginning of the end of censorship merely on the grounds that its representation of sexuality might offend. The end came with *Memoirs* v. *Massachusetts* (383 U.S. 413) in 1966. In this decision, the Supreme Court examined John Cleland's *Memoirs of a Woman of Pleasure*, better known as *Fanny Hill*, first published in 1750, and ruled that to be judged obscene, a book must be "utterly without redeeming social value" – meaning that the material lacks serious literary, artistic, political, or scientific value.

The debate over the nature of the obscene cannot easily be resolved – and perhaps law is not always, or ever, the best place for that resolution. The persistent popularity of *Lolita* suggests that even when we are horrified by the capacity of human nature to harm the vulnerable, we are nevertheless fascinated by the brilliance with which the predator justifies his desire. Just as Humbert is tormented by his desire, as is Lolita, the reader is tormented by the belief that we can understand the pervert. In *Lolita*, the development of what Foucault calls a "forensic subjectivity" in fictional characters now extends to the reader and the narrator, Humbert Humbert, whose obsessive concern with his own motives and justifications is nowhere balanced by that nineteenth-century omniscient narrator who provided the reader with the solace of an ordered and commonsensical understanding of the world. The reader is also obsessively concerned with her motives and justifications: She not only has no way of arriving at a resolution to the crisis, but her own moral and aesthetic judgments are under suspicion. The tables have been turned – we, the readers, are now under suspicion and yet there seems, Kafkaesque-like, no law (of morality, of interpretation, or of representation) but what we imagine it to be, no judgment but of our own making. As such, we find ourselves colluding with the narrator, who likewise seems to exist in a solipsistic universe where individual desire makes up the rules and deceit is the name of the game.

The "conning" begins in the novel's Foreword, in which the editor, John Ray, Jr., Ph.D., explains that Humbert Humbert's confession to the murder of Lolita's lover came into his hands through Humbert's lawyer. This use of the double-voiced narrative – the notional narrator speaks through the *persona* of the editor – recalls the way in which Defoe was able both to criticize and yet also authorize the narrative of Moll Flanders. Indeed, there is much about *Lolita* that recalls the eighteenth-century's fascination with criminal biographies and murderer's confessions, as well as mid-nineteenth-century Newgate novels and sensation novels. Not the least part of that fascination is the reader's covert wish to be horrified and excited by the lurid details of the crime. Indeed, part of the function of Ray's Foreword is to seduce the reader into accepting the narrative that follows as a "true confession," as the narrative of Humbert Humbert's obsession with Lolita, written over fifty-six days while Humbert is imprisoned awaiting trial for murder.[61] For that seduction to work we have to have some trust in Dr. Ray, that he is who he says he is: the author of a book titled *Do the Senses Make Sense?*, friend and relation of H. H.'s lawyer who handed over the confession, and resident of Widworth, Massachusetts. This elaborate construction of verisimilitude was apparently so convincing to an English publishing company that they decided to separate the Foreword from the novel, discarding it in favor of one written by Martin Amis, the English novelist! Not only did they deprive the reader of the necessary ludic introduction to Humbert's own verbal gamesmanship but they also removed the information in the original Foreword that announced that both protagonists, Lolita and Humbert, were already dead.[62] Such knowledge is not incidental to the way in which one reads Humbert's confession but crucial to our concern with law's capacity to provide justice for the victim and punish the victimizer.

For the alert reader, the Foreword is littered with clues to its fabricated nature: for example, the way the editor's initials double his "junior" relationship to the narrative – that is, John Ray is J. R. who is thus also a "Jr." Such verbal play reminds us of another double name, the narrator's pseudonymous Humbert Humbert. The uncertain status of the Foreword as an accurate rendering of the relationship between the "editor" and the narrator of the confession is duplicated in the confusion of the reader over the moral status of Humbert's relationship with Lolita: As a judge and jury listen to render judgment, so we read to know what is legally and morally acceptable and what is illegal and immoral, what is normal, and what is perverse. This "bright line" version of events is, of course, precisely what H. H. spends considerable skill rejecting as an accurate description of the world he once inhabited with Lolita, or, indeed, the world he inhabits even when he is in prison charged with a murder of which he is obviously guilty. The psychosis from which H. H. suffers can find expression only in a narrative that Ray believes will become "a classic in psychiatric

---

[61] For a subtle analysis of the relationship between confession and the law, see Peter Brooks's *Troubling Confessions* (Chicago: University of Chicago Press, 2000), especially his argument that "our social and cultural attitudes toward confession suffer from uncertainties and ambivalences. And...these uncertainties and ambivalences should indicate that confession is a difficult and slippery notion to deal with" (3).

[62] Lolita dies in childbirth and Humbert Humbert dies of a heart attack a few days before his trial was about to start.

Imagining the Law

circles" and one that Ray insists is a "tragic tale" that moves "unswervingly to nothing less than a moral apotheosis."[63] Ray prepares the reader for moral ambivalence: we can recognize that H. H. is both a "shining example of moral leprosy" and yet also a writer who can "conjure up a tendresse, a compassion for Lolita that makes us entranced with the book while abhorring its author."[64] Our dilemma as readers is, of course, echoed in the law's attempt to distinguish pornography from art – both terms that come culturally laden with an already overdetermined weight of legal, moral, and aesthetic bias.

Thus Ray both does and does not serve the normalizing role of an editor – one whose admonitory voice "allows the reader to resist being absorbed by the fictional lures of a particular genre: . . . the liberating effect of criminal transgression, and the devious and furtive lubricity of sexual intrigue."[65] The reader's ethical ambiguity about Ray is reinforced by the "fancy prose style" that Humbert adopts in his confession that is, like so much else in this novel, both what it claims to be – a narrative of transgression and guilt – and yet simultaneously a denial of that narrative genre.[66] Humbert seduces the reader into "playing the game" of turning a perversity into a "tendresse," and of coming to acknowledge the aesthetic beauty of a representation with which Humbert enchants even those who wish to condemn him.[67] We are thus both witnesses and accomplices to the representation of a "crime" that becomes harder and harder to delineate. We are invited, as readers, to play detective and follow the clues left by Humbert in which he appears to "confess": He offers us hints, clues, tormenting half-truths, and sometimes, even straightforward plot summary – "something bad is about to happen," he might say. The very nature of language itself, Nabokov suggests, unsettles the social and moral certainties upon which law and legal decisions depend, just as it unsettles the representation of a verisimilitudinous reality.

The acute reader is thus torn between seduction and detection, between yielding to the desire for a coherent narrative (for something that makes sense) and resisting the deception. One is called upon, however, to decide in the end: Is Humbert mad and therefore unreliable, or only pretending to be mad and therefore unreliable in different ways as the teller of his own story? Or, and this is the most radical possibility, are the conventional distinctions between madness and sanity, between perverse and normal sexuality, between the illegal and the legal, themselves unreliable categories through which to make sense of the world?

---

[63] Vladimir Nabokov, The Annotated Lolita, Alfred Appel, Jr., ed. (New York: Vintage, 1991) 5.

[64] Ibid., 5.

[65] William B. Warner, Licensing Entertainment: The Elevation of Novel Reading in Britain, 1684–1750 (Berkeley: University of California Press, 1998) 151.

[66] Lolita, 9.

[67] One well-known example is H. H.'s reflection on Lolita's previous sexual experience and the difference between "the rapist" and "therapist."

Postscript

The centrality that nineteenth-century novelists accorded law's empire in their fictional world has not been displaced in the twentieth and twenty-first centuries. On the contrary, it seems that representations of law and law's effects have increased exponentially and that legal narratives now dominate the literary (and media) marketplace. Moreover, it is now generally accepted that law is not simply a technique or an objective body of knowledge but is, like the novel, a distinctive way of representing the world. The interpretation of laws, as well as legal practices and the role of law in constructing a just society, are open to debate and, like literature, subject to those laws (ethical and aesthetic) that govern imagined realities. We have, it seemed, come full circle and returned once again to that ancient apprehension that the imaginary contaminates the search for truth that the law must pursue. In this contemporary version of the dilemma, however, it is precisely this contamination (or more positively, this complexity) that constitutes the focus both of literary representations of the law and the law's interrogation of its own standing in culture.

9

Imagining Law as Film (Representation without Reference?)

Richard K. Sherwin

Today we have law on the books, law in action, and now, law in the image... Law lives in images that today saturate our culture and that have a power all their own.
– Austin Sarat[1]

What has film to do with law? Film can be about law, or ostensibly about law. It can reenact famous cases and controversies, or focus on various features of the legal system. Law films can turn viewers into mock jurors, investigators, and advocates. They can show us how the adversarial process reconstructs historic reality inside the courtroom, and how it enacts a dramatic reality of its own. Films can also use any of these topics as a pretext for launching a different sort of story altogether, a melodrama say, or a mystery, in which law serves as no more than a prop or plotting device. Just as law stories may set a story in motion that ultimately has little to do with law itself, the converse is also true. Films not apparently about law may provide insights into analytical methods, social values, and community aspirations that lie at the heart of the legal mind and culture.[2] The quest for justice, and how it goes astray, the clash between vengeance and mercy or between the formality of rules and the free play of equity, the struggle to solve a mystery amid the infinite complexities of human

---

[1] Austin Sarat, "Imagining the Law of the Father: Loss, Dread, and Mourning in the Sweet Hereafter," *Law and Society Review* 34 (2000) 3, 9, 39.

[2] As Carol Clover writes, "Trials are already movie-like to begin with and movies are already trial-like to begin with... the plot structures and narrative procedures (even certain visual procedures, in film and television) of a broad stripe of American popular culture are derived from the structure and procedure of the Anglo-American trial... this structure and these procedures are so deeply embedded in our narrative tradition that they shape even plots that never step into a courtroom, and that such trial-derived forms constitute the most distinctive share of Anglo-American entertainment. Carol Clover, "Law and the Order of Popular Culture" in Austin Sarat and T. R. Kearns, eds., *Law in the Domains of Culture* (Ann Arbor: University of Michigan Press, 1998), 99–100. On this analysis, even in films without trials "the narrative machine underneath the manifest plot, whatever its label, is the trial. There may be no trial in the movie, but there is a trial underneath and behind it; the movie itself mimics the phases, logic, and the narrative texture of the trial." Ibid. at 220.

motivation and the recursive contingencies of time and circumstance – each of these themes has a place in the legal process. Each may just as readily unfold in a courtroom drama, a Western, a gangster film or, for that matter, a film noir or even a comedy.[3]

If we take law films seriously, if there is no pretext about their relevance to law, or if the pretext gives way under force of analysis to themes close to law's heart, we will find that film has much to tell us about the way we understand (or wish to perceive, or fear to learn about) the way our legal institutions function. Films may readily serve as barometers of juridical success and failure. In the archive of law films, for every heroic juror we will find a corrupt one, for every triumph of the rule of law and justice we will find a failure that returns, like Banquo's ghost, to haunt our collective imagination, a specter in search of relief from some unredressed wrong. Perhaps this time, in this dramatic reenactment, we will see how we might have gotten it right. Perhaps we will learn, as if for the first time, how we got it wrong to begin with. Films preach as well as teach. A film may glorify a particular legal institution, practice, or ideal, or cynically mock defects and abuses of power that plague the system. A film may also mimic or parody legal reasoning, perhaps in deference to an absurd, surreal, or acausal universe far removed from the rational one that law typically takes for granted.[4]

In the foregoing examples, the predominant focus is on law in film. The matter of interest here is less the utility or meaning of the film work to lawyers or judges than

---

[3] Consider, for example, classic films like *Gone with the Wind* (1939), *Casablanca* (1942), and *Shane* (1953) that reflect the good guy/bad guy, character-driven, hero-wins-in-the-end genre of melodrama, a classic plot form that typifies the way jurors think about accidents in tort cases. (See Neal Feigenson, "Accidents as Melodrama," *New York Law School Law Review* 43 [1999–2000]: 741.) Or consider films such as *The Maltese Falcon* (1941), *Murder on the Orient Express* (1974), and *Seven* (1995), which exemplify the linear-causal, deductive and inductive reasoning style of the "whodunit," a well-worn plot structure favored by prosecutors in closing argument at trial; or films like *Star Wars* (1977), *The Lord of the Rings Trilogy* (2001–2003), and *Spider Man* (2002), which exemplify the universal story form of the hero quest, a form criminal defense lawyers typically favor and emulate in court. (See Anthony Amsterdam and Randy Hertz, "An Analysis of Closing Arguments to a Jury," *New York Law School Law Review* 37 [1992]: 55.) Consider also films as diverse as *Rear Window* (1954), *Rashomon* (1950), and *Memento* (2000), which tell us about the way memory, critical reflection, and emotion work together, oftentimes unreliably, in the reconstruction of past events, and/or films that examine the core structure and norms of human judgment, such as the tension between mercy and retribution in films such as *Death and the Maiden* (1994) and *Unforgiven* (1992), or unadulterated revenge in films like *Taxi Driver* (1976), *Death Wish* (1974), and *Batman Begins* (2005), or consider films that explore the rule of law without law, as in the *Godfather* (1972), or the consequences of rule breaking in films such as *Pan's Labyrinth* (2006) and *Jumanji* (1995), or films that tell us about the founding of communities (*Red River* [1948]), the abuse of power (*One Flew Over the Cuckoo's Nest* [1975]), or the irrational nature of (Kafkaesque) bureaucratic "justice" (*Brazil* [1985]). Finally, consider a film comedy like *Annie Hall* (1977) that through a humorous and shrewd juxtaposition of spoken and interior monologues provides a model for a trial lawyer's visualization in court of the hidden thoughts that contradicted and mitigated the legal effect of his client's own words. (See Philip Meyer, "Desperate for Love: Cinematic Influences Upon a Defendant's Closing Argument to a Jury," *Vermont Law Review* 18 [1994]: 721.)

[4] See Richard K. Sherwin, *When Law Goes Pop* (Chicago: University of Chicago Press, 2000) 106–39.

Imagining Law as Film (Representation without Reference?)

the effort to understand some new social, political, psychological, or historical aspect of law. There is, however, another way to think about the relationship between law and film, and that is to see "law as film." Viewing law as a particular kind of visual cultural representation raises questions of a different sort, such as: How does the introduction of film and other forms of visual representation inside the courtroom – either as visual evidence, visual argument, or simply by visualizing the legal process itself[5] – affect legal practice, theory, and pedagogy? How might new visual legal methods influence the perception of truth and justice in court and in the court of public opinion? What if the shift from text to sound and image prompts alternative forms of cognition, inculcating new habits of perceiving (truth) and feeling (that a just result has been attained)? I shall contend that, ultimately, law *as* visual representation leads us beyond the rubric of law and film to a more expansive formulation for law on the screen, perhaps under the rubric of visual legal studies. The latter encompasses visual stills and graphics as well as moving images in a variety of mediations – digital as well as analog, interactive as well as passively projected. Understanding how visual representations are made and construed, how they generate meaning and move the will of the viewer – whether on the basis of explicit or implicit reasons, or on the strength of largely unconscious mental associations, moods, memories, and feelings – has now become an inescapable part of what it means to practice, teach, and theorize law in the digital age of audiovisual representation.

Significant changes in visual communication technologies alter the way we record, remember, and ultimately make sense of reality. The shift from the linear logic of words to the associational logic of visual montage[6] is only one example. No form of communication operates in a semiotic vacuum; each adapts to and assimilates emerging forms of communication from other media.[7] As D. N. Rodowick notes, "[C]hanging articulations of the visible with respect to the expressible – shifts in modes of envisioning and representing, positions of seeing and ways of saying – organize relations of knowledge, power, and subjectivity in different ways in different historical societies."[8]

We can only tell (and respond to) the stories we know,[9] or know how to decode. Each medium generates its own set of meaning-making practices and

---

[5] Visualizing the legal process has expanded from televising trials to streaming images of hearings and other legal procedures online.

[6] See generally Daniel Arijon, *Grammar of the Film Language* (Los Angeles: Silman-James Press, 1976).

[7] See Jay David Bolter and Richard Grusin, *Remediation: Understanding New Media* (Cambridge: MIT Press, 2000).

[8] D. N. Rodowick, *The Virtual Life of Film* (Cambridge, MA: Harvard University Press, 2007) 186.

[9] See Robert A. Ferguson, "Story and Transcription in the Trial of John Brown," *Yale Journal of Law and the Humanities* 6 (1994) 37. See also Anthony Amsterdam and Jerome Bruner, *Minding the Law* (Cambridge: Harvard University Press, 2000); Jessica Gurley and David K. Marcus, "The Effects of Neuroimaging and Brain Injury on Insanity Defenses," *Behavioral Sciences and the Law* 26 (2008) 85, 95 ("Jurors may base their verdicts, at least partially, on their prototypical notions of what they believe a criminal to be rather than focusing solely on the evidence presented to them during the trial").

meaning-construing norms. Film techniques, for example, evolve over time and ultimately become "second nature" as we grow accustomed to meaning-making conventions, and unconsciously assimilate the interpretive tools we need to make sense of what appears on the screen. Adapting Robert Cover's famous formulation to contemporary cultural conditions, we may now say that for every constitution there is not only a textual epic but also a cinematic and perhaps even a multiplayer interactive one.[10] Once viewed in the context of the narratives, films, and digital (algorithmically generated) representations that give it meaning, law becomes "not merely a system of rules to be observed," and not simply "a world in which we live,"[11] but many different worlds, each reflecting deep structures within the operating system or organizational logic of the communicative medium in which law's meanings unfold.

Law performs its meanings in a shared, public world that is constituted (and reconstituted) through an overlapping network of discrete cultural and cognitive practices, social institutions, and inherited textual and audiovisual sources.[12] For us to understand the internal logics of law's order we must become mindful of the various media in which that order is enacted. Each medium enjoys strengths and weaknesses that others do not. For example, words may assert logical propositions and deploy them in a more rigorous argumentative form than visual images, whereas visual images may more effectively produce verisimilitude and thereby evoke more compelling perceptual, cognitive, and emotional responses than words alone.

The stories we tell and the way that we tell them differ from one medium to another. Thus, to the extent that law performs its meanings through narrative and image,[13] its fate remains closely tied to the way in which a given medium codes the meaning-making process. For example, if the grammar of film has taught us to instantly recognize the visual code of close-ups, cross-cutting, and montage (through which new meanings emerge from the juxtaposition of discrete images), the digital grammar of computer-generated imaging has taught us similarly to internalize the interactive code of the interface along with the command-and-control conventions of rip, burn, interact, resynchronize, upload, and resend.[14] Law's entanglement in

---

[10] Robert Cover, "Nomos and Narrative," *Harvard Law Review* 97 (1983) 4.

[11] Ibid.

[12] These are what anthropologist Don Handelman refers to as the discrete logics of organizational design. See Don Handelman, *Models and Mirrors: Towards an Anthropology of Public Events* (New York Berghahn Books, 1998) xi–xii.

[13] See, e.g., Richard K. Sherwin, "The Narrative Construction of Legal Reality," *Vermont Law Review* 18 (1994) 681; Peter Brooks and Paul Gewirtz, *Law's Stories: Narrative and Rhetoric in the Law* (New Haven: Yale University Press, 1998).

[14] On the emerging digital culture of command and control, see Rodowick, *The Virtual Life of Film*, 174 (noting that, before the digital screen, "[we] express a will to control information and to shape ourselves and the world through the medium of information.") There, is, however, a price to be paid for this new sense of empowerment. Immersion in virtual worlds generates a form of monadism in which "there is no present other than mine, the one I occupy now" and "no presence other than myself." Ibid., 172. In short, other minds and worlds "have become 'information.'" Ibid., 175. See also Alexander Galloway, *Gaming: Essays on Algorithmic Culture* (Minneapolis: University of Minnesota

Imagining Law as Film (Representation without Reference?) 245

the changing patterns of our "second nature" means that law cannot escape the dominant epistemological anxieties that may afflict a given medium. Thus we are led to ask, what becomes of law when, following the path of contemporary politics and marketing, it too flattens out on the electronic screen? What is the life of law like when it is lived cinematically? Once immersed in the flow of infinitely manipulable digital information, does the law join the expanding regime of "representation without reference?"[15] By entering a virtual realm of algorithmically coded, mathematically generated digital simulacra – copies of copies, without originals; free floating signifiers, without a signified – will legal reality also bear witness to a newly emerging baroque style or aesthetic? If law does begin to emulate purely ornamental forms, does it thereby come to resemble Kafka's law, a law that, as Gershom Scholem put it, remains valid but lacks significance?[16]

As a performance – a way of both constituting, and being in, the world – law exposes itself to new ethical and ontological possibilities as well as uncertainties. For example, who do I become when I watch a film, or a video, or a digital reenactment of an airplane crash on a computer screen? What time do I occupy?[17] What identity do I assume? Do I vicariously occupy the lived experience of a real passenger, as if viewing an amateur video? Or is the terror I feel more akin to the titillating thrill that comes from watching a scene in some action-packed feature? Or is it perhaps more like the denatured experience of being an avatar in a video game? Once we recognize the extent to which differences in media matter for law, ontological concerns may also give way to metaphysical ones. For example, as we increasingly question, in baroque fashion, how real is the reality we see on the screen, and how real the seer, we may find ourselves entering into a labyrinth of worlds within worlds – or is it perhaps dreams within dreams? – seeking a code by which to measure or otherwise discern the proper criteria for lived (waking?) reality. These epistemological,

---

Press, 2006) 87 ("While the disciplinary societies of high modernity were characterized by more physical semiotic constructs such as the signature and the document, today's societies of control are characterized by immaterial ones such as the password and the computer.") As Deleuze notes, what we are witnessing here is a shift in the meaning of control from "discipline" (in Foucault's sense) to information freeways constituted by computer networks: "In making freeways, for example, you don't enclose people but instead multiply the means of control... people can drive infinitely and 'freely' without being at all confined yet while still being perfectly controlled. This is our future." Galloway, *Gaming*, 87–8 (quoting Deleuze).

[15] Gregory Ulmer, "The Object of Post-Criticism," *The Anti-Aesthetic*, Hal Foster, ed. (New York: The New Press, 1983) 92.

[16] See Gershom Scholem, ed., *The Correspondence of Walter Benjamin and Gershom Scholem 1932–1940*, Anson Rabinbach, trans. (Cambridge: Harvard University Press, 1992) 142 (describing the "nothingness of revelation" as "a state in which revelation appears to be without meaning, in which it still asserts itself, in which it has validity but no significance"). See generally Richard K. Sherwin, "Law's Beatitude," *Cardozo Law Review* 24 (2003) 683, 685.

[17] For an example of the conflation of diverse time frames by way of a multimedia montage used in a summation at trial, see Richard K. Sherwin, Neal Feigenson, and Christina Spiesel, "Law in the Digital Age: How Visual Communication Technologies are Transforming the Practice, Theory, and Teaching of Law," *Boston University Journal of Science and Technology Law* 12 (2006): 245–6.

ontological, and metaphysical issues arise from law's migration to the screen and its concomitant assumption of those qualities (and anxieties) that characterize the virtual life of cinema.[18] The cultural shift from the rule of the written or spoken word to that of the visual or digital image compels us to view the pursuit of truth and justice in our time from a radically different perspective than the one we inherited from the European Enlightenment.[19] Suffice it to say, queries like these are suggestive of the new look of cinematic jurisprudence in the digital age.

In our time, and for the foreseeable future, the world itself has become a picture.[20] The proliferation of law in film, on television, in mass-market video games, and on the Internet, has, as Austin Sarat observes, "altered and expanded the sphere of legal life."[21] Today, people everywhere look for reality on the screen, and reality, in turn, assumes the look that the screen provides. To be sure, the two-way traffic between law and popular culture may be managed in either direction for a broad range of strategic purposes. Consider, for example, a blockbuster film such as *Erin Brockovich* (2000). The film's strong proenvironment and anticorporate greed message played out not only in film theaters (as well as on private screens at home) but also as part of an independent political campaign featuring the real Erin Brockovich. Appearing in a series of television advertisements, Brockovich enhanced her public advocacy against proposed tort reform legislation by rechanneling the aura of celebrity that she gained from Hollywood star Julia Roberts' film portrayal of her. Nor is this an isolated instance of the life of law imitating art. Consider, for example, Errol Morris's docudrama, *The Thin Blue Line* (1988), which was based on a real homicide case. The film attracted sufficient public attention to prompt a reopening of the case as a result of which Randall Dale Adams, a one-time resident of Texas' death row, was ultimately set free.[22] When the life of the law imitates the art of film,

[18] Rodowick, *The Virtual Life of Film.*

[19] See Costas Douzinas and Lynda Nead, *Law and the Image* (Chicago: University of Chicago Press, 1999) 19–67.

[20] Austin Sarat, Lawrence Douglas, and Martha Umphry, eds., *Law on the Screen* (Stanford: Stanford University Press, 2005) 1.

[21] Ibid.

[22] See also *Paradise Lost: The Child Murders at Robin Hood Hills* (1996) and the popular television series (featuring the use of forensic evidence at trial) *CSI.* Regarding the latter, see Paul Rincon, "CSI Shows Give 'Unrealistic View,'" BBC News, Feb. 21, 2005, available at http://news.bbc.co.uk/1/hi/sci/tech/4284335.stm (quoting forensics expert Max Houck); Richard Willing, "CSI Effect," *U.S.A. Today,* posted August 5, 2004 at http://www.usatoday.com/life/television/news/2004–08-05-csi-effect:

> The shows – CSI and CSI: Miami in particular – feature high-tech labs and glib and gorgeous techies.... The programs ... foster what analysts say is the mistaken notion that criminal science is fast and infallible and always gets its man. That's affecting the way lawyers prepare their cases, as well as the expectations that police and the public place on real crime labs. Real crime-scene investigators say that because of the programs, people often have unrealistic ideas of what criminal science can deliver.

Imagining Law as Film (Representation without Reference?)

judgments involving aesthetics, box office marketing, and the power of the state grow intimately entangled. This phenomenon presents distinct dangers. Recall, for example, the interlocking set of relationships that emerged during the latter half of the twentieth century involving arms manufacturers, the military establishment, and civilian leadership. President Dwight Eisenhower famously labeled this the "military-industrial complex" and warned against the serious risk that it posed in terms of skewing a nation's public agenda. In similar fashion, more recently a powerful confluence of legal and judicial proceedings, film and television "experts," and a sophisticated polling capacity poses a significant risk of skewing the policymaking and governing process. Political scientist Douglas Reed calls this extraconstitutional regime "the juridico-entertainment complex."[23] As Reed notes, the (con-)fusion of law, politics, and the entertainment industry "transforms legal proceedings and legal conflict into consumable commodities that purport to educate and enlighten but simultaneously titillate, amuse, and otherwise entertain a mass audience."[24] In this respect, among others discussed in this chapter, we may agree with those who say, these days "there's no business that's not show business."[25] And show business, when it comes to law, involves a good deal more than amusement.

In what follows, I will trace three separate (albeit interwoven) strands of the law and film movement. In the first part, I will address the various ways in which the study of law *in* film can help us to enlarge our understanding of what law is or should be or is at risk of becoming in our time. In the second part, I will discuss the consequences for law of changes in our storytelling and mimetic practices from words alone to words mingled with sounds and moving images. Here we examine law *as* film, which is to say, law as it is transformed by cinematic practices. In the third part, I will shift from a mostly descriptive and pragmatic assessment of law's migration to the screen to a more abstract jurisprudential perspective. Here we consider both the epistemological and ethical ramifications of the cinematic coding of legal reality.

See also Janine Robben, "The 'CSI' Effect: Popular Culture Finds the Justice System," *Oregon State Bulletin* 66 (2005): 8, 9. For a conflicting take on this phenomenon, see Tom Tyler, "Viewing CSI and the Threshold of Guilt: Managing Truth and Justice in Reality and Fiction," *Yale Law Journal* 115 (2006): 1050.

23 Douglas Reed, "A New Constitutional Regime: The Juridico-Entertainment Complex," in *Popular Culture and Law*, Richard K. Sherwin, ed. (Hants: Ashgate, 2006) 253–63. See also Ray Surrette, "Predator Criminals as Media Icons," *Media, Process, and the Social Construction of Crime*, Gregg Barak, ed. (London: Routledge, 1994) 131 ("The crimes that dominate the public consciousness and policy debates are not common crimes but the rarest ones. Whether in entertainment or news, the crimes that define criminality are the acts of predator criminals").

24 Reed, "The Juridico-Entertainment Complex," 253. See generally Sherwin, *When Law Goes Pop.*

25 See Bernard Schmitt, David Rogers, and Karen Vrotsos, *There's No Business That's Not Show Business: Marketing in an Experience Culture* (New Jersey: Prentice Hall, 2004); see also Gretta Rusanow, *Knowledge Management and the Smarter Lawyer* (New York: ALM Publishing, 2003). See generally, Stuart Ewen, *PR! A History of Spin* (New York: Basic Books, 1996).

In particular, I will address the impact on the practice and theory of law of the semiotic shift from film as a photographic medium (i.e., celluloid reacting to light) to visual representations based on digital or computational code (i.e., the digital image as a mathematically generated simulacrum). I will close with some thoughts on the future of the law and film movement and the need for an interdisciplinary approach to visual literacy as a prerequisite to professional competency for lawyers in the twenty-first century.

Law in Film

[T]he moviemaker's art is not all that different from the lawyer's – especially the courtroom advocate's. Both must capture, in a very short space, a slice of human existence, and make the audience see a story from their particular perspective. Both have to know which facts to include and which to leave out; when to appeal to emotion and when to reason; what to spoon-feed the audience and what to make them work out for themselves; when to do the expected and when the unexpected; when to script and when to improvise. Judge Alex Kozinski[26]

What films can show us about law, and about law's performance of truth and justice in a given historical, cultural, or dramatic context, is as rich as it is varied. To illustrate the point, consider the range of scholarly approaches and insights prompted by a single film. I have in mind Sidney Lumet's classic law film, *12 Angry Men* (1957). In this film, the viewer is thrust into the gritty – bare, steaming, claustrophobically[27] cramped – reality of a New York City jury room on "the hottest day of year." It's a murder case, and judging by the initial eleven-to-one vote to convict, it seems that the prosecution has done its job well. There are two alleged eyewitnesses, a murder weapon (a switchblade), and a motive (the victim was the defendant's father, who had repeatedly beaten him). Yet, as deliberations proceed, this initial image of certainty will shatter in the jurors' minds, along with a host of preconceptions, self-deceits, and in one instance repressed personal pathology. All of this comes about as a result of a lone holdout, juror #8, played by Henry Fonda. His stubborn insistence that "questions" about the case remain to be addressed launches the group on their journey of collective soul searching and individual self-discovery. Along the way, the specter of a death sentence yields to acquittal through the intervention of reasonable doubt.

---

[26] Foreword to Paul Bergman and Michael Asimow, *Reel Justice* (Kansas City: Andrews and McMeel, 1996) xi.

[27] The director made shrewd use of wide-angle lenses to facilitate this claustrophobic effect. See Sidney Lumet, *Making Movies* (New York: Vintage, 1996).

Imagining Law as Film (Representation without Reference?)

The deliberations that lead these jurors to their ultimate judgment sweeps across a broad range of legal as well as social, economic, psychological, and cultural issues. No wonder these men are angry. It is not simply a product of the harsh physical conditions in which they must face one another (and themselves). It is also a direct offshoot of what they bring to the table. These jurors are a diverse lot, and their vastly different backgrounds soon lead to conflict and misunderstanding. They do not always speak the same language or operate from the same premise or motive. Juror #10, for instance, asserts that the defendant (a minority, perhaps Puerto Rican) is "lucky" to have gotten a trial at all and that people of his class and ethnicity are "born liars,"[28] or as juror #4, the coldly logical stockbroker, puts it: "He was born in a slum. Slums are breeding grounds for criminals. I know it. So do you." Yet, we also see how the life experience of juror #5, who grew up in a neighborhood like the defendant's, can help the other jurors understand how the murder weapon, a switchblade, is used – a fact that places at least one aspect of the prosecutor's case in doubt. In similar fashion, other jurors contribute their share to the deliberation process, like the artist who has painted near the elevated train that runs by the murder scene. He knows that the train's deafening roar would make it hard to overhear a conversation as it passed by, as one eyewitness claims to have done. Juror #2, an elderly man, helps the others understand why someone his age might crave the attention that testifying in an important murder case brings.

Just as there are differences in what each juror knows (or presumes), so, too, there are differences in how they think and how they express what they know. For juror #8, for instance, the very absence of any doubt whatsoever among the witnesses regarding what they heard or saw gives rise to "a peculiar feeling," as if something was not quite right. By contrast, juror #3, insists, "[y]ou can't refute facts," apparently not sensing the need to think about what constitutes a fact or how it acquires meaning in a particular context. Or consider juror #6 who, in response to juror #8's doubts ("It's not so easy for me to raise my hand and send a boy off to die without talking about it first"), articulates an opposing concern: "Supposing you talk us all outa this, and the kid really did knife his father?" Juror #10 goes a step further. What if, he worries, the search for motives to explain (or explain away) some of the trial testimony lands them in a mire of relativism: "You're making out like it don't matter what people say . . . What you want to believe, you believe, and what you don't want to believe, so you don't. What kind of way is that?"[29] In sum, whether it is the force of logic ("I think there's enough doubt to make us wonder")[30] or unadulterated passion ("Every

---

[28] Barbara Allen Babcock and Ticien Marie Sassoubre, "Deliberation in 12 *Angry Men*," *Chicago-Kent Law Review* 82 (2007) 636, n. 12.

[29] Ibid., 655.

[30] Ibid., 656.

one of you knows this kid is guilty! He's got to burn! We're letting him slip through our fingers here!"), each juror brings to the task of deliberation a distinct set of socioeconomically and culturally constructed assumptions and prejudices together with his or her own rhetorical and cognitive styles and psychological predispositions. Reflecting the latter, consider the sports enthusiast who will vote guilty just to avoid missing a ballgame for which he has purchased tickets;[31] or the troubled father whose irreconcilable anger toward his own estranged son plays out as displaced rage against the young defendant; or the wily, coldly cynical ad man to whom everyone seems cut from the same cloth, tailored to suit any calculating, self-interested Machiavellian for whom all the world's a stage on which an endless charade, full of deceit and manipulation, plays out. ("You know what the soft sell is? Well you got it," he tells juror #8, taking [falsely] the other's measure as one of his own, a fellow con artist worthy of sharing secrets of the trade ["I've got a different technique. Laughs, drinks, jokes, tricks... hit 'em where they live, that's my motto"]).[32]

So, what might a film such as this tell us about law, lawyers, and the legal system? As it turns out, a great many things. Indeed, the scholarly response to this film may serve as an illustrative model of that strand of the law and film movement known as "law in film." Consider the possibilities:

1) Films help us to model legal ideals, one of which surely is the liberal ideal of jury deliberation and the collective as well as personal act of taking responsibility. As one commentator put it, 12 Angry Men allows us to explore "the evil of indifference"[33] and teaches that "great evil can be avoided through small acts of individual responsibility."[34]

2) Films also help us to provide a basis for empirically testing popular beliefs and opinions about law, lawyers, and the legal system – including whether our ideals are actually being put into practice. Indeed, the data concerning holdouts such as juror #8 in 12 Angry Men suggest that the phenomenon the film describes is in fact highly unlikely in real life.[35]

3) Films provide an opportunity to show changes in cultural climate, including shifts in shared values, preferences, beliefs, and mood. For example, contrary to the image of the lone dissenting juror as hero in 12 Angry Men, more

---

[31] The sports enthusiast is not alone; his desire to get the tiresome talking done with as soon as possible is also shared by the garage manager and messenger service owner. Ibid., 894.

[32] Ibid., 819.

[33] Ibid., 887.

[34] Ibid., 895.

[35] Ibid., 897 ("Social scientists' empirical studies suggest that whenever the vote is 11–1 or 10–2, the holdout juror (or jurors) usually capitulates").

Imagining Law as Film (Representation without Reference?)

recent depictions of similar juror conduct carry a distinctly different valence. A likelier image today is that of the lone juror as villainous outlier, the anarchical nullifier.[36] This shift is consistent with a distinctly different normative landscape in which, as one commentator asserts, the ideal of popular sovereignty has passed,[37] perhaps leaving, as another notes, nothing in its place but an elaborate game of charades.[38]

4) Films can serve as a springboard to "corrective critique" provided that legal scholars point out popular misconceptions and mistakes about law and its processes. For example, it has been suggested that the jurors in 12 *Angry Men* not only reached the wrong result,[39] but also that the film itself misleads its audience by uncritically depicting (and perhaps even deliberately encouraging) unlawful juror conduct.[40]

5) Film analysis may also be used to stage cultural critiques from a variety of perspectives. For example, one commentator has criticized 12 *Angry Men* for suggesting that the criminal justice system is so enfeebled, so profoundly unreliable as a whole, that it takes not only heroic lone jurors, but also organized "innocence projects" to root out factual innocence.[41] At least one basis for this allegedly widespread misconception (regarding systemic injustice) has been laid at the feet of popular culture itself.[42] From yet another cultural

---

[36] See Jeffrey Abramson, "Anger at Angry Jurors," ibid., 595, 602, ("Instead of hero, the holdout has become a villain blamed for a supposed surge in hung juries. Instead of the embodiment of reasonable doubt, the holdout is variously described as 'unreasonable,' 'unreachable,' 'eccentric,' and 'disengaged'"). For additional insight into law films as cultural barometer, see Richard K. Sherwin, "Cape Fear: Law's Inversion and Cathartic Justice," *University of San Francisco Law Review* 30 (1996) 1023.

[37] David Ray Papke, "12 *Angry Men* Is Not An Archetype: Reflections on the Jury in Contemporary Popular Culture," *Chicago-Kent Law Review* 82 (2007) 735.

[38] See Bruce Hay, "Charades: Religious Allegory in 12 *Angry Men*," ibid., 811.

[39] Ibid., 713 ("The jury erred badly"); ibid., 691 ("A careful review of the evidence and the jury's analysis of the evidence suggest that the twelve angry men may have produced an injustice: specifically, they many have acquitted a guilty man").

[40] Ibid., 718 ("The jury is dysfunctional. They have caustic arguments, not careful discussions. Worse, they reach a verdict based upon evidence that was neither introduced nor discussed in court. The film presents a veritable buffet of juror misconduct." This kind of misconduct, in which vigilante jurors must fill in for incompetent officials, has been favorably depicted in other films." See, for example *Suspect* [1995].) See also Charles Weisselberg, "Good Film, Bad Jury," *Chicago-Kent Law Review* 82 (2007) 723 (delineating five instances of juror misconduct in the movie).

[41] Ibid., 665.

[42] Ibid., 685 ("This loss of confidence [in the criminal justice system] is also quite regularly expressed by prospective jurors in a form some commentators have dubbed 'the CSI effect' [referring to a popular television series featuring new technologies in criminal science investigation, particularly DNA forensics] in which prospective jurors indicate their confidence in the system is so low that they could not convict anyone without irrefutable forensic evidence").

perspective, 12 *Angry Men* has been viewed as a presentation of "sons subject to paternal brutality . . . and of the very real possibility of sons murdering their brutal fathers." In this view, the film confronts us with "the law's complex relationship to reason and violence."[43]

6) Films also provide a basis for conducting jurisprudence in a new key. A critical analysis of film can generate not only novel styles of theorizing, but also novel claims for theory itself. For example, in his interpretation of 12 *Angry Men*, Bruce Hay leads readers through a mystery narrative by the end of which the film emerges from its cleverly concealed "tricks" as an allegorical performance of Christian ministry.[44]

7) Films may also serve as a basis for cross-cultural analysis. For example, in Japan, Shun Nakahara crafted a remake of 12 *Angry Men* as a comedy that nevertheless imparted a serious message, namely: that "Japanese citizens too can rise to the challenge of dispensing group justice."[45] In Germany, a film titled *Die Konferenz* invited viewers to judge, along with the teachers who constituted the jury-like conference, whether the sexual relationship that took place between two students was a rape or an expression of love. "As in 12 *Angry Men*," one commentator notes, "where the defendant's guilt remains ultimately open, *Die Konferenz* at best suggests a 'reasonable doubt' as to [the boy's] guilt."[46] 12 *Angry Men* was first screened in Soviet Russia in 1961. Under its influence, young intellectuals during the thaw of the 1960s advocated the power of the individual to resist the majority and prevail, and in 1993 and 1994, when significant law reforms were underway in Russia, older lawyers

---

[43] Ibid., 864.

[44] Ibid., 860–1 ("That's the thing about the soft sell: when it's done right, people don't know it's happening. If this film is done right, audiences will love it without fully knowing why. They will christen it America's #1 law film, never realizing what a clever, elegant trick they've fallen for." For other examples of cinematic jurisprudence, see Sherwin, *When Law Goes Pop*; Sherwin, "Anti-Oedipus, Lynch: Initiatory Rites and the Ordeal of Justice," in Sarat et al., *Law on the Screen* at 106; and Sherwin, "Nomos and Cinema," *University of California Los Angeles Law Review* 48 (2001) 1519. See also Peter Brooks, "Lawyers, Law, & the Movies: The Hitchcock Cases," *California Law Review* 86 (1998) 211, 232 (noting that law and film scholarship serves as fertile ground for critical theories).

[45] *Chicago-Kent Law Review* 82 (2007) 758.

[46] Ibid., 781. See generally Stefan Machura, "An Analysis Scheme for Law Films," *University of Baltimore Law Review* 4 (2007): 329, 343 ("The impact of American movies on international audiences is so strong that many European films do not depict the authentic legal system and culture of their respective countries. Instead, they mix elements, for example, using the phrase 'your honor,' depicting cross-examinations American-style, and using other features of adversarial trials"). See also Margaret Y. K. Woo, "Law and Discretion in the Contemporary Chinese Courts," *University of Arkansas at Little Rock Law Review* 25 (2003) 665 (describing how cinema can reflect complexities in the lawyer–client relationship that are often absent from traditional legal discourse).

Imagining Law as Film (Representation without Reference?)

and jurists noted the film's influence on their support for the reintroduction of the jury trial in Russia.[47]

8) Finally, films may be used as an aid in law teaching, whether it concerns doctrinal law,[48] insights into visual storytelling practices,[49] or legal ethics.[50] In the commentary on *12 Angry Men*, for example, scholars have explained the difference between circumstantial and direct evidence,[51] how "verdict-driven" deliberations differ from the "evidence-driven" kind,[52] and how a more effective *voir dire* process "might have exposed some of the prejudices of the twelve angry men."[53]

In sum, a scholarly engagement with "law in film" can tell us a good deal about a broad range of issues from a rich variety of disciplinary, rhetorical, and substantive perspectives. We also see that great films, like notorious trials, are irreducibly overdetermined. There is something in the visual work itself that transcends any given interpretation.[54] What that overarching factor might be, and how we account for the irreducibility of visual meaning to propositional content, goes to the very nature of visuality itself. This may be studied through an analysis of the various social, historical, cultural, cognitive, and technological elements that constitute visual mediation. How we understand visual images and what they represent depends to a considerable extent upon what kind of screen we have in mind – and what sort of knowledge and mode of being in the world a given screen experience invites (and precludes).[55] This observation points up the ontological and epistemological as well as the ethical dimensions of law and cinema studies and signals the transition from "law *in* film" to "law *as* film," which is the subject we take up next.

---

[47] *Chicago-Kent Law Review* 82 (2007) 795. A stage version of the film was presented in 2002, with great success.

[48] See Steve Greenfield, Guy Osborn, and Peter Robson, *Film and the Law* (Oxford: Hart Publishing, 2008) 6–11; James Elkins, "Reading/Teaching Lawyer Films," *Vermont Law Review* 28 (2004): 813.

[49] See, e.g., Avi Stachenfeld and Christopher Nicholson, "Blurred Boundaries: An Analysis of the Close Relationship Between Popular Culture and the Practice of Law," *University of San Francisco Law Review* 30 (1996) 903; Philip Meyer, "Desperate for Love: Cinematic Influences Upon a Defendant's Closing Argument to a Jury," *Vermont Law Review* 18 (1994) 721; Richard K. Sherwin, "The Narrative Construction of Legal Reality," 681.

[50] See, e.g., James Elkins, "Popular Culture, Legal Films, and Legal Film Critics," *Loyola of Los Angeles Law Review* 40 (2007) 745, 782; John Osborne, "Atticus Finch – The End of Honor," *University of San Francisco Law Review* 30 (1996) 1139.

[51] *Chicago-Kent Law Review* 82 (2007): 701.

[52] Ibid., 560.

[53] Ibid., 629.

[54] Richard K. Sherwin, "What Screen Do You Have in Mind?" *Studies in Law, Politics, and Society*, Austin Sarat, ed. (Amsterdam: Elsevier, 2008); Richard K. Sherwin, "Law, Metaphysics, and the New Iconoclasm," *Law Text Culture* Vol. 11, (University of Wollongong, 2007) 70–105.

[55] Kenneth Burke, *Language as a Symbolic System: Essays on Life, Literature, and Method* (Berkeley: University of California Press, 1966) 449 ("A way of seeing is also a way of not seeing").

Law as Film

[T]he cinema disturbs one's vision. The speed of the movements and the rapid change of images force men to look continually from one to another. Sight does not master the pictures, it is the pictures which master one's sight. Franz Kafka[56]

With the close-up, space expands, with slow motion, movement is extended. The enlargement of a snapshot does not simply render more precise what in any case was visible, though unclear: it reveals entirely new structural formations of the subject. Walter Benjamin[57]

We make our tools and our tools make us. W. J. T. Mitchell[58]

Studying law films not only teaches us about public expectations and beliefs regarding law, lawyers, and the legal system generally, but it also provides insights into the cognitive tools and cultural templates that people bring into courtrooms, polling booths, and other sites where legal meanings are elicited, debated, and perhaps transformed. Everyone bears the imprint of the culture into which he or she is born and raised. Each of us inherits and constantly renews an archive of cultural knowledge and a repertoire of communicative practices. There are scripts for negotiating certain kinds of social interactions, there are character types for helping us to recognize who we are dealing with, and there are story forms at hand that help us to make sense of the situations we confront either in person, or vicariously through various audio and visual media (such as radio, film, television, video games, and the Internet).[59] It should not prove surprising, therefore, to find trial lawyers importing popular film stories and characters as well as familiar cinematic styles into their courtroom practices.[60]

---

[56] Franz Kafka, in Gustav Yanouch, *Conversations with Kafka* (New York: New Directions, 1971) 88–9.

[57] Walter Benjamin, "The Work of Art in the Age of Its Reproducibility," *Walter Benjamin: Collected Writings Volume 3 1935–1938*, Howard Eiland and Michael Jennings, eds. (Cambridge, MA: Harvard University Press, 2002) 101. See also Orit Kamir, "Why 'Law and Film' and What Does It Actually Mean?" *Continuum: Journal of Media and Cultural Studies* 19 (2005) 265 (noting that "California's pioneering antistalking legislation had in mind fictional archetypal images rather than the actual offenders; no attempt was made to investigate and analyze the real social phenomenon of stalking").

[58] W. J. T. Mitchell, *The Reconfigured Eye* (Chicago: University of Chicago Press, 1992) 59.

[59] See, e.g., Jerome Bruner, *Beyond the Information Given: Studies in the Psychology of Knowing* (New York: W. W. Norton & Co., 1973); Jerome Bruner, *Acts of Meaning* (Cambridge: Harvard University Press, 1990); Roger Schank and Robert Abelson, *Scripts, Plans, Goals, and Understanding: An Inquiry into Human Knowledge Structures* (Hillsdale, NJ: Lawrence Erlbaum, 1977); Gerd Gigerenzer, Peter M. Todd and the ABC Research Group, *Simple Heuristics that Make Us Smart* (Oxford: Oxford University Press, 2000); Richard Nisbett and Lee Ross, *Human Inference: Strategies and Shortcomings of Social Judgment* (New York: Prentice Hall, 1985).

[60] Whether it is courtroom references to Oliver Stone's *Natural Born Killers* (see, e.g., *Beasley v. State*, 269 Georgia 620, 627 [1998]) or to Francis Ford Coppola's malevolent organized crime characters from *The Godfather* (see, e.g., *Commonwealth v. Graziano*, 331 N.E. 808 [Mass. 1975]; Jeremiah Donovan, "Some Off-the-Cuff Remarks about Lawyers as Storytellers," 18 *Vermont Law Review* 18 [1994] 751,

Imagining Law as Film (Representation without Reference?)

Once we assimilate the communication tools of everyday life they become second nature to us; which is to say, they become invisible. These unconscious habits of meaning making make up what we call common sense.[61] Whether accurate or not, these are the familiar images and associations that we carry around in our heads.[62] They include popular images of lawyers, criminals, and the legal system. For good or for ill, these are the materials with which trial lawyers will have to work (or work around). Lawyers cannot function effectively without an adequate understanding of the dominant sources of cultural meaning together with the dominant styles and modalities of communication in the communities in which they practice.[63] Put simply, they must know not only how meanings are made, but also, and arguably more importantly, how meanings are received.[64] When it comes to law on the screen, it's not simply a matter of what you show, it's what people see (or think they see) as well as what they feel, associate to, or identify with, or discount in the process of reaching a judgment in a particular case. The literacy skills needed to meet the demands of a particular communication medium are crucial to advocates and audiences alike.[65] In short, the stories we hear and see are not simply a matter of content or genre; the medium in which they are conveyed matters.[66] As Wallace Stevens put it, "things as they are are changed upon the blue guitar."[67]

The way we respond to visual images is different, as a perceptual and cognitive matter, than the way we respond to words alone.[68] Law on the screen privileges meaning

---

753 [referring to prosecution's invocation of images from the *Godfather* in *United States v. Bianco*, No. H-90–18 {AHN} Connecticut, July 16, 1991)], the fact remains that in adversarial legal systems law is performed as a theater of battle.

[61] See Richard K. Sherwin, "Dialects and Dominance: A Study of Rhetorical Fields in the Law of Confessions," *University of Pennsylvania Law Review* 136 (1988) 729.

[62] See Vicki Smith, "Prototypes in the Courtroom: Lay Representations of Legal Concepts," *Journal of Personality and Social Psychology* 61 (1991) 857; Al Ries and Jack Trout, *Positioning: The Battle for Your Mind* (New York: McGraw-Hill, 1986).

[63] See, e.g., Anthony G. Amsterdam and Randy Hertz, "An Analysis of Closing Arguments to a Jury," *New York Law School Law Review* 37 (1992): 55; Neal Feigenson, *Legal Blame: How Jurors Think and Talk About Accidents* (Washington, DC: American Psychological Association, 2000).

[64] See, e.g., Frank Luntz, *Words That Work: It's Not What You Say, It's What People Hear* (New York: Hyperion, 2006).

[65] Notably, literacy in this sense entails an understanding of what we think about as well as the kinds of tools we use (within a given medium) to think with. As Stachenfeld and Nicholson put it, "the best courtroom stories, and therefore performances, are almost mythic in structure: good vs. evil, man vs. nature, big vs. small, innocence vs. deceit, etc." Stachenfeld, "Blurred Boundaries," 905.

[66] Ibid. ("Every culture has certain boundaries or parameters that define the acceptable style or language of presentation within that group").

[67] Wallace Stevens, "The Man with the Blue Guitar" in *The Collected Poetry of Wallace Stevens* (New York: Vintage, 1990).

[68] See Sherwin et al., "Law in the Digital Age" (2007). Renowned Swedish film director Ingmar Bergman once wrote that in film he found "a language that literally is spoken from soul to soul in expressions that, almost sensuously, escape the restrictive control of the intellect." From Ingmar Bergman, "The Snakeskin," *Sight and Sound* (August 1, 1965), online at: http://www.bergmanorama .com/bergman_snakeskin.htm.

256   Richard K. Sherwin

making through associational logic that operates, in large part, subconsciously, through its emotional appeal. A viewer might be aware that an image is strongly linked to a particular emotional response without knowing or understanding just what the connection is. In this respect, then, visual images tend to capitalize on the power of people's intuitive, *gestalt* emotional responses to shape their judgments. These effects operate beneath the radar of awareness and are thus less amenable to critical scrutiny and counterargument.[69] It is also notable that visual images tend to have more impact than nonvisual expressions of the same information. This is because they tend to be more vivid and more lifelike. Studies show that people respond to photorealistic pictures as they would to the real thing.[70] For example, viewers of an IMAX movie of a roller coaster ride or, for that matter, of an unstable, camcorder-based film like *Cloverfield* (2008), may experience a sense of dizziness that words alone could never induce.

Words are obviously constructed by the speaker and thus are immediately recognized as abstractions. A word is unlikely to be mistaken for a window. By contrast, photorealistic photographs, videos, film, as well as digital reenactments can appear to be caused by the outside world, as if untouched by human mediation or authorial interpretation.[71] The human brain takes in visual information all at once. This

---

[69] At the same time, it may also be the case that a sudden insight, or *gestalt*, might also occur as an act of *recognition* of that which is already known on a profound level by the viewer. As Jennifer Deger observes: "The power of recognition – the moment of insight when one sees beyond what is already known – arises from the way it allows us to *glimpse something more, something new, yet nonetheless somehow known or true.* As a technology of showing, the camera thus brings an ontological charge of truth far exceeding the verisimilitude of the 'realistic' likeness . . ."). Jennifer Deger, *Shimmering Screens: Making Media in an Aboriginal Community* (Minneapolis: University of Minnesota Press, 2006) 19.

The filmic function of "presencing" might operate on a representational or a symbolic level. For an example of the latter, consider Renaissance symbolic painting, such as Botticelli's *Primavera*. As Charles Dempsey observes regarding the Greek rhetorical term *ekphrasis*: "It is a rhetorical means of persuasion, and indeed a means of setting before the eyes and making present the reality that lies behind the actual experience of the thing described." Charles Dempsey, *The Portrayal of Love: Botticelli's Primavera and Humanist Culture at the Time of Lorenzo the Magnificent* (Princeton, NJ: Princeton University Press, 1992).

[70] Tom Gunning, "An Aesthetic of Astonishment: Early Film and the (In)Credulous Spectator," *Viewing Positions: Ways of Seeing Film*, Linda Williams, ed. (Rutgers, NJ: Rutgers University Press, 1995) 114, explains how audiences for Lumiere's *Arrival of a Train at the Station* were simultaneously terrified by the impression that the train was headed straight for them and pleased by their appreciation of film's *trompe l'oeil* capabilities. For research indicating that photographs can provoke emotional responses similar to those aroused by the real thing that in turn affect legal judgments, *see* Kevin S. Douglas, David R. Lyon, and James R. P. Ogloff, "The Impact of Graphic Photographic Evidence on Mock Jurors' Decisions in a Murder Trial: Probative or Prejudicial?" *Law and Human Behavior* 21 (1997) 485.

[71] This is sometimes referred to as "indexicality." See Rodowick, *The Virtual Life of Film*, 9–10, 106 ("The photograph is a receptive substance literally etched or sculpted by light forming a mold of the object's reflected image . . . Computer-generated images, alternatively, are wholly created from algorithmic functions . . . Digital media are neither visual, nor textual, nor musical – they are simulations . . . Weakening or eliminating the indexical powers of photography shifts the balance, then,

Imagining Law as Film (Representation without Reference?)

wealth of data can lead jurors and judges to believe that they have all the information there is to be had, and thus disincline them to pursue the matter further. Held in the grip of moving images, critical thinking is discouraged or effectively disabled; it is enough simply to keep up with the visual flow. Because pictures cannot be reduced to explicit verbal propositions, some of their meaning always remains implicit. This represents a convenient opportunity for advocates who might well prefer to leave an intended meaning unspoken – particularly when evidentiary rules or social conventions forbid making the message explicitly.[72]

In addition, construing visual meaning from the screen readily lends itself to what literary theorists call "intertextual" references.[73] By referring to other works, other genres, even other media, screen images cue the audience's cultural knowledge and allow them to draw on that implicit knowledge in responding to what they see.[74] Of course, words can do this too, but pictures can do it more effectively because they do it unconsciously, in a way that embeds the borrowed cultural value invisibly in the visual representation of the picture's ostensible subject matter.

Finally, cinematic representations favor particularities over abstractions. This has legal consequences. For example, stories driven by particular characters and dramatic events tend to emphasize individual agency and simplified (monocausal) explanations for the consequences of particular actions. As a result, systemic reasons for bad outcomes – such as market incentives for particular kinds of behavior or flaws in bureaucratic decision-making processes – receive short shrift on the screen. The same may be said for more complex (multicausal) explanations that get in the way of dramatic visual storytelling. In short, cinematic narratives mimic the often reality-distorting tendencies of the mind to simplify accounts and attribute blame in precisely these ways.[75] In assessing the impact of visual communication on law we must also be attentive to the largely unconscious process through which we make mental (as well as tactile or affective) associations to the images we see.[76] Although

between causation and intention"); cf. Roland Barthes, *Camera Lucida: Reflections on Photography* (New York: Hill and Wang, 1982) 39 ("In every photograph there is the stupefying evidence of this-is-what-happened-and-how"). *See also* Jennifer L. Mnookin, *The Image of Truth: Photographic Evidence and the Power of Analogy*, 10 *Yale Journal of Law and the Humanities* 1 (1998) 1, 16–17 (referring to O. W. Holmes's description of the photograph as "a mirror with a memory"); Jennifer L. Mnookin and Nancy West, "Theaters of Proof: Visual Evidence and the Law in *Call Northside 777*," *Yale Journal of Law and the Humanities* 13 (2001) 329.

72 Sherwin et al., "Law in the Digital Age," 243–4.

73 Jonathan Culler, *The Pursuit of Signs* (Ithaca: Cornell University Press, 2002) 100–18.

74 See Neal Feigenson and Richard Sherwin, "Thinking beyond the shown: implicit inferences in evidence and argument," *Law, Probability, and Risk* 6(1–4) (New York: Oxford University Press, 2007) 295–310.

75 See Feigenson, *Legal Blame.*

76 See, e.g., Laura Marks, *The Skin of the Film* (Durham: Duke University Press, 1999); Vivian Sobchack, *Carnal Thoughts: Embodiment and Moving Image Culture* (Berkeley: University of California Press, 2002); David F. Marks, "On the Relationship Between Imagery, Body, and Mind," *Imagery: Current Developments* P. J. Hampson, D. F. Marks, and J. T. E. Richardson, eds. (London and New York: Routledge, 1990) 1–38.

we may be aware of experiencing a particular emotion in response to an image or series of images, the precise nature of the connection usually remains obscure. If we cannot account for its source, however, the emotion we experience remains less susceptible to deliberate critique and counterargument.[77]

Skillful legal advocates, like their counterparts in politics and advertising, have learned how to exploit these features of visual communication. The rules of evidence and the ideals of deliberation that govern the legal process must now operate in the context of new audiovisual and increasingly digital communicative practices. This raises novel legal questions. For example, is a computer-generated animation (reenacting an accident, say, or a crime) just another evidentiary illustration or is it something qualitatively different?[78] Might there be something so compelling about a digitally simulated reality (not to mention three-dimensional or more fully immersive simulations)[79] that place it beyond the ordinary bounds of demonstrative evidence?[80] Is it even within the ken of jurors' ordinary common sense to follow judicial instructions to use a visual only as "illustrative" of an expert's opinion rather than as documentary evidence that helps to "prove" a particular party's theory of the

[77] For additional analysis and specific examples of the use of visuals in court (for both descriptive and argumentative purposes), see Sherwin et al., "Law in the Digital Age." There is an ongoing debate about whether visual images *can* be arguments. See, e.g., David Fleming, "Can Pictures be Arguments?" *Argumentation and Advocacy* 33 (1996) 11–22 (asserting that pictures cannot serve as arguments). For a contrary position, see J. Anthony Blair, "The Rhetoric of Visual Arguments," in Charles A. Hill and Marguerite Helmers, *Defining Visual Rhetorics* (New Jersey: Lawrence Erlbaum, 2004) 41; and David Birdsell and Leo Groarke, "Toward A Theory of Visual Argument," *Argumentation and Advocacy* 33 (1996) 1–10.

[78] See, e.g., *Sharon Roy v. St. Lukes Medical Center & Shekhar Sane, MD*, Wisconsin Court of Appeals, District One, Northwestern Reporter 2d 741 (2007): 256 (court decision comparing a computer-generated animation that had been presented as demonstrative evidence at trial to an expert's hand-drawn illustrations during his testimony to depict his party's case theory). See also *Commonwealth v. Serge*, Supreme Court of Pennsylvania, Atlantic Reporter 2d 896 (2006): 1170 (opining that "a CGA [computer-generated animation] should be treated equivalently to any other demonstrative exhibit or graphic representation"). Other courts, however, have articulated a more searching attitude toward demonstrative evidence, particularly reenactment evidence. See, e.g., *Sommervold v. Grevlos*, Supreme Court of South Dakota, Northwestern Reporter 2d 518 (1994): 737 ("The impact of video reenactment is substantial. When people see something on television, they think it is real even when it is not").

[79] See Darius Whelan, "The Bloody Sunday Tribunal Video Simulation," *Visual Practices Across the University*, James Elkins, ed. (Munich: Wilhelm Fink Verlag, Paderborn, 2007) 100. See also: http://www.bloody-sunday-inquiry.org.uk.

[80] Demonstrative evidence is used at trial, typically to supplement expert witness testimony, to help the trier of fact understand the matter at issue. This kind of evidence is meant to be illustrative, it is not meant to be used as substantive proof of the fact asserted. It may consist of a chart, a diagram, or computer-generated animations. Demonstrative evidence of this sort is generally admissible if it is judged fair and accurate, helpful to the jurors' understanding of the issues raised, and if the probative value outweighs any possible prejudice. See generally Gregory Joseph, "A Simplified Approach to Computer-Generated Evidence and Animations," *New York Law School Law Review* 43 (1999–2000) 875.

Imagining Law as Film (Representation without Reference?)

case?[81] For example, a juror might technically obey a judicial instruction not to use illustrative visual evidence as proof of what it depicts, but can we realistically expect that juror to dispel every trace of the emotional impact that comes from "watching" a murder, or seeming to occupy the cabin of an airplane as it crashes to earth?[82]

The debate about the adequacy of current evidentiary rules in the age of computer-generated images remains at a very early stage of development.[83] Some commentators have expressed confidence in the adversarial process[84] whereas others have expressed specific concerns.[85] Without question, the capacity of the legal system to adapt to the demands and novelties of cinematic evidentiary and argumentative representations in court (and out) will depend upon the capacity of lawyers, judges, and law teachers to cultivate new standards of visual literacy as an integral part of lawyering in the digital age. The expectation of jurors, like the public in general, to assimilate information from electronic screens will only grow over time. Lawyers will need to grasp the craft as well as the tactical utility of visualizing their case theories. Moreover, if the adversarial ideal of testing truth claims in open court is to be maintained, lawyers will have to expand their capacity to cross-examine what's on the screen as well as who is in the witness stand.[86] Likewise, judges will need to develop a deeper appreciation of how traditional notions of authentication and prejudice apply to a broad range of cinematic representations in court.

In sum, film literacy as a matter of legal practice requires a conscious expansion of the tools in the jurist's toolkit. Minding the law in the digital age involves new and largely invisible meaning-making practices. Just as reading films has become second

---

[81] Compare *Bruton v United States* (United States Reports 391 [1968]: 123), where the U.S. Supreme Court held that asking jurors to disregard that part of a codefendant's confession that implicated Bruton constituted a "mental gymnastic" that jurors simply could not perform.

[82] See generally Leonie Huddy and Anna Gunnthorsdottir, "The Persuasive Effects of Emotive Visual Imagery: Superficial Manipulation of the Product of Passionate Reason?" *Political Psychology* 21 (2000) 745.

[83] See Neal Feigenson and Meghan Dunn, "New Visual Technologies in Court: Directions for Research," *Law and Human Behavior* 27 (2003) 109, 110; Saul M. Kassin and Meghan A. Dunn, "Computer-Animated Displays and the Jury: Facilitative and Prejudicial Effects," *Law and Human Behavior* 21 (1997): 269; and Fredric I. Lederer, "Courtroom Technology and Its Educational Implications," *Virginia Education & Practice* 8 (1998): 3.

[84] See, e.g., Brian Carney & Neal Feigenson, "Visual Persuasion in the Michael Skakel Trial: Enhancing Advocacy through Interactive Media Presentations," *Criminal Justice* 19 (2004) 22, 23.

[85] See generally Jessica Silbey, "Judges as film critics: New approaches to film evidence," *University of Michigan Journal of Law Reform* 37 (2004): 499 ("Courts fail to encourage the evaluation of film as substantive evidence, subject to rigorous testing for the truth of its assertions.").

[86] For example, in the original state criminal trial, the prosecutor of the Los Angeles police officers who surrounded and beat motorist Rodney King utterly failed to address the way in which the defense had thoroughly altered the meaning and impact of George Holliday's videotape of the encounter. After digitizing Holliday's images, the defense team was able to replay the same images – slowed and carefully choreographed to support the defense theory of self-defense. See Sherwin, "The Narrative Construction of Legal Reality."

nature because the code (one might even say, the camera) is already inside our heads, the same may now be said for reading the computer screen. The digital interface and the concomitant cultural expectation of "command and control" over the information that appears on the screen is also inside our head. How this technology-spawned second nature and its imperatives (i.e., its internal logic or code) will play out in the legal culture remains to be seen, but play out it shall.[87] This eventuality calls for critical thinking regarding the larger meaning and impact of law's migration to the screen. What do we know, or think we know, who do we become, and what kind of shared social reality among others is emerging as part of the unfolding virtual life of law? These more abstract, theoretical queries signal our transition to the third strand of law and film studies, namely: "cinematic jurisprudence."

Cinematic Jurisprudence: The Virtual Life of Law

[R]epresentation without reference is a description of the way film [...] functions as a "language," receiving exact copies of sights and sounds... only to re-motivate them as signifiers in a new system. Gregory Ulmer[88]

[E]very epoch is defined by its own practices of knowledge and strategies of power, which are composed from regimes of visibility and procedures of expression. D. N. Rodowick[89]

Law lives in images the way images live on the screen. Linking law with film presumes a distinct way of meaning-making. It expands the rhetorical domain of generating social worlds and the ethical one of defining our proper place within them. As Jennifer Deger writes, "These technologies do not simply produce multiple versions of 'reality,' they constitute the very grounds of what is knowable."[90] As Annette Hamilton has noted, "from the viewpoint of the emergent visual-aural culture of the twenty-first century, 'what's on' creates the very grounds of what is known and hence finally for what 'is.'"[91] Increasingly, theorists of film are taking note of the "carnate sensuality" of the film experience. As Sobchack puts it, "The flesh is intrinsic to the cinematic apparatus, at once its subject, its substance, and its

---

[87] Indeed, this development is already underway. Consider, for example, the British murder trial during which jurors requested, and received from the judge, a DVD containing the visual evidentiary record for the case. Accordingly, during deliberations, jurors would presumably be free to rearrange the evidence in any manner they preferred (competing trial lawyer narratives to the contrary notwithstanding). See Richard K. Sherwin, "Visual Literacy in Action: Law in the Age of Images," *Visual Literacy*, James Elkins, ed. (New York and London: Routledge, 2008) 190–2.

[88] Gregory Ulmer, "The Object of Post-Criticism," 92.

[89] Rodowick, *The Virtual Life of Film*, xi.

[90] Deger, *The Shimmering Screen*, xxv.

[91] Annette Hamilton, "The National Picture: Thai Media and Cultural Identity," *Media Worlds: Anthropology on New Terrain*, F. Ginsburg, L. Abu-Lughod, and B. Larkin, eds. (Berkeley: University of California Press, 2002) 152–70.

Imagining Law as Film (Representation without Reference?)

limit."[92] In the experience of film "we are caught up without a thought (because our thoughts are elsewhere) in the vacillating and reversible sensual structure that both differentiates and connects the sense of my literal body to the sense of the figurative bodies and objects I see on the screen."[93]

In other words, although it is the case that film viewers are in a certain sense passive, or only partially fulfilled sensually, it is also the case that the viewer's sensing capacity is enhanced. In Sobchack's apt expression, at the movies we "feel ourselves feeling." We become "not only the toucher but also the touched."[94] In short, it is through the sensorium of the body that the film viewer experiences what is in play on the screen. It is perhaps here that the senses become "their own theoreticians."[95] Through mimesis, or mindfulness, we open up to the presence of objects and others before us and are led to appreciate the dynamic, open-ended process of *construction* through which we seek meaning.[96] In some cases, this may lead us to experience anew deep values that invest discrete human relationships with significance in a given social and cultural context.[97] In other cases, however, we may simply encounter the embodiment of sensation for its own sake.

Computer-based visual digital culture introduces its own distinct meaning making forms and practices and its own set of epistemological strengths and dangers. These developments include: remediation,[98] disintermediation,[99] hypermediation,[100] and a variety of screen interactive practices (such as burning, remixing, multiplayer gaming, and wiki coproductions, to name a few). It is important to understand the constitutive and mimetic power and effects of these novel forms of digital meaning-making. Digital communication technologies, much like Cover's Decalogue,[101] have

---

[92] Vivian Sobchack, *Carnal Thoughts: Embodiment and Moving Image Culture* (Berkeley: University of California Press, 2004) 56, 61.

[93] Ibid., 77.

[94] Ibid.

[95] Michael Taussig, *Mimesis and Alterity: A Particular History of the Senses* (London: Routledge, 1992) 253.

[96] See Richard K. Sherwin, "Sublime Jurisprudence: On the Ethical Education of the Legal Imagination in Our Time," *Chicago-Kent Law Review* 83 (2008) 1157.

[97] This is the shared epiphany that ethnographer Jennifer Deger brilliantly documents in her book, *Shimmering Screens*. Guided by an aboriginal mentor and filmmaker, Deger helped to produce a well-received documentary, *Gularri: That Brings Unity*. The film incorporated inherited clan wisdom and ritual in a visual commemoration that, in aboriginal eyes at least, reactivated, as if for the first time, the visible and invisible sources of knowledge and values that have held together aboriginal clan groups over many generations. For an example of similar cultural evocations see Krzysztof Kieslowski's *The Decalogue* (Poland: Image Entertainment, 1988–89), discussed in Richard K. Sherwin, "Law's Enchantment: The Cinematic Jurisprudence of Kieslowski," in Michael Freeman, *Law and Popular Culture* (Oxford: Oxford University Press, 2005), 87–108.

[98] See Bolter and Grusin, *Remediation*.

[99] See John Seely Brown and Paul Duguid, *The Social Life of Information* (Cambridge, MA: Harvard Business School Press, 2002).

[100] See Ann Wagner, *Images in Law* (London: Ashgate Publishing, 2006).

[101] Robert Cover, "Nomos and Narrative."

their own world-building (and perhaps world-altering) potential.[102] It is also important to bear in mind the extent to which the scopic regime of the computer screen may differ from film experience. For example, in film the image streams forward in time. Whether the editorial expansion and contraction of experience operates through flashbacks, flash forwards, or freeze-framing, whether it deploys fast motion or slow motion, film nevertheless invites us into what may be phenomenologically described as *presencing*, a sense of coming into being and signifying that irreversibly moves forward in time. The film experience thus creates its own subjective temporality, what Sobchack describes as "a presence in the present" that is informed by film's connection to "a collective past and an expansive future."[103] In addition, photographic film is analogical; that is to say, it is isomorphic with an originating image.[104] There is a trace causally linked to an object. This leads to the peculiar ontology of film: The object that film presents is present only spatially; it is temporally absent, locked forever in the past. Thus as Rodowick puts it (following Stanley Cavell), the world viewed by way of film is a world from which we are ineradicably removed, screened off from.[105] In the gap between spatial presence and temporal absence the film viewer experiences the peculiar longing for reality that is characteristic of existential alienation. Therein lies the crux of film's drama.

Digital representation is different from film. It breaks the link of physical causality. The objective world must now be encoded in algorithmic form. Light is no longer transformative (in the way that it physically changes photochemically sensitive celluloid); rather, light itself must be transformed and quantified, it must be symbolically coded. This abstract symbolic information then recodes reality in a way that simulates our cognitive preferences. The resulting image, however, is cut off from, or discontinuous with, physical time and space.[106] Rather than a trace, the digital image is a mathematical calculation. In a digitally coded world, only the impression of movement and duration remains. They are simulations. If the ontological challenge peculiar to photographic film consists in the experience of seeking to recapture time lost, in the digital visual domain this is no longer the case. In digital reality, there is no other time than the now I occupy, and there is no other presence than myself.[107]

---

[102] See Yochai Benkler, *The Wealth of Networks* (New Haven: Yale University Press, 2006).

[103] Sobchack, *Carnal Thoughts* at 151. This sense of film's temporality is experienced in the cinematic subject as part of the viewer's mimetic sensorium, what Merleau-Ponty has referred to as the "flesh of the body" through which we experience the "flesh of the world" and its mimetic representations. See Maurice Merleau-Ponty, *The Visible and the Invisible* (Chicago: Northwestern University Press, 1964).

[104] See Rodowick, *The Virtual Life of Film* at 53.

[105] Ibid., 72.

[106] Ibid., 117.

[107] Ibid., 172.

Imagining Law as Film (Representation without Reference?) 263

On the electronic screen we confront a concatenation of discrete images that self-present like pearls on an endless string, each one an insular, freestanding moment, a monadic "now."[108] Each of these momentary presents invites the viewer to experience its own instantaneous stimulation, a sensation without past or future. The algorithmically generated, dematerialized digital domain takes us into an electronic world that is "spatially decentered, weakly temporalized and quasi-disembodied (or diffusely disembodied)."[109] We are thus encouraged to dissolve the body into an inhuman digitized sensorium, a constellation of simulations (or simulacra) rather than a copy of an original. In place of the temporal flow of photographic film here we find ourselves immersed in and adrift on endless currents of contiguous data, momentary inputs, and transient sensations. And each digital (algorithmically constructed) present may be isolated, copied, recombined, and replayed at will.

In short, the irreversible narrative temporality of film is alien to the perfectly fungible, digital scopic regime. In the digital domain of the Internet, for example, dispersal and diffusion tend to displace temporal continuity. As a consequence, the experience of a temporally stable mimetic identification, together with the affective investments that such stability invites and allows, may be eroded, if not lost altogether. To the extent one is confronted within the digital domain by the weighty emotional charge of solicitude toward another's suffering or need, the opportunity and temptation to quickly surf away – in search of a new image stream, a new game, or a new thread of conversation – readily arise.[110] The digital spectacle is, in this sense, reminiscent of the self's narcissistic dissolution in the kinetic stimulation of efflorescent baroque representation with its promise of delight amid endlessly proliferating decorative form. This baroque efflorescence (or lightness of being) may obscure the kind of face-to-face encounter upon which ethical reality depends.[111] In other words, the hyperflat screen of the digital baroque risks foreclosing an experience of transcendent otherness. In the digital simulacrum there may be no way out of the monadic sensorium of subjective sensation and self-absorption.[112] Within the immanent order of digital baroque ornamentation, we may find no

---

[108] As Kracauer has written, "the ornament is an end in itself." Siegfried Kracauer, *The Mass Ornament* (Cambridge: Harvard University Press, 1995) 76.

[109] Sobchack, *Carnal Thoughts* at 53.

[110] To be sure, the psychological and ethnographic research on self and community in virtual worlds has barely begun. Some preliminary studies, however, suggest that existing massive multiplayer games online or communities within persistent virtual worlds may not be so easy. Significant emotional investment in a virtual identity (or 'avatar') and in online social communities may serve as a counterpoint to the instability and transience of virtual identities and social connections online. See Julian Dibbell, *My Tiny Life: Crime and Passion in a Virtual World* (New York: Henry Holt, 1998); Jack Balkin and Beth Noveck, *The State of Play: Law, Games, and Virtual Worlds* (New York: NYU Press, 2006); Clay Shirky, *Here Comes Everybody* (New York: Penguin Press, 2008).

[111] See Emmanuel Levinas, *Totality and Infinity* (Pittsburgh: Duquesne University Press, 1969).

[112] See Haruki Murakami, *Hard-Boiled Wonderland and the End of the World* (New York: Vintage Books, 1991). See also Rodowick, *The Virtual Life of Film* at 172.

staging area for transcendent experience or knowledge beyond the sensorial eye. This discouragement of self-demotion in the service of mimetic identification with the other may carry severe ethical consequences. If there is nothing to constrain the monadic will to command and control the flow of digital information on the screen, in whatever form it may take, how does the self-absorbed subject decenter itself sufficiently to identify with the plight of others? And without the capacity for such self-transcending responsiveness to (and responsibility for) others, what then becomes of justice?

As the previous discussion may suggest, law on the screen gives rise to a distinct form of jurisprudence. On the one hand, visualizing legal reality vastly expands the perceptible range of truthful details, from picturing underground chemical seepage to functional magnetic resonance images showing subtle changes in brain physiology. The visual image also provides access to emotional realities that help us understand individual actions and their impact on others. On the other hand, however, vivid images prompting any kind of emotional intensity are far likelier to gain and hold attention on the screen. Uncritically viewed, visualizing reality under the auspices of law risks authorizing fleeting sensation, emotional regression, collective fantasy, and historical amnesia.

Today, our dominant forms of communication are visual and increasingly interactive. Digital technology plays out on the screen and it invites us to play along. As with *YouTube* and virtual worlds online such as *There.com* and *SecondLife.com* along with massive multiplayer games online, the type of mind and culture that is emerging seems to be increasingly driven by speed, multiplicity ("hypermediation"), and easy adaptation to, as well as the felt need to command and control, shifting information flows. This rapid and agile responsiveness increases the range of diverse inputs, but reduces the size of immediately assimilable content to "blog"-able morsels. Contemporary gamers are conditioned to respond swiftly to what they see on the screen, and the tools at their disposal give them the means of doing so. It should not surprise us to see legal institutions, including courtrooms, adapt to contemporary changes in mind and culture to meet shifting expectations regarding the look of information and the methods of using it on the screen.

To the extent that cinema studies will continue to serve as an important cultural and theoretical benchmark for audiovisual reality in the twenty-first century, law's migration to the screen ensures that law and film studies will play a similarly prominent role. At issue here is the need to harmonize three discrete visual codes of meaning-making: 1) the *code of eloquence* (or aesthetics) that teaches us about the nature of beauty and persuasion in the production of compelling visual images; 2) the *code of representation* (or semiotic legitimation) that teaches us standards of the licit and illicit with regard to the reliability or truthfulness of visual signs; and 3) the *code of ethics* that teaches us standards for self-identity and relationships with others: who are we, how do we respond to the needs of others, and how is the least

Imagining Law as Film (Representation without Reference?)

among us affected by the way power flows in society when we live the way law on the screen projects and prescribes? In sum, to speak of law and film today is to speak of not one, but several – at times competing, at other times mutually reconfiguring – scopic regimes, each expressing a discrete cultural form of visuality, and each configuring a particular way of being, and being among others, in the world.

Concluding Observations

The Once and Future Image: Visual Legal Studies in the Digital Age

Rather than erect another hierarchy, it may therefore be more useful to acknowledge the plurality of scopic regimes now available to us. Rather than demonize one or another, it may be less dangerous to explore the implications, both positive and negative, of each. Martin Jay[113]

Once upon a time, the goddess of justice wore no blindfold. Images pervaded the law.[114] But by the end of the fifteenth century, as modernity glimmered on the horizon of Western culture, the blindfold appeared. Lust of the senses, the flesh of the eyes, and the dangerous seductions of the image were, in this way, to be kept at bay.[115] Cartesian rationality, with its characteristically disincarnated, text-driven ("logocentric") and semiotically nominalist way of minding the law, had come into cultural ascendancy. With the advent of modernity, the visual image gave way, as a source of authority, to the printed text. The word of law, it was thought, would avoid the false pretenses and blasphemy of the idolatrous image.[116] But times have

[113] Martin Jay, "Scopic Regimes of Modernity," *Vision and Visuality*, Hal Foster, ed. (New York: The New Press, 1988), 20.

[114] See Martin Jay, "Must Justice Be Blind? The Challenge of Images to the Law," in Douzinas and Nead, *Law and the Image*, at 19.

[115] The image, as a Byzantine iconoclast once said, is like "the flesh of the eye." (See Liz James, "Seeing is believing but words tell no lies: Captions versus images in the *Libri Carolini* and Byzantine Iconoclasm," in Ann McClanan and Jeff Johnson, *Negating the Image: Case Studies in Iconoclasm* [London: Ashgate, 2005] 97.) Of central concern here is the guiding insight that visual images operate in the realm of the body; the knowledge they produce is sensate knowledge. See David F. Marks, "On the Relationship Between Imagery, Body, and Mind," *Imagery: Current Development*, P. J. Hampson, D. F. Marks, and J. T. E. Richardson, eds. (London and New York: Routledge, 1999) 190. ("Tactile epistemology involves thinking with your skin . . . Haptic cinema, by appearing to us as an object with which we can interact rather than an illusion into which we enter, calls upon this sort of embodied and mimetic intelligence.")

[116] Historically, iconoclasm, the fear of images, has emerged as an offshoot of a belief in unmediated reality. If one may encounter God's presence in word or voice, images pose the danger of at least distraction, and at most spiritual blasphemy in that people may mistake the visible icon or image for the transcendent, unrepresentable God. If one were to create a space, in the realm of visual representation, for that which resists representation we would witness what Peter Goodrich calls the "iconography of nothing." See Peter Goodrich, "The Iconography of Nothing: Blank Spaces and the Representation of Law in *Edward VI and the Pope*," Douzinas and Nead, *Law and the Image*, at 100; Sherwin, "Law, Metaphysics, and the New Iconoclasm."

changed, and the visual image is back. The Cartesian foundation that undercut the once prominent role of rhetorical and ethical studies in the traditional, premodern knowledge base of the humanities, has now, in turn, entered a stage of decline.[117]

The twentieth century was fundamentally an audiovisual culture.[118] The twenty-first century will undoubtedly continue to be so. Although cinema studies promises to remain the benchmark for meaning-making practices on the screen for some time to come, new media are rapidly exerting a significant and growing impact on our relationship to the screen.[119] The way we make sense of the true or the real, and the way we make judgments about the ethical and the just, take on new dimensions and face new challenges when significant changes occur in the dominant medium of communication. For example, a law field constituted by rules and principles operates by way of abstract transcendentals, a commonplace of the written word. By contrast, a law field on the electronic screen, constituted by immanent digitized networks operates as a flattened series of discrete and fleeting insights, impressions, relational possibilities, and affective intensities, a commonplace of the electronic gaze.[120] It behooves us, therefore, to study with great care the diverse meaning-making practices that make up the archives and repertoires of film, television, and new media (including digital computers and the Internet).

The law and film movement is the natural offspring of these cultural and technological developments. Not surprisingly, a growing number of law schools are including law and film courses in their curriculum.[121] Conferences, scholarly symposia, and publications have featured a broad range of issues in this emerging field.[122] Increasingly, the law and film movement is taking on global interest.[123] As new forms

[117] See, for example, Stephen Toulmin, *Cosmopolis: The Hidden Agenda of Modernity* (Chicago: University of Chicago Press, 1990).

[118] Rodowick, *The Virtual Life of Film*, at 186.

[119] Ibid., 86–7 ("Cinema will increasingly become the art of synthesizing imaginary worlds, numerical worlds in which the sight of physical reality becomes increasingly scarce").

[120] The so-called posthuman turn in cybernetics posits a virtual, algorithmic reformulation of what we regard as embodied existence in real life. As N. Katherine Hayles puts it: "The posthuman view privileges informational pattern over material instantiation, so that embodiment in a biological substrate is seen as an accident of history rather than an inevitability of life . . . The posthuman subject is an amalgam, a collection of heterogeneous components, a material-informational entity whose boundaries undergo continuous construction and reconstruction." N. Katherine Hayles, *How We Became Posthuman* (Chicago: University of Chicago Press, 1999) 2–3.

[121] Michael Asimow at UCLA Law School, James Elkins at West Virginia School of Law, Peter Goodrich at Cardozo Law School, Laurent Mayali at UC Berkeley Boalt Law School – to name but a few.

[122] See, e.g., "Symposium, Picturing Justice: Images of Law and Lawyers in the Visual Media," *University of San Francisco Law Review* 30 (1996) 891–1248; "Symposium, Law and Popular Culture," *UCLA Law Review* 48 (2001) 1293; "Symposium, Law in Film/Film in Law," *Vermont Law Review* 28 (2004) 797; "Symposium, *Law and Film*," *Legal Studies Forum* 24 (2000) 559; "Symposium, *Documentaries & the Law*," *Fordham Intellectual Property Media & Entertainment Law Journal* 16 (2006) 707. For a comprehensive catalogue of law and film scholarship, go to: http://tarlton.law.utexas.edu/lpop/.

[123] See, for example, Stefan Machura and Stefan Ulbrich, "Law in Film: Globalizing the Hollywood Courtroom Drama," *Journal of Law and Society* 28 (2001) 1117–32.

Imagining Law as Film (Representation without Reference?)

of visual technologies begin to pervade law school classrooms, as they already have law offices and courtrooms, law's life on the screen will undoubtedly become an integral part of its pedagogical, practical, and jurisprudential reality. To a growing extent, the stories lawyers know and tell, and the way they tell them, bear the signs of a global cinematic or audiovisual culture.

Law and film studies, and its possible future incarnation in the more expansive field of visual legal studies, must encompass old and new visual media alike – which is to say, photographic film and video, as well as digital (computation-based) cinema. The objectives of this scholarly movement are varied. Through interpretive studies, scholars of law on the screen study how public expectations and beliefs are being shaped and informed by popular visual media. These cultural sources also may be mined for their pedagogical and prescriptive content, whether as sites of popular resistance to legal authority, mass cultural manipulation, or as exemplars of new forms of affirmation and utopian striving. Through empirical studies, scholars seek to understand and assess new visual strategies of evidentiary representation and persuasion. Finally, as an ethical or prudential matter, a matter let us say of jurisprudential wisdom, by learning more about the meaning-making tools that help to shape and inform the screen-based realities in which we live, we stand a better chance of mastering, rather than passively mimicking, the aesthetic forms and organizational logic (or codes) that our tools tend to enact.

So what, then, may be said about the future of the law and film movement? In the years ahead, we will no doubt continue to grapple with how law, lawyers, and legal institutions are being depicted in film (and on television, and blogs, and multiplayer games, and Internet websites of all sorts). We will continue to learn about popular and mass culture and by extension about law and the professional identity of lawyers as they are seen through the lens of cinematic storytelling. We will continue to internalize these lessons and turn them into pragmatic insights of craftsmanship as we learn more about how best to optimize the lawyer's cinematic and digital toolkit of visual rhetoric. Legal scholars will continue to learn more about the various ways in which power operates in society, particularly as we reflect on the technological means of cultural production and distribution, and on how control (of mind and culture) may be exercised by the digital codes we unwittingly absorb from our interactions with electronic screens. These issues are crucial to the continued flourishing of democracy in the digital age because they address elementary concerns about who owns culture, and who is free to use it, in what manner, and to what end. The way we visualize the ongoing tension between the commonwealth of culture and the private domain of marketable goods and services will no doubt play a part in that conflict's ultimate resolution.

In sum, law and film studies, broadly conceived, serves as a vital scholarly platform from which to launch practical, theoretical, and ethical queries that are central to the humanities of the twenty-first century. At the same time, however, we must never forget that in one crucial respect law remains unlike other disciplines in the humanities. The particular ways of being and being among others that law imagines are policed, and ultimately enforced, by the power of the state. In this respect, the ethical responsibility that attends thinking about the theory and craft of law – including the institutions, communication technologies, and rhetorical practices through which law's performances are realized – can hardly be overstated. In law's cinematic dreams begin responsibilities, and so we continue to ask: What does the image on the screen allow us to know? Who does it invite us to be? And what social world, what *nomos* or legal reality does it call into being (or cast into oblivion)?

10

Law and Television: Screen Phenomena and Captive Audiences

Susanna Lee

Various journalists and scholars have described the now well-known "*CSI* effect." Max Houck, director of forensic business development at West Virginia University, has said, "The *CSI* effect is basically the perception of the near-infallibility of forensic science in response to the TV show."[1] I would like to use this perception as a point of entry into the complex relationship between law and television. What is interesting about the *CSI* effect is not so much that television shows like *CSI* have altered public perception of the way the law does (or should) work, but that the step from the role of television spectator into the role of juror should seem so natural in the first place. Television has been altering audience expectations since its inception, but there is no "*House* effect," no "*ER* effect," no "*Boston Public* effect." Why is it in the domain of the law that viewers feel implicated in – and drawn to comment on – the preservation of law's correct operation? The answer to this question comes in part from the fact of the jury system, which gives real individuals an actual active voice in determining legal outcomes. Most crimes, though, do not go to trial, and most jurors who serve do not end up on murder trials. The presence of the *CSI* effect has also to do with the ways in which law on television interpolates the viewer: at once as a singular witness, and also as a potential stand-in for a crucial enforcer.

As Richard Sherwin notes in his contribution to this volume, "A law field constituted by rules and principles operates by way of abstract transcendentals, a commonplace of the written word. By contrast, a law field on the electronic screen,

---

[1] "Everyone's an Expert: The CSI Effect's Negative Impact on Juries," Jeffrey Heinrick, http://www .cspo.org/documents/csieffectheinrick.pdf. "The *CSI* effect can best be described as a phenomenon where television "educated" jurors are more likely to not convict someone who is guilty because procedures and techniques they observed from the fictional television show were not applied in the case. Max Houck, Director of the Forensic Science Initiative at West Virginia University, says 'The CSI effect is basically the perception of the near-infallibility of forensic science in response to the TV show.' The *CSI* effect is a recent phenomenon that can be attributed to the influence of mass media. The term started appearing in legal lexicon in 2003; roughly 3 years after the show and its spin-offs became wildly popular television options for the American public."

constituted by immanent digitized networks operates as a flattened series of discrete and fleeting insights, impressions, relational possibilities, and affective intensities, a commonplace of the electronic gaze." The creation of policy (abstract transcendentals) is a largely behind-the-scenes act, resulting in an operational framework. The enforcement of the law is an active and energetic phenomenon. The characteristics and consistency of enforcement as represented on the electronic screen are of particular importance because televised "discrete and fleeting insights" and "relational possibilities" are the sole means by which many of us access the law field. Furthermore, these are also the sole means by which viewers access any field on television. These are television's stock in trade, whether in the realm of law or of anything else.

There are structural and schematic ways in which a subject's position with respect to the law is similar to the viewer's position with respect to television conventions. Both relationships have a passive element of spectatorship/receptivity and an active element of conformity/validation. To participate in a society (a nation) is to accept its laws. To join a television audience is to accept its conventions. The similarities would seem to expire there, because television viewers are usually not enjoined to enter and become part of the television world. At times, however, this enjoining does happen, and it happens in the realm of the law.

One could start by wondering why the law is so richly represented on television. One response to this would be that law's compact and infinitely repeated economies of crime and punishment, investigation and resolution, pursuit and arrest, tort and compensation, conflict and denouement, are well suited to the repetitive and short-form nature of the small screen.[2] Furthermore, because the form that legal procedure has on television is in a schematic sense the form that it really does have, viewers are sometimes less conscious that television is in fact not just the first, but sometimes the only place that they observe law enforcement in action. What viewers "know" about legal procedure and law enforcement professionals, that is, comes in large part from television – both because it is represented there and because the short-form nature of television traces in a schematic sense – and so presents as familiar and possible and normal – the repetitive resolution of crimes, investigations, and trials.[3]

Another reason for the popularity of programs about law is that law gives an actual active role to the voice of the people. More specifically, it gives an actual active voice to people who have spent a significant amount of time listening to the case be presented. Spectatorship in juries leads up to the moment of announcing the verdict. Spectatorship among television viewers leads up to the moment of watching

---

[2] See for instance Carol Clover, "Law and the Order of Popular Culture," in *Law in the Domains of Culture*, ed. Austin Sarat and Thomas Kearns, eds. (Ann Arbor: University of Michigan Press, 1998).

[3] The influence of television on public perception of law enforcement is of interest also to police. See for instance Roger Schaefer, William Vanderbok, Eugene Wisnoski, "Television Police Shows and Attitudes toward the Police," *Journal of Police Science and Administration* 7(1), 1979, 104–13.

Law and Television: Screen Phenomena and Captive Audiences 271

the verdict. The *CSI* effect, then, is a small although radical movement from outside the television to inside: television viewers emulating television juries. In one sense, this movement enacts a vision of being heard as a member of the public in a legal forum.[4] In another, it enacts a vision of crossing the line from outside to inside the television. In short, the *CSI* effect represents the intersection of viewership, creativity, and good citizenship: a vision of moving from seeing to doing and from viewing to creating.[5] With that intersection in mind, one could wonder why the *CSI* effect is remarkable in the first place. Television programs about the law and legal procedures routinely encourage and celebrate the active role of the observant individual. The lone person peering into a microscope, noticing one discrepancy, cracking the case, bursting into the courtroom, punishing the murderer – this is a dramatic commonplace and it amounts to a television convention of watching and then, again and again, turning that perspicacity to good dramatic and legal effect.

To return to the point about spectator participation in the law being structurally similar to spectator participation in television conventions, there are particular characteristics of the television-viewer connection that make those similarities possible. Most scholarship about screen representations of law and legal procedure concentrates on film, and on the one hand, of course, television, a visual medium, has much in common with film: camera angles, manipulation of lights, constructed narratives, the same "discrete and fleeting insights and affective intensities" present in cinema. Television also has certain features that are peculiar to it alone, and because of these features, the individual is interpolated as both viewer and legal subject – or perhaps it would be more precise to say that because of these features, "viewer" and "legal subject" have come to share numerous characteristics.

For one, television literally comes into the home, which film does not do, or at least, does not do in its original form. This entry into the home breeds familiarity or rather the illusion of familiarity. Furthermore, television shows banality, mundane daily life, and the domestic sphere. It is possible for a program to run for years, for instance, with no other set than the characters' living room and kitchen. Along with

---

4   This vision, I think, can particularly take hold in the United States, which, being both democratic and enormous, celebrates the force of the individual voice even as the sheer number of voices and the scale of the population tend to dilute that force.

5   Austin Sarat, Lawrence Douglas, and Martha Umphrey write, "The moving image attunes us to the "might-have-beens" that have shaped our worlds and the "might-bes" against which those worlds can be judged and toward which they might be pointed. *Law on the Screen* (Stanford: Stanford University Press, 2005) 2. The *CSI* effect, like *Law and Order*'s reputation for realism, rests on the idea of turning a "might-have-been" into a "might-be." The *CSI* effect represents the idea that Morson's "sideshadow" could become the actual fact: that a narrative could jump the track and arrive at another ending, specifically, an ending illustrated on television, and that *CSI* effect, like *Law and Order*'s appeal, represents the idea that the audience could jump its track, moving from the narrative course of its reality into the alternate course proposed on television.

the domestic scenes, we have the fact that television operates on a much smaller scale than movies. The screen is smaller, in most cases, and situated literally more on our level: we do not need to gaze upward at a television screen. Television is much less commanding, or at least less palpably so. Furthermore, television is a short-form medium. Programs are an hour or a half-hour long, and even that duration is interrupted by commercials. It does not seem to call for much attention and the viewer need not wait long for the episode's resolution.

In addition to these features, there are other elements of television that bring television viewership in line with legal subjectivity (a combination feeling, I would propose, of being protected and at the same time empowered or validated by the law). The first of these features is the advent of syndication reruns, TiVo®, and other recording devices. Television even without TiVo was constant and continuous, but with TiVo, viewers can watch what they want when they want: spectatorship on demand. For this reason, nothing on television seems valuable or singular: when programs are advertised as television "events," for instance, the viewer knows that this word is out of place. There is nothing special about the time of the event (it can be recorded), and increasingly, there is nothing special about the place (television can be watched in restaurants, at doctor's offices, and on handheld devices anywhere at all).[6] Even someone who does not have TiVo can watch television reruns endlessly: the "marathon" is a commonplace.[7] The second such feature is the advent of reality television. This is a peculiarly televisual phenomenon in itself – no one has had the idea to make a "reality movie" – and this is in part, I think, because of increasing audience participation in television. John Caldwell wrote in *Televisuality* (published in 1995, before reality television became the industry that it is now):

> Well before America was wired for electronic and digital interactivity, reality programming had gotten the viewer off the couch and on the phone. With the success of tabloid cop shows, interactivity – a market-proven embellishment from the well-oiled and lucrative cable ghettos of Christian television – spread across the channel spectrum. The activated televisual viewer was now neither the proverbial housewife nor the distracted consumer of academic theory, but a vigilante – a televisual bounty hunter energized by patriotic appeals to American morality, law and order.[8]

[6] "Television does not turn people into zombies. Viewers do not absorb its images as if by hypodermic injection. Yet television continues to be influential because it remains part of so many hours, more than any other activity except sleep and work." Mike Budd, Steve Craig and Clay Steinman. *Consuming Environments: Television and Commercial Culture.* (London: Rutgers, 1999) 1.

[7] See Walter Benjamin, *Art in the Age of Mechanical Reproduction.* One wonders what Benjamin would make of a *Law and Order* marathon.

[8] John Thornton Caldwell, *Televisuality: Style, Crisis, and Authority in American Television* (New Brunswick: Rutgers University Press, 1995) 259–60. See also Jessica Fishman, "The Populace and the Police: Models of Social Control in Reality-Based Crime Television." *Critical Studies in Mass Communication* 16 (1999) 268–88.

Law and Television: Screen Phenomena and Captive Audiences

Fourteen years later, countless reality shows depend on audience opinion: vote by text message! The *CSI* effect is not at all astonishing when placed in this context: What could be more appealing and seemingly appropriate than voting someone off the proverbial island in a real, moral, law-and-order-boosting, crime-fighting forum?

John Caldwell writes of the development of television since the 1980s, "With increasing frequency, style itself became the subject, the signified, if you will, of television. In fact, this self-consciousness of a style became so great that it can more accurately be described as an activity – as a performance of style – rather than as a particular look," and then, "Conceived of as a presentational attitude, a display of knowing exhibitionism, any one of many specific visual looks and stylizations could be marshaled for the spectacle. The process of stylization rather than style – an activity rather than a static look – was the factor that defined televisual exhibitionism."[9] In modern television, it is not just the producer who participates in this "performance of style," but also the viewer, imbued with (apparently legitimate) authority by the blurring of lines between viewer world and television world.

If in the foregoing citation we replace the word "style" with "law" or "rule of law" and "particular look" with "particular law," then we can begin to see the intersections between law and television. To explain, I have said that television conventions (domestic forum, viewer participation, short form, and repetition) have paved the way for juries/viewers to expect the same combination of drama and resolution in actual legal proceedings. The question remains, however: Why *do* television conventions take root? Why do viewers care, not just enough to watch the program, but to absorb its conventions and (in the case of the *CSI* effect) apply them to reality? What is really at stake? To answer this, I would propose that the relationship between television and law can be understood as symbiotic. Television, that is, is invested in the coherence of its representations of the law because in all its programming, in all its conventions, television is invested in, relies on, the very coherence that the law represents. Viewers care about coherence in television because they care about its model and signified, namely coherence in law.[10] Law represents, stands for, promises, depends on, and therefore raises the stakes of coherence and predictability. Television on its own (as if television could be on its own) would have nothing at stake, but people do in fact want the law to function. Television performs that functioning and so becomes a model for it – not just in programs about the law, but by extension, in programs of all sorts.[11] The *CSI* effect would then allow the viewer to close the loop: to ensure

---

[9] Caldwell, 5.

[10] As Carol Clover writes, "This structure and these procedures [of trials] are so deeply embedded in our narrative tradition that they shape even plots that never step into a courtroom; and . . . such trial-derived forms constitute the most distinctive share of Anglo-American entertainment." Clover, 99–100, cited in Sarat, Douglas, and Umphrey, 5. This structure does more than provide a shape: it provides weight.

[11] It would seem that a similar wish applies to the functioning of medical science and diagnostic techniques: thus the popularity of *House* and other such programs.

that actual real-life law continues to function as a reasonable model for the televisual conventions – conventions that, although fictitious, do respond to an actual wish of viewer/citizens to live within a sound social frame, and at the same time to imitate, stand for, and perhaps even be the sort of person who assures the soundness of that frame.[12]

At this point, I want to talk about two long-running programs that present the law to the viewing public: *Law and Order* and *Cops*. I will talk about how these programs bridge the gap between the law and the viewer with a double offering. On the one hand, the viewer is invited to sense a greater familiarity and comfort with legal and law-enforcement professionals and their procedures. On the other hand, the viewer is invited to find something in those professionals to admire and with which to identify. That something, I would argue, is a way of being in the world, a way of relating to and in fact managing reality. This in essence is what television producers do, and on the other end, what television viewers do, when they choose to have the television on. The way in which television law provides a model of relating to reality reveals in turn the enchanted place that the law and its professionals occupy in the cultural imagination – a place of both mastery and security, of authority and protection.

Law and Order

In this section, I examine the most popular of American television crime dramas, *Law and Order*, to discover how the American viewing public relates – or rather wishes it related – to crime and violence. I will talk particularly about the idea of spectatorship and about the fantasy of menace and protection that this drama represents.[13]

---

[12] Richard Sherwin describes television conventions as influencing the ways lawyers must present cases: "The principal storytellers of our culture today are television and film. Effective storytelling in these media is highly dependent upon visual and aural cues. The legal storyteller must have a sophisticated understanding of mass communication in order to grasp how truth, law, and justice are constructed in the popular imagination. Only then can she effectively tell her story before a particular lay audience." Sherwin, "Picturing Justice: Images of Law and Lawyers in the Visual Media." *University of San Francisco Law Review* 30, 4 (1996) 892. An effective legal argument would thus take into account standards of verisimilitude established by and through television: "We study the popular imagination because it is an important source of law: from the voters who put lawmakers and judges in power, to jurors who determine truth and justice in jury rooms across the nation. And just as it is the lay public from whom law's legitimacy ultimately derives, so too it is the public's continued belief and acceptance upon which law's legitimacy depends. It is the people who in anger may repudiate the law of the state, who may even make their own law from the streets." (Ibid., 898) Austin Sarat, Lawrence Douglas, and Martha Umphrey point to Gary Saul Morson's notion of "sideshadowing" to discuss television's projection of "alternative realities." *Law on the Screen*, 1.

[13] Reprinted with changes from Susanna Lee, "These are Our Stories: Trauma, Form, and the Screen Phenomenon of *Law and Order*." *Discourse: Journal for Theoretical Studies in Media and Culture* 25, 1 & 2. Copyright © 2004 Wayne State University Press, with the permission of Wayne State University Press.

Law and Television: Screen Phenomena and Captive Audiences 275

In modern television crime drama, detectives and prosecutors are as much witnesses as they are creators of legal resolution. Satisfactory resolution is indeed often impossible. In *Law and Order*, for instance, even when a murderer is punished, the prosecutors often ruminate on the ephemeral nature of judicial victories, on the certainty that injustices must continue to arise.[14] On the other hand, even when the murderer goes unpunished and justice unserved (which is common), these characters remain reassuring and caring presences. Television crime drama combines these contradictory elements – the repeated articulation of law's limitations and the reassuring presence of the detective/witness.

Every episode of *Law and Order* starts with a low male voice-over pronouncing these words: "In the criminal justice system, the people are represented by two separate but equally important groups: the police who investigate crime and the district attorneys who prosecute the offenders. These are their stories." In this discussion, I want to underscore the idea that this is a drama of human stories, and, what is more, stories about those who "represent the people." With this focus – because *Law and Order* is as much about how humans respond to crime as it is about the schematic or judicial resolution of social disorder – the show enacts a particular sort of postmodern tension. It combines an uncontainable rush of violence or disorder or menace with the assurance that someone (detective, author, narrator) is watching and producing narrative form. This combination remains dramatic rather than formulaic (or dramatic though formulaic) because the principal tension of *Law and Order*, for the viewer and for the detective character, comes not just from the suspense of the criminal investigation and the legal proceedings. It comes also from a vaster psychic and social precariousness: the incertitude of whether the detectives and prosecutors – and by extension the judicial system, the public, and the narrative itself – can remain intact in the face of relentless violence and disorder. The working through and witnessing of crime becomes itself a drama and a crucial element of the modern television drama.

The police and prosecutors are the people in our culture who, when a crime is committed, "respond" to the scene. In *Law and Order*, the strongest trait of these characters is a steadiness of tone and appearance. For one, there are few extremes of emotion, raised voices, shouting, stuttering, insulting, or storming around. There is a fundamental impassiveness to even the most empathic and troubled of *Law and Order* faces. This evenness, accentuated by the camera's steady focus, has become more and more established in the series' nineteen years. In the first episode (1990), the detectives are shouting at each other in the office, the lieutenant discloses that he is a recovering alcoholic, and the District Attorney remembers aloud his own alcoholic father. In later episodes, even in episodes later that same season, there is no

---

[14] See Timothy Lenz, *Changing Images of Law in Film and Television Crime Stories* (New York: Peter Lang, 2003) 157.

shouting. Characters muse on personal memories but these musings, more sparse, are part of an abstract philosophical and ethical contemplation rather than the other way around. Alcoholism and divorce and even tragedy stand in the characters' pasts but are absorbed and worn with calm. At no time do we see homes, cars, friends, families, pets, or paychecks; personal lives take place entirely off-screen.[15] Precisely for this reason, their stories ("these are their stories"), as human stories – as emotional stories – are rather static. The true spectacle in this series, the principal story told, is not the professionals' dramatic response to crime, but the absence of response – the absence of psychic commotion or unrest.

Law and Order has been called the most realistic of television crime dramas. The question thus presents itself: What in this television scenario – police and prosecutors who respond in deadpan tone, maintain even facial expressions, an invariable demeanor of wise detachment, and, for the women, immaculately combed hair, even outside in the wind – seems so true that viewers across the country embrace it as a realistic portrait of crime and the criminal world? Indeed, throughout *Law and Order*, not just the prosecutors, but every character, from the random couple who finds the body, to the witnesses, to the medical examiner, to the initial suspects and their families, to the courtroom spectators, to the incidental characters and bureaucracies that furnish information, to the juries, to the foreperson with the verdict, looks on with detachment, with evenness. The people standing around watching as suspects are hauled into the police car sometime in the initial half hour invariably look as though they were watching a television episode being filmed on their street, rather than watching an actual friend or acquaintance being arrested. To understand the nature of the show's realism, we remember one of its opening lines, "the people are represented." Assistant District Attorney Jack McCoy does shake his head at murders in his world the way the public shakes its head at murders in the actual world – on the one hand because *Law and Order* does take its stories from the news ("ripped from the headlines"), so the public and the characters are in a sense witnessing the same murders, and furthermore because they are witnessing them in the same way: as detached spectators. I would propose that it is not disturbing or alienating or even particularly surprising to see the characters' impassive regard because this regard mirrors the way the television public accesses violence: by watching it from a distance. Most television spectators never do witness a killing, or find a corpse, or even see a suspect being arrested, so murder, familiar as it is to viewers, is always already murder on television. It is because of this media-based or media-created distance that the impassive prosecutors can "represent" the viewer. We as spectators can relate to this remove because it is the way we relate to violent crime and the subsequent legal proceedings – because, for most viewers, that relationship is based upon spectatorship.

---

[15] I am talking here about the original *Law and Order*, not *Law and Order: SVU* or *Law and Order: Criminal Intent*. These latter have come increasingly to incorporate the personal lives of the characters.

In discussing violence as a primarily *spectacliste* phenomenon, I am not suggesting that television spectators are universally removed from the realities of violence. First, in cities, suburbs, farms, and everywhere, domestic violence, as much a menace to society as street violence, is more common than television would have us think, and exponentially more common than dramatic gun battles. Second, there are numerous places in this country where street violence is an everyday occurrence, where interaction with the criminal justice system is a norm rather than an aberration, and where public discourse about violence is therefore more depressed or resigned than dramatic or inflamed. New York City, where *Law and Order* is set, contains some of these places. The point is that most residents of this country, and most spectators of *Law and Order*, do not have regular contact with police and prosecutors. Even those who do see shootings and robberies on their streets generally still see their first murder on television, not on their block. Whether or not there is cause and effect in these enactments of violence is the subject of much media criticism, and much has been written about the derealization produced in television. On the basis of sheer numbers, *Law and Order* addresses the viewer, as most crime television addresses the viewer, as spectators who know about violence from watching it on television or reading about it in the news.

The unconscious equation of violence and legal response thereto with televised images sustains the realism of other *Law and Order* conventions. One of these is the use of location cards. For instance, when a possible witness is found in upstate New York, the lieutenant proposes, "Why don't you take a ride up to Albany?" One second later (boom boom): "Albany" comes onto the bottom of the screen. This instantaneous word-made-flesh does not correspond to the way real people experience the world, but it does correspond to the way real people experience, or read, criminal investigations and legal proceedings. Whether on television or in the newspaper, violence – and law's response to it – is most often a matter of words and pictures. What is more, it is words and pictures set out in a reasonable narrative order. So it is with every incident in the news, but in the case of crime and punishment, that conventional coherence is the *sine qua non* of viewers' access to the event.

It makes sense, given the viewer's own "remove," that the characters' emotional distance from the crimes represented resonates as realistic. The reason that it also resonates as dramatic is that when we see violence presented in the newspapers or on television in a coherent manner, we know that that coherence is a form imposed. Indeed, that sense of underlying disorder stands as the implied *raison d'être* of the imposed form. The representation of violence on television suggests, in an Althusserian turn, the incomprehensible menace that it contains.[16] Budd, Craig,

---

[16] As Althusser wrote in *Ideological State Apparatuses*, Marx's insistence that "the ultimate condition of production is the reproduction of the conditions of production" holds for ideological as well as industrial productions; and for ideological state apparatuses, including television, a fundamental condition of production is subject interpellation. Althusser writes, "There is no ideology except for concrete subjects, and this destination for ideology is only made possible by the subject" (170). And,

and Steinman point out in *Consuming Environments*: "How many of us who find *ER* or *NYPD Blue* "realistic" have experience in an emergency room or a big-city police department? In fact, most of us get most of our information about such "real" situations not from real life but from television, movies, and books."[17] It is true that the codes of representation depend on television conventions: as John Sumser puts it, the "symbolic environment presented on television has been molded not only by the medium and the genre, but by the preexisting symbolic environment."[18] The police station in *NYPD Blue* looks "real" because the same or similar set was used for various other shows: a visual realist precedent has been set. When *ER* or *NYPD Blue* presents itself as realistic, however, it does not just imply that this is how an emergency room or police station really looks or operates. *Law and Order* does not just imply that this is how courtrooms and the legal proceedings that happen there really operate: that implication would not be enough to make the program compelling. It implies that the courtroom is a vitally important site of confrontation with disorder and danger: that we can experience something there that cannot be accessed otherwise, that there stands there a reality more primal, more fundamental, more complicated, than could be found elsewhere.

Law and Order's steadiness of focus is a dramatic occurrence because television representation of crime does not just bring to us what we would otherwise not see and does not just bring it to us contained, but implies that what it contains would, without that containment, be devastating or at least unmanageable for us. Jack McCoy's serious face carries the implication of turbulence confined. The fact that his even expressions seem both familiar and troubled is a testament to the intimation of disorder beneath coherent representations – especially beneath representations whose coherence is openly and entirely fictitious. It is also a testament, I think, to the sense of unreality that comes from living in a violent culture while rarely seeing acts of violence firsthand. That sense of unreality, a combination of distance and immediacy, is present for most Americans; it is born of the disconnect between what is lived on a daily basis and what is seen on television. This disconnect goes hand in hand with that described by Sherwin, when he contrasts "abstract transcendentals, a commonplace of the written word" to the "affective intensities" represented on television. Television brings what is distant closer, and, in turning word into image, renders the abstract concrete. Even if those transmissions were unproblematic, which

---

"All ideology hails or interpolates concrete individuals as concrete subjects, by the functioning of the category of the subject" (173). *Law and Order* interpolates its viewers as subjects in danger. It does not just respond to a wish for judicial and psychic protection but creates and perpetuates that wish. Louis Althusser, "Ideology and Ideological State Apparatuses." *Lenin and Philosophy and Other Essays*. (London: New Left Books, 1971).

[17] *Consuming Environments*, 108.

[18] John Sumser, *Morality and Social Order in Television Crime Drama*. (Jefferson: McFarland, 1996) 45. In this sense, convention in television is similar to precedent in law: past becomes foundation.

they are not, the fact that television is a commercial enterprise whose principal products are dramatization and coherence would indicate that it cannot be trusted. It cannot be trusted, that is, as a transparent window, a disinterested vehicle, an armored car bringing us the real.[19] One wonders what is lost as well as what is created through television conventions – much as we might wonder, as *Law and Order* in fact encourages us to, what is lost and what is created through broad insistences on procedure and precedent.

Television both threatens the spectator and stands as protector – were it not for television, crime and violence and a disorderly world might come upon us unexpected, or these menaces might remain unseen, operating under our noses, and we in ignorance; which would be worse? As Avital Ronell wonders in "TraumaTV": "What is television covering?"[20] "What video teaches, something that television knows but cannot as such articulate, is that every medium is related in some crucial way to specters."[21] The same can be said, of course, for the law itself, and particularly for the police. Were it not for the law, and for public respect for the law, formlessness and danger could loom. Yet, interestingly, law in *Law and Order* often *is* the villain. The fourth amendment, for instance, looms frequently as a wrench in the wheels of justice, a victory of technicality over substance. That victory, as much as it might frustrate the characters, worry the viewers, and inflame potential jurors, represents a coherence that the characters are loath to abandon. Just as the immovable fourth amendment is described by some judges as a necessary impediment ("and what if everyone decided to trample on the constitution?"), so the simplifications of television itself both protect from and block reality.

This brings us to another feature of *Law and Order. Law and Order*, with its even-tempered characters and violence contained, provides something other than narrative coherence: it represents a sense of psychic protection. The fact that Jack McCoy's detachment seems familiar corresponds to a wish that violence in person could really be the same as violence at a distance: a wish that for the calm and the wise, the actual experience of violence could really be the same as watching it on television, and that the specter of disorder could be a manageable one. To cast this implication in more psychological terms, I would propose that the steadiness of the characters, their psychic distance, couched as it is in a frame of realism, responds to a public desire to suppose that if it were faced with actual violence, if it did encounter corpses, murderers, recalcitrant witnesses, lost evidence, unscrupulous defense attorneys, bored judges, a flawed or inadequate judicial system, and a cynical public, it would be able to respond with composure. We the spectators could really be the people who "represent us," who stand as our protectors.

---

[19] See *Consuming Environments*.
[20] Avital Ronell. *Finitude's Score* (Lincoln: University of Nebraska Press, 1994) 309.
[21] Ibid., 313.

John Sumser writes about the rise of the courtroom drama: "Once trial is brought in as the natural consequence of arrest . . . the adventure is tamed, routinized, bureaucratized, and subordinated to the culture of the law. The second thing is that moral certainty is lost." And then: "The transition from moral certainty to moral ambiguity is basically . . . from a theory of social types (that we are one thing or another) to the idea of social roles (that who we are is situationally defined)."[22] Sumser is correct in saying that there is no conceptual or ethical resolution at the end of the courtroom drama. The one-hour drama form remains intact and it must contain something, reinforce something, represent some sort of certainty. Previously, the position of strength to which one returned was the triumph of good over bad, detective over criminal, social order over social chaos. Now, I argue, the fantasy of resolution presented by the crime drama is psychic rather than conceptual or social. On screen in *Law and Order* is a fiction of human rather than social response to trauma – a microcosmic *mise en scène* of personal resistance to trauma and violence.

Philip Lane writes of *Homicide*: "The detectives of *Homicide* are very cool at the scene of a crime. They talk philosophy, engage in nonsensical repartee, discuss personal relationships and problems while standing over a corpse. They appear to be objective observers of a crime scene; but, in fact, their daily dosage of death eventually gets to them."[23] In *Law and Order*, that dosage (and *Law and Order* has had the much longer run) does not "get to" the detectives. There is no accumulation of trauma, no boredom, no hardness, no increase or decrease in the capacity for empathy.[24] Again and again, the camera remains focused on one face long enough to see an unwavering steadiness of regard, serious but not cold. The pain of violence, of contact with victims and sociopaths, never contaminates the characters' attendance record at the job or pushes them into a morass of depression or makes them uninterested in or hardened to human concerns. This vision in which social consciousness, ethical responsibility, and a fountain of calm flow forth from a seemingly inexhaustible source represents a vision of security – the sort of character that we would want to represent us in the judicial but also, and more importantly, in the figural sense. It is a testament, I propose, to the way we would want to witness and master a culture of violence.[25]

---

[22] Sumser, 161.

[23] Philip J. Lane "The Existential Condition of Television Crime Drama." *Journal of Popular Culture* 2001 Spring; 34(4) 137–51, 146.

[24] On the relationship of empathy and trauma, see Dori Laub and Nanette Auerhahn, "Knowing and not knowing massive trauma: Forms of traumatic memory." *International Journal of Psychoanalysis* 1993 (74) 287–302; Dori Laub and Susanna Lee, "Thanatos and massive psychic trauma: The impact of the death instinct on remembering and forgetting," *Journal of the American Psychoanalytic Association* 51 (2) Spring 2003: 433–64. Here again, I am talking about the original *Law and Order*. Subsequent permutations such as *Law and Order: SVU* have represented and even thematized police "battle fatigue."

[25] Geoffrey Hartman describes the psychic menaces posed by a violent culture: "One of the simplest axioms of psychoanalysis holds that hyperarousal leads to trauma or inappropriate psychic defenses – it seems clear enough that, while human responses are not uniform, and our psyches are quite resilient,

Law and Television: Screen Phenomena and Captive Audiences

The *Law and Order* characters represent a fantasy of psychic intactness and empathic presence in the face of relentless violence. This intactness is their contribution to society, their act of protection. What is it that they do, precisely? How do they convey this sense of protection? They cannot convict every murderer, and even when a conviction is made, it is invariably presented as a drop in the ocean. What these characters do, I propose – and here we return to the notion of calm spectatorship discussed in the first part of this chapter – is listen. For each shot of a character speaking, the reverse shot, of another listening, is implied. Their faces remain earnest, just on this side of burdened, concentrated on their interlocutors. The characters' consistent eye contact with their off-screen interlocutor (not us, but positioned somewhere near us) reminds us of their empathic presence. At no time do the characters break down during the process of listening. One does not get the sense that they are more tired of listening now than they were six or ten years ago, nor does it seem that their aplomb indicates an "inappropriate psychic defense." Instead, their listening remains at once comforting and dramatic. "I'm listening," says Jack McCoy in episode after episode, thus inspiring the murderer to reveal the truth he has been seeking. To understand the nature of this listening (which I would suggest is connected to the *CSI* effect – there is a reason why television viewers believe that they will be heard), we turn to another character in the *Law and Order* cast: Dr. Skoda.

At times, an episode requires that a state-appointed psychiatrist evaluate a suspect. This person's function, at least while he is on the state clock, is to evaluate and ensure the proper judicial response to the perpetrator. Yet, as therapist, he must maintain the empathic presence required in the therapeutic role, and as such has an important function in the psychic economy of *Law and Order*. The detachment of a policeman, a prosecutor, and a therapist complement one another in this series to form a fantasy of witnessing (indeed, the demeanor of the police and the prosecutors – a composed posture, smoothly articulated responses, an even voice, a steady gaze – is nearly identical to that of the psychiatrist). The policeman and the prosecutors are there to maintain social order. The therapist is there to exude empathic presence. Yet, this psychiatrist differs significantly from the traditional therapist. Because he is there to evaluate perpetrators, not to provide therapeutic

---

this intensification has its impact and must be thought about." Among these "inappropriate psychic defenses" is an unreality effect: "What can keep addicted viewers, especially younger ones, from a more fatal 'suspension' which consists in looking at everything live as if it were a reality that could be manipulated?" *Law and Order* shows us a way of responding to trauma that avoids both these pitfalls. At issue here, as Sumser proposed in his discussion of social roles, is a contamination, an inner amorphousness, a sense that one is susceptible to the winds of situation. Of some concern (and this is Sumser's focus) is that one could, in a particular situation, slide into the social role of murderer and be unable to discern right from wrong. At the same time, it is just as troubling to envision sliding into the social and psychic role of victim, being overwhelmed, losing the battle with formlessness. Geoffrey Hartman, "Memory.Com: Tele-Suffering and Testimony in the Dot Com Era." *Raritan: A Quarterly Review* 2000 Winter; 19(3) 1–18.

treatment, his empathy has no obvious outlet. His empathy is not for the prisoners, whom he sees in most cases only once, nor for the victims, who are dead, nor for their families, whom he never meets, nor for his other actual patients, if he has any. We never see him in any other therapeutic capacity. When he is finished evaluating the suspect, he walks away, blending into the crowd in the District Attorney's office. His empathic force, then, like the empathic force of the police and the prosecutors, is by implication for the rest of the cast, and for us. The fact that he is a doctor without patients means that he can use his empathic presence for the people and "those who represent them."

To return to the television conventions that encouraged the *CSI* effect: some of *Law and Order*'s more fictitious elements consist of scenes of being heard, being listened to – scenes of being in the presence of an empathic interlocutor. Some lawyers say that one of the most fictitious elements of this drama is the lawyers' bravado in front of judges. A lawyer whose oration on justice would bring him a contempt citation in the real world sometimes manages, on television, to move a brick wall. The parameters of justice, or of one human life, can be altered, it seems, through capable "representation." Here too, in a curious sense, spectator realities morph into television fantasies. We who watch television and read the papers really do speak with righteous frustration about the iniquities of the justice system. We really do react with indignation at the way certain cases proceed. We speak thus with one another, around the dinner table or at parties, but we would not do so in front of a judge – even if we found ourselves in front of a judge, which most of us never do, other than during jury duty: not the time for an oratory. There is no actual public forum for such social and ethical criticism; none, at least, in which that criticism has immediate and desirable practical consequences.

Another fiction that *Law and Order* puts forth is that of the force of the individual voice or the natural participation of the individual in the public sphere. Each episode opens with two people finding the body. We see them see the body, then we see the body, and then, in a cut, we see the policemen standing over the body. We assume that the people have called the police to report what they have found, and sometimes we see their cell phone, but the call itself, the substance of the conversation, is never shown. Instead, we get the sense that an encounter with crime naturally and instantaneously summons the calm and responsive police. In the first episode, the opening credits came on before the police appeared: subsequent episodes eliminated this delay and had the police come before the credits. The rapid succession of appearances (there is not even a "boom boom" before the police arrive) implies an immediate and seamless protection.

Law and Order represents a fantasy of dealing with violence. It has lasted for nineteen seasons and counting because neither the characters nor the narrative form have crumbled: because it raises the menace of psychic and social disorder – ever so slightly – and then contains it, again and again. The therapist makes a

Law and Television: Screen Phenomena and Captive Audiences

diagnosis (insane or not? capable or not to stand trial?) and with this diagnosis, with this understanding, the prosecutors are more able to determine the suspect's future. This power, this connection of therapeutic comprehension to legal authority to narrative determination, responds to a fantasy that composure and comprehension would translate into an actual mastery of the experience. Dick Wolf, producer of *Law and Order*, likens the show to Campbell's soup as he explains, "People feel comfortable going to something they know about. It attracts you because you know what you're getting."[26] *Law and Order's* therapist, and the police and prosecutors who represent us, incarnate a spectacle of psychic and judicial form-giving power that is a crucial part of "what you're getting." The combination of narrative form and psychic solidity constitutes the dreamed-of response to a violent culture, fusing empathic presence to a subtle talent for shaping and containing reality.

Cops

I turn now to another equally long-running television program whose job it also is to represent law enforcement to viewers. This is *Cops*: representing and mediating an uneasy relationship between the individual and the law since 1989.

It has been said – with some derision – that *Cops* is designed to advertise and normalize the experience of living in a police state – the intended audience for that normalization being the law's subjects. It is not a secret that the police departments and the individual officers filmed have the last word on what material goes into the program.[27] It is not an accident that we never see police brutality, for instance. It is not an accident that when we see officers talking among themselves, we see a quasiparental care and concern, rather than disgust or apathy or contempt. This show, I will propose, serves a double purpose: to model individual authority even as it works to domesticate, or render less intimidating, the police.

Aaron Doyle wrote that *Cops* appeals to an audience who identifies with the authoritarian position: "Reality programs like *Cops* 'were most enjoyed by viewers who evidenced higher levels of authoritarianism, reported greater punitiveness about crime.'"[28] Jessica Fishman described the police officer as standing "between archetypal conflicts of good against evil, an agent of the state fighting in the struggle of civilization against savagery."[29] The question, then, as this program enters its twentieth year: What is the attraction? I propose it has to do with where the domestic (the officer as familiar, as community participant) meets the powerful (the officer

---

[26] Interview with Neal Baer, Executive Producer of *Law and Order: SVU*, February 5, 2003.

[27] Aaron Doyle, *Arresting Images*. (Toronto: University of Toronto Press, 2004) 50–3.

[28] Doyle, 56

[29] Jessica Fishman, "The Populace and the Police: Models of Social Control in Reality-Based Crime Television." *Critical Studies in Mass Communication* 16 (1999) 273–4.

as manipulating, indeed literally writing, dramas of crime and punishment). Let us look at the opening sequence of the show.

The opening credits of *Cops* use a pop reggae song, "Bad Boys" (Whatcha gonna do . . . when sheriff John Brown come for you. . . . Bad boys, bad boys, whatcha gonna do, whatcha gonna do when they come for you) accompanied by vignettes of arrest. Among these vignettes are a man being wrestled to the ground by several policemen, an officer chasing a suspect, a man shrugging sheepishly as he fails a sobriety test, a bored-looking woman in handcuffs leaning against a car. While the song still plays, we see the word "COPS" in black on a background of flashing blue and red lights, while a booming and theatrical male voice announces: "*Cops* is filmed on location with the men and women of law enforcement. All suspects are innocent until proven guilty in a court of law." The flashing lights and the booming voice suggest one part circus and one part late-night talk show. On the one hand, we see the police as spectacle, as entertaining actors willing to delve into the realm of the unsavory and absurd. On the other hand, we see the police as active, aggressive, and energized. The "bad boy" of the song's title is as much the officer as it is the suspect.

The fact of a television program that celebrates the idea of living in a police state even as it discloses the artificial showmanship of that celebration, and that exalts the authority and energy of the individual officer even as it renders him a fallible subject, reveals a curious ambivalence about the law and about the police. More precisely, I propose, it demonstrates a public fascination with (and at the same time considerable ambivalence about) a scenario in which personal drive fuses with, or morphs into, public authority. In the end, a fundamental element of the authoritarianism that Doyle perceives is precisely a fantasy about that fusion. It is a fantasy about authority as fun – that fun being connected to merely *having* professional authority, and more specifically, to having that authority emerge from one's personal inclinations and caprices.

As Fishman writes: "*Cops* offers a profile of a profession, not a person. The stories told celebrate the collective agency of the fraternal order, making the character and personal history of individual officers irrelevant. . . . *Cops* creates an abstracted form of heroic consistency. The individual cast of heroes varies, but the 'good guy' remains an interchangeable police-hero."[30] What is on parade in this opening "Bad Boys" sequence, I want to propose, is not just a profession, as Fishman wrote, but a profession in which personal excitement and energies are inextricably inscribed. The *Cops* officers are individuals who can be counted on to put aside nervousness and fear to subdue the criminal element in a community. Yet, these are people who care about the community, and whose very decision to enter the police force – that bastion of the impersonal and professional – is a consequence of that caring.[31] That

---

[30] Fishman, 273.
[31] That caring, of course, could have been developed through watching television.

Law and Television: Screen Phenomena and Captive Audiences

caring, in turn – its intensity and its scope – is necessarily inflected by the professional experience. Officers sometimes remark that when they are out on the street, they see elements of society that the average person does not see. The behavior to which the police are exposed as a function of their profession then influences their personal impressions about criminals: personal impressions that then in turn underscore and shore up – and in some sense constitute – the professional mission.[32]

When the police officer arrests someone on the program, he does not spout emotion or articulate his contempt for criminals. (Or rather, he might, but if he does, that outburst is edited out of the program). The less emotional he seems, the better. It has to be clear, that is, or has at least to appear probable, that the arrest is about the application of the law rather than about the personal caprices of the officer. The police officer in other words must appear to be the *vehicle* of the law, not its writer, nor even its interpreter. Yet, he is the only representative of the law that we see.

The officer's professional function is at once a transcendence of his personal feelings about social order and criminality (he is a professional) and – paradoxically – an enactment of them (he cares about the community and his professional actions proceed from that caring). This sense of enactment, or instantaneous movement from personal into professional, is underscored for instance in the course of officer monologues. In one episode, for instance, the officer muses on the town she patrols; "I like to go hiking; I like to walk on these trails. I'm on my way to a pizza place where a fight has broken out, and the suspect is in the parking lot." There is a seamless transition from the police as person to the police as professional. The candor of the former invites us to trust the authority of the latter – even as that same authority led us to trust that candor in the first place. The result of these transitions is a seemingly constitutive connection of personal to professional: of human individual to legal vehicle.

Cops may be the profile of a profession rather than a person in the sense that we do not have a back story, we do not see homes and families, we do not see civilian clothing, and the intention of the program is to showcase the police corps, not the individual. Of course, we do nonetheless see a person, a named person, who represents the police. This person acts as the episode's principal character, even its hero, and also as its narrator. This Möbius strip of the personal and the professional is represented in the program's narration and in its very process of production. Narrative shape in *Cops* comes from two sources: the running monologue of the police officer and the editing of the footage. When we examine that narrative shape, we find

---

[32] "Social science studies of police behavior tell us that police believe they have the capacity to recognize criminals on sight (Scheingold 100). This can, of course, be a self-fulfilling prophecy, since police tend to find crime wherever they look for it." Judith Grant, *Prime Time Crime: Television Portrayals of Law Enforcement*. See Stuart Scheingold, *The Politics of Law and Order: Street Crime and Public Policy* (New York: Longman, 1984).

how many voices, personae, roles, and levels of authority the officer incarnates. This multiplicity is worth discussing because it mirrors the complicated and contradictory position of the police in our actual society.

To put the officer's television role in literary terms, he is a character who pauses at times to author, or at least to narrate, the very drama in which he has a part. To put it another way, he is a narrator who stands by turns in the shoes of character and author. The policeman finds the suspect and determines how to pursue him. He performs the arrest and brings the suspect to the police station to be processed. On top of this, he provides the narration and supervises the editing process.[33]

On the one hand, *Cops* tells the story of a law enforcement officer arresting a criminal. On the other hand, it tells the story of a law enforcement officer turned narrator scripting a drama of – and a reasonable narrative for – the arrest that he is performing as he performs it. The fact that the officer appears as both character and narrator represents, or mirrors, his embodiment of both the personal and the professional. On the one hand, that is, *Cops* tells the story of a character acting in a law enforcement drama. On the other hand, it tells the story of a narrator dedicated to rendering that act comprehensible. Then, in parallel: *Cops* tells the story of a professional. At the same time, it shows a person dedicated to making the professional conduct go in a certain direction. Because the officer's monologue is the only narrative voice that the viewer hears, and because the voice-over precedes, accompanies, and reviews the relevant action, there is something almost constitutive in the officers' expressions of suspicion, displeasure, determination to capture, and so forth. The editing – and we understand that both the arrest and the monologue are edited – has the double purpose of providing form to both (arrest and monologue), and of weaving them into an organic-seeming whole.

Here, I want to refer back to the opening credits, and their reminder to the viewer that "suspects are innocent until proven guilty in a court of law." This reminder promises on the one hand to eliminate any possible vigilante justice on the part of the policeman: the court is there as a corrective. On the other hand, because these same opening credit shots, namely the background against which the statement is made,

---

[33] Russian Formalists, writing about narrative construction, differentiated between the subject and the fable, or the plot and the story. As Tzvetan Todorov wrote, "They distinguished, in fact, the fable (story) from the subject (plot) of a narrative: the story is what has happened in life, the plot is the way the author presents it to us. The first notion corresponds to the reality evoked, to events similar to those which take place in our lives; the second, to the book itself, to the narrative, to the literary devices the author employs. In the story, there is no inversion in time, actions follow their natural order; in the plot, the author can present results before their causes, the end before the beginning." Tzvetan Todorov, *The Poetics of Prose*, Richard Howard, trans. (Ithaca: Cornell University Press, 1977) 45. In the program, the officer supervises the "story": the course of the arrest. He also supervises the "plot," narrating it and overseeing the editing process that makes the arrest play as reasonable and coherent. He then explains that (edited) arrest to the camera, ensuring that manipulation of the plot become itself an organic-seeming part of the story. In this sense, the officer has in effect a totalizing presence, as actor and director, character and author.

Law and Television: Screen Phenomena and Captive Audiences

show suspects running from police, stumbling drunkenly out of cars, grumbling as their bag of marijuana is found, we get the sense that innocence and guilt and courts of law are unessential technical terms and that we are already seeing all that we really need to know. These criminals do not appear smart and devious enough (or wealthy enough to engage lawyers devious enough) to make their actions seem blameless. The only way these charges are going to be dropped is if the police are disbelieved – and in the case of these particular suspects, who will disbelieve a policeman when the entire situation is on tape?[34] The existence of the show (even if that show is artificial) renders the "innocence until proven guilty" beside the point. We already have in hand plot and story: this is all the investigation we need, all the proof we need.

Cops tells the story of the mantle of authorship being reclaimed by the policeman – reclaimed in the sense that the officer apprehends the subject, and reclaimed in the sense that the officer accompanies that apprehension with a developing story. Indeed, the mere fact of the editing, the dramatic frame, constitutes another level of narration, another form-giving stratum that deploys and shores up the officer's powers. Add to this the fact that the police have the last word on what is and is not included in the program, and we have an endless but ultimately closed circle of police influence.

One question that this mastery of plot and narrative then raises is: What does this show do for its viewers, and more specifically, for its viewers as legal subjects? Is the idea of the police as powerful really so attractive to viewers as to carry the show through twenty years of production? Do that many viewers want to be policemen, or to identify with policemen, or to push others around? I would propose that this program appeals for the same reason *Law and Order* appeals: it represents characters in control of realities around them, and at the same time of their own image, their own apparent emotions. In this sense, the "authoritarian" impulse that Doyle notices (a punitive nature) meets the impulse to construct and master one's own image, à la reality television. Another question that must be asked of this program, though, is one that *Law and Order*, with its gravitas and solemn formula, manages to avoid: How are so many viewers able to watch this program without balking at its over-the-top performativity? *Cops* is a deliberate public relations phenomenon, a carefully constructed and pruned product.[35] The opening credit sequence is almost parodic, both in its music video look and in the scenes it represents: How does this jibe with the "authoritarianism" that the show purports to celebrate?

---

[34] As Judith Grant writes, "Even the initial shots of decadence shown at the outset prepare the viewer for crime. Thus, the basic premise of American law – presumed innocence – is immediately and repeatedly called into question by *Cops*." Judith Grant, "Prime Time Crime: Television Portrayals of Law Enforcement," *Journal of American Culture* 15(1) 2004, 57–68, 61.

[35] Doyle writes for instance that for every hour of the program that the audience sees, the makers of the show film 60 to 100 hours of footage.

Even as it advertises the power of the police and illustrates the pleasures of heightened personal authority, I would venture that *Cops* serves another important social function – not in spite of, but precisely *because* of its often absurd nature. Since 2001, increases in homeland security have paralleled inventions in real crime television: as the actual law gets more restrictive, dramatic representations of individuals outside the control of the law increase, as do dramatic representations of law enforcement subduing such individuals.[36] This growth in real crime programming has two principal effects. First, when television programs such as *Cops* show individuals who contravene the law in ways purely domestic (speeding, public drinking, fighting, drug possession, disturbing the peace), we are seeing an almost anachronistic category of criminal – the one who does nothing to threaten infrastructure and institutions.[37] There are no references here to conspiracies or to terrorism or to large-scale destruction and violence; indeed, what is offered here is a markedly more comforting and familiar image of criminality. More than this, however, it offers a comforting and familiar image of law enforcement. In a world where increasingly, crime evokes terrorism and law enforcement evokes national security, these shows offer a refamiliarization, a redomestication, both of the rule of law and of criminality – a hometown portrait of that which we have otherwise come to see as mythic and inscrutable.[38]

The advent of Homeland Security as a law enforcement category has subtly but certainly altered the way people regard and communicate with law enforcement of all sorts. An increase in federal regulations since September 11 means that the average citizen has more encounters with law enforcement, but it also means that

---

[36] Examples include *Speeders, Most Shocking: Police Chases, Fist Fights and Amazing Crashes, Forensic Files, Inside American Jail, Disorder in the Court,* etc. http://www.trutv.com/index.html#.

[37] The suspects on *Cops* are the precise opposite of the shady and inscrutable villains of 1950s Hollywood and of early twenty-first-century White House press releases. Subdued and frightened in ponytails and exercise pants, frequently inarticulate, these suspects seem more than anything to threaten themselves. A reality cop show that has more in common with *Nanny 911* than it does with dramatic fictional crime showcases a sort of fantastically nonthreatening familiarity with crime.

[38] *Cops* reruns appear on the "TruTV" channel. That channel's motto reads "Not Reality. Actuality." This is a curious nondistinction seemingly born of the public's overload on reality television. But what does it mean? On the one hand, this is a nod to the fact that "Reality" (think of *Real Housewives*) means outsize, vulgar, farcical, ridiculous, narcissistic, and self-parodic. Whereas "actuality" and "reality" appear in the dictionary as definitions of one another, "actuality," unblemished by the ridicule that has tainted "reality," is more clinical and less sentimental. "Actuality" would thus claim to mean what "reality" once meant: a glimpse at what is actually (currently, really, simply) going on. At the same time, the speed with which "reality" became outsize, thus creating the need for a clean-up in the form of "actuality," indicates the inadequacy of mere reality as a spectacular phenomenon. Reality needs a frame, the show needs a beginning and an end, and while they are at it, a conflict and a denouement – even though not every half-hour of real life, indeed not even most half-hours of real life, have a conflict or a denouement. *Cops* then stands on a surreal edge of American appetites: the desire to render reality dramatic, and the desire to retreat from the high anxiety that has resulted from a decade of precisely that dramatization.

Law and Television: Screen Phenomena and Captive Audiences

those encounters are detached from their specific communities and even from their specific participants. That is, when someone is stopped for speeding or fighting, the conversation is about the infraction at hand. When someone is stopped and asked to remove their shoes at the airport, there is no conversation because the reason for the search, the referent, the regulation, is detached from the searcher (it does not depend on any finding of probable cause) and almost always completely detached from the searchee (who in most cases has nothing to hide). In the case of this latter encounter, wherein searches take place in obedience to federal law without there being a present cause for alarm, the experience is necessarily rather depersonalizing both for the law enforcer and especially for the subject.[39]

Now, this sort of quasipunitive, ostensibly necessary, but in fact completely arbitrary imposition of regulation has long been familiar to minorities, who for instance find themselves stopped driving through a primarily white neighborhood not because of their actions, but because of an officer's ideas about the possibility of actions. Subsequent searches and arrests have nothing to do with, are in fact surreally removed from, the individual at hand. That surreal remove, so familiar to victims of profiling and so utterly problematic as a way of imposing regulation, is now a nearly universal norm for encounters with law enforcement: a norm that causes people to expect to be treated as suspects, as subjects, rather even than members of a society.

What *Cops* does for the viewer, then, is represent law enforcement entrenched within its communities, rather than connected to some omnipotent but fundamentally distant federal mandate. The program represents law enforcement focused on what an individual suspect is actually believed to have done, rather than on what that suspect might do in the future. B. Keith Crew writes of police procedurals, "it would be totally incongruous, for example, for Perry Mason or Matlock to get one of their clients on a technicality; these sleuthing defense attorneys always prove the client's innocence, usually by discovering the real murderer."[40] By the same token, it would be totally incongruous for the police officers of *Cops* to arrest or search someone on a technicality; cases of mistaken identity or erroneous arrest or judicial overreaction do not appear on the show because this would amount to

[39] Michel Foucault, in *Discipline and Punish*, explains that the phenomenon of punishment is not just a consequence of contravening regulations; rather, it precedes disobedience and acts as an instrument of regulation itself. He writes, "The art of punishing, in the régime of disciplinary power, is aimed neither at expiation, nor even precisely at repression. The perpetual penalty that traverses all points and supervises every instant in the disciplinary institutions compares, differentiates, hierarchizes, homogenizes, excludes. In short, it *normalizes*." Michel Foucault, *Discipline and Punish: The Birth of the Prison*. Alan Sheridan, trans. (New York: Vintage Books, 1995) 183. That normalization (that amounts to depersonalization) turns the encounter with law enforcement into an uncanny phenomenon.

[40] B. Keith Crew, "Acting Like Cops The Social Reality of Crime and Law on TV Police Dramas," *Marginal Conventions: Popular Culture, Mass Media, and Social Deviance* (Bowling Green: Bowling Green State University Popular Press) 131–44, 133.

the police going over the heads of the suspects, as it were, overwriting rather than responding to the realities at hand.

In addition to the very fact of the focus on community-based policing, there are some cinematographic elements of *Cops* that suggest a desire to understand or, more strongly, to domesticate the law enforcer. The camera, for instance, often follows directly behind the police officers in the program. This is a point of view that one rarely sees in real life because police officers, for obvious reasons, prefer to watch their own backs and those of others, rather than the other way around. So on the one hand, that camera position allows the viewer to see what the officer sees, and to stand in his or her (usually his) shoes. On the other hand, the viewer also sees the officer seeing, and can thus scrutinize both officer and officer's vision from a privileged angle.

In addition to the camera angle, merely watching the police officers race in their cars from one scene to another – although this is how they will catch their suspect – subverts their absolute omnipotence and raises the question of who or what drives the course of the episode. Once the policeman enters the scene, he takes control of what happens to the suspect, both in the legal sense (the suspect either will or will not go to prison) and in the narrative sense (he will be represented as a sympathetic character, a menace, a pitiable loser, etc.). Until that moment of capture, it is the fleeing criminal who determines the course of the story – literally, because they are in the front car or escaping on foot. The policeman goes where the suspect goes and then tries to round him up: those moments of chase are moments without control, without authority. The police will prevail – but, significantly – and here is the way in which the very existence of the program deconstructs its intended purpose – viewers know that this is not because the police always prevail, or always can, but because this is a program edited to show the police prevailing.

If *Law and Order* creates the market conditions for its own success with its repeated introductions and subsequent suppressions or mediations of traumatic experience, *Cops* creates the market conditions for its own success with its curious balance of the authoritarian and the fallible. It advertises the authority and assurance of the police, but as it does so, it reminds the viewer that the police need their authority and assurance advertised. It reminds viewers, in other words, of the very fallibilities that the program is designed to dispel, and of the very showmanship that it uses to dispel them. As such, it has opposite tensions to attract its various viewers or rather to attract each viewer in various ways: desire to see in the program assurance of the police's power (and perhaps a promise that that power could belong to them), and desire to see in the program assurance of the police's continuing mortality (as evidenced in its continuing need for jazzy promotion). As in the case of the audience of *Law and Order*, these two impulses collide in the same viewer: a viewer pleased to see the law function in a strict manner, but hesitant about the absolute authority that the police can exercise.

Conclusion

The *CSI* effect with which we started can be understood as part of a natural movement of social thought into and out of the law. The *CSI* effect, in other words, can be understood not as an anomaly but as an emblem of the usual and necessary practice of bringing "outside ideas" to bear on the law. Studies of law and television might not show television as being particularly "inside"; rather, they show as unreliable the distinction between the inside and the outside when it comes to the form and function of the law.

William McNeil writes in his introduction to *Lex Populi: The Jurisprudence of Popular Culture*, "The various media highlighted in this book not only reach a much larger audience than standard legal texts, but potentially, and even more democratically, they also help restore topics of jurisprudential important – justice, rights, ethics – to where they belong: not with the economists, not with the sociologists, not even with the philosophers, but rather with the community at large."[41] This is a striking statement, not because of the professions it names but because of those it does not name: lawyers, prosecutors, judges, police, and legal scholars. The omission of those categories suggests to me the provocative notion that law as a discipline, and "thinking like a lawyer" as a concept, is in fact a compendium of other disciplines and other thoughts, other intellectual vistas, other social roles. (McNeil talks of 'reading jurisprudentially,' but that adverb is already a hybrid).[42] In other words, interdisciplinarity is fundamental to studies of law not because it is a new vogue and not even because it can "enrich" legal studies, but because the law (and thus legal studies) is porous and thus interdisciplinary by nature. As a concept and as a product, law is a synthesis of perspectives sociological, anthropological, economic, narratological, and so on. Although in a very different way, television convention too is such a hybrid product. Television representations of the law, then, bring this hybridity into sharp focus. By analyzing television representations of law, we can understand what viewers believe the law to be, want the law to be, and what the law in fact *is*. The value of television studies as a subset of cultural legal studies thus resides in television's role as a kaleidoscopic window onto both law and viewer/subject.

---

[41] William McNeil, *Lex Populi: The Jurisprudence of Popular Culture* (Stanford: Stanford University Press, 2007) 2. See also *Television and Common Knowledge*, Jostein Gripsrud, ed. (London: Routledge, 1999).

[42] McNeil, 2.

11

Imagining the Law

Art

Christine Haight Farley[1]

Street photographer Philip-Lorca diCorcia took candid images of passers on the streets of New York City without their knowledge. From twenty feet away, he operated a system of strobe lights and a camera attached to construction scaffolding aimed toward a fixed point on the sidewalk. Eighty-four-year-old Erno Nussenzweig, a retired diamond merchant from New Jersey, was one such passerby who had his image captured. DiCorcia selected Nussenzweig's image, along with sixteen others of the numerous photographs taken over a two-year period, edited them and blew them up into 48- by 60-inch posters, which he sold for between $20,000 and $30,000 each. Nussenzweig, as an Orthodox Hasidic Jew and member of the Klausenberg Sect – which was nearly eliminated during the Holocaust – possessed a deeply held religious conviction that diCorcia's use of his image violated the second commandment's prohibition against graven images. Nussenzweig sued diCorcia for invasion of privacy.

In dismissing the suit in 2006, a New York court determined the photograph in question to be "art," and thus immune from such challenges.[2] In so concluding, however, the case prompts further inquiries. How was the court able to make this determination when so many art experts are confounded by the question of what is art? What guidance, if any, does the law offer in making these determinations? Should these determinations be made by law? Has the law adopted an aesthetic theory? How does law appreciate the creative acts of the photographer? Does law appreciate the power of the image and should it police that power? These are some of the questions provoked be the curious interactions between art and law that some scholars have sought to explore.

---

[1] Professor and Associate Dean for Faculty and Academic Affairs, American University, Washington College of Law. I am indebted to the terrific research skills of Adriane Grace and Jessica Bryant. Please send comments to cfarley@wcl.american.edu.

[2] *Nussenzweig v. diCorcia*, 11 Misc.3d 1051(A), 814 N.Y.S.2d 891 (N.Y. Sup. 2006).

Imagining the Law

Rather than comprehensively surveying this broad field, this chapter will indicate the kind of scholarly work that has been done at the various points where law and art meet. It first suggests the different areas of law that regulate – protect or censor – art. I then tease out the major themes and subjects that dominate art law. The focus, however, is on the way that law imagines art – even the status of images within law, and the way that law is imagined in art.

Art is in fact regulated in multiple ways – it is not apart from the law. The interactions between law and art are spread across a variety of legal disciplines including contract law, tort law, constitutional law, criminal law, intellectual property law, tax law, commercial law, and international law. Within these domains law regulates the international movement of art during times of war and peace and is utilized to preserve art and cultural property. Law regulates artists' business relationships with commissioners, sellers, and purchasers and is brought to bear on museums. Of course the state is present here too when it censors art, regulates obscenity, and selectively funds public art. Law seeks to be instrumental in our cultural policies by rewarding creation and prohibiting copying.

Thus, there is no body of law that is "art law"; rather, the law encounters art as random, seemingly isolated events. Any discussion of art law, therefore, is usually focused on the treatment of art within one area of the law. As used in this chapter, "art law" will refer to the broad array of legal issues raised by art, artists, and the art world.

The subject of art law is inherently cross-disciplinary because it is situated between disciplines. Of course, art itself is of interest and concern to a variety of disciplines, implicating the disciplines of anthropology, art history, archeology, museum studies, arts administration, history, and philosophy, among others. When law is included, the list of other disciplinary approaches to consider also includes criminology, economics, and development studies, among others. The multidisciplinary approaches used by researchers and decision makers are recognition that the problems that art law disputes raise are too complex for a single disciplinary approach.

Spread as it is across so many diverse areas of the law, art law, as a field of study appears haphazard and incoherent. At first glance, it would seem not to possess any unifying themes that could bring it together in some meaningful or useful way. A casual observer may wonder what art law is other than the study of what happens to art in various areas of the law. As Stephen Weill, one of the early practitioners of art law, stated, art law is a fascinating subject to study if only because of the "extraordinary dramatis personae by which [art objects] are surrounded."[3] However it is not the artists and collectors who are the most interesting subjects in these legal interactions. It is the art and our relationship with art that is a worthy subject of scholarly attention.

---

[3] Stephen E. Weil, "Introduction: Some Thoughts on 'Art Law,'" 85 *Dickinson Law Review* 555, 558 (1980).

Art is different. As a society, we imbue artworks and cultural objects with our values and aspirations in a way that is different from our relationship with all other things, save perhaps sports teams. We reflect onto art objects fundamental attitudes about culture and society. These reactions to art occur regularly and seem natural. For the most part they go unexamined; however, legal determinations about art often push these ideas about art to the surface. When the object of the legal dispute happens to be art, participants tend to argue that artworks should be subject to special legal rules or that standard legal rules should be given particular interpretations when they are applied to artworks. At base, the only justification for these special approaches is that art occupies a different and unique space in our society vis à vis other objects and practices.

Relative to other subjects of Law and Humanities research, scholarship on law and art is a fairly recent development: It has a life of less than fifty years. Although there are some early scattered accounts of particular issues in art law, the 1970s saw a sharp increase in scholarly attention to the special problems of the art world.[4] In 1971, *The Visual Artist and the Law* treatise was published defining the field for practitioners.[5] In 1979, Stanford professors John Merryman and Albert Elsen first published *Law, Ethics, and the Visual Arts*, a more scholarly survey of the issues presented when law and art collide.[6] This work opened up the field to further study and this attention by an established legal scholar and an established humanities scholar gave gravitas to the subject. Following this work, art law has gained an increasing acceptance as a valid course of study in law schools, graduate programs, and undergraduate studies. More recently, art law has received increased attention from practitioners, students, and scholars due in part to the enormous growth of the art market – both the legal investment market and the multibillion dollar annual international illicit trade. In addition to the financial high stakes, the current art markets arouse interest by raising questions about history, ownership, and cultural identities as they reveal narratives such as the restitution of Nazi-looted art and poor, "art-rich" countries exporting art to rich, "art-poor" countries.

Because the intersection of art and law is so rich and interesting, many published works in the last thirty years provide accounts of what happens when the law addresses art. For the most part these accounts are not theoretically based, and they are not addressed to larger phenomena in law. This chapter seeks to organize the scholarship on law and art under central themes that have concerned scholars (and only

---

[4] Franklin Feldman and Stephen E. Weil, *Art Works: Law, Policy, Practice* (New York: Practicing Law Institute 1974); Scott Hodes, *What Every Artist and Collector Should Know About the Law* (New York: E. P. Dutton 1974).

[5] *The Visual Artist and the Law* (New York: Associated Council of the Arts, 1971).

[6] John Henry Merryman and Albert Elsen, *Law, Ethics, and the Visual Arts* (Philadelphia: University of Philadelphia Press, 1979).

Imagining the Law

scholarship that can be so organized is included): studies of the law as art, the law of art, the law of creativity, and the collision of art and law. Because of the impossibility of providing an exhaustive survey, this chapter instead suggests the most significant branches, texts, and authors in the field. I then concentrate on a few key areas of inquiry: law and its relationship to creative cultural practices and, more specifically, aesthetic judgments rendered in the domain of law and art.

The Law of Art and the Art of Law

This chapter will be devoted mostly to scholarship on the law's treatment of art or the law of art. I pause here, however, to note that some scholars have chosen to look at the relationship from the opposite direction: at the art of law. This body of work can further be divided into scholarship that looks at law as an artistic form, and scholarship that investigates art's depiction of law and finally, law's fascination with the image.

On the relationship between art and law, some scholars have suggested that law is a form of art.[7] Akin to a law and literature analysis, some scholars argue that what lawyers and artists do is the same. James Boyd White, for example, refers to the legal practitioner "as an artist" and certain legal problems as "high art."[8] Those who assert that there is an aesthetic value in the work of lawyers consider the use of rhetoric only a starting point. Oftentimes, legal writing is so well crafted and stylized that it becomes an art form. In this vein, Nathaniel Berman compares legal modernism and artistic modernism as expressed in Pablo Picasso's Les Demoiselles d'Avignon.[9] Thus some easily conclude that law is "an artistic venture, and the lawyers' craft embodies the aesthetic principles that define beauty in art."[10] Beyond rhetoric, there

---

[7] See, e.g., Gary Bagnall, *Law as Art* (Aldershot: Dartmouth Publishing, 1996); David Kennedy, "Critical Legal Theory" in *Law and the Arts* 124, Susan Tiefenbrun, ed. (Westport: Greenwood Press, 1999).

[8] James Boyd White, *The Legal Imagination*, xxv (Chicago, University of Chicago Press 1985). See also Alfred C. Aman, Jr., "Celebrating Law and the Arts," 2 *Green Bag* 2d 129, 130 (1999). Apparently, Holmes disagreed stating, "Law is not the place for the artist or the poet." Daniel J. Kornstein, "The Double Life of Wallace Stevens: Is Law Ever the, 'Necessary Angel,' of Creative Art?," 41 *New York Law School Law Review* 1187, 1193 (1997) (as quoted in Oliver Wendell Holmes, Jr., The Profession of the Law: Conclusion of a Lecture Delivered to Undergraduates of Harvard University, February 17, 1886, in *The Essential Holmes: Selections from the Letters, Speeches, Judicial Opinions, and Other Writings of Oliver Wendell Holmes Jr.*, 218, 218, Richard A. Posner, ed. (1992)).

[9] Nathaniel Berman, "Modernism, Nationalism, and the Rhetoric of Reconstruction," 4 *Yale Journal of Law and Humanities* 351, 358–60 (1992).

[10] Kara Abramson, "'Art for a Better Life': A New Image of American Legal Education," 2006 *Brigham Young University Educucation and Law Journal* 227, 252 (2006). Those who have written about the distinctions between law and art tend to reinforce conventional and dichotomous images of both. For instance, Wendy Nicole Duong argues that art is creative and therefore not as concerned with arriving at a theory or conceptualization as law is. Art is prompted by emotion, whereas law is prompted by knowledge. Artistic creation is a subconscious, often spontaneous, impulse, whereas lawyers are

is metaphor, form, imagery, and symbolism,[11] as well as simplicity, elegance, and coherence.[12]

Perhaps more significant in pushing the argument that law itself is an aesthetic creation is the scholarship that investigates the aesthetic attributes of law. Here scholars discern aesthetic arrangements in law. Pierre Schlag, for example, reveals recurring forms in law that shape its understanding and practice.[13] Related is the work that explores the structural similarities between art and law in projecting their own systems of ordering. These scholars also push the analogy in likening law to art in the way both bring a sense of order to human experience.[14]

Other aspects of law have been considered as an art form such as the performance of law as art.[15] Here scholars have looked at the physical space, décor, and other visual cues that contribute to the symbol and ritual of the public practice of law.[16] The architecture of legal institutions, especially the stylized – usually neoclassical – buildings that house law courts, is examined as nonneutral space through which the law simultaneously derives its power, distance, and authority. Thus, these scholars analyze the court house as a ceremonial monument dedicated to an ideological function. The totality of art and architecture organizes the visitor's experience into an activity comparable to a religious ritual.[17] Its decorative language can be seen as functioning as an iconographic program. The significance of these programs lies in their ability to evoke a mythic or historical past that informs and justifies the values celebrated in the ceremonial space. In this light, it is difficult to imagine how such an actively constructed environment can be seen as neutral space.

For example, David Evans analyzes the architecture of the Inns of Court by using concepts of bodily disunity derived from psychoanalysis, and Linda Mulcahy looks at

---

trained to be deliberative, logical, and rational. Wendy Nicole Duong, "Law is Law and Art is Art and Shall the Two Ever Meet? Law and Literature: The Comparative Processes," 15 *Southern California Interdisciplinary Law Journal* 20–4 (2005). This theme of art as law's opposite will be taken up later.

[11] Desmond Manderson, *Songs Without Music: Aesthetic Dimensions of Law and Justice*, ix (Berkeley: University of California Press, 2000).

[12] Janice Toran, "'Tis a Gift to be Simple: Aesthetics and Procedural Reform," 89 *Michigan Law Review* 352 (1990).

[13] Pierre Schlag, "The Aesthetics of American Law," 115 *Harvard Law Review* 1047 (2002). See also Brian E. Butler, "Aesthetics and American Law," 27 *Legal Studies Forum* 203 (2003).

[14] Hilde Hein, "Law and Order in Art and Law," *Law and Literature Perspectives*, Bruce L. Rockwood ed. (New York: Peter Lang Publishing, 1996) at 113; Kornstein, supra note 8, at 1240.

[15] See, e.g., Costas Douzinas, "The Legality of the Image," 63 *Modern Law Review* 813 (2000); Costas Douzinas, "Law's Fear of the Image: Whistler v. Ruskin," 19 *Art History* 353 (1996).

[16] See Peter Goodrich, "The Iconography of Nothing: Blank Spaces and the Representation of Law in Edward VI and the Pope," *Law and the Image: The Authority of Law and the Aesthetics of Law*, Costas Douzinas and Lynda Neal, eds., 89–114, at 206 (Chicago: University of Chicago Press, 1999); Peter Winn "Legal Ritual," *Law and Aesthetics*, Roberta Kevelson, ed., 401–42 (New York: Peter Lang Publishing, 1992).

[17] The word basilica was first used to denote a courthouse, as in the basilica in Pompeii.

Imagining the Law

the design of modern courtrooms and its effect on the notion of participatory justice.[18] Piyel Haldar describes how the ornamental aspects of the courtroom represent the rhetorical category of the English common law.[19] Katherine Fischer Taylor's analysis of France's 1849 Festival of Justice postulates that it was necessary for the republic to define visually postrevolutionary justice.[20] Jonathan Rosenbloom analyzes trends in courtroom and courthouse architecture in the United States as a reflection of American legal ideology, finding that its continuity demonstrates a durability in American legal culture but that recent changes to a more corporate architecture show that public perceptions of the legal system are changing.[21]

Another aspect of the visual ceremony of law that has been studied is judicial portraiture. The conventions used within the genre of the judicial portrait include large-scale depictions, ascending perspective, ceremonial dark robes, and large, folded hands. Robert Ferguson's reading of the portrait of Justice Holmes reveals how these common images can be built up like a legal argument, and yet appear completely noncontroversial.[22]

A related, and perhaps broader, scholarly concern is how law is depicted in art. Here, the visible symbols of the authority of law are analyzed as the iconography of law.[23] As with the previous scholarship, some scholars are interested in examining the works of art used in legal spaces to illuminate the ways in which legal systems have relied on images to consolidate their power and project their authority within concrete legal spaces, whereas others explore what pictures of law reveal about perceptions of law at the time the picture was produced.[24]

---

[18] See, e.g., David Evans, "Theatre of Deferral: The Image of the Law and the Architecture of the Inns of Court," 10 *Law Critique* 1 (1999); Linda Mulcahy, "Architects of Justice: The Politics of Courtroom Design," 16 *Social and Legal Studies* 383 (2007).

[19] See e.g., Piyel Haldar, "The Function of the Ornament in Quintilian, Alberti, and Court Architecture," *Law and the Image: The Authority of Art and the Aesthetics of Law*, Costas Douzinas and Lynda Nead eds., 117–36 (Chicago: University of Chicago Press, 1999).

[20] Katherine Fischer Taylor, "The Festival of Justice: Paris, 1849," *Law and the Image: The Authority of Art and the Aesthetics of Law*, Costas Douzinas and Lynda Nead, eds., 137–77 (Chicago: University of Chicago Press, 1999).

[21] Jonathan D. Rosenbloom, "Social Ideology as Seen Through Courtroom and Courthouse Architecture," 22 *Columbia-VLA Journal of Law and the Arts* 463 (1998).

[22] Robert A. Ferguson, "Holmes and the Judicial Figure," 55 *University of Chicago Law Review* 506 (1988); Mitchel de S.-O.-l'E. Lasser, "Judicial (Self-) Portraits: Judicial Discourse in the French Legal System," 104 *Yale Law Journal* 1325 (1995).

[23] See, e.g., R. J. Schoeck, "The Aesthetics of the Law," 28 *Am. J. Juris.* 46 (1983); Bernard S. Jackson, "Envisaging Law," 7 *International Journal for the Semiotics of Law* 311 (1994).

[24] Ana Laurel Nettel, "The Power of Image and the Image of Power: The Case of Law," 21 *Word and Image* 136 (2005). Nancy Illman Meyers also looks at artistic representations of justice and the history of law that can be found in art. Nancy Illman Meyers, "A Painting and Accompanying Essay: Painting the Law," 14 *Cardozo Arts and Entertainment Law Journal* 397 (1996). Ultimately the author concludes that law and art have long been linked together because art draws on law for inspiration but the author proposes that, by drawing on art, law could have an even stronger voice.

Foremost is the ubiquitous, large, female form of Justice, draped in white robes, eyes blindfolded and armed with a sword in one hand and scales in the other, who has been the subject of much scholarly attention. Cathleen Burnett, for instance, explores how the deliberate use of the figure of the Greek goddess relates to the generalized notion of justice.[25] Dennis Curtis and Judith Resnik trace the strategic deployment and didactic power of the imagery of Justice from a wide-eyed Goddess to today's blindfolded protector of impartiality before the law.[26] After assessing the virtues and vices of the blindness of justice – that it works toward partiality but eliminates particularity – Martin Jay suggests a creative tension between a seeing and a blind Justice.[27]

The interplay between law and art is more complicated than the use of art as an instrument of law's force. If the law has recognized the potential for art, it has also recognized its danger. No one better expresses the law's long-standing ambiguous relationship with imagery than Costas Douzinas:

> Law's deep ambiguity to images remains intact. The power of spiritual, edifying icons is celebrated and put into effect in every courtroom, in the wigs, the robes, and the other theatrical paraphernalia of legal performance and in the images of sovereignty and justice that adorn our public buildings. The fear of idols is encountered in the renunciation of rhetoric and imagery in legal doctrine and theory, in the claim that reason alone without the contamination of eloquence and passion, oratorical excess and casuistry can deliver justice, in the disassociation between law and aesthetics symbolized by the defeat of images. Finally, fear of idolatry is seen in the denunciation of those figures of seduction and corruption: women, jesters, children – those who do not think like others.[28]

Thus, according to Douzinas, the law possesses a conflicting view of the image as both something to restrict, but also something that can be used to maintain the "social bond."

Protecting Culture

If there is any dominant legal policy that accounts for the myriad interactions between law and art, it is that the law generally promotes the production and preservation of art. The logic is that the more art that exists in a society, the better, and so

---

[25] Cathleen Burnett, "Justice: Myth and Symbol," 11 *Legal Studies Forum* (1987).

[26] Dennis E. Curtis and Judith Resnik, "Images of Justice," 96 *Yale Law Journal* 1727 (1987).

[27] Martin Jay, "Must Justice Be Blind? The Challenge of Images to the Law," *Law and the Image: The Authority of Art and the Aesthetics of Law*, Costas Douzinas and Lynda Nead, eds., 19 (Chicago: University of Chicago Press, 1999).

[28] Costas Douzinas, "The Legality of the Image," 63 *Modern Law Review* 813–31 (2000); Costas Douzinas, "Law's Fear of the Image: Whistler v. Ruskin," 19 *Art History* 353, 387 (1996).

Imagining the Law

its creation should be promoted and its integrity protected, rather than impeded by law.[29]

Although the law may seek to promote creativity overall, each branch of law that addresses art has its own distinct objectives, which are usually not articulated but implied and may involve a diverse set of concerns such as public morality, commercial morality, stabilizing meaning, or quieting title.[30] These objectives may be unique to art disputes or they may be more generally applicable to disputes in that area of law. If the latter, the presence of art will invariably add significance to the law's objective.

In recent years, the interest in cultural property, artifacts, and ancient art has increased dramatically. "Cultural property" refers to any items that have "artistic, archaeological, ethnological, or historical interest."[31] With this newfound appreciation for cultural property and ancient art have also come a variety of problems: black markets rooted in the looting, theft, and illegal trade of antiquities. In response, legal academics have formulated various approaches and theories in their attempt to affect policy, which would curb and eventually terminate the illicit trade of cultural property. The world of legal academia is largely split, however, on how cultural property should be treated, and the scholarship in this field often yields opposing or contradictory approaches in how to deal with cultural property and the issues surrounding it.

The world of cultural property law was largely defined first by John Henry Merryman, one of the founding fathers of art law.[32] In principally dealing with the restitution of cultural objects, he etched out the two schools of thought in this area: cultural internationalism and cultural nationalism. Cultural nationalism is premised in the notion that cultural property belongs "at the place, or among the descendants of the culture of its origin."[33] Conversely, the cultural internationalist school subscribes to the notion that the trade of cultural property should emulate that of any other goods, and in turn, should be freely traded.[34] Further, cultural

---

[29] See, e.g., *Mazer v. Stein*, 347 U.S. 201, 219 (1954) ("[t]he economic philosophy behind the clause empowering Congress to grant patents and copyrights is the conviction that encouragement of individual effort by personal gain is the best way to advance public welfare through the talents of authors and inventors in 'Science and useful Arts'").

[30] See, e.g., Paul Kearns, *The Legal Concept of Art* 58 (Oxford: Hart Publications, 1998) (discussing the interplay of art and the objectives of law, where an artist's objective is to create freely, the objectives of the law are to protect and promote public morality).

[31] John Henry Merryman, "Two Ways of Thinking About Cultural Property," 80 *American Journal of International Law* 831, 831 (1986).

[32] See, e.g., John Henry Merryman, *Thinking About the Elgin Marbles: Critical Essays on Cultural Property, Art, and Law* (Boston: Kluwer Law International, 2000).

[33] John Henry Merryman, *Law, Ethics, and the Visual Arts* 5th ed., 342–3 (Alphen aan den Rijn: Kluwer Law International, 2007).

[34] John Henry Merryman, "Two Ways of Thinking About Cultural Property," 80 *American Journal of International Law* (1986).

property should be enjoyed and viewed by all cultures, as art belongs to all people as a common heritage.

Today, Patty Gerstenblith's scholarship dominates this field.[35] Arguing from what Merryman describes as a cultural nationalist perspective, Gerstenblith suggests that there is a public interest in restitution because theft and looting of antiquities results in the loss of context of the object, which results in a loss of valuable information archaeologists use to study the characteristics of a society, and undocumented antiquities allow for fakes and forgeries to inhabit archival spaces.[36] Gerstenblith argues for the restitution of antiquities to the original owners and for export restrictions for cultural property to curb looting. Conversely, Gerstenblith's critics claim that restitution is not in the public interest because encouraging cultural objects to remain in the country of origin is anti-internationalist.

To delve deeper into the competing claims of the cultural internationalist and nationalist theories, Derek Gillman looks at the philosophical underpinnings of cultural heritage by considering the place and value of culture in both ancient and modern societies.[37] Looking at ways in which the idea of heritage has been constructed, he notes the importance of cultural roles and narratives, which often exclude as much as they include. This leads to a consideration of how value is assigned to cultural activities and objects. Arguments for the preservation of heritage now provide the grounds for controlling both the export of works of art and what may be done to historic buildings. In democratic nations, periodic clashes between "heritage" and private rights reflect an ongoing tension within public policy about the respective importance of communities and individuals.[38]

Law and Creativity

One area of law that has frequent interactions with artworks is intellectual property law. Here the law is more explicit about its objective. Copyright law in particular seeks to promote the creation of new artworks by incentivizing that activity through the offer of legal protections that promise economic rewards.

The interactions between art and law here therefore elucidate how law understands and defines creativity. Even as the law seeks to promote creativity, however,

---

[35] See, e.g., Patty Gerstenblith, "The Public Interest in the Restitution of Cultural Objects," 16 *Connecticut Journal of International Law* 197 (2001).

[36] Patty Gerstenblith, "The Public Interest in the Restitution of Cultural Objects," 16 *Connecticut Journal of International Law* 197, 198–200 (2001).

[37] Derek Gillman, *The Idea of Cultural Heritage* (Leicester: Institute of Art and Law, 2006).

[38] The issue of cultural property, the debates, and conflicting perspectives that it has incited continue to produce scholarship in the field of art law. For a condensed spectrum of the literature and thought in this area, Kate Fitz Gibbon describes the expansion of cultural property law and case law with regard to ownership of foreign art by museums and private collectors in her book *Who Owns the Past? Cultural Policy, Cultural Property, and the Law* (New Brunswick: Rutgers University Press, 2005).

Imagining the Law

numerous scholars have noted that law's relationship with this concept is ambiguous. For example, Roberta Rosenthal Kwall, who is primarily concerned with artists' moral rights, argues that artistic creativity and innovation are intrinsically motivated, but that the law fails to recognize this intrinsic dimension and only recognizes the resulting creation.[39] Kwall maintains that artists create out of inspirational (even spiritual) motivation. The law, however, based as it is on the concept of natural law and utilitarianism, deemphasizes the intrinsic process of creation and instead emphasizes the idea of economic reward.[40]

For others, the problem is less that the law is ineffective at promoting creativity, but that it demands a particular conception of creativity, one in which creativity is presented as a constant and stable subject[41] and thus suffers from "a certain dullness of meaning."[42] This is in contrast to what modern and postmodern artists have done in challenging and reconstructing the concept of creativity.

Additional critiques of law's concept of creativity are aimed at what its standard requires. The critique, in short, is that law sets the creativity bar too high. Although copyright law demands only a "modicum of creativity"[43] and explicitly refuses to distinguish between high and low authorship, at base in demanding originality, it requires independent creation. As a result, copying becomes an activity denigrated by law, whereas in art, copying is ever present and can clearly be detected in chains of acknowledged masterpieces. Thus for artists, copying is a means connecting the present with a past and then with the future, and "[t]o deny artists the right to copy is to deny their right to be creative."[44]

For many, the restrictions that the law imposes by way of its creativity threshold are unjustifiable as they constrain creative, cultural practices. These scholars argue that intellectual property law fails to take account of the development of contemporary art practices. These practices then serve to remind us that copyright law is unable to accommodate new forms of cultural expression.[45] For instance, in conceptual art, where the idea itself constitutes the work, and the work may be the result of a simple

---

[39] Roberta Rosenthal Kwall, "Inspiration and Innovation: The Intrinsic Dimension of the Artistic Soul," 81 *Notre Dame Law Review* 1945 (2006). See also Jane C. Ginsburg, "The Right to Claim Authorship in U.S. Copyright and Trademark Law," 41 *Houston Law Review* 263 (2004).

[40] Roberta Rosenthal Kwall, "Inspiration and Innovation: The Intrinsic Dimension of the Artistic Soul," 81 *Notre Dame Law Review* 1945, 1983 (2006).

[41] *The Construction of Authorship: Textual Appropriation in Law and Literature*, Martha Woodmansee and Peter Jaszi, eds. (Durham: Duke University Press, 1994).

[42] Kathy Bowrey, "Who's Painting Copyright's History?," *Dear Images: Art, Copyright, and Culture*, Daniel McClean and Karsten Schubert, eds. (London: Ridinghouse, 2002) at 272.

[43] *Feist Publications, Inc., v. Rural Telephone Service Company, Inc.*, 499 U.S. 340, 345 (1991).

[44] Karsten Schubert, "Raphael's Shadow: On Copying and Creativity," *Dear Images: Art, Copyright, and Culture*, Daniel McClean and Karsten Schubert, eds. (London: Ridinghouse, 2002) at 372.

[45] Johnson Okpaluba, "Appropriation Art: Fair Use or Foul?," *Dear Images: Art, Copyright, and Culture*, Daniel McClean and Karsten Schubert, eds. (London: Ridinghouse, 2002) at 200.

choice, law's creativity standard is unaccommodating.[46] Another contemporary art practice that is often used by scholars to bring law's creativity standard into focus is appropriation art. Appropriation artists explicitly challenge conventional notions of authenticity and originality. These moments in art history announce the obsolescence of the legal conception of creativity. Rather than incentivizing this art, in some instances the law forbids it. Thus critics here urge that the law needs to better understand the creative process and adopt a more nuanced understanding of the nature of cultural transformation. Otherwise, the law's mode of resolving disputes involving art such as appropriation art amounts to "objectifying and reifying cultural forms – freezing the connotations of signs and symbols and fencing off fields of cultural meaning with 'no trespassing' signs."[47] Obviously law's ability to stabilize the meaning of cultural forms in this way may be seen as a boon for certain owners, but it creates a tension with its objective to promote cultural production.

Some scholars suggest that the law ought to be able to sort out creative copying from noncreative copying.[48] Paul Edward Geller proposes that rather than a total ban on copying, the law consider "a spectrum of copying: starting with mechanical or rote copying, graduating to knowledgeable reworking and culminating in innovative recasting." This proposal, however, assumes that a simple tweaking of doctrine is all that is necessary to open law to the more nuanced and variable understanding of creation that art requires.

These critiques demonstrate the apparent limits to the legal protection of contemporary art forms. For critics such as John Carlin, copyright law constrains the impulse of modern artists to use, refer, quote, challenge, and praise the imagery that pervades the visual environment, thus placing unacceptable limitations upon artistic activity and free expression.[49] These constraints frustrate the law's apparent purpose. According to Susan Scafidi, "The unregulated freedom to engage in cultural appropriation may be as powerful a stimulus to creativity as the promise of protected economic rewards."[50]

So rather than fulfilling its objective of promoting creativity, law assumes a restrictive relationship with artistic practices. For Daniel McClean, this constraint amounts

---

[46] Nadia Walravens, "The Concept of Originality and Contemporary Art," *Dear Images: Art, Copyright, and Culture*, Daniel McClean and Karsten Schubert, eds. (London: Ridinghouse, 2002) at 175.

[47] Johnson Okpaluba, "Appropriation Art: Fair Use or Foul?," *Dear Images: Art, Copyright, and Culture*, Daniel McClean and Karsten Schubert, eds. (London: Ridinghouse, 2002) at 217.

[48] Paul Edward Geller, in *Dear Images: Art, Copyright, and Culture*, Daniel McClean and Karsten Schubert, eds. (London: Ridinghouse, 2002) at 27 ("courts apply tests which are far too rigid, failing to distinguish between 'creative' copies that build on the original and literal or 'close' copies which do not").

[49] John Carlin, "Culture Vultures: Artistic Appropriation and Intellectual Property Law," 13 *Columbia-VLA Journal of Law and Arts* 13, 103 (1988).

[50] Susan Scafidi, *Who Owns Culture: Appropriation and Authenticity in American Law* (New Brunswick: Rutgers University Press, 2005).

Imagining the Law

to an "'intrusion' of law into the hallowed sphere of artistic production" and the concomitant fear of "state restrictions on artistic freedom and individual creativity."[51] He notes the pervading view that "law is perilously out of step with" contemporary art practices in which "the readymade imagery and materials of our culture" are used and recontextualized "thereby calling into question the values of originality and authorship upon which both modernist aesthetics and copyright law are seemingly built."[52] The law's restrictions on creativity are also "realistically unsustainable, as the proliferation of reproduction in the digital environment renders legal mechanisms for controlling information redundant."[53] The law's "apparent miscasting of the diverse impulses and purposes that motivate artistic copying" are therefore an opportunity lost in promoting the arts.[54]

My own research has suggested that the law has a restrictive view of creativity and innovation. My investigations of the interactions between law and cultural practices in which the cultural practice has been either sanctioned, or not, as legally acceptable creativity, reveals the law's action in these contexts of evaluations. For instance, in considering whether or not traditional Aboriginal art presented the requisite authorship for copyright protection, the law had an opportunity to elevate *the selection* of the presentation of particular traditional motifs among numerous others as a creative contribution.[55] Again when considering whether photographs evidenced the presence of the author, the law had an opportunity to declare *the selection* of particular scenes among many others captured by the camera a creative act.[56] And when considering whether appropriationist art revealed the authorship of the appropriator, the law had the opportunity to regard *the selection* of particular preexisting cultural materials to recontextualize among a nearly infinite inventory as a creative choice.[57] The law, however, resists these invitations to place a greater value on selectivity; instead continuing to demand greater innovation. This causes judges to strain legal doctrines to argue why authorship is present in cases where it had not been previously perceived, as was the case in each of the preceding examples. Thus these case studies highlight the law's intuitive tendency to employ a restrictive model of authorship. For instance, the examples discussed demonstrate that judges often demand authorial contributions to be innovative, aesthetically pleasing, and manually produced even when there is no legal authority for the imposition of these

---

[51] Daniel McClean, *Dear Images: Art, Copyright, and Culture*, Daniel McClean and Karsten Schubert, eds. (London: Ridinghouse, 2002) at 11.

[52] Ibid., 12.

[53] Ibid., 15.

[54] Ibid., 22.

[55] Christine Haight Farley, "Protecting Folklore of Indigenous Peoples: Is Intellectual Property the Answer?," 30 *Connecticut Law Review* 1 (1997).

[56] Christine Haight Farley, "Copyright Law's Response to the Invention of Photography," 65 *University of Pittsburgh Law Review* 385 (2004).

[57] Christine Haight Farley, "Judging Art," 79 *Tulane Law Review* 805 (2006).

restrictions. These instances present the law with challenges to perceive authorship more broadly. In each, however, the law rejects the opportunity to accept the author's act of selection as an original, creative contribution.

There is more work to be done here. It would be interesting to compare the different understandings of the nature of cultural transformation that law and art maintain. To better understand each conception of "transformation," it may be useful to investigate the ways both art and law draw from their respective disciplinary histories, the particular cultural moment in which the articulation occurs, as well as the way those expressions (the specific art object or legal enactment, for example) contribute to the creation and, finally, transformation of that cultural sensibility. For example, law maintains an idea of art that depends on the equation of creativity with originality. Perhaps in stating a requirement that art be transformative, an important, but implicit, corollary is also being articulated. That is, although art transforms, law maintains. If so, then the examples of selectivity and appropriation as modes of artistic creativity are interesting. After all, these modes are not recognized by law as artistic acts. Perhaps these modes are understood by law within its own practices particularly in regard to law's use of precedent. Perhaps law understands its own use of precedent as compared with its rulings on the degree of originality required for something to be considered art and to be owned.

If intellectual property law seems ineffective at incentivizing cultural production, it is quite superb at maintaining control of the meaning of particular cultural forms. After all, the selection and representation of works in new contexts can significantly undermine any stabilized meaning. Thus in the intellectual property regime, the property that can be owned are ideas. As law is predicated on categories of private property and originality that artists and theories of art are bound to challenge, law does not so much protect freedom of artistic expression as property interests in art.[58] For example, Kembrew McLeod analyzes the way the law has allowed for the private ownership of a vast array of things including hip-hop music and third-world culture.[59] Related research on commercial appropriation of traditional cultural expressions highlights communities' desire to take back their cultures and use the tools of intellectual property to prevent outsiders from poaching and altering their cultural symbols. These scenarios, however, demonstrate the limits of intellectual property protection. In numerous cases, what is desired is the protection and containment of ideas. As I have explored elsewhere, in the case of traditional cultural expressions, what is often desired by the local communities is the prohibition on any derivation in the presentation of traditional designs. My research has also shown how often what photographers want to own is the scene before the camera, rather than the particular

[58] Anthony Julius, "Art Crimes," in *Dear Images: Art, Copyright, and Culture*, Daniel McClean and Karsten Schubert, eds. (London: Ridinghouse, 2002) at 495.

[59] Kembrew McLeod, *Owning Culture: Authorship, Ownership & Intellectual Property* (New York: Peter Lang Publishing, 2001).

Imagining the Law

expression of that scene that they have captured. Similarly in contemporary art, the artists of works appropriated into new works seek to use the law to prevent their work from being recontextualized. None of these protections should be possible under legal doctrines that aim to leave ideas in the public domain. Nevertheless, these cultural moments teach that a stronger set of intellectual property rights attach more readily when culture is presented as self-contained and fragile. The harm in strengthening these protections is made clear only when we see culture as robust and fluid.

There has been much scholarly attention devoted to both law's insistence on creativity, and the particular conception of creativity upon which it insists. Thus, artists, as both the creators and the users of protected works, may benefit or be burdened by the law. As Michael Spence has suggested, "It all depends upon the ways in which she creates and appropriates."[60] In the end, "there may be little to gain, and a lot to lose," for artists from the operation of law in these areas.[61] Therefore, in addition to presenting a conflicting relationship between law and creativity, this body of research also raises a larger point about a potential conflict between law and art that is more general in nature.

The Art–Law Collision

Much scholarship in this area is concerned with a perceived collision between the practices of art and law. An unexamined storyline pervades this perception: "Over the centuries, the art world has developed its customs and practices for the most part without any regard for possibly relevant legal principles."[62] Similarly, it is thought, as the preceding section demonstrates, that the legal world has developed its rules and standards without any input from artists, but then something occurs that causes these two separate worlds to collide. What is discovered in this interaction is that the two worlds are incompatible.[63] Moreover, some conclude that "when the two collide, [art] is the invariable loser."[64]

Just as aesthetics is often criticized for lagging behind art, many observe that law lags behind both art and aesthetics.[65] This means that when law attempts to utilize aesthetics, the conflict is extreme. Outmoded theories of art that never adequately

---

[60] Michael Spence, "Justifying Copyright" in *Dear Images: Art, Copyright, and Culture*, Daniel McClean and Karsten Schubert, eds. (London: Ridinghouse, 2002).

[61] Ibid., 392.

[62] Susan Scafidi, *Who Owns Culture: Appropriation and Authenticity in American Law* (New Brunswick: Rutgers University Press, 2005).

[63] Apparently not everyone agrees. Paul Edward Geller asserts, "It is a misunderstanding to assume that copyright, and art are necessarily in tension." Paul Edward Geller, in *Dear Images: Art, Copyright, and Culture*, Daniel McClean and Karsten Schubert, eds. (London: Ridinghouse, 2002) at 30.

[64] Anthony Julius, "Art Crimes," in *Dear Images: Art, Copyright, and Culture* (Daniel McClean and Karsten Schubert, eds., 2002) at 495.

[65] Anthony Julius, "Art Crimes," in *Dear Images: Art, Copyright, and Culture* (Daniel McClean and Karsten Schubert, eds., 2002) at 495.

explained contemporary art practices even in their prime may be employed by law. The effect then is a crystallization of law's proscriptions and a concomitant disavowal of their relevance by artists.

Although never fully unpacked, these views are usually premised on the following conventional understandings of both art and law. First, art and law belong in separate cognitive and intellectual spheres. Second, art and law exist in polarity where law is objective and art is subjective. Third, law is about precedent whereas art is about the evolution of ideas. Finally, law is about uniformity, whereas art is unique.[66]

For many scholars, this potential conflict is absolutely fundamental. Some see the conflict as occurring because the legal culture "demands solution," whereas art "defies definition."

> The artist's vocation calls him to creation, not regulation. In art he expresses and is free until a legal mind, allocated to protect potential viewers of his art, directs the need of society to clamp him down, relying on its own judgment within the bounds of a given legal framework.[67]

Paul Kearns sees law as "coercion to bring about conformity," whereas art is unique "by its nature" and is fundamentally unable to conform to law's dictates.[68] Similarly, McClean finds "fundamental and insurmountable differences" in the manner in which legal and aesthetic judgments are made.[69] The law requires certainty, whereas art is comfortable with instability. Likewise, Scafidi worries that even the most "well-intentioned legal protections may [unwittingly] provoke ossification" because "culture is naturally fluid and evolving."[70]

Art creates conflict for law because it has the tendency to expose law's certainty as masking necessary ambiguities, as the case that began this chapter illustrates. It disrupts law's dominion over complexities by demonstrating its elastic discourses and definitions. Law struggles to reduce these complex ideas to neat and finite categories with practical effects. Law, for its part, is the powerful oppressor of art's uncategorical distinctiveness.[71] Law imposes its multi-pronged and multi-factored tests, and ignores nonlegal assistance for fear of appearing to need other aid. At its best, law searches in vain for the ideal legal criteria that will delineate the conceptual complexities involved in disputes over art, when instead it requires an altogether more flexible structure that avoids any set criteria.

In contrast, Douzinas reminds us that sometimes art is as, if not more, rule-bound than law. The conflict between art and law is only visible when the "the law of the art"

---

[66] Paul Kearns, *The Legal Concept of Art* (Oxford: Hart Publications, 1998) at 7.

[67] Ibid., 58.

[68] Ibid., xv.

[69] Daniel McClean, *Dear Images: Art, Copyright, and Culture*, Daniel McClean and Karsten Schubert, eds. (London: Ridinghouse, 2002) at 18.

[70] Susan Scafidi, *Who Owns Culture: Appropriation and Authenticity in American Law* (New Brunswick: Rutgers University Press, 2005).

[71] Paul Kearns, *The Legal Concept of Art* (Oxford: Hart Publications, 1998) at xv.

Imagining the Law

is forgotten. In exposing how law uses its dichotomous relationship with art, Douzinas challenges the conventional acceptance of art as frivolous and radically subjective, and law as its opposite. Furthermore, in this relationship, law achieves power by presenting itself as a discourse with dominion over other discourses, interpretive at base, and self-sufficient. When we take into account their disciplinary history, however, art and art theory can be seen as being equally interested in demarcating categories such as genre and form and delineating boundaries between art and nonart. Instead of finding commonalities, art and law are set off against each other in ways that produce suspicion, envy, and contempt between the two.

What is Art?

Because of society's special relationship with art and underlying belief that law should treat art differently, whether or not a disputed object is a proper inhabitant of the category of art becomes critical to the legal resolution. Whether or not special approaches should be taken hinges on the answer to this question. These disputes then routinely involve resolutions of the definition of art, although rarely is this definitional question addressed explicitly. Thus, in these instances, the "What is art?" question – so contentious in other disciplines – emerges in the context of law.

One avenue of scholarly inquiry has looked at how, when, and why these definitional questions are addressed in the law and whether legal definitions of art are being produced. As the preceeding section demonstrates, many scholars conclude that legal and artistic determinations should not be merged and that judges should refrain from indulging in subjective aesthetic determinations.[72] These scholars are in step with most of the judiciary. Judges repeatedly declare their neutrality and

---

[72] The following commentators, although not expressing a unified view, have each made statements to the effect that law and aesthetics should not be joined. See, e.g., Amy M. Adler, "Post-Modern Art and the Death of Obscenity Law," 99 *Yale Law Journal* 1359, 1377–8 (1990) ("Because many contemporary artists are so estranged from lay notions of what constitutes 'art' courts might refuse to recognize them as artists"); Keith Aoki, "Contradiction and Context in American Copyright Law," 9 *Cardozo Arts and Entertainment Law Journal* 303, 303–4 (1991) (suggesting that aesthetic determinations made by judges in copyright law have led to "confusing, inconsistent, and erratic decisions"); Robert C. Denicola, "Applied Art and Industrial Design: A Suggested Approach to Copyright in Useful Articles," 67 *Minnesota Law Review* 707, 708 n. 10 (1983) (agreeing with the wisdom of the *Bleistein rule* and arguing for legal tests that avoid the subjectivity of aesthetics); Leonard D. DuBoff, "What Is Art? Toward a Legal Definition," 12 *Hastings Communications and Entertainment Law Journal* 303, 350–1 (1990) (stating that "the legal definition of art greatly depends upon who is doing the defining" and that precise definitions of what constitutes a work of art "would not do justice to the diverse interests involved"); Lindsay Harrison, "The Problem with Posner as Art Critic: Linnemeir v. Board of Trustees of Purdue University Fort Wayne," 37 *Harvard Civil Rights Civil Liberties Law Review* 185, 203 (2002) ("The consequences of judges playing art critic in the context of First Amendment law are...grave"); J. H. Reichman, "Design Protection in Domestic and Foreign Copyright Law: From the Berne Revision of 1948 to the Copyright Act of 1976," 1983 *Duke Law Journal* 1143, 1165 (arguing that copyright decisions should be made independently of any judgment as to the aesthetic merits of the work at issue).

restraint in the face of an opportunity to engage in such activity.[73] Many scholars use Justice Holmes' famous quote from *Bleistein v. Donaldson* regarding the dangers of law delving into the analysis of art as a starting point in assessing the rationales advanced as to why courts should not make aesthetic determinations.[74]

> It would be a dangerous undertaking for persons trained only to the law to constitute themselves final judges of the worth of pictorial illustrations, outside of the narrowest and most obvious limits. At the one extreme some works of genius would be sure to miss appreciation. Their very novelty would make them repulsive until the public had learned the new language in which their author spoke. It may be more than doubted, for instance, whether the etchings of Goya or the paintings of Manet would have been sure of protection when seen for the first time. At the other end, copyright would be denied to pictures which appealed to a public less educated than the judge. Yet if they command the interest of any public, they have a commercial value – it would be bold to say that they have not an aesthetic and educational value – and the taste of any public is not to be treated with contempt.[75]

[73] See, e.g., Smith v. Goguen, 415 U.S. 566, 573 (1974) ("What is contemptuous to one . . . may be a work of art to another"); Cohen v. California, 403 U.S. 15, 25 (1971) ("One man's vulgarity is another's lyric"); Mazer v. Stein, 347 U.S. 201, 214 (1954) ("Individual perception of the beautiful is too varied a power to permit a narrow or rigid concept of art."); Pivot Point Int'l, Inc. v. Charlene Prods., Inc., 372 F.3d 913, 924 (7th Cir. 2004) ("This approach necessarily involves judges in a qualitative evaluation of artistic endeavors – a function for which judicial office is hardly a qualifier"); Bucklew v. Hawkins, Ash, Baptie & Co., 329 F.3d 923, 929 (7th Cir. 2003) ("Any more demanding requirement would be burdensome to enforce and would involve judges in making aesthetic judgments, which few judges are competent to make"); Martin v. City of Indianapolis, 192 F.3d 608, 610 (7th Cir. 1999) ("We are not art critics, do not pretend to be and do not need to be to decide this case"); Finley v. NEA, 100 F.3d 671, 688 (9th Cir. 1996) (Kleinfeld, J., dissenting) ("'Artistic excellence' and 'artistic merit' are also vague, and could not be proper criteria for censorship or discrimination in an entitlement program"), rev'd, 524 U.S. 569 (1998); Brandir Int'l, Inc. v. Cascade Pac. Lumber Co., 834 F.2d 1142, 1145 n.3 (2d Cir. 1987) ("We judges should not let our own view of styles of art interfere with the decision-making process in this area"); Gracen v. Bradford Exch., 698 F.2d 300, 304 (7th Cir. 1983) (Posner, J.) ("Judges can make fools of themselves pronouncing on aesthetic matters"); Hoepker v. Kruger, 200 F. Supp. 2d 340, 352 (S.D.N.Y 2002) ("Courts should not be asked to draw arbitrary lines between what may be art and what may be prosaic as the touchstone of First Amendment protection"); Yurkew v. Sinclair, 495 F. Supp. 1248, 1254 (D. Minn. 1980) ("Courts are ill equipped to determine such illusory and imponderable questions"); Esquire, Inc. v. Ringer, 414 F. Supp. 939, 941 (D.D.C. 1976) ("There cannot be and there should not be any national standard of what constitutes art"), rev'd, 591 F.2d 796 (D.C. Cir. 1978); United States v. Ehrich, 22 C.C.P.A. 1, 13 (1934) ("I freely admit, and I think my very sincere associates would do the same, that I know no more about artistic merit than does the average layman, and what might appeal to me as being an artistic creation of great merit, if appearance alone controlled, might not meet the test at all, and vice versa"); Parkersburg Builders Material Co. v. Barrack, 192 S.E. 291, 293 (W. Va. 1937) (describing aesthetics as an "essentially speculative" discipline that offers little guidance except "the infinite variations of taste and preference").

[74] See, e.g., Costas Douzinas, "The Aesthetics of the Common Law," 17 *Studies in Law Politics and Society* 3 (1997); Christine Haight Farley, "Judging Art," 79 *Tulane Law Review* 805 (2006); Alfred C. Yen, "Copyright Opinions and Aesthetic Theory," 71 *Southern California Review* 247, 301 (1998).

[75] Bleistein v. Donaldson Lithographing Co., 188 U.S. 239, 251–2 (1903).

Imagining the Law

Aesthetic judgments are considered subjective and therefore jurisprudentially undesirable; however, decisions about what is and is not art are mandated by the law in a wide range of areas. Some commentators have therefore concluded that some areas of law require courts to make aesthetic choices.[76] Despite the ubiquitous axioms to the contrary, aesthetic judgments are often implicit and, sometimes even explicit, in the law in areas as diverse as obscenity, copyright, customs, and tax. In other areas, legal determinations are inevitably and necessarily entangled with aesthetic judgments. In these instances, the law needs to determine whether the disputed object is art. My own work examines the extent to which the law inescapably must take on these questions.[77]

The resistance on the part of courts and legislatures to devise a definition of art is somewhat understandable considering the difficulty philosophers, scholars, and artists have had in pinning down this phenomenon. The "What is art?" debate has raged for centuries without a definitive resolution. If the law has conceded the impossibility of defining hard core pornography, it is logical also to acknowledge the impossibility of devising a definition of art. Nevertheless, the discussion engendered by the debate about line drawing in the case of pornography has been rich and not fruitless. Moreover, because our cultural policies want to put art in a privileged position, the legal category of art is unavoidable.

In determining art status, courts have found an easy proxy: the status of the artist. Whereas the art status of the object in question is fraught, determining the status of the artist in question is relatively straightforward. Thus, the status of the artist plays into the analysis even where it has no role. The successful claimants in indigenous art disputes resemble the successful claimants in historical photography disputes, which resemble the successful claimants in postmodern art disputes: they best mimic the Romantic author. They are individuals who act like individuals; they suppress the collaborative or group nature of their artistic production. Thus in my own research, the Aboriginal artist Milpururu shares these critical characteristics with the nineteenth-century photographer Napoleon Sarony. They are both the first practitioners of their craft to be designated as authors by the law even if that meant denying the corporate nature of their production. Although judges might be criticized for relying too heavily on an artist's status, what this reliance reveals is the necessity to rely on something objective. At least an artist's status can be confirmed in litigation. In this way, the law influences the understanding of art outside

---

[76] See, e.g., Raymond M. Polakovic, "Should the Bauhaus Be in the Copyright Doghouse? Rethinking Conceptual Separability," 64 *University of Colorado Law Review* 871, 873 (1993) (asserting that the Copyright Act requires courts to separate aesthetic and useful elements of a useful article); Alfred C. Yen, "Copyright Opinions and Aesthetic Theory," 71 *Southern California Law Review* 247, 301 (1998) ("The existence of copyright makes subjective judicial pronouncements of aesthetic taste necessary").

[77] Christine Haight Farley, "Judging Art," 79 *Tulane Law Review* 805 (2006).

the legal context. Artists must translate their story into law's image of the artist to succeed.

Although work here demonstrates that courts are forced to decide the "What is art?" question on a regular basis, significantly, courts try hard not to do so. They may avoid an explicit discussion of this question and decide the case by methodically analyzing another issue, or they may simply mask this determination, hoping to obscure it in the course of their denials. These conflicts raise questions about law's effectiveness in avoiding subjective determinations.

Courts' explicit resistance to engage in aesthetic analysis only masks that they do so nonetheless. Sometimes the law requires courts to decide definitively what art is, and other times, courts are not required to reach this determination, but allow themselves to be guided by their aesthetic judgments. As a result of this concealed approach, courts employ a variety of problematic techniques to avoid addressing these determinations head on. Thus when courts do make decisions regarding art, they often engage in deflection, denial, and disguise. Ultimately, in several cases courts' responses track various aesthetic theories. Courts seem to assume and enforce particular conceptions of art that they neither commit to paper nor stoop to justify, perhaps because they themselves fail to recognize what is happening. I contend that courts adopt aesthetic theory intuitively, even as they remain seemingly ignorant of that body of scholarship. Ironically, the lure of objectivity may have drawn courts further inward into the subjective realm.

My work argues that law should explicitly look to aesthetics for assistance in resolving cases in which the determination of an object's art status is necessary. Aesthetics offers the law a rich and vibrant debate about both the nature of art and definitional approaches. This engagement does not require that one particular definition of art should be privileged in all cases. Such an approach would reify this definition through the practice of precedent. Instead, courts should import the discourse as a whole to facilitate their analysis of what may or may not be art in particular cases. Rather than selecting just one strain of aesthetic theory, that is, courts should recognize the contested nature of various views on aesthetics. The result would be more open and thoughtful resolutions of these cases. Instead of denying that a difficult question confronts them, courts could take comfort in the rich discourse on the subject that precedes them. Although the aesthetic determinations in these cases may still be extremely controversial, participants and observers would at least be clear on the approach adopted by the court.

Writing about *Whistler v. Ruskin*, Douzinas describes how aesthetic considerations took center stage in the case. Even though each litigant had a very different view of how aesthetics considerations should be used to make an ultimate judgment, both agreed that law was "the proper forum for deciding the truth in art." As one who has investigated the supposed art-law conflict, Douzinas argues "the modern order

Imagining the Law

of images is always accompanied by laws and regulations" and by a "code that tells us how to . . . understand the image, how to link the sign, visual or graphic, with its signatum and stop its endless drifting."[78] The case, however anomolous in its explicit embrace of an aesthic debate, demonstrates that a court can open itself to this nonlegal aid without being mired in subjectivity.

Conclusion

This brief introduction to the scholarly intersection of art and law suggests the kind of work that has been done at the various points where law and art meet and the themes and subjects that dominate art-law. The opportunities for further scholarship on this relationship are most exciting where the disciplines meet. For instance, there is a growing body of scholarship directed at artistic portrayals of law, and this is the place where the two disciplines can usefully collaborate. Legal scholars can borrow art historical interpretive theories, whereas art historians can adopt a critical and theoretical engagement with the law.

Although some have written about the mutual influences that art and law have had on each other, in my mind, what is most critically missing from this scholarship is an investigation of the correspondence between law and culture. In particular, almost completely absent is an account of the impact of law on artistic practices. As has been shown, some critiques of law suggest that certain artistic practices challenge legal concepts or that the law is in conflict with understandings in the art world. Conversely, some scholars have investigated how a cultural practice finds its way into law's embrace. The next step, however, is to consider the cultural consequence, if any, of the law's rejection or embrace of an art form.

Some scholars explore the mutual influences of law and art. Examining a variety of instances in which law interacts with art reveals how the interactions leave both institutions changed. For example, in the work on intellectual property law and folklore, scholars demonstrate that the accommodation of indigenous art within the intellectual property regime has an effect on copyright law. Notions of group rights and originality, for instance, are challenged. Likewise, the application of copyright law to indigenous art has an effect on our understanding of that art. To be successful in this arena, the art needs to be translated in terms we understand and value. Thus, the individuality and ingenuity of the artist is more apparent. My work on copyright and photography makes a similar contribution. There we see that copyright law's response to the invention of photography left a lasting impression both on the reading of photography and on our concept of the author in copyright law.

---

[78] Costas Douzinas, "The Legality of the Image," 63 *Modern Law Review* 813, 830 (2000).

There has been some work toward an analysis of how the law has been affected by specific points of contact between art and law. Less work, however, has focused on the affects, if any, on artistic practices when legal concepts rigidly undermine them. Perhaps work of this kind may reveal that art is solidly resistant to perceived conflicts with law, or perhaps it may reveal that these conflicts provide artists with a galvanizing oppositional force.

PART IV

LINGUISTIC, LITERARY, AND CULTURAL PROCESSES IN LAW

12

Language

Penelope Pether

As I began to write this chapter, the intersections of law and language, more or less insistently visible in my quotidian scholarly and teaching praxis, were brought sharply into focus. I had for a semester been working collaboratively with a faculty colleague and two students on a clinical legal education project, my first direct involvement in live client clinical rather than simulation-based skills training.

As the spring semester began, the event to which our work had been directed, an asylum application hearing, took place in an ICE[1] "family shelter" in rural Pennsylvania, where the clients had been detained for some months. They were able to see each other, it is true, and the shelter was evidently preferable[2] to the jails in which they could well have been held, but although they could spend their days together, they were housed at night in separate cells (or rooms or dormitories) for men on the one hand, and women and children on the other. This situation complicated what "family" might be thought to signify in context – the enabling of what I will call familial, if not domestic or sexual, intimacy. So too the term "shelter" was complicated by its rendering, in context, euphemistic: "[t]he Berks County facility, a former nursing home in Leesport, Pa., about 50 miles northwest of Philadelphia, is 'less jail-like,' [than the notorious Hutto family shelter in Texas].... [However, i]t is part of a larger juvenile facility housing U.S. citizens charged with or convicted

---

[1] This is the acronym for the Immigration and Customs Enforcement, a subdivision of the U.S. Department of Homeland Security, formed from parts of the previous Immigration and Naturalization Service and U.S. Customs.

[2] "Separation and threats of separation were used as disciplinary tools on [illegal immigrant/undocumented alien] adults and children" housed in ICE's two "family shelters," one in Texas and one in Pennsylvania, noted Lutheran Immigration and Refugee Service and the Women's Commission for Refugee Women and Children in a February 2007 report, and indeed threats that our male client would be moved to a jail were used, effectively, to "discipline" him. See Pauline Gamboa, "Report condemns centers for illegal-immigrant families: In Texas, detainees are held in 'prison,'" *San Diego Union-Tribune*, Feb 22, 2007: http://www.signonsandiego.com/uniontrib/20070222/news_1n22immig.html.

315

of crimes."[3] The carceral institution, prison, asylum, school, or "shelter," indeed provides shelter. It also enables, indeed, makes inevitable, surveillance, or discipline, and in turn punishment.

The "family shelter," officially the "Berks County Shelter Care Facility,"[4] is a detention facility for "aliens" who have been apprehended by law enforcement officers while "unlawfully" or "undocumented" in the United States, and who constitute what are recognized as "families." Our clients were an opposite sex married couple with a child; the shelter also houses women and their children.

It was unsurprising to learn as I researched this chapter that the "family shelter" is also used as what I have learned to call a "juvenile detention facility": it is built, configured, furnished, and staffed in ways that are familiar to me from investigating the treatment of incarcerated juvenile offenders in Australia more than two decades ago. An occasion for shock and outrage, although not on reflection surprise, was offered when, after our clients had been granted asylum by an Immigration Court judge, the corrections staff departed from their usual practice of preparing to release our clients at the point within the next twenty-four or so hours that their paperwork was completed.

Our clients, we were told, would be held indefinitely, potentially for up to six months, because the ICE corrections staff needed "third-agency clearances" from institutions such as the CIA, the FBI, the ATF, and the NSA, indicating that they were "not interested" in them. Although these clearances had been applied for some months earlier, they had not yet, we were told, been received. It could not be reliably anticipated when they might be received.

Asked whether the authority to continue to detain our clients was contained in a regulation, the ICE corrections staff supervisor told us that it was contained in an email, or at least that was what he thought, and conceded that it was possible that he might be able to find it, and if so, and if its readership was not restricted to ICE staff, he might be able to provide us with a copy. Asked if the authority of the putative email applied to all persons granted asylum, he indicated that it applied, for example, to Iraqis, Moroccans, and Syrians; he conceded in response to a question about whether it applied to persons from "Middle Eastern" nations that yes, it applied to persons from "suspect" nations.

This was not the only point in the day, or indeed in carriage of the matter, when culturally resonant and significant signifiers, tropes, and narratives were both visible and deployed. The student representatives had invoked the "breakdown of the rule of law," evidently with some persuasive effect, in closing argument. The male client, it had emerged when we had "mooted" examination-in-chief and cross-examination, was the thing all trial lawyers hope their client will prove to be if he or she takes

[3] Ibid.
[4] Ibid.

Language

the stand: a "good witness," able to perform truth, or its simulacrum. In asylum law, where the rules of evidence do not apply, credibility both of client witness and of stories he or she in various ways tells – about self and belief, about "his or her" culture, "their" culture, and "ours," and about persecution and trauma, past and anticipated – is everything in seeking a favorable exercise of the discretionary jurisdiction to grant asylum.

There are other aspects of law, including of some of its doctrines, in which language is especially visible. Privilege, among other things, prevents me from relating to my readership the evidence that had enabled our clients to be granted asylum; it does not, however, block the transmission of what the dean of our law school said when I told him about the "third-agency release" regime. It was what I learned as a lawyer to call "words to the effect of" "[a]nd let me guess, [the clients] were in [the trouble that was the basis for the grant of asylum] because they helped the Americans?"

In the event, the clients were released from the facility four days after the grant of asylum, after an Associated Press journalist had manifested interest in the circumstances in which they were being detained. The release was remarkable because there was an alternative reason offered by the ICE corrections staff to hold them in detention after the grant of asylum: the ICE lawyer had reserved his right to appeal,[5] and because ICE had thirty days to lodge an appeal, we were told, they could not be released before the expiration of that period, even, presumably, if the elusive "third-agency clearances" arrived.

So much for acronym, euphemism, context, signifiers, and what they signify, writing, positive law and its bureaucratic and institutional simulacra, institutional and disciplinary discourses, surprise, its absence, familiarity, shock, and outrage; and cultural stories, tropes, schemas, or plausible narratives, like the performance of both truthfulness and trauma, or what we might call their discursive construction; and the sites where law and language are evident kin. What of law and language? What does telling stories about law, including the genre of "war stories," suggest about this aspect of the interdisciplinary field constituted by law and humanities work? After all, "'[c]ollecting stories,'" Ewick and Silbey write, in one of a group of recent thoughtful critical studies of law and language that complicate the distinction between linguistic humanities and linguistic human science method, "and 'having

---

[5] He had explicitly done so because the judge had granted the adult clients asylum, rather than withholding deportation, the alternative relief available in cases where asylum is not available because the asylum seeker has a firm offer of asylum from another nation. Although the ICE lawyer conceded that there was no such firm offer in evidence here (and thus inferentially that his basis for seeking a withholding order was flawed), he nonetheless argued that withholding was the appropriate relief for the adult clients, apparently on the grounds that because the (lacking) offer, had it been made provided discretionary grounds for refusing asylum, and made it explicit that if withholding rather than asylum had been ordered, he would not have reserved the right to appeal.

conversations' is not the usual way of describing social science research."[6] More to the point, all of these aspects of the writing about law might equally be found in other sociocultural institutions and their discourses.

Beyond registering that the body of work on law and language that proceeds from the premise that language is but a medium of transmission for the substance of law has been left methodologically behind by contemporary law and language scholarship, this much might also be said: This survey of the state of contemporary humanistic Law and Language scholarship suggests four main conclusions.

The first is that much of value in this body of work involves applying linguistic humanities and/or critical linguistic human sciences methodology to the work of legal institutions, discourses, and texts, and could equally be replicated in "and language" interdisciplinary work in other professions, practices of subject formation, disciplines.

Next, some of it – and the scholarship of Peter Goodrich stands out in particular here – is about the unique or distinctive relationships between law and language. That said, this chapter's third conclusion about law and language scholarship and the praxes that might be informed by it is that much is yet to be done in the subdiscipline of scholarship concerning itself with the unique or distinctive insights that might emerge from interdisciplinary inquiries into "law"[7] grounded in the work of influential theorists of language and discourse. A cursory sampling of such scholars working in the post- and neostructuralist language studies traditions might range from Derrida and Foucault and Irigaray to Halliday, Kress, and Threadgold to Badiou and Lacan and Kristeva. There are likewise possibilities for interdisciplinary work in law and language that might be potentiated by the development of Peircean semiotics and the linguistic philosophy of Searle and, to a lesser extent, Austin.

This in turn suggests survey's fourth conclusion: That to the extent that there is an aspect of law and language scholarship that is presently significantly underdeveloped, it is the interrelationships among theories of language, of subject formation, and of law. Lines of inquiry exploring this question might be generated by work drawing on sources that include Husserl's phenomenological theorization of meaning and language and its account of the communicating subject, and Bourdieu's work on both discourse and subject formation.

The balance of this chapter will be divided into six main sections that in turn map distinctive subtypes of Law and Language scholarship: "Humanism and its Supplements"; "Instrumental/Phenomenal"; "Philosophy/Theory"; "Pedagogy

---

[6] Patricia Ewick and Susan S. Silbey, *The Common Place of Law: Stories from Everyday Life* (Chicago and London: The University of Chicago Press, 1998) xii.

[7] It might – aptly – be said that "Law" is the privileged element in this dyad: that my focus is on what language scholarship can tell us about law, rather than what legal scholarship can tell us about language. I would concede the point: In context, law is the privileged object of interdisciplinary inquiries around which the *Introduction* is focused and which it both reproduces and constructs.

Language   319

and Subject Formation"; "Practice"; and "Culture." I have endeavored to select both representative and significant scholars to exemplify general arguments, with inevitable omissions.

Humanism and Its Supplements

Although for those inclined to value disciplinary and subdisciplinary borders of the kinds signaled by some of the subdivisions in this *Introduction*'s table of contents, James Boyd White and Richard Weisberg might be most obviously thought of as leading "Law and Literature" scholars, because they have both made significant contributions to contemporary Law and Language scholarship.

Boyd White's first book, *The Legal Imagination*,[8] is a liberal humanist manifesto in the form of a textbook designed to educate law students about what it has traditionally meant in post-Langdellian U.S. legal education "to learn to think and speak [and read and write] like a lawyer,"[9] and what it might mean if the student learned through the cultivation of the imagination and through reflection to develop his "ability to make sense out of what he does by looking beyond it"[10] to the practice of analysis of the canonical literary texts White excerpts. Although the book is organized around law and language, then, White also aims for a version of that which I have suggested still waits to be done in studies of law and language, which is to theorize the connections among law, language, and subject formation.

In *When Words Lose Their Meaning: Constitutions and Reconstitutions of Language, Character, and Community*,[11] White models the reading, writing, and legal professional subject formation that he attempts to instill in *The Legal Imagination*, "the double activity of claiming meaning for experience and of establishing relations with others in language,"[12] and in *Heracles' Bow*, White's project of constructing an heuristic for a certain kind of normative reading and writing the law is articulated more explicitly as "a kind of legal identity worked out in [the] performance" of reading and writing.[13] He also makes plain his liberal humanist commitments in a critique of (critical) legal and literary theory, claiming for us all a "common birthright," an (implicitly shared) "ordinary language," and an "individual mind."[14]

Thus White's praxiological and otherwise open-textured account of the legal professional subject's mediation between self and tradition and self and community

---

[8] *The Legal Imagination: Studies in the Nature of Legal Thought and Expression* (Boston and Toronto: Little Brown and Company, 1973).

[9] Ibid., xix.

[10] Ibid., xx.

[11] (Chicago and London: The University of Chicago Press, 1984).

[12] Ibid., x.

[13] Ibid., ix.

[14] Ibid., x.

in the interests of enabling justice depends upon liberal humanist assumptions about subjects, communities, culture, and the world. White arguably fails to make a normative case for liberal humanism, except for a brief defense in *Justice as Translation*[15] of his method, and the (sometimes apparently magisterial) worldview from which it proceeds and that it reflects. Despite White's move in his most recent three books to further his account of the relations among law, language, and legal subjects, in exploring questions of authority, justice, and power, the assumptions about norms and communities that impel White's body of work also limit it.

In *Acts of Hope: Creating Authority in Literature, Law, and Politics*,[16] White makes a case for both just authority and a reading and writing practice that might bring it into being. *The Edge of Meaning*[17] sees White write of lawyers as living "constantly at the edge of language, the edge of meaning, where the world can be, and must be, imagined anew," well or badly,[18] and of legal language as having characteristic "restraints" and "enablements," of law work as potentiating both subject formation and world-making.[19] *Living Speech*[20] turns to what White, following Simone Weil, calls the force that stands opposed to the possibility of both love and justice: denying the humanity of other human beings. White argues that law can be at best a "counterforce" of inhumanity in the guise of state power, at least a site for generating a critique of the empire of force, imagining its opposite.[21]

Nonetheless, for those not working in the liberal humanist tradition, White's project is arguably compromised by assumptions about what he and his readers have in common, and that imaginative reflection on the law which draws on intertextual resources taken from canonical literature will lead to common judgments about what law omits and fails to do. These assumptions also include an imagined audience of autonomous individual subjects, "free" and "responsible,"[22] endowed with agency and able to discern the difference between their authentic voice and that used in professional roles, and what is presented as a purely ethical project of self-shaping through a certain type of intellectual commitment, cerebral rather than embodied, that of Boyd White's imagined "ideal student,"[23] to learning to "read and write well."[24]

White shares with Richard Weisberg both an interest in legal subject formation and an assertive normative vision. Although for White the legal subject's engaging

---

[15] *Justice as Translation: An Essay in Cultural and Legal Criticism* (Chicago and London: The University of Chicago Press, 1990).

[16] (Chicago and London: The University of Chicago Press, 1994).

[17] (Chicago and London: The University of Chicago Press, 2001).

[18] Ibid., 223.

[19] Ibid., 224.

[20] *Living Speech: Resisting the Empire of Force* (Princeton and Oxford: Princeton University Press, 2006).

[21] Ibid., 10.

[22] Ibid., xxxv.

[23] Ibid., xxiii.

[24] Ibid., xxxi.

Language 321

law and language is a positive project in ethical self-shaping, Weisberg develops a phenomenological account of legal subjectivity infected with corrupt rhetorical and hermeneutic practices, depicting "legality" – a "relativistic *method* of ordering reality through language" – as "the controlling principle in modern society,"[25] and theorizing "considerate," or deceptive, communication, a characteristic of legal rhetoric that both masks the viciousness of the "protagonist as lawyer" of the modern fiction he interprets and enables that protagonist to urge his audience on to atrocity.

Poethics[26] claims that law and literature are "our culture's two most central narrative endeavors,"[27] and its project is reinvigorating a humanist legal ethics. The phenomenological and theological grounds for Weisberg's account of the ethical lawyer – theorized in *Poethics* – and his inhumane other, suggested in *The Failure of the Word*, become manifest in *Vichy Law and the Holocaust in France*, which grimly documents practices that seem the paradigm of Robert Cover's thesis in "Violence and the Word,"[28] that legal language is distinctive because of its essential relationship with state violence, its operation on "the field of pain and death."[29]

Shifting ground from Cover's sweeping indictment of law as such, Weisberg assigns significant responsibility for the persecution of French Jews under Vichy Law to legal texts, whether Vichy statutes, judicial opinions, or scholarship, to the lawyers who produced them and thus mobilized a violent and specifically legal "exclusionary discourse," and to French jurisprudential discourses on positive law and on what he argues is a constitutional antisemitism, or antisemitic constitutionalism; but also to a specific textual – hermeneutic – practice, which he argues distorts the egalitarian foundational texts of the modern French nation, and names "the [French] Catholic method of reading legal texts."[30] This insidiously familiar mode of textual practice[31] reinterprets what is for Weisberg a stable and authoritative foundational text and thus corrupts the lawyer whose professional subject formation might have otherwise inoculated him against "traditional kinds" of antisemitism and "virulent racism."

Weisberg's thesis depends on a relationship between legal texts and subjects, to be sure, but leaves untheorized the subject formation of those French lawyers who resisted rather than became complicit with the dictates of Vichy. Although his reflexively authoritarian originalist paradigm for reading the law partakes in the explicitly theological, it also manifests humanistic influences both in its egalitarian

---

[25] *The Failure of the Word: The Lawyer as Protagonist in Modern Fiction* (New Haven and London: Yale University Press, 1984) xi–xii.

[26] *Poethics and Other Strategies of Law and Literature* (New York: Columbia University Press, 1992).

[27] Ibid., xiv.

[28] Robert Cover, "Violence and the Word," *Yale Law Journal* 95 (1986): 1601.

[29] Ibid.

[30] Richard Weisberg, *Vichy Law and the Holocaust in France* (New York: New York University Press, 1996) 428–9.

[31] Ibid., 428–9.

rhetoric and in its commitment to using exegetical method to derive ethical lessons for lawyers from studying legal texts.

Significant "supplementary" models of humanist law and language scholarship are offered by Austin Sarat and by Robin West. Sarat takes his orientation from Cover's "Violence and the Word," arguing that modern law is "built on representations of aggression, force, and disruption, of aggressive acts. . . . [a]nd, once built, . . . traffics in violence every day"; that "[v]iolence, as both a linguistic and physical phenomena, as fact and metaphor, is integral to the constitution of modern law."[32] As Sarat's law and language work is both oriented and framed by his scholarly expertise in state and human violence, criminal law, and the death penalty, so his account of law and language is grounded, like Weisberg's, in an egalitarian politics formed against the background of the constitutive race relations of the United States. Drawing on the work of scholars from critical theoretical rather than liberal humanist traditions, his situated case study of Elaine Scarry's thesis that "the courtroom and the discourse of the trial provide one particularly important site to observe the way violence and pain 'enter language,'"[33] is nonetheless profoundly humanist in its attempt to put "violence and pain into discourse," and thus "know . . . [the] full measure [both of violence] and the pain it inflicts."[34]

West likewise takes her orientation from "the [national] past, at which time subordination was entrenched, and entrenched in the very traditions that formal equality so vigorously promotes,"[35] but her distinctive progressive "care feminist" ethical humanism offers a different perspective on law and language. West is less concerned than Weisberg and Sarat about law's service of state violence, more concerned by "the absence of a political state [shaped by law] . . . that gives rise to the subordination of others, through fratricidal, infantile violence."[36] Her critique of "liberal legalism's"[37] dominant discourses of "the meaning of the Rule of Law, the content and purpose of our rights, and the moral mandate of formal equality,"[38] leads her to propose both a critique of CLS and critical/left legal scholarship's textualist strategies for destabilizing those dominant discourses and their related institutional and disciplinary practices, and a radical reimagining of "legal justice." The latter takes its cue from Hobbes, arguing for the "attempt to construct, through law . . . not . . . the unleashing of free individual choice unfettered by an oppressive state, but the necessary conditions of cooperative community life." West concludes that "the point of

---

[32] Austin Sarat, "Speaking of Death: Narratives of Violence in Capital Trials," *The Rhetoric of Law*, Austin Sarat and Thomas R. Kearns, eds. (Ann Arbor: The University of Michigan Press, 1994) 135, 136.

[33] Ibid., 139, quoting Elaine Scarry, *The Body in Pain* (New York: Oxford University Press, 1985) 10.

[34] Sarat, "Speaking, of Death," 139.

[35] Robin West, *Re-Imagining Justice* (Aldershot: Ashgate, 2003) 8.

[36] Ibid., 9.

[37] Which she identifies as conservative. Ibid., 8.

[38] West, *Re-Imagining Justice*, 8.

Language   323

the Rule of Law . . . is not to frustrate politics, but to enable it. And politics, on this
view, . . . is the means by which communities and individuals create meaning."[39]

Instrumental/Phenomenal

Although Peter Goodrich catalogues sixteenth-century English texts on legal rhetoric, grammar, and lexicon among the heterogeneous sources of the common law
tradition,[40] the genre of modern texts seeking to account for the relationships
between law and language includes work characteristically done by linguists and
other social scientists, particularly linguistic anthropologists, psychologists, and sociologists, which provides analytical accounts of distinctively legal language and language usage by lawyers and in legal institutions.

These texts' generic features include deterministic histories of English or Anglo-
American legal language and usage, criticisms of complex or obfuscatory legal
language that either foreshadow or document the Plain Legal Language movement,
discourses on clarity and precision, and some relatively undertheorized or selectively
theorized legal linguistic hermeneutics. Tiersma's *Legal Language*[41] is both more
sophisticated in approach and wider ranging in content than is typical of the genre,
considering issues of power, race, class, and the performance and coding of "truth"
in legal discourse. Solan and Tiersma's *Speaking of Crime: The Language of Criminal Justice*[42] moves beyond analyzing "language crimes" to identify some especially
critical sites for the operation of semantics and hermeneutics in the criminal procedural arena, and provides a brief account of some aspects of contemporary linguistic
theory implicated in studies of legal language.

More commonly, however, these texts tend to the "commonsense" and commonplace in their accounts of the relationships between law and language, largely viewing
law and language as implicated but distinct phenomena and practices, rather than
understanding law as essentially or substantially discursive, and to the extent that
they do the latter, not moving far beyond observations about the language-saturated
work of practicing lawyers, and collapsing the category "law" with that of positive
law's legal texts. An example of the largely unexplored possibilities and significant
methodological limitations of this work can be found in law and language law reform
projects such as the U.S.-based efforts to redraft pattern jury instructions in according
to plain language or psycholinguistic principles.

Arguably humanistic in orientation, in that they proceed from an assumption
that redrafted texts will be democratizing and will enhance just outcomes in legal

---

[39] Ibid., 9.
[40] Peter Goodrich, *Languages of Law: From Logics of Memory to Nomadic Masks* (London: Weidenfeld
& Nicolson, 1990) 66–7.
[41] Peter M. Tiersma, *Legal Language* (Chicago and London: The University of Chicago Press, 1999).
[42] (Chicago and London: The University of Chicago Press, 2005).

processes, jury instruction reform projects are limited in their goals because of their assumptions both that the law is "there" to be translated and that jury instructions are not embedded in cultural contexts. Thus if juries decide rape cases according to the influence of cultural stories about sex, gendered sexuality, and what passes for the performance of integrity or plausibility in patriarchal culture; and criminal defendants whose cultural performances of innocence or guilt differ from those prevalent in dominant culture are convicted at high rates because of such cross-cultural dissonance, simplified jury instructions are likely to have little influence on outcomes, as on "justice."

A distinctively humanistic body of this reform-based law and language work is directed to nonstandard English speakers, and addresses cross-cultural communication, including translation in legal settings and cross-cultural legal education. Susan Berk-Seligson's *The Bilingual Courtroom: Court Interpreters and the Judicial Process*[43] is an especially thorough and carefully framed analysis of how this aspect of language practices in legal contexts implicates legal power and produces "law," and might inhibit or enable the possibility of justice that is at the heart of the humanist law and language scholarship considered *supra*. Much remains to be done, however, to theorize relationships among law, socioeconomic and cultural power, and race, class, and ethnicity, particularly in the context of the inculcation of legal literacy in what is, perhaps especially in the United States, a strongly monocultural academy.

The rhetorician of law Marianne Constable's *Just Silences*, informed by speech act theory, addresses "the [many] silences of law" that "gesture not only toward the justice to be found in laying claim to voice and to the power to be had in speech, but also towards the possibilities of justice that lie in silence."[44] Historically situated "at a juncture in the history of relations of law and justice, a moment in which the justice of law lies as much if not more in the silences of positive law as in its speech,"[45] in times when there may be "no justice to speak of," Constable's text theorizes relations among law, language, violence, society and subjects, and justice.

Constable's project points toward a significant division in law and language work, which frequently also fractures around the subject formation of the scholars involved, primarily linguists on the one hand, and on the other, legal scholars or those whose interdisciplinary work may be grounded in the methodology of sociology or rhetoric or philosophy, but whose subject is more or less exclusively law or justice. On the one hand, there are scholarly anatomies, the technical applied studies. On the other, there are profound inquiries, jurisprudential projects, philosophical inquiries about law, which always, whether explicitly or not, also generate questions about what

---

[43] (Chicago and London: The University of Chicago Press, 1990, rev'd. ed., 2002).
[44] Marianne Constable, *Just Silences: The Limits and Possibilities of Modern Law* (Princeton: Princeton University Press, 2005) 8.
[45] Ibid., 178.

Language   325

Constable identifies as the "precarious and open" future of the "traditional concerns of jurisprudence – law and its relation to justice."[46]

Another relatively visible tension in the differing strands of work done in law and language scholarship emerges around the division between more or less purely formal scholarship and theoretical interdisciplinary law and language scholarship which enables understandings of how law is constituted; how it functions; and how it might be imagined into being in differing ways. Thus its explicit or implicit *telos* is transforming law in the interests of enabling justice, troubling the superficial split between applied and theoretical work in this interdisciplinary field.

A version (itself complicating) of this difference of view might be found by contrasting Jack Balkin's highly technical domestication of Derridian thought on language and subjects,[47] which skirts Derrida's critique of hierarchy, subordination, and "the metaphysics of presence," and detaches Derrida's work from the realm of the ethical, with Drucilla Cornell's account of a principled common law method, derived from Peirce's pragmatic linguistics, oriented to change.[48] Like Constable, she finds the possibility of hope, the possibility of justice, in law's silences, gaps, and aporias, on its margins, and above all in its subjects, and the kind of law they might imagine and bring into being:

> Power, of course, plays a crucial role in designating both who is to decide what is better and on what criterion that decision should be based. But the reality that there are embodied ideals that guide the interpretive process in art or in law imposes at least some limit on what those in power can impose. That such ideals can be constituted against the endless power bargaining of actual individuals is the hope of constitutional government. It is a hope, however, that depends on interpreters of the law for its reality against those who say it is only wishful thinking. Of course, if we *accept* that law is nothing more than power, then there is always the possibility that this is what law will become. This is just a possibility, not a mandate of faith.[49]

Yet another complication of demarcations is indirectly raised by Constable's method. What is "language," for the purposes of considering interdisciplinary relations that might exist or be forged between law and language? Is it something profound, recognized in absences as well as in articulation and inscription? Does it include only matters like grammar, syntax, and lexicon? Does it extend to differing formulations of discourse, itself a contested term? If so, how might it be demarcated from studies

---

[46] Ibid., 178.

[47] J. M. Balkin, "Deconstructive Practice and Legal Theory," *Law and Language*, Frederick Schauer, ed. (New York: New York University Press, 1993) 385.

[48] Drucilla Cornell, *Transformations: Recollective Imagination and Sexual Difference* (New York and London: Routledge, 1993) 23–44.

[49] Ibid., 39.

of narrative on the one hand and rhetoric on the other? What are the relationships among meaning, interpretation, and language?

Philosophy/Theory

A text that illustrates the complexity of drawing lines of this last kind while at the same time suggesting, as Constable's work likewise does, the difficulty of dividing instrumental and philosophical accounts of the relationship between law and language, is *Law's Stories*,[50] whose project is framing law as "stories, explanations, performances, linguistic exchanges – as narratives and rhetoric."[51] Catharine MacKinnon's brief, often excoriating terminal reflection on the volume ranges from acute insights into the allure of "felt verisimilitude"[52] and its lack in constructing legal authority; legislation as a genre "predicated on elided voices";[53] legal canonicity; the structural privileging of some voices, accounts, and interpretations and subordination of others; the textual politics of legitimating commonplaces of judicial discourse; and the situated history of legal narrative scholarship. Her insistence is on grasping the multiple connections among law, language, and the reality of inequality, the imbrication of power and ethics in any employment of language in law, primary or secondary.

A skeptical intervention in distinctively philosophical law and language scholarship – in its own way as provocative as MacKinnon's – is Brian Bix's monograph, *Law, Language and Legal Determinacy*.[54] Bix makes a case for the inadequacy of philosophies of language to generate philosophies of law because of law's normative and political dimensions, as he explores questions of legal authority, the lawmaker's intention, and the determinacy rather than the indeterminacy of law.

The stakes of philosophical law and language scholarship are most forcefully advanced in acutely political accounts, like MacKinnon's, of the relationships of law and language. By contrast, Schauer's *Law and Language*[55] treats the relation as a formal one, both because of what Schauer concludes law and language have in common – a distinctive institutional generality[56] – and because of the functions language plays in the dispute resolution that Schauer locates at the core of the enterprise "law." For all that Schauer defensively characterizes the law and language interdiscipline as fragmented or incoherent,[57] his editorial focus is narrow, even

---

[50] Peter Brooks and Paul Gewirtz, eds., *Law's Stories: Narrative and Rhetoric in the Law* (New Haven and London: Yale University Press, 1996).
[51] Ibid., 2.
[52] Ibid., 232.
[53] Ibid.
[54] (Oxford: Clarendon, 1993).
[55] Frederick Schauer, ed., *Law and Language* (New York: New York University Press, 1993).
[56] Ibid., xi–xii.
[57] Ibid., xiv.

Language

within the relatively circumscribed domain of a particular debate about law that is usefully framed through thinking about theories of language: that centering on the indeterminacy thesis.

Two especially important contributions to theorizing the relationships between law and language are the work of the late Robert Cover, and *Deconstruction and the Possibility of Justice*,[58] taking its title from a talk given by Derrida at Cardozo Law School, and including an essay based on that talk, "Force of Law: 'The Mystical Foundation of Authority.'"[59] Many writers on law and language, including Cornell and Constable, invoke Cover's "Violence and the Word,"[60] which opens, famously, thus:

> Legal Interpretation takes place in a field of pain and death. This is true in several senses. Legal interpretive acts signal and occasion the imposition of violence upon others: A judge articulates his understanding of a text, and as a result, somebody loses his freedom, his property, his children, even his life. Interpretations in law also constitute justifications for violence which has already occurred or which is about to occur. When interpreters have finished their work, they frequently leave behind victims whose lives have been torn apart by these organized, social practices of violence. Neither legal interpretation nor the violence it occasions may be properly understood apart from one another.[61]

Like Constable and Cornell, Cover engages with the possibility of justice, "the projection of an imagined future upon reality:" that on his account resists the coupling of the practices of interpretation and violent domination that is the law of tyranny, "insisting... that if there is to be continuing life, it will not be on the terms of the tyrant's law."[62] Cover's most forceful jurisprudential insight, however, is in his thesis both that legal interpretation is "rendered as part of... [an] act of state violence,"[63] and that it is necessary that "death and pain are at the center of legal interpretation" because the alternative, that they exist "within our polity but outside the discipline of the collective decision, rules and the individual efforts to achieve outcomes through those rules," is "truly unacceptable."[64]

This text is noteworthy not merely for its influence on law and language scholarship but also for its account of the significance of embodied law: "the normative world-building that constitutes 'Law' is never just a mental or spiritual act," Cover writes. "A legal world is built only to the extent that there are commitments that place

---

[58] Drucilla Cornell, Michel Rosenfeld, and David Gray Carlson, eds., *Deconstruction and the Possibility of Justice* (New York and London: Routledge, 1992).

[59] Ibid., 3–67.

[60] Robert M. Cover, "Violence and the Word," 95 *Yale Law Journal* (1985–86): 1601.

[61] Ibid., 1601.

[62] Ibid., 1604.

[63] Ibid., 1628.

[64] Ibid., 1628.

328   Penelope Pether

bodies on the line."[65] Elsewhere in his distinctively linguistic jurisprudence Cover explores the relationship between constitutional texts and the "epics" that locate and give meaning to them, constituting the *nomos*, the normative universe, which we inhabit,[66] and, crucially, argues that "[t]he uncontrolled character of meaning exercises a destabilizing influence upon power."[67]

This last insight encapsulates a central concern of many of the essays in *Deconstruction and the Possibility of Justice*, especially Henry Louis Gates' at once skeptical and engaged inquiry into the actual possibility of racial justice in a nation whose judiciary "remains entrapped in a pre-modern.... episteme"[68] in an essay that fore-shadows the current interest in the possibilities of binary economics for slavery reparations in the United States.

Derrida's own contribution to the collection is a particularly significant text for law and language scholarship, engaging, like Cover's equally seminal essay, with law's violence, in Derrida's case in exploring the relations between law and justice in the interests of change, a task motivated by the interpretive "task and responsibility"[69] occasioned by the Holocaust. Grounded in significant part in the work of Emmanuel Lévinas, Derrida's essay, the metasubject of which is the work of interpretation, engages the paradox of the impossible condition of justice, "address[ing] oneself to the other in the language of the other."[70] It lays bare the state's fear "of fundamental, founding violence, that is, violence able to justify, to legitimate,... or to transform the relations of law,"[71] through performing a close (deconstructive) reading of Walter Benjamin's "Critique of Violence."

Drawing significantly on Lévinas, and also on Lacan, Cornell's contribution to *Deconstruction and the Possibility of Justice* brings Derrida's thought and Luhmann's systems theory into engagement in exploring "why the conditions of women's inequality," and in particular, their inequality at law, "are continually *restored*."[72] Luhmann's account of "structural coupling," read through Lacanian psychoanalytic theory, gives Cornell a basis for supplementing Pateman's account of the sexual contract to understand the mechanisms that reproduce sex hierarchy and women's inequality. Deconstruction, the "philosophy of the limit," and Lévinasian ethics are means to theorize the disruption of the present system, the possibility of hope.

---

[65] Ibid., 1605.

[66] Cover, "Nomos and Narrative," 97, 4.

[67] Ibid., 18.

[68] Henry Louis Gates, "Statistical Stigmata," in Cornell et al., eds., *Deconstruction and the Possibility of Justice*, 330–45, 335.

[69] Jacques Derrida, "The Force of Law: The 'Mystical Foundation of Authority,'" in Cornell et al., eds., *Deconstruction and the Possibility of Justice*, 3–67, 63.

[70] Ibid., 3–67, 17.

[71] Ibid., 3–67, 35.

[72] Drucilla Cornell, "The Philosophy of the Limit: Systems Theory and Feminist Legal Reform," in Cornell et al., eds., *Deconstruction and the Possibility of Justice*, 68–91, 68.

Language

329

Some equally ambitious philosophical inquiry into some aspects of the relationships between law and language can be found in Habermas's application in *Between Facts and Norms*[73] of his "theory of communicative action"[74] to generate a model of law, adapting the work of Searle, Austin, and pragmatist philosophers of language to theorize a legal discourse that will both function in pluralist postmodern societies and mediate the tension between facts and norms that characterizes both law and this way of thinking about language. A counter theory to that advanced by Habermas is Teubner's model of autopoetic law,[75] also based on Luhmann's systems theory, which begins its theorizing of law based on an account of law's self-referentiality and hence a claim for its unpredictability. This is affirmatively a theory of law *qua* law: it rejects the sociology of law's claims to know the "truth" that legal knowledge obscures just as it rejects claims to legal coherence.

Although Teubner's autopoetic theory of law and language lacks the insistently political thrust of Habermas' work, it does have a place for human subjects, albeit one that inadequately engages questions of power, law, and legal subject formation and agency:

> It is not only the elements of the system [of autopoetic law], the legal acts, that are involved in the process of self-reproduction; elements, structures, processes, boundary, identity, function, and performance all play their part. Human agents play an important double role in this process. They function as semantic constructs of the legal system and as independent autopoetic (psychic) systems in the environment of the law.[76]

Teubner's theory thus flags a significant tension in law and language scholarship in that it has a paradoxical kinship with "instrumental" law and language work that owes its origins to Realist legal thought, and its successor Law and Society scholarship. Offering accounts of the "truth" of "law" or legality or legal processes or the operation of legal institutions drawn from other disciplines, and implicitly predicated on understanding those disciplines as truth procedures, it thus differs fundamentally from work in the critical theoretical tradition, which provides supplementary rather than totalizing accounts of law, often passing judgment on law, while refusing to foreclose the "possibility of justice."

Peter Goodrich is arguably the most significant contemporary scholar of linguistic jurisprudence working in the critical theoretical tradition. His *Reading the*

---

[73] Jürgen Habermas, *Between Facts and Norms: Contributions to a Discourse Theory of Law and Democracy*, William Rehg, trans. (Cambridge: MIT Press, 1993).

[74] Advanced in Jürgen Habermas, *The Theory of Communicative Action*, Vols. I and II, Thomas McCarthy, trans. (Boston: Beacon Press, 1984, 1987).

[75] Gunther Teubner, *Law as an Autopoetic System*, Anne Bankowska and Ruth Adler, trans. (Oxford and Cambridge: Blackwell, 1993).

[76] Ibid., 26.

Law[77] is many things, among them a theoretically sophisticated history of legal discourse that seeks to "outline and question" "prevalent" modes of reading, writing, laying down, interpreting, and understanding law that do not register, or acknowledge, or accept that to understand law's "effective social meaning and practice, its history and empirical readings," entails an understanding that "the process of reading is an inherently social and political activity," which "constitutes a preferred text and actively selects and privileges meanings and accents."[78] It is also a radical pedagogical text, as the heteroglossic pun constituted by its title suggests. *Reading the Law's* most significant contributions to the philosophy of Law and Language are its genealogy of modern common law, its account of the relations between law and writing, and its theorizing of hermeneutic and rhetorical law-reading practices, the former complicit with law's claims to totalizing authority, the latter making visible the way legal authority does its work.

In *Languages of Law*[79] Goodrich both anatomizes and advances a radical critique of the common law tradition as one confined to the surface that is law's language. Goodrich seeks to "understand the religious life of the law, of the institution, as an historical ruin, as the legible surface or marked text of a lived world," and thus to deconstruct, reinhabit, and change law.[80] This text proposes a genealogy of common law legal subjectivity, concerning itself with the material and embodied histories of legal discourse, "the historical and ontological issue of how law is lived, what are its habitual forms, what is the deep structure that allows its repetition in ever different forms."[81] Goodrich problematizes orthodox understandings of the relationship between law and language, concluding with an account of the aesthetics of signs and images of law detached from the "logics of memory," exceeding the scene of writing and testifying to an impoverished tradition, a broken down, fragmented, proliferating law, a puppet of the state and technique of governance, powerful in its very arbitrariness, "a law of masks."[82]

In *Law in the Courts of Love*,[83] the record of a literary psychoanalysis of law, Goodrich constructs a supplementary history of literary and legal texts that constitute "minor jurisprudences."[84] Frequently linguistic in focus, they do not pretend to cover the field, but rather represent "the strangeness of language and so the possibilities of

---

[77] Peter Goodrich, *Reading the Law: A Critical Introduction to Legal Method and Techniques* (Oxford: Basil Blackwell, 1986).

[78] Ibid., v.

[79] Peter Goodrich: *Languages of Law: From Logics of Memory to Nomadic Masks* (London: Weidenfeld and Nicolson, 1990).

[80] Ibid., viii.

[81] Ibid., 2.

[82] Ibid., 11.

[83] Peter Goodrich, *Law in the Courts of Love: Literature and Other Minor Jurisprudences* (London and New York: Routledge, 1996).

[84] Ibid., 2.

Language

interpretation as also of plural forms of knowledge,"[85] all in aid of reconnecting law with "subject, person, . . . emotion," and thus enabling "the dialogue or the attention to singularity which justice or ethics requires."[86] In assembling this "glossary of the phantoms" that law has discarded,[87] invoking the canons it has suppressed, Goodrich insists on law's dependence on subjects for its existence and on its recognition of this relationship if it is to do justice, passes judgment on the impoverishment of legal scholarship, and explores "the relationship of law to writing and of justice to genre."[88] He argues for "using the literary genre of law to reinstate the uncertainty and the undecidability of the writing of law":

> The reason and the value of such suspension or aporia in relation to judgment is a question of justice, of attention to the particular. In this aspect suspension of judgment opens up the possibility to recognize and in some sense account for the desires of the subject that writes and of the subject judged. That subjectivities motivate both judgment and the writing of law is a theme closer to literature than to legal doctrine within the contemporary order of disciplines. It implies a recognition of the phantasmatic character of legal practice, of the bridging of the unbridgeable gap between norm and judgment, rule and application.[89]

In *The Laws of Love*[90] Goodrich furthers his radical pedagogical project, constructing an alternative jurisprudence, a legal text of his own, a "case law of love,"[91] eloquent, ethical, and good humored. This is both scholarly guerilla assault on and satirical mirror for the common law his earlier books anatomize: death-driven, it is closed, detached from bodies and from history, from ethics and others, rather than open to eloquence and relations with the other disciplines and bodies of knowledge that might inform – and transform – it.

Pedagogy and Subject Formation

Scholars of the pedagogy of rhetoric/composition in the U.S. university can identify two distinct models of the teaching and learning of tertiary literacy. One is grounded in psycholinguistics and treats the inculcation of such literacy as the task of composition generalists. The other, the best known of which is located at Cornell University, treats discipline-specific literacy as imbricated with the modes of

---

[85] Ibid.
[86] Ibid., vii.
[87] Ibid., 3.
[88] Ibid., 6.
[89] Ibid., 8.
[90] Peter Goodrich: *The Laws of Love: A Brief Historical and Practical Manual* (Basingstoke and New York: Palgrave Macmillan, 2006).
[91] Ibid., xiv.

reasoning and inquiry specific to that discipline, and thus most appropriately taught by highly expert scholars and teachers of the discipline.

There are some similarities discernible in the split between the vast majority of "Legal Writing" programs in U.S. law schools, where teachers of legal writing are constructed as legal literacy specialists, and teach in standalone courses, and the few law schools where introductory instruction in legal literacy is "integrated" with a doctrinal subject. There is arguably no genuine law school equivalent to Rhetoric/Composition's Cornell model of inculcating foundational disciplinary literacy, Boyd White's pedagogy of law and its disciplinary literacy as profoundly imbricated being characteristically confined, where it is practiced, to the upper level optional J. D. curriculum.

Although Boyd White's method might offer a richly humanistic vision of the possibilities of foundational legal disciplinary literacy pedagogy, it fails to register the necessary violence of disciplinary formation and the grinding instrumentalism that both confines and thus often characterizes this pedagogy. Two related insights remain more or less completely unexplored in the literature on law, language, and the pedagogical contribution to legal professional subject formation.

The first suggests that accounts of teacher–student power relations that assume that discursive and institutional power is possessed exclusively by the teacher, merit troubling in the context in which disciplinary literacy is taught and learned in law schools, where most of those teaching foundational legal literacy are relatively discursively and institutionally powerless. The second suggests supplementing the critical work on legal education's monocultural and monological discourses with studies explicitly focused on the monological legal literacy generally institutionalized in law schools' "Legal Writing" curricula and pedagogy. There is perhaps a particular utility in such work in the context of legal education in the United States, with an African-American population with a history of vexed and complicated relations with legal texts and power on the one hand, and with literacy more generally, often imbricated with law, on the other. Although there is a developed literature on the gendered politics of employment in the legal writing professoriate, there are few reflections on questions of the operation of aspects of sex, race, class, and power in the inculcation of foundational disciplinary literacy in law. Such work might explore Robert Cover's insight that "the uncontrolled character of meaning exercises a destabilizing influence upon power"[92]; and that of the editors of *Words That Wound*,[93] that conventional (say Marxian) accounts of unequal power relations are unstable, and that the discourse of oppression is available for rhetorical use, as

---

[92] Robert Cover, "The Supreme Court, 1982 Term: Foreword, *Nomos* and Narrative," 97 *Harvard Law Review* (1983): 4, 18.

[93] Charles R. Lawrence III, Mari J. Matsuda, Richard Delgado, and Kimberlè Williams Crenshaw, *Words that Wound: Critical Race Theory, Assaultive Speech, and the First Amendment* (Boulder, San Francisco, and Oxford: Westview Press, 1993).

Language

when "[t]he privilege and power of white male elites is wrapped in the rhetoric of politically unpopular speech [and] . . . [t]hose with the power to exclude new voices from the official canon become an oppressed minority."[94]

Elizabeth Mertz's *The Language of Law School: Learning to "Think Like a Lawyer*,"[95] the most systematic account to date of the position of legal literacy in law school pedagogy and legal professional subject formation, is alert to questions of sex, race, and power. It asks hard questions, albeit ones arguably anchored, despite their frequent critical edge, in a (left) liberal intellectual tradition, about the possible "limits that legal epistemology may place on law's democratic aspirations," and about "whether legal training itself may impact the democratizations of the legal profession," and thus the nation more generally.[96]

Mertz concludes that "linguistic ideologies" transmitted through "microlevel processes in language" both structure and are formed by "the social uses of language and text in legal contexts,"[97] that legal epistemology and the processes of legal training are intimately connected, and indeed that "the acquisition of lawyerly 'thinking' . . . [is] an initiation into a particular linguistic and textual tradition."[98] Her judgment is that the inculcation of this tradition is transformative of the orientation of law students to the world in general, and law and society in particular, and that although viewed across the legal academy it is neither seamless nor homogeneous, its investments are not neutral, but rather tend to construct a worldview respectful of authority and convinced by the premises and perspective of formal equality. At least this is frequently the case for those students whose embodiment and acculturation – in terms of race, class, and sex – conforms to that of the student subjects around whom the durable Langdellian paradigm of U.S. legal education was constructed. A particular strength of her study, offering radically transformative possibilities to critical legal educators, is its nuanced awareness of the contexts – present and erased, systematic and variable – in which legal literacy is inculcated, and legal professional subjects, with their "shared epistemology"[99] formed in a culture that they form in their turn.

From Theory to Practice

There is a difference discernible, although not always easily demarcated, between the scholarship discussed in this section and that in the second section, *supra*. The scholars whose work is discussed here seek to account for the uses of their theoretical

---

[94] Ibid., 15.
[95] (Oxford and New York: Oxford University Press, 2007).
[96] Ibid., 3.
[97] Ibid.
[98] Ibid., 4.
[99] Ibid., 207.

premises and disciplinary method and then to deploy theory in praxis as they read their sociocultural data. With some exceptions, those whose work is analyzed in the second section are less concerned to either account for or frame an argument for their method, and characteristically treat their interpretation of data and the lines of reform that it opens up as self-evident.

Some of Mertz's most significant early interdisciplinary work in law and linguistic anthropology was her coauthored article with Lisa Frohmann on the limits of liberal legal reform of the law on sexual violence, and work in this tradition provides the most developed and potentially transformative case study of praxiological law and language work. Another significant contributor to the law and language scholarship on gendered violence is Kim Lane Scheppele, who draws attention to the instability and malleability of evidence in the context of rape trials, and the ways in which certain types of testimony, performances of identity, and dominant contextual cultural discourses enable the construction of "facts" that "are presented as natural and interpreted as truth," and are enabled to do "much misogynistic work . . . in the construction of 'reality.'"[100]

Gary LaFree's *Rape and Criminal Justice: The Social Construction of Sexual Assault*[101] is a relatively sophisticated, book-length study of how every aspect of rape prosecutions, including victim decisions to report, depend on the perceived fit between social data and "criminal labels [that] depend on definitions constructed through social interaction,"[102] but is methodologically limited by its binary account of the "socially constructed" and the "real" worlds in which law and language, culture, narrative, and interpretation do their work. Matoesian's *Reproducing Rape*,[103] arguably the most significant book-length study of the intersections of law and language in an especially linguistically charged subfield of law and legality,[104] argues that "language functions [in rape trials] as the symbolic embodiment of social values, as a strategic instrument of domination and . . . as a sequentially organized inference generating machine," characteristically "transforming women's experience of rape . . . into consensual sex through the social organization of courtroom talk."[105] Matoesian is evidently aware of the blind spot in much of the law and language scholarship on rape: its failure to theorize the problem of the production of "truth" in the project of generating counterdiscourses to those that dominate culture and law.

---

[100] "Just the Facts, Ma'am: Sexualized Violence, Evidentiary Habits, and the Revision of Truth," 37 *New York Law School Law Review* (1992): 123, 123.

[101] (Belmont: Wadsworth, 1989).

[102] Ibid., 66.

[103] Gregory M. Matoesian, *Reproducing Rape: Domination Through Talk in the Courtroom* (Chicago: The University of Chicago Press, 1993).

[104] Another especially thoughtful contribution to this genre is Andrew E. Taslitz's *Rape and the Culture of the Courtroom* (New York and London: New York University Press, 1999).

[105] Matoesian, *Reproducing Rape*, viii.

Language   335

The essays collected in Robert Post's *Censorship and Silencing: Practices of Cultural Regulation*[106] take language theory as a starting point for well-theorized, sophisticated, praxiological law and language scholarship. In a uniformly thoughtful and thought-provoking collection, Schauer's "The Ontology of Censorship,"[107] Sanford Levinson's theorizing of "The Tutelary State,"[108] and contributions by Judith Butler[109] and Wendy Brown[110] on the censor's vocabulary and silence and freedom, respectively, stand out. Butler's theorizing of agency, postsovereign subjects, speech and power is a particularly helpful contribution in an interdisciplinary field in which accounts of subjectivity, power, and agency are both rare and thin. Brown's skeptical exploration of "practices of freedom"[111] and "the rhetorical purchase of confessional discourse in a postfoundational epistemological era"[112] leads her to warn

> if the silences in discourses of domination are sites for insurrectionary noise, if they are corridors to be filled with explosive countertales, it is also possible to make a fetish of breaking silence. It is possible too that this ostensible tool of emancipation carries its own techniques of subjugation – that it converges with unemancipatory tendencies in contemporary culture, establishes regulatory norms, coincides with the disciplinary power of ubiquitous confessional practices; in short, feeds the powers it meant to starve,[113]

and to inquire "whether our contemporary crisis of truth has not been displaced into an endless stream of words about ourselves, words that presume to escape epistemological challenges to truth because they are personal or experiential?"[114]

George Marcus's perceptive and provocative account of the "rigorous economy of knowledge, the distribution and restriction of which shape the main institutions of social control in . . . [indigenous Australian] communities"[115] makes a signally critical theoretical contribution to a body of work on law and language and indigenous Australian subjects' encounters with invader law, to which the forensic linguist Diana Eades is arguably the leading contributor. Her work on the ways in which speakers of Aboriginal English experience and are structurally discriminated against

---

[106] Robert C. Post, *Censorship and Silencing: Practices of Cultural Regulation* (Los Angeles: Getty Research Institutes, 1998).

[107] Ibid., 147–68.

[108] "The Tutelary State: 'Censorship,' 'Silencing,' and the 'Practices of Cultural Regulation," ibid., 195–220.

[109] Judith Butler, "Ruled Out: Vocabularies of the Censor," in Post, *Censorship and Silencing*, 247–59.

[110] Wendy Brown, "Freedom's Silences," in Post, *Censorship and Silencing*, 313–27.

[111] Ibid., 313.

[112] Ibid., 320.

[113] Ibid., 314.

[114] Ibid.

[115] George E. Marcus, "Censorship in the Heart of Difference: Cultural Property, Indigenous Peoples' Movements, and Challenges to Western Liberal Thought," in Post, *Censorship and Silencing*, 221–42, 236.

Penelope Pether

in the legal system is both theoretical and applied: She has given expert evidence in defense of Aboriginal English speakers charged with criminal offenses, and her scholarship has had significant impacts on the way some Australian lawyers and judges engage with indigenous Australian speakers of Aboriginal English.

Culture

Some scholars who undertake specifically cultural studies of law and language are more attentive to the relations between language and subjects, or "bodies and languages," as Alain Badiou dismissively puts it, than others. They register that the scholar and the teacher and their writing do work in the world that may conserve the status quo, or enable or make change. Eades' uses the purchase enabled by interdisciplinary expertise in making strategic intervention in the cultural and material politics of contemporary Australia and its vexed race relations. Mertz's account of the socialization of lawyers through linguistic ideologies and the microprocesses of what she argues is a distinctively linguistic disciplinary pedagogy is especially attentive to situated questions of the relations among law, language, power, and culture.

Cultural studies of law impelled by the psychoanalytic jurisprudence scholar and legal philologist/historian Pierre Legendre, and the situated specificity of Peter Goodrich's recent life as a legal scholar and teacher trained in Europe in the post-structuralist tradition and now living and working in the institutional and psychic spaces of U.S. law, are the ground for the essays collected in *Law, Text Terror*.[116] The contributors to this volume – working in both common and civil law traditions – explore the intersections of law's various textual practices and legal (including citizen) subject formation, with an eye to rebuilding a lost – or realizing an imagined – tradition of a legal literacy that is at once scholarly and profoundly politically engaged with the world.

Anton Schütz reads textual artifacts in search of "the history of [a culture's] unrealized possibilities," and maps as he imagines "the corridor of a culture's projected possibilities (and dangers) at a particular moment of its trajectory."[117] Schütz acutely renders a Legendrian genealogy of modern Western Christian epistemology and its "unrelenting need . . . for a position of internal outsider, or hostage."[118] Marinos Diamantides' social psychoanalytic account of the ways in which relationships among subjects, bodies, and texts construct the sovereign subjects of contemporary Western and Islamic states constitutes a forceful intervention in

---

[116] Peter Goodrich, Lior Barshack, and Anton Schütz eds., *Law, Text, Terror: Essays for Pierre Legendre* (Abingdon and New York: Glasshouse, 2006).

[117] Anton Schütz, "Structural Terror: A Shakespearean Investigation," in Goodrich et al. eds., *Law, Text, Terror*, 71–92.

[118] Ibid., 81.

Language 337

twenty-first-century postcolonial global politics.[119] Other insistently situated recent work in textual cultural studies of law includes essays on the texts of the "War on Terror," Joseph Pugliese's, "Abu Ghraib's Shadow Archives,"[120] and Nina Philadelphoff-Puren's, *"Genre's Judgment: Discrediting Torture Testimony in the War on Terror,"*[121] although their critical vision of the tension between law and the "possibility of justice" is markedly less optimistic than that of the editors of *Law, Text/Terror*.

Conclusion(s)

Differences are discernible in the orientation and theories and practices of law and language scholarship and pedagogy across institutional sites and national borders, then. Sharper divisions manifest themselves between reform-oriented scholars, whether committed to versions of liberal legalism or working in critical theoretical traditions, and those scholars who diagnose the violence of the law, its texts, and the practices associated with those texts, while at once – at least implicitly – desiring something other.

Both critique and change require subjects, and the most notable gap in contemporary law and language scholarship lies in how adequately to account for subjects, and thus for agency and cultural reproduction and change, in accounts of the relationships between law and language. Lines of profitable future scholarly inquiry in law and language thus include attempts to think through the relations among subject formation, language, and law, which might be informed by accounts of embodied subjects, language, and subject formation of the kinds generated by Husserl, whose work, like Derrida's account of "fresh judging," is especially promising for theorizing a transformative theory and practice of judgment. So, too, the formation of legal professional subjects might be accounted for by bringing together Bourdieu's account of the making of subjects through their embodied experience of worlds that they in turn shape with Derrida's distinctively linguistic account of the "force of law." Bourdieu's theory of subject formation, for all its careful complicating of the impasse between formalist and instrumentalist jurisprudential thought, lacks a clearly articulated model for engaging legal institutions, discourses, and subjects in the project of shifting forms of social power. Thus studies of the possibilities for productive change offered by inscribing the facticity of law in action in its textual practices, troubling both doctrinalism and the presently dominant models for the construction of professional legal identity, are called for.

---

[119] Marinos Diamantides, "Towards a Western-Islamic Conception of Legalism," in Goodrich et al. eds., *Law, Text, Terror*, 95–118.

[120] 19 *Law and Literature* (2007): 247–76.

[121] 19 *Law and Literature* (2007): 229–45.

My text engages "the sense of an ending" as it began, with accounts of – and linguistic interventions in – acute and yet abiding crises in law, its institutions and discourses, and the proliferating spaces at once beyond and constituted by law, jurisdictions of exception. At its most productive, such scholarship and its pedagogy not only perform gestures of demystification of legal power, and law's many instantiations of the violence with which Robert Cover identified it, enabling a searching engagement with "the disparate ways in which law posits legal subjects, and extends and consolidates state power."[122] Carefully theorized and situated, insisting on engaging politics and law, it also charts ways for law and its subjects to use power, do justice.

[122] Nasser Hussain, *The Jurisprudence of Emergency: Colonialism and the Rule of Law* (Ann Arbor: The University of Michigan Press, 2003) 70.

13

Interpretation

Francis J. Mootz III*

> It is in fact the genius of law that it is not a set of "commands," but a set of texts meant to be read across circumstances that are in principle incompletely foreseeable.... It is this fact that gives rise to the intellectual and ethical life of legal thought and argument.
> – James Boyd White[1]

Interpretation is a ubiquitous feature of legal practice. Nevertheless, the relationship between law and interpretation is troubled. Simply put, legal actors find it difficult to acknowledge the centrality of interpretation given the manner in which the validity of the legal system is established. The traditional account of legal practice insists that lawyers read statutes and precedents to recover the meaning embedded in them and then apply these determinate meanings to the case at hand. Under this account, there generally is no need for "interpretation," an activity that suggests that the law is ambiguous and requires the active participation of the lawyer or judge to render the law meaningful for the case at hand. This account is deemed necessary to underwrite the rule of law because it insists that preexisting legal rules are applied rather than fashioned in the course of the application.

Of course, even under this traditional account, interpretation is inevitable because individual laws sometimes are opaque and not easily applied, but this interpretive activity is regarded as a regrettable necessity that exists on the fringes of law's primary practice of unproblematic application. The precedent-respecting common law

---

* I wish to thank Jack Balkin and Christopher Green for commenting on a draft, and Brian Bix for his careful and detailed suggestions. None of these generous colleagues are to blame for any remaining errors of fact or judgment. I also wish to thank Matthew Anderson for his editorial suggestions and encouragement.
[1] James Boyd White, "What Can a Lawyer Learn from Literature?," *Harvard Law Review* 102 (1989) 2014–47, 2035 (reviewing Richard Posner, *Law and Literature: A Misunderstood Relation* [Cambridge, MA: Harvard University Press, 1988]).

approach in the United States is premised on the belief that judges can understand the plain meaning of the language in prior opinions apart from particular social contexts, and then apply it to present disputes in the course of articulating timeless principles. As law entered the age of statutes and regulations, originalist and plain meaning approaches to these written artifacts developed along similar lines. Much of constitutional theory is grounded in the rhetoric of using strategies designed to absolve the judge of the power and responsibility to make constitutional law. Notwithstanding these earnest efforts to deny or corral interpretation, courts in all of these domains continue to decide, sometimes with a five-to-four vote over a strenuous dissent, that reasonable minds could not differ about the meaning of the law for the case at hand.

Contemporary work in hermeneutical philosophy, literary theory, and rhetoric has undermined the strategies by which law traditionally has proclaimed its independence from the complexities of interpretation. In this chapter I will adumbrate some of the major themes of, and issues arising out of, these initiatives for law and legal theory. The chapter provides a brief account of some recent scholarly developments in hermeneutical philosophy and connects these developments to the various legal contexts to which they speak. The first section considers a variety of theoretical approaches to interpretation by grouping them according to broadly shared characteristics. Natural law theorists approach questions of legal interpretation from a distinct perspective that seeks to displace legal interpretation with an inquiry into objective moral truths. Scholars who embrace the analytical perspective that is predominant in the Anglo-American tradition regard interpretation as a set of recognized moves within legal practice that may be described accurately but not directed by a methodology grounded in theory. Many contemporary theorists regard a legal text as a means to transmit information, and from this communication orientation argue that the locus of meaning is found in the original intentions of the author(s) or in the original public understanding of the words in the text. Finally, the broad-based "hermeneutic turn" has influenced theorists who regard interpretation as a fundamental feature of knowledge generally, and of legal practice more specifically, and who draw on contemporary European philosophy to articulate the hermeneutical situation of legal actors.[2]

The second section of the chapter describes how different legal contexts shape interpretive practices. Although necessarily brief, this discussion reaffirms my thesis that legal hermeneutics should speak not only to ontological or epistemological

---

[2] I have defined each school in the broadest manner in this introduction for the purpose of providing an initial orientation. In a chapter of this length it is impossible to describe the complexities of any one school of theory regarding the question of interpretation, and so I certainly do not pretend to provide a definitive picture of legal theory generally. In the text I will focus my study by choosing one or more theorists from each school of legal theory to serve as a concrete, but not necessarily representative, instance of that school of thought.

Interpretation 341

accounts of legal reasoning but to legal practice as well. The private law of contracts confronts one group of interpretive dilemmas, and different issues arise in the domain of public law with regard to the interpretation of judicial precedents, statutes, constitutions, and treaties. The space constraints of this chapter permit only a brief sketch of how the imperatives of these distinct forms of legal practice connect to broader theoretical debates.

My discussion unavoidably is overly intellectualized, which suggests incorrectly that I believe academic theories of meaning are more important than practices of meaning-making by legal actors. My own theoretical commitments lead me to conclude that a full theoretical consideration of legal interpretation must include detailed examination of the practice in question, and so I shall take account of legal practice to the extent feasible. The growing awareness of the relationship between interpretation and law is not solely an academic concern. The practical demands of modern legal systems have pushed legal practice more expressly into the realm of interpretation, even if legal practitioners generally remain uninterested in the intricacies of the theoretical debates. Consequently, it makes good sense to begin this chapter with a simple example of how law has dealt with interpretive principles and theories. I set the stage for my discussion by recounting the historical trajectory of the parol evidence rule in contract law as an example of the increasing visibility of the role of interpretation in law.

Common law courts have long understood the importance of permitting parties to define their obligations under a contract in a manner that is both secure and certain. The "freedom of contract" encompasses not only the "freedom *to* contract," but also the "freedom *from* contract." Parties are free to limit their consensual liability by carefully circumscribing the parameters of their agreement. The parol evidence rule facilitates this important goal by providing that the written memorial of an agreement cannot be undermined by alleged prior agreements that conflict with the memorial, and also prevents enforcement of prior agreements if they are not reflected in a written memorial that constitutes the complete and exclusive agreement of the parties. The classical common law approach to the parol evidence rule employed the infamous "four-corners" rule, under which a written memorial was presumed to be the complete and exclusive statement of the agreement of the parties if it imported a contractual agreement "on its face." Because this rule deviated so dramatically from actual communication patterns in commercial transactions, a number of courts eventually refined their approach and established the new polestar of the parties' intent with respect to the memorial. If the parties intended the memorial to be final as to some terms, it was so construed; if the parties intended the memorial to be final as to all of the terms of their agreement, it was so construed. The evidence of the circumstances attending the creation of the written memorial is indispensable to making this determination, and so no written memorial can be "self-executing" for parol evidence purposes.

In a related and parallel vein, a number of courts moved from a classical "plain meaning" approach to interpreting the words in a written memorial of the agreement (which amounted to the belief that "interpretation" was unnecessary) to a much more nuanced "context approach" according to which courts read the words within the context of their use by the parties to the contract. This shift followed the broader move away from legal language as a freestanding object to an understanding that legally effective language (such as a memorial of a contractual agreement) serves as a token of legally effective behaviors and commitments that must be investigated in their full complexity. These two developments converge in the "interpretation" exception to the parol evidence rule, which opens many avenues for lawyers to secure the admission of parol evidence by arguing that it is offered for the purpose of interpreting the writing (as broadly construed under the "context approach") rather than seeking to supplement it with additional terms. The tenacity with which some courts continue to cling to more traditional applications of the parol evidence rule indicates the angst occasioned when legal actors confront the full scope of the interpretive nature of law.

This doctrinal example from private law reveals that the issues surrounding legal interpretation flow from two primary questions. First, one must determine the contours of the "object" of interpretation. Originally, courts considered a writing to be an objective fact in the world for purposes of the parol evidence rule, such that this physical entity was the sole focus of interpretation. Today, courts regard a writing as only the gateway to a more contextual inquiry into the relationship between the parties. Interpretation becomes more far ranging when its object is a relationship between parties that includes, but also extends beyond, the language that they have used in structuring the relationship.

Second, one must determine the "goal" of interpretation. The parol evidence rule provides a relatively simple example in this respect because it is now relatively unproblematic to assume as a normative matter that courts should enforce the parties' reasonable expectations engendered by objective manifestations of their intended commitments in a contract. This principle changes in other private law contexts, such as interpreting a will according to the testator's intentions. The goal of interpretation is more complex when the text to be interpreted is a constitution, statute, or judicial precedent. Contract interpretation affects parties to the contract, whereas interpretation of an authoritative legal text affects all those subject to the law. Thus, litigants must address not only whether the object of interpretation extends beyond the legal text, they also must resolve the normative goal of the interpretative practice: Is it to recover the original meaning intended by the authors, to enforce the objective meaning that the text had at the time of enactment, to elucidate the meaning that best implements the underlying purpose of the provision, to do justice according to the text as filtered through contemporary values, or some other goal?

Interpretation

Theoretical Approaches to Interpretation

The issues and problems relating to interpretation and law have not arisen in the modern research university but instead have persisted for millennia. In the Western tradition, Ancient Greece and Rome provide enduring exemplars of attempts to address these issues. Aristotle famously discusses equity as a necessary feature of legal practice to soften the harshness of general rules and to make justice possible. Cicero's discussions of the role of the orator in law and civic life provide a different angle, but one that equally shapes contemporary thinking. It is common for scholars to note these classical touch points before turning quickly to the Enlightenment as the source of our modern traditions.

Patrick Nerhot reminds us that we err by fast-forwarding from the ancient polis to the modern state. In the early centuries of the second millennium a "premodern theologico-juridical episteme" emerged in which religious thinking was "totally impregnated with legal culture just as legal thought is bathed in religious culture."[3] These entwined practices defined truth and authenticity for the community. The great schism of the Protestant Reformation effected a fundamental shift in this defining reality, moving away from the authority of the author as secured by patristic practices and toward the discovery of truth through direct investigation of authoritative texts. Reformulated in a philological manner, this development appeared to "undermine theology at its root," but Nerhot argues that the practices of the jurist provided an abiding link with previous traditions:

> His work is always to reconstitute the truth of something that happened, on the basis of every type of record, written or spoken evidence. His instrument, proof, is a translation of the way we know nature: the jurist's interpretation and argumentation thus come to apply that science, which characterises a society and institutes the signs one must know how to interpret.[4]

The following brief account must necessarily ignore the historical depth and breadth of interpretive practices in law, and so it pays to recall at the outset what must be omitted. Legal interpretation is not just a matter of technique or theory, but rather is a long-standing practice intertwined with other practices relating to fundamental norms of the community and its disciplining epistemologies.[5]

---

[3] Patrick Nerhot, *Law, Writing, Meaning: An Essay in Legal Hermeneutics*, Ian Fraser, trans. (Edinburgh: Edinburgh University Press, 1992) 63–4.

[4] Ibid., 115.

[5] For an excellent and succinct historical overview of interpretation generally, and the development of legal interpretation more specifically, see Charles Collier, "Law as Interpretation," *Chicago-Kent Law Review* 76 (2000) 779–823. Perhaps the most insightful scholar to address law's historical entanglement with a wide variety of interpretive practices and regimes is Peter Goodrich, whose erudite and sophisticated work includes "Amatory Jurisprudence and the *Querelle Des Lois*" *Chicago-Kent Law Review* 76 (2000) 751–78; *Law in the Courts of Love: Literature and Other Minor Jurisprudences*

Law as the Dictates of Natural Law

Natural law theories no longer are a predominant force in the secular political realm, but they cast a long shadow. In its most dogmatic form, natural law is not an interpretive theory so much as a claim that interpretations of legal texts are subordinate to objectively discernible moral dictates. Cicero famously offered a succinct definition of pre-Christian natural law based on the Stoic tradition, arguing that natural law is universal, eternal, and unchanging and that these characteristics of reality follow from the fact that natural law is authored and administered by a deity.[6] This philosophy was easily accommodated by Christianity and propagated by the Roman Empire, blossoming centuries later when Aquinas famously differentiated eternal law, natural law, and positive law. He argued that God's divine will is beyond our ken but that we are capable of determining the objective conditions for human flourishing through the use of reason because – to borrow Paul's words – the natural law is written in our hearts.[7] The collapse of the traditional natural law project leaves us in an ontological gap that we now seek to fill by interpreting texts that are legitimated through positive political theory rather than moral correctness.[8] In this respect, natural law theory precedes and is an alternative to the modern interpretive approach to law.[9]

The "new natural law," exemplified in the work of John Finnis, purports to render Aquinas sensible to our secular and rationalist age by arguing that certain basic and incommensurable goods are elements of human flourishing because they arise from a shared human nature. He claims that these goods serve as the basis for ethical decision making through the exercise of shared practical reasoning.[10] The new natural law speaks to interpretive theory to the extent that one believes that the

---

(London: Routledge Publishing, 1996); and "Historical Aspects of Legal Interpretation," *Indiana Law Journal* 61 (1986) 331–54.

[6] Cicero, *De Re Publica*, Clinton Walker Keyes, trans. (Cambridge, MA: Harvard University Press, 1928), III, xxii.33.

[7] Romans 2:14–15, *The New American Standard Bible* (1995).

[8] Peter Goodrich describes the plight of contemporary legal theory with concise accuracy: we have abandoned natural law foundations originally constructed in ecclesiastical venues only to find that the project of developing a secular legal language capable of transforming the management of social conflict into questions of technical rationality is doomed to failure. Goodrich, *Law in the Courts of Love*, 160–1. More recently, Steven Smith has described "law's quandary," arguing that legal reasoning is constituted by a generalized appeal to something beyond immediate, positive legal practice – something analogous to religious ontology – but that we expressly disavow such an ontological grounding. Steven D. Smith, *Law's Quandary* (Cambridge, MA: Harvard University Press, 2004).

[9] The theological roots of classical natural law thinking provide a helpful analogy for contemporary theorists engaged in disputes about legal hermeneutics, inasmuch as the contrast between the tradition-based project of Catholic and Jewish thinkers and the text-based projects of Protestant thinkers illuminates many questions and problems very similar to those discussed by legal theorists.

[10] John Finnis, *Natural Law and Natural Rights* (Oxford: Oxford University Press, 1980). See also Robert P. George, *In Defense of Natural Law* (Oxford: Oxford University Press, 1999).

Interpretation

interpretation of legal texts includes practical reasoning about the grounds for human flourishing. Heidi Hurd draws this connection by arguing that theorists who embrace moral realism and the connection between law and morality should embrace a fundamental change in legal interpretation. Claiming that law has authoritative status only to the extent that law is "a source of education about antecedently existing moral obligations" and "its ability to inspire insight into genuine truths," Hurd urges theorists to reject a communication model of legal authority and its attendant theories of interpretation and instead to focus on the ways in which legal texts can foster the discernment of moral truths.[11]

Lloyd Weinreb's classical understanding of natural law as *nomos* relates to legal interpretation in a different manner. Weinreb argues that morality is a fact of the social world, but morality does not provide specific answers to legal or moral questions.[12] Natural law is not the guarantor of correct moral and legal judgment, Weinreb explains; rather, it is the ground from which moral and legal judgment issues and against which such judgment is assessed. Seemingly irreconcilable disputes about how to balance liberty and equality demonstrate that natural law does not succeed as a hermeneutical method, but they do evidence the deep *nomos* of communal life that enables us to attribute responsibility and desert in the course of legal interpretation.[13]

We may conclude that the natural law tradition, even in its contemporary manifestations, is not primarily concerned with interpretive practice as much as with establishing some manner of ontological claim. Natural law theorists inquire into a preinterpretive reality, although their work might hold significant implications for theories of legal interpretation. If nothing else, interpretation is a pressing question in legal theory precisely because the vast majority of legal theorists have rejected natural law foundations and adopted some version of legal positivism, in which law is a textual communication that must be interpreted. We now turn to theories that begin with the premise that law is embodied in texts to be interpreted, rather than in the ontology of social life or in the power of human reason.

---

[11] Heidi Hurd, "Interpreting Authorities," *Law and Interpretation: Essays in Legal Philosophy* 405–32, Andrei Marmor, ed. (Oxford: Clarendon Press, 1995) 432; Heidi Hurd, "Sovereignty in Silence," *Yale Law Journal* 99 (1990) 945–1028. Hurd suggests that the "claim that interpretation necessarily aims to recapture authorial intentions is simply an artificial limitation on the meaning of the term 'interpretation,' and that a more capacious sense of interpretation as recuperating the moral purpose of legislation would provide more guidance than theories built on a notion of law as the communication of a rule." Ibid., 1027.

[12] Lloyd Weinreb, "The Moral Point of View," *Natural Law, Liberalism, and Morality: Contemporary Essays* 195–212, Robert P. George, ed. (Oxford: Oxford University Press, 1996) 208–9: "Natural law doesn't provide moral truths, it just rebuts skepticism and existentialism."

[13] Lloyd L. Weinreb, *Natural Law and Justice* (Cambridge, MA: Harvard University Press, 1987) 224–66. Weinreb argues that particularly vexing legal problems – such as affirmative action – are amenable to more satisfactory resolution if we accept his natural law account, Lloyd L. Weinreb, *Oedipus at Fenway Park: What Rights Are and Why There Are Any* (Cambridge, MA: Harvard University Press, 1998), and so his work is expressly intended to assist with difficult interpretive problems in law.

Analytical Legal Positivism and Linguistic Philosophy

H. L. A. Hart famously secured the standing of legal positivism when many theorists concluded that he overcame Lon Fuller's minimalist procedural approach to natural law theory.[14] It is well known that Hart's analytical legal positivism was premised on a position quite close to the linguistic philosophy of the later Wittgenstein, developed in the course of reworking Austin's legal positivism.[15] One might question Hart's confidence in being able to accomplish this task,[16] but his efforts have had enormous influence. Stated succinctly, Hart assumed that language has core meanings that can be applied to situations without difficulty or need for active efforts of interpretation, but in difficult cases on the fringe the meaning of a governing phrase must be interpreted and, after a point, simply would be exhausted.[17] This forms the basis of

---

[14] H. L. A. Hart, "Positivism and the Separation of Law and Morals," *Harvard Law Review* 71 (1958): 593–629; Lon L. Fuller, "Positivism and Fidelity to Law – A Reply to Professor Hart," *Harvard Law Review* 71 (1958) 630–72.

[15]

> There are obvious parallels between Hart's approach and that of Wittgenstein: in their discussions of philosophy as a type of therapy, their attempts to avoid metaphysical questions and explanation, and their emphasis on defeasibility as an important, if not central, aspect of concepts. As an historical matter, however, Hart's approach probably derives from J. L. Austin and the advocates of "ordinary language philosophy" at Oxford. The similarities between Hart's work and Wittgenstein's ideas may be explained by the influence of Friedrich Waisman on Hart (as well as by a convergence of ideas between Austin and Wittgenstein).

> Brian Bix, "Questions in Legal Interpretation," *Law and Interpretation: Essays in Legal Philosophy* 137–54, Andrei Marmor, ed. (Oxford: Clarendon Press, 1995) 138. Andrei Marmor draws a tighter link between Hart and Wittgenstein:

> > I would suggest that as someone who has learnt from (the later) Wittgenstein, Hart would have avoided any attempt to construct what is usually called a *theory* of meaning for a natural language.... Hart seems to share Wittgenstein's view that an adequate account of meaning and language must not obscure the fact that the meaning of the words we use is completely overt and manifest in their use.

> Andrei Marmor, *Interpretation and Legal Theory* (Portland, OR: Hart Publishing, 2nd rev. ed. 2005) 101.

[16] One commentator notes that Hart often writes as if he simply is applying the unproblematic tenets of modern linguistic philosophy to the study of law without acknowledging that all "the most interesting products of linguistic philosophy, and philosophy of language in general, are extremely controversial. It takes careful argument to distinguish between insights and misconceptions, and it is controversial whether jurisprudence has been advanced by any of Hart's claims about language." Timothy A. O. Endicott, "Law and Language," *The Oxford Handbook of Jurisprudence and Philosophy of Law* 935–68, Jules Coleman and Scott Shapiro, eds. (Oxford: Oxford University Press, 2002) 966.

[17] Brian Bix reports that Hart expressed in a letter to him that he intended his discussion of the open texture of language, and its resulting "partial indeterminacy," to be a general description of language rather than a theory that pertained only to legal regulation. Brian Bix, *Law, Language, and Legal Determinacy* (Oxford: Clarendon Press, 1993) 24, n. 79. Bix provides a helpful summary of Hart's position in the first chapter of this work, entitled "H. L. A. Hart and the "Open Texture" of Language." Ibid., 1–28.

Interpretation

347

Hart's famous distinction between core and penumbra, as explored in his celebrated discussion of the hypothetical ordinance forbidding vehicles in the park.

Hart sharpened his analysis by responding to Dworkin's interpretive critique of analytical legal positivism in his posthumous postscript to *The Concept of Law*. Hart argues that he does not promote a reductionist plain-meaning approach to language, and he does not ignore the role that principles play in judicial interpretation.[18] Instead, he argues that Dworkin's grand interpretive theory that there is always a "right answer" is counter factual. Existing legal systems exhibit a pattern within the community of socially recognized rules that are neither self-executing nor can they definitively address all cases within their purview.[19] Hart reaffirms his central argument that the law can run out,[20] but he agrees that the judge is not without constraint of any kind when she fills the gap.[21] He argues against Dworkin's position by insisting that the judge's selection between competing principles is the moment when the judge creates the law of the case, and that Dworkin's judge Hercules could discover a definitive correct answer to resolve hard cases only in the impossible circumstance that "for all such cases there was always to be found in the existing law some unique set of higher-order principles assigning relative weights or priorities to such competing lower-order principles, would the moment for judicial law-making be not merely deferred but eliminated."[22]

Brian Bix assesses Hart's approach to language in light of the need for legal determinacy, concluding that a legal system cannot simply follow the interpretation of legal texts because other values are always implicated in legal decisions.[23] Law is a normative discourse, Bix emphasizes, and so legal meaning cannot simply follow the interpretation of the linguistic meaning of legal texts. For example, courts are empowered to determine when it is appropriate to go beyond the legislature's intent, which is just to say that legal norms sometimes override what might be the accepted linguistic meaning of legal rules.[24] Bix contends that Hart is perhaps best read as

---

[18] H. L. A. Hart, *The Concept of Law*, Penelope A. Bulloch and Joseph Raz, eds. (Oxford: Clarendon Press, 2nd ed., 1994) 248.

[19] Ibid., 267.

[20] Ibid., 252.

[21] Ibid., 273–4. In this way, Hart began to frame a tentative answer to earlier critics who found his analysis frustratingly vague on the question of whether the judge was constrained by techniques of legal reasoning – which calls into question whether the judge is really unconstrained by law in developing her response to the case – or whether the judge was radically free to decide on the result in the case – which calls into question whether this process is really rational rather than just an assertion of authority. See, for example, Michael Martin, *The Legal Philosophy of H. L. A. Hart* (Philadelphia: Temple University Press, 1987) 49–77.

[22] Hart, *The Concept of Law*, 275.

[23] Bix writes: "The role of language in 'easy cases' is thus at best one factor among many, for the clarity of a legal rule's application to some case *as a matter of language* is neither sufficient nor necessary for the case to be an easy one." Bix, *Law, Language, and Legal Determinacy*, 181.

[24] Ibid., 178–9.

promoting a practice-based theory of law that eschews metaphysical debates about the nature of constructs such as "legislative intent" in favor of examining how claims about legislative intent are used in legal discourse.[25]

Legal positivists following Hart generally remain agnostic about theoretical debates concerning the genuine goal of interpretation, focusing instead on how the law works in practice. Adopting the general perspective of ordinary language philosophy as developed in his day, Hart did not claim to develop or follow a theory of legal language; rather, he sought to understand how law operated given what he assumed were the widely understood limitations of language. His answer, that judges find meanings in texts but also engage in creative but constrained gap filling to effectuate the implications of legal texts for individual cases, might appear undertheorized, but a strong argument may be made that theory will not resolve the matter definitively and that legal theorists are best counseled to direct their attention elsewhere.[26]

Andrei Marmor has perhaps done more than any other analytical philosopher to develop a robust philosophy of legal interpretation. Marmor takes seriously Ronald Dworkin's challenge to positivism rooted in a theory of law as interpretation, and he acknowledges that interpretation "is part and parcel of the legal *practice*" and so it is necessary for legal philosophers to develop "a philosophical account of what it is to interpret the law."[27] Marmor, however, makes clear that interpretation is occasioned only by hard cases, when following the rule manifest in the text becomes problematic for some reason.[28] When confronted with a hard case, Marmor rejects the notion that judges always should follow a particular interpretive theory such as discerning and then following the drafters' original intent; rather, judges should carefully work within the scope of their comparative institutional competence.[29]

Analytical legal positivists caution against the urge to theorize interpretive practices in law rather than tending to those practices. Nevertheless, intense theoretical battles have been waged in recent decades to establish the proper interpretative methodology. We turn now to consider the competing theories that work from the assumption that legal texts are communicating a meaning that must be retrieved by the interpreter.

---

[25] Bix, "Questions in Legal Interpretation," 140–2.

[26] Joseph Raz has maintained Hart's distinction between applying a legal rule and creatively filling the gaps in the law, with the latter not reducible to a methodology of good judgment. Joseph Raz, "Why Interpret?," *Ratio Juris* 9 (1996) 349–63.

[27] Marmor, *Interpretation and Legal Theory*, 45.

[28] Ibid., 118. Thus, judges can follow the legal rules embedded in statutes with no need to engage in a complex interpretive strategy such as intentionalism. Ibid., 121.

[29] See ibid., 119–30 (Chapter 8: Legislative Intent and the Authority of Law) and 141–69 (Chapter 9: Constitutional Interpretation).

Interpretation

Law as Communication: Originalism, Intentionalism, and Textualism

Against Hart's relative agnosticism, many theorists have debated the proper manner of interpreting legal texts in the shadow of a simple proposition: that legal texts are communicative events that should be interpreted in light of this function by uncovering a meaning that exists prior to the interpretation. There are two primary variations on this theme that often generally are characterized as "originalism." First, some theorists argue that the legal rule should be regarded as a communication by its drafters, in which case the text means precisely what its drafters intended to communicate. Aptly characterized as "intentionalism," this theory claims the virtue of identifying a univocal meaning for all legal rules, even if that meaning is not always easy to determine. In the face of substantial theoretical and practical critiques, many originalists have more recently rejected the project of uncovering the subjective intentions of the drafters and instead argue that the meaning of a legal text just is the publicly understood meaning of the text at the time of its adoption. This move from intentionalism to "textualism"[30] attempts to shore up the ability of legal interpretation to be determinate. Although neither approach lives up to its promise of determinacy when subjected to the demands of practice, both have been highly influential and continue to shape the judicial discourse about interpretation.

A. *Intentionalism*

Francis Lieber was one of the most important hermeneutical theorists in America during the nineteenth century. His text, *Legal and Political Hermeneutics*, brought German philosophy to bear on developing legal practices in the new constitutional republic.[31] Even if he now is "famous for being forgotten,"[32] Lieber's translation of the romantic tradition of German hermeneutics to the American setting provided the intellectual basis for the intentionalist approach to interpretation. Lieber sought to preserve the rule of law by identifying and clarifying the "immutable principles and fixed rules for interpreting and construing" the law.[33]

---

[30] The term "textualism" is sometimes used to refer to a theory that texts can have a "plain meaning" that is understood by the reader without need for extratextual resources. I will not discuss this "plain meaning" fantasy of avoiding the need for interpretation; although it lives on in legal dictum, it is recognized as fantasy by virtually all sophisticated lawyers and theorists.

[31] Francis Lieber, *Legal and Political Hermeneutics, Or, Principles of Interpretation and Construction in Law and Politics with Remarks on Precedents and Authorities* (Boston: Charles C. Little and James Brown, enlarged ed., 1839) (Buffalo, NY: William S. Hein & Co., 1970 reprint).

[32] Michael Herz, "Rediscovering Francis Lieber: An Afterword and Introduction," *Cardozo Law Review* 16 (1995) 2107–33, 2107. Herz introduces an excellent symposium issue dedicated to exploring the relevance of Lieber's book for contemporary debates: "Symposium on Legal and Political Hermeneutics," *Cardozo Law Review* 16 (1995) 2107–351.

[33] Lieber, *Legal and Political Hermeneutics*, viii.

Lieber begins with the observation that words convey the thoughts of other persons who otherwise are inaccessible to us and that the "true sense" of words is "the sense which their author intended to convey."[34] With the exception of the self-contained symbolic realm of mathematics, language always requires interpretation to discern correctly the author's intention.[35] A strictly literal reading of the words of the text can be misleading because it threatens to wrench them from the sense intended by the author.[36] Thus, Lieber viewed intentionalism as a bulwark against a crude "plain meaning" approach to interpretation.

Even after being interpreted properly, though, Lieber acknowledges that the text might be subject to overriding considerations. He uses the term "construction" to refer to the activity of applying the intended meaning to the case at hand by means of norms and principles that are not specified by the specific meaning of the text.[37] The art of hermeneutics requires both interpretation and construction.[38] Although he recognizes that construction is dangerous because it goes beyond the univocal meaning of the text,[39] Lieber insists that the dynamic character of society makes it undesirable to have the author's intended meaning govern unforeseen situations, "as if the human mind could be permanently fettered by laws of by-gone generations."[40] Construction is inevitable in a legal system, but Lieber advocates a restrained approach by judges to preserve the continuity provided by the abiding singular meaning of the text.[41]

As Lieber was articulating the philosophical bases for intentionalism, his honesty and attention to pragmatic considerations simultaneously undermined its utility. If construction is a necessary element of legal practice, then the intended meaning of the text can provide only a veneer of determinacy and objectivity. Deciding when to construe a legal text in a manner that departs from its intended meaning is not something that is controlled by the text itself, and so Lieber recognizes that every construction has the potential to undermine the rule of law. Lieber recognized that no rule could prevent this excess and so his pragmatic response was simply to caution interpreters.

---

[34] Ibid., 23. Thus, there can be only one true meaning of a text – that intended by the author – and to speak of a sentence having two meanings "amounts to absurdity." Ibid., 86.

[35] Ibid., 39–40.

[36] Ibid., 66–8. Lieber argues that an interpreter must use good faith in searching for the intended meaning, and that interpretations generally should coincide with common sense on the assumption that this reflects the intent. Ibid., 93–9. Or, by way of summary, "In doubtful cases, therefore, we take the customary signification, rather than the grammatical or classical; the technical rather than the etymological. That which is probable, fair, and customary, is preferable to the improbable, unfair and unusual." Ibid., 120.

[37] Ibid., 56.

[38] Ibid., 64.

[39] Ibid.

[40] Ibid., 135.

[41] Ibid., 121–2, 136.

Interpretation

Lieber's theoretical groundwork provided the vocabulary that we continue to use in theoretical discussion. In a number of provocative books, Raoul Berger famously argued that the intentions held by the constitutional framers were historical facts that established the meaning of the Constitution. Two successive books in the 1970s seemingly established that his methodology rose above politics by adhering to the true meaning of the Constitution. Arguing against the Nixon administration's efforts to establish a broad-based "executive privilege" that was not grounded in the Constitution, Berger's approach was cheered by the American left.[42] A few years later when he argued that much of the Warren Court's jurisprudence was illegitimate in light of the intended meaning of the Fourteenth Amendment, Berger was regarded as a spokesperson for the American right.[43]

Berger's work became the basis for a broad-based effort by conservative politicians, judges, and scholars to turn back the perceived liberal activism of the Warren and Burger courts and to thwart what they perceived as the antidemocratic practice of amending the Constitution by means of judicial review.[44] The idea, however, that judicial practice could be restrained effectively by requiring recourse to the drafters' intentions was subjected to withering theoretical and practical critiques that appeared to relegate intentionalism to the dustbin of legal theory.[45] What could it possibly mean to determine the "intended" meaning of a document written by a group of people 200 years earlier and then effectuated by votes in various states and subsequently amended after a wrenching civil war? Some theorists still insist that the true meaning of a text just is the meaning intended by its author, but this approach no longer has substantial influence.

---

[42] Raoul Berger, *Executive Privilege: A Constitutional Myth* (Cambridge, MA: Harvard University Press, 1974).

[43] Raoul Berger, *Government by Judiciary: The Transformation of the Fourteenth Amendment* (Cambridge, MA: Harvard University Press, 1977).

[44] Edwin Meese III, "The Supreme Court of the United States: Bulwark of a Limited Constitution," *South Texas Law Review* 27 (1986) 455–66 (articulating the policy reasons for the adherence to original intent as part of President Reagan's conservative approach to government). Key political statements regarding the Reagan administration's originalist theories and competing speeches by several judges are included in *Originalism: A Quarter-Century of Debate*, Stephen G. Calabresi and Antonin Scalia, eds. (Washington, DC: Regnery Publishing, Inc., 2007) 47–112.

[45] See Paul Brest, "The Misconceived Quest for the Original Understanding," *Boston University Law Review* 60 (1980) 204–38 (describing the multiple difficulties in determining the drafters' intentions); Ronald Dworkin, "The Forum of Principle," *New York University Law Review* 56 (1981) 469–518 (arguing that judges are political actors even when purporting to locate original intent); Mark V. Tushnet, "Following the Rules Laid Down: A Critique of Interpretivism and Neutral Principles," *Harvard Law Review* 96 (1983) 781–827 (arguing that originalism is rendered incoherent by its own premises); H. Jefferson Powell, "The Original Understanding of Original Intent," *Harvard Law Review* 98 (1984) 885–948 (arguing that an originalist theory was self-defeating because the drafters did not endorse originalism); Paul Finkelman, "The Constitution and the Intentions of the Framers: The Limits of Historical Analysis," *University of Pittsburgh Law Review* 50 (1989) 349–98 (arguing that historical inquiry cannot resolve how we should rule ourselves).

B. *Textualism*

More recently, a "new originalism" has spread across the legal academy like a prairie fire. Interestingly, the modern impetus for (which is not to say the leading light of) this theoretical movement is a sitting judge, albeit a former law professor. Supreme Court Associate Justice Antonin Scalia has argued that legal texts – statutes and constitutions alike – should not be interpreted according to the presumed intentions of the drafters, but rather in accordance with how the text would have been understood at the time of its enactment.[46] The goal of this strategy is to avoid the hopeless search for the subjectively held intentions of the drafters in favor of specifying the objective fact of how ordinary readers would have understood the text at the time it was enacted.

Political scientist Keith Whittington provided one of the first detailed defenses of textualist "new originalism" as an approach to constitutional meaning.[47] Whittington argues that modern theorists have erred by trying to reduce all of Constitutional practice to interpretation, rather than recognizing that interpretation is a judicial function that is only one part of constitutional rule. In Whittington's terminology, constitutional interpretation is the search for the meaning in the text, whereas constitutional construction is a creative political act that necessarily goes beyond the meaning of the text.[48] Judges are empowered to interpret the text according to the meaning that it held at the time of enactment, but only political actors (such as administrative agencies or the legislature) are empowered to construe the Constitution to deal with gaps or to elaborate its meaning.[49] He grounds this approach in

---

[46] Justice Scalia criticizes those who would treat statutes differently from the Constitution, stating: "What I look for in the Constitution is precisely what I look for in a statute: the original meaning of the text, not what the original draftsmen intended." Antonin Scalia, "Common Law Courts in a Civil Law System: The Role of the United States Federal Courts in Interpreting the Constitution and Laws," *A Matter of Interpretation: Federal Courts and the Law* 3–47, Amy Gutman, ed. (Princeton, NJ: Princeton University Press, 1997) 38.

[47] Keith E. Whittington, *Constitutional Interpretation: Textual Meaning, Original Intent, and Judicial Review* (Lawrence, KS: University Press of Kansas, 1999); Keith E. Whittington, "The New Originalism," *Georgetown Journal of Law and Public Policy* 2 (2004) 599–613.

[48] Whittington (*Constitutional Interpretation*, 5) explains:

> As the name suggests, constitutional interpretation is a fairly familiar process of discovering the meaning of the constitutional text. The results of this process are recognizable as constitutional law, capable of being expounded and applied by the courts. Though still concerned with the meaning of the text, constitutional construction cannot claim merely to discover a preexisting, if deeply hidden, meaning within the founding document. It employs the "imaginative vision" of politics rather than the "discerning wit" of judicial judgment. Construction is essentially creative, though the foundations for the ultimate structure are taken as given. The text is not discarded but brought into being.

[49] Ibid., 9. On the role of democratically responsive actors to engage in constitutional construction, see Keith E. Whittington, *Constitutional Construction: Divided Powers and Constitutional Meaning* (Cambridge, MA: Harvard University Press, 1999).

Interpretation 353

democratic legitimacy: interpretation is the discovery of what past democratic activities mean, whereas construction is a democratically sanctioned activity that accords with but extends beyond the meaning of the constitutional text.[50]

Textualism appears to offer a reasonable means of addressing the most vexing issues in constitutional theory. There is no counter majoritarian difficulty because judges legitimately play a vital role by striking down unconstitutional statutes and regulations according to objective criteria. There is no fear of tyrannical judges because they are constrained to interpret the constitutional text in accordance with its original public meaning and are not permitted to amend the meaning through flexible interpretive standards.[51] The theory does not rest on an implausible view of mechanical jurisprudence, inasmuch as Whittington agrees that discovering the original meaning requires an artful practice that will be filled with controversy and dissent.[52] The theory is not guilty of bootstrapping because it acknowledges that originalism is not an interpretation of the original public meaning of the Constitution but rather is a construction of American constitutionalism grounded in political theory and prudential reasoning.[53] Finally, the theory avoids allegations of consigning politics to the "dead hand" of previous generations because judicial interpretation respects democratic choices and is supplemented by constitutional construction by political actors to address pressing issues not resolved by interpretation.[54]

The allure of the "new originalism" has been strong.[55] Perhaps the most interesting development has been Jack Balkin's announcement that he adheres to new originalism, that originalism does not conflict with the notion of a living constitution, and that *Roe v. Wade* is defensible on originalist grounds; all this despite his standing as a leading liberal constitutional theorist who cut his scholarly teeth writing about semiotics and deconstruction.[56] Balkin argues that originalists (often unwittingly)

---

[50] Whittington, *Constitutional Interpretation*, 110–59 (Chapter 5: Popular Sovereignty and Originalism).

[51] "The definition of a single interpretive method ... not only allows the various participants in the dialogue to speak intelligibly to one another but also provides the framework for judicial accountability. Recognized interpretive standards allow criticism of the Court." Ibid., 14.

[52] Ibid., 4, 174–5.

[53] Ibid., 15.

[54] Ibid., 204–8. Whittington uses Lieber's vocabulary of "interpretation" and "construction," but he emphasizes that he rejects Lieber's willingness to permit courts to engage in the full range of constitutional rule. Ibid., 221, n. 3. The linchpin of his theory is that courts may not engage in constitutional construction under the guise of interpreting the constitution. Ibid., 12.

[55] The growing literature includes "Symposium," *George Washington Law Review* 66 (1998) 1081–1394; Randy Barnett, *Restoring the Lost Constitution: The Presumption of Liberty* (Princeton, NJ: Princeton University Press, 2004); John O. McGinnis and Michael B. Rappaport, "A Pragmatic Defense of Originalism," *Northwestern University Law Review* 101 (2007) 383–97; and Lawrence B. Solum, "Semantic Originalism" (May 28, 2008) available at SSRN: http://ssrn.com/abstract=1120244.

[56] See Jack M. Balkin, "Abortion and Original Meaning," *Constitutional Commentary* 24 (2007) 291–352 ("Abortion") and Jack M. Balkin, "Original Meaning and Constitutional Redemption," *Constitutional Commentary* 24 (2007) 427–532 ("Constitutional Redemption").

confuse the original meaning of the text with a supposition of how the text was expected to be applied; in effect, he indicts their tendency to slip from textualism to intentionalism.[57] If theorists resolutely attend to the original meaning of the constitutional text at the time of its enactment, Balkin insists, they will find that original meaning of originalism "is actually a form of living constitutionalism."[58] This is true because the Constitution is comprised of both rules and principles, and the original meaning of a principle such as "equal protection of the laws" is capacious enough to permit judicial elaboration in accordance with changing social contexts as long as we do not limit the principle by construing it in terms of how the drafters anticipated that it would be applied in the future.[59]

Balkin distinguishes the original meaning of the text from its application to the case at hand, which appears to parallel Whittington's distinction between interpretation and construction. Balkin, however, argues that judges should engage in constitutional construction in the course of applying textual principles to new situations, whereas Whittington argues that constitutional construction is reserved to the democratic branches of government. Whether the text embodies a clear principle with uncertain application (underdetermined meaning) or an unclear principle (vagueness), Whittington argues that when judicial interpretation fails to answer the question before the court it should reveal as much constitutional meaning as exists and then defer to political construction. Both claim the mantel of a textualist approach to originalism, but a huge gulf remains between Balkin's effort to demonstrate the constitutional legitimacy of *Roe v. Wade* under the original understanding of principles announced by the Privileges and Immunities clause and the Equal

---

[57] Balkin, "Abortion," 292–3. Balkin adopts the line of argument that Ronald Dworkin has long pressed against originalists by accusing them of slipping from "semantic originalism" to "expected application originalism." See Ronald Dworkin, "Comment," in *A Matter of Interpretation: Federal Courts and the Law* 115–27, Amy Gutman, ed. (Princeton, NJ: Princeton University Press, 1997); Ronald Dworkin, *Justice in Robes* (Cambridge, MA: Harvard University Press, 2006) 117–39. In fact, we can assume that virtually all theorists would ostensibly accept Balkin's position (Marmor, *Interpretation and Legal Theory*, 155–60), but Balkin renews Dworkin's point that originalists tend to slip into an illegitimate mode of considering how the drafters would wish their words to be applied.

[58] Balkin, "Constitutional Redemption," 449.

[59] This same distinction might be characterized with Gottlob Frege's terminology of sense and reference. Christopher R. Green, "Originalism and the Sense-Reference Distinction," *St. Louis University Law Journal* 50 (2006) 555–627. "The Justices' failures to appreciate the difference between the meaning historically *expressed* by constitutional language, on the one hand, and the tangible outcomes *accomplished* by that language, on the other hand, lead to a frustrating dynamic.... I will here defend an answer based on Frege's sense-reference distinction: the *sense* of a constitutional expression is fixed at the time of the framing, but the *reference* is not, because it depends on the facts about the world, which can change." Ibid., 559–60. In turn, this distinction is similar to John Stuart Mill's terminology of connotation and denotation, and Rudolph Carnap's terminology of intensions and extensions. Ibid., 561.

Interpretation

Protection clause and Whittington's insistence that when interpretations of the text do not provide an answer the matter must be left to politics.[60]

The underlying premise of the diverse perspectives discussed previously, including Marmor's elaboration of a legal hermeneutics congenial to analytical legal positivism, is the idea that legal interpretation is founded on communication in a text that precedes the interpretation. This Anglo-American tradition in the philosophy of language has been challenged by contemporary European philosophers working in philosophical hermeneutics, semiotics, and deconstruction, to which we now turn.

The Hermeneutical Turn in Law and Philosophy

Francis Lieber translated nineteenth-century German hermeneutical philosophy to the developing American legal culture, but contemporary hermeneutics has changed substantially since his day.[61] In his early lectures, Martin Heidegger's creative reading of Aristotle as providing a "hermeneutics of facticity" set the stage for the development of a philosophical hermeneutics.[62] Philosophical hermeneutics breaks with parochial attention to interpretation within particular disciplines and investigates the hermeneutical mode of being that girds all inquiry and understanding as an active involvement in the world rather than a "presuppositionless apprehending of something presented to" a self-contained subject as an object.[63] Put simply, Heidegger

[60] The existence of this gulf and the blurred lines that demarcate it are revealed in two critiques of Balkin's position. Mitchell Berman challenges Balkin from a nonoriginalist position, asking why constitutional principles should be interpreted in accordance with the original meaning of the principle embedded in the text rather than in accordance with the principles as understood in contemporary society, but he interprets Balkin's reply as agreeing that constitutional principles are a matter of contemporary elaboration in a manner that the text can bear. Mitchell N. Berman, "Originalism and its Discontents (Plus a Thought or Two About Abortion)," *Constitutional Commentary* 24 (2007) 383–404, 392–3, 402. On the other hand, Randy Barnett challenges Balkin from an originalist position by cautioning him against finding principles in the text, constructing constitutional doctrine on the basis of those principles, and then applying the doctrine and principles in contemporary contexts without returning to the text as the ultimate arbiter: "It is the text, properly interpreted and specified in light of its underlying principles, *not the underlying principles themselves*, that are to be applied to changing facts and circumstances by means of constitutional doctrines." Randy E. Barnett, "Underlying Principles," *Constitutional Commentary* 24 (2007) 405–16, 413. Nevertheless, Barnett concludes that Balkin has embraced the originalist method and is concerned only with those who might misread him as adopting a position that authorizes the contemporary elaboration of constitutional principles. Ibid., 416.

[61] Francis J. Mootz III, "The New Legal Hermeneutics," *Vanderbilt Law Review* 47 (1994) 115–43 (reviewing *Legal Hermeneutics: History, Theory, and Practice*, Gregory Leyh, ed. (Berkeley, CA: University of California Press, 1992).

[62] Martin Heidegger, *Phenomenological Interpretations of Aristotle: Initiation into Phenomenological Research*, Richard Rojcewicz, trans. (Bloomington, IN: Indiana University Press, 2001); Martin Heidegger, *Ontology: The Hermeneutics of Facticity* (Bloomington, IN: Indiana University Press, 1999).

[63] Martin Heidegger, *Being and Time*, John Macquarrie and Edward Robinson, trans. (New York: Harper & Row, 1962) 192.

rejects that idea that a reader confronts a text like a freestanding object that has an objective meaning prior to the interpretive event. Heidegger's impact on the philosophy of interpretation is most evident in the diverse (and somewhat contesting) philosophical projects undertaken by Hans-Georg Gadamer, Paul Ricoeur, and Jacques Derrida.[64]

Gadamer contends that interpretation is a way of being rather than a conscious activity taken up when a text proves to be vague or ambiguous, concluding that "understanding is always interpretation."[65] He defines interpretation as a (never complete) fusing of the horizons of the text and reader, with the former having an effective history constituted by past interpretations and the latter having a prejudiced forestructure of meaning that confronts the text in the form of a question. From this, Gadamer concludes that understanding occurs only through application, that there is no pregiven meaning of the text that can be understood in the abstract and then later applied to a given situation.[66] Legal hermeneutics is exemplary in this regard because a "law does not exist in order to be understood historically, but to be concretized in its legal validity by being interpreted,"[67] with the result "that discovering the meaning of a legal text and discovering how to apply it in a particular legal instance are not two separate actions, but one unitary process."[68] Gadamer responds to the persistent demand that theorists provide a scientific account of how there can be objective meaning by arguing that legal interpretation exemplifies why this fantasy can never be fulfilled.[69]

---

[64] I shall concentrate on Gadamer's influence due to space constraints, and in recognition that deconstructive approaches differentiate themselves precisely by seeking to problematize the question of interpretation rather than seeking to develop a different understanding of interpretation.

[65] Hans-Georg Gadamer, *Truth and Method*. Joel Weinshiemer and Donald G. Marshall, trans. (New York: Continuum, 2nd rev. ed. 1989) 307. Gadamer continues:

> Our consideration of the significance of tradition in historical consciousness started from Heidegger's analysis of the hermeneutics of facticity and sought to apply it to a hermeneutics of the human sciences. We showed that understanding is not a method which the inquiring consciousness applies to an object it chooses and so turns it into objective knowledge; rather, being situated within an event of tradition, a process of handing down, is a prior condition of understanding. *Understanding proves to be an event*, and the task of hermeneutics, seen philosophically, consists in asking what kind of understanding, what kind of science it is, that is itself advanced by historical change.

[66] Ibid., 309.

[66] Ibid., 307–11.

[67] Ibid., 309.

[68] Ibid., 310.

[69] In an encyclopedia entry on "Interpretation," Gadamer condenses his extended argument in *Truth and Method*, ibid.,324–41, regarding the exemplary status of legal hermeneutics. Gadamer writes:

> In light of this issue, the venerable tradition of juristic hermeneutics attains a new life and relevance. Within the dogmatics of modern law this tradition could only play a troubling role, seeming like a never completely avoidable stain on a self-fulfilling dogmatics. Nevertheless, one should make no mistake: jurisprudence is a normative discipline and performs the necessary

Interpretation

Ronald Dworkin generally is regarded as a hermeneutical thinker in this vein, and in *Law's Empire* he cites Gadamer approvingly.[70] In fact, though, Dworkin does not embrace the ontological claims girding philosophical hermeneutics; rather, he proposes an interpretive ethic that he regards as politically superior to the rule-focused practice described by legal positivists.[71] Dworkin has been a powerful force in jurisprudence because he charts a distinctive course between the semantic sterility of much of legal positivism and the unpersuasive claims of natural law theorists, arguing that judges are engaged in an interpretive activity that continually refines legal principles in the context of individual cases by ensuring that their decisions fit within the existing legal framework and reach morally correct results. Toward this end, Dworkin expertly deconstructs the analytical distinction between simply applying the law and creatively filling the gaps, arguing that judges should expressly adopt an interpretive ethic that identifies general principles within the legal corpus into which their decision must fit, and then works to ensure that the law has normative

> dogmatic function of supplementing the law. As such, it performs an indispensable task, because it bridges the unavoidable gap between the universality of settled law and the concreteness of the individual case. In this regard, we should remember that Aristotle in his *Nicomachean Ethics* already staked out the hermeneutical space within legal doctrine for this process with his discussion of the problem of natural law and the concept of *epieikeia* [decency; *epieikes*, decent people]. Also, if we think back on the history of this concept, we find that the problem of an understanding exegesis [*verstehen Auslegung*] of the law is indissolubly linked with application.

> Hans-Georg Gadamer, "Classical and Philosophical Hermeneutics," *The Gadamer Reader: A Bouquet of the Later Writings* 44–71, Richard E. Palmer, trans. and ed. (Evanston, IL: Northwestern University Press, 2007) 59–60. Gadamer emphasizes that Heidegger changed the intellectual landscape fundamentally. The efforts by Emilio Betti and others to preserve the romantic and idealist tendencies of nineteenth-century hermeneutical philosophy could not answer the essential questions raised by philosophical hermeneutics.

>> For instance, the basically psychological underpinnings of hermeneutics during the period of German idealism proved to be dubious. Is the meaning of a text really exhausted by arriving at the meaning that was psychologically "intended" by the author, the *mens auctoris* [mind of the author]? Is understanding to be conceived of as nothing more than the reproduction of the author's original production? It is quite clear that this view cannot hold true in the case of juridical hermeneutics, which manifestly exercises a creative legal function.

> Ibid., 57.

[70] Ronald Dworkin, *Law's Empire* (Cambridge, MA: Harvard University Press, 1986) 55, 62.

[71] In one of his important early essays on this topic, Dworkin argued that judges "develop a particular approach to legal interpretation by forming and refining a political theory sensitive to those issues on which interpretation in particular cases will depend; and they call this their legal philosophy. Any judge's opinion about the best interpretation will therefore be the consequence of beliefs other judges need not share." Ronald Dworkin, "Law as Interpretation," *Critical Inquiry* 9 (1982) 179–200, 196. Most recently, Dworkin describes his interpretive approach in terms of a constellation of choices regarding semantics, jurisprudence, doctrine, and adjudication. Dworkin, *Justice in Robes*, 1–35. Dworkin admits that he cannot compel other theorists to adopt his approach by appealing to a demonstrable constitutional method, ibid., 127, but he is unmindful of the degree to which he shares substantial ground with his positivist opponents in his understanding of interpretation as a matter of politics or style.

justification while maintaining institutional integrity. There are no "gaps" in this account, because Dworkin believes that judges are inevitably engaged in an interpretive, normative, and political undertaking such that the resolution of difficult cases is not a different kind of practice.

Although appealing, in the end Dworkin's approach fails to realize the benefits claimed at the opposite ends of the spectrum that he bisects: his theories are a bit too grand to map onto the practice of law in any convincing manner, but at the same time his discussion of principle pales in comparison to the robust moral realism of natural law. Although Dworkin has identified good reason to reject both poles of the contemporary debate between positivists and natural law adherents, we might conclude that a more radical hermeneutical approach is required to secure his theoretical gains.[72] For example, Patrick Nerhot challenges the intellectualist assumption that legal interpretation is employed by a herculean judge drawing upon preexisting norms and a fixed conceptual structure, arguing instead that law is a rhetorical-hermeneutical activity all the way down.[73]

> What is it that is being interpreted in legal science? The idea currently accepted by legal practitioners interpreting the law is that interpretation relates to entities prior to all legal activity, which are imposed on all such practitioners: legal norms. These are posited as preconstrued, and antecedent to any research (whether for identifying or for interpreting the rule); the rule, "the norm," is the *starting-point* for thinking on what the law "says." The rule speaks to us; interpretation consists in understanding what it is saying to us. Contrary to this conception, we shall say that *the legal rule, far from being the starting-point, is a result; and specifically, that of the activities, in the broad sense, of the interpreter.*[74]

[72] Bernard S. Jackson, "Semiotics and the Problem of Interpretation," in *Law, Interpretation, and Reality: Essays in Epistemology, Hermeneutics, and Jurisprudence* 84–103, Patrick Nerhot, ed. (Dordrecht: Kluwer Academic Publishing, 1990) 84 (arguing for a semiotic correction of Dworkin's "rationalist model of interpretation").

[73] Nerhot writes:

> Theory sometimes loses sight of the banal fact that at the origin there is the social problem and not a normative category; in other words that legal principles are never static elements of a scholastically constructed edifice, but topics, selection criteria of the legal assessment. Through interpretation the principal emerges, with the special feature that legal hermeneutics has a practical purpose. Thus the anticipated representation of the result that the interpreter supposes to be legally relevant before asking any interpretive question at all delimits the scope and direction taken by the interpretive methods . . . Understanding of the rule develops in the hermeneutic circle as the relationship between the question asked and the solution pursued, and this circle, far from being closed on itself, is a *continuous creation* . . .

Nerhot, *Law, Writing, Meaning,* 41. He summarizes by emphasizing that "what we call 'the law' corresponds to the historical space where legal experience is developed and expresses those principles." Ibid., 42.

[74] Patrick Nerhot, "Interpretation in Legal Science: The Notion of Narrative Coherence," *Law, Interpretation, and Reality: Essays in Epistemology, Hermeneutics, and Jurisprudence* 193–225, Patrick Nerhot,

Interpretation   359

Legal practice is an argumentative and creative activity in which invention plays the primary role rather than discovery. Nerhot insists that law is interpretive, but we must understand this claim in a deep sense that all argumentation is interpretive.[75]

In my work I have tried to make good on the radical claims of philosophical hermeneutics for legal theory.[76] This is not to say that hermeneutical insights generate a unique interpretive method; in fact, just the opposite is true. Accepting the ontological claims that human understanding is interpretive and that interpretation never involves a freestanding object subjected to the analytical gaze of a disinterested interpreter holds significance primarily because it cautions against the theoretical urge to methodize legal practice. There is a positive lesson as well: An interpreter will approach a text differently if she takes to heart the lessons of philosophical hermeneutics. Rather than Dworkin's Hercules believing that he can discern the best means of advancing the law with coherence and integrity, Gadamer's Hermes is wary of being more than an imperfect messenger who must recognize the need to place his own presuppositions at risk in response to the legal tradition.

"Putting at risk" is the guiding normative implication of critical hermeneutics, providing an alternative account of integrity to which judges should aspire. Gadamer writes:

> Hermeneutic philosophy understands itself not as an absolute position but as a way of experience. It insists that there is no higher principle than holding oneself open in a conversation. But this means: Always recognize in advance the possible correctness, even the superiority of the conversation partner's position. Is this too little? Indeed, this seems to me to be the kind of integrity one can demand only of a professor of philosophy. And one should demand as much.[77]

Should we not demand such integrity from legal actors as well? The integrity called for is more than polite listening, but less than a virtuoso performance by the expert judge; it is a self-effacing response to the constantly renewed truth of tradition that contains the resources for critical insight.[78]

---

    ed. (Dordrecht: Kluwer Academic Publishers, 1990) 196. In contrast, even Dworkin's capacious constructivist view of legal principle appears to unfold against an abiding backdrop of morality.

[75] Ibid., 200–1.

[76] Francis J. Mootz III, *Rhetorical Knowledge in Legal Practice and Critical Legal Theory* (Tuscaloosa, AL: University of Alabama Press, 2006); Francis J. Mootz III, "A Future Foretold: Neo-Aristotelian Praise of Postmodern Legal Theory," *Brooklyn Law Review* 68 (2003) 683–719; Mootz, "The New Legal Hermeneutics"; Francis J. Mootz III, "The Ontological Basis of Legal Hermeneutics: A Proposed Model of Inquiry Based on the Work of Gadamer, Habermas, and Ricoeur," *Boston University Law Review* 68 (1988) 523–617.

[77] Hans-Georg Gadamer, "On the Origins of Philosophical Hermeneutics," *Philosophical Apprenticeships* 177–93, Robert K. Sullivan, trans. (Boston, MA: The MIT Press, 1985) 189.

[78] Although Gadamer casts interpretation as a dialogic fusion of horizons with a traditionary understanding, his philosophical approach provides a firm basis for understanding the inevitability and limits of critical thinking about the tradition if one engages in a hermeneutic dialogue.

The judicial virtues implied by the ontological claims of philosophical hermeneutics are not foreign to legal practice, but humility and "putting at risk" is rendered more difficult in the age of theory and judicial methodology. Although philosophical hermeneutics teaches that originalism is a false ideal, it recognizes the historicity of all understanding; although it rejects the subject-centered approach by Dworkin, it recognizes the ethical dimension of interpretation; and although it denies the timeless truths of natural law philosophy, it accepts the power of the experience of truth that exists beyond methodological understanding. Ironically, perhaps the closest affinity exists between analytical legal philosophy and philosophical hermeneutics, if we construe them as dividing the labor of legal scholarship between sociological description of practice and philosophical inquiry into the nature of that practice.

Interpretation in Specific Legal Contexts

My overview of the competing theories of interpretation has not attended sufficiently to the specific legal contexts in which the interpretation takes place. In this section I compare the private law task of interpreting a contract to the public law task of interpreting constitutions, statutes, and regulations, with the aim of confirming that interpretation is first and foremost a practice that is only later theorized.

Contract Law

When the object of interpretation is a memorial of a contractual agreement, the courts are concerned with adjudicating the rights and duties of the two parties to the contract. One of the guiding themes of contract law generally is the protection of reasonable expectations, and over time this value has been vindicated in connection with contract interpretation. Originally, courts adopted a subjective approach to interpretation and concluded that if the minds of the parties had not met there could be no agreement, as evidenced in the famous case of *Raffles v. Wichelhaus*.[79] This view of contract interpretation might be plausible with regard to face-to-face negotiations that are akin to a conversation, in which one understands the other party only if one understands what that person is intending to say. With an increasing

> The dialogical character of language . . . leaves behind it any starting point in the subjectivity of the subject, and especially in the meaning-directed intentions of the speaker. Genuinely speaking one's mind has little to do with a mere explication and assertion of our prejudices; rather, it risks our prejudices – it exposes oneself to one's own doubt as well as to the rejoinder of the other.
>
> Hans-Georg Gadamer, "Text and Interpretation," *Dialogue and Deconstruction: Gadamer-Derrida Encounter* 21–51, Diane P. Michelfelder and Richard E. Palmer, eds. (Albany, NY: SUNY Press, 1989) 26. See Francis J. Mootz III, "The Quest to Reprogram Cultural Software: A Hermeneutical Response to Jack Balkin's Theory of Ideology and Critique," *Chicago-Kent Law Review* 76 (2000) 945–89.

[79] 159 Eng. Rep. 375 (1864).

Interpretation

number of commercial deals concluded solely through written documentation, through intermediaries, and over a period of time, contract scholars argued that courts should enforce the "objective" meaning of the contract documents, which is to say that contracts should be enforced according to how a reasonable person would understand the documents.[80] This approach culminated in the first Restatement of Contracts declaring that the meaning of an integrated memorial of a contract might be something that neither of the parties intended nor understood.[81] When the document was not an integration of the contract it was to be interpreted in accordance with "the meaning which the party making the manifestations should reasonably expect that the other party would give to them," thereby effectuating the principle of reasonable expectations directly.[82]

Despite the superficial appeal that an integrated memorial of a contract ought to be interpreted objectively rather than attempting to "bend what he said to what he wanted,"[83] it was a triumph of theory over common sense to suggest that the parties might commit themselves to an agreement that meant something that neither party intended. The modern approach to contract interpretation adopts a "modified objective" theory grounded in the reasonable expectations of the parties as determined by the context of their agreement. As reflected in the Restatement (Second) of Contracts, interpretation of the words used by parties to the agreement is now uniformly governed by a determination of their shared meaning or meanings which they had reason to understand.[84]

We can return for clarification to the example with which we opened this chapter: the parol evidence rule. The modern approach freely admits parol evidence to interpret a writing adopted by the parties as a complete integration of their agreement, and under the Uniform Commercial Code a broad category of evidence is freely admissible to determine the scope of the parties' agreement.[85] Moreover, any

---

[80] "For each party to a contract has notice that the other will understand his words according to the usage of the normal speaker of English under the circumstances, and therefore cannot complain if his words are taken in that sense."

Oliver Wendell Holmes, "The Theory of Legal Interpretation," *Harvard Law Review* 12 (1899) 417–20, 419.

[81] See Restatement of Contracts §226, comment b (the meaning of language used "is not necessarily that which the party from whom the manifestation proceeds, expects, or understands") and Restatement of Contracts §230, comment b (an integrated memorial of a contract "may have a meaning different from that which either party supposed it to have").

[82] Restatement (First) of Contracts §233.

[83] Holmes, "The Theory of Legal Interpretation," 417.

[84] Restatement (Second) of Contracts §§201–203.

[85] The canonical case under the UCC is *Nanakuli Paving & Rock Co. v. Shell Oil Co.*, 664 F.2d 772 (9th Cir. 1981), in which the court determined that the parol evidence rule is not implicated by the admission of evidence of course of performance, course of dealing and usage of trade to establish that the price term "posted price at time of delivery" in fact represented the agreement of the parties that the price term would be "posted price at time of delivery, but no higher than the posted price at the time of contracting."

relevant evidence is admissible to determine if the parties intended a writing to be a complete integration of their agreement.[86] Most courts have rejected a simple rule-based effort to construe the meaning of written memorials in favor of understanding contractual meaning as a contextual fact, leading them to investigate the objectively manifested intentions of the parties rather than making presumptions that any documents generated by the parties were complete and intended to speak for themselves.[87]

Arthur Corbin summarized his elegant approach to these matters as a cultivation of the good sense of the common law rather than as a theoretical insight to be brought to bear on the law.

> All rules of interpretation, whether stated by a court or by a writer, are mere aides to the court, the lawyer, and the layman, in ascertaining and enforcing the intention of the parties. No supposed rule should be given any respect when it fails of that purpose.

> I shall continue to do my best to clarify the process and the law of interpretation, of both words and acts as symbols of expression; to demonstrate that no man can determine the meaning of written words by merely glueing his eyes within the four corners of a square of paper; to convince that it is men who give meanings to words and that words in themselves have no meaning; and to demonstrate that when a judge refuses to consider relevant extrinsic evidence on the ground that the meaning of written words is to him plain and clear, his decision is formed by and wholly based upon the completely extrinsic evidence of his own personal education and experience.[88]

Given that the reference to the parties' intentions is to be understood in accordance with the modified objective approach that Corbin championed, it is evident that Corbin appreciated the complexities of language and interpretation. In his discussion of the parol evidence rule, Stanley Fish happily skewered the ideologically driven efforts by Judge Kozinski to resist the need for interpretation of written agreements

---

[86] Restatement (Second) of Contracts §210.

[87] For the connections between the context rule of interpretation and the parol evidence rule in the common law, see *Berg v. Hudesman*, 801 P.2d 222 (Wash. *en banc* 1990). For the connections as recognized under the Uniform Commercial Code, see §2–202, Comment 1 ("This section definitely rejects: (a) Any assumption that because a writing has been worked out which is final on some matters, it is to be taken as including all the matters agreed upon; (b) The premise that the language used has the meaning attributable to such language by rules of construction existing in the law rather than the meaning which arises out of the commercial context in which it is used; and (c) The requirement that a condition precedent to the admissibility of [extrinsic evidence] is an original determination by the court that the language used is ambiguous.")

[88] Arthur L. Corbin, "The Interpretation of Words and the Parol Evidence Rule," 50 *Cornell Law Quarterly* (1964) 161–90, 171, 164.

Interpretation   363

and lauded the ability of most legal practitioners to cobble together workable rules that accept both the inevitability and instability of interpretation.[89] His praise of legal practice is vintage Fish:

> The failure of both legal positivists and natural law theorists to find the set of neutral procedures or basic moral principles underlying the law should not be taken to mean that the law is a failure, but rather that it is an amazing kind of success. The history of legal doctrine and its application is a history neither of rationalistic purity nor of incoherence and bad faith, but an almost Ovidian history of transformation under the pressure of enormously complicated social, political, and economic urgencies, a history in which victory – in the shape of *keeping going* – is always being wrested from what looks like certain defeat, and wrested by means of stratagems that are all the more remarkable because, rather than being hidden they are almost always fully on display. Not only does the law forge its identity out of the stuff it disdains, it does so in public.[90]

The interpretation of contracts is an immense subject that connects with the theories of interpretation discussed previously, but we might close by agreeing with Fish that the common law has displayed an amazing capacity to get the work of interpretation done without being frozen by indecision or being hamstrung by the felt rhetorical necessity to claim constantly that its amazing feats are unproblematic.

Statutory Law

Interpreting statutes and regulations presents a different question entirely because the interpretation is binding on all persons subject to the rule rather than just two parties to a contract. At the height of the objective approach to interpretation of contracts, Holmes argued that there is no difference: "Different rules conceivably might be laid down for the construction of different kinds of writing. Yet in fact we do not deal differently with a statute from our way of dealing with a contract. We do not inquire what the legislature meant; we ask only what the statute means."[91] As courts moved to a contextual approach to meaning that embraced the modified objective

---

[89] Stanley Fish, "The Law Wishes to Have a Formal Existence," *There's No Such Thing as Free Speech and It's a Good Thing Too*, 141–79 (Oxford: Oxford University Press, 1994) 144–7. Fish criticizes Kozinski's opinion in *Trident Center v. Connecticut Gen. Life Ins. Co.*, 847 F.2d 564 (9th Cir. 1988), in which Kozinski criticizes the landmark development of the parol evidence rule by the Supreme Court of California in *Pacific Gas & Electric, Co. v. G.W. Thomas Drayage & Rigging Co.*, 68 Cal. 2d 33 (1968).

[90] Ibid., 156. Fish argues that the development of the parol evidence rule is a wonderful example of the law building the road upon which it is traveling, creating a formal existence on the run, so to speak, rather than finding it already given. Ibid.

[91] Homes, "The Theory of Legal Interpretation," 419.

theory, Corbin argued that statutes required the same recuperation of manifested intentions as contracts.[92] Nevertheless, the public law character of statutory text has certainly shaded how it is interpreted.

The interpretation of statutes in the United States has a long history that is shaped by the English common law legacy and the peculiarities of American legal history.[93] In the common law era English courts viewed statutes as isolated efforts to articulate the principles of the common law, and so they construed statutes narrowly against established common law doctrines. In the democratic ethos of nineteenth-century America, judges were regarded with suspicion and accused of undermining legislation with their exercise of "equitable interpretation," but courts generally continued to interpret statutes narrowly even without a guiding theoretical dogma. In the twentieth century, judges more readily acknowledged the primacy of legislation, but focused on effectuating the purpose of statutes rather than attending only to a claimed "plain meaning." Despite the sometimes dogmatic claims of theorists and commentators, judges for the most part have assumed a partnership with legislatures and sought pragmatic solutions to problems of interpretation that often employed an eclectic mix of interpretive strategies responsive to the comparative institutional competencies.[94] William Popkin describes the modern theoretical focus by most commentators as displaying a lack of faith in "ordinary judging" by attempting to cabin judgment with purportedly objective principles.[95]

[92] Corbin, "The Interpretation of Words and the Parol Evidence Rule," at 187–8. Corbin rejects the claim that the plain meaning of the statute constructs a "semantic stone wall" that a judge should obey, pointing out the existence of plain meaning is predicated on the judge's unexamined assumptions and context rather than seeking the context in which the statute was written. Statutes never announce their own ambiguity; rather, Corbin writes, ambiguity is apparent only after examining the statute in contextual detail. Corbin essentially argues for a purposivist approach to legislative intent.

[93] The brief historical overview in this paragraph is drawn from William D. Popkin, *Statutes in Court: The History and Theory of Statutory Interpretation* (Durham, NC: Duke University Press, 1999).

[94]

> When the common law was dominant, courts developed various approaches that allowed them to shape statutory meaning based on the assumption that legislatures did not always get things right and needed a lot of help making law, reinforced in the latter part of the nineteenth century by split between law and the people. Increased legislative competence forced courts to be less arrogant regarding statutes and their own lawmaking potential, and this change in attitude eventually evolved into purposive interpretation in which the judge's creative role could be grounded in affirmative assumptions about creative legislation and about the link between the law and the people that was supposed to exist in a democracy.

> Ibid., 149. In a similar vein, William Eskridge argues that in the first thirty years of the new Republic the courts used an eclectic blend of text, history, purpose, context, and norms to interpret statutes, underscoring the extent to which theory-driven approaches are a relatively new phenomenon. William N. Eskridge, Jr., "All About Words: Early Understandings of the 'Judicial Power' in Statutory Interpretation, 1776–1806," *Columbia Law Review* 101 (2001) 990–1106.

[95] Popkin, *Statutes in Court*, 151–255.

Interpretation   365

The infamous case of *Rector, Holy Trinity Church v. U.S.*[96] is a watershed for contemporary statutory practice and theory. Justice Brewer sought to avoid the plain meaning of a statute prohibiting a corporation from making a contract with a foreign alien to perform work and then assisting in his importation because the Court did not believe that the statute should apply to a church that hired a pastor from England. The majority opinion evidences the eclectic approach by considering the language of the statute in context, the purpose of the statute, and the legislative history. The Court famously concluded with a wholly intentionalist argument, suggesting that the United States is a Christian nation and it would be absurd to impute an intention to the legislature to forbid churches from hiring ministers from abroad. In this case, one might argue that the Court was working in partnership with the legislature in the manner of "ordinary judging," but the extent of its equitable reshaping of the patent rule suggested that courts might be free to import all manner of bias through the guise of interpretation.

A short time later Roscoe Pound argued that statutory law is properly conceived as the communication of author's intent and that deviating from the "genuine" interpretation of this fixed, historical fact is to engage in spurious interpretation.[97] As in the *Holy Trinity Church* case, Pound's insistence on following the intentions of the drafters is embedded in an argument that heeds the plain meaning of the statute and the context of enactment as revealing its underlying purpose. The reference to legislative intent is ubiquitous in the reported cases, but it is apparent that courts have used this concept in imprecise, contradictory, and changing ways even as they have sought to secure a determinate guide for interpretation. We might say that the constant reference to "intent" as cover for the practice of ordinary judging has created a quagmire into which modern theorists have fallen. The question is whether the lawyers and judges have been pulled in with them.

Attempting to escape the confused notions of an "intent" or "purpose" that guides interpretation, Justice Scalia has adopted a textualist approach to interpreting statutes and sought to provide a model to reorient statutory interpretation. He agrees that statutes must be read within their legal context and rejects the idea that judges can refer simply to a literal reading of the specific language of a statute, but his focus is the narrow question of the ordinary meaning of the words used at the time of the enactment. He recoils from the general practice of looking to the legislative history to discern the subjective intentions of the drafters and the purpose of the statute in question, arguing that these open-ended and unreliable concepts permit judges too

---

[96] 143 U.S. 457 (1892).
[97] "The object of genuine interpretation is to discover the rule which the law-maker intended to establish; to discover the intention with which the law-maker made the rule." Roscoe Pound, "Spurious Interpretation," *Columbia Law Review* 7 (1907) 379–86, 381.

much leeway in deciding cases, and – even if these concepts are constraining – are not democratically and constitutionally validated. His erstwhile opponent in many decisions is Justice Stevens, who uses a variety of traditional approaches to statutory interpretation in an effort to effectuate the underlying purpose.[98]

Justice Scalia is not an unadorned textualist, however. As a textualist he readily endorses the grammatical canons of construction although he is far more wary of substantive canons that tip the scales of judgment when a statutory text is opaque.

> To the honest textualist, all of these preferential rules and presumptions are a lot of trouble. It is hard enough to provide a uniform, objective answer to the question whether a statute, on balance, more reasonably means one thing than another. But it is virtually impossible to expect uniformity and objectivity when there is added, on one or the other side of the balance, a thumb of indeterminate weight.... Can we really just decree that we will interpret the laws that Congress passes to mean less or more than what they fairly say? I doubt it. The rule of lenity is almost as old as the common law itself, so I suppose that is validated by sheer antiquity.[99]

And in fact, Justice Scalia relies on the rule of lenity despite its conflict with the textualist theory of meaning.[100] More generally, he is criticized for not using the

---

[98] A few classic examples illustrate this divide. In *Green v. Bock Laundry Machine Co.*, 490 U.S. 504 (1989) the Court considered a rule of evidence that permitted the introduction of the criminal convictions of a witness so long as the probative value outweighed any prejudice to the "defendant." The case involved a civil plaintiff who was injured while on work release, and the court below held that the prejudicial effect of introducing evidence of his criminal history was irrelevant because he was a plaintiff in the case. Writing for the Court, Justice Stevens engaged in a lengthy and detailed reconstruction of the drafting history of the rule to determine that Congress was attempting to protect criminal defendants from prejudice. Justice Scalia concurred, but chastised the majority for its inquiry. Scalia argued that the court should consider extratextual materials only to confirm that the literal reading of the rule was absurd, and then interpret the text by doing the least violence to it. He insisted that the Court focus first on the words of the text as ordinarily understood, and only if that leads to an absurdity should the Court engage in the benign fiction that the statute should be read to cohere with related areas of law. Finally, Justice Blackmun in dissent argued for an expansion of the protective aspects of the rule by applying it to all parties, basing his analysis on the policy underlying the gradual liberalization of the rule over time.

The different approaches to statutory interpretation often are claimed to be the basis for different results. In *Chisom v. Roemer*, 501 U.S. 380 (1991), the Court considered whether the Voting Rights Act relating to the election of "representatives" applied to judicial elections. Justice Stevens' majority opinion drew on the remedial purpose of the act to conclude that the use of the term "representative" rather than "legislator" was intended to apply to judicial elections. Justice Scalia dissented, arguing that the word "representative," as ordinarily understood, does not apply to judges and then criticizing the Court for broadening the scope of the act under the guise of interpretation to serve as a generalized weapon to combat discrimination.

[99] Scalia, *A Matter of Interpretation*, 28–9.

[100] For recent cases, see *United States v. Santos*, 128 S. Ct. 2020 (2008) (Scalia, J., concurring); *Begay v. United States*, 128 S. Ct. 1581 (2008).

Interpretation

textualist approach rigorously, suggesting that it does not provide the objective or determinate answers that he claims.[101]

There can be no doubt that textualist arguments hold great sway in the academy and for certain judges, but the practice of deciding cases tends to undermine the desire for theoretical purity. Justice Scalia gave rise to the modern textualist movement, but his work as a judge suggests that even the most ardent proponent cannot help deviating at times. William Eskridge has articulated a "dynamic" approach to statutory interpretation that has served as the theoretical counterweight to Justice Scalia's textualist revolution.[102] Drawing on contemporary philosophical hermeneutics, Eskridge contends that judges generally use practical reasoning and a variety of interpretive strategies to determine the meaning of the statute for the case at hand in light of the character of interpretation.[103] He summarizes, with coauthor Philip Frickey, his central conclusions:

> First, statutory interpretation involves creative policymaking by judges and is not just the Court's figuring out the answer that was put "in" the statute by the enacting legislature. An essential insight of hermeneutics is that interpretation is a dynamic process, and that the interpreter is inescapably situated historically.
>
> Second, because this creation of statutory meaning is not a mechanical operation, it often involves the interpreter's choice among several competing answers. Although the interpreter's range of choices is somewhat constrained by the text, the statute's history, and the circumstances of its application, the actual choice will not be 'objectively' determinable; interpretation will often depend on political and other assumptions.
>
> Third, when statutory interpreters make these choices, they are normally not driven by any single value... The pragmatic idea that captures this concept is the "web of beliefs" metaphor... [ed. note: they then argue that another helpful metaphor is Charles Peirce's contrast of a chain of arguments no stronger than the weakest link and a cable woven from various threads.] In many cases of statutory interpretation, of course, the threads will not all run in the same direction. The cable metaphor suggests that in these cases the result will depend upon the strongest overall combination of threads.

---

[101] Randy Barnett, "Scalia's Infidelity: A Critique of Faint-Hearted Originalism," 75 *University of Cincinnati Law Review* (2006) 7–24; Jack Balkin, "Abortion," 297 (arguing that Justice Scalia is forced to adopt a "faint-hearted originalism" because he begins with an overly narrow conception of originalism that would lead to unacceptable results).

[102] William N. Eskridge, Jr., *Dynamic Statutory Interpretation* (Cambridge, MA: Harvard University Press, 1994); William N. Eskridge, Jr., "Gadamer/Statutory Interpretation," *Columbia Law Review* 90 (1990) 609–81; William N. Eskridge, Jr., "Dynamic Statutory Interpretation," *University of Pennsylvania Law Review* 135 (1987) 1479–1555.

[103] Eskridge, *Dynamic Statutory Interpretation*, 55–7; William N. Eskridge, Jr. and Philip Frickey, "Statutory Interpretation as Practical Reasoning," *Stanford Law Review* 42 (1990) 321–84.

Our model holds that an interpreter will look at a broad range of evidence – text, historical evidence, and the text's evolution – and thus form a preliminary view of the statute. The interpreter then develops that preliminary view by testing various possible interpretations against the multiple criteria of fidelity to text, historical accuracy, and conformity to contemporary circumstances and values. Each criterion is relevant, yet none necessarily trumps the others.[104]

Eskridge contends that dynamic statutory interpretation is a descriptive account of how judges resolve interpretive problems, but also that it is normative to the extent that it cautions against unrealistic efforts to reduce statutory interpretation to a single valence.[105] Courts rarely endorse Eskridge's dynamic approach expressly, but he would argue that the great weight of legal practice supports the hermeneutic understanding of statutory interpretation as practical reasoning.

[104] Eskridge and Frickey, "Statutory Interpretation as Practical Reasoning," 345, 347–8, 351, 352.

[105] The evolution of the "pragmatist" Judge Posner might be a case in point of this kind of practical reasoning. Although strongly committed to an interpretive perspective guided by economic theory, Judge Posner more recently has embraced the necessity of practical reasoning and ordinary judging in at least some cases where the literal meaning of the statute is not in question. Richard Posner, *Overcoming Law* (Cambridge, MA: Harvard University Press, 1995); Richard Posner, *The Problems of Jurisprudence* (Cambridge, MA: Harvard University Press, 1990). Against Judge Easterbrook's willingness to affirm a sentence of twenty years for the sale of LSD under a criminal statute that was (in the case of LSD, bizarrely and almost certainly mistakenly) geared toward weight rather than dosage, Judge Posner expressly and eloquently argued for a broad view of interpretation that utilized the tools of ordinary judging.

> Well, what if anything can we judges do about this mess? The answer lies in the shadow of a jurisprudential disagreement that is not less important by virtue of being unavowed by most judges. It is the disagreement between the severely positivistic view that the content of law is exhausted in clear, explicit, and definite enactments by or under express delegation from legislatures, and the natural lawyer's or legal pragmatists' view that the practice of interpretation and the general terms of the Constitution (such as "equal protection of the laws") authorize judges to enrich positive law with the moral values and practical concerns of civilized society.
>
> . . . .
>
> The literal interpretation adopted by the majority is not inevitable. All interpretation is contextual. The words of the statute – interpreted against a background that includes a constitutional norm of equal treatment, a (closely related) constitutional commitment to rationality, and evident failure by both Congress and the Sentencing Commission to consider how LSD is actually produced, distributed, and sold, and an equally evident failure by the same two bodies to consider the interaction between heavy mandatory minimum sentences and the Sentencing Guidelines – will bear an interpretation that distinguishes between the carrier vehicle of the illegal drug and the substance or mixture containing a detectable amount of the drug. The punishment of the crack dealer is not determined by the weight of the glass tube in which he sells the crack; we should not lightly attribute to Congress a purpose of punishing the dealer in LSD according to the weight of the LSD carrier. We should not make Congress's handiwork an embarrassment to the members of Congress and to us.

United States v. Marshall, 908 F.2d 1312, 1334–5, 1337–8 (7th Cir., 1990) (Posner, J., dissenting).

Interpretation

Constitutional Law

Even if one believes that legislation is a democratically sanctioned communication of a rule that must be followed, the Constitution presents a different case. As the constituting document of the polity, it gestures toward timeless and enduring principles that can provide stability to society over time. A constitution that required constant emendation to deal with changes in society would not be constituting a polity as much as serving as a super-statute. On the other hand, a written constitution must mean more than an invitation for judges to rule as they deem best.

There have been various interpretive approaches to the Constitution that reflect its status as a founding document for the polity. John Hart Ely famously argued that the Constitution should be interpreted in a manner that reinforces democratic responsiveness,[106] Ronald Dworkin contended that moral reasoning is at the root of constitutional interpretation,[107] and Randy Barnett has sought the "lost constitution" that instituted libertarian rights and limited government.[108] The complexity and diversity of constitutional litigation is such that it is difficult enough for courts to attempt to articulate a unified approach to the First Amendment, let alone an overriding interpretive approach to the Constitution. The encrustation of precedent appears to be relatively resilient against the contemporary quest for a unified theory of interpretation that produces a method or approach that renders decisions more predictable and legitimate. The Court famously refused to overrule *Roe v. Wade*[109] in the interest of doctrinal purity, citing the need to respect the settled expectations engendered by precedents and acknowledging that constitutional interpretation requires reasoned judgment rather than recovery of a fixed and unchanging meaning.[110]

In a remarkable case decided in 2008, though, the Court openly confronted the question of the interpretative principles that guide adjudication of constitutional rights because it was faced with a rare case involving an Amendment that had not been interpreted extensively by the Court. In *District of Columbia v. Heller*,[111] the Supreme Court determined by a five-to-four vote that a District of Columbia law effectively banning private ownership of handguns violated the Second Amendment, holding that the Amendment protected an individual right to own handguns for

---

[106] John Hart Ely, *Democracy and Distrust: A Theory of Judicial Review* (Cambridge, MA: Harvard University Press, 1980); John Hart Ely, "Toward a Representation-Reinforcing Mode of Judicial Review," 37 *Maryland Law Review* (1978) 451–87.

[107] Ronald Dworkin, *Freedom's Law: The Moral Reading of the American Constitution* (Cambridge, MA: Harvard University Press, 1986).

[108] Randy Barnett, *Restoring the Lost Constitution: The Presumption of Liberty* (Princeton, NJ: Princeton University Press, 2005); Randy Barnett, *The Structure of Liberty: Justice and the Rule of Law* (Oxford: Oxford University Press, 2000).

[109] 410 U.S. 113 (1973).

[110] *Planned Parenthood of Southeastern Pennsylvania v. Casey*, 505 U.S. 833 (1992).

[111] 554 U.S. – (2008) (slip. op.)

the purpose of self-defense. The opinions in the case illustrate a sharp contrast between application of the new textualist methodology to the Constitution and more traditional inquiries into purpose and precedent.

Justice Scalia's majority opinion provides the first thoroughly new textualist reading of the Constitution by the Court. He begins with the central textualist tenet – that meaning precedes application – by spending more than fifty pages analyzing the "meaning of the Second Amendment" before turning "finally to the law at issue here."[112] Combing the historical record to determine how the famously ungrammatical and ambiguous Amendment[113] would have been understood by the public at the time of its adoption, Justice Scalia concludes that it means that individual citizens have a right to own handguns for their personal defense.[114] His opinion breaks down the single sentence of the Amendment to its constituent clauses, which are defined by reference to dictionaries from the period. The Court struck down the gun control legislation for violating a constitutional right, acknowledging that the rampant urban violence in Washington, D.C. might lead some to believe that a right to own guns is anachronistic, but concluding nonetheless "that it is not the role of this Court to pronounce the Second Amendment extinct."[115]

There are immediate and obvious contradictions raised by Scalia's attempt to provide a genuinely textualist interpretation of the original meaning of the Second Amendment. He begins by ignoring the prefatory clause regarding the Militia until after determining the meaning of what he construes to be the operative clause, although he provides no objective grammatical or historical justification for this approach.[116] He rejects the arguments of professional linguists expressed in an amicus brief and assumes that there can be a truth of the matter to historical research.[117] After determining the original meaning of the Amendment he then asks whether any precedents foreclose the application of this meaning, suggesting that *stare decisis* might trump the original meaning to some extent.[118] He acknowledges that the right is not unlimited, and that there will be exceptions for restricting ownership by persons who are mentally ill or convicted felons, and for restricting possession of handguns in government offices or schools, but again the historical record appears to provide

[112] Ibid., 2, 56. This is a weak rhetorical device rather than a phenomenology of the act of decision making, of course, because the entire historical discussion is oriented around the notion that ownership of a weapon to protect one's home was an understood meaning of the Amendment. In other words, it would be utterly fantastic to assume that Justice Scalia would have written these same fifty pages describing the original meaning of the Amendment if he had no idea of the nature of the dispute before the Court!

[113] The Second Amendment provides, in full: "A well regulated Militia, being necessary to the security of a free State, the right of the people to keep and bear Arms, shall not be infringed."

[114] *District of Columbia v. Heller*, 554 U.S. at 8–15 (slip. op.).

[115] Ibid., 64.

[116] Ibid., 3–5. Justice Stevens chides the majority for this approach, arguing that it is a legitimate move for an advocate, but not for a judge. Ibid., 8–9 (Stevens, J., dissenting).

[117] Ibid., 15–16.

[118] Ibid., 47.

Interpretation 371

no justification for these potential exceptions.[119] It takes little effort to see the cracks in Justice Scalia's effort to hew to the original public meaning and nothing more, even if one grants that determining the original public meaning is appropriate.

Justice Stevens dissented based on an interpretation of the Amendment grounded in its text, history, and the *Miller* precedent that permitted the banning of sawed-off shotguns because there was no nexus with militia service.[120] His dissent centers on a historical understanding that the purpose of the Amendment was to ensure that the new federal government could not oppress the states by regulating ownership of weapons by able-bodied white males, who comprised each state's militia.[121] The opinion is shaped by Justice Scalia's historical bent, but it seeks a higher level of generality. Rather than determining how individual words and phrases would have been understood at the time of enactment, Justice Stevens inquires into the original understanding of the purpose of the Amendment. Justice Breyer's dissent is more openly critical of the new textualist methodology and the lack of definitive evidence for Justice Scalia's claim that self-defense is a core value of the Amendment, leading him to conclude that the new originalist project is bankrupt, even as it triumphs in this case.[122]

---

[119] Ibid., 54–5. Justice Scalia suggests, "There will be time enough to expound upon the historical justifications for the exceptions we have mentioned if and when those exceptions come before us," ibid., 63, but it is curious how he came up with his admittedly incomplete list in textualist fashion if he had not already consulted the historical sources. The early case law interpreting *Heller* already is drifting away from the perceived solid ground of an original understanding of the amendment. See, e.g., *U.S. v. Knight*, – F. Supp. 2d –, 2008 WL 4097410 (D. Me. 2008) (upholding statutory prohibition on the possession of firearms by a person under a restraining order regarding domestic violence). A prominent judge on the conservative Court of Appeals for the Fourth Circuit has chastised Justice Scalia's opinion for its activist character, going so far as to proclaim that *Heller* is guilty of the same sins as *Roe v. Wade*, 410 U.S. 113 (1973). J. Harvie Wilkinson III, "Of Guns, Abortions, and the Unravelling of Law," *Virginia Law Review* (2009).

[120] *Heller*, at 8–9 (Stevens, J., dissenting).

[121] Ibid., 26–7 (Stevens, J., dissenting). In other words, Justice Stevens is making an argument that combines originalism and purposivism, claiming that the "proper allocation of military power in the new Nation was an issue of central concern for the Framers" that led to the enactment of the Second Amendment.

[122]

At the same time the majority ignores a more important question: Given the purposes for which the Framers enacted the Second Amendment, how should it be applied to modern-day circumstances that they could not have anticipated? Assume, for argument's sake, that the Framers did intend the Amendment to offer a degree of self-defense protection. Does that mean that the Framers also intended to guarantee a right to possess a loaded gun near swimming pools, parks, and playgrounds? That they would not have cared about the children who might pick up a loaded gun on their parents' bedside table? That they . . . would have lacked concern for the risk of accidental deaths or suicides that readily accessible loaded handguns in urban areas might bring? Unless we believe that they intended future generations to ignore such matters, answering questions such as the questions in this case requires judgment – judicial judgment exercised within a framework for constitution analysis that guides that judgment and which makes its exercise transparent. One cannot answer those questions by combining inconclusive historical research with judicial *ipse dixit*.

Ibid., 43 (Breyer, J., dissenting).

The dissenting opinions are equally open to criticism. They too look to history, but they do so in a manner that appears to provide greater ability to adapt the text to modern problems; however, they provide no convincing explanation as to why they do not simply operate at a general level of constitutional values and adopt the best approach to the problem at hand. If history is inconclusive, why must it play such a large role in their opinion? The case, then, appears to be a battle between the faint-hearted originalists and the faint-hearted purposivists.

The *Heller* case is interesting precisely because it pits competing approaches to constitutional interpretation against each other in legal practice, rather than in the self-referential world of academia. The case makes clear that new textualism has a very real effect on legal practice and strongly influences even the dissenters. Under the stresses of a real case, however – and particularly the institutional constraints of the appellate process – the case seems to confirm that no theory can deliver a knockout punch that eliminates the art of judging.

At this point it pays to return to the level of theory and reconsider its connections to the practice of constitutional decision making. If the practice of new originalism is a political approach to constitutional practice, this begs the question: How can we judge this practice if there is no theoretically secured notion of the nature of the constitution and the legitimate means of interpreting it? As mentioned previously, there is a (perhaps surprising) confluence of some forms of analytical legal positivism with philosophical hermeneutics in describing the role of theory for legal philosophers. I explore this connection within the scope of constitutional theory and practice as a means of bringing my analysis full circle.

Joseph Raz promotes an exclusive positivism that locates the validity of legal rules in social fact rather than normative evaluation. There is much that can be said about legal rules by a positivist, but when considering constitutional law as the ground of such rules he concludes that constitutions are "self-validating. They are valid just because they are there, enshrined in the practices of their countries," but he also immediately modifies this stark approach with an important qualification:

> As long as they remain within the boundaries set by moral principles, constitutions are self-validating in that their validity derives from nothing more than the fact that they are there. It should be added that this conclusion follows *if morality underdetermines* the principles concerning the form of government and the content of individual rights enshrined in constitutions.[123]

In other words, the opacity of morality provides a wide arena within which a constitutional tradition may develop, and within this arena the "constitution of a country is a

---

[123] Joseph Raz, "On the Authority and Interpretation of Constitutions: Some Preliminaries," in *Constitutionalism: Philosophical Foundations* 152–93, Larry Alexander, ed. (Cambridge University Press, 1998), 173.

Interpretation 373

legitimate constitution because it is the constitution it has."[124] The founding fathers have an important practical and symbolic value, but – especially with respect to older constitutions – their intentions and understandings cannot legitimately claim supremacy in guiding the interpretation of the constitution.[125]

Raz argues that contemporary decision makers owe no obeisance to past understandings of the Constitution, and insists that constitutional interpretation always blends a conserving and innovating function. Because these features cannot be strictly differentiated in a particular interpretive act, there can be no theoretical prescription for constitutional practice: "There is little more that one can say other than 'reason well' or 'interpret reasonably.' What little there is to say consists mainly of pointing out mistakes that have been made attractive by the popularity among judges, lawyers, or academic writers."[126] Although constantly revised through interpretation, the original Constitution is not discarded any more than the constant adaptation of a house over two centuries means that the original house has disappeared; Raz makes clear that interpretive development does not entail a loss of identity.[127]

Raz's conceptual approach coincides with Gadamer's ontological account of understanding. Gadamer dismisses the methodologies of intentionalism and new originalism as false ideals – mistakes that have been made attractive, in Raz's phrasing – that mask the reality that every interpretation is application within a particular context that cannot hew to some supposed previously existing meaning of the text. Constitutional practice simply exists, and the hermeneutical discernment of constitutional meaning cannot be subjected to a method. This does not yield quiescence, but instead invests interpretation with an unavoidable ethical dimension.

Raz and Gadamer echo Jürgen Habermas's efforts to describe law as existing between social fact and moral norm, which is to say that law mediates social organization and moral norms.[128] Habermas, however, defends a discourse theory of law rooted in his theory of communicative action, reaching beyond the more

---

[124] Ibid.

[125] Ibid., 69, 76.

[126] Ibid., 180.

[127] Ibid., 191.

[128] It is surprising that Raz does not draw explicitly from Habermas's detailed work, in which Habermas describes how "mediation through law serves the role of concretizing moral principles – that is, of giving them the concrete content they must have in order for people to be able to follow them." Jürgen Habermas, *Between Facts and Norms: Contributions to a Discourse Theory of Law and Democracy*, William Rehg, trans. (Cambridge, MA: The MIT Press, 1996) (1992) 172. Habermas makes just this point against the backdrop of a broad survey of continental and Anglo-American political and legal theory. To manage the dissensus resulting from the collapse of a unified lifeworld and the plurality of lived experience, Habermas contends that law serves "as a transformer in the society-wide communication circulating between system and lifeworld," ibid., 81, or as described by Talcott Parsons, as a "transmission belt." Ibid., 76. Law serves an important function by relieving citizens of the burden of acting morally in the face of the unprecedented cognitive, motivational, and organizational demands of the modern, fractured world. Ibid., 114.

modest implications of the conceptual work by Raz and the ontological explorations of understanding by Gadamer. Habermas regards Gadamer's hermeneutics as implausible in the fragmented post-Enlightenment world, and he criticizes legal positivism for restricting the role of rationality too severely.[129] Rather than Dworkin's monological Hercules, Habermas insists that legal argumentation validates legal practice if it is dialogically grounded and the society embodies the material features to sustain such a discourse.[130] Habermas is the most prominent defender of a post-Enlightenment and postmetaphysical philosophy of meaning that provides more than minimal guidance to legal practice.[131] Whether Habermas or anyone else can succeed in this endeavor is philosophically contested and one of the great questions facing contemporary legal theory.

Conclusion: The Future of Scholarship on Interpretation

Interpretation is Janus-faced. It preserves and innovates; it recovers and projects; it acknowledges and creates. As a result, legal interpretation unavoidably is a high-wire act without a safety net. Preservation and stability are vitally important values, but the need to apply the law in new contexts and under changed circumstances is no less important. There can be no calming of this hermeneutical anxiety – no stabilization of interpretive vertigo – achieved through practical engagement or theoretical reflection. The future is interpretation, but it is an uncertain future that we must cobble together as we move forward in both practical and theoretical ways.

The scholarship on legal interpretation would benefit by undertaking several initiatives that move beyond the debates described in this chapter. Most important, scholars should pursue a more robust description of the hermeneutical situation in which interpreters find themselves. This is not to call for a naturalistic inquiry in the sense of reductionist empiricism, but rather to promote bringing cognitive studies, psychology, sociology, linguistics, and other disciplines to bear on elucidating hermeneutical capacities. Nietzsche described our nature as interpretive, but we have only begun to understand this feature of human nature. Hermeneutical philosophy should chart a place between Heideggerian mysticism and linguistic scientism, bringing interdisciplinary knowledge to bear on interpretation as an embodied experience. This project is anticipated by philosophical hermeneutics, which rejects the

---

[129] Ibid., 199–203.

[130] Ibid., 222–7.

[131] Habermas concludes that certain rights follow from the discourse principle, including those oriented to establishing the private autonomy of legal persons as potential addressees of the law, rights that secure equal opportunity to participate in the processes of opinion and will formation that generate legitimate law, and rights to the provision of living conditions that enable the exercise of rights. Ibid., 122–31. This stands in contrast to Raz and Gadamer.

Interpretation 375

idea that interpretation is simply a strategy or methodology that one may employ to investigate objects.

This philosophical reorientation would have significant effects in legal studies, not the least of which would be to clarify that originalism is a political theory rather than a theory of interpretation and that it must be judged politically. More generally, regarding interpretation as a way of being rather than a conscious activity would explode the assumption that legal actors can step outside the hermeneutical uncertainty of ordinary life and adopt a "legal" point of view that resolves the dilemmas of interpretation. The result should be to integrate studies of legal interpretation with inquiries into judgment, discernment, and understanding in different venues. This would not deny the importance of the legal context, but rather would reject the dogma that the legal context is able to tame or escape the hermeneutical situation.

By focusing on the hermeneutical situation, scholars would be able to highlight the full ethical dimension of interpretation. Too many theories of interpretation attempt to quell uncertainty by regarding interpretation as a rule-bound activity that could be judged as easily as determining whether a baker properly followed a recipe. Certainly there is skill and judgment involved in baking, but if one is constrained to follow a recipe there clearly is a metric against which to judge the performance. In contrast, there is no recipe for interpretation, which is to say that there is no methodology against which interpretive performances may be judged. Interpretation is a judgment made without benefit of a metric, and so this activity is ethical in a much deeper sense than the ethical obligation to follow authoritative procedures. Future scholarship should explore the moral agency that exists because of, and not despite, the fact that socially constructed actors work within long-standing narrative discourses. The irreducible fact is that this activity always demands the exercise of creative judgment, even if the actor denies this ethical moment.

My suggested course of inquiry goes against the grain of most legal scholarship, and even most philosophy, but a bold reorientation is precisely what we require. By adopting a phenomenological approach to the interpretive nature of our existence and then tracing the effects of this mode of being for legal practice, scholars have the best chance for overcoming the destructive disjunction of theory and practice that mars most academic inquiry. As things stand now, when reflecting on the current situation we might indict interpretive theory for attempting to arrest the activity of interpretation, to constrain an unruly play by posting boundaries and prescriptions from outside the practice. Under this view, legal practice is dynamic, supple, and precognitive, even if it cloaks its activity with a superficial obeisance to the theoretical model of the day (whether it be original intent, textualism, or consequentialism). It is equally plausible that we might indict practitioners for plodding along by repeating mantras that have no conceptual integrity or practical utility. Under this view, legal theory is an insightful corrective, even if it hides its practical effect behind academic jargon that purports to rise above mundane matters.

The dilemma of contemporary legal hermeneutics is that both views are correct. The play of interpretation occurs, in part, in the interplay of theory and practice. The future of legal interpretation is a continuation of this frustrating dance, which lacks both a rhythm and an end. By focusing on the hermeneutical situation we might eliminate the gulf between theory and practice, but not the challenge of interpretation. Theorists and practitioners perennially claim that they have unlocked the secret of interpretation. To do so, however, would mean the end of history and the denial of the future.

14

Narrative and Rhetoric

Ravit Reichman

To speak of law in terms of rhetoric is already, in some sense, to court redundancy. Law is, after all, a matter of persuasion, and distinguishing law from rhetoric thus amounts to the impossible task – to call up Yeats's famous line in "Among School Children" – of "know[ing] the dancer from the dance."[1] Yet despite this intimate, indeed inseparable connection that would lead one to the conclusion that law *is* rhetoric, discussions of law nonetheless often failed to take this affinity into account, assuming instead a transparency through which law emerged as a distinct and discrete entity, a truth to be discovered and described in language rather than a state of affairs that language itself brings into being. Moreover, the idea that law is about (or indistinguishable from) rhetoric conjures negative images of fast-talking lawyers, murky jargon, and the seduction of virtuoso performances at the expense of plain truth. To think of law in terms of rhetoric, Austin Sarat and Thomas Kearns have noted, might "seem to let law off too easily by displacing the question of justice."[2] In so doing, it places law in a position that simultaneously acknowledges and disavows its dependence on rhetoric. Sarat and Kearns thus observe, "It appears, then, that to insist on the importance of the rhetoric of law is to highlight an opposition with law's conception of itself."[3]

This chapter will highlight several key approaches to law and rhetoric since their appearance – or more accurately, resurgence – in the 1970s. Then, drawing on these critical perspectives, I consider a moment of legal decisionmaking alongside a contemporaneous work of literature. Taken together, I will suggest, the legal and literary texts reveal the tension between the rhetorical heft of law – a matter,

---

[1] W. B. Yeats, "Among School Children" (1928), *The Collected Poems of W. B. Yeats*, Richard J. Finneran, ed. (New York: Macmillan, 1989) 217.

[2] Austin Sarat and Thomas R. Kearns, "Introduction," *The Rhetoric of Law*, Austin Sarat and Thomas R. Kearns, eds. (Ann Arbor: University of Michigan Press, 1996) 2. See also *Law's Stories: Narrative and Rhetoric in the Law*, Peter Brooks and Paul Gewirtz, eds. (New Haven: Yale University Press, 1996).

[3] Sarat and Kearns, 2.

377

ultimately, of *substance* rather than style – and the law's imagined need for (and insistence upon) silencing the force of such rhetoric. This tension ultimately reveals the catastrophic results of the law's self-imposed blindness to its own cultural work.

I begin with the observation that the attention to legal rhetoric represents a resurgence because the close relation between law and rhetoric has roots as ancient as the Greeks and Romans, from Aristotle and Isocrates to Cicero and Quintillian. It seems only fitting, then, that the twentieth-century emergence of scholarship on law and rhetoric often looks to ancient Greek literature to theorize the central place of rhetoric in the work of law. The modern turn to rhetoric owes much to James Boyd White, whose work on legal discourse, beginning in 1973 with *The Legal Imagination*,[4] laid a critical foundation for law and humanities scholarship, often drawing upon classical texts such as Homer's *Iliad*, Euripides's *Alcestis*, Aeschylus's *Oresteia*, Plato's *Gorgias* – and ranging widely from these ancient works to much later writers such as Dickens, Lawrence, Joyce, and Proust, all of which he reads alongside a wealth of legal opinions. Approaching law "as a kind of rhetorical and literary activity,"[5] he insists that this endeavor amounts to more than viewing law as the art of persuasion (though it is this art, too, for White), and seeing it rather as "that art by which culture and community and character are constituted and transformed."[6] This does not mean, however, that we ought to seek out stability (such as the Framers' intent in the Constitution) with a view to strengthening community, legal or otherwise. "To conceive of the law as a rhetorical and social system," White concludes, "as a way in which we use an inherited language to talk to each other and to maintain a community, suggests in a new way that the heart of law is what we always knew it was: the open hearing in which one point of view, one construction of language and reality, is tested against another."[7] Legal and literary uncertainty thus proves more constitutive of community than unwavering interpretations that remain impervious to conversation, disagreement, and reconsideration. "The multiplicity of readings that the law permits," for White, "is not its weakness, but its strength, for it is this that makes room for different voices, and gives a purchase by which culture may be modified in response to the demands of circumstance."[8] A focus on rhetoric thus becomes the closest (perhaps even the surest) approximation of a guarantee that culture, in law as in life, remains fluid rather than coalescing into a static object with no capacity to stimulate communities of citizens, readers, and human beings.

---

[4] James Boyd White, *The Legal Imagination* (Chicago: University of Chicago Press, 1973).
[5] James Boyd White, *Heracles' Bow: Essays on the Rhetoric and Poetics of the Law* (Madison: University of Wisconsin Press, 1985), x.
[6] Ibid., xi.
[7] Ibid., 104.
[8] Ibid., 104. White here positions himself against Stanley Fish's claim in *Is There a Text in this Class?: The Authority of Interpretive Communities* (1980), which submits that readers rather than texts determine meaning.

Narrative and Rhetoric

What does it mean, then, to read the law rhetorically? As Marianne Constable asks more broadly, "How *do* rhetoricians attend to language?" Her answer offers an ambitious itinerary for reading within and beyond the law:

> They read. They listen. They read very carefully. They read texts for what they say; and they read texts for what they don't say. They read the words of a text; they listen for its silences. They wonder, for instance, about phrases like "law is too important to leave to the lawyers," a phrase with a lovely alliterative lilt. But does the phrase mean that *law* is too important to leave to the lawyers, but that it is all right to leave some less important nonlaw to lawyers (and what might that be?). Does it mean that law is too *important* to leave to the lawyers, rather than too interesting or enriching or complicated (and how is it important)?[9]

Posing and answering such questions may well lead to legal reform in the view of some critics, but for Stanley Fish, they expose an inherent impotence in what rhetorical analysis specifically, and theory generally, can achieve. As he sees it, the law can never escape its own rhetoricity, which is both a good and bad thing. Once we acknowledge that "we live in a rhetorical world,"[10] we can no longer insist on the distinction between theory and practice or thinking and acting. Theory, in other words, cannot be coopted by actors with a wider agenda, because that agenda is, in the first place, no more and no less than rhetoric.[11]

Fish's position on law's rhetorical condition has been accused of being resolutely apolitical, ignoring the contexts of power and authority in which legal language occurs (to which Fish replies, "I am not denying that theory can have political consequences, merely insisting that those consequences do not belong by right or nature to theory, but are contingent upon the (rhetorical) role theory plays in the particular circumstances of a historical moment"[12]). In demanding that rhetoric, in the form of theory or philosophy, produce material change in the world, Fish insists, we do little more than mix our metaphors, imposing agency where none exists. Thus, "bourgeois capitalist societies are not propped up by philosophy, but by the material conditions of everyday life – by the means of production, by the patterns of domestic relations, by the control or dissemination of information, etc. It is when those conditions are altered or removed that the cultural practices of

---

[9] Marianne Constable, *Just Silences: The Limits and Possibilities of Modern Law* (Princeton: Princeton University Press, 2005), 17.

[10] Stanley Fish, *Doing What Comes Naturally: Change, Rhetoric, and the Practice of Theory in Literary and Legal Studies* (Durham and London: Duke University Press, 1989) 25.

[11] For an excellent analysis of Fish's position, see Adam Thurschwell's "Reading the Law," in *The Rhetoric of Law*, Austin Sarat and Thomas R. Kearns, eds. (Ann Arbor: University of Michigan Press, 1996) 275–332.

[12] Fish 28.

bourgeois capitalist society will tremble; all that will tremble when the hit parade of theory undergoes a change is the structure of philosophy departments."[13]

This position has, of course, flown in the face of a wide swath of legal scholarship that holds that such "change in philosophy departments" cannot but produce meaningful transformation elsewhere – that ideology is not just another instance of rhetoric but a place where social (read: material) sea changes begin. Duncan Kennedy, for example, writing from the vantage of Critical Legal Studies, points out that Fish's "mode of 'always already constrained'... was patently a constraint that couldn't exclude ideology."[14] Objecting to the sense of futility at work in Fish's "always already" strategy, Kennedy contends "that some part of judicial law making in adjudication is best described as ideological choice carried on in a discourse with a strong convention denying choice, and carried on by actors many of whom are in bad faith."[15] The task of rhetorical analysis with regard to law – which Kennedy and others[16] insist needs to be recognized as qualitatively (that is, practically) different from such analysis elsewhere – should therefore be to expose and ultimately transform legal decisions:

> My idea is that real experiences of constraint, represented (by song and story) in culture, legitimate and reinforce judicial authority in law-making situations where the imagery of constraint gets at only part of what is going on. In other words, one of the consequences of the *reality* of constraint is the mystification of choice, controversy, and ideology in adjudication, of situations in which constraint is only part of the story.[17]

Challenging such authority means identifying the rhetorical moves that legal discourse makes – its rhetoric of neutrality and inevitability, for instance – to obscure its own capacity to act in the world, a concealment that I shall examine in specific terms at the end of this chapter.[18] In a related vein, Austin Sarat has marshaled rhetorical strategies in his critique of the death penalty in the United States, and his attention to narrative has at its foundation the abolition of capital punishment. As Sarat argues in *When the State Kills*, "State killing depends on flattened narratives of criminal or personal responsibility of the type found in melodrama and

---

[13] Fish, 28.

[14] Duncan Kennedy, A *Critique of Adjudication {fin de siècle}* (Cambridge, MA: Harvard University Press, 1997) 24.

[15] Ibid., 4.

[16] See also Roberto Mangabeira Unger, *The Critical Legal Studies Movement* (Cambridge, MA: Harvard University Press, 1983); Mark Kelman, A *Guide to Critical Legal Studies* (Cambridge, MA: Harvard University Press, 1990); *Politics, Postmodernity, and Critical Legal Studies: The Legality of the Contingent*, Costas Douzinas, Peter Goodrich, Yifat Hachamovitch, eds. (London and New York: Routledge, 1994).

[17] Kennedy, 4.

[18] For a rhetorical treatment of CLS as an aesthetic genre in its own right, see David Luban's *Legal Modernism* (Ann Arbor: University of Michigan Press, 1994).

Narrative and Rhetoric

responds to insistent demands that we use punishment to restore clarity to the moral order."[19] His readings, which set legal language on the death penalty in dialogue with cultural and literary texts, look to restore to these narratives a robustness, and to show how this "restored clarity" in fact distorts the broader cultural discourse around executions. Sarat, like the scholars of Critical Legal Studies and in marked contrast to Fish, insists that examining the rhetorical contingencies of our legal judgments enables us to lay bare, revisit, and potentially recast our ideological and legal commitments.

Beyond Legal Reform

The sense that law's rhetoric demands that we think both ethically *and* politically figures centrally in the work of legal scholar Robert Cover. Indeed, if there exists a text that nearly all scholars of law and humanities acknowledge as central to their respective practices, it would be Cover's path-breaking article in the *Harvard Law Review*, "Nomos and Narrative" (1983). Cover situates law squarely within the realm of storytelling, refusing to draw disciplinary lines between one form of narrative and another. The normative world or *nomos* that we inhabit, he argues, cannot be neatly severed from other narratives that together shape our sense of reality; as such, "law and narrative are inseparably related."[20] Narrative's rhetorical force, in other words, is precisely what makes us believe or doubt, comply or resist: "Law may be viewed as a system of tension or a bridge linking a concept of reality to an imagined alternative – that is, as a connective between two states of affairs, both of which can be represented in their normative significance only through the devices of narrative."[21] For Cover, the possibility of such alternatives comes down to far more than the bare facts of legal decisions; rather, a *nomos* forms or transforms when we throw the weight of words behind our actions. Thus, Cover mounts a forceful attack on the Supreme Court's 1983 decision to revoke Bob Jones University's tax-exempt status on the grounds that its refusal to admit students in interracial relationships or marriages ran counter to public policy. The decision was right, Cover acknowledges, but the narrative through which the Court articulated it was wrong – a sign of "wary and cautious actors, some eloquence, but no commitment."[22] The court had an opportunity not just to hand down a ruling but to set forth a commitment to equality among all races; instead, it took shelter in the logistics of the Internal Revenue Service, with the result

---

[19] Austin Sarat, *When the State Kills: Capital Punishment and the American Condition* (Princeton: Princeton University Press, 2002) 14.

[20] Robert Cover, "Nomos and Narrative," *Narrative, Violence, and the Word: The Essays of Robert Cover*, Martha Minow, Michael Ryan, and Austin Sarat, eds. (Ann Arbor: University of Michigan Press, 1993) 96.

[21] Ibid., 101.

[22] Ibid., 172.

that "the grand national travail against discrimination is given no normative status in the Court's opinion, save that it means the IRS was not wrong" (170).

In another landmark piece, "Violence and the Word," Cover turned to the way in which legal language can never be severed from the violence it does. The duty of narrative, in this case, is not to disavow this violence. Given that violence and language cannot be uncoupled under the rule of law, it becomes all the more urgent and necessary that we put it squarely in our midst, rather than writing it out of legal discourse and so relegating it to the status of an unstated fait accompli. Language here confers upon law a particular *tone*: the tone of resignation, even of mourning, that arises from articulating the violence that we do even as we are in the act – an inevitability for Cover – of doing it. Such injury cannot be resolved; the most we can do is to narrate it, to give it voice as an indelible residue rather than an unfortunate by-product of the law.

Pressing this matter further, Wai Chee Dimock submits in *Residues of Justice* that justice is always a site of residue because it marks a point of intersection and entanglement of a range of discourses, "a zone marked above all by the transparent relation between the various descriptive languages on its behalf."[23] The law's rendering of justice leaves a residue that needs to be negotiated, expressed, and drawn out in fiction. Dimock reads Herman Melville, Walt Whitman, Kate Chopin, and other nineteenth-century American writers not as thematic depictions of law but as meditations on justice, and particularly "its historically problematic relation to the densities and textures of human lives." By this she means that in literature, justice emerges as "an *incomplete* dictate, haunted always by what it fails to encompass."[24] To read the law rhetorically thus amounts to reading it through the fictions of what it omits:

> Literary justice is a point of commensurability rationally arrived at, but it is simultaneously registered as a loss, a strain, a necessary abstraction that necessarily does violence to what it abstracts. Such an image of justice, sedimented out of the cognitive conundrums of a different tradition and carrying with it a different vocabulary, a different language with which to describe the world and what matters in that world, must stand as a supplement and a corrective to any legal or philosophical propositions.[25]

This perspective of the necessary supplement similarly informs Nan Goodman's work in *Shifting the Blame*, which also looks to American literature to imagine the possibilities – and the roads not taken – of legal decisions. Examining specifically the development of tort law in the nineteenth century, her readings of writers such

[23] Wai Chee Dimock, *Residues of Justice: Literature, Law, Philosophy* (Berkeley and Los Angeles: University of California Press, 1996) 8.
[24] Ibid., 9.
[25] Ibid., 9–10.

Narrative and Rhetoric

as James Fenimore Cooper, Mark Twain, and Stephen Crane seek "to identify the contingencies rather than the exigencies of legal history – the possibility, in short, that legal history in general, and the notion of liability under negligence in particular, need not have taken the path it did."[26]

Approaches such as those of Fish, Cover, Dimock, and Goodman illustrate one of the critical strains of rhetorical readings of law: the turn away from conceiving of literature as instrumental to law. To analyze law rhetorically, literarily, such accounts imply, does not mean making claims about legal reform, even as it involves imagining counterfactual situations of what *might have* been. We might thus take Paul Kahn's exhortation in *The Cultural Study of Law* as equally relevant to the rhetorical study of law: "The project of a cultural study of law starts only with the establishment of an imaginative distance that shakes off the scholarly compulsion to point the way toward reform."[27] Resisting expectations to justify a more literary methodology by setting it in the practical terms of legal reform, these interpretative strategies change the terms of legal interpretation precisely in refusing to make pronouncements as to what the law *should* be. As such, they take up the challenge issued by Kahn, who insists on the centrality of fiction to cultural legal work:

> A cultural approach sees that all of law's texts, including those of the legal scholar, are works of fiction. Calling them fiction allows us to see simultaneously the power of law's rule and its contingent character. By abandoning reform, the cultural study lowers the stakes by marginalizing itself. We too must lower the stakes by marginalizing ourselves, if the study of law is to free itself from the practice of law.[28]

The marginal position that Kahn calls for pertains, of course, specifically to scholars in law schools; in other fields of study – literature, rhetoric, psychology, and philosophy, among others – the place of this margin (and its existence to begin with) would be entirely different. The claim here remains a critical thread through much of the scholarship on law and rhetoric, which positions itself not in the service of jurisprudence but in the thick of a wider cultural field in which law enters as one force among many other competing or compatible discourses.

Speech Acts, Omissions, and Silences

In elucidating the ways that rhetoric actively shapes a legal world, critical engagement with legal rhetoric has consistently affirmed a central tenet of language

---

[26] Nan Goodman, *Shifting the Blame: Literature, Law, and the Theory of Accidents in Nineteenth-Century America* (Princeton: Princeton University Press, 1998) 8.
[27] Paul W. Kahn, *The Cultural Study of Law: Reconstructing Legal Scholarship* (Chicago and London: University of Chicago Press, 1999) 6.
[28] Ibid., 139.

philosopher J. L. Austin, whose work on language arguably underpins all scholarship on law and language. Austin's concept of speech acts, advanced in his influential book *How To Do Things With Words*, proposes that language has the capacity not just to describe the world but also to actively call it into being.[29] Some utterances can be categorized as descriptive ("The house is red") and can be deemed true or false, whereas others fall outside such a rubric. Statements such as "I sentence you to life in prison" does not describe something so much as *enact* it; it is a *performative* utterance by virtue of creating the very conditions it articulates. The influence of Austin's work can hardly be underestimated; in its wake, scholars from a range of perspectives have pursued the myriad ways that legal discourse creates the very world that it describes, as well as how language can be a source of injury or repair. At the heart of this work lie political concerns that engage questions of race, gender, sexuality, class, and power.

Critical Race Theorists, for example, identify in such ideas a radical potential for political change, drawing upon them to argue for restricting First Amendment rights in the interest of protecting defenseless groups and individuals from the damages of hate speech. In their introduction to the volume of essays *Words That Wound*, Charles R. Lawrence, Mari Matsuda, Richard Delgado, and Kimberlè Crenshaw maintain, "Critical race theory names the injury and identifies its origins, origins that are often well disguised in the rhetoric of shared values and neutral legal principles."[30] Law's rhetoric, in other words, conceals latent prejudices and hostilities that surface in the controversies surrounding the law's protection or prosecution of hate speech. The task of getting underneath this neutral, polished language to take seriously the need to protect people from words that wound – rather than protecting those who utter them – cuts to the very heart of both legal and academic language.[31] The discourse in support of protecting hate speech, they submit, bears disconcerting resemblance to arguments against policies such as Affirmative Action: "The chief spokespersons for this more refined sentiment against persons and voices that are new and unfamiliar to the campus and intellectual discourse are not the purveyors of gutter hate speech. They are polite and polished colleagues. The code words of this backlash are words like merit, rigor, standards, qualifications, and excellence."[32]

---

[29] J. L. Austin, *How To Do Things With Words* (Cambridge, MA: Harvard University Press, 1962).

[30] Charles R. Lawrence III, Mari J. Matsuda, Richard Delgado, and Kimberlè Williams Crenshaw, "Introduction," *Words That Wound: Critical Race Theory, Assaultive Speech, and the First Amendment* (Boulder, CO: Westview Press, 1993) 13.

[31] Patricia Williams's pathbreaking *The Alchemy of Race and Rights: Diary of a Law Professor* (Cambridge, MA: Harvard University Press, 1991) challenges this neutral, "reasoned" discourse by attempting to produce "a genre of legal writing to fill the gaps of traditional legal scholarship" (7), weaving autobiography with meditations on such legal issues as property, equal opportunity, slavery, and privacy. For a penetrating discussion of Williams's book, see Barbara Johnson, "The Alchemy of Style and Law," in *The Rhetoric of Law*, Sarat and Kearns, eds. 261–74.

[32] Lawrence, Matsuda, Delgado, and Crenshaw, *Words That Wound*, 14.

Narrative and Rhetoric

Building on the arguments of Critical Race Theorists, Judith Butler maintains "that the citationality of discourse can work to enhance and intensify our sense of responsibility for it. The one who utters hate speech is responsible for the manner in which such speech is repeated, for reinvigorating such speech, for reestablishing contexts of hate and injury. The responsibility of the speaker does not consist of remaking language ex nihilo, but rather of negotiating the legacies of usage that constrain and enable that speaker's speech."[33] Butler criticizes the Critical Race Theorists, however, for their willingness to find in law – which itself participates in the production of hate speech – a progressive means by which to legislate hate speech, which ultimately points to a misplaced "faith in the resignifying capacities of legal discourse."[34] The most radical potential for dismantling the injurious effects of such language, for Butler, lies in rhetoric itself rather than in the law's policing of rhetoric – by which she means in a reappropriation and resignification of language. If there is something like "redemption" for such linguistic acts – which we might take to mean that certain terms, epithets, verbal abuses are reclaimed and subsequently transformed – Butler locates it in the power of music, literature, or art rather than in law:

> The aggressive reappropriation in the rap of, say, Ice T becomes a site for traumatic reenactment of injury, but one in which the terms not only mean or communicate in a conventional way, but are themselves set forth as discursive items, in their very linguistic conventionality and, hence, as both forceful and arbitrary, recalcitrant and open to reuse.[35]

Butler believes, moreover, that not only language but also silence functions in crucially rhetorical ways to create legal, political, or social subjects. Injurious language such as hate speech can subjugate the people at which it is aimed, but "one can be interpellated, put in place, given a place, through silence, through not being addressed, and this becomes painfully clear when we find ourselves preferring the occasion of being derogated to the one of not being addressed at all."[36]

Butler shifts the critical focus away from law by arguing that language such as hate speech has been reappropriated most meaningfully outside law's purview, and by questioning whether legal remedies have the capacity to overhaul, overcome, or confront in any deep sense, such language at all. In doing so, she puts pressure on approaches that look to the language *of* law, suggesting instead a more antagonistic dynamic between artistic speech (Ice T's rap as an appropriation and judgment of hate speech) and legal language (prosecuting hate speech in the courts). If her

---

[33] Judith Butler, *Excitable Speech: A Politics of the Performative* (New York and London: Routledge, 1997) 27.

[34] Ibid., 98.

[35] Ibid., 100.

[36] Ibid., 27.

discussion of silence similarly imagines the lack of address beyond the strictly legal sphere, the work of Peter Brooks and Marianne Constable returns silence to law's framework, positing it as a crucial and persistent dimension of our relationship to jurisprudence and situating it squarely within law's bounds. For both Brooks and Constable, a speech act like the *Miranda* rights becomes fertile ground on which to parse our culture's assumptions and expectations of justice. Brooks reads the "right to remain silent" against the speech that law demands or exacts, namely the confession. Treating confession as a complex rhetorical thicket rather than a plumb line to truth, Brooks points out that confessions do not necessarily do what we expect them to do: "You may damn yourself," he writes, "even as you seek to exculpate yourself."[37] *Miranda v. Arizona* (1966), Brooks observes, does not resolve the problem of confession so much as expose its complexity: "The *Miranda* warnings, then, are to set the conditions in which the voluntary confessional narrative can unfold – or fail to unfold."[38] Because the speech act of confession itself proves at all moments tenuous and unpredictable, silence only underscores its fundamental instability: "You may be in a situation of damning yourself if you do confess or if you don't confess."[39]

The demand for speech that characterizes the dominant understanding of positive law across a range of disciplines (among them, legal studies, sociology, and political theory) has eclipsed, in Marianne Constable's assessment, the radical potentiality of silence within the law. Challenging the primacy of loquaciousness over silence entails emphasizing that "the justice of modern law lies precisely in positive law's ostensible silences," by which she means that "the conditions of justice . . . cannot be stipulated or definitively pronounced."[40] This does not imply, however, that they are unavailable; Constable's argument turns on the *readability* of silence and the conviction that, rather than pointing to the limits of law, such instances constitute possibilities for rather than absences of justice. From her perspective, then, the promise of *Miranda v. Arizona* "comes from the opportunity for silence that a felicitously issued warning offers to an accused who finds himself in the extraordinary circumstance of being asked to speak in conditions in which ordinary conditions of speech no longer seem to apply."[41] To create the optimal conditions for the speech act that *Miranda* encourages – the uncoerced, legally admissible confession – means to open up an alternative of silence. If, as Constable maintains, "the utterance of the [*Miranda*] warning ["You have the right to remain silent"] marks the formal

---

[37] Peter Brooks, *Troubling Confessions: Speaking Guilt in Law and Literature* (Chicago: University of Chicago Press, 2000) 6.

[38] Ibid., 17.

[39] Ibid., 23.

[40] Marianne Constable, *Just Silences: The Limits and Possibilities of Modern Law* (Princeton and Oxford: Princeton University Press, 2005) 8.

[41] Ibid., 173.

Narrative and Rhetoric

entry of the accused into the legal process,"[42] then sanction for this process rests on the freedom (and, more critically, the *right*) to say nothing. Whether this silence paves the way for justice or injustice remains undecidable in practice; in principle, however, it may just be the best that the legal system can produce.

For Shoshana Felman, silence also marks the point at which a legal event moves out of its enclosed juridical context – the courtroom, lawyers, judges – and into the wider cultural realm. In *The Juridical Unconscious*, Felman considers the example of a witness at the Eichmann trial who fainted on the stand and could therefore no longer be considered a valid witness from the point of view of the law. The cultural life of this moment, however, proved another matter: everyone in Israel remembered K-Zetnik's collapse in court as the most searing, representative moment of the trial; the event, in effect, became *synonymous* with the trial from a cultural standpoint. Drawing a distinction between legal and artistic evidence, she proposes, helps us to grasp how "it was precisely through K-Zetnik's *legal muteness* that the trial inadvertently *gave silence a transmitting power*, and – although not by intention – managed to transmit the legal meaning of collective trauma with the incremental power of a work of art."[43] The instant that the witness ceases to speak – the instant of traumatic silence – is precisely the point, for Felman, where culture and law intersect. Silence, which to some may seem like the absence of rhetoric, here works in a pointedly rhetorical way to create the conditions by which legal experience enters the wider cultural in a transformed and lasting way.

Our culture's experience of law, as Cover, Brooks, Constable, and Felman suggest, begins in and unfolds through rhetoric. This experience acquires shape, moreover, whether or not one sets foot in a courtroom or comes face to face with a police officer. It is buoyed by language from its most ordinary to its most literary guises; to speak of law's rhetoric thus means to address its myriad iterations and omissions, its echoes from legal opinions to novels to newspaper reports and overheard conversations. With this sensibility in mind, I would like now to turn to a landmark opinion of American law and to consider its implications in light of rhetoric.

Between Rhetoric and Fiction: *Plessy v. Ferguson* and the Construction of Race

If rhetorical readings of law have called attention not only to language but also to silence, I propose to examine one case in particular, *Plessy v. Ferguson* (1896), which I approach as a paradigmatic example of the potency such readings can offer. I conclude the discussion of *Plessy* by considering its relationship to Robert Louis

---

[42] Ibid., 167.
[43] Shoshana Felman, *The Juridical Unconscious: Trials and Traumas in the Twentieth Century* (Cambridge, MA: Harvard University Press, 2002) 154. Emphasis in the original.

Stevenson's *Dr. Jekyll and Mr. Hyde* (1886), a connection that I intend as suggestive rather than exhaustive. I pair these texts in hopes that the resonances between them intimate avenues for continued and future inquiry into the literary dimensions of jurisprudence. *Plessy*, moreover, offers particularly fertile ground for rhetorical reading because it began as a planned challenge to Louisiana's law requiring African Americans and whites to ride in separate railway cars. Seeking to contest this law, a committee of Louisiana citizens, the majority of whom were of mixed race, chose a light-skinned black man named Homer Plessy to deliberately violate the enforced separation. *What* happened – itself a rhetorical gesture intended to signify, to deliver a message – thus turned out to be secondary to the language that gave this "what" legal shape and traction; the premeditated event served as a pretext, in other words, to the rhetorical intervention offered by Plessy's attorney, Albion Tourgée. What makes this case ripe for a rhetorical reading is precisely this history as a staged intervention into the law – as an explicit attempt *to retell the story of race* by exposing the arbitrariness of racial classifications and to narrate identity in terms other than those of the physical (that is, visible) world. Racial identity itself is thus installed in the wider fabric of storytelling, and the story it presents turns out to have surprising implications for the difficult concepts – at once separate and conjoined – of race and identity.

On June 7, 1892, Homer Plessy boarded a train, sat in a whites-only compartment, and announced to the conductor that he was, contrary to appearances, black. Plessy was forcibly removed from the train, arrested and briefly jailed. Nearly four years later, on May 18, 1896, his case reached the U.S. Supreme Court, which upheld the appellate court's decision, ruling that Louisiana's Separate Car Act did not violate the Thirteen and Fourteenth Amendments outlawing slavery and guaranteeing due process and equal protection under the law, respectively. The opinion created the legal conditions for the Jim Crow south, enforcing the separate-but-equal logic that held sway until *Brown v. Board of Education* overturned it in 1954.[44]

In his preliminary statement of the case's facts, Justice Henry Billings Brown, who authored the majority opinion, called attention to the defense's claim that Plessy, "*instead of pleading* or admitting that he belonged to the colored race . . . declined and refused, *either by pleading* or otherwise, to admit that he was *in any* sense or *in any* proportion a colored man."[45] The repetition in this seemingly straightforward account already suggests an unwieldiness, even a confusion, about the nature of Plessy's offense. If his violation consisted of willfully sitting in the wrong

---

[44] For a succinct account of the case and related documents surrounding it, see *Plessy v. Ferguson: A Brief History with Documents*, Brook Thomas, ed. Bedford Series in History and Culture (Boston and New York: Bedford Books, 1997).
[45] 163 U.S. 537 at 539–40 (1896). Emphasis added.

Narrative and Rhetoric

compartment, why does the stress fall on the observation that "instead of pleading," he rebuffed, "either by pleading or otherwise," to declare his race? It becomes difficult to tell, in this narration, whether the breach consisted of an act or an omission. In his majority opinion, Brown would reiterate the plaintiff's refusal to speak, stating that although Plessy had been assigned to the appropriate railway car for his race, "he insisted upon going into a coach used by the race to which he did not belong. Neither in the information nor plea was his particular race or color averred."[46] The sense of disapproval rehearsed by the Court turns on the fact that Plessy would not say what was demanded of him, namely that he was black. The phrasing here suggests that *any* words to that effect – "by pleading or otherwise," "in any sense or in any proportion" – would have sufficed.

Of course, Plessy *had* to announce his race, because to all appearances he looked white. Brown's opinion notes further that "petitioner was seven-eights Caucasian and one-eighth African blood; that the mixture of colored blood was not discernible in him; and that he was entitled to every right, privilege, and immunity secured to citizens of the United States of the white race; and that, upon such theory, he took possession of a vacant seat in a coach where passengers of the white race were accommodated, and was ordered by the conductor to vacate said coach."[47] The conductor (who had been alerted to the plan beforehand) had, in fact, asked the neatly dressed passenger with the first-class ticket, "Are you a colored man?" To which Homer Plessy replied, "Yes." Why, then, does the opinion elide Plessy's own admission? The legally induced silence – which seems as salient as it is as it is resounding – ushers in a muteness about race that the court must fill with the demand for "pleading or otherwise" (what, we might ask, would this "otherwise" entail?), the insistence upon something more: an unequivocal expression of racial difference, perhaps; an expression of shame or remorse.

In rejecting the prosecution's argument that the Louisiana law mandating separate railway cars did not violate the Constitution, *Plessy* takes pains to disavow its own legal potency, positing it as at most a reinforcement of the status quo. "A statute which implies merely a legal distinction between the white and colored races – a distinction which is founded in the color of the two races, and which must always exist so long as white men are distinguished from the other race by color – has no tendency to destroy the legal equality of the two races, or reestablish a state of involuntary servitude."[48] Law, in this sense, "merely" reflects the world it inhabits, and it can no more avoid this reflection than it can alter the hard fact that some people are born white and others black. To insist on separate-but-equal as "merely

---

[46] 163 U.S. 537 at 541 (1896).
[47] 163 U.S. 537 at 542 (1896).
[48] 163 U.S. 537 at 543 (1896).

a legal distinction" is thus to resist the notion that legal pronouncements have force beyond the descriptive (or at most, conservative). The problem that remains unspoken here, however, is the specificity of Plessy's case: this particular plaintiff, after all, was able to board the whites-only car in the first place because he *could not be distinguished* from a white man. If the "merely legal" distinction simply codifies what everyone can see, then this distinction becomes impossible to maintain when blackness is invisible.

Yet even as the Court asserts that segregated railway cars do not compromise legal equality, it does entertain the possibility that inequality might exist in a fictional realm – and can therefore be rejected out of hand. If inferiority exists, Brown writes, it is as a delusion chosen by, rather than forced upon, blacks. "We consider the underlying fallacy of the plaintiff's argument to consist in the assumption that the enforced separation of the two races stamps the colored race with a badge of inferiority. If this be so, it is not by reason of anything found in the act, but solely because the colored race chooses to put that construction upon it."[49] In positing inferiority as little more than a phantasmatic projection, the court places blame for this imagined status squarely on the shoulders of African Americans, whose impoverished or paranoid imaginations blind them to the neutral light of separate-but-equal. The Constitution guarantees blacks civil and political protection. The social world, however, stands outside this sphere, beyond the province of legislation: "If one race be inferior to the other socially, the Constitution of the United States cannot put them upon the same plane."[50] W. H. Auden parodied legal tautology in his poem "Law Like Love" (1939) with the laconic pronouncement, "Law is The Law,"[51] and we might recognize some of this line's insularity in the *Plessy* majority's logic. If "Law is The Law" – no more and no less – then its reach cannot possibly extend beyond its self-contained sphere; one should not expect the law of the land to be the custom of the country.

Suspecting, perhaps, that such reasoning may prove unsatisfying, the Court offers yet another scenario, one that might be taken (in the wake of its previous claim) as a counterfactual: "The argument also assumes that social prejudices may be overcome by legislation, and that equal rights cannot be secured to the negro except by an enforced commingling of the two races. We cannot accept this proposition. If the two races are to meet upon terms of social equality, it must be the result of natural affinities, a mutual appreciation of each other's merits, and a voluntary consent of individuals."[52] Legal pronouncements, Brown reasons, do not have the power

---

[49] 163 U.S. 537 at 551 (1896).
[50] 163 U.S. 537 at 552 (1896).
[51] W. H. Auden, "Law Like Love," *Collected Poems*, Edward Mendelson, ed. (New York: Random House, 1991) 263.
[52] 163 U.S. 537 at 551 (1896).

Narrative and Rhetoric

to force individuals together in any material, practical sense; the Supreme Court's word cannot be set on par with the world in which it is spoken. As Paul de Man put it, "No one in his right mind will try to grow grapes by the luminosity of the word 'day.'"[53] De Man goes on to note, however, that life would be inconceivable without the structure lent by narrative, because "it is very difficult not to conceive the pattern of one's past and future existence as in accordance with temporal and spatial schemes that belong to fictional narratives and not to the world."[54] In *Plessy*, the Supreme Court assumes the literalist posture without heeding de Man's second proposition about life's tightly bound relation to narrative. If one "cannot grow grapes by the luminosity of the word 'day,'" then in the Court's view, one cannot cultivate a social world by the light of the legal word.

In ostensibly mitigating its authority by asserting its position as one of constraint, the Supreme Court takes pains to draw a sharp line between the rhetorical act (passing for white when one is black) and the legal distinction, which is objective ("founded in the color of the two races") and permanent ("must always exist so long as white men are distinguished from the other race by color"). Perhaps the most complex and subtle rejoinder to this resistance to rhetoric – and the strongest appeal to self-determination of one's racial identity – takes the form of the prosecution's assertion of the harm done to Plessy. In arguably his most creative legal gambit, Tourgée insisted that the injury to his client consisted of damage to his reputation as a black man who passed for white. As a consequence, the Separate Car Act compromised his earning potential – the potential property – that he would have enjoyed with that reputation intact. Justice Brown engaged and dismissed the argument in the following terms:

> It is claimed by the plaintiff in error that, in any mixed community, the reputation of belonging to the dominant race, in this instance the white race, is *property*, in the same sense that a right of action, or of inheritance, is property. Conceding this to be so, for the purposes of this case, we are unable to see how this statute deprives him of, or in any way affects his right to, such property. If he be a white man and assigned to a colored coach, he may have his action for damages against the company for being deprived of his so-called property. Upon the other hand, if he be a colored man and be so assigned, he has been deprived of no property, since he is not lawfully entitled to the reputation of being a white man.[55]

Plessy v. Ferguson, quite unexpectedly, turns out to be a case about property law, invoking Lockean ideas of property in one's body – and refiguring, too, the painful

---

[53] Paul de Man, "The Resistance to Theory," *The Resistance to Theory* (Minneapolis: University of Minnesota Press, 1986) 11.

[54] Ibid., 11.

[55] 163 U.S. 537 at 549 (1896).

memory of the slave *as* property. The Court, however, overlooks the multiple layers of this argument, just as it bypasses the concept of reputation that Tourgée posits and replaces it with an altogether different understanding. In Tourgée's account, reputation operates independently from either a biological or a legal determination of race; it is chosen, self-fashioned, performed rather than prescribed. It thus becomes the point of resistance to the one-drop rule and serves, more powerfully, as the *legal articulation* (yoked as it is to property) of the rule's arbitrariness. Reputation, the *Plessy* prosecution implies, is social in nature: it traffics in belief rather than knowledge, retaining a rhetorical potential to destabilize, challenge, and expose the fragility of a legal rule. In short, it is not – contrary to the Court's conclusion – something to which one is ever "lawfully entitled." In setting its version of reputation within the framework of legal entitlement, then, Brown's majority opinion refuses to acknowledge the protean concept advanced by the prosecution, relating reputation instead to the legal idea of race. Yet in doing so, it neglected the more troubling question underlying the prosecution's case: If a "merely legal" distinction between black and white cannot destroy legal equality, why would a person's "mere" appearance as a white man prevent him from reaping the *social* (and economic) benefits of his (observed and obvious) skin color? The Court's narrow definition of reputation does not entertain the possibility that reputation rests on anything other than verifiable (that is, biological, one-drop rule-bound) truth. The implications of its holding further imply that in practice, only a white person's reputation can be tarnished; one could not, after all, imagine as a corollary the scenario in which a black man's reputation as a nonwhite could be in any sense compromised.

To consider the rhetoric of *Plessy v. Ferguson* through the lens of the prosecution's claims to reputation and property, then, means to see it as a story of who tells (and in telling, authorizes and owns) the story of personhood. The existence of at least two such stories – one imagined from the white, the other from the African American perspective – emerged most forcefully, of course, in W. E. B. Dubois' *The Souls of Black Folk* (1903) and its articulation of African American double consciousness. As Brook Thomas has argued, "The *Plessy* majority institutionalizes double consciousness as African American identity, an identity that influences the form of at least one strain of the African American literary tradition."[56] Related to the overarching condition of double consciousness, we find the fiction of race at work in *Plessy* in a range of novels about light-skinned African Americans passing as whites, among them William Wells Brown's *Clotel* (1853), James Weldon Johnson's *The Autobiography of an Ex-Colored Man* (1912), and Nella Larsen's

---

[56] Brook Thomas, "*Plessy v. Ferguson* and the Literary Imagination," *Cardozo Studies in Law and Literature* 9 (1): 58 (1997).

Narrative and Rhetoric 393

Passing (1929).[57] Tourgée himself wrote a passing novel, *Pactolus Prime*, six years before the separate-but-equal decision was handed down.[58] Although it seems all too fitting, therefore, to relate *Plessy*'s language to this genre of fiction, I propose to set it alongside a different but no less suggestive text – a close relative, perhaps, of the passing novel. This relative (or strange bedfellow), Robert Louis Stevenson's *Dr. Jekyll and Mr. Hyde*, tells the story of the unsettling double, of inarticulate revulsion and – oddly enough – of property.

Ten years intervene between Stevenson's novella and the Supreme Court's verdict in *Plessy*, and six years separate the fictional story from the historical event of Plessy's fateful train ride. Such a retrospective move from the historical circumstances of *Plessy* to the fictional world of *Jekyll and Hyde* deliberately sets aside more traditional concerns about causality or chronology (Tourgée, put simply, was not "staging" Stevenson in any explicit sense). In doing so, this approach emphasizes law and literature as cultural productions, suggesting (as critical approaches to legal rhetoric have done) that we read them not as mirrors but as prisms through which we can better discern the nuances, fractures, and stakes of the normative worlds we inhabit. That each of these texts comes from a different side of the Atlantic only reinforces the point: These words are shared rather than discrete. In their most sweeping iterations, they shed light on the assumptions that underpin culture (in this instance,

---

[57] We find this double-consciousness and passing enunciated, too, in Paul Lawrence Dunbar's famous poem "We Wear the Mask" (1913):

> We wear the mask that grins and lies,
> It hides our cheeks and shades our eyes –
> This debt we pay to human guile;
> With torn and bleeding hearts we smile
> And mouth with myriad subtleties.
> Why should the world be over-wise,
> In counting all our tears and sighs?
> Nay, let them only see us while
> We wear the mask.
> We smile, but oh great Christ, our cries
> To Thee from tortured souls arise.
> We sing, but oh the clay is vile
> But let the world dream otherwise,
> We wear the mask!

Paul Lawrence Dunbar, *The Collected Poetry of Paul Lawrence Dunbar*, Joanne M. Braxton, ed. (Charlottesville: University of Virginia Press, 1993) 71. Dunbar's poem, also, takes aim at black minstrelsy in the Jim Crow era. For a discussion of the poet in this context, see Blair L. M. Kelley, "Right to Ride: African American Citizenship and Protest in the Era of *Plessy v. Ferguson*," *African American Review* 41:2 (2007), 347–56.

[58] *Pactolus Prime* was published in 1890. For a discussion of Tourgée's novel, see Ch. 3 ("*Huckleberry Finn*; or, Consequences") in Stacey Margolis, *The Public Life of Privacy in Nineteenth-Century American Literature* (Durham: Duke University Press, 2005).

Anglo-American culture), illuminating those preoccupations that exceed national boundaries or historical chronology.

At its most elemental, *Jekyll and Hyde* tells the story of scientific ambition gone awry: Dr. Henry Jekyll discovers a potion that transforms him into the sinister Edward Hyde, the alter-ego who terrorizes the streets of London and eventually overwhelms his creator, who manages to pen a confession of the disastrous experiment just before succumb to his doppelgänger. Stevenson's iconic story has been read variously as an allegory of good versus evil; as a cautionary tale about the pitfalls of science in the Victorian era; as a Freudian narrative about the conflict between ego and id; as a staging of class struggle between the upper-class Jekyll and the working-class Hyde – to name but a few avenues for a text that seems able to contain a seemingly infinite number of interpretive possibilities. In reading this work alongside *Plessy v. Ferguson*, however, I want to consider *Jekyll and Hyde* rhetorically rather than thematically. Rather than treating it as an allegory onto which one might map the Supreme Court's defense of the separate-but-equal doctrine, I will suggest that Stevenson's language of evasion and circumlocution can shed light on the rhetorical complexities that shape the normative universe of *Plessy*. The turn to a nonthematic text is also meant to adumbrate possible directions in future studies of law's rhetoric, encouraging scholarship that moves beyond thematic connections among law and the humanities (connections that, intuitively and not necessarily unwisely, might lead one to read *Plessy* together with one of the "passing" novels mentioned previously). To bypass around the question of theme brings us closer to the rhetoric underwriting the larger moral issues at play in the judgments we make within and beyond the law – a methodology that studies of law and rhetoric, at their most potent, bring into focus.

Having said that, however, it would be hard *not* to note one particular thematic connection, namely that *Jekyll and Hyde*, like *Plessy v. Ferguson*, turns on a pivot of property. In Stevenson's novella, property – in the form of Jekyll's will – structures the text as the portal through which Hyde comes into view. When Jekyll's attorney, Gabriel Utterson, learns to his dismay that one "friend and benefactor Edward Hyde" has been named as the heir to his client's possessions, Utterson finds himself confronted with a problem as mysterious as it is outrageous. "The document had long been the lawyer's eyesore. It offended him both as a lawyer and as a lover of the sane and customary sides of life, to whom the fanciful was the immodest."[59] As the novella's dominant narrative perspective, Utterson launches the tale in the direction of mystery – who exactly is this Hyde? – with the intention of exposing the person named in the will as a wrongful heir.

The problem of uncovering this purported scandal, however, is that nobody seems to know Hyde outside of the reputation that precedes him. His crimes – trampling a young girl and murdering a Minister of Parliament – occur in the presence of

---

[59] Robert Louis Stevenson, *Dr. Jekyll and Mr. Hyde* (1886; New York: Penguin, 1987) 46.

Narrative and Rhetoric

witnesses. Yet despite being seen in these moments, the man appears oddly indescribable; there is something unseemly about him, but his observable qualities do not clarify so much as confound. Early on, Utterson's friend Mr. Enfield paints the elusive figure in a language strained with effort and encumbered by imprecision:

> He is not easy to describe. There is something wrong with his appearance; something displeasing, something down-right detestable. I never saw a man I so disliked, and yet I scarce know why. He must be deformed somewhere; he gives a strong feeling of deformity, although I couldn't specify the point. He's an extraordinary looking man, and yet I really can name nothing out of the way. No, sir; I can make no hand of it; I can't describe him.[60]

Enfield's repetitions amount to a narrative stutter of sorts, a stammer that the "extraordinary looking man," in his silence, refuses to correct. Nor is it corrected later, when Utterson finally meets Hyde and finds himself no more capable of finding words for his discomfort than was his friend:

> Mr. Hyde was pale and dwarfish, he gave an impression of deformity without any nameable malformation, he had a displeasing smile, he had borne himself to the lawyer with a sort of murderous mixture of timidity and boldness, and he spoke with a husky, whispering and somewhat broken voice; all these were points against him, but not all of these together could explain the hitherto unknown disgust, loathing and fear with which Mr. Utterson regarded him. "There must be something else," said the perplexed gentleman. There *is* something more, if I could find a name for it. God bless me, the man seems hardly human. Something troglodytic, shall we say?[61]

The "deformity without any nameable malformation," the disturbance that lies just beneath the surface of speech, both fuels and thwarts the need to come to some sort of judgment about Hyde. We might, however, also conclude that these oblique descriptions – Utterson's utterances – do not describe so much as *judge*; as utterances, that is, they function as speech acts through which he constitutes his subject, and through which he deems him less than human ("troglodytic, shall we say?"). As such, his language evokes a quality that James Boyd White associates with the form of a legal rule, which "appears to be a language of description . . . but in cases of any difficulty . . . is actually a language of judgment."[62] The central problem of *Jekyll and Hyde* thus emerges as a problem of identification rather than identity – not "who is Hyde?" or "where can one find him?" but more urgently: How can one define and ultimately judge this "something" or articulate this "somewhere"? How, in short, can one "specify the point"?

[60] Ibid., 44.
[61] Ibid., 52.
[62] White, *Heracles' Bow*, 65.

With striking resonance, the Supreme Court in *Plessy* sought to describe in law what remained indescribable – beneath the surface, on the tip of one's tongue, invisible to the naked eye – in life. Law provides legitimacy to that "something," but not, I submit, a language for it. The discomfort surrounding this "something" persists in what Homer Plessy does not say (or what Brown's opinion, in any case, omits) and in the Court's expression of the wish that *something* be said. I am not suggesting that Edward Hyde serves as the fictional analogue for Homer Plessy, but that the unnameability and inarticulateness surrounding him stages a profoundly legal conundrum, one that *Plessy v. Ferguson* is unable to work out: the dilemma of mixed race. "There must be something else," Utterson reflects – and so there must. Justice Brown, however, never resolves this something, expressing it instead as the fact of an omission: what the Court imagines that Homer Plessy *might* (and should) have said, which it can only imagine by omitting the answer he in fact *did* give in response to conductor's question. Recounting instead that the plaintiff "declined and refused, either by pleading or otherwise, to admit that he was in any sense or in any proportion a colored man," the opinion ducks and weaves around the arbitrariness of this "any sense" or "any proportion" that the prosecution sought to expose.

We might recognize something of the demand or desire beneath *Plessy*'s surface by setting it against what Stevenson's text *does* supply: a confession. Jekyll's tell-all letter closes the novella by revealing how Hyde came into being, even though it ultimately elucidates the doctor's mysterious creation with little more specificity than either Enfield or Utterson. We know no more of Hyde's interiority or experiences (beyond the few reported crimes he commits, what does he *do* when he is loose in the city?) than we did before. Yet what we do find in these closing words amounts to an explanation and a confession: from the "morbid sense of shame"[63] that opens the letter to its report of Jekyll's descent into madness as he becomes consumed by "the horror of my other self,"[64] we cannot but sympathize with the doomed physician as he takes responsibility for who he is and what he – as both Jekyll and Hyde – has done. What the Supreme Court wants in *Plessy*, I propose, is what readers get in *Jekyll and Hyde*: an expression of shame, a confession of guilt, and a disavowal of – and simultaneous accounting for – one's deeds. That Jekyll's letter reaches Utterson's hands after Hyde's (and thus, Jekyll's) death, of course, suggests that the speech act of this written confession may restore a social order, but that it does so by removing the offending person from it – or more precisely, that order is restored when the individual who upended it willingly *takes himself out* of the social world. No judge, lawyer, police officer, or detective need intervene – and perhaps this self-righting

---

[63] Stevenson, 103.
[64] Stevenson, 122.

Narrative and Rhetoric

moral universe figures, ultimately, as the ground atop which *Plessy v. Ferguson* rests.

It may well be only natural for the law to resist the potency of its own rhetoric. Paul de Man might certainly have suggested as much when he claimed that structuralism, in attempting to model the study of literature after the sciences, attended to only two of the three parts of the medieval trivium of grammar, logic, and rhetoric. Putting grammar and logic at the forefront of their literary analysis, structuralists ultimately elide the crucial third element of rhetoric. Yet it is this element, de Man notes, that presents at once the most difficult – indeed, indeterminable – aspect of reading. Rhetoric makes a text's multiple meanings possible, giving it its complex texture and interpretive life. The resistance to theory, de Man famously argued, can therefore be grasped as a resistance to rhetoric's elusiveness, which is nothing short of a resistance to reading. His emphasis on rhetoric and resistance drives home two critical points: first, "that literature is not a transparent message," and second, "that the grammatical decoding of a text leaves a residue of indetermination that has to be, but cannot be, resolved by grammatical means, however extensively conceived."[65] These residues remain – in literary works, I submit, as in legal narratives – and are bound to produce anxiety. Building on this sensibility, we might say that the resistance to legal rhetoric – the theory that subverts the certainty of both grammar and logic – constitutes a resistance to reading the law, pointing in turn to the impossible wish for transparency in jurisprudence. It directs us, that is, toward a wider cultural and juridical wish for a language that infallibly duplicates the world, and can therefore judge it with unwavering certainty.

[65] de Man, 15.

15

Justice as Translation

Harriet Murav

Translation has been an object of humanistic inquiry going at least as far back as the third century BCE, when the Hebrew Bible was translated into Greek. Walter Benjamin's famous essay "The Task of the Translator," originally published in 1923, praises the interlinear translation of the Bible as the ideal form of translation because it unites freedom and literalness.[1] Freedom and literalness as the twin poles of translation are tied to the definition of translation as the transfer of meaning between two languages, a concept that long dominated the field of translation studies. This notion of translation presupposes a model of language as a transparent vessel of meaning, and a neutral space wherein all languages are similar. Benjamin's praise of interlineal translation, which graphically displays the gap between the two languages calls transparency and even translatability into question. Postcolonial studies challenges the assumption about a neutral space for translation, arguing instead that universalizing neutrality masks the imposition of power of a dominant culture over a weaker one, ignoring the gaps and heterogeneity not only between cultures and languages but also within a single culture. As Talal Asad argued in 1986, "there are asymmetrical tendencies and pressures in the languages of dominated and dominant societies."[2] The problem of rendering a statement in one language into another becomes more difficult if the relations of power between the two languages are uneven. In this context, the something that is invariably lost in translation is more than just a nuance of meaning. Translations into a so-called weaker language may also undermine and invert the original meaning of a text, shifting the balance

---

[1] Walter Benjamin, "The Task of the Translator," *Illuminations*, Harry Zohn, trans. (New York: Schocken Books, 1969) 82. For a study that focuses on the issue of literalness in relation to the cultural significance of the Jews as translators, see Naomi Seidman, *Faithful Renderings: Jewish Christian Difference and the Politics of Translation* (Chicago: University of Chicago Press, 2006).

[2] Talal Asad, "The Concept of Cultural Translation in British Social Anthropology," *Writing Culture: The Poetics and Politics of Ethnography*, James Clifford and George E. Marcus, eds. (Berkeley: University of California Press, 1986) 164.

Justice as Translation

of power in an unforeseen direction.[3] The problem of translation as attending to difference and not sameness is particularly important in the era of globalization, when presumably the differences between cultures pale before the overwhelming similarities produced by the mobility of labor and capital and global insecurity.[4]

These reassessments of translation have important consequences for law and humanities. One of the criticisms of law and literature studies is that regardless of their similarities, law and literature are fundamentally different, because decisions made in legal interpretation have real-life consequences absent in the field of literary interpretation. Another related criticism is that whereas the study of the representation of law in literature may shed light on literature, it offers little help to students or practitioners of law. The conceptualization of translation not as linguistic transfer, but rather, as an act performed in relation to another – to whom one must be faithful yet also betray, whose unique unrepeatable body must be preserved but also destroyed – bridges the gap between the seemingly dissimilar orders of law and translation. Among the studies of law and literature to emerge in recent decades, the question of justice and translation offers a fruitful avenue for exploring the possibility and impossibility of each.

To do so, this chapter examines James Boyd White's *Justice as Translation* (1990) in the context of two other major theoretical works on the same issue: Derrida's "What Is a Relevant Translation" and Lyotard's *The Differend: Phrases in Dispute*. Derrida's analysis and provocative translation of Portia's speech in *The Merchant of Venice* points to an aspect of language that is usually elided: the violence that unfolds even before an utterance is translated across languages. Lyotard's work points to the double bind of a victim whose injury includes the impossibility of bringing her suffering to the knowledge of a tribunal. The rules governing what can be said are not universal, and the "differend" arises when what counts in one "genre" as evidence does not have validity in other genres. The differend describes the limits of a model of justice based on a homogeneous, universal model of the rules governing the production of language. The challenge of the differend has currency in the twenty-first century, and not only in international law having to do with genocide and ethnic cleansing, but also in cases involving the claims made by one people against another within a single sovereign state. This chapter examines the recent

---

[3] Mikhail Bakhtin's work on hybrid speech, in which the boundaries between one's own and another's speech are blurred, and Homi Bhabha's arguments about the subversive force of colonial mimicry are important texts in this connection. See M. M. Bakhtin, *The Dialogic Imagination: Four Essays*, Caryl Emerson and Michael Holquist, eds. and trans. (Austin: University of Texas Press, 1981; and Homi Bhabha, *The Location of Culture* (London and New York: Routledge, 1994). Tejaswini Niranjana directly addresses the issue of colonial translation in *Siting Translation. History, Post-structuralism, and the Colonial Context* (Berkeley: University of California Press, 1992). See also Gayatri Spivak, "The Politics of Translation," *Outside in the Teaching Machine* (New York: Routledge, 1993) 179–200.

[4] See Naoki Sakai and Jon Solomon, eds., *Translation, Biopolitics, Colonial Difference* (Hong Kong: Hong Kong University Press, 2006).

body of writing that has emerged in Australia having to do with the claims made by indigenous peoples, whose tribal law goes unrecognized by state power. I conclude by considering two alternative versions of justice, language, and translation, one from American popular culture, the film *Crash*, and the other from the South African Truth and Reconciliation Commission. My discussion throughout focuses on the problem of the unique body of the text and the person, the subject of translation and the subject of justice.

Translation and Fidelity to the Self

White argues there is no legal action without translation: "At the center of the law is the activity of translation.[5] Translation is not a matter of finding an equivalent in a second language for a term in the original language. Language, in his view, is not a vessel of meanings, intentions, or any other "nonlinguistic material." Translation, it follows, is not the recovery of an original meaning or intention, but rather, "a reciprocal gesture" and a form of response "meant to honor the other and assert the self."[6] Translation, understood in this new sense, not as mastery of another's word, but as an answer to it, can serve, according to White, as "a model of social life," and in particular, a model for law, which is a way of thinking, talking, and acting. The lawyer, White suggests, translates the client's story into the language of the law; the client learns about this other legal language, and together lawyer and client create something new. In the process of making something new, White acknowledges, something will also be lost, just as something is always lost in the process of translation: the law both creates and jettisons possibilities for speech. Nonetheless, appreciating justice as translation offers enhanced possibilities for open-endedness and intersubjectivity among individuals and peoples.

The lawyer and her client, the lawyer explicating expert testimony before the jury, the officer, and a suspect, the judge interpreting a legal opinion, and the heads of state negotiating a treaty – are all engaged in transferring meaning from one type of language to another. Translation comes into play in all these instances because they variously engage the difference between the vernacular and specialized language of the law, the difference between the specialized language of an expert, the specialized language of the law, and the vernacular, the difference between the language of the past and the present, and finally, the difference between two national languages. To appreciate White's book requires, however, that we go beyond the mere enumeration of these legal activities to the broader question of their meaning in relation to the question of justice. (I will borrow White's use of the first-person plural for the time

---

[5] James Boyd White, *Justice as Translation: An Essay in Cultural and Legal Criticism* (Chicago: The University of Chicago Press, 1990), xii.

[6] Ibid., 256, 258.

Justice as Translation

being.) To use language is to perform an act that is "ethical and political in character," because speaking creates a character, a version of the self, and also creates a relation to another, constituting a community (ix). Justice Brandeis, in his dissent in *Olmstead* writes that even though the Constitution does not explicitly say that words are also things that the government cannot seize, protection from unreasonable search and seizure also means protection from government wiretapping. In so doing, Brandeis, according to White is performing an act of translation, carrying meaning from the past to the present. In so doing Brandeis is faithful to the principles of American democracy, if not to the literal terms of the Fourth Amendment.

White seeks to balance fidelity to the self, the past, the text, and "our cultural values" against respect for the other, openness to the future, and the acknowledgment that individuals perpetually re-create themselves, their past, their texts, and their cultural values. Fidelity operates as the limit to open-endedness, as for example, when White says that in the translation from the vernacular to legal language and back again, we ought not to "eliminate our cultural past in favor of an uninformed view of the present." Yet we must also acknowledge that our translations are always approximate, partial, even "contingent."

White gives as an example of the difficulty of translation the first line of Homer's *Odyssey*, "Sing to me of the man, Muse, the man of twists and turns."[7] The original Greek term *polytropon* – "twists and turns" – as White points out, presents a problem, because it can mean both man "suffering many turns" and man "capable of many turns," that is, tricky, "skilled in all ways of contending," as Fitzgerald translates it.[8] Fitzgerald's translation, which emphasizes the capacity for deception, connects Odysseus's description in the opening line to terms that are later used to describe him, such as *poikilomêtis* (full of various wiles).[9] What makes Odysseus and *The Odyssey* worth dwelling on is not so much this problem of translation as it is the problem of fidelity. Odysseus is simultaneously the trickiest, most deceptive, and the most faithful man. He is the most faithful because he endures all the "turns" of his twenty-year odyssey to get back home to Ithaka and Penelope; yet he is also the most unfaithful, not only because he has not been faithful to his wife, but also because only the most cleverly deceptive, wiliest man could escape from the Cyclops' cave (by naming himself "no one") and from all the other hosts who want to make him a permanent guest in one way or another. Finally, only the most long-suffering and trickiest man would be willing to and could figure out the final test that Penelope sets him before permitting him to enter their bedroom. Being faithful means acting as if there are no grounds for faith, being ready to give everything up to prove again (yet again) one's commitment to the other.

[7] Homer, *The Odyssey*, Robert Fagles, trans. (New York: Penguin Books, 1996) 77.
[8] Homer, *The Odyssey*, Robert Fitzgerald, trans. (Garden City, NY: Anchor, 1963) 1.
[9] For the discussion of Odysseus from which I take this point see Nancy Felson, *Regarding Penelope: From Character to Poetics* (Norman and London: University of Oklahoma Press, 1997) 49.

Faithfulness and fidelity do not mean a relation with the past so much as a willingness to break absolutely with the past for the sake of the future in which there is no guarantee of a place for oneself. In his discussion of affirmative action cases such as *Bakke*, White talks about the "opportunity for meaningful action," in other words, looking toward the future and not back toward the wrongful actions of the past, for which responsibility may be disavowed; his notion of fidelity and justice however, stays safely on this side of a boundary that secures a place for the self and continuity with the past. Despite his use of the term contingency, White stays within the territory of what "we" already know. The next two parts of this chapter explore the consequences for justice that White's limited model implies.

Derrida, like White, finds that the activities of law and translation are fundamentally related. In his essay "What Is a 'Relevant' Translation?" – which translates a single term in *The Merchant of Venice* – Derrida argues that "everything" in the play is a problem of translation. Translation, he writes, "is the law, it even speaks the language of the law beyond the law, represented by a woman who is disguised, transfigured, converted, travestied, read translated into a man of law."[10] Whereas White's model of law as translation suggests rational, transparent, univocal speakers negotiating with each other according to their faithful, uncoerced visions of themselves and each other, Derrida's use of the language of travesty and disguise suggests a far greater instability of self and language. Derrida argues that the attempt to come up with the most proper, suitable, pointed, economic, and idiomatic translation necessarily destroys the original even in the effort to preserve it faithfully. Like White, he sees fidelity as a key element in translation and justice, but his model of fidelity more resembles the dialectic interweaving of faithfulness, loss, and betrayal that I described earlier as characteristic for Odysseus.

Derrida writes, "All translation implies an insolvent indebtedness and an oath of fidelity to a given original."[11] The "oath of fidelity" is always impossible to fulfill in translation and in law, as in Antonio's promise to Shylock that should he be unable to pay his debt, Shylock will receive a pound of his flesh. Neither Antonio nor Shylock, however, can be faithful to their bond without giving up their very selves: in Shylock's case, his relation to God, in Antonio's case, his life. Justice and translation demand an impossible fidelity.

The contract between Antonio and Shylock centers on translation in a broader sense: the translation of a pound of flesh into a sum of money.[12] The relation between

[10] Jacques Derrida, "What Is a 'Relevant' Translation?," *Critical Inquiry* 27, Winter (2001) 183.
[11] Ibid.
[12] Derrida here uses Roman Jakobson's model of intersemiotic translation between codes or semiotic systems, one of which may be nonverbal. See Roman Jakobson, "On Linguistic Aspects of Translation," *The Translation Studies Reader*, Lawrence Venuti, ed. (London: Routledge, 2000) 114. White briefly discusses Jakobson's essay without referring to this concept in White, *Justice as Translation: An Essay in Cultural and Legal Criticism*, 251

Justice as Translation

a particular body and an abstract system is the hinge on which Derrida's expanded discussion of translation turns. He emphasizes the tension between "the unique literalness of proper body and the arbitrariness of a general, monetary, or fiduciary sign." In terms of translation in the narrow sense, the unique literalness of a proper body could mean the specific features of a particular word in a particular language, including for instance, its acoustical qualities (what it rhymes with, what it is homophonous with, its light or dark vowels), its grammatical gender, the history of its usage in low or high registers, its usage among specific speakers, and even its "foreignness" in its own language. Translation inevitably destroys these palpable features of the word. Language universalizes; translation adds to universalizing; and translation into legal language universalizes even more. White does not disagree with this characterization, as he says, when a plaintiff and a defendant face each other in court, each must speak in a language not his own. Where White and Derrida dramatically disagree has to do with the consequences of this universalizing trajectory.

Derrida's reading of the trial scene shows the seriousness of the consequences. Shylock refuses the court's offer to increase the payment owed to him, because of the oath he made before God. Portia, disguised as a legal scholar, demands that Shylock show mercy: "Then must the Jew be merciful." Leaving aside the problem of compulsory mercy, I quote Derrida's account of Portia's praise of mercy:

> In the name of this sublime panegyric of forgiveness, an economic ruse, a calculation, a stratagem is being plotted, the upshot of which (you know it well: the challenge to cut flesh without shedding one drop of blood) will be that Shylock loses everything in this translation of transaction, the monetary signs of his money as well as the literal pound of flesh – and even his religion, since when the situation takes a bad turn at this expense he will have to convert to Christianity, to translate himself (*convertere*) into a Christian, into a Christian language, after having been in turn forced, through a scandalous reversal – he who was entreated to be *merciful* – to implore the doge for mercy on his knees.[13]

The allegedly transcendent quality of mercy, which trumps law (Shylock must be merciful, must forgive the debt that is legally owed him), makes possible the application of the harsh penalties of law.

The passage that Derrida translates comes in the speech Portia gives to elaborate her request that Shylock show Antonio mercy. Portia famously says, "And earthly power doth then show likest God's/When mercy seasons justice." Derrida proposes the French word *relever* for "seasons." When Derrida says that mercy *relève* ("relieves") justice, he does so to capture the way Portia's demand that Shylock show mercy lifts justice from the physical and the literal into the elevated realm of spiritual interiority. It universalizes, and in so doing very nearly destroys what it

---

[13] Derrida, "What Is a 'Relevant' Translation?," 189.

allegedly attempts to preserve. The physical and the literal, the unique proper body that corresponds to White's notion of the self is fundamentally at risk in the process of translation. This self, which White says owes itself fidelity and elsewhere says owes itself to assert itself – inevitably must lose itself. Translation brings together the two incommensurate orders – of Christianity and Judaism, of the spirit and the letter, the sign and the body, mercy and law – in such a way as to destroy the original, the self, as in the case of Shylock in *The Merchant of Venice*. What White characterizes as law's "intelligibility," because law translates disagreements into abstract, neutral, and universal terms, Derrida characterizes as law's violence. The demand that Shylock show mercy utterly undermines Shylock's status as a plaintiff. He becomes a victim.

The Other's Word

White and Derrida would agree that translation always involves loss; where they disagree has to do with the quantity, quality, and reparability of the loss. For White, loss is almost an incidental result of law and of translation, even though he characterizes the loss in the following serious terms: "The law builds itself, over time, by discarding possibilities for speech and thought as well as by making them; and what it discards is for some person or people a living language, a living truth."[14] For Derrida, and for Lyotard as well, the loss is not incidental, but foundational, and cannot be repaired as easily as White suggests. Complete transparency is out of the question, argues White, once we give up on the idea of a "superlanguage" into which everything could be translated. White also says that the recognition of the "limited and tentative nature" of judgments that are made does not mean that the process of negotiation should lead participants to cede everything:

> We should not feel that respect for the other obliges us to erase ourselves, or our culture, as if all value lay out there and none here. As the traditions of the other are entitled to respect, despite their oddness to us, and sometimes despite their inhumanities, so too our tradition is entitled to respect as well. Our task is to be distinctively ourselves in a world of others: to create a frame that includes both self and other, neither dominant, in an image of fundamental equality. This is true of us as individuals in our relations with other[s], and true of us as a culture, as we face the diversity of our world. It is analytically true of translation, which owes fidelity to the other language and text but requires the assertion of one's own as well.[15]

In terms of its reflections on communities, the passage suggests a monolithic us and a monolithic them, with the inhumanities and oddness on "their" side. In terms of language, the passage implies a univocality of language and addresser and

[14] White, *Justice as Translation: An Essay in Cultural and Legal Criticism*, 262.
[15] Ibid., 264.

Justice as Translation

a transparent overlap between addresser and language. In other passages in which White uses the term "fidelity," the fidelity was to the self. Here fidelity is to the other, and what is owed the self is "assertion." How the assertion of the self – which the previous passage seems to normalize as a white, Western Christian self confronting the world's diversity – can leave space for fidelity to the other, or lead to justice, is hard to imagine.

Derrida asserts the inevitability of translation's violence, which destroys what it attempts to bring across the boundary separating two languages. Derrida also sees the fundamental operation of law as a kind of violence, the violence that takes place when a concrete particularity, a unique body, is translated into an abstraction, subsumed under a general class. For Lyotard the problem arises when a claim cannot be subject to this process, when the assertion of an injustice cannot come before the law – to put it another way, when the suffering of individuals as singularities cannot be translated into the abstract categories of law. If for Derrida the problem is translation, for Lyotard the problem is the failure to translate; the problem takes place when the gap between the two ways of speaking – the idiom of the sufferer and the language of the law – is too great.

In *The Differend: Phrases in Dispute* Lyotard takes seriously the charge of "Holocaust-denier" Robert Faurisson that the existence of the gas chambers cannot be proved. Lyotard transforms Faurisson's challenge into an inquiry into the evidentiary rules of history that raises questions about the possibilities for justice. His inquiry is particularly relevant for the question about justice as translation because it centers on a problem, or "limit-case" of language, which he calls the "differend." Lyotard defines the differend as follows: "A case of differend between two parties takes place when the 'regulation' of the conflict that opposes them is done in the idiom of one of the parties while the wrong suffered by the other is not signified in that idiom."[16] The Nazi extermination of the Jews is the paradigmatic differend because the rules for establishing the reality of the gas chambers cannot be satisfied; the best victims – "best" in the sense of those best qualified to give evidence – are dead. They are also victims in Lyotard's specific sense of the word because they are deprived of the means of proving that what happened to them was a wrong.

Both White and Lyotard reject the model of language as instrumental communication; both are interested in the ways that language creates a relation between addressor and addressee, although White stresses the agency of speakers, and Lyotard, the agency of language. The important difference between them is that Lyotard, in contrast to White, emphasizes the obstacles that prevent the birth of the relation between addressor and addressee. I open my mouth and speak, but you do not hear

---

[16] Jean-Francois Lyotard, *The Differend: Phrases in Dispute*, Georges Van Den Abbeele, trans., vol. 46, *Theory and History of Literature* (Minneapolis: University of Minnesota Press, 1988) 9.

me; you do not even recognize that I am speaking. There is no contact.[17] What White describes as a benign process, law's creating and discarding possibilities for speech, Lyotard describes in more radical terms as the ever-present loss of the possibility of justice created by a failure of language, a gap between "genres of discourse."[18] White says that if individuals cannot locate themselves in the public language of their societies "the discourse becomes exclusive and authoritarian in character" and "silences" the attempt to express the meanings of their experiences.[19] The silencing is what Lyotard calls a differend and it is always present. White's image of a frame that includes both self and other assumes an even playing field, symmetry across the two parties and homogeneity within both sides and across them. In his analysis of *Robinson*, a Fourth Amendment case involving the right of a suspect against an unreasonable search, White shows that both parties to this and other disputes have to speak in a language not their own. He finds much to praise in this compulsion, seeing in it a greater potential for justice. I will return to this question later, but for now, what is important is the hidden asymmetry of the two speakers: although the police officer is not a lawyer or a judge, she is far more familiar with the language of the law than the suspect. The police officer is, furthermore, an officer of the court. For Lyotard a differend takes place when a plaintiff loses the means to prove that damage was done. "One loses them, for example, if the author of the damages turns out directly or indirectly to be one's judge," writes Lyotard.[20] The case of the officer and the suspect approaches this description.

Lyotard is interested in "a radical critical politics of heterogeneity" attentive to the always-present failures of the system that determines what counts as proof of a wrong.[21] The problem is not merely filling in the gap in existing language with some other idiom, because this substitution would only create new differends. The feeling that "one cannot put it into words," as Lyotard says, cannot be "smothered right away in a litigation." The differend describes gaps within language and within single subjectivities but also the limit between groups of speakers and beings not able to speak (animals are an example of victims, according to Lyotard), those deemed outside the boundaries of acceptable speakers. The differend is "the unstable state

---

[17] To push the metaphor, Derrida's image of translation, in contrast to Lyotard's, focuses on the other end of the life cycle; translation provides only a mournful memory of the (dead) original.

[18] Interview by Gary A. Olson, "Resisting a Discourse of Mastery: A Conversation with Jean-François Lyotard." http://www.jacweb.org/Archived_volumes/Text_articles/V15_I3_Olson_Lyotard.htm. In the same interview Lyotard goes on to say, "There is no language game or genre or discourse which is able to encompass all the different discourses or genres, and there is a real *différend* in which no court or tribunal is able to decide what is best because there is no best way." White similarly argues that there is no single authoritative "superlanguage."

[19] White, *Justice as Translation: An Essay in Cultural and Legal Criticism*, 179.

[20] Lyotard, *The Differend: Phrases in Dispute*, 8.

[21] David Carroll, "Rephrasing the Political with Kant and Lyotard: From Aesthetic to Political Judgments," *Diacritics* 14, no. 3 (1984) 75.

Justice as Translation

and instance of language wherein something must be able to be put into phrases yet cannot be."

How do we know when a differend has taken place? The answer is contained in the question: as soon as we say "we." The instant two or more speakers reach consensus, someone else has been excluded; some injustice has been done, because, as Lyotard writes: "it is in the nature of a wrong not to be established by consensus."[22] The minute there is this community of self and other, this world of ethical relations produced by an act of speech, there is somewhere else another other who is not yet a self who can speak.

Thumbprints and Ashes

When the testimony and the witnesses have been destroyed, as in the Holocaust, a differend has taken place. The differend, however, is not limited to Auschwitz. A recent body of writing has emerged in Australia and New Zealand that uses Lyotard's model of the differend to critique legal decisions in cases made by indigenous peoples against the state. The apology offered by the Australian government on February 13, 2008, is one of the outcomes of the failures of these cases. Alisoun Neville's analysis of the judgment in *Cubillo v Commonwealth*, which was heard in 2000, uses the differend to examine the failure of the wrong done to two members of Australia's "stolen generation" to translate into legally acceptable proof.[23] In the discussion that follows, I use Neville's analysis, adding comments that highlight the larger issues of this chapter, the problem of justice as translation.

The point is not that Australian law lacks a category for the wrong done when individuals are deprived of parental care or their cultural heritage. Australian law does in fact recognize both these deprivations as harmful: Australia ratified the Convention on Genocide in 1949, and the judge in *Kruger* acknowledged that the case did involve the forcible transfer of children, which, according to Article II of the Convention, is a criterion for genocide. The decision in *Kruger*, however, found the removal of aboriginal children was not done with the intent to harm them, and therefore that genocide had not taken place.[24] Genocide was not the issue in *Cubillo*; however, both plaintiffs described the penalties they endured for attempting to speak their native language while in care and the harmful consequences of losing it. They claimed damages for loss of cultural and other aspects of Aboriginal life and loss of rights under the *Aboriginal Land Rights (Northern Territory) Act 1976*.[25]

---

[22] Lyotard, *The Differend: Phrases in Dispute*, 56.

[23] Alisoun Neville, "Cubillo v Commonwealth: Classifying Text and the Violence of Exclusion," *Macquarie Law Journal* 5, no. 31 (2005).

[24] *Kruger v Commonwealth* ("Stolen Generations case") [1997] HCA 27; (1997) 190 CLR 1.

[25] Jennifer Clarke, "Cubillo v Commonwealth," *Melbourne University Law Review* 25, no. 1 (2001).

The existence of a law establishing a category of wrong does not mean that the wrong can be proved. The plaintiffs in *Cubillo* as well as in other child-removal cases could not show that they suffered a wrong. The court found that what was done was done for their protection. Neville uses Lyotard's differend to show the classificatory schemes brought to bear in the decision did not acknowledge the indigenous sources that were the backbone of the plaintiffs' claim. The wrong suffered by the plaintiffs had no idiom in the language used to adjudicate their case.

I summarize Neville's argument. Under the Aboriginals Ordinance of 1918, the two plaintiffs, Lorna Cubillo and Peter Gunner, were removed from their families' care (in 1947 and 1956) and placed in church-run missions. Neville writes, "They sought damages from the Commonwealth for their removal from their families and culture... for their experiences of abuse in those missions, and for the trauma, illness, loss of culture and rights to land said to result from these events." The case was dismissed. The differend arises, according to Neville, because the language by means of which the harm was perpetrated, the language of the law and the state that removed the children, is the same language in which the plaintiff's case against the state was adjudicated. The harm could not be phrased in terms of indigenous law, tradition, and culture. The language gap that is at issue here is not the gap between speech and silence, but the gap between what counts as evidence, or, more precisely, how evidence is differently ranked by the two cultures leading to the plaintiffs' victimization.

One of the crucial moments of the case has to do with the question of oral versus documentary evidence: Indigenous culture highly values oral testimony, whereas Australian law privileges documentary evidence. Peter Gunner's mother affixed her thumbprint to the document of removal, thereby, according to the court, consenting to her son's removal. The court ranked the documentary evidence more highly than the oral testimony given by witnesses who said that an attempt was made to hide the child from the officers, including blackening his face with ash to conceal his light skin. The removal, according to the plaintiffs, was part of a systematic attempt to separate part European children from indigenous populations. What might have been read as acquiescence in the face of intimidation was read instead as consent, and even, a request for removal. The judge's summary of his decision specifically regarding Peter Gunner reads: "Most importantly, there was his mother's thumbprint on a form of request that asked that Peter be taken to St Mary's and given a western education. I have concluded that Peter went to St Mary's at his mother's request."[26]

The thumbprint, which everyone has, but is unique in each case, is a substitute for the personal signature. Whether the appearance of a thumbprint on a document is

---

[26] *Cubillo v Commonwealth* (includes summary dated 11 August 2000) [2000] FCA 1084 (11 August 2000) Last Updated: 11 August 2000. Available at: http://www.austlii.edu.au/au/cases/cth/federal_ct/2000/1084.html.

Justice as Translation

necessarily an indication of freely given consent, however, is another matter. As Irene Watson, writing in *The Indigenous Law Bulletin* puts it: "Will judges of the future interpret these agreements to mean that the natives have given their consent, as in *Cubillo*. But how free and informed and without duress have these processes been?"[27]

The Biometrics of Exclusion

The judgment in *Cubillo* emerges out of a broader legal framework that failed to grant Aboriginals legal status. As Paul Havemann writes, "The legal fiction that Australia was *terra nullius* (land of no one) justified the territorial acquisition of this continent and expropriation of Australia's Indigenous people, denied their personhood, culture, and governance systems, and legitimated their exclusion."[28] The debate about "law and exclusion" has received a new and important impetus from the work of Giorgio Agamben, whose argument about the fundamental operation of the political challenges the model of justice as translation. White's model only speaks to those who are inside the protected zone of law, deliberation, courts, and political life generally. His argument about a frame that includes both self and other reveals a blind spot about how the frame is created in the first place. Agamben's 1995 *Homo Sacer: Sovereign Power and Bare Life* argues that political life depends on what it places on its boundary, mere biological life. The conventional definition of the realm of politics (and justice) splits off the living being who has language – who can, according to Aristotle, as Agamben points out, deal with the "just and the unjust" – from those animal and less than fully human beings who merely have voice. The problem is that the boundary between the two realms is unstable, creating a "zone of indistinction." Human life can go either way, either toward political life or bare life, and this is what sovereign power decides. It is not only that citizens may suddenly find themselves in a vegetative or migratory, alien enemy, or stateless condition, deprived of language or rights and the opportunity of being heard. The use of Mrs. Gunner's thumbprint indicates a more generalized threat to the status of citizens as speakers. Judge O'Loughlin decided that the thumbprint, as the substitute for a signature, was a form of consent. The thumbprint in this interpretation resembles a speech act. The thumbprint, however, also contains biometrical data that may be used in the absence of speech giving consent. In this instance, the thumbprint is a record of a body and not an act of speech. When visitors to the United States give their thumbprints or when travelers pass through airport security devices that record, among other things, their temperatures, they are not giving consent to anything. They are not speaking at all. Information has been removed from them in

---

[27] Irene Watson, "There Is No Possibility of Rights without Law: So until Then, Don't Thumb Print or Sign Anything!," *Indigenous Law Bulletin* 44, no. 5 (2000).

[28] Paul Havemann, "Denial, Modernity, and Exclusion: Indigenous Placelessness in Australia," *Macquarie Law Journal* 57, no. 5 (2005).

such a way as to diminish their status as speakers; they more resemble the animals whom Lyotard says are victims. The harvesting of biometrical data potentially exiles everyone to the zone of indistinction between those who can speak and those who merely have voice. The singularity of the individual's unique, proper body, as Derrida says in his description of the word to be translated – here is translated into abstract data. Wiretapping without a warrant, as in White's example of *Olmstead*, is benign in comparison.

In *Cubillo*, Peter Gunner's mother was compelled to speak in a language not her own not only because of the compulsion to give consent, but to give it in the form of the substitute signature, the thumbprint on the document requesting that her child be removed from her care. The consequence was that harm was done to herself, her child, and to justice. White finds, in contrast, that the compulsion imposed on both parties in a dispute to speak in a language not their own advances the possibility of justice:

> The language is artificial, in the sense that it is made by the Court, not the parties: its terms are not those in which either the officer or the citizen would naturally talk . . . But it is possible that the officer, the suspect, and those who readily identify with either, can find in that language an expression or recognition of what they regard as their important and legitimate concerns . . . One of the functions of the law is indeed to provide a rhetorical coherence to public life by compelling those who disagree about one thing to speak a language which expresses their actual or pretended agreement about everything else. In this way the law makes the disagreement both intelligible and amenable to resolution, it establishes in the real world an idealized conversation.[29]

To assess more fully the potential for "justice as translation" realized in the instance White describes, when the two speakers are compelled to speak in a language not their own, I turn to two compelling and conflicting examples, the first from an award-winning American film and the second from the South African Truth and Reconciliation Commissions.

The Officer and the Suspect

Paul Haggis's 2005 film *Crash* offers repeated scenes of an officer and a suspect. For White, the compulsion to speak in the language of the law (a language that is not customary for either the officer or the suspect in *Robinson*) offers an enhanced opportunity for community and for justice. *Crash* offers a different perspective on this issue. The film, set in Los Angeles, tells the interlocking stories of a dozen characters from different racial and ethnic backgrounds, including police detective Graham Waters, played by Don Cheadle, police officers John Ryan (Matt Dillon) and

---

[29] White, *Justice as Translation: An Essay in Cultural and Legal Criticism*, 179.

Justice as Translation

Tom Hanson (Ryan Phillippe), TV director Cameron Thayer (Terrence Howard) and his wife, Christine (Thandie Newton), Cameron's brother Peter (Larenz Tate), Anthony, (played by rap star Ludacris), District Attorney Rick Cabot (Brendan Fraser), and his wife Jean (Sandra Bullock).

The narrative device of the film is the car: love, violence, crime, and rescue all take place in cars; the car crash brings to a head the conflicts between the characters, and the racial, ethnic, class, and sex tensions that underlie their collisions. As Don Cheadle's character says in the opening: "We crash into each other so we can feel something." Peter and Anthony carjack the District Attorney's black Navigator, and even though his partner tells him it is not the same car, Officer Ryan pulls over Cameron and Christine in their black Navigator and subjects Christine to a search that amounts to a sexual assault. The pretext is that the two white officers have seen what they take to be Christine performing fellatio on her husband, the Terence Howard character. Officer Ryan threatens to book them, but Cameron apologizes for the crime he did not commit, and the couple leaves. Later in the film, the Matt Dillon character saves Christine from her overturned car, which is about to explode. In order to be saved, Christine must submit once again to the touch of the white officer.

Crash has been criticized for its failure to see race in systemic terms. The film offers the universalized values of common humanity, realized through personal connections made between characters, as a solution to entrenched racist attitudes.[30] In the rescue scene, the camera positions the couple, the rescuer and the victim, as if in the act of making love, the black man, the character Cameron Thayer is excluded from the picture, literally and metaphorically. He is outside the frame.

The film, however, notwithstanding the criticism of its portrait of racial dynamics emphasizes Cameron Thayer's problems as a black man in the eyes of whites. Cameron Thayer faces humiliation at work when white producer Fred, played by Tony Danza, criticizes the way a black character on the show they are working on stops sounding "black":

> This is gonna sound strange, but is Jamal seeing a speech coach or something?
> What do you mean?
> Have you noticed, uh . . . This is weird for a white guy to say,
> but have you noticed he's talking a lot less black lately?
> No, I haven't noticed that.
> Really? Like in this scene, he was supposed to say, "Don't be talkin' 'bout that."
> And he changed it to,
> "Don't talk to me about that."
> Wait a minute. You think because of that, the audience
> won't recognize him as being a black man?[31]

---

[30] See, for example Hsuan L Hsu, "Racial Privacy, the L.A. Ensemble Film, and Paul Haggis's Crash," *Film Criticism* 31, no. 1–2 (2006).

[31] http://www.script-o-rama.com/movie_scripts/c/crash-script-transcript-paul-haggis.html.

This set of exchanges captures the problem of universalizing language, which does not permit code switching. White concedes that the language of law is an artificial language, and that speaking it is the result of the law's force: to have their day in court, both parties in a legal dispute are compelled to speak this language. Regardless of the artificiality and compulsion, White finds a positive potential: "It is possible that the officer, the suspect, and those who readily identify with either, can find in that language an expression or recognition of what they regard as their important and legitimate concerns." The problem is that, as *Crash* so effectively shows, as in the scene with Terrence Howard (Cameron Thayer) and Thandie Newton in their car, the black man is always a suspect and his attempt to speak in a language that is "not customary" to him – in the TV studio scene earlier, "less black" – is a provocation to whites. White goes on to say that the universality of legal language, which belongs to no one and everyone, "provide[s] a rhetorical coherence to public life." The question is: coherence and cohesion for whom? When Cameron agrees to redo the scene according to Fred's wishes, he says, "We don't have a problem." This is not the "we" that speaks to and in so doing, creates the community, as in White's use of the term; in contrast, this "we" expresses compliance. The demand for coherence, the reliance on an already given intelligible script, forestalls the possibility of creating anything new. Derrida's analysis of *The Merchant of Venice* shows that the universalizing instance that is language destroys the unique proper body; Shylock, who must show mercy, must convert. In *Crash* the problem unfolds from the other direction. Jamal *may not* convert, may not speak in another language. The violence of prohibition is the same as the violence of compulsion.

Indeed, by the end of the film, the force of the pedagogical exercise in language hits home. Anthony and Peter attempt to carjack Cameron's black Navigator, but while driving the car Cameron gets Anthony's gun away from him. The police, including the Ryan Phillippe character, Officer Tom Hanson and his new partner, pursue them. The officer and the suspect confront one another in a driveway festooned with Christmas decorations, which offer an ironic commentary on the failure of a miracle to take place. Terrence Howard's character stops the car and gets out, this time playing a new version of Cameron, whose speech and body language now conform to the script of how black men talk. In the next exchange, Cameron uses obscene language to talk back to the officer, Tom's new partner. In response to the order to get on his knees, Cameron says:

> You get on your knees
> and suck my fucking dick!
> Do I look like
> I'm fucking joking with you?
> That's what you look like,
> a fucking joke to me.

Justice as Translation

This man is making threatening gestures.
Threatening gestures?
You wanna see a threatening gesture?
I got a threatening gesture.[32]

Officer Hanson, shocked and confounded by the scene that is taking place intervenes by shouting at his partner, "I know this man, " and by announcing "this man is not armed." What Officer Hanson does not know, of course, is that Cameron happens at this moment to be carrying Anthony's gun, stuck in his belt. In this scene Tom unwittingly plays out the script in which whites "know" and are able to recognize blacks. The Terrence Howard character learns to "talk black" and is rewarded by being saved by a white officer, the Ryan Phillippe character. This scene is a part of a public life that is coherent and intelligible, precisely because it is a replay of countless other scenes just like it. In *Crash* and in other instances of American culture, the scene of the officer and the suspect precludes the possibility of anything that is new, and therefore precludes the possibility of justice.

Speaking in a Language Not Their Own: South Africa

This chapter has used *The Odyssey*, Derrida's reading of *The Merchant of Venice*, Lyotard's concept of the differend, legal cases arising from Australia's "stolen generation," the problem of biometrics, and the film *Crash* to challenge White's model of "justice as translation." These instances show the equal violence of the compulsion to speak and the compulsion not to speak. When a community relies on a grounded notion of self, text, and past, to which fidelity is owed, the script does not change, and justice is not enhanced. The demand for coherence polices shifts in language, those unruly translations of self into other terms. Intelligibility provides a screen that makes it impossible to see outside the frame or to hear a wrong for which no idiom has yet been created. White's justice relies on a notion of self whose boundedness, self-knowledge, and stability are the grounds for the gesture toward the other that he defines as translation. Derrida, Lyotard, and other theorists of politics and language argue that this very concept of an already given self, prior to language and prior to the other, is an obstacle to justice. White, to be sure, acknowledges a central role for language in the constitution of the self. He writes, for example, "What we call the self is in part of the history of a perpetual, and in principle unstable negotiation between the languageless experience of the organism and its language."[33] How the languageless organism "negotiates" is a problem that goes unexplored in White, but is the basis for Agamben's distinction between mere biological life and political life.

---

[32] Ibid.
[33] White, *Justice as Translation: An Essay in Cultural and Legal Criticism*, 35.

The larger point is that White fails to engage the challenge that his own definition of self-presents to his argument about justice as translation. Communication, says White, is "a performance in relation to others that has an ethical and political character."[34] If language is indeed not a vessel of intention or meaning, according to Derrida, Lyotard, and others, one of the things it performs, or, brings into being, in response to another is the "self." The absence of the self in the first place and the bringing to language of the self in response to another mean that fidelity to the self is tied to the denial of the self and its claims in the same way that translation is a betrayal of the original. By agreeing to take the test that Penelope presents to him, Odysseus is in effect denying his own twenty-year effort to get home to her. He has to start all over again.

The relation with the other that makes the "I" take place brings with it a tremendous risk. As Thomas Keenan writes, "The other implies the possibility of the dispropriation of oneself and one's rights and property."[35] Mark Sanders' reading of the South African Truth and Reconciliation Commission hearings in light of Keenan's argument shows how translation puts into practice this radically altered, highly mediated version of self, and in so doing, creates the possibility for justice.

Sanders emphasizes that the translation at the hearings of the Commission set in motion the exile, displacement, and dispropriation of the self. The witness speaks in response to the questioner, and interpreters simultaneously translate the questions and answers. Interpreting the scene of translation, Sanders writes:

> Witness and questioner alike are heard in a language not their own. Response, responsiveness, responsibility – all appear paradoxically to require the apparatus of removal or displacement from self.[36]

The displacements and substitutions include the victims and the perpetrators, the living and the dead (for example, when witnesses seek something on behalf of the dead), and among questioners, witnesses, and their interpreters. The interpreters reported that in describing an episode of torture and saying "I" in the place of the victim was an extraordinarily powerful experience:

> What really gets to you . . . is that you are always talking in the first person . . . If a Zulu-speaking victim says 'They connected the electrodes to my private parts and turned on the current' then that is what the translator says in English, Afrikaans, or Tswana. His private parts become your private parts. His pain is yours. If you are saying 'I' then your brain is telling you it is you.[37]

---

[34] Ibid., ix.

[35] Thomas Keenan, *Fables of Responsibility: Aberrations and Predicaments in Ethics and Politics*, Werner Hamacher and David Wellbery, eds. *Meridian: Crossing Aesthetics* (Stanford: Stanford University Press, 1997) 39.

[36] Mark Sanders, "Reading Lessons," *Diacritics* 29, no. 3 (1999): 4.

[37] Stephen Laufer, "The Burden of Evidence," *Leadership* July 1997, p. 88 cited by Ibid. 16.

Justice as Translation

Translation alters the translator's "I" by throwing a neurological switch. Justice, says White, is a "matter of relations" between people, but his model of a neutral, universal language and an a priori self mean that the script defining the relations between people has little chance to create something new. For White, the self takes place as the product of a negotiation between the body and language. For Sanders, in contrast, translation produces a vastly altered self, displaced across bodies and languages.

This shift from an atomistic to a more collective vision is important. Sanders uses the concept of *ubuntu* to get at a model for the relations between people that approximates justice. Sanders understands *ubuntu* not in the trivial sense of group solidarity but in a far more radical sense. He writes, "The being-human of a human being is realized through his or her being (human) through human beings."[38] It is not mere respect for the other that is implied here but rather the risk of the loss of self in the face of other human beings on whom my humanity depends.

It is important to clarify what Sanders is not saying about justice as translation. He is not saying that economic compensation is inappropriate in cases such as those heard by the Truth and Reconciliation Commission, or that everyone's voice was heard at the hearings. He is not talking about the restoration of the self of the torture victim through the recovery of voice, and he is not making an argument about greater empathy through storytelling. Justice as translation in the Truth Commission is not about the transfer of an idiolect, a uniquely private language into an abstract universal into which all human beings have to translate themselves. It is not about settling a dispute between two individuals by compelling them to speak in the neutral language of the law, and therefore maintaining the coherence of public life. This chapter has tried to show the pitfalls involved in such an approach. Justice as translation could be the singular but repeatable instance in which the unique proper body transfers itself into the suffering of another unique proper body through language: "If you are saying 'I' then your brain is telling you it is you."

---

[38] Ibid., 13.

16

The Constitution of History and Memory

Ariela Gross

Almost twenty years ago, the historian Pierre Nora wrote about the growing number of "lieux de mémoire" – museums, monuments, and memorials – where postmodern society situates public remembrance of traumatic or triumphant events. Yet he devoted little sustained attention to what may be the quintessential *lieu de mémoire* today, the courtroom or truth commission hearing room. Traces of our contemporary obsession with the encounter among law, history, and memory are everywhere. It is a rich bonanza for lawyers: writing new constitutions for new republics, staffing international tribunals for war criminals, and taking testimonies for truth commissions. Much of the enthusiasm for legal strategies to "come to terms with" the past draws on individual psychoanalytic metaphors for collective traumas, and relatively simplistic theories of historical practice, law, and narrative – whether that personal narrative will humanize law, or that justice will be secured by the search for historical truth.

This chapter will discuss efforts by scholars of law and the humanities to address law's relationship to history and collective memory, often through the lens of psychoanalytic or literary theory. This work began with a focus on trials of war criminals, especially Holocaust perpetrators, and has developed to consider alternative political and legal mechanisms to address a shameful past, such as truth commissions, apologies, and reparations, with growing attention to the aftermath of apartheid in South Africa, as well as the legacy of slavery and the slave trade in the United States, Europe, and Africa.

The vast body of work about remembering the mass atrocities of the twentieth century – the Holocaust and apartheid, especially – centrally concerns itself with the relationship between law/justice (trials, truth commissions, and constitutions, in particular) and the history and memory of those atrocities. Some of this work is quite practical: Do truth commissions help uncover the truth about atrocity? What is the best way to frame a truth commission? Some of it is also highly theoretical, including subtle and sophisticated treatments of the contemporary obsession with memory, and

416

The Constitution of History and Memory

the obsession with the obsession with memory, and how to understand memory's relation to history and to the postmodern self. Yet little of this work theorizing history and memory has taken seriously the legacy of slavery and colonialism as crimes against humanity, as epitomized by Pierre Nora's seven volumes on "lieux de mémoires" with only a single article devoted to France's colonies. Thus, these two fields of academic endeavor have remained quite separate.

So far, the new surge of scholarship on the memory of slavery and the slave trade has not engaged with law to the same extent. Most social scientists have concentrated on drawing the connections between collective memory of slavery and black (or African-Caribbean, or African, or African-American) identity, and historians have chiefly been engaged in a work of excavation, drawing public attention to the slave past. The kind of critical debates that have arisen in the mass-atrocity context about the dangers of too much memory have not played a large part in this literature. Even more surprisingly, although much of the public discussion about remembering slavery and the slave trade has dealt with the possibilities and pitfalls of turning to law to repair the harms of slavery – whether through commemorative laws or through some form of reparations – very little academic writing has contended critically with the relationship between law and the history or memory of slavery.

What has the new (almost entirely Anglophone) "interdiscipline" of Law and Humanities contributed to these burgeoning fields? Although some legal scholars have tried to apply the social science of collective memory and cultural trauma in a fairly straightforward way to thinking about law and the best ways to achieve justice and mend society, legal humanists are also trying to go beyond practical questions of whether law can do a good job of constructing collective memory or preserving history, or whether justice can be done, to analyze the ways law, history, and collective memory interact. They draw on close readings of trials or truth commission hearings, and literary or filmic representations of trials, to analyze the formation of national identity and the shaping of collective memory through legal processes. So far, however, most Law and Humanities scholars, as well, have focused on the mass atrocities of the twentieth century, and in particular the Holocaust. What little Law and Humanities work has touched on the memory of the United States' racial past has focused on the meaning of the Constitution in light of the memory of Reconstruction. Therefore, this chapter will end by sketching some possibilities raised by the juxtaposition of theoretical insights on law, history, and memory from the twentieth-century mass-atrocity context, with questions regarding the history and memory of slavery in the United States and the international slave trade, and in particular, the question of reparations for slavery.

The Turn to Memory Studies in the Humanities

The rise of collective memory as an object of study in the last two decades can be traced to several sources: the sociology of Maurice Halbwachs; Pierre Nora's

418 Ariela Gross

influential *Lieux de Mémoire*; psychoanalytic approaches to history; Jewish history; the history of nationalism; and the ferment stirred up by certain public events, such as the "Historians' Debate" in Germany and the trial of Klaus Barbie in France.

Sociologists were the first to name "collective memory" as distinct from individual memory. Maurice Halbwachs coined the term to emphasize the way even individual memories are formed socially, through families, religious communities, and even social classes. Most scholars who have taken Halbwachs' conception as a starting point define collective memories as "collectively shared representations of the past."[1] The social science of collective memory and cultural trauma shows the centrality of collective memory to the reproduction of society and the formation of identity. This work emphasizes that in the aftermath of "collective trauma," it is dangerous for a society to "repress" the trauma; society needs to make it part of collective memory to move forward. Sociologists and political scientists have generally seen political trials and truth commissions from this perspective as valuable tools in the creation of collective memory.[2]

Pierre Nora's influential work on sites of memory emphasizes the materiality of collective memory creation at particular cultural locations – from children's books to archives to new media. Nora's Europe-centered view traces the proliferation of commemorative sites to the rise of the modern nation state and the end of shared traditions of memory. Nora refers to this replacement of traditional rituals with public, official memory-making as the "patrimonialization of history," by which "national pasts" are transformed "into 'heritage' cultures."[3]

[1] Wulf Kansteiner, "Finding Meaning in Memory: A Methodological Critique of Collective Memory Studies," *History and Theory* 41 (May 2002) 179–97, at 181.

[2] Maurice Halbwachs, *On Collective Memory* (Chicago: University of Chicago Press, 1992) showing how memory is socially constructed, especially connected to particular places/locations; collective memory as central to the reproduction of society, formation of identity; Ron Eyerman, "The Past in the Present: Culture and the Transmission of Memory," *Acta Sociologica* (2004), at 160 discussing cultural trauma, "a dramatic loss of identity and meaning, a tear in the social fabric, affecting a group of people who have achieved some degree of cohesion"; Jeffrey Alexander, "Toward a Theory of Cultural Trauma," in Jeffrey C. Alexander, et al., *Cultural Trauma and Collective Identity* (Berkeley: University of California Press, 2004) "Cultural trauma occurs when members of a collectivity feel they have been subjected to a horrendous event that leaves indelible marks upon their group consciousness, marking their memories forever and changing their future identity in fundamental and irrevocable ways," 1; "there is an increasing body of literature that addresses the effects of the repression in terms of the traumas it caused. The aim is to restore collective psychological health by lifting societal repression and restoring memory," 7; W. James Booth, *Communities of Memory: On Witness, Identity, and Justice* (Ithaca: Cornell University Press, 2006) presenting a positive view of memory as identity, necessary to creating community, doing justice.

[3] Pierre Nora, "Between Memory and History: Les Lieux de Mémoire," *Representations* 26 (Spring 1989) 13–4. See also Nancy Wood, *Vectors of Memory: Legacies of Trauma in Postwar Europe* (Oxford and New York: Berg Publishers, 1999) 31–2. Kerwin Klein puts forward "several alternative narratives of the origins of our new memory discourse" to that offered by Nora: one attributes the rise of memory discourse to "the modernist crisis of the self in the nineteenth century;" another "sketches a tale in which Hegelian historicism took up premodern forms of memory that we have since modified through

The Constitution of History and Memory

Some historians have also applied psychoanalytic theory to the study of the past, and especially "the past in the present," to draw the links between history and memory. In the United States, perhaps the leading practitioner of psychoanalytic history has been Dominick LaCapra. LaCapra's project is to apply psychoanalytic concepts like transference, repression, acting out, and working-through to collectivities and to allow memory to be a starting point for mourning.[4] To LaCapra, public memory guides historians to ask the right questions, and good history helps a nation with its memory work, allowing the nation to work through the traumatic event collectively, come to terms with shameful episodes, and take a stand in favor of justice for the future.[5]

In addition to its roots in psychoanalysis, some of the inspiration for this kind of history of memory can be found in Benedict Anderson's conception of "invented traditions."[6] Anderson describes nation building through what an earlier generation of scholars might have termed "myth making." For example, Yael Zerubavel's *Recovered Roots* traces the formation of Israeli national identity through the creation of collective memories of heroic pasts, like the Bar Kokhba Revolt or the martyrs at Masada.[7]

Finally, there is also an important tradition of tracing the relationship between history and memory in Jewish history. In *Zakhor: Jewish History and Jewish Memory* (1996), Yosef Yerushalmi explored the puzzle that Jews are commanded to remember, yet "nowhere is it suggested that [Israel] become a nation of historians," and

---

structural vocabularies. A fourth implies that memory is a mode of discourse natural to people without history, and so its emergence is a salutary feature of decolonization. A fifth claims that memory talk is a belated response to the wounds of modernity." Klein, "On The Emergence of 'Memory' in Historical Discourse," *Representations* 69 (Winter 2000) 127–50.

[4] LaCapra sees this kind of history of memory, and historical memory work, to be answering the call of the philosopher Jurgen Habermas, who took a public stand during the famous "Historians' Debate" in Germany in the 1980s in favor of an "obligation that we in Germany have – even if no one else any longer assumes it – to keep alive the memory of the suffering of those murdered by German hands, and to keep it alive quite openly and not just in our own minds." According to LaCapra, Habermas theorized a new relationship between history and public memory: "Habermas's arguments indicate that a historical consciousness ideally performs critical work on memory in order to undo repression, counteract ideological lures, and determine what aspects of the past justifiably merit being passed on as a living heritage. Conversely, the workings of memory, including its significant lapses or repressions, help to delineate significant problems for historical research and criticism." Dominick LaCapra, *History and Memory after Auschwitz* (Ithaca: Cornell University Press, 1998) 43.

[5] Ibid., 63–4. See also Wood, *Vectors of Memory*, 40 ("Habermas believes that only memory's constant performativity in the public sphere can generate in individuals a subjective foundation receptive to the kind of critical memory-work in which he believes the German national polity must constantly engage"). This public "working-through" is of "collective liability," *not* guilt. Ibid., 44.

[6] Benedict Anderson, *Imagined Communities: Reflections on the Origin and Spread of Nationalism* (London and New York: Verso, 2006).

[7] Yael Zerubavel, *Recovered Roots: Collective Memory and the Making of the Israeli National Tradition* (Chicago: University of Chicago Press, 1997); see also Nadia Abu El-Haj, *Facts on the Ground: Archaeological Practice and Territorial Self-Fashioning in Israeli Society* (Chicago: University of Chicago Press, 2002).

indeed, Jewish history is a very new field. Traditions, remembrance, and memory took the place of historiography for centuries of Jewish life. "Only in the modern era do we really find, for the first time, a Jewish historiography divorced from Jewish collective memory and, in crucial respects, thoroughly at odds with it. To a large extent, of course, this reflects a universal and ever-growing modern dichotomy."[8] Thus, Jewish history, itself a relatively new field, has always been self-consciously concerned to distinguish itself from collective memory, and more recently, to trace the history of Jewish memory. When coming to terms with the Holocaust became a pressing matter on the agenda of many European nations and the United States in the 1970s, there was a natural historiographic tradition for Holocaust studies to draw on.[9]

Debating the Turn to Memory

The sharpest critique of memory studies within history, but also of the rise of commemoration in the public sphere, comes from historian Charles Maier, who suggests that our society's "pathological" fixation on memory is related to a politics of victimhood, in which identity as a people is linked to a traumatic past. In an influential article entitled "A Surfeit of Memory?", Maier warns that memory work can become an end in itself rather than a means to a goal.[10] Maier refers to memory as an "addiction" that "can become neurasthenic and disabling."[11] He attributes the

[8] Yosef Yerushalmi, *Zakhor: Jewish History and Jewish Memory* (Seattle: University of Washington Press, 1996) 93. Yerushalmi ends *Zakhor* with a quotation from Borges' *Funes the Memorious* about the dangers of too much memory, yet in a postscript on "forgetting," Yerushalmi writes, "Historiography, I will continue to insist, cannot be a substitute for collective memory, nor does it show signs of creating an alternative tradition that is capable of being shared. But the essential dignity of the historical vocation remains, and its moral imperative seems to me now more urgent than ever . . . I will take my stand on the side of 'too much' rather than 'too little,' for my terror of forgetting is greater than my terror of having too much to remember." Ibid., 116–17.

[9] Yet the Holocaust appears to present to Jewish history a decisive rupture in that dichotomization. Saul Friedlander discusses the German "historians' debate" as evidence that "when past and present remain interwoven, there is no clear dichotomy between history and memory." Friedlander sees the Shoah as an "unmasterable past" that leads to "the inability to say, the apparent pathology of obsessive recall, the seemingly simplistic refusal of historiographical closure." Despite the increasing identification of the Shoah with Jewish and Israeli national identity, "its interpretation is increasingly multifaceted and lacking in consensual interpretation." Friedlander notes that this is a true departure from the Jewish tradition presented by Yerushalmi in *Zakhor*, in which catastrophic events were routinely integrated into the tradition "through a set pattern of archetypal responses." By contrast, Friedlander argues, fifty years after the Holocaust, "no mythical framework seems to be taking hold of the Jewish imagination, nor does the best of literature and art dealing with the Shoah offer any redemptive stance. In fact, the opposite appears to be true." Saul Friedlander, *Memory, History, and the Extermination of the Jews of Europe* (Bloomington: Indiana University Press, 1993) 32, 62.

[10] Charles S. Maier, "A Surfeit of Memory? Reflections on History, Melancholy, and Denial," *History and Memory* 5 (Winter 1993) 138.

[11] Ibid., 141.

The Constitution of History and Memory

turn to memory to disillusion with the future, "the late-twentieth-century diminution of what we believe politically possible, our age of failing expectations."[12] What has been lost, according to Maier, is the possibility of a shared political future based on collective institutions.[13] We have replaced such a vision with loyalty to fragmented ethnic identity groups, based on memories that "exclude others who do not share a group's particular past."[14]

Defenders of the turn to memory, Dominick LaCapra and Michael Roth, actively celebrate the sacred aspect of memory and disparage critics as themselves "fixated" or "obsessed." In particular, LaCapra insists that professional historians need to pay attention to the questions raised by collective memory. He believes that the turn to memory can be explained by the social trauma of the Holocaust, the individual trauma of widespread child abuse, and by the proliferation of first-person testimonies.[15] Michael Roth argues that even if Maier is correct, we need "to understand why claims to remember how one has been oppressed have extraordinary power at particular times for particular purposes." Although he acknowledges, "the cultivation of traumatic memory can lead to a harvest of hatred and violence," he also argues that memory "can be used to expand that group of people who count for us, those who we do not consider merely strangers."[16]

Ultimately, there is a contrast between the way a national identity is created around a positive memory, even one of martyrdom – the Confederate soldier, the Masada fighters – as opposed to the memory of a shameful past. The commemorative narratives Yael Zerubavel writes about are invented traditions starkly in counterpoint to the Holocaust story. Yet Habermas and others believe that it is possible for a nation to discipline itself to memory work that involves acknowledging guilt rather than triumph and that Germany has to some extent succeeded in doing so. Historians of memory defend this effort and argue that historians should remain engaged with memory.

Relationship between History and Memory

In all of this debate, still very much an open question is the relationship between history and memory. Some historians use the term "memory" to refer to official,

---

[12] Ibid., 143.

[13] Ibid., 147.

[14] Ibid., 148–50. See also Wood, *Vectors of Memory*; Henry Rousso, *The Haunting Past* (Philadelphia: University of Pennsylvania Press, 2002) 19, "Jewish identity cannot be eternally rooted in the suffering of an older generation, a generation which will soon become ancestral. Sooner or later, Jewish identity must have a new project that points it toward the future, giving it an active, forward-looking content. After all, the state of Israel is in large part built against this image of the Jew as victim."

[15] LaCapra, *History and Memory after Auschwitz*, 8–16.

[16] Michael S. Roth, *The Ironist's Cage: Memory, Trauma, and the Construction of History* (New York: Columbia University Press, 1995) 12.

public efforts at commemoration, others to more amorphous, popular understandings of the past. Conventional historians of memory tend to draw a relatively sharp dichotomy between history, as practiced by historians according to professional norms, and collective memory, more of a vernacular or folk representation of the past. United States historian Ira Berlin sees the relationship between history and memory as one of inevitable conflict. Professional historians' understanding of history as contested, contingent, and incomplete put them "on a collision course with popular understanding, which is prone to fix institutions in time and place and to see events marching inevitably forward to the present, thus accentuating aspects of the past that shape contemporary life."[17] He emphasizes a series of dichotomies: history is skeptical, "memory presumes the truth;"[18] history is global; memory is local;[19] history and memory "speak past one another."[20] Another historian of the United States David Blight defines *"History – what trained historians do"* as "a reasoned reconstruction of the past rooted in research; it tends to be critical and skeptical of human motive and action, and therefore more secular than what people commonly refer to as memory. . . . *Memory*, however, is often treated as a sacred set of potentially absolute meanings and stories, possessed as the heritage or identity of a community."[21] Memory, then, can only be the object of history, although public history may attempt to shape collective memory.[22]

Some critics of "memory studies" argue that there is no meaningful separation between history and memory; both are simply representations or interpretations of the past, and "memory" is just another word for popular culture, or perhaps for "public history." Others suggest that the line between history and memory is blurred, that the two overlap, but that there is still a meaningful distinction.[23] Even some who distinguish between history and memory consider professional history a subset of the general category of memory. Michael Roth agrees with Nora that historical consciousness has to some extent replaced traditional forms of memory, but Roth believes that in this modern stage, the writing of history itself can become "one of the crucial vehicles for reconstructing or reimagining a community's connections to its traditions," especially for subaltern groups. Thus, historiography is a kind of substitute for collective memory, in terms of creating a usable past. Yet he also believes that to the extent grave traumas such as the Holocaust make the past "unmasterable,"

---

[17] Ira Berlin, "American Slavery in History and Memory and the Search for Social Justice," *The Journal of American History* 90 (No. 4, 2004) 1263.

[18] Ibid., 1265.

[19] Ibid.

[20] Ibid., 1267.

[21] David W. Blight, *Beyond the Battlefield: Race, Memory, and the American Civil War* (Amherst: University of Massachusetts Press, 2002) 2.

[22] Ibid., 224.

[23] See, e.g., Rousso, *The Haunting Past*, 8–9; Berlin, "American Slavery in History and Memory;" Blight, *Beyond the Battlefield*.

The Constitution of History and Memory

this is both an obstacle and a spur to historians to engage with public memory.[24] LaCapra criticizes historians' tendency to either conflate memory with history or to lock memory and history in a binary position, "rather than implicate" memory "in a more problematic, mutually questioning relation to" history.[25] Gabrielle Spiegel likewise warns of the dangers of the "current tendency to theorize a reciprocal conversion of memory into history and history into memory"[26] because memory "cannot be severed from its sacral and liturgical – its 'commemorative' – contexts" and made analytical.[27] Most scholars end up with some kind of admonition for historians and memory-makers to be informed by one another.

How Does Law Shape Memory?

As legal scholars have turned to look at history and memory, most have kept a practical and normative focus on the best way for a society to achieve justice and healing after traumatic events. Law and Humanities scholars, however, have also analyzed descriptively the various ways law shapes collective memory, interpreted legal texts as sites of memory, or compared them to literary models of memory.[28]

How Do Societies Use Law to Reform the Past?

American legal scholars became interested in history and memory primarily in the context of "transitional justice," legal responses to regime change or democratization in formerly unjust societies. Some have tried to apply these insights more broadly

---

[24] Rousso, *The Haunting Past*, 10.

[25] Ibid., 16.

[26] LaCapra, *History and Memory after Auschwitz*, 20; Gabrielle M. Spiegel, "Memory and History: Liturgical Time and Historical Time," *History and Theory* 41 (2002) 160.

[27] Spiegel, "Memory and History," 161–2.

[28] Recent works in the law and society tradition include Inga Markovits' article on selective memory in East Germany, and Savelsberg and King's more general essay on law and collective memory. Markovits describes the way law can shape history and collective memory through legal decisions of what to keep in archives. Savelsberg and King essentially offer a catalog of law's effects on collective memory, including: shaping history in courts of law; selectivities in law's construction of history; law's interaction with other social institutions; complementary or alternative mechanisms such as truth commissions; as well as indirect effects: the regulation of mnemonic content by law; structuring historical memories by controlling access to archival information; and the dissemination of knowledge. A somewhat unusual example of a primarily descriptive piece that also takes a normative stand is Brian Havel, "In Search of a Theory of Public Memory: The State, the Individual, and Marcel Proust," *Indiana Law Journal* 80 (2005) 605, which discusses the way the Austrian government uses public law to establish the official memory of Austria as a victim of the Nazis. He shows that states use law for myth-making, but the professional practice of historiography, because its method is revisionism, makes it unlikely to offer an alternative. Havel draws on Halbwachs for the concept of nonofficial "collective memory" as a counterpoint to official public memory, but then turns to literature, using Proustian "transcendent memory" to pose individual affective memory as a better alternative to the official story.

to a variety of societies, including the United States, that have not undergone such radical regime changes – or at least, not recently. Marc Galanter, in an essay about "reforming the past," looks at "ordinary practices of justice" in the private law contexts of property, tort, contract, and criminal law, to help us think about new practices of transitional justice, which "elevate the themes of memory, witness, and redemption over the closure and finality that are a major component of the law."[29] Galanter maps out the axes along which to classify the universe of old wrongs, as well as issues regarding the class of wrongdoers, the class of victims, the forum to adjudicate their claims, and the standards by which to judge them.[30] Finally, Galanter catalogues a series of responses: "doing the right thing belatedly," "setting the record straight," apology, commemoration, restitution, token payment, programmatic reconstruction, or full reparations.[31]

Like Maier, Galanter argues that the new interest in reforming the past stems from contemporary politics, but he has a rosier view of its sources; he believes that post-1960s critical views of established authority, an "extension of the frontiers of empathy," and "optimism about institutions" lead us to enthusiasm for righting old wrongs. At the same time, he notes that hopefulness about corrective justice goes hand in hand with "pessimism about comprehensive distributive justice." This is akin to Maier's belief that we focus on righting individual or group wrongs of the past when we have given up hope for transformative collectivist politics in the future.[32] Yet, despite all of Galanter's reservations, he believes we really have no choice but to pursue these flawed efforts.[33]

Robert Gordon considers transitional societies' responses to an unjust past, and in particular, the historical narratives in which these responses are embedded. In these narratives, "the period of injustice usually figures as a deviation from, or a distortion of, the history that should have happened instead."[34] Gordon distinguishes among three approaches to historical injustice: narrow-agency framing; broad-agency approaches; and structural responses. Narrow-agency models focus on compensating, correcting, or punishing wrongs by specific perpetrators to specific victims. Broad-agency approaches focus on correcting or compensating harms to entire groups by collective or state entities. Finally, structural models aim to alter entire systems or institutions in a "forward-looking" manner rather than focusing on liability looking to the past. Gordon characterizes the most "radical proposals" of American Reconstruction as structural ones: the confiscation of slaveholders'

---

[29] Marc Galanter, "Righting Old Wrongs," *Breaking the Cycles of Hatred: Memory, Law, and Repair*, Martha Minow, ed. (Princeton, NJ: Princeton University Press, 2002) 107, 110.

[30] Ibid., 117.

[31] Ibid., 118–19.

[32] Ibid., 121.

[33] Ibid., 123–4.

[34] Robert W. Gordon, "Undoing Historical Injustice," *Justice and Injustice in Law and Legal Theory*, Austin Sarat and Thomas Kearns, eds. (Ann Arbor: University of Michigan Press, 1996) 35.

The Constitution of History and Memory

property and redistribution of land to ex-slaves. "The results of Allied occupation 'democratization' policies in Germany were more mixed – and still very much disputed among historians."[35] Denazification was an "expensive fiasco."[36] Gordon ends by analyzing America's "Second Reconstruction," again coming down in favor of structural, forward-looking approaches to affirmative action over reparations.

Political scientists, as well, show new interest in reparation, restitution, and historical justice. Janna Thompson, for example, writes a "defence of historical obligation and entitlement... grounded in a conception of a society or nation as an intergenerational community."[37] Likewise, some critical race scholars have insisted that law can reform the past through reparations to injured communities and that scholars can assist through telling stories that give voice to those communities' collective memories. For example, Sharon Hom and Eric Yamamoto view courts as one arena for "the struggle over recognition of competing collective memories." They argue that "through those struggles we have the potential to remake our, and society's, understandings of justice – for good or ill."[38] They reinterpret the case of *Rice v. Cayetano* through this lens; in that case, the U.S. Supreme Court recited its version of Hawai'ian history, in effect denying Hawai'ian collective memory. The case resulted in injustice to native Hawai'ians, in part because of the way it "remembered" Hawai'ian history. "Justice claims of 'right' start with struggles over memory... The construction of collective memory implicates power and culture... of which legal process, and particularly civil rights adjudication is one, but only one, significant aspect."

All of these works critically examine political and legal efforts to use law to achieve historical justice in one way or another. For the most part, they come out of the "transitional justice" literature, but these are also pieces that put the issues facing nations in transition in a broader context, side by side with the challenges facing any society, including the United States, when it faces its unjust past.

What Are the Limitations of Trials in Shaping Public Memory and Reforming the Past?

A great deal of the writing on law, history, and memory has focused on trials, especially trials for mass atrocities, and the limitations of criminal prosecution as a vehicle

---

[35] Ibid., 46.

[36] Ibid., 47.

[37] Janna Thompson, *Taking Responsibility for the Past: Reparation and Historical Injustice* (Malden, MA: Blackwell Publishers, 2002), xvii. See Elazar Barkan, *The Guilt of Nations: Restitution and Negotiating Historical Injustices* (New York: W. W. Norton & Co, 2000); Nigel Biggar, ed., *Burying the Past: Making Peace and Doing Justice after Civil Conflict* (Washington, DC: Georgetown University Press, 2001).

[38] Sharon Hom and Eric Yamamoto, "Collective Memory, History, and Social Justice," *UCLA Law Review* 47 (August 2000) 1764.

both for the creation of history and collective memory and for doing justice in the aftermath of such collective trauma.

Several scholars devote attention to the mismatch between a criminal trial, organized around the rights of the defendant, and the societal goal of shaping collective memory about a past atrocity. Zealous advocacy by defense counsel will (and should) challenge state efforts to shape collective memory. Mark Osiel, in a seminal work on trials of mass atrocities, warns that such trials "unwittingly provide more *mis*education than accurate historical instruction."[39] In a number of trials, a major problem has been that the charge of the court is much more limited or narrow than the scope of the atrocity. For example, the International Military Tribunal at Nuremberg had jurisdiction to focus on the Nazis' "aggressive war" as opposed to all of their crimes against humanity, so the prosecutors had "to weave the Holocaust into a larger story that was primarily about perverted militarism."[40] This misfocus also affected historiography, "skew[ing historians'] analysis in favor of what came to be known as the 'intentionalist' interpretation of the period. This focus subtly drew attention away from institutional dynamics and the 'machinery of destruction,' particularly the crucial role of minor bureaucrats and functionaries at all levels of German society."[41] By looking at top leaders, "the courts not only missed the macropicture: the story of mass collaboration and institutional support for administrative brutality. They also missed the micropicture: the story of the victims – the human experience of uncomprehending suffering that official brutality produced."[42]

This problem, of missing both the larger and the smaller picture, also arose in the most recent criminal trials based on crimes of the Holocaust, which took place in France: the trial of Klaus Barbie in 1987; the trial of Paul Touvier in 1994; and the trial of Maurice Papon in 1997–8. All three were prosecuted long after the crimes they committed during World War II, but each presented unique problems. Barbie was known as the "Butcher of Lyon" and presented the most clear-cut case of personal responsibility for the deaths of Jews in concentration camps. Touvier was in the SS, but his main function had been as part of the *milice* who were trying to wipe out the Resistance. Finally, Papon was a Vichy bureaucrat. His trial was the most controversial because it implicated the entire Vichy regime – he was being tried less as an individual than as a representative of the faceless bureaucracy. His prosecution also raised the mismatch between France's law about crimes against humanity, which seemed to require collaboration with the Germans, and the actual crimes that were probably committed.[43]

---

[39] Mark Osiel, *Mass Atrocity, Collective Memory, and the Law* (New Brunswick, NJ: Transaction Publishers, 1997) 82.
[40] Ibid., 96.
[41] Ibid., 100.
[42] Ibid., 103.
[43] Ibid., 110.

The Constitution of History and Memory

Historians have weighed in on the public debate in France on the role of the trial in preserving and creating public memory and history. Most famously, Henry Rousso, the author of *The Vichy Syndrome*, a blistering critique of French society's collective forgetting of the Vichy regime's collaboration in Nazi crimes, refused to participate in the trials of Touvier and Papon, writing publicly to the Papon court when subpoenaed by the defendant. In *The Haunting Past: History, Memory, and Justice in Contemporary France*, Rousso explained why he disapproves of criminal trials of aging Nazis. Rousso argued that it distorts historians' search for truth to be expert witnesses in such trials and deplored the "judicialization" and moralization of history entailed in the use of law to revisit a shameful past. Rousso voiced the fear that by "judicializing" the past, courts affirm an "illusion that the verdict delivered will take the place of 'history as the world's court of judgment.'"[44] Indeed, law is presented as an alternative – a bad alternative – to historiography, attempting to render a verdict on the past. Although it is acceptable for criminal trials to render individual verdicts of guilt, and to establish boundaries between "good and evil, the tolerable and the intolerable, the permissible and the punishable," trials should not try to render a verdict on an entire era. The goals of "belated reparation" or "catharsis on a national scale" are illicit or at least ill advised.[45] As a narrower matter, he argued that historians should not be expert witnesses at such trials because it is misleading to present general historical context for a case when one is not tying that context to the specifics of the individual, given that his freedom hangs in the balance, and when one's testimony will give the impression that the part stands for the whole and vice versa.[46]

Others who have written about the French trials similarly criticize the mismatch between law and history, as well as the inability of law to "serve the needs of history, memory, and justice simultaneously." Nancy Wood concludes that even "if we accept that 'working-through' a traumatic past is a precondition of the moral health of democratic states," at some point the process "demand(s) some form of provisional closure so that it does not become an end in its own right, preventing future-oriented perspectives that are also vital to social dynamism."[47] Similarly, Leila Sadat Wexler

---

[44] Rousso, *The Haunting Past*, 50.

[45] Ibid., 56–7.

[46] See also Richard Evans, "History, Memory, and the Law: The Historian as Expert Witness," *History and Theory* 41 (No. 3, 2002) 326–45 (reviewing Rousso).

[47] Wood, *Vectors of Memory*, 115, 136, following Maier, she finds that sometimes "memory's performativity has served primarily as grist to the mill of identity-politics, encouraging a retreat from, rather than participation in, 'transformative politics.'" See also Jean-Paul Jean and Denis Salas, *Barbie, Touvier, Papon . . . Des procès pour la mémoire* (Paris: Editions Autrement, 2002) ≪La justice entre Histoire et Mémoire≫ Richard J. Golsan, *The Papon Affair: Memory and Justice on Trial* (New York: Routledge, 2000). "Today, Everything Converges on the Haunting Memory of Vichy," interview with Pierre Nora in *Le Monde*, October 1, 1997, reprinted in Golsan, *The Papon Affair*, at 171 (Nora attributes the fact that Vichy does not die to two international phenomena beginning 1967–8, "the creation of a special

argues that Paul Touvier's trial was an unsatisfactory vehicle for reexamining the Vichy period. The court was ill equipped to evaluate history, and, given the ill-fitting aims of a criminal trial, there was always the danger that Touvier would be acquitted and, by implication, Vichy France as well.[48]

How Can Trials Shape Memory and National Identity in a Meaningful Way?

Substantial numbers of scholars remain optimistic about the possibilities for public trials of shameful national events to contribute to national identity formation, to social solidarity, to collective memory formation, and to some kind of historical justice. Mark Osiel argues that criminal trials for mass atrocities can "contribute significantly to a certain, underappreciated kind of social solidarity." The defense tells the story as a tragedy, the prosecutors as a morality play; the task of comparative historical sociology, according to Osiel, is to understand why these narrative tropes are used and to assess their success in influencing collective memory. He hopes to use this analysis of law's influence on collective memory to help design future prosecutions.[49] Osiel argues that law can play "a significant role in the process of 'mastering the past,'" and that it did so in Germany, with the prosecution of concentration camp guards in 1964 and 1975–81. "In German public awareness, these trials effected a symbolic severing of ties to the past."[50] Thus, Osiel appears to believe that trials can help make it possible to "break with the past, through guilt and repentance," although he acknowledges the difficulty for courts in balancing individual justice for the criminal and the goal of shaping collective memory for the larger society.[51]

Most of the interventions of Law and Humanities scholarship into the debates about trials of mass atrocities have taken a favorable view of the possibilities of law's engagement with history and memory. For example, Lawrence Douglas views trials of Holocaust perpetrators as serving a salutary pedagogical purpose; however, he sees trials of Holocaust deniers negatively because of their implications for freedom of expression.[52] Looking at the Nuremberg trial, as well as the trials of Eichmann, Demjanjuk, Barbie, and Holocaust denier Ernst Zundel, Douglas's concern is less

---

Jewish identity, and the creation of an identity belonging to one generation whose beginning was marked by the events of May 1968."

[48] Leila Sadat Wexler, "Reflections on the Trial of Vichy Collaborator Paul Touvier for Crimes against Humanity in France," *Law and Social Inquiry* 20 (No. 1, 1995) 191–221, 225.

[49] Osiel, *Mass Atrocity, Collective Memory, and the Law*, 3.

[50] Ibid., 192–3.

[51] Ibid., 292.

[52] Lawrence Douglas, *The Memory of Judgment: Making Law and History in the Trials of the Holocaust* (New Haven: Yale University Press, 2001).

The Constitution of History and Memory

whether trials do justice to the defendant than whether trials do justice to the crimes of the Holocaust. He judges trials in terms of the way they teach history and shape collective memory, which he considers the central reason such trials are staged. For example, Gideon Hausner, the Israeli attorney general in the Eichmann trial thought it would help young Israelis answer, "How did they allow themselves to be led like lambs to the slaughter?"[53] In other words, trials offer "didactic legality." Some scholars "argue that the procedural norms that govern a criminal trial render it a flawed tool for comprehending traumatic history."[54] Trials are too individualized, too focused on pathology, and cannot comprehend mass bureaucratic murder. Yet Douglas tries to show "the intense, creative labors of the law to master the problems of representation and judgment posed by the Holocaust."[55] Douglas shows the ways in which the Eichmann trial showcased stories that "buttressed a specifically Israeli ideology of nationhood and Jewish identity."[56] He concludes, "My criticisms notwithstanding, I believe the Eichmann trial and aspects of Nuremberg possessed greatness – as dramatic and necessary acts of legal and social will – that fully justified their historic undertaking."[57]

Leora Bilsky's analysis of Israeli "political trials" is one of the most nuanced efforts to address the relationship of law to collective memory with the tools of legal and literary theory. She defines a "political trial" as one in which "political authorities seek to advance a political agenda through criminal prosecution," but not necessarily a show trial in the sense that there is "no element of risk about the outcome." Her question is whether a trial can transform national consciousness and promote democratic politics. She distinguishes political trials in Israel from "transitional" trials in postauthoritarian societies: "My claim in a nutshell is that the Zionist revolution did not end with the Declaration of Independence and the establishment of the State of Israel but has continued for the last fifty years, transformed through 'constitutional moments,' many of them involving a transformative trial."[58]

---

[53] Ibid., 3.

[54] Ibid.

[55] Ibid., 4.

[56] Ibid., 158.

[57] Ibid., 261. Douglas has also written in a law and literature mode about the role imaginative literature can play, along with law, in "safeguarding historical truth." He writes that the novel *Wartime Lies*, written by a lawyer, "vindicates the prerogatives of fiction . . . less because it provides a poignant narrative of the Holocaust, than because it defines, in exemplary fashion, the limits of such representations – whether imaginatively or juridically conceived." Lawrence Douglas, "Wartime Lies: Securing the Holocaust in Law and Literature," *Yale Journal of Law and the Humanities* 7 (No. 2, Summer 1995) 369.

[58] Leora Bilsky, *Transformative Justice: Israeli Identity on Trial* (Ann Arbor: University of Michigan Press, 2004) 7.

In Bilsky's chapter on the trial of Kastner, she gives a literary reading of Halevi's opinion, which likened Kastner's deal with the Germans to the Faustian contract with Satan; she argues that Halevi used the contract metaphor to focus on collaboration with Eichmann as a *choice*, a Faustian bargain. This narrative draws on the image of Jews as world conspirators. Supreme Court Justice Agranat reversed Halevi's decision, and also reordered the time frame of his narrative through administrative law doctrine.

Bilsky also distinguishes contrasting historical narratives between Hausner and Arendt in the Eichmann trial: Hausner wanted to give victims a chance to tell their stories on a public stage, to develop a more tolerant society in Israel. Arendt had a more universal narrative: "Transitional trials proceed on two levels. On one level, the judges ascertain the guilt of the defendant as in ordinary criminal trials. But on the other level their judgment is also a performative act through which society's collective identity is formed in opposition to an Other (the defendant) whose values are contrasted with the fundamental values of society."[59] Bilsky both uses the tools of narrative theory to analyze the trials as cultural performances and judges the success of these trials in national identity formation and collective memory creation.

Other Law and Humanities scholars who take a more skeptical view of trials as vehicles for memory creation have taken different approaches. One of the most interesting is that of Devin Pendas, who critically analyzes the claim that trials for mass atrocity serve a pedagogical function, "engendering a historical narrative of truth."[60] Pendas argues that such a function depends on the public reception of these trials, and he finds that there was a great deal of public ambivalence toward the Auschwitz trials. Much of this ambivalence he attributes to a doctrinal problem with German criminal law, the distinction between two types of homicide based on the motivations of the perpetrator: Totschlag, which is murder; Mord – homicide for "base motives," which has no statute of limitations. Thus trials of Auschwitz guards had to be prosecuted as "Mord," but focusing on the motives of individuals and the most "inhuman" atrocities made it easy for the public to distance themselves from the crimes of the Holocaust. Other scholars take at face value the pedagogical function of trial narratives, but analyze those narratives to pronounce moral judgment on them. Guyora Binder, for example, critiques both Klaus Barbie's prosecutors for defining Jews as unique sacrificial victims of Nazism, and Vergès, his defense attorney, a well-known anticolonialist who drew on a French leftist tradition that Binder finds,

---

[59] Ibid., 117.

[60] Devin O. Pendas, "'I didn't know what Auschwitz was': The Frankfurt Auschwitz Trial and The German Press, 1963–1965," *Yale Journal of Law and the Humanities* 12 (Summer 2000) 397.

The Constitution of History and Memory

like "Holocaust Judaism," to be a "symptom[s] of a common culture of despair that paralyzes moral choice in the wake of Nazi atrocities."[61]

Can Truth and Reconciliation Commissions Overcome the Limits of Law?

Although legal scholars are ambivalent about the possibility of justice through criminal trials, they are almost universal in their praise for truth and reconciliation commissions as alternative paths to restorative justice. Truth commissions appear to offer not only the possibility of uncovering more of the history of evil regimes and the crimes they committed but of honoring the collective memory of victims, and even healing victims, perpetrators, and the society itself. In legal scholarship on truth commissions, especially by scholars of law and literature, we see sometimes romantic and sometimes hardheaded assessments of the power of storytelling. This work melds psychoanalytic and social work approaches to trauma with literary romanticism and narrative theory.[62]

In one of the most influential works by a legal scholar on transitional justice, *Between Vengeance and Forgiveness*, Martha Minow compares trials, truth commissions, and reparations in a broad international context. Minow asks what paths lie "between vengeance and forgiveness, *if legal and cultural institutions offered other avenues for individuals and nations?* . . . [Legal institutions] need to ask, what would it take . . . to come to terms with the past, to help heal the victims, the bystanders, and even the perpetrators? What would promote reconstruction of a society devastated by atrocities?" Although Minow notes that trials have the advantage of creating a permanent record, they are also flawed by their dependence on political actors for their operations and resources, as well as the problems of "fairness, neutrality, and

---

[61] Guyora Binder, "Representing Nazism: Advocacy and Identity at the Trial of Klaus Barbie," *Yale Law Journal* 98 (May 1989) 1344, 1372–3. Other Law and Humanities scholarship about trials includes studies of trials of Holocaust deniers. See, e.g., Lawrence McNamara, "History, Memory, and Judgment: Holocaust Denial, The History Wars, and Law's Problems with the Past," *Sydney Law Review* 26 (2004) 353, on the *Irving v. Lipstadt* libel case and Australia's "History Wars," a vociferous public debate about the history of Australia's conquest of Aboriginal peoples. See also Shoshana Felman, "Forms of Judicial Blindness: Traumatic Narratives and Legal Repetitions," *History, Memory, and the Law*, Austin Sarat and Thomas Kearns, eds. (Ann Arbor: University of Michigan Press, 2002) applying psychoanalytic and literary theory to the O. J. Simpson trial.

[62] On the power of storytelling and the possibility that narrative and literature can humanize law, see Shulamit Almog, "Healing Stories in Law and Literature," *Trauma and Memory: Reading, Healing, and Making Law* in Austin Sarat et al., eds. (Stanford: Stanford University Press, 2007) 307; Shoshana Felman and Dori Laub, *Testimony: Crises of Witnessing in Literature, Psychoanalysis, and History* (New York: Routledge, 1992); Kathryn Abrams, "Hearing the Call of Stories," *California Law Review* 79 (July 1991) 971; Robin West, *Narrative, Authority, and Law* (Ann Arbor: University of Michigan Press, 1993).

predictability posed by retroactive application of norms."[63] By contrast, Minow finds that the "potential restorative power of truth-telling, the significance of sympathetic witnesses, and the constructive roles of perpetrators and bystanders each suggest promising features of a truth commission."[64] Although she notes the criticism that this therapeutic approach "seems to ignore politics, shortchange justice issues, and treat survivors and their recovery as a means toward a better society rather than as persons with dignity and entitlements to justice," she nevertheless thinks truth commissions may promote justice even more effectively than trials if we consider "restoring dignity to victims" and promoting reconciliation as goals of justice.[65]

Political theorist Jean Bethke Elshtain argues in favor of the South African Truth and Reconciliation Commission's version of reconciliation, not as a demand for victims to forgive nor for perpetrators to express remorse or apologize, but only to tell the truth, to acknowledge the harms of the past, and to "bring matters into a framework within which conflicts can be adjudicated short of bloodshed and in the name of cooperation and tolerance."[66] Elshtain and other advocates of truth commissions argue that reconciliation itself is a form of justice – restorative rather than retributive or punitive justice, that holds out the hope of breaking the cycle of violence.

André du Toit, a participant in the South African Truth and Reconciliation Commission process, argues that the South African understanding of reconciliation shifted over time from a more political meaning (enabling former victims and perpetrators to work together in a new polity) to a more religious and therapeutic sense (expressing remorse and forgiveness, to achieve personal healing), especially because of the influence of Archbishop Desmond Tutu. Later in the process, the quasijudicial and adversarial procedures of amnesty hearings took center stage. The final stage was the publication of the Truth and Reconciliation Commission Report, in which data processing and corroboration of statements actually led the Truth and Reconciliation Commission to make victim and perpetrator "findings"; however, it is unclear what legal standing these findings have. The operative notions of truth and justice in the Truth and Reconciliation Commission process, according to du Toit, were truth as acknowledgment and justice as recognition.[67]

---

[63] Martha Minow, *Between Vengeance and Forgiveness* (Boston: Beacon Press, 1998) 21.

[64] Ibid., 65.

[65] Ibid., 80, 88–9.

[66] Jean Bethke Elshtain, "Politics and Forgiveness," *Burying the Past*, Neal Biggar, ed., 59.

[67] Andre du Toit, "Experiments with Truth and Justice in South Africa: Stockenström, Gandhi, and the TRC," *Journal of Southern African Studies* 31 (No. 2, June 2005) 440–1. See also Cynthia E. Milton, "At the Edge of the Peruvian Truth Commission: Alternative Paths to Recounting the Past," *Radical History Review* 98 (Spring 2007) 3–33; Jacqueline Rose, "Apathy and Accountability: South Africa's Truth and Reconciliation Commission," *Raritan* 21 (No. 4, 2002) 175–95; Beth Rushton, "Truth and Reconciliation? The Experience of Truth Commissions," *Australian Journal of International Affairs* 60 (No. 1, 2006) 125–41; Jay A. Vora and Erika Vora, "The Effectiveness of South Africa's Truth and

The Constitution of History and Memory

Numerous political theorists have joined the chorus of voices praising truth commissions. The basic descriptive work is Priscilla B. Hayner's *Unspeakable Truths*. Hayner describes the "turn toward truth" as "partly due to the limited reach of the courts, and partly out of a recognition that even successful prosecutions do not resolve the conflict and pain associated with past abuses."[68] She defines truth commissions as temporary bodies, officially authorized by the state, that "focus on the *past*" and "investigate a pattern of abuses over a period of time, rather than a specific event."[69] Such commissions are set up to "respond to the needs and interests of victims," to "outline institutional responsibility and recommend reforms," to "promote reconciliation," and to contribute to, rather than to replace, other forms of justice.[70] Hayner insists that there is no "trade-off" between truth and justice, given the difficulties and costs of reaching justice through prosecutions of wrongdoers. Although in certain cases (El Salvador), a truth commission led to blanket amnesty, in other cases, truth commissions have forwarded information to the justice system for prosecution. Even with an amnesty in place, as in Chile, the truth commission was a source for some names of perpetrators.[71] Hayner also argues that some victims will find testimony healing, even if others feel worse afterward.[72] Hayner argues that truth should not be a substitute for justice, but can be a complement, and that we cannot assume healing and catharsis from truth telling, but that healing and reconciliation may be the result, if truth commissions are well-designed.

Robert Rotberg notes that most scholars of law and politics "affirm truth commissions as a modern instrument capable of strengthening civil society and providing restorative justice," yet there are also critics who warn that the search for "truth" can mask or suppress healthy political conflict.[73] Amy Gutmann and Dennis Thompson, in "The Moral Foundations of Truth Commissions," argue that reconciliation as forgiveness is "a utopian aim, and not even a positive one." In their view, democracies should foster political disharmony rather than agreement on one historical truth. They also criticize the "historicist" justification of truth commissions, that such commissions are the best way to uncover facts about the shameful past that would otherwise be buried, on the grounds that such commissions will unduly focus on a single history rather than a multiplicity of competing interpretations. Gutmann

---

Reconciliation Commission: Perceptions of Xhosa, Afrikaner, and English South Africans," *Journal of Black Studies* 34 (No. 3, 2004) 301–22.

[68] Priscilla B. Hayner, *Unspeakable Truths: Confronting State Terror and Atrocity* (New York: Routledge, 2001) 14.

[69] Ibid.

[70] Ibid., 28–30.

[71] Ibid., 97.

[72] Ibid., 152–3.

[73] Robert I. Rotberg, "Truth Commissions and the Provision of Truth, Justice, and Reconciliation," 10–11, *Truth v. Justice: The Morality of Truth Commissions*, Robert I. Rotberg and Dennis Thompson, eds. (Princeton, NJ: Princeton University Press, 2000).

and Thompson suggest, "The aim of truth-seeking, with its strong intimations of singularity and finality, is not the most appropriate model for political judgment in an emerging democratic society." Instead there should be an "assumption of ongoing disagreement and continuing conflict." They note the "remarkable section of [South Africa's Truth and Reconciliation Commission's] *Final Report* entitled 'The Commission's Shortcomings'" as a salutary feature because it contains within itself the acknowledgment of its own flaws and the recognition that there is not one historical "truth."[74]

Some analysts of truth commissions specifically address the potential for truth commissions to tell good histories – and even for historical production to be a form of justice. Charles Maier argues that truth commissions can produce material for historians and that doing justice and doing history can complement one another.[75] In a chapter entitled "Historical Justice," Ruti Teitel goes even farther, exploring the possibility that "historical accountability [could be] a corrective, ushering in liberalization," or that "collective history making regarding the repressive past [could] lay the necessary basis for the new democratic order."[76] Although she warns of the danger in confusing history with a single truth, she also traces the historical narratives at work in various trials and truth commissions to assess whether they achieved some form of historical justice. For example, she examines the links between successive Holocaust criminal trials and shifts in Holocaust historiography. First, Nuremberg shaped memory of the Nazis for a long time by its focus on "aggressive war" and military leaders. Then, the Eichmann trial "coincided with Raul Hilberg's *The Destruction of the European Jews*."[77] Later a historiographic focus on the lower echelons of wrongdoers led to the trials of Touvier, Papon, and others.

Teitel also puts truth commissions in context, comparing them to the realistic alternatives; truth commissions were an antidote to impunity in Latin America and South Africa. She concludes that the truth process has virtues: Historical justice as a way of setting the record straight gives victims some reparation and "delineates a line between regimes."[78] Teitel also applies literary analysis to the question, arguing that the narrative of historical justice in transition is one of tragedy narrowly averted – a tragedy-romance in which "an awful fate is averted, as in a dramatic narrative,

---

[74] Amy Gutmann and Dennis Thompson, "The Moral Foundations of Truth Commissions," 32–5, *Truth v. Justice*, Rotberg and Thompson, eds. Other critics, particularly among legal scholars, focus on individual criminal justice, warning about the dangers of amnesty for perpetrators. Kent Greenawalt argues that amnesty for murderers or torturers is immoral. Sandy Levinson sees amnesties by truth commissions as a special form of plea bargaining. Kent Greenawalt, "Amnesty's Justice," 189–210, *Truth v. Justice*, Rotberg and Thompson, eds.; Sanford Levinson, "Trials, Commissions, and Investigating Committees: The Elusive Search for Norms of Due Process," *Truth v. Justice*, Rotberg and Thompson, eds., 211–34.

[75] Charles Maier, "Doing History, Doing Justice: The Historian and the Truth Commission," *Truth v. Justice*, Rotberg and Thompson, eds., 18.

[76] Ruti G. Teitel, *Transitional Justice* (Oxford and New York: Oxford University Press, 2000) 69.

[77] Ibid., 74.

[78] Ibid., 90.

The Constitution of History and Memory

by the introduction of a magical switch." She compares the transitional narrative to romances such as the Jacob-Esau story or Shakespeare's *The Tempest*, the movement from exile to home. Yet Teitel, like most students of truth commissions, remains optimistic.

What Are the Limitations of Truth Commissions?

Whereas Teitel and Minow are unabashed supporters of the truth and reconciliation process, a few law and literature scholars evince more ambivalence about truth commissions, in part because they question the power of narrative and testimony, both for the victim and for society. Mark Sanders' literary rendering of the South African Truth and Reconciliation Commission's work sees the process as ambiguous but ultimately offering healing through mourning. He writes: "The dominant tendency among scholars interpreting Truth Commission testimony has been to point to the inadequacy of the commission's procedures in allowing stories to be told, or to its facilitating only certain kinds of stories ... the problem may not always lie solely with the legal body and its rules and procedures. Although it is clear enough in traumatic cases that a quasi juridical hearing may do nothing to mend the break between recollection and observation, either for the witness or for the inquiry, it is not obvious that it will fail to do so *because* of its demand for particular evidence."[79] Of course, there were inadequacies to the human rights framework: "Speaking as a witness before the commission implied being enjoined to frame one's testimony according to the demands of universal human rights. As a perpetrator or a victim, one testified to a transgression of human rights ... Soliciting testimony in this way revealed ambiguities in cases that did not fit, in an obvious way, into the paradigm of human rights that guided the commission's work."[80] Denials of funeral rites violated custom but not law, for example. Sanders suggests that the truth commission offered the possibility of mourning, forgiveness, reparation – the very antithesis of apartheid, which he portrays as a denial of mourning and condolence.

Julie Stone Peters offers perhaps the most brilliant example of a literary critique of law's potential to heal a society through the use of narrative.[81] Peters critiques the assumption that narrative will humanize, that we can get catharsis and redress from giving testimony to atrocities. Peters is skeptical about the psychoanalytic model of trauma and repair as well as what she considers the naïve belief in the healing power of storytelling. She presents a tale of the narrative foundation for "rights" in the Enlightenment era, the moment at which early advocates for human rights first made

[79] Mark Sanders, *Ambiguities of Witnessing: Law and Literature in the Time of a Truth Commission* (Stanford: Stanford University Press, 2007) 8.

[80] Ibid., 60.

[81] Julie Stone Peters, "'Literature,' the 'Rights of Man,' and Narratives of Atrocity: Historical Backgrounds to the Culture of Testimony," *Yale Journal of Law and the Humanities* 17 (Summer 2005) 253.

436   Ariela Gross

the spurious connection among humanitarianism, narrative, and rights/justice. She
notes ironically the fact that even poststructuralists such as Jacques Derrida and
Gayatri Spivak have climbed on the human rights bandwagon. Critiques of rights
that are mainstream in the domestic context are left at the doorstep of international
human rights work.

Finally, several legal scholars and political theorists have also considered the usefulness of government apologies. Martha Minow considers that apology is valuable
both because it indicates "full acceptance of responsibility by the wrongdoer" and
because it gives the victims the power to accept or reject it.[82] Elazar Barkan and
Alexander Karns argue that although apology seems like a flaccid remedy, it "has great
flexibility and potential when considered as part of a larger framework of transitional
justice."[83] They compare Australia's apology to the Aborigines to Gover's apology
to Indians on behalf of the BIA. Ruti Teitel calls the transitional apology "a leading ritual of political transformation."[84] She traces executive apologies historically
through monarchies and now in democracies; at last, apologies have gone global, as
epitomized by Kofi Annan's apology to Rwanda on behalf of the United Nations.

The New Frontier in Memory Studies: Slavery and the Slave Trade

How Can We Remember a Centuries-old History?

In recent years, the United States has seen an outpouring of public remembrances
of slavery – museum exhibits, films, and other public efforts to recapture the history
and memory of slavery – and a growing academic focus on recovering the memory
of slavery in the United States, North as well as South. This new public attention
to slavery has not been limited to one side of the Atlantic. Recent anniversaries
of the abolition of the slave trade in the United Kingdom and of slavery in the
French colonies have been the occasion for public commemorations of the trade
and its abolition, and historians have begun to write about their experience of
involvement in such commemorations. Most of this writing describes, and to some
extent critiques, recent efforts to overcome the forgetting of slavery and advocates
for better ways to bring public memory in line with history. Some of this work itself
historicizes collective memory, narrating as an intellectual history the changing
images of slavery over time. Overall, however, it remains relatively undertheorized
in terms of the relationship between history and collective memory, the definition
of "memory," and the potential of public memory to heal a society or lead to social

---

[82] Minow, *Between Vengeance and Forgiveness*, 115.

[83] Elazar Barkan and Alexander Karn, "Group Apology as an Ethical Imperative," *Taking Wrongs Seriously: Apologies and Reconciliation*, Elazar Barkan and Alexander Karn, eds. (Stanford: Stanford University Press, 2006).

[84] Ruti Teitel, "The Transitional Apology" in *Taking Wrongs Seriously*, 101.

The Constitution of History and Memory

justice. Although this new attention has led to some public debate about the role of law in the memory of slavery – most particularly in France, which declared slavery and the slave trade to be crimes against humanity in a 2001 law – most academic writing on the subject has not focused on law. Slavery is a crime with no perpetrators to try, and although some institutions have attempted something like truth commissions on slavery, reparations talk has yet to become wholly mainstream, and to the extent that in France law has become a site of memory, mainstream historians have lined up against it.

Although sociologists have concentrated primarily on the relationship between African-descended people's collective memory of slavery and the formation of black identity, historians have been writing about the history of collective *forgetting* of slavery. David Blight's *Race and Reunion* and Nina Silber's *The Romance of Reunion* tell the story of the U.S. North and South united in the post–Civil War era by a joint commitment to white supremacy and to burying the memory of slavery. Joanne Pope Melish and Brown University's Committee on Slavery and Justice remind us of the way New Englanders and other Northerners "disowned" their own history of slavery.[85] Other historians have begun to write about the new flood of public memory work about slavery, primarily in a celebratory fashion, but also in an attempt to historicize it as connected to contemporary civil rights struggles.[86] Ira Berlin notes that public debate over the relationship between Thomas Jefferson and Sally Hemings and the huge success of the New York Historical Society's exhibit on slavery demonstrates that "slavery has become a language, a way to talk about race in a society in which race is difficult to discuss."[87] Similarly, French historian Alyssa Sepinwall celebrates new efforts to remember the French history of enslavement

---

[85] Ron Eyerman, *Cultural Trauma: Slavery and the Formation of African American Identity* (Cambridge and New York: Cambridge University Press, 2001); Iyunolu Folayan Osagie, *The Amistad Revolt: Memory, Slavery, and the Politics of Identity in the United States and Sierra Leone* (Athens, GA: University of Georgia Press, 2000); Saidiya Hartman, "The Time of Slavery," *The South Atlantic Quarterly* 101 (No. 4, Fall 2002) 757; Shelley Fisher Fishkin, "Race and the Politics of Memory: Mark Twain and Paul Laurence Dunbar," *Journal of American Studies* 40 (No. 2, 2006) 283; Elizabeth Rauh Bethel, *The Roots of African-American Identity* (New York: St. Martin's Press, 1997); Berlin, "American Slavery in History and Memory," 1251–68; Fredrick Harris, "Collective Memory, Collective Action, and Black Activism in the 1960s," *Breaking the Cycles of Hatred: Memory, Law, and Repair*, Martha Minow, ed. (Princeton, NJ: Princeton University Press, 2002); Julie Saville, "Circuits of Memory: Modern Routes to Slave Pasts," *Georgia Historical Quarterly* 83 (No. 3, 1999) 539; W. Fitzhugh Brundage, ed., *Where These Memories Grow: History, Memory, and Southern Identity* (Chapel Hill: University of North Carolina Press, 2000); David Blight, *Race and Reunion: The Civil War in American Memory* (Cambridge, MA: Harvard University Press, 2002); *Slavery and Justice*, Report of the Brown University Steering Committee on Slavery and Justice (2006); James Oliver Horton and Lois E. Horton, eds., *Slavery and Public History: The Tough Stuff of American Memory* (New York: The New Press, 2006).

[86] See, e.g., Ira Berlin, "American Slavery in History and Memory," at 1, connecting the new public "engagement over the issue of slavery" to "a crisis in American race relations" that makes engagement with the past especially important in struggles for justice.

[87] Ibid., 19.

and disparaging the "amnesia" about slavery that formerly governed. She argues that francophone history teaching is far behind Anglophone writing in its lack of attention to the Haitian Revolution or an Atlantic perspective more generally. The 2004 CAPES examination, for students going into teaching in France, focused on the years 1773 to 1802, excluding 1804 from consideration.[88]

Taking a more critical view, Elizabeth Kowaleski Wallace examines fiction, museum exhibits, and films in the United Kingdom that focus on the history of the British slave trade, and finds that many of these efforts to shape collective memory so emphasize the victimization of Africans that they "play" into stereotypes of dehumanized slaves, ineffectual subjects rendered passive, weak, and silent through their enslavement." She also raises questions about whether it is possible to "convey the extraordinary human affliction" of the slave trade through a memorial "without... potentially cheapening the experience or suggesting that it can be vicariously assumed?" She concludes that the most successful efforts to remember slavery are those that "remain self-conscious about themselves as expressions" and, through a balanced depiction of slaves' victimization and resistance, "allow" people to recognize both the human capacity for evil and the human ability to retain agency."[89]

Christine Chivallon describes the public memory work about the slave past in Bristol, United Kingdom, passing "from silence to 'too much memory.'" She compares this surfeit of memory with the absence of memory at another slave trading post, Bordeaux, France.[90] France has commemorated slavery by celebrating the Republican abolition, especially the white abolitionist leader Victor Schoelcher. Jacques Chirac, then president, gave a speech at the commemoration that referred to abolition as a "founding act" that "reinforced the unity of the Nation."[91] By contrast, Chivallon suggests that Bristol city may have even gone too far in reshaping its public history to put its grand houses and personages in the context of the slave trade. Public controversy ensued over taking down the statue of Colston, an early leader who had also been a slave trader; eventually this was resolved by an explanatory plaque.[92]

---

[88] Alyssa Sepinwall, "Atlantic Amnesia? French Historians, the Haitian Revolution, and the 2004–2006 CAPES Exam." See also Rex Nettleford, "The Haitian Revolution and the Struggle Against Slavery: Challenges to Knowledge, Ignorance, and Silence," *International Social Science Journal* 58 (No. 188, 2007) 202; Nicolas Argenti and Ute Röschenthaler, "Between Cameroon and Cuba: Youth, Slave Trades, and Translocal Memoryscapes," *Social Anthropology* 14 (No. 1, 2006) 33–47; Jean-Michel Deveau, «Silence and Reparations,» *International Social Science Journal* 58 (No. 188, 2007) 248.

[89] Elizabeth Kowaleski Wallace, *The British Slave Trade and Public Memory* (New York: Columbia University Press, 2006) 207–8, 212.

[90] Christine Chivallon, "Bristol and the Eruption of Memory: Making the Slave-Trading Past Visible," *Social and Cultural Geography* 2 (2001) 347–61.

[91] Ibid., 350.

[92] See also Catherine Reinhardt, *Claims to Memory: Beyond Slavery and Emancipation in the French Caribbean* (New York: Berghahn Books, 2006) 153, describing the commemoration of slavery in the former French colonies of Martinique, Guadeloupe, and Haiti.

The Constitution of History and Memory

In Africa, there has been increased tourism to slave trade sites, a rise in commemorations of the slave trade in museums and anniversary ceremonies, as well as a growing discourse of reparations, including demands for apology, debt forgiveness, and other forms of repair. Historians outside the United States who have chronicled this memory work with regard to the slave trade have taken a somewhat more sophisticated approach to the divisions between professional historiography and public memory work. For example, several scholars have critiqued the commemorations at African slave trade sites. Ralph Austen compares African and African American memory of the slave trade. He tells the story of Ndiaye, a Senegalese man who worked to have the Maison des Ésclaves at Gorée restored, turned it into a pilgrimage destination for African Americans, and now exaggerates the story of the "Door of No Return" in his tours. United States historian of the slave trade Philip Curtin denounced Ndiaye's project as a "hoax" and a "scam," and his words were reported in the French newspaper *Le Monde*. This criticism caused such a firestorm of controversy, that eventually a conference was held on Gorée Island in April 1997 to repair the damage. African critics of empirical work on the slave trade insist on a larger historical context and more use of African oral tradition to give meaning to the numbers. Austen tries to bridge divisions between professional historians and this memory work by drawing on Eric Williams, the most powerful black figure in slave trade historiography.[93]

The historian Emmanuel Akyeampong also writes about the slave trade in terms of both history and memory. He describes the upsurge of slave-trade tourism in Ghana, turning slave trade castles and forts into World Heritage Sites maintained by UNESCO funds. In his story, he links the Anlo people's effort to have the village of Atorkor declared an international slave-history site to another recent development, the new international media attention to ritual female bondage in the Volta and Greater Accra regions of Ghana. He argues that slaveholding is an embarrassing memory in Anlo – there are still current distinctions made between descendants of free persons and slaves, and a "complex identity politics about how people choose to present themselves in the present and reflect on their past."[94] Thus, although oral traditions of the Atorkor slave story persist in song, people prefer to keep these memories in the private domain, rather than publicizing them to attract tourists. This complicates any effort to draw political analogies between contemporary and historical slavery in the region.

An American literary scholar, Saidiya Hartman, has written some of the most incisive criticism of the memory work going on at tourist sites of the slave trade in

---

[93] Ralph Austen, "The Slave Trade as History and Memory: Confrontations of Slaving Voyage Documents and Communal Traditions," *William and Mary Quarterly* 58 (Third Series, No. 1, January 2001) 229–44.

[94] Emmanuel Akyeampong, "History, Memory, Slave-Trade, and Slavery in Anlo (Ghana)," *Slavery and Abolition* 22 (No. 3, December 2001) 18.

Ghana from a U.S. perspective. She describes the experience of African American tourists "returning" to Africa to grieve for the slave trade. Her own reaction was anger at the sentimentalized staging of the "Door of No Return," in which the tour guide declared, "It is not really the Door of No Return because now you are back!"[95] Yet she also envied the other women on her tour their tears. She finds it "difficult, if not impossible, to separate the mourning that exceeds tourism from the contained catharsis promoted by it."[96] Hartman affirms that mourning at these memory sites can center the tragedy of the slave trade in public consciousness; yet at the same time, "the work of mourning is not without its perils, chief among these are the slippage between responsibility and assimilation and witnessing and incorporation."[97] Hartman asks whether there is a "necessary relation between remembrance and redress?" Is it possible to reach any kind of redemption by "working through" the past?[98] Nevertheless, she concludes that such representations of the past are necessary but require critical engagement rather than "facile invocations of captivity, sound bites about the millions lost."[99]

All of this writing about slavery remains very much in the domain of memory work – whether telling the history of collective memory and forgetting of slavery, drawing the links between collective memory of trauma and identity formation, or lauding the work of memory recovery. Unlike in the context of twentieth-century mass atrocities, there has been little scholarship that stands outside of this memory work to critique the efforts to shape collective memory or the historical narratives at play in political or legal debates. Few critical voices have suggested problems with the way we are remembering slavery, or the costs of remembering slavery, for example. Little of this work has engaged with law, in part because legal efforts to redress slavery seem utopian or remote.

How Does the Public Memory of Slavery Shape the Law?

In a recent essay, I have written about the public memory of slavery and its relation to legal responses to slavery's legacy in the United States. The essay details the competing historical narratives in the public political sphere and in jurisprudence regarding redress for racial injustice based in slavery. The resurgence of memory of slavery can play out in both conservative and liberal modes, as can a turn to popular constitutionalism. I begin by examining three chief strategies in conservative historical argument: first, depicting slavery as part of a teleological progression toward

[95] Hartman, *The Time of Slavery*, 766.
[96] Ibid., 769.
[97] Ibid., 771.
[98] Ibid., 773.
[99] Ibid., 774.

The Constitution of History and Memory 441

freedom, glossing over the Jim Crow era and postslavery racial injustice; second, portraying slavery and Jim Crow as temporary deviations from a continuous American tradition of freedom and color blindness; and third, decoupling slavery from race by arguing that slavery was not caused by racism, and emphasizing the blacks who owned or traded slaves and the whites who did not.[100]

The essay then canvasses several approaches to history among liberals or radicals who defend efforts to redress racial injustice: first, an emphasis on the legacies of slavery, and in particular on the continuing harms of the Jim Crow era; second, a progressive view of American history, emphasizing the "living Constitution," not as ratified in 1787 but as it has evolved over the last two centuries to embody antisubordination principles; and third, a history of the interdependence of black slavery and white freedom and privilege. The "remember Jim Crow" story is an effective counterpoint to the "slavery to freedom" story, and yet it has rarely been elaborated to argue against the celebration of antislavery as the Christian West's gift to the rest of the world. The "living Constitution" view is opposed to the "continuous color blindness" history that celebrates the 1787 Constitution, yet most proponents of the evolving Constitution do not directly dispute the view that slavery was a temporary aberration from a continuous color-blind principle. Finally, the most promising and least-developed historical narrative is the "black slavery/white privilege" story, which counters conservatives' strategy to "decouple slavery from race."

I also consider two other liberal or radical approaches to history, neither of which is represented in judicial opinion but both of which have found articulation among legal academics: first, a more pessimistic approach, in some ways an antiprogressive view of history, emphasizing the static nature of racism and inequality in the United States; second, a more optimistic embrace of "popular constitutionalism" for alternative visions of the Constitution (in some ways building on the liberal justices' version of "living constitutionalism").

I conclude by suggesting that to strengthen arguments in favor of remedies for racial injustice, liberals must not only refute the conservative histories but build on histories of slavery, antislavery, and movements for racial redress "from the bottom up." Furthermore, I argue that even structural, forward-looking remedies require historical grounding. The most compelling historical narratives are those that emphasize the links between black slavery and white freedom, as well as the connections between the relatively recent injustices of the Jim Crow era and the inequality that continues today.

This essay is one of the first efforts to consider explicitly the relationship between law and the memory of slavery.

---

[100] Ariela Gross, "When Is the Time of Slavery? The History of Slavery in Contemporary Legal and Political Argument," *California Law Review* 96 (February 2008) 283.

Reconstructing the Constitution of History and Memory

Although less explicitly focused on the memory of slavery, several U.S. legal scholars have trained their attention on the history and memory of Reconstruction and the Civil War, seeking to recapture the meaning of the Constitution through the lens of a recovered history. Akhil Amar first paved the way for rereading the Constitution through the lens of the history of slavery and Reconstruction with his neo-originalist reading of the Thirteenth Amendment. Richard Primus and Norman Spaulding have extended his approach, reconstructing the meaning of federalism and other basic constitutional structures by reimagining the history of Reconstruction from the perspective of the freed slaves, rather than the Northern Democratic version of history espoused by the post–Civil War Court. Both Mark Graber and Pamela Brandwein, political scientists, have begun to critique the way constitutional scholars use the history of *Dred Scott* and Reconstruction to argue for their own interpretive theories. All of this work points to the possibility of a constitutional discourse that is historicist without being originalist.[101]

Norman Spaulding explores the architectural theory of "countermonument" to imagine ways of interpreting the Constitution, not through traditionally didactic memory, with its "authoritarian propensity," but in a less reductionist way. Spaulding argues for the "deep legal and political salience" of collective memory, and writes, "It is primarily the courts that bear the explicit institutional burden of collective memory." Courts are "mnemonic institutions par excellence." Can courts use the method of countermemory, as other lieux de mémoires, like countermonuments, have done? "Can a constitution be written or read against itself? Or is constitutional law accessible only in monumental form, with all its didactic, demagogic, and amnesic liabilities?" Spaulding argues that the Reconstruction Amendments should be interpreted as countermonuments: "monuments against the axioms that justified slavery," an interpretation hinted at by Thurgood Marshall's assertion that the Constitution did not survive the Civil War. According to Spaulding, this mode of interpretation, applying the method of countermemory, requires more rigorous memory work than traditional monuments, resisting "the dependence of collective memory on didactics and collective amnesia."[102]

---

[101] Akhil Amar, "Child Abuse as Slavery: A Thirteenth Amendment Response to *DeShaney*," *Harvard Law Review* 105 (April 1992) 1359; Richard Primus, "The Riddle of Hiram Revels," *Harvard Law Review* 119 (April 2006) 1680; Norman W. Spaulding, "Constitution as Counter-Monument: Federalism, Reconstruction, and the Problem of Collective Memory," *Columbia Law Review* 103 (December 2003) 1992; Mark Graber, *Dred Scott and the Problem of Constitutional Evil* (Cambridge: Cambridge University Press, 2006); Pamela Brandwein, *Reconstructing Reconstruction: The Supreme Court and the Production of Historical Truth* (Durham, NC: Duke University Press, 1999). This brief discussion is drawn from Ariela Gross, "When Is the Time of Slavery? The History of Slavery in Contemporary Legal and Political Argument."

[102] Spaulding, "Constitution as Counter-Monument," 2000–3.

The Constitution of History and Memory

Spaulding finds just such didactics and collective amnesia in American memory of the Civil War, the revising of that war into the "war between 'brothers' rather than between – as they briefly were – two sovereign nation-states." Just as public monuments have accepted this essentially Southern version of the war and of Reconstruction as a regrettable and corrupt period of readjustment, the Supreme Court, in its recent federalism decisions, has forgotten "the structural significance of the Civil War and Reconstruction Amendments." This forgetting stems from a desire for closure, just as many Northerners as well as Southerners desired an end to "the Negro question" after the Civil War. "If this corrupt desire for closure indeed lies behind the survival thesis; then it is not unfair to conclude, having begun to emerge more than a century later from the atrocities of segregation and racial oppression invited by the Compromise of 1877, that the federalism revival is chillingly amnesic."[103]

How can constitutional interpreters resist this kind of forgetting? Spaulding suggests that we must accept Marshall's invitation to "remember something we have always already forgotten." The three aspects of War and Reconstruction of which he reminds federalism revivalists all challenge the "monumentalist narrative of reassuring fratricide supporting the survival thesis": "(1) the fact of secession, with its deep roots in robust antebellum federalism principles; (2) the fact of federal coercion in the ratification of all three Reconstruction Amendments by southern states; and (3) the original Thirteenth Amendment, which would have avoided war by canonizing robust federalism and guaranteeing the right to slavery." If we remember these events, Spaulding argues, we cannot share the Court's monumentalist interpretation of the relationship between the states and the federal government.[104]

Richard Primus has also undertaken a project of memory work, recovering a forgotten episode in Reconstruction history, to challenge and reshape constitutional interpretation. Primus tells the story of the Senate debate over seating Hiram Revels, an African American from Mississippi, who may or may not have been born a citizen, depending on whether the senators considered the *Dred Scott* case (holding that free blacks could not be citizens) to be good law. In the debate, some Republicans argued that *Dred Scott* had never been good law, whereas some Southern Democrats believed that it was still good law. Ultimately, Revels was seated. Primus argues that the significance of the debate can be understood if we view it in the context of transitional justice, and therefore, we should interpret the Reconstruction Amendments as the product of transition.

Primus suggests "two deeper and potentially more satisfying justifications (than those offered at the time) for seating Revels. The first is that the Civil War and Reconstruction nullified antebellum legal authority limiting the rights of African

[103] Ibid., 2005–6, 2036.
[104] Ibid., 2026, 2036–7.

Americans to a greater extent than was codified in the Thirteenth, Fourteenth, and Fifteenth Amendments. The second is that once black men were recognized as equal participants in the American polity, the legitimacy of the (amended) Constitution rested less on its 'democratic' pedigree and more on other considerations, including substantive justice and the subjective identification of citizens with the regime – factors that would be enhanced by seating Revels and vitiated by barring him." In the first view, "we can understand the Civil War and Reconstruction as having nullified aspects of the prior legal order that harmed African Americans." This understanding stems not only from a reading of the Amendments but of the entire historical context, "a narrative, or a set of images, with a social meaning that speaks to the changed status of black Americans and says more than the Amendments say on their own." In the second view, Reconstruction was "an incompletely democratic expansion of the polity that required further extension as a matter of transitional justice."[105]

Finally, several authors draw on the work of philosopher Walter Benjamin to offer new possibilities for the interpretation of the Constitution in light of history and memory. Amy Kapczynski contrasts the method of "redemptive history" to both "historicism" and "progressivism," which she sees as dominating contemporary American constitutionalism. "Constitutional historicism is preoccupied with returning to the past" whereas progressivism "is preoccupied not with the past but with the future." What are the problems with these two modes? "First, historicism attributes a false certainty to its history, and by doing so, fails to take responsibility for its own acts of interpretation. Second, in order to defend its conflation of the past and authority, historicism reduces history to heritage. It thus serves the victors of the past, and undermines historicism's claim to the contemporary legitimacy that it seeks." By contrast, the problem with progressivism is the belief in human perfectibility and its inevitability.[106]

As alternatives, Kapczynski offers several examples, foremost among them reckoning with the "legacy of slavery in our nation's constitutional and political life." She contrasts the progressive view with "Saidiya Hartman's attempt to theorize the period of Reconstruction from the point of view of the freed slaves," for whom slavery did not come to an end in 1865. Kapczynski proposes "redemptive history" as an alternative, using "the past to free up rather than constrain interpretation, to make new meanings in the present, rather than reiterate meanings that were ostensibly fixed in the past." As examples of redemptive approaches, she includes Norman Spaulding's work as well as that of other historians, such as Reva Siegel and Risa

---

[105] Primus, "Riddle of Hiram Revels," 1703, 1709–10, 1716.
[106] Amy Kapczynski, "Historicism, Progress, and the Redemptive Constitution," *Cardozo Law Review* 26 (February 2005) 1044–5, 1063.

The Constitution of History and Memory

Goluboff, who explore forgotten constitutional meanings and paths not taken in legal and constitutional history.[107]

Can Law Help the United States to Redress Slavery?

Although my essay looks at the narratives about slavery embedded in legal debates about affirmative action and other programs of racial remediation that could be conceived broadly as redress for the slave past, the last decade has also seen the rise of a public discourse specifically focused on slavery reparations. Academic writings in favor of reparations are the only works to take seriously a turn to law to redress the history and memory of slavery. Most of the new writing, however, takes the form of advocacy, making the case for or against reparations; a few pieces either tell the history of the debate or analyze the arguments on both sides. At this stage, however, with a few exceptions, very little has been written that critically approaches reparations or redress claims in terms of the relationship among law, history, and memory.

Why reparations talk now? One answer is that reparations has been an ever-present demand in African American politics but has only received public attention at certain moments. Historians Martha Biondi and Mary Frances Berry have recently published histories of black reparations movements, beginning with that of Callie House and the campaign for ex-slave pensions after the Civil War. Civil rights activists from Martin Luther King, Jr. to black nationalist leaders demanded reparations for slavery.[108] Reparations discourse may appear more prominent today to the extent that other avenues to racial justice have been closed off. Al Brophy, in *The Cultural War over Reparations*, argues that reparations debates represent "another front on . . . the culture wars."[109] They remain enormously divisive, with great majorities of African Americans supporting apology and compensation for slavery but only tiny minorities of whites. To the extent that affirmative action and other programs of the Second Reconstruction have faded and come under attack, reparations appears no less radical or viable, no less divisive, and potentially energizing. Claims for reparation have also gone hand in hand with public educational efforts for "historical justice." For example, the Brown University Committee on Slavery and Justice

---

[107] Ibid., 1091, 1102. But see Christopher Tomlins' critique of Kapczynski in Christopher Tomlins, "The Strait Gate: The Past, History, and Legal Scholarship," unpublished paper on file with author, on Walter Benjamin and legal history.

[108] Martha Biondi, "The Rise of the Reparations Movement," *Radical History Review* 87 (Fall 2003) 5–18; Mary Frances Berry, *My Face Is Black Is True: Callie House and the Struggle for Ex-Slave Reparations* (New York: Knopf Publishing Group, 2005).

[109] Alfred L. Brophy, "The Cultural War Over Reparations for Slavery," *DePaul Law Review* 53 (Spring 2004) 1181.

coupled historical research on Brown's role in slavery and the slave trade with an apology for the university's complicity, and efforts to inaugurate programs of redress.

An emphasis on the continuing legacies of slavery animates all arguments in favor of reparations for slavery, but, in the United States, these have taken three forms with regard to legal claim: debt (contract), unjust enrichment (restitution), or corrective justice (tort). All three of these legal and moral approaches rely on a version of history in which slavery is the direct cause of continuing harm. Some reparations advocates focus on continuing racial harms; others draw causal connections between slavery and present-day inequality involving cultural or material deprivations inherited by the descendants of ex-slaves.

The idea of a debt to be repaid is based not only in the history of slavery and its legacy but also on the history of ex-slaves' claims for compensation. In *The Debt: What America Owes to Blacks*, Randall Robinson argues most forcefully: "Black people worked long, hard, killing days, years, centuries – and they were never paid . . . There is a debt here."[110] Similarly, Charles Ogletree, Jr., the Harvard Law professor who has coordinated recent reparations litigation efforts, argues that reparations require "acceptance, acknowledgment, and accounting" for the debt of slavery.[111] This argument builds not only on the history of slavery and its legacy, but also on the history of ex-slaves' claims for compensation for stolen labor, beginning with the demands of ex-slaves for "forty acres and a mule," through the ex-slaves' pension movement of the late nineteenth century.

The legal principle of restitution or unjust enrichment involves not a debt for a voluntarily assumed obligation, like a contract, but rather the disgorgement of a benefit it would be unjust to retain. The remedy of restitution focuses not on the loss to the slave but on the benefit to the slaveholder. In this sense, restitution may be a better model for slavery reparations than debt. Thus, legal commentators have been attracted to unjust enrichment theory. Robert Westley writes, "Belief in the fairness of reparations requires at the intellectual level acceptance of the principle that the victims of unjust enrichment should be compensated."[112] Those who advocate an unjust enrichment theory also focus on history but turn their lens toward the history of institutions and corporations that benefited from slavery. The recent efforts by universities to acknowledge the role that slavery and the slave trade

---

[110] Ibid., 207.

[111] Charles J. Ogletree, Jr., "The Current Reparations Debate," *U. C. Davis Law Review* 36 (June 2003) 1055. For an early exponent of this position, see Vincene Verdun, "If the Shoe Fits, Wear It: An Analysis of Reparations to African Americans," *Tulane Law Review* 67 (February 1993) 597.

[112] Robert Westley, "Many Billions Gone: Is It Time to Reconsider the Case for Black Reparations?," *Boston College Law Review* 40 (December 1998) 436. See also Hanoch Dagan, "Restitution and Slavery: On Incomplete Commodification, Intergenerational Justice, and Legal Transitions," *Boston University Law Review* 84 (2004) 1139; Andrew Kull, "Restitution in Favor of Former Slaves," *Boston University Law Review* 84 (2004) 1277; Emily Sherwin, "Reparations and Unjust Enrichment," *Boston University Law Review* 84 (2004) 1443.

The Constitution of History and Memory

played in building the institutions partake of this approach, as do lawsuits aimed at insurance companies such as Aetna that benefited from insuring the lives of slaves.[113] Some also widen the lens to paint a broad picture of white privilege and benefit; for example, the sociologist of race Joe R. Feagin emphasizes the "transgenerational transmission of wealth" and "labor stolen under slavery" as well as government programs that benefited only whites, such as the Homestead Act and a variety of New Deal programs.[114]

Finally, some advocates of reparations for slavery view it as morally necessary as a matter of corrective justice broadly conceived, as a remedy for the harms of slavery and its aftermath, akin to a tort remedy rather than damages for breach of contract. A corrective justice argument too depends heavily on drawing the causal connections between past and present, the harms of slavery and the harms of today.[115]

Some critics of reparations, especially those focused on the terrible harms of Jim Crow, have raised concerns about the exclusive focus on reparations for slavery, as opposed to more recent harms. The first major academic treatment of reparations, Boris Bittker's *The Case for Black Reparations*, published in 1973, concluded that reparations should be paid for the harms perpetrated on African Americans under Jim Crow in the recent past, and for as specific claims as possible. More recently, Emma Coleman Jordan has urged reparations advocates to concentrate on the crime of lynching as a way to avoid the "formidable obstacles and conceptual challenges" of a slavery reparations strategy.[116] Sociologist Ira Katznelson describes the period "when affirmative action was white" by characterizing the mid-twentieth-century programs of the New Deal, especially Social Security and the GI Bill, as a massive wealth transfer to white Americans for which blacks should be repaid.[117]

Shifting the temporal focus from slavery to Jim Crow not only reduces the practical problems of lawsuits, as Jordan emphasizes, but undermines the moral weight of the "no liability" argument against reparations. As Bittker wrote, "This preoccupation with slavery, in my opinion, has stultified the discussion of black reparations by implying that the only issue is the correction of an ancient injustice, thus inviting the reply that the wrongs were committed by persons long since dead, whose profits

---

[113] "U-Va. Expresses Regret Over Past Link to Slavery," *The Washington Post*, April 25, 2007, B6; "Brown Focuses on Ills of Slavery," *The Providence Journal* (Rhode Island), February 25, 2007, A1; "Slavery Funds Helped Found Brown University," *The New York Sun*, October 19, 2006, 6.

[114] Joe R. Feagin, "Documenting the Costs of Slavery, Segregation, and Contemporary Racism: Why Reparations Are in Order for African Americans," *Harvard BlackLetter Law Journal* 20 (Spring 2004) 55–62.

[115] For the best summary of reparations arguments, see Brophy, "The Cultural War Over Reparations for Slavery"; Alfred L. Brophy, "Some Conceptual and Legal Problems in Reparations for Slavery," *New York University Annual Survey of American Law* 58 (2003) 497.

[116] Emma Coleman Jordan, "A History Lesson: Reparations for What?" *New York University Annual Survey of American Law* 58 (2003) 557.

[117] Ira Katznelson, *When Affirmative Action Was White: An Untold History of Racial Inequality in Twentieth-Century America* (New York: W. W. Norton & Co., 2005).

may well have been dissipated during their own lifetimes or their descendants', and whose moral responsibility should not be visited upon succeeding generations, let alone upon wholly unrelated persons . . . to concentrate on slavery is to understate the case for compensation, so much so that one might almost suspect that the distant past is serving to suppress the ugly facts of the recent past and of contemporary life."[118]

Critics of slavery reparations who urge reparations for Jim Crow also fear that a focus on slavery will minimize continuing racial harms, allowing us to believe that injustice was part of the deep past. These critics urge us to remember Jim Crow and argue that the most direct cause of present-day inequality are these more recent harms. Some also contend that the harms of slavery are too great to be remedied: "There is no adequate rejoinder to losses on this scale," writes Ira Katznelson. "In such situations, the request for large cash transfers places bravado ahead of substance, flirts with demagoguery, and risks political irrelevance."[119]

By contrast, reparations advocates argue that removing slavery from the set of harms to be redressed "eliminates the most compelling basis for claims and damages" and deals the reparations movement "a near-fatal blow."[120] This debate may be unresolvable, as people come to it with very different moral intuitions about where the most compelling claims for redress lie.

Elazar Barkan chronicles the rise of claims for reparation for slavery around the world in 1990s, especially after Japanese Americans won reparations for internment.[121] An apparently spontaneous movement for reparations in 1993 occurred when a significant number of blacks withheld taxes, calling it reparations for slavery. Affirmative action could be seen as restitution, but it is also most constitutionally vulnerable on those grounds. Paul Starr proposes a "national endowment" for blacks: Barkan believes that perhaps that could be the basis for affirmative action as restitution.[122] Is restitution a copout, an easy way for rich nations to remake their past? "Successful restitution . . . transforms a traumatic national experience into a constructive political situation. By bringing a conflict to closure and opening new opportunities while creating new rights, it facilitates changes in national identities

---

[118] Boris I. Bittker, *The Case for Black Reparations* (New York: Random House, 1973) 9–12.

[119] Katznelson, *When Affirmative Action Was White*, 157–8.

[120] Rhonda V. Magee, Note: "The Master's Tools, from the Bottom Up: Responses to African-American Reparations Theory in Mainstream and Outsider Remedies Discourse," *Virginia Law Review* 79 (May 1993) 901, "[The] post-slavery focus, though it may appeal to some pragmatists, eliminates the most compelling basis for claims and damages. The reparations argument derives considerable moral and emotional power from the 'super-wrong' propagated by the institution of slavery, and any presentation of the case for reparations which concedes the impracticality of remedying the injury caused by slavery has likely dealt itself a near-fatal blow.")

[121] Barkan, *The Guilt of Nations*.

[122] Ibid., 296.

The Constitution of History and Memory

and is becoming a force in resolving international conflicts."[123] Roy L. Brooks argues that most progress on rights comes in times of war, so maybe also with the "war on terror," it will be possible to advance the cause of apology or reparations for slavery.[124]

Stephen Best and Saidiya Hartman, in "Fugitive Justice," come closest to a Law and Humanities reading of narratives of reparation or redress. They convened the "Redress Project" at the University of California Humanities Center to address "questions of slavery, fugitive forms of justice, and the role of history in the political present." They asked, "Why is justice fugitive?" Why was it elusive even "from within the crucible of slavery and at the height of the slave trade?" "Is this elusiveness then an index of the incommensurability between grief and grievance, pain and compensation?" "What is the time of slavery?" Is slavery in the present, "a death sentence reenacted and transmitted across generations?" They focus on the impossibility of adequate redress, the violence of slavery that is "ongoing and constitutive of the unfinished project of freedom."[125]

Thus, they critique recent efforts to win reparations through lawsuits as emblematic of political resignations, in essence suits for "back wages," aimed at corporations who benefited from slave labor rather than the "racial state" that made it all possible with its "slaveholders' constitution." Locked into a "liberal legal conception of law and property," recent efforts for slave reparations have lost sight of the gap between grief and grievance, all that has been lost that can never be compensated or restored. This emphasis on mourning and condolence suggests a way of thinking about reparation that might draw on the critical readings of truth commissions and trials. Law has a role to play in shaping history and memory, but law cannot remake the past.[126]

Can Law Redress the Slave Past in France?

In 2001, France became the first of the former slaveholding nations to declare slavery and the slave trade a "crime against humanity" in the "loi Taubira." This law decreed that slavery and the slave trade should be taught in public schools, commemorated in museums and monuments, and otherwise be a subject of public education and memory. While historians of slavery advocated for this law, and since its passage have worked on committees and in research groups to effectuate its goals, other historians publicly opposed the Taubira law, lumping it together with laws against Holocaust denial and other "historical" laws in a public "call for the liberty of history" (appel de la liberté de l'histoire). These historians argue that "history is not a religion" and

[123] Ibid., 345.
[124] Roy L. Brooks, "The New Patriotism and Apology for Slavery," *Taking Wrongs Seriously*.
[125] Stephen Best and Saidiya Hartman, «Fugitive Justice,» Special Issue on Redress, 92 (No. 1, Fall 2005) *Representations* 3–4.
[126] Ibid., 6–9.

450   Ariela Gross

that the state should have no role in declaring historical truth. Pierre Nora and other historians of memory have been leaders in this effort to separate law from history and memory.

In France, as in the United States, the politics of commemoration implicate contemporary racial politics. The campaign to recognize publicly France's role in the slave trade, which culminated in the 1998 commemoration of the 150th anniversary of the abolition of slavery in the French colonies, was spearheaded by a black movement that modeled itself on the Holocaust reparations movement.[127] The date for the 1998 commemoration occasioned vociferous public debate: April 27, the first day chosen, was the day in 1848 that the Republicans, led by Victor Schoelcher, abolished slavery. Many advocates of commemoration found this date too celebratory because it "emphasized only the positive aspects of *Républicain* historiography," ignoring the reestablishment of slavery. Conflict also arose within the black movement over its relationship to the French Jewish community. Radicals argue not only that there is a direct analogy between the slave trade and the Holocaust, but take it farther to compare Zionism with Nazism. The recent public controversy over comedian Dieudonné M'Bala, M'Bala's "Isra-Heil" exemplifies this black supremacist trend. By contrast, moderates "seek to use slavery as a starting point for organizing their community as a political lobby"; that is the goal of the Conseil Représentatif des Associations Noires (CRAN), a center-right umbrella group. Camus concludes: "'Black consciousness' has emerged around the issues of slavery and cultural/racial domination, and today it plays an important role in the fundamental transformation of French society from an assimilationist into a multicultural society."[128]

At the same time, despite the overwhelming passage in Parliament of the Taubira law, all elected officials have hastened to clarify that they do not support either apology or any form of reparations for slavery. Among academics, A. F. Ade Ajayi argues in favor of reparation; he compares the French situation with that of the United States and finds slavery both a crime and a sin, focusing on church involvement.[129] By contrast, Michel Giraud, while chronicling the fact that the moral reparation of calling slavery a crime against humanity has led to claims for material reparations, finds it unlikely that there will be material reparations because slavery is too distant temporally to justify reparations. He argues that France should focus on

---

[127] Jean-Yves Camus, "The Commemoration of Slavery in France and the Emergence of a Black Political Consciousness," *The European Legacy* 11 (No. 6, 2006) 647–55, at 648–50. COFFAD, the Collectif des Filles et Fils d'Africains Déportés, is modeled on the Jewish Association des Fils et Filles des Déportés Juifs de France, led by the Klarsfelds. Ibid., 651.

[128] Ibid., 649–50, 652, 654. See also Salah Trabelsi, "Memory and Slavery: The Issues of Historiography," *International Social Science Journal* 58 (No. 188, June 2006) 237–43; Anthony Holiday, "Slavery and Denial," *International Social Science Journal* 58 (No. 188, June 2006) 203–14.

[129] J. F. Ade Ajayi, "La politique de Réparation dans le contexte de la mondialisation," *Cahiers d'Études africaines* 44 (No. 173, 2004) 41–63.

The Constitution of History and Memory 451

inequality as a problem for the future, rather than approaching justice by looking backward.[130]

Conclusion

As nations turn a critical eye on their own pasts, scholars have begun to ask whether we have an obsession with memory or an obsessive fear of it. Although historians of memory urge a joining of history and memory, allowing collective preoccupations to shape historiography as we attempt to introduce new historical interpretations to a public audience, legal scholars are asking whether law can help. Can law repair traumatic memories or establish historical justice? Can law reform the past?

With regard to the Holocaust and South African apartheid, as well as other twentieth-century mass atrocities, trials of perpetrators and truth commissions have been the most common legal efforts to repair the past, although apologies and limited forms of reparation have also been attempted. Scholars of Law and Humanities have subjected both of these legal forms to intense scrutiny, analyzing trial narratives for the way they shape and distort history and transform national identities. Truth and reconciliation commissions have emerged as the chief humanistic alternative, with scholars posing the possibility that testimony and storytelling can heal victims, offer "restorative justice," and repair the social fabric.

What about slavery? There has been a great deal of public memory work recently with regard to slavery, especially histories of memory and forgetting, and calls to join history to memory. This approach to history and memory is more overtly political, an effort to shape contemporary politics in favor of affirmative policies to further civil rights and social justice for the descendants of slaves by recalling – and demanding repair for – past injustice. So far, fewer concerns have been voiced about a surfeit of memory of slavery, although perhaps this is what is being expressed in the political conservatives' narratives warning of the dangers of identity politics or a "politics of victimhood." Finally, although reparations for slavery lurk on the horizon as a logical outgrowth of the turn to memory, reparations discourse has yet to become mainstream.

Law has yet to become a chief site of memory for the slave past. Trials of perpetrators are impossible, although there are beginning to be a few quasitruth commissions – for example, Brown University's Committee on Slavery and Justice, or the truth commissions focused on twentieth-century racial atrocities in the United States, as have taken place in Tulsa, Oklahoma, and Rosewood, Florida, to investigate racial cleansings in the 1920s. Yet, because big political questions in the United States always become constitutional questions, most scholars who have thought about law,

---

[130] Michel Giraud, "Le passé comme blessure et le passé comme masque," *Cahiers d'Études africaines* 44 (No. 173, 2004) 65–79.

history, and memory have constitutionalized the issues, reimagining the meaning of the Constitution as a way to achieve historical justice. By contrast, in France, questions of identity and memory are nationalized through commemorative laws, yet many historians of memory have resisted treating slavery comparably to other crimes against humanity. The discourse of reparations exists in both countries, but despite renewed academic attention, it remains marginal. The next stage of public discourse about slavery will be to consider seriously what harms of the past can be redressed and which legal strategies hold out danger as well as promise.

PART V

INSTITUTIONAL PROCESSES

17

Trials*

Lindsay Farmer

From the "Trial of the Century" to the Century of the Trial

On January 31, 2005, the "trial of the century" began in Santa Barbara, California, as pop star Michael Jackson was accused of conspiracy to abduct a child, as well as various other lewd acts against children.[1] At the same time, on the other side of the world, another "trial of the century" was already in progress, that of Slobodan Milosevic, the former president of Serbia, before the International Criminal Tribunal for the former Yugoslavia for crimes against humanity and genocide.[2] This trial followed on the heels of yet another "trial of the century" – the trial of two Libyan men in Camp Zeist, the Netherlands, accused of murdering the passengers of Pan Am flight 103 by exploding a bomb over Lockerbie, Scotland.[3] This trial took place only a few years after the trial of O. J. Simpson for murder in 1995, a trial that was in its time widely claimed to be the trial of the century – albeit a different century. Indeed, it is possible to find the claim being made about large numbers of trials going back to the early years of the twentieth century – although in these earlier cases the claim is more often made by later commentators than contemporary observers. Thus other candidates for the "trial of the century" include variously the trial of Julius and Ethel Rosenberg (1951), the Nuremberg trials (1945), the Scopes "Monkey" trial (1925), the trial of Leopold and Loeb (1924), and back to the trial of Harry Thaw (1906) – and large numbers of trials in between. That we cannot know which criminal trial was

---

* My thanks to Sarah Armstrong and Peter Goodrich for help and suggestions.
[1] *People v. Jackson* 2005 (http://en.wikipedia.org/wiki/People_v._Jackson; http://www.courttv.com/trials/jackson/). Jackson was eventually acquitted after a trial lasting four and a half months.
[2] This trial began on February 12, 2002, and ended with the death of Milosevic from a heart attack in March 2006: http://hague.bard.edu/.
[3] *HM Adv v. Al Megrahi*, http://www.scotcourts.gov.uk/library/lockerbie/index.asp (Judgment and appeal). The trial lasted thirty-nine weeks and led to the conviction of one of the accused and the acquittal of the other: http://news.bbc.co.uk/1/hi/in_depth/scotland/2000/lockerbie_trial/default.stm.

455

the trial of this, or any other century, has not hindered the rush to label trials in this fashion.[4]

It is easy to make fun of this need to attach the epithet trial of the century to any particular legal proceedings. Beyond the attempt to build up the profile or significance of the event, to attract viewers or readers, it does raise some more serious underlying issues. Why has this epithet come to be seen as being of particular significance? Why is it that trials of the century seem to be occurring ever more frequently? Is there something about this century – I speak here of the "long" twentieth century, extending from the 1890s to present day – that accords special significance to criminal trials?

One answer to these questions is that trials matter because they are always about more than the particular case; they reveal something about the time and culture in which they take place. This is commonly understood to be true of historical trials, with the transcripts of trials offering an unparalleled documentary record of how people lived in particular times and places.[5] Moreover trials, whether criminal or civil, have always seemed to offer access to a deeper understanding of the society within which they take place. They have been moments of confrontation between established power and the citizen, or between individuals, that have the potential to throw new light on social or political relations or reveal something hidden beneath the surface of conventional social interaction. This is partly a result of legal procedures, particularly in common law systems, where trials take the form of a publicly staged contest, but it is also because trials have in an important sense been designed to do just this. The staging of the trial, from the language used to the legal rituals to the symbols of justice and the architecture of the courtroom, seeks to represent the law in a certain way, to legitimize the exercise of state power and present a certain image of the community of law. These features of trials, which have to a large extent been neglected in standard legal and sociological accounts of the trial, have provided the main points of interest for scholars of Law and the Humanities. Thus a trial might be dubbed a trial of its century because it crystallized a particular kind of social conflict or dispute,[6] because it laid down the template for succeeding trials,[7] or because it symbolized something particular about the age.[8] There is arguably

---

[4]   See e.g., MSNBC poll at http://www.law.umkc.edu/faculty/projects/ftrials/Todaysurvey.html.

[5]   For celebrated examples see Natalie Zemon Davies, *The Return of Martin Guerre* (Cambridge, MA: Harvard University Press, 1983); Partha Chatterjee, *A Princely Impostor? The Strange and Universal History of the Kumar of Bhawal* (Princeton, NJ: Princeton University Press, 2002).

[6]   See e.g., http://www.law.umkc.edu/faculty/projects/ftrials/century.html (Doug Linder on the Scopes Monkey trial [1925]).

[7]   See e.g., the claim made about the trial of Harry Thaw (1906): Linda Deutsch, "Trials of the Century," *Loyola of Los Angeles Law Review* 33:2 (2000) 743.

[8]   This is a claim commonly made about the Nuremberg trials. See e.g., Shoshana Felman, *The Juridical Unconscious: Trials and Trauma in the Twentieth Century* (Cambridge, MA: Harvard University Press, 2002) 3–7.

Trials

something more at stake, however, when contemporaries describe the trials of their own time in this way, for going beyond the simple hyperbole of the claim, it requires a certain amount of self-consciousness, the belief that *this* trial is capable of revealing a truth about *our* society and *our* time.

In this chapter I shall argue that there is something distinctively modern about this sensibility, and that – to turn the phrase around – our age can be understood as the century of the trial. This is not to claim that trials did not take place before this (they plainly did), or that they were not significant, but that over the course of the twentieth century the trial has come to be accorded a particular kind of significance. This is reflected both in the fact that trials have come to be understood as a particular kind of social, political, and cultural event, and in the fact that resort to a trial has come to be understood as *the* means of resolving certain kinds of conflict.[9] One of the aims of this chapter is to explore why this should be so – what it is about trials in modernity that has led to them being accorded this particular significance and meaning. I shall argue that one of the main reasons that the trial is able to perform these diverse social functions and has become the repository of social meaning is linked to the form of the modern trial. This chapter will first identify the principal features of the modern adversarial criminal trial – what I shall call the "reconstructive" trial – because I shall go on to argue that the social and cultural role of the trial is closely linked to this form. It will then look at three particular themes that have been addressed by writing in Law and Humanities to show how these are linked to and reflect this modern sensibility.

The Reconstructive Trial

It is well known that the use of public punishment declined sharply in the first half of the nineteenth century, as the old system of exemplary and severe punishment was replaced by new institutions of policing and punishment.[10] This development was driven in large part by the desire to make punishment more certain and effective, but it also required that the legitimacy of the criminal justice system be established on a new basis. Critics of the English Bloody Code were concerned not only that the use of capital punishment was ineffective in deterring crime, but also that the public

---

[9] This is particularly obvious in the recent development of international criminal courts, a development that might be traced back to the trials at Nuremberg. It can also be seen in the recent trial of Saddam Hussein. The development of the "didactic" trial is traced in Lawrence Douglas, *The Memory of Judgment: Making Law and History in the Trials of the Holocaust* (New Haven: Yale University Press, 2001).

[10] Michel Foucault, *Discipline and Punish: The Birth of the Prison* (London: Penguin, 1977) Part I; V. A. C. Gatrell, *The Hanging Tree: Execution and the English People 1776–1868* (Oxford: Oxford University Press, 1994); John Beattie, *Crime and the Courts 1660–1800* (Princeton NJ: Princeton University Press, 1986).

display of authority involved in the spectacle of the scaffold was too easily subverted, as the condemned refused to display the necessary contrition and the behavior of crowds became increasingly difficult to manage. Reformers argued that the criminal justice system resembled a lottery in which few offenders were detected, fewer still convicted, and where capital punishment was inflicted mainly on those unfortunates who did not have the social resources to make a successful plea for mercy.[11] Thus, in the early part of the nineteenth century the Bloody Code was repealed to be replaced by organized police forces and new forms of punishment, principally the penitentiary but also the use of transportation, which offered the possibility of more certain detection and the more measured infliction of punishment. As part of this process punishment became a secret process, increasingly hidden behind the walls of the prison, operating on the soul or mind rather than the body of the condemned person.

Yet the decline of the scaffold as the principal symbol of criminal justice and the move to secret punishments did not mean the decline of symbolism altogether, but rather that different institutions acquired a symbolic importance. This is recognized even in Foucault's classic account of the birth of the prison:

> Now the scandal and the light are to be distributed differently; it is the con- viction itself that marks the offender with the unequivocally negative sign: the publicity has shifted to the trial, and to the sentence; the execution itself is like an additional shame that justice is ashamed to impose on the condemned man; so it keeps its distance from the act, tending always to entrust it to others, under the seal of secrecy.[12]

In this new regime it was the public trial that took on a new importance for the legitimacy of the system. The authority of the criminal law could not be based on the personal authority of the judge, the widespread use of mercy, and the terror of the scaffold. Justice was instead to operate through the impersonal application of predetermined (and less severe) laws, introducing distance, uniformity, and impar- tiality in place of the interplay of severity and mercy.[13] The trial was central to

---

[11] On the image of the lottery and the reform movement, see David J. A. Cairns, *Advocacy and the Making of the Adversarial Criminal Trial* (Oxford: Oxford University Press, 1998) ch. 3.

[12] Foucault, *Discipline and Punish*, 9–10. He goes on to argue that the criminal trial develops a new focus on the accused person, looking behind their acts to the pathologies of their character. Although this might be true of French criminal procedure, it is clearly not the case in the English adversarial trial, where a consequence of the reform of the criminal law was the silencing of the accused. For an account that develops Foucault's argument in relation to French criminal procedure, see Katharine F. Taylor, *In the Theater of Criminal Justice* (Princeton, NJ: Princeton University Press, 1993), Introduction.

[13] Randall McGowen, "The Image of Justice and Reform of the Criminal Law in Early Nineteenth- Century England," *Buffalo Law Review* 32 (1983) 89–125; Douglas Hay, "Property, Authority, and the Criminal Law" in D. Hay et al., *Albion's Fatal Tree: Crime and Society in Eighteenth-Century England* (London: Allen Lane, 1975).

Trials

this as a means of displaying the legitimate consequences of a criminal act, the representation of punishment as an idea – staging questions of individual guilt and innocence – although its symbolic role was to increase in inverse proportion to its practical importance to the criminal justice system as the nineteenth century saw the increasing development of forms of summary and informal justice that sought to bypass the full adversarial criminal trial.[14] There was a double principle of publicity at work, with the publicity of the penal norm linked to a new form of procedural publicity in the trial.[15]

Central to the establishment of the trial as a principal symbol of the criminal justice system was the emergence, over the course of the nineteenth century, of a new kind of trial – the reconstructive trial. This form of the trial, which had fully emerged in Anglo-American jurisdictions by the end of the nineteenth century, is one in which all the principal characteristics of the contemporary adversarial trial had developed. The trial was organized as a contest between two sides, with the aim of arriving at a final outcome – the verdict – based on proof beyond reasonable doubt. The process was organized around the reconstruction of the event, through the presentation of direct and circumstantial evidence in specially designed courtrooms, and the testing of the reliability of testimony through cross-examination and debate.

In England the emergence of the reconstructive trial was linked to the passing of the Prisoners' Counsel Act in 1836, which granted all those accused of felonies the right to a full legal defense, thereby formally instituting (at least the possibility of) a fully contested adversarial trial.[16] If, however, the 1836 act laid the foundations for the reconstructive trial, its development over the next seventy years was less the consequence of particular legal reforms than the coming together of a range of legal and extralegal factors. These factors combined to extend the duration of trial and to shift its focus onto the increasingly detailed reconstruction of the crime and the state of mind of the accused at the time that the crime was committed. Of course, the jury trial has always been reconstructive to some extent – concerned with the proof of past facts – but what was novel about the emergent trial was that its focus moved from the testing of strength or the assessment of character to the systematic

---

[14] See R. M. Jackson, "The Incidence of Jury Trial during the Past Century," *Modern Law Review* 1 (1937), 132. On the rise of plea bargaining, see George Fisher, *Plea Bargaining's Triumph* (Stanford: Stanford University Press, 2003); Michael McConville and Chester Mirsky, *Jury Trials and Plea Bargaining: A True History* (Oxford: Hart Publishing, 2005).

[15] See also Taylor, *Theater* 22. In nineteenth-century France there was a rebuilding of courthouses to present the trial as spectacle or theater: "reviving iconicity when its traditional subject, the ruler, had been displaced by a diffuse new subject, the public" (xxi).

[16] Hitherto only those accused of treason were entitled to counsel, following the Treason Act of 1696. In practice lawyers had become more involved in defense work, but this was only partial and not formally recognized by law. On the 1836 act see Cairns, *Advocacy*, ch. 4; Allison N. May, *The Bar and the Old Bailey 1750–1850* (Chapel Hill: University of North Carolina Press, 2003); John H. Langbein, *The Origins of Adversary Criminal Trial* (Oxford: Oxford University Press, 2003).

and detailed reconstruction of the event.[17] This in turn relied on the development of techniques for interrogating witnesses and collecting information in the attempt to extend the actuality of the past into the present, to make the court "witnesses" to the truth of the event, judging an accused on the basis of what was seen in the courtroom.[18] This was not, of course, an exact reproduction of the event, reflecting the fact that the purpose of the trial is not only to investigate/establish the truth, but also to dramatize it.[19] The form of the trial that emerged following the 1836 act cannot, as is contended by the leading historian of the criminal trial, be explained by the claim that it was simply a matter of "testing the case" of the prosecution.[20] It reflected a more complex process in which the way that crimes were proved was changed, for which reason it is better to understand it as the "reconstructive trial." To understand this we must look more closely at, among other things, the question of how the prosecution sought to establish the truth of their case, at the staging of this truth and at the process of judgment.

An understanding of the staging of the trial is necessary to see both how the elements of the trial could combine and contribute to the overall image of justice and how the trial was linked to the broader transformations in the enforcement of the criminal law. This is not to suggest that there was a conscious attempt to make the courtroom theatrical or to increase the drama of the trial.[21] Historians of the English adversarial process have drawn attention to the muted nature of the nineteenth-century trial – the fact that there seemed to have been a deliberate eschewing of publicity, that flamboyant or overdramatic advocacy was frowned upon, and that the courtroom was organized so as to minimize dramatic potential.[22] This should not lead us to conclude, however, that trials were not still in an important sense staged. The reconstructive trial was never exclusively about the identification and punishment of wrongdoers; it was always also about other things. In the procedures and rules for the determination of truth, the standing of the various actors, the kinds of questions that can be determined, and in its relation to the broader criminal justice system, the trial is always something more than a simple legal procedure for the

---

[17] For discussion of the longer history of the jury trial, see Antony Duff, Lindsay Farmer, Sandra Marshall, and Victor Tadros, *The Trial on Trial III: Towards a Normative Theory of the Criminal Trial* (Oxford: Hart Publishing, 2007) ch. 2.

[18] For fuller discussion of the reconstructive trial, see Lindsay Farmer, "Responsibility and the Proof of Guilt" in M. D. Dubber and L. Farmer, *Modern Histories of Crime and Punishment* (Stanford: Stanford University Press, 2007).

[19] Vismann, following Pierre Legendre, suggests that the purpose of the trial is that of registering the event in discourse: Cornelia Vismann, "'Rejouer Les Crimes.' Theater vs. Video," *Cardozo Studies in Law and Literature* 13 (Spring 2001) 119 at 125.

[20] Langbein, *Origins*, ch. 5.

[21] Which is not to say that trials did not have a dramatic potential and were frequently compared with a form of theater. See *infra* pt. III.

[22] See Taylor, *Theater* 13 also comparing it to a protestant meetinghouse. She also notes that the English courts limited public access and interest through the charging of an admission fee.

Trials

determination of guilt and innocence. It is a communicative process, which might either conflict with or reinforce the image of a universal and impartial legal order.[23] It is a form of public ritual of shaming or degradation.[24] It is also an imaginative space in which complex stories are told and new forms of subjectivity and responsibility are constructed and contested.[25] The question of staging, then, is concerned with the trial as a legal and social event and the way that this changes over time: the way that reality is reconstructed and represented in the courtroom;[26] the relationship between substance and procedure; between written and unwritten laws;[27] the distribution of roles, burdens, presumptions; and even the way that the courtroom is spatially organized to represent the authority of the law.[28] Thus, even in the absence of conscious attempts to stage or dramatize the law, it is nonetheless the case that the criminal trial was ordered to establish the truth in a certain way and to present the accused, the judge, and the law in such a way as to perform certain social functions.[29]

What, then, are the distinctive features of the reconstructive trial? First, by the first half of the twentieth century the trial had been thoroughly professionalized, dominated by lawyers, police, and expert witnesses and oriented toward the effective processing of criminal cases. The position of the accused was relatively weak: permitted to testify on oath but under conditions that would limit the effectiveness of that testimony and that could undercut protections such as the right to silence or privilege against self-incrimination. Second, trials were increasingly long. Lengthy trials were not unknown before 1900, but until the latter part of the century trials would rarely last longer than a day, partly because of legal constraints, such as the

---

[23] cf., Doreen McBarnet, *Conviction! Law, the State, and the Construction of Justice* (London: Macmillan, 1981) on the ideology of triviality.

[24] See David Garland, *Punishment and Modern Society* (Oxford: Oxford University Press) 70 ff.; Harold Garfinkel, "Conditions of Successful Degradation Ceremonies," *American Journal of Sociology* (1956) 420–4. This leaves open the important question of how the ritual is structured, as it is not enough merely to invoke the social importance of ritual.

[25] Lisa Rodensky, *The Crime in Mind: Criminal Responsibility and the Victorian Novel* (Oxford: Oxford University Press, 2003); John Bender, *Imagining the Penitentiary: Fiction and the Architecture of Mind in Eighteenth-Century England* (Chicago: University of Chicago Press, 1987).

[26] See e.g., Lance Bennet and Martha Feldman, *Reconstructing Reality in the Courtroom: Justice and Judgment in American Culture* (New Brunswick, NJ: Rutgers University Press, 1981).

[27] See Martha Merrill Umphrey, "The Dialogics of Legal Meaning: Spectacular Trials, the Unwritten Law, and Narratives of Criminal Responsibility," *Law and Society Review* 33 (1999) 393–423; Martin Wiener, "Judges v. Jurors: Courtroom Tensions in Murder Trials and the Law of Criminal Responsibility in Nineteenth-Century England," *Law and History Review* 17 (1999) 393.

[28] See Clare Graham, *Ordering Law: The Architectural and Social History of the English Law Court to 1914* (Aldershot: Ashgate, 2003).

[29] For more general discussion see Michel Foucault, "Truth and Juridical Forms" in Paul Rabinow (ed.), *Essential Works of Foucault 1954–84. Vol. 3 Power* (ed. James D. Faubion) (New York: New Press, 2000) 1–89; Faubion J. Francois, "Aveu, Verite, Justice et Subjectivite. Autour d'un enseignement de Michel Foucault," *Juridiques* 7 (1981) 163–82.

need to confine the jury, but mainly because there were fewer witnesses called.[30] By the end of the century it was becoming commonplace for certain trials – particularly those for serious crimes or where there was a certain notoriety attached to the accused or the victim – to last for a week or more. This has now become routine, even for relatively minor crimes, with trials for more serious crimes lasting for a month or longer. One of the principal reasons for this was the greater number of witnesses being produced as the police effectively took over the prosecution process.[31] More organized police detective work and a more professional defense meant that greater numbers of potential witnesses were contacted and required to appear at trial. These witnesses testified to their respective roles in the discovery of the crime, or their relation to the accused or victim, and through the accretion of such detail the prosecution would seek to reconstruct both the crime and the motives of the accused. Certain key witnesses shaped the process of reconstruction. The authority of the professional detective and the scientific expert was central to the interpretation of the evidence of the crime.[32] Thus, the case that was being tested was more than a matter of simple legal fact, as one side was backed by the authority and organization of the police, such that the defense was placed in the position of responding to an account that had already been organized by the police and prosecution. Finally, the increasing importance of lawyers had the effect of throwing the spotlight on the character and personality of certain lawyers, making some (notably Edward Marshall Hall in England and Clarence Darrow in the United States) into minor celebrities to the extent that it came to be widely believed that certain lawyers could influence the outcome of cases through a peculiar alchemy of personality, rhetoric, and theater.

We can make a number of more specific remarks about the staging of the reconstructive trial, introducing themes that will be taken up later in the chapter. First, although the reconstructive trial relies on proof beyond reasonable doubt as the basis for conviction – "a common, honourable, and anonymous regime of truth for a supposedly universal subject"[33] – the increasing duration and complexity of the processes of reconstruction poses particular problems for the use of evidence, potentially undermining the epistemological basis of the trial. This is in part connected to uncertainties around the nature of evidence itself, as debate has raged in

---

[30] The rule that a jury, once empanelled, had to be detained and prohibited fire, food, and drink was reformed by the Juries Act of 1870. See David Bentley, *English Criminal Justice in the Nineteenth Century* (London: Hambledon, 1998) 63–4, 275–7.

[31] Although prosecution was private in name until 1985, in practice the police had taken over prosecution by the late nineteenth century.

[32] On the rise of expert testimony generally, see Carol Jones, *Expert Witnesses: Science, Medicine, and the Practice of Law* (Oxford: Clarendon, 1994).

[33] Michel Foucault, *Abnormal: Lectures at the Collège de France 1974–1975* (London: Verso, 2003) 8. For further debate on the meaning of "beyond reasonable doubt" see Barbara Shapiro, "The Beyond Reasonable Doubt Doctrine: 'Moral Comfort' or Standard of Proof," *Law and Humanities* 2:2 (2008) 149–73 and James Q. Whitman, "Response to Shapiro," *Law and Humanities* 2:2 (2008) 175–89.

Trials 463

the theoretical literature over the relative merits of direct and circumstantial evidence and the kinds of inferences that can be drawn from them.[34] As important as these debates are, it is arguable that a greater challenge is inherent in the process of reconstruction itself. As the trial gets longer and increasing amounts of evidence are led, the problem becomes that of how to manage the uncertainty (or doubt) that inevitably accompanies this process. The question is that of how to interpret the evidence that is being presented, a process that increasingly privileges the experts and police who structure and interpret the case – although this is in turn exacerbated by the ability of wealthy defendants to use their resources to "spin-out" the trial by leading greater amounts evidence and exhaustive challenges to the prosecution case.[35] This can lead to a deep skepticism about the capacity of the trial to establish any kind of true account where there seems to be no absolute criteria for the establishment of truth and to the extent that much seems to depend on the resources (in terms of power or money) of the participants.[36] Equally, however, the ability to generate certainty – and to convince a jury – under these conditions can be understood as depending not only on the deduction of conclusions from the proof of facts but also the capacity to generate a plausible or convincing narrative of the event at issue. Reconstruction then has come to be understood primarily as a process of imaginative understanding. This process has clear affinities with literary forms such as detective fiction – the denouement by the master-detective can be compared with counsel's summing up to the jury – with both relying on similar literary tropes and rhetorical devices.[37] This account of the relationship between truth and the trial has been one of the most influential and important strands within Law and Humanities thinking about the trial and will be discussed further.

Second, the reconstructive trial led to the recognition of a new kind of subjectivity. Although the trial was concerned principally with the reconstruction of the event, the early-nineteenth-century reforms opened up a space in which questions of guilt, intention, and evidence could be examined more fully than hitherto.[38] Defense

---

[34] Barbara Shapiro, *"Beyond Reasonable Doubt" and "Probable Cause." Historical Perspectives on the Anglo-American Law of Evidence* (Berkeley: University of California Press, 1991). Ch. 4 documents the acceptance of circumstantial evidence. See also Alexander Welsh, *Strong Representations: Narrative and Circumstantial Evidence in England* (Baltimore: Johns Hopkins University Press, 1992); Jan-Melissa Shramm, *Testimony and Advocacy in Victorian Law, Literature, and Theology* (Cambridge: Cambridge University Press, 2000).

[35] A problem that is referred to by Langbein as the 'wealth effect'; *Origins*, 331–4.

[36] The classic account is Jerome Frank, *Courts on Trial: Myth and Reality in American Justice* (Princeton: Princeton University Press, 1949).

[37] See now Kate Summerscale, *The Suspicions of Mr Whicher: A Shocking Murder and the Undoing of a Great Victorian Detective* (New York: Walker & Co., 2008) for a popular account of the relationship between trials and detective fiction.

[38] See J. P. Eigen, *Unconscious Crime: Mental Absence and Criminal Responsibility in Victorian London* (Baltimore: Johns Hopkins University Press, 2003) 158–60.

counsel were able to explore new means of avoiding liability, leading to developments in the scope of defenses such as insanity and the recognition of the relevance of other forms of mental abnormality to criminal responsibility. As the century progressed, the trial became increasingly concerned with the character and motives of the accused, reflecting a new awareness of the relevance of mental states to the construction of criminal liability, as well as a developing fascination with the character of the individual criminal.[39] While this might appear to reflect a new liberal political sensibility – a respect for the individual subject – the form that this took suggests a rather more ambiguous account. The trial is apparently based on the idea that witnesses can testify about their own experience, that facts can speak for themselves, and that the court can in turn interpret this evidence to reach a verdict. However, the increasing complexity noted previously, combined with anxiety about the truthfulness of testimony, has tended to undermine this idea of the transparency of fact in the trial process: evidence was not what it seemed; confessions were unreliable; and the oath was no guarantee of truth.[40] Appearances, then, were to be distrusted and there was a need for evaluation both of evidence and the way it was delivered because reality was not transparent. Consequently more attention was given to the question of how unreliability or guilt would manifest itself in the person of the witness or accused. In a lecture delivered in 1906, for example, Freud addressed the question of the "growing recognition of the untrustworthiness of statements made by witnesses" and the need to recognize objective signs by which truthfulness could be established.[41] The awareness of the complexity, and often opacity, of motives and desires threw new emphasis on the skill of examining and interpreting the behavior of suspects and witnesses. Texts such as Gross' popular manual on criminal psychology, translated into English in 1911, explicitly tutored legal professionals on such topics as how to interpret mental states from the outward appearances of witnesses and suspects.[42] Detective fiction also popularized such work, tutoring the

---

[39] See e.g., Martin Wiener, *Reconstructing the Criminal: Culture, Law, and Policy in England 1830–1914* (Cambridge: Cambridge University Press, 1990); Rodensky, *Crime in Mind.*

[40] James Oldham, "Truth-Telling in the Eighteenth-Century English Courtroom," *Law and History Review* 12 (1994) 95 at 100–1; Wendie Schneider, "Perjurious Albion: Perjury Prosecutions and the Victorian Trial," *Law and History*, Andrew Lewis and Michael Lobban, eds. (Oxford: Oxford University Press, 2004); Theodor Reik, *The Compulsion to Confess: On the Psychoanalysis of Crime and Punishment* (New York: Farrar, Strauss, & Cudahy, 1959). The link between psychoanalysis and law is also explored in Peter Brooks, *Troubling Confessions: Speaking Guilt in Law and Literature* (Chicago: Chicago University Press, 2000).

[41] S. Freud, "Psycho-Analysis and the Establishment of Facts in Legal Proceedings," *Standard Edition of the Complete Psychological Works of Sigmund Freud*, vol. 9 (London: Hogarth Press, 1959).

[42] Hans Gross, *Criminal Psychology: A Manual for Judges, Practitioners, and Students* (Boston: Little, Brown, & Co., 1911) esp. pt. I Title A, Topic 3. See also Hugo Münsterberg, *On the Witness Stand: Essays on Psychology and Crime* (New York: Doubleday, Page & Co., 1909). See also Clare Valier, "True Crime Stories: Scientific Methods of Criminal Investigation, Criminology, and Historiography" *British Journal of Criminology* 38 (1998) 97–8.

Trials

reader in signs of guilt, so that the criminal juror could scrutinize the words, actions, and demeanor of the accused to see what was being hidden.[43] Thus a "hermeneutics of suspicion" was institutionalized in certain features of the reconstructive trial.[44]

Third, the reconstructive trial took place in a new kind of space, as courtrooms were redesigned and rebuilt. This space was a means both of projecting a new image of legal authority and of the authority of judges and lawyers and of structuring communication within the trial.[45] These changes are summarized in a recent study of English courtroom architecture:

> There is a shift from multi-purpose to single-purpose buildings, from movable furnishings to fixed fittings and a greater elaboration of architectural decoration; from open access to restricted circulation and segregated accommodation; from the general and the public to the specific and the private.[46]

The impact of this was to underline a strict segregation between public and restricted areas. In the United Kingdom, it became common for there to be a passage from below the dock, through which the prisoner could be brought into court; the lawyers' quarters (robing rooms, judges' chambers) were separated by walls and corridors from the public parts of the court, distancing them from the public and even their own clients; there were separate waiting rooms for witnesses, and corridors so that they could be taken to and from the courtroom without encountering others; and jury members were clearly segregated from the general public through the use of special entrances and accommodation. These courtrooms were designed to facilitate the specialized functions of criminal justice through the efficient flow of different groups and individuals around the central space of the courtroom. At the same time, the move to specialized accommodation sought to enhance the majesty of the law by the adoption of styles of architecture and ornament that projected the order and authority of the law.[47] It is in this period that we see the courtroom

---

[43] See Farmer, "Responsibility," 56–7 on the demeanor of Dr Crippen at his trial. The question of demeanor was also addressed by Charles Dickens after observing the trial of Dr. William Palmer, the notorious poisoner; see "The Demeanour of Murderers," *Household Words* (1856) 504–7.

[44] The term comes from Paul Ricouer and is discussed in Matt Matsuda, *The Memory of the Modern* (Oxford: Oxford University Press, 1996) ch. 5, and Elisabeth Strowick, "Comparative Epistemology of Suspicion: Psychoanalysis, Literature, and the Human Sciences," *Science in Context* 18 (2005) 649–69. For further discussion see Lindsay Farmer, "Arthur and Oscar (and Sherlock): The Reconstructive Trial and the 'Hermeneutics of Suspicion,'" *International Commentary on Evidence* (2007) (Article 4).

[45] Robert A. Ferguson, *The Trial in American Life* (Chicago: Chicago University Press, 2007) 28 refers to the "aesthetic element of control in legal procedure."

[46] Graham, *Ordering Law* 29; Martha J. MacNamara, *From Tavern to Courthouse: Architecture and Ritual in American Law 1658–1860* (Baltimore: Johns Hopkins University Press, 2004). See also Taylor, *Theater.*

[47] Although making little attempt to match the imposing theatricality of the rebuilt *Palais de Justice* in Paris: see Graham, *Ordering Law*, 328.

beginning to take on its recognizably contemporary form: the vertical organization of the seating that reflected the hierarchical arrangement of participants, from judge to clerks to lawyers; there was also, in a significant move, dedicated space for members of the press. Significantly, however, as Taylor points out, members of the public were physically removed from the courtroom, sitting in galleries isolated from and overlooking the floor of the court, underlining the fact that their presence was for the purpose of observation rather than participation.[48] The public face of the trial was important, but the public themselves were often considered to be something of an inconvenience.[49]

The reconstructive trial as it developed over the course of the "long" twentieth century has become both the typical trial and the typical symbol of the criminal justice system. Actual trials or fictional representations of trials take this as their model and are judged to be more or less effective according to the staging of the trial, the truths that it reveals, and its social function. These are the themes that have dominated studies of the trial in Law and Humanities.

Themes in the Study of Trials

The Trial as Theater

Many critics have pointed to the relationship between theater and the trial. If, as Friedman has suggested, early trials were more like sermons than dramas with the outcome being known in advance, the reconstructive trial releases the dramatic potential because the outcome is now uncertain.[50] This relationship, however, should be understood as going beyond the trivial sense of trials being a source for drama or courtrooms as a setting for dramatic moments to seeing judicial proceedings as a type of theater. In the words of Ball:

> The live presentation of cases in the courtroom, although a means to the end of judgment, is also an end in itself. Trials and oral arguments are as essential to the judicial system as performance is to drama.[51]

It is thus argued that trials and theater share an underlying structural similarity and perform overlapping functions in the symbolic representation of conflict and its

[48] Taylor, *Theater*, 13–14 draws a contrast with the French courtroom where the public occupied part of the court and participated in the proceedings.

[49] See e.g., James Fitzjames Stephen, *A History of the Criminal Law of England* (London: Macmillan, 1883) I, 516 suggesting that the necessary degree of publicity could be secured by admitting members of the press only.

[50] Lawrence M. Friedman, "On Stage: Some Historical Notes About Criminal Justice," *Social Science, Social Policy, and the Law*, Patricia Ewick, Robert A. Kagan, and Austin Sarat, eds. (New York: Russell Sage Foundation, 1999) 77.

[51] Milner S. Ball, "The Play's the Thing: An Unscientific Reflection on Courts Under the Rubric of Theater," *Stanford Law Review* 28:1 (1975) 81–115 at 82.

Trials 467

resolution.[52] This points then to the importance of orality and immediacy – that all the actors in the drama that is the trial must be present and that judgment, whether by judge or jury, is to be based on what has taken place within the spatial and temporal limits of the courtroom. It also points to the irreducible element of performance in the trial – that trials are always at least a reenactment or reconstruction – even though, as I will suggest later, the content of this performativity is constrained in important ways in the reconstructive trial. This theme, it should be noted, is also closely linked to other strands of Law and Humanities scholarship that have sought to recover the visual, the rhetorical, and the symbolic in the study of law.[53]

This analogy rests on a number of general features relating to the staging of trials and to the authority and legitimacy of the institution of law.[54] First, there is the sense in which the courtroom is a theatrical space. This space is organized to permit certain kinds of communication as well as to reinforce the dignity of the law.[55] Participants in the trial speak from assigned positions; there are rituals of performance in such things as the entry of the judge, the swearing of oaths and the delivery of the verdict; and participants are rehearsed in delivery, posture, and demeanor. In this sense, then, "a courtroom is much more than a backdrop or occupied space; it is the controlling presence that codes all effort and recognition at trial."[56] Second, the trial follows a particular format that plays out like the conventions of a kind of drama. In the Anglo-American trial this is organized as a form of stylized conflict or confrontation; in other systems the criminal trial is a more formal confrontation between state and citizen. It is central to this that the behavior of the actors in the trial is governed by understandings of the roles that they are playing, conventions about who may speak and when, and of the kind of language that is acceptable. These, it has been contended, are central to the encouragement of disinterestedness and lack of prejudice, an acting out of impartiality.[57] Third, the performance is always for an

---

[52] Goodrich points out that these are related to the general theme of jurisdiction as the power of enunciating law and grounding legality in visible legitimacy: Peter Goodrich, "Screening Law," *Law and Literature* 21:1 (2009) 1–23 at 7–8. Vismann, "Rejouer les Crimes," 127, points out that calling trials theater is only possible after both domains have been differentiated, so that the latter can become a metaphor for the former. See also Julie Stone Peters, "Legal Performance: Good and Bad," *Law, Culture, and the Humanities* 4 (2008) 179 at 180–1.

[53] See Goodrich, "Screening" for a recent discussion, or more generally Alain Supiot, *Homo Juridicus: On the Anthropological Function of Law* (London: Verso, 2007) pt I.

[54] See Ball, "The play," 83–97. cf. Ferguson, *Trial in American Life*, ch. 2 listing the characters in the trial: judge, prosecuting attorney, defense counsel, jury, defendant, victim, courtroom.

[55] See also Linda Mulcahy, "Architects of Justice: The Politics of Courtroom Design," *Social and Legal Studies* 16 (2007) 383; Judith Resnik and Denis Curtis, "Representing Justice: From Renaissance Iconography to Twenty-First-Century Courthouses," *Proceedings of the American Philosophical Society* 151 (2007) 139.

[56] Ferguson, *Trial in American Life*, 30

[57] Ball, "The play" 100–1. Ferguson, *Trial in American Life*, 16, suggests that these create a zone where procedural correctness and final decision making meet and protect one another; cf. Peters, "Legal Performance," 192–3.

audience. This is true both in the specific sense that there is always an audience that is internal to the trial – the jury – and that the trial is a public trial, open to the public or its representatives (and, of course, that the jury are representatives of the community). The drama and suspense in the trial may derive from the need to attend on, and convince, the jury, but more generally the principle of publicity is to allow the participation of the public in the trial process and to make legal institutions answerable to the wider community. In this sense the public trial ensures not merely that justice be seen to be done (as if the being seen were more important than the being just), but that there can be no proper justice without this element of openness to the public.[58]

These three features are in turn dependent on a wider conception of a (frequently idealized) political community, founding a normative claim about the institution of law and its legitimacy. For American lawyers, in particular, this has its roots in the formulation of de Tocqueville that the trial is a political institution, in the sense that it is a means by which the community, in the form of the jury, can hold the state or public authority to account.[59] Thus, Burns' influential account is grounded in a kind of Fullerian sense of the importance of the trial as a central part of the enterprise of subjecting oneself to the governance of rules – and one that is reliant to a very great extent on (counterfactual) claims about the commitment, honesty, and ethical attitude of the participants.[60] Likewise Ferguson's analysis of the trial in American life places the trial at the center of the republic of laws, seeing high-profile trials as sites for the dramatization and resolution of social and political conflict.[61] Such claims are problematic, either because they conflict so sharply with the reality of criminal justice (and the panoply of devices available to the state to manage delinquents and ensure that their cases need not come to trial) or because they seem to be a more accurate description of a set of institutions that were characteristic of early-modern states, rather than the late-modern bureaucratic-administrative state. Even if we accept this kind of idealized account, it is important to note that the idea of the trial as a form of political theater also carries certain risks.

The first set of risks relates to the essential fragility of the trial as theater. If it becomes too predictable or a form of morality play or show trial, then the enhanced theatricality may come at a cost to the trial itself. The point has been explored specifically in relation to political trials, but it is equally true of the more mundane

[58] Discussed in Duff et al., *The Trial on Trial III*, ch. 9.

[59] Alexis de Tocqueville, *Democracy in America* (New York: Harper Perennial Modern Classics, 2006) I, 293–5.

[60] Robert P. Burns, *A Theory of the Trial* (Princeton: Princeton University Press, 1999); Lon L. Fuller, *The Morality of Law* (Cambridge, MA: Harvard University Press, 1969) 145.

[61] Ferguson, *Trial in American Life*, 1: "Courtroom trials are central ceremonies in the American republic of laws." His historical account stresses the republican tradition in courtroom rhetoric, and even the failures of the law (e.g., convicting the innocent) are ultimately seen as its long-term successes because of the lessons learned.

Trials 469

everyday business of the criminal justice system. If there is no opportunity to contest the charges, if the outcome is known in advance, if the aim of the trial is understood to be the delivery of a political message rather than a judgment of liability, then the trial will have failed – and may also be bad theater.[62] This is not to say that trials may not also be didactic – to establish certain facts as a matter of historical record and to demonstrate the power of law to call those responsible to account – but, as Douglas argues, the trial must also do justice, making "visible and public the sober authority of the rule of law."[63] There is also a risk that the actors in the trial, and in particular the accused, will not cooperate. In his analysis of the trial of Adolf Eichmann, Douglas points out that the defendant was extraordinarily obedient, respecting the conventions of the courtroom and participating in the process of his own conviction.[64] Yet if the defendant refuses to cooperate in this way, denying or refusing the authority of the court, then the trial itself can be put at risk, with heavy-handed attempts to reassert order or silence the accused, creating a different kind of theater.[65]

The second set of risks relates to the process of representation of law in terms of both the form and content of the trial. As we have noted, the reconstructive trial was concerned with control of the process of representation – reconstructing the courtroom to display the symbols of legal authority in a certain way and limiting and controlling public participation and access. As many commentators have pointed out, however, many modern trials – and particularly high-profile trials – have been turned into a kind of spectacle.[66] Media accounts play down the tedium and legal minutiae of the proceedings in favor of moments of drama and tension. There is a relentless focus on the character and personalities of the participants, making celebrities of criminals and defense lawyers along the way. These accounts are less concerned with the careful building of a case or the dignity of legal judgment than in bringing out the conflict and the human interest in the law, less concerned with law than entertainment. In certain cases the battle has come to be fought not only in the courtroom, but also in the media, displacing the distinctions between

---

[62] Otto Kirchheimer, *Political Justice: The Use of Legal Procedure for Political Ends* (Princeton: Princeton University Press, 1961).

[63] Douglas, *Memory of Judgment*, 3; cf. Hannah Arendt, *Eichmann in Jerusalem: A Report on the Banality of Evil* (London: Penguin, 1994) 233: "The purpose of a trial is to render justice, and nothing else."

[64] Lawrence Douglas, "Perpetrator Proceedings and Didactic Trials" in R. A. Duff et al., *The Trial on Trial II: Judgment and Calling to Account* (Oxford: Hart Publishing, 2006) 203.

[65] Lahav terms this "rough theater": Pnina Lahav, "Theater in the Courtroom: The Chicago Conspiracy Trial," *Law and Literature* 16 (2005) 381–474 at 394–405. For a more theoretical analysis see Emilios Christodoulidis, "The Objection that Cannot be Heard: Communication and Legitimacy in the Courtroom" in R. A. Duff et al., *The Trial on Trial I: Truth and Due Process* (Oxford: Hart Publishing, 2004).

[66] The best discussion of this is in Richard Sherwin, *When Law Goes Pop. The Vanishing Line Between Law and Culture* (Chicago: Chicago University Press, 2000).

inside and outside the court.[67] The media, and especially TV cameras, have entered the courtroom, a development that inevitably has an effect on the conduct of the participants.[68] Most crucially, though, this changes the nature of public involvement as the media takes the proceedings outside the courtroom. For the most part the public are no longer participating as active citizens but are passive consumers of information; the judgment of the public is not based on what is experienced in the courtroom but what is seen and heard in the media; the ability of judge and counsel to control and orchestrate the process of interpretation and judgment is inevitably diluted.[69] Although this might enable the law to reach a new audience, at the same time it becomes harder to differentiate law from other forms of entertainment. Because the public is constructed as a new kind of jury, this undoubtedly has an impact on the legitimacy of the institution.[70]

Truth and Communication

The adversarial criminal trial rests on a central paradox. Its stated purpose is agreed to be the determination of matters of past fact, yet it is frequently asserted that the procedures of the trial are designed rather to impair than to assist in the discovery of truth.[71] It suffers, it is alleged, from a "truth deficit."[72] The trial, it is argued, is by its nature a contest or battle between prosecution and defense to convince judge or jury, who are neutral between the parties. In this contest, structured by evidential rules and presumptions, the prosecution should seek to demonstrate beyond reasonable doubt that the accused committed the crime charged, whereas the defense attornies seek to raise doubts about the prosecution case. Neither side is under an obligation to discover or present the "truth" to the court, and indeed the duty of the judge, as referee, is to ensure only that the rules are respected and that the decision of

---

[67] Peter Goodrich, "Europe in America: Grammatology, Legal Studies, and the Politics of Transmission," *Columbia Law Review* 101:8 (2001) 2033–84 at 2075.

[68] For a full discussion of the development and legal issues, see Ferguson, *Trial in American Life*, ch. 8.

[69] Antoine Garapon, "Justice Out of Court: The Dangers of Trial by Media," *Law as Communication*, David Nelken, ed. (Aldershot: Dartmouth, 1996); Cornelia Vismann and Sara Ogger, "Tele-Tribunals: Anatomy of a Medium," *Grey Room* 10 (Winter 2003) 5–21; Peters, "Legal Performance" 195–200.

[70] Linda Mulcahy, "The Unbearable Lightness of Being? Shifts Towards the Virtual Trial," *Journal of Law and Society* 35 (2008) 464–89; Vismann, "Rejouer les Crimes"; Peter Gewirtz, "Victims and Voyeurs: Two Narrative Problems at the Criminal Trial," *Law's Stories: Narrative and Rhetoric in the Law*, Peter Brooks and Peter Gewirtz, eds. (New Haven: Yale University Press, 1996). Goodrich, "Europe in America," 2075–6 argues, by contrast, that the "videosphere" can liberate the law by taking it out of the hands of the lawyers and freeing it from the text.

[71] See e.g., Frank, *Courts on Trial*; William Pizzi, *Trials Without Truth* (New York: New York University Press, 1999). Alternatively it is sometimes asserted that an adversarial procedure driven by the interest of the parties is in fact the best method of discovering the truth. For a discussion of the "received view" of the trial that takes this as its starting point, see Burns, *Theory*, ch. 1.

[72] See Langbein, *Origins*.

Trials 471

the jury is justifiable on the basis of facts presented in court. The truth, should it be discovered, may be seen as a by-product of a process in which counsel pursue their clients' interests: "The advocate in the trial . . . is not engaged much more than half the time – and only then coincidentally – in the search for truth."[73] This is frequently contrasted with the inquisitorial process of civilian systems, a form of criminal procedure that is said to be exclusively oriented toward the discovery of the truth, though at the cost of placing greater power in the hands of agents of the state.[74] A verdict in an adversarial trial may thus, at best, be described as accurate based on the evidence presented rather than as expressing any truth.

What sort of truth is being talked about in these accounts? This is rather harder to determine, but it seems that there is a rather naïve belief in the capacity of the trial to uncover "what really happened" – a standard against which there must always be a truth deficit. However, what we see here is not necessarily institutional failure but a failure to understand the institution properly. Although this account captures one important feature of the adversarial trial – the importance of conflict and confrontation – it does so at the cost of ignoring the more complex relations between trials and truth. The trial is concerned with truth but in a range of different ways – in the sense that it is concerned with a certain way of knowing (what are relevant facts?), of proving (what counts as proof?), of judging (how do we distinguish between truth and falsehood?) and of behaving (how is one true to oneself and to the court?) – that in each case are subtly different. The verdict, moreover, must be true, rather than merely accurate, to the extent that it makes a claim about the condemnation of the wrongdoer, the standing of the community to call them to account, and the legitimacy of the trial itself.[75] Thus it would appear that the trial, while explicitly disclaiming any relationship to truth, nonetheless operates on the basis of diverse, possibly even divergent, understandings of truth. In this sense the discovery of "what really happened" is at best a very thin account of the relationship between trials and truth. The paradox here is that although the reconstructive trial imposes a "what really happened" framing narrative onto events, which seems to reduce the truth claims at stake in the trial, in practice it also seeks to establish much more – not only "whodunit" but why and how as well. Thus, rather than suffering from a truth "deficit," the reconstructive trial generates an excess of possible truths.

Laws of evidence and criminal procedure reflect understandings of how a fact can be proven and constrain the process of interpretation. It is central to the ideals of openness and accountability that govern the reconstructive trial that the verdict must be related to the evidence presented in the courtroom – even if the interpretation of

[73] Marvin E. Frankel, "The Search for Truth: An Umpireal View," *University of Pennsylvania Law Review* 23 (1975) 1031 at 1035.

[74] The classic analysis is in Mirjan Damaska, "Evidentiary Barriers to Conviction and Two Models of Criminal Procedure," *University Pennsylvania Law Review* 21 (1973) 506.

[75] See Duff et al., *Trial on Trial III*, pt. II esp. ch. 3 and 5. For a different view see Burns, *Theory*, ch. 8.

evidence is mediated through lawyers and other experts. This can easily be seen by looking at characteristic features of the criminal trial, which in different ways certify the relationship of words to reality.[76] The oath, even in a secular world, is a way of guaranteeing the seriousness (if not the credibility) of the speaker, and the rituals of testimony make speech acts identifiable. The claim of the witness to credibility is based on the relationship between speaker and hearer, tested in the process of cross-examination (by contrast, say, to scientific truth claims). Thus the adversarial process puts a particular stress on the orality of proceedings because the presence of the witness (who may only testify about what they have personally seen), and the obligation on them to present their testimony in open court, with opportunity for cross-examination, is understood as the best method of assessing the truth or falsity of their words.[77] Rules on the relevance or exclusion of certain types of evidence are based not only, or even primarily, on the desire to protect the accused – although it is often suggested that a proper understanding of the trial requires the acknowledgment that truth be subordinated to the aim of protecting the accused – but on concerns about the reliability of the testimony that would be produced under certain conditions.[78] Legal presumptions or rules relating to, say, causation or the inference that a certain state of mind existed, are based on the codification of commonplace assumptions about the world (or, at least, assumptions that are commonplace among lawyers!). The importance of interpretation, moreover, means that it is important to take into consideration understandings of the probity of lawyers, their duties to the court, and more general conceptions of credibility, probability, and fairness. Burns, for example, argues that the ethical and moral significance of the trial is deeply embedded in the practices and procedures of, and in the attitudes of the participants toward, the institution. His account accordingly provides a detailed examination of how a case is constructed, of procedural, evidential, and ethical rules, and ultimately of the place of the trial in a network of social and political institutions.[79] This leads him to see the truth of verdicts as linked to a series of features internal to the trial process. Central to his account, and to much recent analysis of trials, is the importance of narrative as a way of ordering, understanding, and judging the world.[80]

Narrative may be understood as operating within the trial in a number of different ways.[81] First, narratives can provide a basic way of making sense of the facts presented in the trial, understanding facts and drawing inferences about relationships between

---

[76] Richard Fenn, *Liturgies and Trials: The Secularization of Religious Language* (London: Blackwell, 1982) 51.

[77] See Ian Dennis, *The Law of Evidence*, 3rd ed. (London: Sweet & Maxwell, 2007) 12.

[78] John C. Smith, "Evidence in Criminal Cases," *The Handbook of the Criminal Justice Process*, Michael McConville and Geoffrey Wilson, eds. (Oxford: Oxford University Press, 2002) 184.

[79] Burns, *Theory*, ch. 3–5.

[80] Ibid., ch. 6 and 8.

[81] The classic account is Bennett and Feldman, *Reconstructing Reality*, ch. 1.

Trials 473

them. These stories are then a way of sorting out information – in testimony, in the summations of counsel and judge, and (no doubt) in the deliberations of the jury.[82] Narrative, in this initial sense, takes particular prominence in the reconstructive trial because of its role in solving problems of information overload. Second, narrative can impose normative constraints on the understanding of evidence: they are "everyday communication devices that create interpretive contexts for social action."[83] Stories must be plausible, they must be consistent with other evidence, and they must be coherent.[84] Ambiguities or inconsistencies are grounds for reasonable doubt, and thus it is not surprising that in the adversarial trial the strategies of lawyers are frequently directed at either the creation of a "good" story or the exposure of such ambiguities. Third, these narratives are worked out in a process of communication or dialogue, structured by legal procedure in a particular way in the trial.[85] Fourth, it is claimed that narratives are a way of anchoring legal questions in everyday understandings of the world. This may relate to the understanding of certain legal concepts, such as fault or causation, but it may also be a way in which social prejudices are used to judge or explain the actions of those involved. This last sense also points to the way in which the meaning in the trial draws on and appeals to broader social and cultural understandings – of actions, of explanation, and of the institution of the trial itself.[86] Umphrey, for example, has shown how the defendants were able to appeal to a sense of the "unwritten law" to defeat the attribution of criminal liability, arguing that the trial is a forum "which mediates the relation between formal legal rules and the unofficial world of norms, customs, common sense, and social codes."[87]

As in the discussion of trials as theater, we should note that this understanding of the trial in terms of narrative carries significant risks, as well as potential benefits, for the legitimacy of the trial. This is especially clear if we read the discussion of narrative through the account of the reconstructive trial because this showed how the trial developed so as to limit or constrain certain kinds of communication and to control the process of representation. This may also be a particular problem in notorious or spectacular trials in which the most intractable social and cultural conflicts play out. Here, as Sherwin notes, "The trial is no longer about factual truths only; its truths have become symbolic."[88] One danger here is that in aiming to address or resolve broader truths the trial may subordinate both the relevance and content of truth to those aims. Alternatively, if it seeks to acknowledge that there might be other truths – of

---

[82] See essays in Brooks and Gewirtz, *Law's Stories*.

[83] Bennett and Feldman, *Reconstructing Reality*, 7.

[84] Bernard Jackson, *Law, Fact, and Narrative Coherence* (Liverpool: Deborah Charles, 1988).

[85] Umphrey, "Dialogics of Legal Meaning"; Martha M. Umphrey, "Fragile Performances: The Dialogics of Judgment in 'A Theory of the Trial,'" *Law and Social Inquiry* 28 (2003) 527–32.

[86] This is a theme of both Ferguson and Burns.

[87] Umphrey, "Dialogics of Legal Meaning."

[88] Sherwin, *When Law Goes Pop*, 74.

474 Lindsay Farmer

the historian or scientist, or higher "moral truths" – in this multiplication of truths, the law may be emptied of content.[89] This leads into the discussion of the final theme, the social function of trials.

The Social and Cultural Functions of the Trial

A final major theme in writings about trials has been their social function in the resolution of social conflict or as part of a process of social healing. This might be thought to be simply a matter of resolution through the verdict of the court, or the condemnation of the wrongdoer, but the claim is broader than this. It is often suggested that the trial can represent a kind of therapeutic closure for the victim of crime, not only through the verdict, but because the victim is given an opportunity to tell his or her story.[90] It has also been argued that the role of trials in the resolution of conflict – particularly in notable or spectacular trials but also in the use of quasi-juridical *fora* such as Truth Commissions – reaches far beyond even this.[91] Thus, for example, Berman has argued that beyond the immediate verdict, a trial can "allow the community to domesticate chaos by providing a consensus explanation of social reality to replace what would otherwise seem to be frightening and uncontrollable activity."[92] Trials "create a mythic arena for expressing the great tensions and moral battles of the community."[93] Likewise for Ferguson, "the ideal trial moves from contest towards ritual in communal acceptance of the result achieved in court," with trials offering the opportunity for the resolution of conflict through appeal to and the construction of larger narratives about the republic of laws.[94] This also points to the way that notable trials come to be thematized around the dramatization of particular cultural fears or "invisible worlds."[95] Thus, Ferguson argues that among the features

---

[89] Douglas, "Didactic Trials."

[90] For a critical discussion of the healing power of testimony see Julie Stone Peters, "Literature, the Rights of Man, and Narratives of Atrocity: Historical Backgrounds to the Culture of Testimony," *Yale Journal of Law and the Humanities* 17 (2005) 253–83.

[91] The discussion of Truth and Reconciliation Commissions goes beyond the immediate scope of this chapter. For discussion of the issues of truth, memory, and social reconciliation see Emilios Christodoulidis and Scott Veitch, eds., *Lethe's Law: Justice, Law, and Ethics in Reconciliation* (Oxford: Hart Publishing, 2001).

[92] Paul Schiff Berman, "Rats, Pigs, and Statues on Trial: The Creation of Cultural Narratives in the Prosecution of Animals and Inanimate Objects," *New York University Law Review* 69 (1994) 288 at 292.

[93] Ibid., 293.

[94] *Trial in American Life*, 21–4. It is interesting to note that both Berman and Ferguson draw on the work of social anthropologist Victor Turner in making these claims.

[95] Peter Charles Hoffer, "Invisible Worlds and Criminal Trials: The Cases of John Proctor and O. J. Simpson," *American Journal of Legal History* 41 (1997) 287 at 291. cf., Lahav, "Trials as Theater," 392–4: trials contain archetypal motifs that galvanize the collective imagination – so as to "burst the shell of analytic language and cerebral discourse" (324).

Trials 475

that make certain trials high profile or notable are that the conflict reaches beyond the particular dispute, that it causes a social shock or surprise that the society must address, and that it invokes the symbolism and imagery of personality, allowing members of the community to identify with or judge the participants.[96] In less hyperbolic terms we might say that trials can crystallize particular social conflicts, which the participants in (and observers of) the trial draw on and appeal to this broader culture and that the cultural life of the trial often continues long after the final verdict.[97] Notorious trials may thus be understood as double trials: about both the particular event, as well as what it means for the event to have taken place at all.[98]

This theme has been taken up in a distinctive way in the work of Felman who argues that in modernity trials have become central to the response to major social traumas.[99] She links, in particular, the discovery of trauma in psychoanalytic theory as a new dimension of social experience, the spread of large-scale atrocities, and the resort to law as a means of coping with the traumatic legacies and collective injuries left by these events.[100] This articulation between trials and traumas was institutionalized in the wake of the Nuremberg trials, as new crimes and forms of trial were recognized in international law. This historical argument – that law has in fact been used as a response – becomes a normative argument for how trials should be used – as a tragic drama capable of leading to collective catharsis.[101] In these trials, she suggests, although the law is initially called upon to address claims of individual guilt and innocence, it finds itself responding to larger (unconscious) historical traumas. In reenacting the trauma, the trial dramatizes and generalizes the conflict, giving public voice and witness to individual trauma, and thereby enabling resolution. The narrative truth of the accounts of the victims transcends the legal forum and the conscious ends of the institution of the trial to provide a broader form of recognition and reconciliation.

---

[96] *Trial in American Life*, 2–3, although it is not clear why the iconography of a notable trial should be limited to personality and identification, and Ferguson does not provide an historical account of how these forms of identification developed.

[97] It is also, of course, important to understand how trials are thematized by the broader culture. See Sherwin, *When Law Goes Pop*; Lindsay Farmer, "'With all the Impressiveness and Substantial Value of Truth': Notable Trials and Criminal Justice, 1750–1930," *Law and Humanities* 1:1 (2007) 57–78; Shani d'Cruze, "'The damned place was haunted': The Gothic, Middlebrow Culture and Inter-War Notable Trials" in *Literature and History (Third Series)*, 39. One could just as easily look at literary or cinematic representations of the trial, see e.g., Franco Moretti, *Signs Taken for Wonders: On the Sociology of Literary Forms* (London: Verso, 1983) ch. 5 on detective fiction; Jonathan H. Grossman, *The Art of Alibi: English Law Courts and the Novel* (Baltimore: Johns Hopkins, 2002); Rodensky, *Crime in Mind*.

[98] Sherwin, *When Law Goes Pop*, 77.

[99] Felman, *The Juridical Unconscious*. See also Mark Osiel, *Mass Atrocity, Collective Memory, and the Law* (New York: Transaction, 1997) and Douglas, *The Memory of Judgment*.

[100] *The Juridical Unconscious*, 2.

[101] Ibid., 162.

These are large claims and I want to conclude this section by identifying two critical concerns. The first is that although a trial may well present opportunities for insight, engagement, and reconciliation, there is no guarantee that these will be taken up. We must beware confusing the potential of the trial with its actuality. Sherwin, for example, has argued that when confronted by large social or cultural conflicts, the response of the law is mainly one of evasion and the failure to engage with cultural anxieties.[102] This may in part be a limitation deriving from the structure of the reconstructive trial itself. As I suggested previously, the trial institutionalizes a "hermeneutics of suspicion," that nothing can or should be taken at face value, and this may limit the opportunities for identification or empathy with witnesses or an accused. More often than not this will create distance, leading to criminals being seen as an "other" and making the trial like a ritual of degradation reaffirming the authority of the law. When, moreover, this kind of identification does take place, as in the trial of Harry Thaw discussed by Sherwin, it may do so on the basis of prejudice, sentimentality, and moral indignation rather than appeal to the higher values represented by the republic of laws – a tendency that may be exacerbated by new media representations of the trial.[103] Second, this points to broader limitations on what we might hope to achieve through resort to law and the institution of the trial.[104] Although trials provide a public response to wrongdoing, it is not clear that they can either establish the truth about or ascribe responsibility for large-scale wrongdoing in a way that transcends the bounds of individual agency. Likewise, although closure for the victim may be an important side effect, it should never be allowed to become the main aim of the trial for the reason that it may conflict with the central aim of publicly calling an offender to account for their wrongdoing. We should be especially wary here of moving from the historical claim that certain trials have offered this kind of truth or closure, to either the assumption that this must therefore be true of all trials or to the normative claim that it is proper or justified for the trial to do so.[105]

The Century of the Trial?

For Hannah Arendt, a major factor in the widespread interest in trials in the nineteenth century was the public fascination with the achievements and failures of

---

[102] *When Law Goes Pop*, ch. 4. Ferguson does concede that trials that capture the imagination tend to divide sharply along the axes of contest and ritual. A ritual without contest can also be empty, losing sight of the individuals at the center of the process in the rush to judgment: *Trial in American Life*, 21.

[103] See also Peters, "Legal Performance," 197.

[104] See the discussion in Duff et al., *Trial on Trial III*, ch. 10. See also Scott Veitch, "Judgment and Calling to Account: Truths, Trials, and Reconciliations" in R. A. Duff et al., *The Trial on Trial II*, at 163–70.

[105] For an account that is sensitive to the limits of the law see Douglas, *The Memory of Judgment*.

Trials 477

the rule of law.[106] Over the course of the twentieth century the focus of this interest has shifted from the rule of law to a fascination with character, conflict, and, ultimately, to the trial as entertainment. This is, at least in part, a consequence of the subtle reorderings of the criminal trial that took place over the course of the nineteenth century. The formation of the reconstructive trial, indeed, has fostered the tendency, which has gone more or less unchecked in certain jurisdictions, to allow the indefinite expansion of relevant subject matter and evidence so long as the parties can afford it. These have operated to throw a particular focus on to lawyers and judges as interpreters of the evidence and as principal figures in the dramaturgy of the trial. They have at the same time led to a new fascination with character – of the motivations of the accused, the story of the victim and the response of both to the experience of the trial itself. Trials are reported in the press as they happen, even televised in some jurisdictions, and reporters scrutinize every action of the parties involved. The public that consumes these trials sits as a jury in judgment not only of the accused but also of the trial itself. For these reasons alone we might characterize our century as the century of the trial. In concluding, however, I want to offer two further remarks as to how this fascination reflects a distinctively modern sensibility.

First, as we have noted, the claims about the truth established by the trial go well beyond the claim that the aim of the trial is merely to establish as a matter of legal record that a certain person is guilty as charged. In our age we look to trials to tell us much more: to tell us about their motivations and character; to establish an official historical account of certain events; to give voice to forgotten or silenced victims; and to reveal truths about human character and affairs. The trial is not merely a place where these stories can be heard but is also seen as an institution that can reveal further truths about our society and ourselves. The trial is thus invested with a significance that goes beyond being an institution where wrongdoers are called to account or conflicts resolved. However, in a society obsessed by celebrity, gesture, and character, the trial may be doing little more than reflecting our own obsessions. The problem is that of how to maintain the seriousness of the institution in the media age. Second, this belief in the significance of trials fosters a desire for further significant trials or conflicts, encouraging a resort to law and the belief that trials are an appropriate response to everything from minor crimes to major atrocities. The repeated claims that particular trials will be the trial of the century reflect the desire to continue to invest trials with this meaning. The danger is that in doing so we overload the institution in such a way as to undermine its effectiveness.

[106] *The Origins of Totalitarianism* (New York: Harcourt Brace Jovanovich, 1973) 91.

18

Testimony, Witnessing

Jan-Melissa Schramm

"Testimony" is a richly multivalent term. It describes the statement of a witness in court, "offered as evidence of the truth of that which is stated;"[1] but it is also a profession of religious faith, and a story habitually narrated in the first person by those who seek to bear witness to the role of traumatic events in the formation of larger historiographical narratives. This is the essential ambiguity of the term "testimony": That it not only encompasses narratives of personal experience, which require no immediate external verification, but that it also seeks to be regarded as a species of evidence – that it is articulated in a public forum with a view to establishing its "truth."[2] Indeed, jurists acknowledge that there is a sense in which testimony is the sole medium of judicial evidence: Putative distinctions between testimony and circumstantial or documentary evidence founder upon the requirement that documents and things produced in court must nevertheless be described (and their provenance accounted for) by a witness.

The centrality of testimony to the trial process has ensured the emergence of cogent rules to test its validity, which often operate simultaneously to suppress its similarities to narrative fiction and story. Current Anglo-American law is concerned to establish the competence and compellability of a potential witness to the fact at issue: Competence relates to whether or not a party may be permitted to testify, and compellability refers to whether or not that party may be forced to do so by the service of witness summons and the provision of sanctions in the event that such a summons is ignored. Further rules seek to guarantee the reception of only that testimony which is deemed voluntary and freely given, and, at first glance, this evidentiary apparatus seems rather straightforward. In Peter Brooks's terms:

[1] Colin Tapper, *Cross and Tapper on Evidence*, 7th ed. (Oxford: Oxford University Press, 2007) 57.
[2] For this reason, "testimony" in this chapter is taken to refer to prose narratives: oral and written and factual and fictionalized. On the whole, poetry as a genre is less explicitly dependent upon the vocabularies of fact and evidence.

Testimony, Witnessing 479

Since the law implicitly recognizes the power of story-telling, it has been intent, over the centuries, to formalize the conditions of telling – to assure that narratives reach those charged with judging them in certain rule-governed forms. Against what may often appear as the fragmented, contradictious, murky unfolding of narrative in the trial courtroom stand formulas by which the law attempts to impose form and rule on stories. The judge must know and enforce these rules. And when stories are culled from the trial record and retold at the appellate level, it is to evaluate their conformity to the rules ... So it is that the law has found certain kinds of narrative problematic and has worried about whether they should have been allowed a place at trial or what place they should have been allowed. All the rules of evidence, including the much-debated exclusionary rule, touch on the issue of rule-governed story-telling.[3]

As Brooks goes on to note, however, a deeper investigation disturbs the distinction between admissible narratives and those that cannot fit comfortably into the recognized taxonomies of the "rule-governed forms." Although the current rules of competence and compellability are of comparatively recent construction, many cases continue to arise in which neither the admissibility of a certain narrative nor indeed its voluntariness are considered to be self-evident. The anxieties of the earlier debates about the status of eyewitness evidence remind us that the law is profoundly "transactional" – in Paul Gewirtz's analysis, "not just a directive but an activity involving audiences as well as sovereign law-givers"; such a perspective "sees laws as artefacts that reveal a culture, not just policies that shape a culture."[4] A perusal of eighteenth- and nineteenth-century sources reveals both the complexity of early modern legal process and the profound interrelation of literary, legal, and theological epistemologies in the age that witnessed the rise of the legal profession: Modern practice would do well to continue to attend to the resonance of these debates.

A Brief History of English Trial Procedure

The English common law trial is a fact-finding forum that has long privileged orality, cross-examination, and adversarial exchange, and hence it has been dependent for many centuries on the testimony of witnesses. Those who give evidence to a common law court have traditionally had to be *"un oyant et veyant,* a hearer and seer ... one who could say, as the witnesses to courts in older times always had to say, *quod vidi et audivi*; it must not be testimony at second hand."[5] Historians have related the

---

[3] Peter Brooks, "The Law as Narrative and Rhetoric," *Law's Stories: Narrative and Rhetoric in the Law*, Peter Brooks and Paul Gewirtz, eds. (New Haven and London: Yale University Press, 1996) 19–20.

[4] Gewirtz, "Narrative and Rhetoric in the Law," *Law's Stories*, Brooks and Gewirtz, eds., 3.

[5] James Bradley Thayer, *A Preliminary Treatise on Evidence at the Common Law* (London: Sweet & Maxwell, 1898) 518–9. A longer version of this account is found in Jan-Melissa Schramm, *Testimony and Advocacy in Victorian Law, Literature, and Theology* (Cambridge: Cambridge University Press, 2000) 48–56.

emergence of the rules of evidence to the demise of any widespread communal belief that the truth of a matter may be divinely revealed: The rise of the trial as a model of inquiry in which facts are determined by a jury of epistemologically competent lay-people can be positioned alongside the disuse of more primitive ideas of trial that presupposed miraculous intervention to establish innocence, such as ordeal by fire or water (the Anglo-Saxon manner) or by battle (the Norman practice).[6] In 1215, the Church prohibited recourse to the ordeal as a type of proof and by 1220 the trial jury had emerged (from embryonic beginnings perhaps two decades earlier) to determine the culpability of those named by a presenting jury.[7] The medieval jury was a self-informing body chosen from the local area in which an offense or disagreement occurred and its members accumulated information about the fact at issue themselves.[8] Consequently, historians claim that early modern jurors functioned essentially as witnesses; they "were primarily called, not to consider the evidence put before them, but to disclose to the court what they thought of the matter."[9] As a verdict could then be reached on the basis of their knowledge of the defendant and the circumstances of the case, rules governing the admissibility of the evidence tendered to the court were superfluous. The demise of the self-informing jury seems to date from around 1500, although vestiges of the medieval practice appeared occasionally in criminal cases conducted in Tudor and Stuart times.[10] Once it was established that the jury's attention should be restricted to the evidence presented to the court by various witnesses, then a new judicial sensitivity to questions of witness competence and credibility began to appear; documentary evidence receded in significance (particularly in the criminal courts) and means were gradually devised to test the admissibility and relevance of witness narratives.

The history of the reception of eyewitness testimony in early modern trials is thus inseparable from that of the jury as an independent forum for the discovery of fact and the so-called lawyerization of the (criminal) trial in the late eighteenth and early nineteenth centuries. This process of professionalization coincided with, and was in turn sustained by, rigorous developments in standards of proof: Barbara Shapiro has shown that although the term "fact" was developed in medieval trial process to refer to a human act or deed (frequently criminal) within the province of the jury to determine, it was appropriated by the discourse of natural philosophy in the

---

[6] See Julius Stone, *Evidence: Its History and Policies*, rev. by W. A. N. Wells (Sydney: Butterworth, 1991) 1–11; Thomas A. Green, *Verdict According to Conscience: Perspectives on the English Criminal Trial Jury 1200–1800* (Chicago: University of Chicago Press, 1985) 3–27.

[7] Green, 3 and 11–4.

[8] See Green, 16–20, Stone, 12–9; Thomas A. Green and J. S. Cockburn, eds., *Twelve Good Men and True: The Criminal Trial Jury in England, 1200–1800* (Princeton: Princeton University Press, 1988) 358–99.

[9] Stone, 18.

[10] Stone, 20–3. See also William Blackstone, *Commentaries on the Laws of England*, 4 vols. (Oxford: Clarendon Press, 1765–1769) vol. III, 359–60 and 374–5.

Testimony, Witnessing

seventeenth century to describe "things" and yoked in perpetuity to empirical notions of evidence, experiment, and experience.[11] From there, the idea of "fact" spread infectiously into the other nascent discourses of the day – including historiography, the newspapers, and the early novel. The dominance of the rhetoric of fact in turn supplanted other vocabularies that purported to lay claim to narrative reliability: Brooks and Peter Goodrich have both argued that the law's increased reliance on the epistemologies of proof promoted by the Royal Society and the philosophy of Locke was accompanied by a tendency to disavow its early origins in Aristotelian rhetorical theory[12] – the development of rigorous professional ideas of proof, precedent, and practice left little room for reminders of shared roots in storytelling and the classical dramas of recognition.

The reform of trial process occurred gradually throughout the Enlightenment and the early nineteenth century. Eighteenth-century trials, particularly in relation to criminal matters, were often short, combative, and confrontational: John Beattie has estimated that the average duration of a hearing for a capital charge in the period was thirty minutes.[13] Attempts by historians to trace a genealogy of the earliest rules of evidence – the "forms" (in Brooks's terms) that governed these oral exchanges – have drawn scholarly attention to the nonfictional writings of Henry Fielding, author and magistrate (1707–1754). Discussion of one of the earliest formal rules of evidence has been located in his prosecutorial treatise, *An Enquiry into the Causes of the Late Increase of Robbers* (1751), in which he calls for the abolition of the requirement that the evidence of accomplices be corroborated. Frustrated by the wiles of the street gangs with whom he engaged in daily judicial battle, Fielding argued that the reception of accomplice testimony should be a question of credibility for the jury rather than a question of competence (that is, whether or not the jury was entitled to hear the evidence in the first place).[14] This vivid portrait of prosecutorial anxiety plunges us straight into the heart of heated juridical debate about the efficacy of an exclusionary regime of evidentiary assessment.

The list of people unable to give sworn evidence in legal proceedings at the beginning of the nineteenth century was a lengthy one. In *The Law of Evidence*

---

[11] Barbara Shapiro, *The Culture of Fact: England 1550–1720* (Chicago: University of Chicago Press, 2001).

[12] See Brooks, "The Law as Narrative and Rhetoric," and Peter Goodrich, *Law in the Courts of Love: Literature and Other Minor Jurisprudences* (London and New York: Routledge, 1996).

[13] John Beattie, *Crime and the Courts in England 1660–1800* (Oxford: Clarendon Press, 1986) 378. See also Beattie, "Scales of Justice: Defence Counsel and the English Criminal Trial in the Eighteenth and Nineteenth Centuries," *Law and History Review* 9 (1991) 221–67; Stephan Landsman, "The Rise of the Contentious Spirit: Adversary Procedure in Eighteenth-Century England," *Cornell Law Review* 75 (1990) 497–609; and John Langbein, *The Origins of Adversary Criminal Trial* (Oxford: Oxford University Press, 2003).

[14] Henry Fielding, "An Enquiry into the Late Increase in Robbers," *An Enquiry into the Late Increase in Robbers and Related Writings*, Malvin R. Zirker, ed. (Oxford: Clarendon Press, 1988) 158. See Langbein, *Origins*, 25–8.

in Victorian England, Christopher Allen agrees with the observation of the Common Law Commissioners in their Report of 1852–3 that the distinguishing feature of Victorian trial process was "the extent to which it prevented witnesses from testifying."[15] Most suspicion was directed toward the motive of self-interest, and as a consequence, the parties to a civil case (and indeed, anyone who would benefit financially from the proceedings) were prevented from testifying (on the grounds that their interest in the outcome of proceedings rendered their evidence unreliable). In criminal cases the position was inconsistent: Prosecution witnesses could verify their evidence with access to the oath in Tudor legal process, but this right was only extended to witnesses for the defense in 1702. The eighteenth-century version of the felony trial has been described by John Langbein as the "accused speaks" model (in which access to the speech of the prisoner was crucial to the finding of fact),[16] but even while the assessment of his story was deemed essential to the verdict, the accused himself was still denied access to the oath. Felony trial procedure was reformed in 1836 with the enactment of the Prisoners' Counsel Act, which extended full legal representation to those accused of serious crime, yet the retention of counsel effectively silenced the accused – judicial rules of practice that appeared in 1837 ensured that the court would only hear one voice on behalf of the defense: either the accused or his counsel, but not both.[17] As a consequence, the Victorian courtroom (like the Victorian novel) was the locus of particular anxiety about the types of "truth" generated by first-person, layman's speech, and the third-person voice of the professional legal representative. That the first-person speech of the unrepresented accused had to be offered to the court unsworn further complicated judicial attempts to assess its reliability.

The history of evidence can be read as an account of progressive secularization, but scriptural mandates continued to influence the emergent body of enlightenment procedure that replaced the mechanisms of ordeal and trial by battle. Although English procedure abjured the Romano-canonical requirement that two witnesses were necessary for conviction and insisted instead on the sufficiency of a voluntary confession to found a verdict, witness testimony did require the verification of the Christian oath of truthfulness.[18] Non-Christians were traditionally regarded as incompetent to give evidence as they were unable to take the oath – although the position of foreign witnesses was treated with some sensitivity in the case of *Omychund* v. *Barker* (1744) 1 Atk. 22 when other cultural equivalents of the English oath were recognized in

[15] Christopher Allen, *The Law of Evidence in Victorian England* (Cambridge: Cambridge University Press, 1997) 1.

[16] Langbein, *Origins,* ch. 1.

[17] On the enactment and implementation of the Prisoners' Counsel Act, see Langbein, *Origins,* and David J. A. Cairns, *Advocacy and the Making of the Adversarial Criminal Trial 1800–1865* (Oxford: Oxford University Press).

[18] On the status of pre-trial confessions in the period, see Henry Joy, *On the Admissibility of Confessions and Challenge of Jurors in Criminal Cases in England and Ireland* (Dublin: Milliken, 1842).

Testimony, Witnessing

the interests of promoting international trade. For local religious nonconformists, however, restrictions remained: Quakers, Moravians, Separatists, and children were all regarded as incompetent witnesses in the eighteenth century by virtue of their inability to subscribe to the terms of the oath. It was Jeremy Bentham, in his rigorous endeavors to found legal process upon scientific and utilitarian principles, who did most to illuminate the absurdities of this system. In *A Rationale of Judicial Evidence* (1827), he argued that the continuing usage of the exclusionary scheme amounted to a "mendacity licence" issued by the courts to perpetuate the commission of crimes: "[e]xclusion put upon all persons of this or that particular description, includes a licence to commit, in the presence of any number of persons of that description, all imaginable crimes."[19] Instead, he argued for evidentiary inclusivity: "The rule will be, – Let in the light of evidence. The exception will be, – Except where the letting in of such light is attended with preponderant collateral inconvenience, in the shape of vexation, expense, and delay." Regarding the competence of witnesses he concluded: "In principle, there is but one mode of searching out the truth – see everything that is to be seen; hear every body who is likely to know anything about the matter; hear everybody, but most attentively of all, and first of all, those who are likely to know most about it, the parties."[20]

Increasingly, Benthamite approaches to rational enquiry prevailed. Legislative reforms in 1828 and 1833 allowed Quakers, Moravians, and Separatists to give evidence in criminal matters after making a solemn affirmation in lieu of an oath.[21] The Evidence Act of 1843 ensured that prior convictions for criminal activity became a question of credibility rather than competence and enabled people with a pecuniary interest in the outcome of civil proceedings (other than the parties themselves) to give evidence.[22] The most significant changes were implemented by the Law of Evidence Amendment Act of 1851, which rendered the parties in civil proceedings competent to testify on their own behalf.[23] Repeated attempts were made in subsequent decades to create parity in criminal proceedings, but it was not until 1898 that the Criminal Evidence Act empowered defendants to give sworn evidence on their own behalf should they choose to do so.[24]

The Continental Tradition and the Status of Confession

Continental European trial process remained closer to its Romano-canonical inheritance than its English counterpart and tended to prioritize pre-trial investigation: In

---

[19] Jeremy Bentham, *A Rationale of Judicial Evidence, Specially Applied to English Practice*, 5 vols. (London: Hunt & Clarke, 1827) vol. IV, 490–2.

[20] Bentham, vol. V, 743.

[21] 9 Geo. IV, c. 32, and 3 & 4 Will. IV, c. 49.

[22] 6 & 7 Vict., c. 85.

[23] 14 & 15 Vict., c. 99.

[24] 61 & 61 Vict., c. 36.

French procedure (for example), oral exchange, cross-examination, and adversarial combat were traditionally regarded as less important than the provision of written evidence and the supervisory role of the judge. The assessment of evidence was also traditionally governed by a complex arithmetical formula (the so-called system of statutory proofs), which tended to attribute a fixed value to testimony in the event that it was seen as directly relevant to the fact at issue. The logical attractions of the arithmetical model were debated at various stages of the English reform process (see for example the discussion in W. M. Best's lucid *Treatise on the Principles of Evidence*[25]), but the English distrust of judicial torture, which could be invoked to effect a more full disclosure of the facts and thus an alleged "improvement" in the quality of testimony, usually resulted in a principled rejection of this format.[26] Indeed, anxieties were heightened by the impact of the French Revolution itself (1789–94) and concomitant fears that violent social unrest could spread across the Channel.

Although Revolutionary interference with legal structures radically reshaped trial process (and led, ultimately, to the abolition of the statutory system of proofs[27]), historians and literary critics have also drawn attention to the ways in which the Revolution itself was sustained by testimonial writings that nurtured popular enthusiasm for republican ideals. Jean-Jacques Rousseau's *Confessions*, published posthumously in two parts, 1782–88 used the direct immediacy of the first-person voice to generate a distinctive radical sensibility. A secular response to the *Confessions* of St. Augustine, Rousseau's *Confessions* adopted an unprecedented tenor of narrative transparency, arguing for a complete equation of inner character and textual representation:

> Que la trompette du Jugement dernier sonne quand elle voudra, je viendrai, ce livre à la main, me presenter le souverain juge . . . j'ai dévoilé mon intérieur tel que tuétre éternel l'as vu toi-même.[28]

Rousseau asserted that the composition of the text was inspired in part by his urge to atone for an injury inflicted upon an honest serving girl whom he wrongly blamed for a theft he had himself committed in younger years:[29] He thus tethered the production of first-person narrative to the generative capacities of shame and guilt.[30] For Brooks, this problematizes any sense in which a confession can be considered fully voluntary: for Gregory Dart, the implications are political – Rousseau "implicitly

---

[25] (London: Sweet, 1849) 68–92.

[26] On the interrelationship of the two, see John H. Langbein, *Torture and the Law of Proof: Europe and England in the Ancien Régime* (Chicago: University of Chicago Press, 1976; repr. 2006) ch. 1.

[27] Langbein, *Torture*, 11.

[28] Jean-Jacques Rousseau, *Les Confessions* [1782–88] (Gallimard, 1959) 33–4.

[29] Ibid., 127–8.

[30] On the implications of this association for contemporary legal procedure, see Peter Brooks, *Troubling Confessions: Speaking Guilt in Law and Literature* (Chicago: University of Chicago Press, 2000).

Testimony, Witnessing

represented the autobiographical subject as an anticipation, in individual form, of the transparency and virtue which would be the defining feature of the ideal political community of the future."[31] We hear echoes of this in English utopian writings of the period – for example, in William Godwin's definition of sincerity as a civic value. Writing in his *Enquiry Concerning Political Justice, and its Influence on General Virtue and Happiness* (1793), Godwin observed, "'An upright man,' it has sometimes been said, 'ought to carry his heart in his hand.' He ought to have an ingenuousness which shrinks from no examination. The commerce between his heart and his tongue is uniform. Whatever he speaks you can depend upon to be the truth and the whole truth."[32]

The disillusionment that followed the Reign of Terror was to reveal the tragic flaws in this idealistic promotion of personal transparency on both sides of the Channel, and subsequent deployments of the first-person confessional form in England must be read as self-consciously aware of the genre's political heritage. In his novel *Caleb Williams* (1794), Godwin produced a painfully ironic commentary on the shortcomings of his theories of political and linguistic sincerity: so too, William Wordsworth's epic poem *The Prelude* (1805, revised 1850), which adopts the confessional form to display the maturation of a poet's mind, must be read as bravely experimental, because, in Dart's terms, "fully-wrought autobiography was, at least during the early years of the nineteenth century, a dangerously radical form in both Britain and France, not least because of its continuing potential to challenge existing notions of the relationship between private reflection and public politics, the individual personality and history."[33] The suspect nature of the form was confirmed by Thomas De Quincey's *Confessions of An English Opium-Eater* (1827), which reminded its readership of the strong association between guilt, transgression, and first-person narration promulgated a hundred years earlier by the likes of Daniel Defoe. The generic distinction between fact and fiction, autobiography and the novel, had long been problematic, but practitioners of both genres expressed concern about the type of material confessed by the narrating subject and its impact upon the implied audience.

Testimony, Fiction, and the Law

Although the Revolutionary upheavals of the 1790s enhanced English anxieties about the reliability of speech, homegrown reservations concerning the value or desirability of transparent subjectivity – and the related trope of narrative sincerity – had

---

[31] Gregory Dart, *Rousseau, Robespierre, and English Romanticism* (Cambridge: Cambridge University Press, 1999) 9.

[32] William Godwin, *Enquiry Concerning Political Justice, and its Influence on General Virtue and Happiness*, 2 vols. (London: Robinson, 1793) vol. I, 275.

[33] Dart, 180.

long been expressed. The cultural preference for a vocabulary of plain fact that eschewed ornament had traditionally been associated with Puritanism and the work of the Royal Society in the seventeenth century: In Michael McKeon's influential analysis, this "negative capability" was associated with a reaction against rhetoric's power to generate opinion rather than knowledge.[34] In *A Culture of Fact*, Shapiro rightly notes, "[a]ll the discourses of 'fact' became suspicious of rhetoric and often voiced this suspicion in connection with announcing their dedication to the norm of impartiality."[35] This celebration of "artlessness" or the language of "plain fact" can be seen in some of the earliest English novels: Samuel Richardson's *Pamela* (1740) and *Clarissa* (1748) both suggest that their eponymous heroines "speak and write the sincere dictates of [their] hearts:"[36] for Pamela and, particularly, the persecuted Clarissa, speech is "the heart's dictation"[37] and the creditworthiness of the girls' accounts of their trials at the hands of Mr. B – and Lovelace is tested in forums that closely model themselves on the eighteenth-century court. Both novels enact "gendered competitions for credibility"[38] and are deeply engaged with the juridical discourse of their day. Literary critics such as Terry Castle and Judy Cornett argue that *Clarissa* in particular "exposes the fundamental assumptions underlying the Lockean framework of eighteenth-century evidence law." Her story is a study of the ways in which "power relations define the interpretation of evidence":

> Because the type of experience assumed by Gilbertian evidentiary principles was not neutral and universally available to all knowers, it inscribed culturally determined power relations within the eighteenth-century law of evidence. Thus Clarissa's story exposes what Gilbert's scheme obscures: the inadequacy of the Lockean model of cognitive self-sufficiency for knowers who are innocent and powerless.[39]

If sincerity prevails in *Pamela*, it is weakened by Fielding's vitriolic parody *Shamela* (1741), which suggests the performative self-construction of the epistolary narrative, and the trope is defeated altogether (in worldly terms) in *Clarissa* – although

---

[34] Michael McKeon, *The Origins of the English Novel, 1600–1740* (Baltimore: Johns Hopkins University Press, 1987) 104–5 and 109. See also Steven Shapin, *A Social History of Truth: Civility and Science in Seventeenth-Century England* (Chicago: University of Chicago Press, 1994).

[35] Shapiro, 29.

[36] Samuel Richardson, *Clarissa* [1748] (Harmondsworth: Penguin, 1985) 240.

[37] Terry Castle, *Clarissa's Ciphers: Meaning and Disruption in Richardson's Clarissa* (Ithaca: Cornell University Press, 1982) 67.

[38] See Schramm, *Testimony*, 83–9.

[39] Judy Cornett, "The Treachery of Perception: Evidence and Experience in *Clarissa*," *University of Cincinnati Law Review* 63 (1994), no. 1, 165–93 at 190–2. See also Castle, 54–7; and Elizabeth Judge, "Character Witnesses: Credibility and Testimony in the Eighteenth-Century Novel" (D. Phil. Dissertation, Dalhousie University, 2004). Lord Geoffrey Gilbert's *The Law of Evidence*, first published posthumously in 1754, depended heavily upon Lockean psychology (although Gilbert's attention was directed largely to documentary rather than oral evidence).

Testimony, Witnessing

the evidence of the heroine's model death encourages the reader to dwell on her reward in the life to come. Subsequent novels such as Laurence Sterne's delightfully experimental *Tristram Shandy* (published in nine volumes, 1759–69) suggested the impossibility of efforts to represent the "life and opinions" of a chosen subject. Although endlessly diverting, Tristram's fictional autobiography proves difficult to start and, indeed, almost impossible to finish, as one cannot realistically narrate one's own conception, birth, or death. The assumed correspondence between thought and speech, so central to claims for the reliability of the first-person form, is thus subject to a rather harsh interrogation.

That engagement with the law affects both fictional content and narrative form is an axiom of critical study of the English novel. The common interest in content enjoys a long history. The accusation and trial of the protagonists were dominant motifs in the earliest Greek romances (the Helleno-Roman narratives perfected during the period of the so-called Second Sophistic, i.e., the first two centuries AD). Yet, in Mikhail Bakhtin's terms, the trials that conclude ancient tales such as *Kleitophon and Leucippe* and *The Adventures of Callirhoe* "are somewhat external and formal, leaving little imprint upon the psychological makeup of the protagonists... the hammer of events shatters nothing and forges nothing – it merely tries the durability of an already finished product. And the product passes the test."[40] Renaissance dramatists reworked and extended plots of tragic and comic recognition borrowed from the classical tragedians, pioneering in the process a new forensic vocabulary based on theological notions of trial, Aristotle's *Poetics*, and the language of the Inns of Court, where many of these plays were first performed. The interest in crime was foregrounded by the appearance of the recognizably modern English novel in the early eighteenth century. Texts such as Daniel Defoe's *Moll Flanders* [1722] were closely allied to the nonfictional form of the criminal biography (confessional morality tales sold around the foot of the scaffold on days of public executions), and Defoe may well have tried to appeal to the biography's established readership by allowing some of the same narrative patterns to shape his own work (albeit with significant departures, most notably in respect to narrative closure). Fictional fascination with transgression and its punishment (either earthly or divine) generates what Patrick Brantlinger has identified as the double dynamic of much eighteenth- and nineteenth-century fiction: The reader can identify within the text both the celebration of criminal propensity (particularly when articulated in the first-person form) and the conservative policing and expulsion of such elements at the point of narrative closure with the reassertion of economic and Providential order.[41]

---

[40] Mikhail Bakhtin, *The Dialogic Imagination: Four Essays*, Caryl Emerson and Michael Holquist, trans. (Austin: University of Texas Press, 1981; repr. 1998) 48.

[41] Patrick Brantlinger, *The Reading Lesson: The Threat of Mass Literacy in Nineteenth-Century British Fiction* (Bloomington: Indiana University Press, 1998) 77–83. See also D. A. Miller, *The Novel and the Police* (Berkeley: University of California Press, 1988).

Similarities of literary and legal structure and form are inseparable from a consideration of content. In his seminal study *The Rise of the Novel*, Ian Watt reminds us of the epistemological assumptions shared by readers and jurors:

> The novel's mode of imitating reality may...be equally well summarised in terms of the procedures of another group of specialists in epistemology, the jury in a court of law. Their expectations, and those of the novel reader coincide in many ways: both want to know all the particulars of a given case – the time and place of the occurrence: both must be satisfied as to the identity of the parties concerned, and will refuse to accept evidence about anyone called Sir Toby Belch or Mr. Badman – still less about a Chloe who has no surname and is "common as the air"; and they also expect the witnesses to tell the story in "his own words."[42]

Although Watt's analysis can be criticized – for his elevation of the genre of realistic writing above other forms less indebted to the discourse of empiricism and for the exceptions that undermine his thesis that the novel "arises" as a consequence of the union of Protestantism and capitalism (*Don Quixote*, for example)[43] – his insight into the nature of the reading process has engendered a number of valuable studies that have affirmed the intense interrelationship of literary, legal, and theological language in the period. Alexander Welsh, author of the seminal study, *Strong Representations: Narrative and Circumstantial Evidence in England* has drawn attention to this pronounced discursive engagement by uncovering what he calls "the evidentiary basis of...realism."[44] Just as the Royal Society yearned to generate experimentally verified factual information about the physical world, the law courts sought to establish facts of human action, and rationalist theologians sought to verify the facts of the New Testament record, so too the novel dramatized what John Bender has called acts of "ongoing probabilistic judgement" that generated vicarious knowledge for the attentive reader.[45] As standards of proof underwent modulation and both juridical and creative authors wrestled with definitions of doubt, both legal treatises and the novel sought to establish what was sufficient evidence to found a conviction of belief (in guilt or simply in the existence of a fact). Curiously, authors of fiction who were simultaneously employed in the legal profession (or its margins) changed stance as they moved genre. Fielding, author of the notoriously prosecutorial *Enquiry into the Causes of the Late Increase in Robbers*, frequently and somewhat unexpectedly drew attention to the plight of the wrongly accused in his fiction. *Tom Jones* [1949]

---

[42] Ian Watt, *The Rise of the Novel* (London: Chatto & Windus, 1957) 31.

[43] See Margaret Anne Doody, *The True Story of the Novel* (London: Fontana, 1996; repr. 1998) 1–2.

[44] Alexander Welsh, *Strong Representations: Narrative and Circumstantial Evidence in England* (Baltimore: Johns Hopkins University Press, 1992) 49.

[45] John Bender, "Novel Knowledge: Judgment, Experience, Experiment," in Clifford Siskin and William Warner, eds., *This Is Enlightenment*, forthcoming from University of Chicago Press, 2010.

Testimony, Witnessing

has been described as a submission for the defense, and the history of the novel as a genre has been labeled "the art of alibi."[46] That Tom Jones can be redeemed from the fate suggested by the template of the criminal biography – that he is a man "born to be hanged" – illuminates not just the triumph of one protean literary genre over its less sophisticated relative but also the curiously compromised nature of the commentary that the literary text can offer upon the law. In Ian Bell's words:

> The comic novel becomes...a kind of moot, a hypothetical working out of test cases, or a forensic tribunal without the pressure of immediate judgement or the painful responsibility of sentencing, to which all the relevant evidence might be presented. The author offers the controlled and disciplined comic novel as a fantastic replacement for the existing tribunals of justice, and, in doing so, finds room for a sustained, slyly insinuated critique of those present institutions.[47]

Consequently authors both denigrate the law and yet appropriate its methodologies for the composition of their tales, a sleight of hand most popularly illustrated in the opening chapter of Wilkie Collins's *The Woman in White* (1860). On the one hand, the case of imposture detailed within the narrative could not be heard in a court of law because the law is always "the servant of the long purse"; but on the other hand, Collins depends upon the presentation of testimony in the courtroom for any claim he seeks to make upon the reader's assent to the tale:

> As the Judge might have heard it once, so the Reader shall hear it now. No circumstance of importance, from the beginning to the end of the disclosure, shall be related on hearsay evidence...Thus the story here presented will be told by more than one pen, as the story of an offence against the laws is told in Court by more than one Witness – with the same object, in both cases, to present the truth always in its most direct and most intelligible aspect; and to trace the course of one complete series of events, by making the persons who have been most closely connected with them, at each successive stage, relate their own experience, word for word.[48]

A number of Victorian authors, such as Collins and his contemporaries William Thackeray and Charles Reade, had been called to the Bar prior to cementing their creative reputation, although the author most famous for his satirical portraits of the legal profession at midcentury, Charles Dickens, had instead trained as a legal clerk and then served as a freelance reporter in the Court of Doctors' Commons. Like Fielding, Dickens moved between the prosecutorial position adopted in his editorial and journalistic work, in which he frequently denounced the commercial

---

[46] See Welsh, ch. 3; Schramm, *Testimony*, ch. 2; and Jonathan H. Grossman, *The Art of Alibi: English Law Courts and the Novel* (Baltimore: Johns Hopkins Press, 2002).

[47] Ian Bell, *Literature and Crime in Augustan England* (London: Routledge, 1991) 204.

[48] Wilkie Collins, *The Woman in White* [1860] (Oxford: Oxford University Press, 1996) 5.

self-interest of the legal profession and the consequent rhetorical slipperiness of its practitioners, and the sentimental stance he adopted in his novels, in which he aligned himself with the figure of the wrongfully accused. Dickens's portrait of the notoriously inequitable Court of Chancery in *Bleak House* (1852–53) calls to mind Bakhtin's definition of the professional stratifications of language found within an ostensibly heteroglossic text – "the incorporated languages and socio-ideological belief systems, while of course utilized to refract the author's intentions, are unmasked and destroyed as something false, hypocritical, greedy, limited, narrowly rationalistic, inadequate to reality" (an appropriation that in turn reminds us that "literary language is not self-evident and is not in itself incontestable"[49]). It is perhaps the role of feeling in the formation of judgment (and the ways in which professional rhetoric may or may not legitimately engage with that feeling) that serves as the genuine ideological battlefield of authors and lawyers in the period.

The nineteenth century was characterized by increased specialization of knowledge and greater degrees of professionalization in law, medicine, and science. Insightful critical studies by Richard Sennett and Ronald Thomas have shown that the experience of subjectivity altered in this period: The disciplinary forces of the bureaucratic, industrial state ensured that ideas of character were increasingly replaced by notions of identity based upon documentary material (such as birth and death certificates, and medical records) that were capable of verification only by trained medical and legal personnel.[50] At the same time, authors were now seeking to earn a living from their writing (earlier generations had relied more heavily on patronage and private incomes), and Dickens's work habitually suggests that he envied the status and respectability of the other gentlemanly professions. There is much evidence in fictional texts of a heightened sense of competition between literary and legal discourse in Victorian England. The introduction of the Prisoners' Counsel Act of 1836 brought the work of barristers and literary authors into close and contested proximity.[51] The extension of full legal representation to those accused of felony coincided with the so-called Newgate Novel controversy of the 1830s and early 1840s, which saw novelists such as Dickens, Bulwer-Lytton, and Ainsworth arguing about the ethical implications of the sympathetic representation of criminality in fiction. As both groups spoke on behalf of those accused of transgression and undertook in a narratological defense of violence, this creative engagement – between the

---

[49] Bakhtin, *Dialogic Imagination*, 311–2.

[50] See Ronald Thomas, *Detective Fiction and the Rise of Forensic Science* (Cambridge: Cambridge University Press, 1999) ch. 1; Richard Sennett, *The Fall of Public Man* (Cambridge: Cambridge University Press, 1977).

[51] Whether professional advocacy in the courtroom affected the appearance of free indirect discourse in literature has been the subject of some critical speculation, although important differences between the two types of representation have been identified by Lisa Rodensky in *The Crime in Mind: Criminal Responsibility and the Victorian Novel* (Oxford: Oxford University Press, 2004).

Testimony, Witnessing

forensic advocacy of the courtroom and the narrative advocacy of fiction – influenced both the very material that authors chose to represent in their tales and the formal way in which such material was rendered.[52]

This sense of discursive competition was frequently manifest in ethical terms; authors of imaginative literature often claimed that fiction represented a higher court of appeal than the Old Bailey, and lawyers regularly argued that writers were preoccupied with emotion and sentimentality to the detriment of a proper assessment of the evidence in any given case. In its close attention to the law's ideological and semiotic weaknesses, fiction portrayed itself as a compassionate and equitable forum for the representation of material repressed or excluded by the law. This was often seen in cases in which a witness's testimony had been excluded as inadmissible in a court of law only to form the basis of a prolonged episode in a work of fiction that drew on original trial records (for example, Jo's story in *Bleak House*) – although this opportunity for fictional investigation clearly declined as the exclusionary regime of witness evidence was progressively dismantled. The representation of the law in utilitarian, reductionist terms thus promoted literature's claim to act as an ethical supplement to the legal lexicon[53] and the fictional reproduction of witness testimony was often the venue in which such a struggle occurred.

At stake was the moral influence of rhetoric (both printed and spoken) and in particular, the extent to which the influence of a text may move a potentially transgressive agent to action – barristers allegedly used sham defenses to effect what Anthony Trollope called "the manumission of murderers," but in their last words of confession on the scaffold, killers such as Francois Courvoisier (1840) registered the impact of novels like *Jack Sheppard* on their decision to resort to violence.[54] This self-reflexive debate was refracted in a wide range of novels at midcentury: Elizabeth Gaskell's *Mary Barton* (1848) addresses the perceived amorality of advocacy, and enthusiastic announcements of a defendant's innocence (and concomitant rejections of legal assistance) are to be found in George Eliot's *Felix Holt* (1866), in Charlotte Yonge's *The Trial* (1864), and in Dickens's *Posthumous Papers of the Pickwick Club* (1836–7, albeit in a breach of promise of marriage case) and *Bleak House*. *Bleak House* depicts George Rouncewell's vigorous denial of both guilt and legal assistance when wrongfully charged by Inspector Bucket with the murder of

---

[52] See Schramm, *Testimony*, 1–23, ch. 3; and "'The Anatomy of a Barrister's Tongue': Rhetoric, Satire, and the Victorian Bar in England," *Victorian Literature and Culture* (2004) 287–305.

[53] See, for example, Wai Chee Dimock, *Residues of Justice: Literature, Law, Philosophy* (Berkeley: University of California Press, 1996); Peter Goodrich, *Law in the Courts of Love: Literature and Other Minor Jurisprudences* (London: Routledge, 1996), and Dieter Paul Polloczek, *Literature and Legal Discourse: Equity and Ethics from Sterne to Conrad* (Cambridge: Cambridge University Press, 1999).

[54] Anthony Trollope, *Orley Farm* [1862] (London: Folio, 1993) 86. On Courvoisier's trial, see Schramm, *Testimony*, ch. 3; Cairns, ch. 5; and Allyson May, *The Bar and the Old Bailey, 1750–1850* (Chapel Hill: University of North Carolina Press, 2003) ch. 4.

Tulkinghorn. Expressing Dickens's own anxieties about the morality of advocacy (which can be located in his pseudonymous letters to the *Morning Chronicle* as early as 1840), George sees the representation of his interests by another as opening up the possibility of a sham defense, which could lead in turn to an acquittal based upon a technicality. Instead, George wants his innocence established on substantive grounds: "I must come off clear and full or not at all." True, transparent innocence should establish itself despite the manipulation of evidence by the prosecution, and there must be an authentic correspondence between testimony and verdict:

> [W]hen I hear stated against me what is true, I say it's true; and when they tell me, "whatever you say will be used," I tell them I don't mind that: I mean it to be used. If they can't make me innocent out of the whole truth, they are not likely to do it out of anything less, or anything else. And if they are, it's worth nothing to me.[55]

Unlike the Victorian courtroom, which could not hear the accused if he chose to employ counsel, Victorian fiction insists time and time again on access to the first-person speech of the prisoner at the point at which a verdict is obtained – narrative justice must be substantive as well as apparent.[56] In the age of print culture, nostalgia persists here for the power of the voice, and in particular for an innocence that requires no professional interpretation.[57] The latter is in part indicative of the influence of melodrama, a theatrical form that began in France shortly after the Revolution, and that depended upon "the dramaturgy of virtue misprized and eventually recognized."[58] According to Juliet John, "Dickens's belief in the principles of communality and cultural inclusivity made the notion of a psyche-centred approach to people and society seem individualistic, divisive, and potentially elitist" – consequently, he was drawn to dramatic exaggeration, which delineated clearly between extremes of vice and virtue and which eroded distinctions between high art and popular culture "as a point of ideological principle."[59] That the triumph of the language of fiction (and its domains of affect and sentiment) invariably involved the defeat of the law reveals Dickens's indebtedness to these melodramatic structures of emplotment.

In *Strong Representations*, Welsh argues that the intensity of fiction's engagement with the law was diminishing by the 1870s and that testimony in these later works

---

[55] Charles Dickens, *Bleak House* [1852–3] (Oxford: Oxford University Press, 1948; repr. 1978) ch. Lii, 706–7.

[56] See Schramm, *Testimony*, 180–92.

[57] See Ivan Krielkamp, *Voice and the Victorian Storyteller* (Cambridge: Cambridge University Press, 2006) 1–7.

[58] Peter Brooks, *The Melodramatic Imagination: Balzac, Henry James, Melodrama, and the Mode of Excess* (New Haven: Yale University Press, 1976; repr. 1995) 27.

[59] Juliet John, *Dickens' Villains: Melodrama, Character, Popular Culture* (Oxford: Oxford University Press, 2001) 3, 9.

Testimony, Witnessing

manifests itself in its weaker form as "stories of personal experience."[60] The rationalist phase of theological enquiry (in which religion too was preoccupied with the accuracy of the scriptural record) may also be seen to end at mid-century:[61] Mrs. Humphry Ward's fictional study of the need for a scientific approach to the study of religious testimony, *Robert Elsmere* (1882), is a retrospective account of the turmoil of the previous generation. Aesthetic innovation (in novels such as *Middlemarch* [1872] and the mature works of Thomas Hardy) increasingly arose from the interface of literature and Darwinian science and a concomitant loss of belief in models of theological omnipotence. At the same time, autobiography as a genre outgrew its earlier associations with political upheaval and life-writing enjoyed renewed popularity, independent of any appeal it could make to factual value. Although evidentiary and testimonial material remained of interest to modernist writers of fiction, it was often deployed to suggest the fundamental unknowability of events and their resistance to straightforward interpretation (see, for example, Jim's epistemologically opaque testimony to the enquiry investigating the sinking of the *Patna* in Joseph Conrad's *Lord Jim* (1899) and Adele's agonized inability to account for the episode in the Marabar Caves in E. M. Forster's A *Passage to India* (1924). Yet the power of legal tropes to organize and interrogate human experience persists in contemporary fiction, with writers as diverse as John Banville (*The Book of Evidence* [1989]), Peter Carey (*The True History of the Kelly Gang* [2000]), Richard Flanagan (*Gould's Book of Fish* [2002]), and Elliot Perlman (*Seven Types of Ambiguity* [2003]) all using testimonial form to great effect in narratives that pay homage to their eighteenth- and nineteenth-century fictional predecessors.

The Current Status of Testimony in the Humanities

The evidentiary status of testimony depends upon a foundational question of epistemology – whether "truth" is to be found in the generation of words by the body of the eyewitness or whether the disinterested severance of this connection by professionals best promotes impartial discovery of who we actually are and what we can know. In Samuel Richardson's terms, is "speech the heart's dictation" or is the body capable of some form of automatic writing that is most accurately read by another? Tensions inevitably arise between the novel's intuition that "in a human being, there is always something that only he can reveal, in a free act of self-consciousness and discourse, something that does not submit to an externalizing, second-hand definition"[62] – and the vocabulary of subjectivity in the court reports of the eighteenth and nineteenth

---

[60] Welsh, ch. 5.

[61] See, for example, Mark Pattison, "Tendencies of Religious Thought in England 1688–1750," in *Essays and Reviews* (London: Parker, 1860) 259.

[62] Mikhail Bakhtin, *Problems of Dostoevsky's Poetics*, Caryl Emerson, ed. and trans. (Minneapolis: Minnesota University Press, 1984) 58.

centuries in which the judge regularly calls upon two witnesses to "*give* the accused a character" (in other words, that even identity is something to be attributed to us externally by others). Whereas Michel Foucault privileged confession as a manifestation of authentic self-knowledge, John Kucich reminds us that "the missing piece in [Foucault's] account of confession is an examination of its inherent undependability: the new spaces for lying that it opens."[63] First-person speech must thus be scrutinized with care.

Yet despite these interpretative difficulties (frequently rehearsed in histories of rhetoric), the role of the witness in twentieth-century historiography is well established. For scholars of testimony such as Richard Weisberg and Shoshana Felman, modern history is "an Era of Testimony"[64] – in Elie Wiesel's words, "our generation [has] invented a new literature . . . [w]e have all been witnesses and we all feel we have to bear testimony for the future."[65] Scholars of Holocaust literature define "testimony" as broadly inclusive of both factual accounts of wartime atrocities and fictionalized responses that also seek to bear witness to genocide. For Weisberg, first-person narratives are valuable for the very reason that they tend to "undermine 'authoritative' testimony" promulgated by those in power: "in the context of our own generation, the eye-witness gains credibility just as the political or institutional or cultural account is precisely devalued."[66] The representation of first-person speech, in both fiction and historiography, thus carries great ethical weight: It often purports to inscribe the voice of those at the social margins and is frequently a medium for the articulation of suffering and persecution. As both a story of personal experience and a type of evidence, testimony remains a crucial organizational principle of journalism and a number of narrative art-forms, including autobiography, documentaries, and fiction.

The Current Status of Testimony in the Law

The elimination of the complex rules of exclusion in the course of the nineteenth century also dealt with the worst of the anomalies between civil and criminal trial praxis. Current jurisprudential debate highlights a number of possible developments in the law of evidence that may impact upon the reception of witness testimony – for example, the influential English jurist Colin Tapper includes amongst the most prominent contemporary issues, the increasing tendency to admit evidence and then offer juries guidelines as to the assessment of its weight; the question of whether or

---

[63] John Kucich, *The Power of Lies: Transgression in Victorian Fiction* (Ithaca: Cornell University Press, 1994) 18.
[64] Shoshana Felman and Dori Laub, *Testimony: Crises of Witnessing in Literature, Psychoanalysis, and History* (New York: Routledge, 1992) 5.
[65] Elie Wiesel, ed., *Dimensions of the Holocaust* (Evanston: Northwestern University Press, 1977) 9.
[66] Richard Weisberg, "Editor's Preface," *Cardozo Studies in Law and Literature* 3 (1991) no. 2, i–iii.

Testimony, Witnessing

not the law of evidence can and should be the subject of codification (as undertaken, for example, by Sir James Fitzjames Stephen, whose Indian Evidence Act of 1872 serves as the basis of a number of Evidence Acts throughout the Commonwealth); the impact of European Union law such as the European Convention on Human Rights on domestic legislation and trial process; and the evaluative issues raised by psychological and investigative research into the inherent reliability or otherwise of contentious eyewitness evidence.[67] It is widely recognized by jurists and criminologists, for example, that identification evidence – statements by witnesses that place a particular person at the scene of a crime – is more likely than not to be untrustworthy, less for reasons of explicit mendacity than because of the psychological pressures endured when experiencing or witnessing criminal activity, and the means of assessing the reliability of such material is now the subject of regular academic debate.[68] Although jury deliberation remains a private and privileged activity, and little can thus be known about the ways in which jurors receive such evidence, new studies continue to illuminate the psychology of the witnessing process. In their attention to such issues as agency, audience, duress, voluntariness, mistake, and misapprehension, these studies both pioneer new directions in the law and remind us of the substantial overlap between literary and legal approaches to first-person narration.

[67] Tapper, 1–5, 243–51, 747–66.
[68] See for example, Tom Bingham, "Assessing Contentious Eyewitness Evidence: A Judicial View," *Witness Testimony: Psychological, Investigative, and Evidential Perspectives*, Anthony Heaton-Armstrong et al., eds. (Oxford: Oxford University Press, 2006) 327–43.

19

Judgment in Law and the Humanities

Desmond Manderson

The interdisciplinary temperament of "Law and the Humanities" is both perplexing for law and intriguing for the humanities. This perplexity and this intrigue come to a head precisely over one of the most important institutional necessities and problems of law: judgment. If a text is not a truth but a debate; if it embodies not one story or meaning but many; if a statute, let us say, or a court case cannot be neatly separated from literature, or rhetoric, or politics – then there is literature, and rhetoric, and politics, in every interpretation and in every decision. A philosophical treatise can be subversive, open-ended, and speculative; a literary reading probably should be. A judge, however, must *decide* what this text means, whether this statute applies, who wins, who loses, and even sometimes, who lives and who dies.[1] One of the central questions that the influence of the humanities on law raises is this: how, and with what legitimacy, can judgment take place if the texts on which judges base their decision do not – even in principle, let alone in practice – yield "one right answer." The question of judgment becomes then a serious problem. It is a problem for positivists, of course, who entirely reject this approach to interpretation and meaning. It is no less a problem for scholars of the humanities in law, who have to try to find an answer to it if they wish to be relevant to legal institutions at all.

Over the past few years, as the question of judgment has ever more urgently weighed upon scholars within the broad church of the humanities, at least two kinds of answers have emerged: one broadly speaking influenced by Derrida's later work[2] and the other, equally schematically, taking Heidegger as its point of

---

[1] Austin Sarat, *When the State Kills* (Princeton, NJ: Princeton University Press, 2002).

[2] Jacques Derrida, "Force of Law: The Mystical Foundation of Authority," (1990) 11 *Cardozo Law Review* 919–1045, 959; Jacques Derrida, *Acts of Religion*, Gil Anidjar, ed. (New York: Routledge, 2002), 228–98. See also, for example, *The Gift of Death* (Chicago: University of Chicago Press, 1995); *On Cosmopolitanism and Forgiveness*, Mark Dooley and Michael Hughes, trans. (London: Routledge, 2002).

Judgment in Law and the Humanities

departure.[3] Now these two streams draw very closely on a common intellectual tradition and share many points of similarity. Both, for example, think that positivism is incapable of either adequately describing the nature of legal reasoning or seriously justifying its core claim that law is a system of determinate rules capable of neutral application. Nevertheless I wish to insist in this chapter that the two strands part company on the crucial question of judgment in law.

I have chosen two paradigmatic texts to highlight this comparison: Derrida's "Force of Law," and a recent history of German legal positivism by Roger Berkowitz.[4] The former, of course, is one of the field's seminal contributions. The latter is exemplary, I think, because it addresses the question of judgment and justice explicitly. In so doing it draws out Heideggerian resonances that we find in a number of recent works: in much of Philippe Nonet's extraordinarily imagined work on Heidegger and on the Greeks, in the elegant and persuasive historical work of Marianne Constable's *Just Silences*, in the exceptionally careful scholarship of Mark Antaki's critiques of human rights, and in Richard Weisberg's recent research on Nietzsche, to name but a few.[5] One might go further and note the more general burgeoning of interest within legal academia in not only Heidegger but also Carl Schmitt.[6]

In this chapter I focus on these two divergent paths now open to Law and the Humanities. The key difference between them (although not everyone will agree) lies in the transcendentalism – I would say the Romanticism – of the latter and the pragmatism – I would say the humanism – of the former. I am not content to simply *note* this split. Could a scholar committed to Law and the Humanities sit on the fence, pretending to describe impartially a discourse rather than actively

---

[3] See for example, Ian Ward, *Law, Philosophy, and National Socialism: Heidegger, Schmitt, and Radbruch* (Herbert & Cie Lang AG, 1992); Oren Ben-Dor, *Thinking about Law: In Silence with Heidegger* (Oxford: Hart Publishing, 2007).

[4] Roger Berkowitz, *The Gift of Science: Leibniz and the Modern Legal Tradition* (Cambridge, MA: Harvard University Press, 2005).

[5] Philippe Nonet, "Antigone's Law" (2006) 2 *Law Culture and the Humanities* 314–35; "What is Positive Law?" (1990) 100 *Yale Law Journal* 667; "Technique and Law," *Legality and Community*, Kagan, Krygier, and Winston, eds. (New York: Rowman, 2002); Marianne Constable, *Just Silences: The Limits and Possibilities of Modern Law* (Princeton, NJ: Princeton University Press, 2005); Mark Antaki, "The World(lessness) of Human Rights" (2004) 49 *McGill Law Journal* 203; *Genealogy of Crimes Against Humanity*, unpublished doctoral dissertation, University of California Berkeley, 2005; Richard Weisberg, "Nietzsche's Hermeneutics: Good and Bad Interpreters of Texts," *Nietzsche and Legal Theory: Half-Written Laws*, Peter Goodrich and Mariana Valverde, eds. (New York: Routledge, 2005).

[6] See for example in addition to the previous footnote, Ian Ward, *Law, Philosophy and National Socialism: Heidegger, Schmitt, and Radbruch* (Herbert & Cie Lang AG, 1992); Oren Ben-Dor, *Thinking about Law: In Silence with Heidegger* (Oxford: Hart Publishing, 2007); Gillian Rose, *Dialectic of Nihilism, Post-Structuralism, and Law* (Oxford: Blackwell, 1984); David Dyzenhaus: *Law as Politics: Carl Schmitt's Critique of Liberalism* (Chapel Hill: Duke University Press, 1998); Mark Antaki, "Carl Schmitt's Nomos of the Earth" (2004) 42 *Osgoode Hall Law Journal* 317; Carl Schmitt, *Political Theology: Four Chapters on the Concept of Sovereignty*, George Schwab, ed. (Chicago: University of Chicago Press, 2006); *Legality and Legitimacy* (Chapel Hill: Duke University Press, 2004); Giorgio Agamben, *State of Exception*, Kevin Atell, trans. (Chicago: University of Chicago Press, 2005).

engaging in its evolution? No, I am not a judge hiding my opinions like lingerie beneath the long black robes of law's neutrality.[7] There is an argument in this chapter. First, there is a lot at stake here. The difference between the two strands of antipositivism generated by recent work in Law and the Humanities has profound implications for our understanding of what it means to interpret a law or to make a legal decision. Second, we have both social and intellectual reasons to prefer the humanist perspective to its Romantic alternative. Drawing on the language of deconstruction and the experience of literature that lies at its heart, I want to defend an understanding of the purpose and nature of legal judgment that places as its central concern the provisional and multivocal experience of human discourse. From this we might develop a theory of judgment that is neither positivist *nor* Romantic.

Critiques of Positivism and the Transcendence of Justice

Force of Law

For many years now, legal positivism has come in for a barrage of criticism: first from realists[8] and Marxists,[9] then in the wake of the civil rights movement from feminists and race theorists, and in the 1980s from critical legal studies.[10] The highlight of the past fifteen years has been the contribution of deconstruction[11] to this critique. For Derrida, justice embodies two opposing impulses: equal treatment and singular respect. It expresses an aspiration toward "law or right, legitimacy or legality, stabilisable and statutory, calculable, a system of regulated and coded

---

[7] See "Black Robes with Humans Inside Them," *New York Times*, December 12, 2000, A1.

[8] Karl Llewellyn, *Jurisprudence: Realism in Theory and Practice* (Chicago: University of Chicago Press, 1962); Jerome Frank, *Law and the Modern Mind* (New York: Brentano's, 1930); Julius Stone, *Legal System and Lawyer, Reasonings* (Stanford, CA: Stanford University Press, 1964).

[9] See the discussion in Cameron Stewart, "The Rule of Law and the Tinkerbell Effect: Theoretical Considerations, Criticisms, and Justifications for the Rule of Law" (2004) 4 *Macquarie Law Journal* 135–64; Evgeny Pashukanis, *Selected Writings on Marxism and Law*, P. Beirne and R. Sharlet, eds. (London and New York: Academic Press, 1980).

[10] The citations would be endless: see Jorge Borges, "The Library of Babel" in *Ficciones* (New York: Grove Press, 1962 [1956]) 79–89. Purely for notable illustrations, I refer the reader to the work of Roberto Unger, *Knowledge and Politics* (New York: Free Press, 1984); *The Critical Legal Studies Movement* (Cambridge, MA: Harvard University Press, 1986); Mark Kelman, "Trashing," (1984) 36 *Stanford Law Review* 293; and for feminist critiques of positivism, see the work of Catherine MacKinnon, *Towards a Feminist Theory of the State* (Cambridge, MA: Harvard University Press, 1991).

[11] Derrida, "Force of Law"; Dennis Patterson, ed., *Postmodernism and Law* (Dartmouth: Ashgate, 1994); Allan Hunt, "The Big Fear: Law Confronts Postmodernism," 35 *McGill Law Journal* 507; Jack Balkin, Deconstructive Practice and Legal Theory, 96 *Yale Law Journal* 743 (1987); Costas Douzinas, Peter Goodrich, and Yifat Hachamovitch, *Politics, Postmodernity, and Critical Legal Studies: The Legality of the Contingent* (London: Routledge, 1994); Costas Douzinas, Ronnie Warrington, and Shaun McVeigh, *Postmodern Jurisprudence: The Law of Texts in the Texts of Law* (London: Routledge, 1991).

Judgment in Law and the Humanities

prescriptions"[12] and at the same time the desire for a unique and singular response to a particular situation and person asking for our help. Justice is general *and* unique; it involves treating everybody the same and treating everybody differently, applying the law . . . and not.

> Our common axiom is that to be just or unjust and to exercise justice, I must be free and responsible for my actions, my behaviour, my thought, my decision. But if the act simply consists of applying a rule, of enacting a program or effecting a calculation, we might say that it is legal, that it conforms to law, but we would be wrong to say that the decision was just . . . In short, for a decision to be just and responsible it must, in its proper moment if there is one, be both regulated and without regulation: it must conserve the law and also destroy it or suspend it enough to have to reinvent it in each case.[13]

If we could separate justice from law then this would not pose a problem. Lawyers could just apply the rules, and think about justice on their days off. This is of course the strategy adopted by most standard positivist theories of judgment; but it will not do.[14] Every legal decision requires us to make a judgment as to the applicability of prior general norms to the *necessarily* different and singular situation before us. Although cases in what H. L. A. Hart called the penumbra dramatize it, in fact every case requires us to make the same kind of choice. We must still judge if this unique case is the same as or different from the past, and this is of course the very judgment that the past *cannot ever help us with*. It does not matter whether we are talking about legal judgment in the context of statutory interpretation, a Code, a Constitution, or case law. The necessary passage of time between the enunciation of a norm and its application, and the necessary uniqueness of the present judgment by comparison to its prior instances, inevitably opens up a space for decision.[15]

The paradoxical choice and conflict that judgment always opens up, then, is hardwired into law no less than justice. Both demand of us that we respect the rules in their utmost generality and the individual in his utter specificity: that we attend to the constructive power of the past as a way of controlling the future, and the reconstructive power of the present as a way of reinterpreting that past. This complicated backward-and-forward dynamic is essential to all decision making – to all *reading,* insists the humanities – and no rules could ever tell us exactly how to

---

[12] Derrida, "Force of Law."

[13] Ibid., 961.

[14] H. L. A. Hart, "Positivism and the Separation of Law and Morals," (1957–8) 71 *Harvard Law Review* 593; Joseph Raz, *The Authority of Law* (Oxford: Clarendon Press, 1979); Tom Campbell, *The Legal Theory of Ethical Positivism* (Dartmouth: Ashgate, 1996); Andrei Marmor, "Legal Positivism: Still Descriptive and Morally Neutral" (2006) 26 *Oxford Journal of Legal Studies* 683–704. In some ways, these views all go back to the great work of Hans Kelsen, *General Theory of Law and State*, Wedberg, trans. (1945).

[15] Richard Beardsworth, *Derrida and the Political* (London and New York: Routledge, 1996) 110. Gerald Postema, "On the Moral Presence of our Past," (1991) 36 *McGill Law Journal* 1153–80.

accomplish it. Samuel Beckett wrote, "we are not merely more weary because of yesterday, we are other."[16] Perhaps we are only a little bit wearier than yesterday, or a little bit other, but we can never know without first thinking about it. The judge is bound, says the positivist. The judge is bound to choose, say I.

Accordingly, an element of incalculability, irreducible to formal rules, necessarily enters into the moment of legal judgment. This element continually unsettles our established rules and categories and forces us to reopen their meaning at the very moment we apply them. Neither justice nor law is capable of being reduced to "juridical-moral rules, norms or representations, with an inevitable totalising horizon," some one-way track by which the past could stop us thinking in the present about the future. In law as in language,[17] in philosophy as in literature, such a tyranny is simply not possible. The meaning of a text always has the possibility of changing in light of changed circumstances. This is not a tragedy. On the contrary, as Derrida remarks, "we may even see in this a stroke of luck for politics, for all historical progress."[18]

This is hardly so very different from what was said, fifty years ago, by Lon Fuller. In debating Hart, he too insisted that it is just not *possible* to apply a rule without being forced, in some measure, to consider its meaning in relation to a greater framework or set of principles that are themselves, if they are not to fall foul of the logic of infinite regression, incapable of reduction to a perspicuous form of words.[19] So positivist theories find themselves confronted by a challenge based on the nature of "law" and the nature of "language," a challenge that points to the *illimitable* moment of judgment that lies at the core of legal interpretation.

The problem, not just for lawyers I think but for anyone interested in social justice, is that such an approach to interpretation equally challenges the standard theory of the rule of law. It too sets great store by the idea that judges, in following the law, are simply applying guidelines whose implications are already well known (or at least knowable) by the community.[20] As Hart wrote, "If it were not possible to communicate general standards of conduct which multitudes of individuals could *understand, without further direction,* as requiring from them certain conduct when occasion arose, nothing that we now recognize as law could exist."[21] Accordingly, as

---

[16] Samuel Beckett, *Proust* (London: Grove Press, 1957 [1931]) 3.

[17] Jacques Derrida, *Of Grammatology*, Gayatri C. Spivak, trans. (Baltimore: Johns Hopkins University Press, 1976 [1967]).

[18] Derrida, "Force of Law," 949.

[19] Lon Fuller, "Positivism and Fidelity to Law: A Reply to Professor Hart," (1957–8) 71 *Harvard Law Review* 630.

[20] H. L. A. Hart, *Concept of Law* (Oxford: Clarendon Press, 1960), and 'Positivism'; Heydon Dyson, "Judicial Activism and the Rule of Law" (2003) 23 *Australian Bar Review* 110; John Gava, "Another Blast from the Past or Why the Left Should Embrace Strict Legalism" (2003) 27 *Melbourne University Law Review* 7.

[21] Hart, *Concept*, 121. Italics added.

Judgment in Law and the Humanities

Langille observes, if "language is indeterminate, unstable, subject to manipulation and incapable of expressing rules and principles which constrain judges... the law is a failure on its own terms and the virtues of the rule of law are impossible to secure."[22] To the extent that the rule of law involves certainty of judgment,[23] the implications of connecting law to the humanities, and jurisprudence to continental philosophy, are problematic to say the least.

This chapter is not interested in looking at positivist responses to this critique.[24] Yet although I find myself persuaded by Derrida's approach to the problem of judgment, there is nevertheless plenty here that still troubles me. Practically, what can the rule of law mean in light of this critique? Philosophically, what are the implications of this account of justice? If judgement involves "madness," "a moment of undecidability"[25] in which the judge merely intuits what true justice demands referable to nothing but his own manifest sense of it, like some invisible trump, what then? Have we simply replaced the positivists' tyranny of the text with a priesthood of judges? Are we replaying the Reformation, which once before pitted direct communication with God against the primacy of the written word – only this time in reverse?

Gift of Science

My concern has been further sharpened by a new historical critique of legal positivism that touches on these very points. *The Gift of Science,* by Roger Berkowitz, offers legal history refracted through Heidegger[26] and stands, I think, for one way in which the challenge that Law and the Humanities poses to the question of legal and institutional judgment might be met. Berkowitz draws on approaches to the relationship of law and justice, which, as I noted earlier, have been developing among a number of writers in recent years. Nevertheless, Berkowitz is my focus here because he directly confronts the question of legal judgment – how is it to be understood and how is it to be justified? In doing so he defends explicitly – perhaps, in fairness to other commentators such as Constable, the word "starkly" would be better – the social and institutional implications of his answers.

---

[22] Brian Langille, "Revolution without Foundation: The Grammar of Scepticism and Law," (1988) 33 *McGill Law Journal* 451, 455.

[23] Lon Fuller, *The Morality of Law* (New Haven: Yale University Press, 1964); Colleen Murphy, "The Moral Value of the Rule of Law" (2005) 24 *Law and Philosophy* 239–62; Tom Campbell, *Legal Theory, and Justice,* 2nd ed. (London and New York: Macmillan, 2001).

[24] But see for a careful reflection on many of these issues, Peter Drahos and Stephen Parker, "The Indeterminacy Paradox in Law" (1991) 21 *University of Western Australia Law Review* 305–19; and "Rule Following, Rule Scepticism, and Indeterminacy in Law: A Conventional Account" (1992) 5 *Ratio Juris* 109–19.

[25] Derrida, "Force of Law."

[26] Berkowitz, *The Gift of Science,* e.g., Introduction.

The Gift of Science studies with great care the German positivist tradition from the late seventeenth century up to the enactment of that pinnacle of legal systematization, the *Bürgerliches Gesetzbuches* (BGB) of 1900. We might summarize Berkowitz's thesis as follows: Modernity in law involves the attempt to do without God as the foundation and origin of law. We see this first in Leibniz, although he remains a transitional figure in many ways (as was Newton in other fields), and then with increasing force in the theorists of German positive law who followed: Svarez, Savigny, and Jhering. Absent God, law ceases to be a coherent entity with an "existence outside of its posited existence in rules, norms, and conventions."[27] This creates a problem for law's authority. Without God – or nature, or tradition, for that matter – who is to say what justice really requires of us?

The answer given in modernity goes by the name of science or, we might say, the objective text.[28] Science is used compendiously here to suggest a way of thinking that has in many fields aimed to provide empirical, verifiable, objective answers to problems, grounded in certainties of logic, reason, and human knowledge. Science is the opposite of faith: It is proof not truth, human not divine. This was the "gift" that was intended to give back to law the sure foundation that had been destroyed.

> Leibniz's introduction of the principle of sufficient reason into jurisprudence promised to give law the scientific grounds for its authority that it so dearly desires... Similarly, law too must have a reason posited for it if it is to exist. Law, in other words, does not exist in and of itself as a natural or traditional insight into what is right and fitting... Law is subordinated to its reasons and justifications.[29]

In place of authority, mere justifications; in place of justice, mere law. In place of *Recht* or *droit*, a coherent body of eternal principles, *gesetz* or *lois*, a vast and constantly expanding list of interdictions and procedures produced in conformity with and changeable by human will. This is the story of modern law from Leibniz to the BGB.

Using the interdisciplinary tools of Law and the Humanities, one could easily expand our perspective and see similar trends throughout the West, as ideas of religious or inherent authority weakened. In classical music, to take one example, we see at the time of the Enlightenment the decline of improvisation and its replacement by increasingly detailed instructions that aim to bind performers to the composer's will. This too reorients authority from the present to the past and from the spirit to the letter of the law; it marks a shift in the locus of meaning from the insightful creativity of the judge/performer to the procedurally legitimated straitjacket imposed

---

[27] Ibid., xvi.
[28] Ibid., 156.
[29] Ibid., 51.

Judgment in Law and the Humanities

by the legislator/composer.[30] Indeed, the Reformation itself was part of this great historical transition from faith to science, from authority to reason, and from judges' responsibility to unique persons to their obedience to general texts.[31]

Berkowitz's arguments go well beyond historical analysis. They concern the present not the past. These arguments are not presented in a systemic form, but they appear insistently throughout the book and reflect a deeply held set of commitments. Berkowitz does us a great service in putting his cards on the table. "The gift of science," he argues, is a poisoned chalice that did and must fail to provide law with the certainty, the decision-making capacity, and the justification that it seeks. One can see in this argument an affinity with the deconstruction of rules and the relationship between law and justice, which we observed earlier. On the one hand, "to say that 'deconstruction is justice'... is to insist, rightly, that law cannot be separated from an ideal of transcendental justice." On the other, it is only once modern law becomes a "product of scientific knowledge... willed, posited, and in need of scientific justification," from which the transcendent element of law has been rigorously excluded, that "the indeterminacy of law comes to be such a forbidding problem."[32]

Berkowitz draws from this several important conclusions that concern not only change but also loss. In the first place, with the rise of positivism we have lost the relationship between law and justice, which for Berkowitz is crucial to the act of judgment. Indeed, the plea to reforge that relationship runs through *The Gift of Science* from its very first sentence: "Justice has fled our world."[33] This justice is posed throughout as "transcendent."[34] The scientific objectivity that modern law promises but fails to deliver suppresses precisely "the legal idea of justice... in its connection with transcendence... the beautiful dream of transcendence."[35] The meaning of justice as transcendence is never adequately explained. We can see it in the context of Derrida or even, perhaps, Fuller. Berkowitz, following Nonet, following Heidegger, goes much further than this. Justice for him imports insight into the "ethical unity" of law.[36]

Justice as law's "ethical unity" appears to transcend not only specific rules but also individual or conflicting interests in favor of the unification of the community. "Active thinking... is irreducible to rules or laws... Similarly, justice demands that man think and in thinking transcend the limits of his unique self and enter into an

---

[30] See Desmond Manderson, "Et Lex Perpetua: Formalism in Law and Music" (1999) 20 *Cardozo Law Review* 1621–48; "*Statuta* v Acts," 7 *Yale Journal of Law and Humanities* (1995) 317–66.

[31] David Trubek, "Max Weber on Law and the Rise of Capitalism" (1972) *Wisconsin Law Review* 720–53; Max Weber, *Law in Economy and* Society (Cambridge, MA: Harvard University Press, 1954).

[32] Berkowitz, *The Gift of Science*, xv.

[33] Ibid., ix; see also, among many examples, xiii, and 159–60.

[34] Ibid., e.g., at x, xiii, xv, 90, 139, and *passim*.

[35] Ibid., 159–60.

[36] Ibid., 108.

ethical community with others. The dream of justice, in other words, is the dream of transcendence."[37]

The second loss is "that law might actually *be* – that it might actually have an existence – outside of its posited existence in rules, norms, and conventions."[38] Here we begin to see the powerful antihumanism of Heidegger, which clearly forms the philosophical spine of these suppositions, as read through Philippe Nonet's influential work on Heidegger and law, to which Berkowitz among others is deeply indebted.[39] Law is "more than human." It is not just our tool to fashion and justify as we wish. On the contrary, it "exists in and of itself," preceding human needs or social ambitions. It is the emanation of an "already presupposed ethical world."[40]

What we have seen so far is that legal judgment, on this view, cannot be tied down to the failed positivist faith in preexisting rules and objectively interpreted texts. What is proposed to replace it is the judge who has a sense of justice that transcends not just the rules, but the human and social world itself. How is this unified ethical world to be discerned? The third loss for Berkowitz, and it is one to which he returns repeatedly, is the "loss of insight." "Natural law . . . previously knowable only through a free and active insight into an incalculable yet manifest sense of divine and human justice, increasingly assumes the character of an instrument of scientifically knowable will." Elsewhere this insight is referred to as "natural" whereas the "scientific knowing of law" is characterized – in language that might recall for us that of Sir Edward Coke – as "artificial."[41] So on this view, true judgment occurs through an "insightful activity of justice"[42] that, as the word implies, is not to be articulated and still less to be justified. It is to be divined.

Divined is the right word. If one wonders who is to be entrusted with this insightful activity, one encounters a fourth loss – that of authority. For Berkowitz, authority, too, is natural and intrinsic. It is the opposite of "legitimacy" that, like rules or the norms of social justice, demands that the judge be held accountable for his decisions by the giving of reasons. Indeed, we need this constant questioning and justification of decisions precisely because "law loses its natural claim to authority."[43] Authority, like justice and insight, does not *require* justification.[44] Instead, it is founded in what is variously called "nature" or "tradition," or "religion." It is "the natural connection with the divine"[45] – note, natural – and law's "necessary connection to the ineffable"[46] – note, necessary – that grants this authority, provides this insight,

---

[37] Ibid., x.

[38] Ibid., xvi.

[39] Ibid., e.g. x, xx, 11, 28. See in particular Nonet, "Antigone's Law" and "Technique and Law."

[40] Ibid., 139, 51, xii.

[41] Berkowitz, 24, 107. See Edward Coke, *Prohibitions del Roy* (1608) 12 Co. *Rep.* 63; 77 E.R. 1342.

[42] Berkowitz, *The Gift of Science*, 16.

[43] Ibid., 7.

[44] Ibid.

[45] Ibid., 159.

[46] Ibid., xvi.

Judgment in Law and the Humanities

comprehends this unity, and imparts this transcendence. The greatest loss in a litany of losses is the loss of God.

Berkowitz does not merely describe a vanished worldview: he advocates its renaissance. The word insight shows us how closely Berkowitz, along with others working in this tradition, allies himself to an approach to law that has been corrupted by positivist science. The scholar who comes in for the most sympathetic attention is Savigny, and in Berkowitz's analysis, the key word that underscores his approval of Savigny is "insight." Savigny fights a rearguard action in attempting to return the practice of insight to law.[47] Throughout, there is a fusion between Savigny's ideas about insight, Savigny as himself blessed with insight, and his approach that merits the accolade "insightful."[48] Nothing could be clearer then, but that the very same insight that marks the prescientific approach to law is the foundation of Berkowitz's own. An intense longing pervades the book, as it is equally clear in Nonet that there "would seem to be a mourning, or, rather, melancholic longing for a lost utopia, a world without the things the law decides."[49]

From Loss to Lack

The Deconstructive Moment

My question is: Is this the shore on which the search for judgment has been beached? Have we escaped the Scylla of formalism only to be cast into this Charybdis of unreason? More specifically, does this version of judgment as transcendence necessarily follow from the critique of positivism I outlined previously?[50] Suppose one accepts that a responsible legal judgment must "be both regulated and without regulation: it must conserve the law and also destroy it or suspend it enough to have to reinvent it in each case."[51] Suppose that some idea of justice is a necessary element of legal interpretation but is indeed irreducible to a Code or *gesetzbuch*. Must one fall back on those figures whose loss Berkowitz mourns: authority unquestioned, justice ineffable, law natural, God? If not, where precisely is the exit ramp?

Many have read Derrida this way. Jack Balkin, for one, insists that justice for Derrida is indeed "transcendent": unreasoned, inexplicable, and instinctive.[52] So too

---

[47] Ibid., 112.

[48] Ibid., 121–9.

[49] Andrew Norris, "Heideggerian Law Beyond Law?" (2006) 2 *Law, Culture, and the Humanities* 341, 348.

[50] Balkin, for one, lumps together all these approaches as species of "anti-humanist philosophy," although the term in relation to Derrida is too bizarre to require further attention here: Jack Balkin, "Deconstruction's Legal Career" (2005) 27 *Cardozo Law Review* 719, 719–20, and *passim*.

[51] Derrida, "Force of Law," 961.

[52] Jack Balkin, "Deconstruction's Legal Career"; "Transcendental Deconstruction, Transcendent Justice," (1994) 92 *Michigan Law Review* 1131; Christopher Norris, *Deconstruction: Theory and Practice* (London: Routledge, 1991).

Gillian Rose takes to task the "new ethics" of "Messianic deconstruction" – by which term she encompasses both Levinas and Derrida – because it disdains justification in favor of a "sacralized polity."[53] In a remark that seems apposite, she proclaims herself committed "to return philosophy from her pathos to her logos."[54] However fair this criticism might be of Levinas[55] or, although with quite other implications, of Heidegger, I think a very different reading of Derrida is possible. It is that reading that I attempt here, drawing in particular on "Force of Law," not to mention his forceful rejection of Searle's criticism of him in the "Afterword" to *Limited Inc.*[56]

The difference between justice-as-transcendence and deconstruction-as-justice can be summed up in a single word. We have not *lost* the foundations of law. We *lack* them. This fantasy of God and unquestionable authority and of law as an eternal truth never existed, although the established order could always be relied upon to insist otherwise. Derrida insists throughout the entire body of his work, in relation to law and otherwise, on the iterability of language that renders necessarily unstable our concepts and ideas; on *différance* that renders infinitely questionable our structures of authority; on the constant collisions and paradoxes not just between our beliefs here in this community and their beliefs over there in that community, but *within* our words and beliefs and faiths and foundations themselves. Contrary to the utopian imagery of Nonet, our tradition was never whole; it was fractured *ab initio*. No one did this to it; it did this to itself. As Barbara Johnson writes in a passage that I take to be the very manifesto of Law and the Humanities:

> The de-construction of a text does not proceed by random doubt or arbitrary subversion, but by the careful teasing out of warring forces of signification within the text itself... It is thus not out of hostility to the moral values of Western civilization that deconstruction has arisen, but out of a desire to understand how these values are potentially already different from themselves. By re-reading the texts of writers and philosophers that have made a difference to Western history, it might be possible to become aware of the repressions, the elisions, the contradictions and the linguistic slippages that have functioned

---

[53] Gillian Rose, *Judaism and Modernity* (Oxford: Blackwell, 1993) 87; *The Broken Middle* (London: Blackwell, 1992) 293. Rose's target here is the work of Emmanuel Levinas but she is also happy to encompass Derrida in a searing critique. For a further discussion of Rose's critique in relation to Levinas and to Derrida, see Desmond Manderson, *Proximity, Levinas, and the Soul of Law* (Montreal: McGill-Queen's University Press, 2006) 73–81, 195.

[54] Rose, *Broken Middle*, 310.

[55] Desmond Manderson, ed., *Essays on Levinas and Law* (London and New York: Macmillan, 2008).

[56] Manderson, *Proximity*, chapter 7; Derrida, "Force of Law"; Jacques Derrida, "Afterword" to *Limited Inc.* (Evanston, IL: Northwestern University Press, 1988). As Pierre Schlag has pointed out to me, it is nevertheless fair to say that Derrida's flirtation with the mysticism of "the madness of decision," no less than his ethereal and abstract discussion of justice, no doubt invite Balkin's interpretation.

unnoticed and that undercut the certainties those texts have been read as upholding.[57]

Deconstruction is relentless in drawing our attention to the conflicts and ambiguities we experience at every moment of our lives.[58] It is dogged in insisting not on the "ethical unity" of principles or texts, but on the contrary in urging us to recognize and to be constantly aware of the politics, the context, and the social implications of any and every such fallacious claim. For me, such an approach pits ethical *against* unity. It stands for the sheer impossibility of foundations, and for the toxic character of any rhetoric that purports to have escaped or preceded or risen above it.

Although we strive to make a judgment on the basis of the case before us and the texts that surround us, in the midst of the contradiction and aporia that deconstruction will not let us forget for an instant, and although the moment of decision that we all face requires us to make that leap without some certain rule to fall back upon, we do not thereby *transcend* the problem of judgment. We savor it; we endure it; we suffer it.[59] This does not provide us with some stable ground, lost or otherwise; it makes us all too aware of the necessary lack of that ground.

In this way, the notion of justice-beyond-the-rules is not a new foundation or a perfected authority but quite the opposite: new justifications and not an end to them, new doubts and not an end to them, new instabilities and not an end to them. Deconstruction suggests to me the need for a constant and unbending vigilance in the face of any claims of transcendence or authority or foundation – precisely to protect justice against its many well-wishers, paramours, and would-be proprietors. At the moment of judgment, these unresolved tensions and uncertainties become part of a never-ending discourse in which we all participate – indeed, in which our participation is unavoidable – and in which the change and argument and doubt surrounding a judgment become not symptoms of its failure but, in a deeper sense, of its success.

The Transcendental Moment

Where one response to the indeterminacy of rules speaks the loss of transcendence, I note a lack. Where Berkowitz grieves that "the whole simply lives no more,"[60] I can only remark that whatever roles the idea of this whole might have served in

---

[57] Barbara Johnson, "The Surprise of Otherness: A Note on the Wartime Writings of Paul de Man," in Peter Collier and Helga Geyer-Ryan, *Literary Theory Today* (Ithaca: Cornell University Press, 1990) 13–21, 18, 21.

[58] See Beardsworth; Johnson; Aletta Norval, "Hegemony After Deconstruction," (2004) 9 *Journal of Political Ideologies* 139–57; Simon Critchley, *The Ethics of Deconstruction*, 2nd ed (Edinburgh: Edinburgh University Press, 2000 [1991]).

[59] Derrida, "Force of Law."

[60] Berkowitz, *The Gift of Science*, 158 quoting Max Weber.

other societies, it has now a fantastic and too often a pernicious quality. Berkowitz presents us with a simple opposition: Either we believe in the "beautiful dream" of "transcendent justice" based on "the ethical unity of law" or we must be satisfied with "modern conceptions of social justice based upon rules."[61] The point of this chapter is to argue that these are not our only choices. The tradition of Law and the Humanities offers a third way. Whereas the Heideggerian move seeks justice outside of or prior to discourse and language, the Derridian move maintains that no such outside exists. *Il n'y a pas de hors-texte.*[62] Whatever legal judgment can achieve – and we agree that objectivity and certainty is not an option – it achieves only through discourse.

When we try to discern what and who will find and realize for us transcendent justice, it is worth noting that Berkowitz typically qualifies the word authority and the word law with "natural." To rediscover the true meaning of law and justice, we must return to nature. Authority is a "natural claim" or a "natural and traditional" one; it acts upon law's "natural connection to truth and justice" as a "natural and traditional" insight.[63] Here is a word with a great and exceptionally problematic pedigree. I doubt that I am alone in being astonished at the amount of justificatory work it performs here. To speak of nature is already to speak of something *outside* discourse, self-evident, authoritative, and beyond reproach.[64] Meanwhile its semantic vagueness allows it to stand for a variety of different ideological positions at once and to slip seamlessly from one to the other.[65] If authority and insight are both natural, well what could be more natural than that? Who, however, is to be the judge of what counts as natural? Who defines nature and according to what terms? Whose interests are favored by nature? Who gets to claim its marvelous, protective mantle and so shield their actions from question? Whose judgments, on the other hand, are reduced to the realm of the unnatural, a word that has not lost its power to silence?[66] "Nature" is the answer to no question; it merely puts an end to questions. It is no wonder that a word such as "discrimination," for example, now carries with it a whole lot of baggage that it did not have back in the good old days when it meant merely the recognition of "natural" distinctions between people. Our disenchantment is not a sign that we have lost something. On the contrary, we have *learned* something about how that word has been wielded by actual persons living in actual societies.

---

[61] Ibid., x, 108.

[62] Jacques Derrida, *Of Grammatalogy* (Baltimore: John Hopkins University Press, 1977) 158.

[63] Berkowitz, *The Gift of Science*, 3, 7, 51–2, 108.

[64] See the deconstruction of nature/culture in relation to Rousseau in Derrida, *Of Grammatology*.

[65] Anne Fernihough, *Aesthetics and Ideology* (Clarendon Press: Oxford, 1993) 32–4, discusses at some length Pierre Bourdieu's analysis of the multiple ideologies embedded in the word "natural." Indeed, see Philippe Nonet on this: "Antigone's Law," 323–4.

[66] Although it is true that Nonet, for example in ibid., insists that our reading of the word nature in relation to the Greeks has, since Hegel, mistaken the meaning and implications of that term, Berkowitz, in a fashion that is crucial to the political and legal argument of the book, nevertheless fuses these different senses and connotations.

Judgment in Law and the Humanities

The Gift of Science presents us with strongly etched dichotomies, one side of which is subject to a very careful historical and social critique, and the other side of which is not analyzed at all but offered up as a fantastic vision. This vision is not only devoid of all history or social context, but fuses together disparate ideas into an imagined "ethical unity." The steady references to authority, justice, or insight as "natural and traditional," "traditional and religious," and so on, mix together justifications based on social practice, history, politics, and ethics.[67] In the process, the deep and immemorial conflict between the claims of nature and tradition and religion disappear, and to believe in one is necessarily to become committed to all. This is what Walter Benjamin meant by "the aestheticization of politics."[68] On one side history, and against it myth.[69] No wonder myth has the inside running. It solves problems aesthetically that remain unsolved in the real world.

Berkowitz's history stops at the high point of German positivism, but it is the history of what came next that interests me. A century ago, German writers overwhelmingly responded exactly as Berkowitz does to the intellectual poverty of positivism. Sometimes termed New Romanticism, the outpouring of writing around the turn of the century, by which Heidegger was profoundly influenced,[70] rejected in almost identical terms the German obsession with mechanics, systems, technology, and positivism. There too we can observe the same fusion of nature, tradition, custom, religion; the same belief in justice as hierarchical and judgment as manifest.[71] The political effects of this revolt against modernity were of course both radical and reactionary:

> But was it not a contradiction to believe simultaneously in a revolutionary yet conservative change? By no means, as long as there was a metaphysical foundation, as long as one's doctrine of revolution did not call for new and radical social and economic reforms. Man did not advance progressively, discarding his traditions as they became useless; rather he was bound by eternal laws that had been established in the past and embodied in tradition . . . [The new Germany] had to revive and make operative in a new age the traditions of medieval messianism.[72]

Berkowitz elegantly retells the history of German positivism and in the process vigorously reenacts the secret history of German New Romanticism. As M. H.

---

[67] Berkowitz, *The Gift of Science*, e.g., 3, 10, 15, 51, 52.

[68] Walter Benjamin, politics and aesthetics.

[69] According to Roland Barthes, among others, myth is precisely the synthesis of conflicting claims through linguistic or semiotics structures: see the seminal essay "Myth Today" in *Mythologies*, Annette Lavers, trans. (New York: Hill & Wang, 1984 [1957]).

[70] Pierre Bourdieu, *The Political Ontology of Martin Heidegger* (Stanford, CA: Stanford University Press, 1991).

[71] George Mosse, *The Crisis of German Ideology: Intellectual Origins of the Third Reich* (New York: Grosset and Dunlap, 1964) e.g., 98, 4–6, 54, 33, 92.

[72] Ibid., 281.

Abrams puts it, the Romantic movement was primarily "a metaphysics of integration, of which the key principle is that of the 'reconciliation' or synthesis, of whatever is divided, opposed, and conflicting."[73]

Thus the three positions become clear. When it comes to legal judgment, positivism rejects the possibility of conflicting or divided interpretations, and deconstruction attempts to embrace the possibility, whereas the New Romantics attempt to reconcile or transcend it.

A Third Way?

The Novel

Certain aspects of the tradition and development of the European novel offer us a good illustration of what a third way might begin to look like. First, this literature's commitment to psychology pricks the hubris of philosophical abstractions. In the voice of women in particular – and the history of English literature in particular, over the past two hundred years, has been the emergence of the voices and the realities of women's lives[74] – we hear a constant reminder of the cruelties and repression sustained by appeals to an authority so vague and entrenched as to remain as imperceptible, irresistible, and omnipresent as the mist.

Hegel famously remarked that women are "the everlasting irony in the life of the community."[75] He was thinking of Antigone and he was right, although he managed to draw from his observation entirely the wrong conclusion.[76] Perhaps the systematic exclusion of women from political and philosophical discourse led them – although of course hardly them alone or all of them – to exhibit a skepticism of grand theories and of the romance of violence and power. Irony, which is one of the gifts of literature, holds our great words and promises up and examines them from a distance; "the distance we are obliged to assume towards our most 'authentic' dreams, towards the myths that guarantee the very consistency of our symbolic universe."[77]

Second, the novel offers us an alternative vision of the nature of judgement. I do not think it is excessive for me to claim that one of crucial features of the novel's

---

[73] M. H. Abrams, *The Mirror and the Lamp: Romantic Theory and the Critical Tradition* (Oxford: Oxford University Press, 1971).

[74] Again it would be ludicrous to provide a reading list, but for notable signposts of this history see Charlotte Bronte, *Jane Eyre* (1847); George Eliot, *The Mill on the Floss* (1860); Virginia Woolf, *To the Lighthouse* (1927), although the point is not about women *writers* but about the representation of the inner lives of women.

[75] G. W. F. Hegel, *The Phenomenology of Spirit*, A. V. Miller, trans. (Oxford: Oxford University Press, 1977) 288.

[76] For feminist critiques, see Kimberley Hutchings, *Hegel and Feminist Philosophy* (Edinburgh: Polity Press, 2002); Susan Easton, "Hegel and Feminism," (1984) 38 *Radical Philosophy*; Alison Stone and S. Sandford, eds., "Hegel and Feminism" (1999) 22 *Women's Philosophy Review*.

[77] Slavoj Zizek, "Superego by Default," *Metastases of Enjoyment* (London: Verso, 2004) 54–85, 82.

Judgment in Law and the Humanities

development has been its polyphonic character. It multiplies voices; it sets characters' perspectives *against* each other; it does not shy away from but embraces the resulting uncertainty. This embrace of uncertainty, particularly in the form of humor, sets it apart from either positivism or Romanticism. Milan Kundera argues that humor is perhaps the most important achievement of the European novel, from *Don Quixote* to the present day.

> Humour: the divine flash that reveals the world in its moral ambiguity and man in his profound incompetence to judge others; humour: the intoxicating relativity of human beings; the strange pleasure that comes of the certainty there is no certainty.[78]

D. H. Lawrence took the argument still further, insisting that "the great discovery" of the novel lay in its fundamental hostility to *any* ideology of unity or of "a presupposed ethical world."

> The novel is the highest form of human expression so far attained. Why? Because it is so incapable of the absolute. In a novel, everything is relative to everything else, if that novel is art at all. Every Commandment that ever issued out of the mouth of God or man, is strictly relative: adhering to the particular time, place and circumstance. And this is the beauty of the novel; everything is true in its own relationship, and no further.[79]

Such narratives, rich, internal, dynamic, and multiple, do not resolve or synthesize tensions but on the contrary bring them out.

> The artist usually sets out – or used to – to point a moral and adorn a tale. The tale, however, points the other way, as a rule ... Never trust the artist. Trust the tale. The proper function of a critic is to save the tale from the artist who created it ... If it be really a work of art, it must contain the essential criticism of the morality to which it adheres.[80]

This is not only compatible with the ideas of deconstruction we have been looking at; it is how deconstruction came to understand the nature of language and judgment in the first place.[81]

---

[78] Milan Kundera, "The Day Panurge no Longer Makes People Laugh," 1–33, *Testaments Betrayed*, Linda Asher, trans. (London: Faber & Faber, 1995), 32–3.

[79] D. H. Lawrence, *Study of Thomas Hardy and Other Essays* (Cambridge: Cambridge University Press, 1985 [1923]) 179; see also 172.

[80] D. H. Lawrence, *Studies in Classic American Literature* (New York: Viking Press, 1964 [1923]) 2.

[81] Jacques Derrida, *Acts of Literature*, Derek Attridge, ed. (London and New York: Routledge, 1992); esp. "Before the Law" 189 and "The Law of Genre" 222.

Justice

The unceasing and incurable struggle with uncertain meaning, multiple perspectives, and ever-changing context is our *true* ethical predicament. We can neither deny it, as the positivists claim, nor transcend it, as the Romantics imply. This takes us back to Derrida's "Force of Law," one of the key texts in the movement of Law and the Humanities. The *tension* between justice as sameness and justice as difference, between judgment as calculation and judgment that recognizes the incalculable and the singular, is irreducible. "Between justice (infinite, incalculable, rebellious to rule and foreign to symmetry) and the exercise of justice as law or right, legitimacy or legality, stabilizable and statutory, calculable, a system of regulated and coded prescriptions"[82] we cannot *choose* because our belief in these two aspects is neither synthesizable into a unity nor prioritizable into a hierarchy.

These inescapable contradictions, however, are not problems for the moment of judgment – they are *productive*. As Derrida points out, responsibility and accountability are not opposites or choices: they are incommensurable forces that provide us with a deeper understanding of each although we are constantly forced to betray them as we attempt to realize them.[83] In language too, communication and expression pull meaning in strictly opposite directions but paradoxically open wide the warp of language to creativity, dialogue, and change.[84] Finally, in his late work on hospitality, he speaks of a "tension at the heart of the heritage" between forgiveness as the unconditional pardon of the guilty as such, and forgiveness as a conditional grant in an economy of repentance.[85]

> These two poles, the *unconditional and the conditional,* are absolutely heterogeneous, and must remain irreducible to one another. They are nonetheless indissociable: if one wants, and it is necessary, forgiveness to become effective, concrete, historic; if one wants it to arrive, to happen by changing things, it is necessary that this purity engage itself in a series of conditions . . . It is between these two poles, *irreconcilable but indissociable,* that decision and responsibilities are to be taken.[86]

Likewise in the moment of legal judgment the words that we are called on to interpret are neither transparent instruction machines, nor yet the memory of essences. Instead they are a polarized field of differences, crackling with energy. There is an inescapable tension – irreconcilable but indissociable – between the prior rule,

---

[82] Derrida, "Force of Law," 959; see also "Before the Law."

[83] Derrida, *Gift of Death.*

[84] Derrida, *Of Grammatology.*

[85] Jacques Derrida, "Forgiveness," *On Cosmopolitanism and Forgiveness,* Mark Dooley and Michael Hughes, trans. (London: Routledge, 2002) 34–5; see also the Introduction by Simon Critchley and Richard Kearney, e.g., at x–xi.

[86] Ibid., 44–5.

Judgment in Law and the Humanities

general and certain, and the question of its application *in this case*. Now this gives no comfort to the positivists who think that the prior rule can be relied upon to simply tell us what is required *in this case*, but neither does it give comfort to the transcendentalists. The beyond-the-rules is not a circuit breaker: it is a circuit *maker*. This tension forces us to rethink our rules, and the meaning we give to our words, and the imagined "essences" of those words, and the purposes served by them: we are forced to reconsider, to question, to doubt. This tension, however, is ended only by a new judgment that attempts to reimpose stability on the legal order.[87] This generates, immediately if not sooner, a new polarity, and new tensions.

Justice, therefore, does not lie in the imperfect legal judgment itself, but rather in the doubt and the challenge that went with it, on the one hand, and the discourse of justification, reason-giving, and resistance that continues the circuit into the future, on the other. Legal judgment is on this view exactly opposite to the closure and finality – the death wish or *Thanatos* of discourse – to which both Romanticism and positivism, in their very different ways, are drawn.

This leads me back to my early puzzle about how to develop a notion of judgment that would give some meaning to the rule of law without falling back into either positivism or Romanticism. As Berkowitz so powerfully shows us, reason in the orthodox structure of positivism is meant to lead to a single right answer to legal judgments, grounded in the faith that logic and science can provide lawyers and citizens with objective and determinate answers to their legal problems. The rule of law, on this understanding, makes a fetish of certainty that sacrifices everything to the tyranny of an ever-growing heap of *gesetz*.[88] I certainly agree that this promise is destined to fail.

It does not follow that we should give up on judgment as the giving of "reasons," now in the plural. The rule of law might instead offer us a promise that decision makers be required to articulate and justify their decisions, and to be challenged on their reasons, forced to question them and think again, without ever simply being able to appeal to their authority or their insight as some kind of ineffable trump. The rule of law cannot deliver a grounded truth about law – nothing can. It can, however, deliver a discourse through which those who judge and interpret the law remain answerable, engaged in a dialogue of listening with those who come before them and after them. When we reflect on whether to apply a rule in some new circumstance, or whether to apply this rule or that, we are forced to think about the notion of justice behind that rule in a way that is not capable of being nailed down in advance. Because justice is unattainable, because there is a necessary imperfection to this process, the obligation to render a judgment is not severable from the obligation to *expose* one's judgment, to explain, justify, and to be criticized for it. Corrigibility

---

[87] Derrida, "Afterword" in *Limited Inc.*, 148.
[88] Berkowitz, *The Gift of Science*, 94–7.

is the soul of justice. Were it not for that, the endless return of deconstruction would be short-circuited by some appeal to a foundation – nature or tradition or authority – that it was Derrida's implacable goal to expose as a metaphysical version of the shell-and-pea trick.

Accordingly, legal judgment is the province of neither technicians nor gurus. It is the province of us all, a ceaseless and participatory social discourse. Without the giving of reasons and the pressure of justification, however provisional and protean, the law would cease to offer us – all of us, whether as citizens or as lawyers or as judges – the possibility of *learning* something new about ourselves and the world. Just as recent trends in literature (the judgment of fiction) have striven to dethrone the solitary genius in favor of readers' active participation in the construction, interpretation, and crucially, the transmission of meaning over time, so too similar trends in our thinking about justice (the judgment of law) have dethroned the solitary judge in favor of citizens' active participation in legal discourse. Just as with literature and philosophy, the influence of the humanities on law makes the process of judgment more contentious and continuous, but at the same time more democratic and more dynamic than ever before.

The word "insight," which is Berkowitz's alternative to rule following, appears a purely *in*-ward process by which one intuits the big picture and discovers what justice just is. To speak of law as an inspired insight "that grows of its own accord" or as a "natural or traditional insight into what is right and fitting," suggests precisely an intuition that comes without the need for interrogation, or modification, or argument, but simply as a divinely ordained fact. Insight is not transformed by argument or effected by resistance – it is "free." Insight is not transformed by time or reflection – it is "manifest" and "divine."[89] Berkowitz's profound hostility to law as "the modern approach of giving reasons and justifications"[90] appears to confirm this reading: reason and justification mark the impoverishment of law.[91] To my way of thinking, *nothing* is free, or natural, or manifest. What we learn about justice, and of course this changes over time in a world of bewildering complexity and constant motion, we earn, like a novel's gradually ramified understanding, precisely through processes of justification and reason-giving.

Insight and reasons are not somehow opposite. On the contrary, they stem from each other. The same is true of teaching, which is not the mere manifestation of insight but its slow emergence under the relentless demands of our students that we give reasons and explain our views. As Tobias Wolff writes, "Teaching made him accountable for his thoughts, and as he became accountable for them he had

---

[89] Ibid., 29, 51, 24.
[90] Ibid., 156.
[91] Ibid., e.g. at 51, 52.

Judgment in Law and the Humanities

more of them, and they became sharper and deeper."[92] Insight is collective, chiseled out of us by the constant demands and interrogations of others; the painful *result* of reasons and not the transcending of them. It is con-science – knowledge shared *with* others – and not, in the old Anglo-Saxon word, "in-wit." Without the giving of reasons there would be no insight at all: not reason – singular – in the limited sense of the authority of pure reason or the dictates of logic, but in the broader sense of reasons – plural – that encompasses the articulation of positions, the challenge of justification, and the to-and-fro of reflection. Justice, similarly, is not a process by which those in authority teach us mortals, but a process by which, under the pressure of reasons and the demands to justify, they come to *learn* from them.[93]

Conclusion

So the two alternatives that Law and the Humanities offer to positivistic theories of judgment, although drawing on a similar heritage, inhabit drastically different worlds. Again, Berkowitz is exemplary in refusing ever to shy away from the logic of his position. Because the nature of the insight into justice is entirely without the trappings of discourse, it "cannot but appear to others as 'lawless caprice.'"[94] Indeed, legal systems that abandon all efforts to justify and to give reasons, and that refuse to open themselves to question, very often resort to some appeal to nature or authority or tradition. I suspect that this moment really does usher in the reign of lawless caprice.

In the moment of judgment, justice is always incomplete or lacking: this lack is its beauty and its strength. Of course living with uncertainty is uncomfortable; thereby we experience judgment not as the manifest knowledge of what is right and fitting, but as the energized field of doubt that requires justification in human terms and in which such justification is *always* inadequate, *always* subject to challenge and revision. This is, perhaps, what the literature of the novel contributes most in our thinking about judgment. It takes the smallness, and the inadequacy, and the goddamn perversity of us, and it does so without yearning for a time when gods and heroes roamed the earth, without ever waxing nostalgic about the whole that lives no more. Instead, these marvelously imagined narratives take our smallness and inadequacy and fragmentation seriously. They make of it something that can be seen, *truly seen* in all its incoherent detail – and something thereby capable at last of being loved.

The rule of law, thus reimagined, is not the outcome of a foundation but a process of continually challenging them; it is governed by reasons but not reason;

---

[92] Tobias Wolff, *Old School* (New York: Vintage, 2003) 181–2. Berkowitz' own vision of teaching seems dramatically different; see 159–60.

[93] Bob Gibbs, "The Other Comes to Teach Me" (1991) 24 *Man and World* 219–33.

[94] Berkowitz, *The Gift of Science*, xvi.

it offers a discourse by which the law learns and not a declaration by which it instructs. Enlivened by literature as well as philosophy, the rule of law becomes a polarity and not a unity; the expression of restless dialogue and never the manifestation of a unifying transcendent insight. This is, of course, all too human and imperfect. Positivism glorifies the inhuman in law so as to eradicate imperfection by removing the judge from judgment. Romanticism glorifies the superhuman in law so as to transcend imperfection by exalting the judge's judgment. Deconstruction, for its part, glorifies nothing *but* this imperfection. Against the gift of science and the siren song of nature, then, Law and the Humanities might defend a rule of law and a theory of judgment full of the beauty and doubt of literature: not a way out, or a way back, but a way in and on.

20

Punishment

Karl Shoemaker

At first glance, it is not clear what precisely the humanities have to offer to a discussion of punishment. Punishment, as the dictionary tells us, is the infliction of pain on account of a wrong.[1] The power to determine what acts are punishable and the corresponding power to inflict pain upon offenders has been, since at least the late Middle Ages in the West, so closely bound up with conceptions of sovereignty and jurisdiction that, along with the power to levy war, a monopoly on punishment is generally considered the defining feature of the modern state.[2] As such, punishment, and the discussions attendant to its procedures, justifications, constitutional limitations, and application have primarily, although certainly not exclusively, resided within the disciplinary domain of law and lawyers.

Law's disciplinary claim on punishment, if never complete, has been substantial within the Western tradition since the Middle Ages. Although this observation may be rather obvious, it is not inevitable that the discipline of law take pride of place in shaping a given culture's discourses and practices of punishment. For example, juridical discussions concerning the principles and application of punishment are surprisingly rare in ancient Roman law, even though the Roman Empire, especially in its late stages, showed a remarkable preoccupation with using punishment to establish and to police the boundaries of social rank. To be sure, the ancient Romans punished with astonishing inventiveness,[3] but in concept and practice, Roman punishment did not bear the imprint of sustained juridical reflection to the extent

[1] The first definition of "pain" in the *Oxford English Dictionary*: "Punishment; penalty; suffering or loss inflicted for a crime or offence."

[2] According to Max Weber's classic description, "a state is a human community that (successfully) claims the monopoly of the legitimate use of physical force within a given territory." *Politics as a Vocation* From Max Webers: *Essays in Sociology*, H. H. Gerth an C. Wright Mills, eds. (Oxford University Press, p. 78; 1958).

[3] A convicted matricide, for example, might be put into a sack with a monkey, a dog, a rooster, and a snake. The sack was then to be thrown in a river, or, where a river was lacking, from a high precipice. *Dig.*, 48.9.9.2.

517

that one finds in late medieval and modern Western law (or, for that matter, in other areas of ancient Roman law).[4] Similarly, early medieval epic poetry offers important insights into understandings of punishment, feuding, and reconciliation in a heroic age for which we have very little by way of legal texts and nothing by way of juridical reflection. Recall, for example, that in *Beowulf* the monstrousness of Grendel is introduced by way of pointing out his fundamental incapacity to engage in the processes of lawful feud and concord that constituted the just resolution of wrongdoing in the world of men.[5] In *Beowulf*, and the world it rendered, punishment was not a matter of legal doctrine expounded by lawyers or imposed by judges. It was, rather, one measure of how a just and noble man addressed his own wrongs and those done against him. So, how did law come to claim priority in the domain of punishment?

In the West, the origins of law's overt disciplinary claim on punishment are often located in the twelfth century.[6] There, jurists in the Roman-canonical tradition ponderously examined questions pertaining to punishment and constructed out of

[4] The classic account of ancient Roman criminal law is Theodor Mommsen, *Romisches Strafrecht* (Leipzig: 1899); See now also, Jill Harries, *Law and Crime in the Roman World* (Cambridge: Cambridge University Press, 2007), who stresses the importance of social attitudes, over against the conservative tendencies of ancient Roman law, in shaping Roman modes of punishment.

[5] *Beowulf*, lines 155–8 (chapter 2) *Francis B. Gummere*, trans. (P. F. Collier & Son, New York, 1910)

> . . . how ceaselessly Grendel
> harassed Hrothgar, what hate he bore him,
> what murder and massacre, many a year,
> feud unfading, – refused consent
> to deal with any of Daneland's earls,
> make pact of peace, or compound for gold:
> still less did the wise men ween to get
> great fee for the feud from his fiendish hands.

[6] There is a sizeable literature. Among the most important works are Richard M. Fraher, "The Theoretical Justification of the New Criminal Law of the High Middle Ages: *Rei publicae interest, ne crimina remaneant impunita*," *Illinois Law Review* (1984), 577–95; and his "Preventing Crime in the High Middle Ages: The Medieval Lawyers' Search for Deterrence," in *Popes, Teachers, and Canon Law in the Middle Ages*, James Ross Sweeney and Stanley Chodorow, eds. (Ithaca: Cornell University Press, 1989) 212–33; Harold Berman, *Law and Revolution; The Formation of the Western Legal Tradition* (Cambridge, MA: Harvard University Press, 1983) 165–98; Edward Peters, "Juristic Theology? Medieval and Early Modern European Perspectives on Punishment," in *Perspectives on Punishment: An Interdisciplinary Exploration*, Richard Mowery Andrews, ed. (New York: Peter Lang, 1997) Stephan Kuttner, "Ecclesia de occultis non judicat: Problemata ex doctrina poenali decretistarum et decretalistarum a Gratiano usque ad Gregorium PP. IX," *Actus Congressus Iuridicis Internationalis* (Rome, 1936) Vol. III, 225–46; and Kuttner's, *Kanonistische Schuldlehre von Gratian bis auf die Dekretalen Gregors IX* (Vatican City: Biblioteca Apostolica Vaticana, 1935); Andre Gouron, "Zu den Ursprungen des Strafrechts: die ersten Strafrechtstraktate," in *Festschrift für Hans Thieme zu seinem 80. Geburtstag* (Sigmaringen: Jan Thorbeck, 1986), reprinted in Andre Gouron, *Études sur la diffusion des doctrines juridiques médivales* (London: Variorum, 1987), IX; Hermann Kantorowicz, *Albertus Gandinus und das Strafrecht der Scholastik*, 2 vols. (Berlin-Leipzig: Walter de Gruyter, 1926).

Punishment 519

the raw materials of scholastic theology, ancient Roman law, ecclesiastical law, royal legislation, and custom an impressive edifice that might be called "a criminal justice system."[7] The result was the articulation of crime and punishment as matters of public interest, a marked tendency to concentrate the power to prosecute and punish crime in official hands, and a preference to assign punishment through procedures that were actively shaped, when they were not actually created, by jurists.[8] In the centuries that followed, the complex of doctrines, procedures, and punishments that had been born in the twelfth-century renaissance of European jurisprudence[9] remained sufficiently within the grip of professional jurists that Cesare Beccaria (1738–94) could introduce his momentous *On Crimes and Punishments* by lamenting the extent to which punishment in his day was determined by resort to "ill digested tomes by obscure commentators who spoke only for themselves."[10] The "obscure commentators" derided by Beccaria were of course the law professors, legal commentators, and judicial officials that had been advising urban and royal authorities in Europe on the development and administration of penal law for more than five centuries. Beccaria and other Enlightenment critics made sport of the gruesome punishments inherited from posterity and the text-bound lawyers and judges who "blandly accepted" them. Together, these critics can share at least some of the credit for the considerable penal reforms that took hold in parts of Europe and the New World in the decades following the publication of *On Crimes and Punishments.*[11] Regardless of how one assesses the success or failure of these penal reforms, which tended to stress the benefit of certain but lenient punishments over the haphazard but spectacular harshness of the old regime, and which helped to pave the way for the metastasization of the modern penitentiary system, the assertion that disciplinary blinders might prevent lawyers from properly understanding the relationship between punishment and society would persist. Durkheim's famous

---

[7] Peters, "Juristic Theology?," 39 (emphasis in original).

[8] It is not possible here to develop the important differences that exist in criminal law and procedure between the English common law and the Roman-canonical tradition, or to note the extent to which the centralization of the power to punish in official hands was an uneven process. On the difference between English and Continental criminal process, see Karl Shoemaker, "Criminal Procedure in Medieval European Law: A Comparison between English and Roman-canonical Developments after the IV Lateran Council," *Zeitschrift der Savigny-Stiftung für Rechtsgeschichte. Kanonistische Abteilung* 85 (1999): 174–202.

[9] See, *Twelfth-Century Europe and the Foundations of Modern Society,* Marshall Clagett, Gaines Post, and Robert Reynolds, eds. (Madison: University of Wisconsin Press, 1966); *Renaissance and Renewal in the Twelfth Century,* Robert Benson and Giles Constable, eds. (Cambridge, MA: Harvard University Press, 1982).

[10] Beccaria, *On Crimes and Punishments and Other Writings,* Richard Bellamy, ed., Richard Davies, trans. (Cambridge: Cambridge University Press, 1995) 3.

[11] M. T. Maestro, *Voltaire and Beccaria as Reformers of Criminal Law* (New York, 1942); and especially Richard Andrews, "The Cunning of Imagery: Rhetoric and Ideology in Cesare Beccaria's *On Crimes and Punishments,*" in *Begetting Images: Studies in the Art and Science of Symbol Production,* Mary B. Cambell and Mark Rollins, eds. (New York: Peter Lang, 1989) 113–32.

account of the crucial function of punishments in stoking and strengthening social solidarity was set in part against (what he perceived to be) the narrow and formalistic understandings of punishment entertained by the jurists.

Nonetheless, it was only with the emergence of the empirical social sciences, in particular criminology and psychology, in the twentieth century that punishment was wrestled from the exclusive disciplinary domain of the jurists. The result in mid-twentieth-century Europe was what some have termed "open warring between lawyers and scientists over who would dominate the problem of crime" and punishment.[12] In the United States, disciplinary disputes over crime and punishment were resolved through a "great compromise" in which law retained sovereignty over the doctrines that determined guilt and responsibility and the social sciences took a more prominent role in the determination of sentences and the administration of punishment, relying on psychology-based strategies of risk assessment, custody, and prison administration.[13] This truce was possible in part because the social sciences were perceived to produce new forms of expertise that challenged law by promising more efficient and rational approaches to disciplining mass society than traditional statutory and doctrinal law were deemed able to provide. Hence, although it may be that, as a discipline, law no longer holds an encompassing claim on how our discourses of punishment are framed, the disciplinary claim has been broken by the empirical social sciences, not the humanities.

So, we are thrown back on the question of what the humanities have to offer to a discussion of punishment, but now with perhaps even less reason for optimism than at the outset. The success of the social sciences in mediating a "great compromise" with the lawyers over questions of punishment serves to highlight the estrangement of the humanities from the disciplines of law and the empirical social sciences, an estrangement that is not restricted to matters of punishment. Estrangement, of course, presupposes prior moments of intimacy between the humanities and law. Historically, there have been moments when the humanistic disciplines formed an important pillar not only of legal education but also of the practice and application of law. In Renaissance Europe for example, grounded learning in humanist culture was considered by some to be as essential as technical expertise for jurists who sought to do justice.[14] Indeed, some historians have identified the abandonment of

---

[12] Jonathan Simon, "Visions of Self-Control: Fashioning a Liberal Approach to Crime and Punishment in the Twentieth Century," in *Looking Back at Law's Century*, Austin Sarat, Bryant Garth, and Robert A. Kagan, eds. (Ithaca: Cornell University Press, 2002) 109–50.

[13] David J. Rothman, *Conscience and Convenience: The Asylum and its Alternatives in Progressive America* (Boston: Little Brown, 1971); David Garland, *Punishment and Welfare* (Brookfield, VT: Gower, 1985); See also, Jim Jacobs, *Stateville: The Penitentiary in Mass Society* (Chicago: University of Chicago Press, 1977).

[14] Guido Astuti, *Mos italicus e mos gallicus: nei dialoghi "de iuris interpretibus" di Alberico Gentili* (Biblioteca della rivista di storia del diritto italiano, Bologno, 1937); Donald R. Kelly, "*Jurisconsultus Perfectus*: The Lawyer as Renaissance Man," *Journal of the Warburg and Courtauld Institutes*, (1988)

Punishment

humanistic educational ideals in the law schools to be a cause of the "lamentable over-severity and brutality with which torture came to be used in the sixteenth and seventeenth centuries" in Europe.[15] In such accounts, the humanistic education of lawyers and judges helped preserve law from the "flowering of cruel justice and of judicial cruelty" that emerged later.[16] Whether the humanistic education can claim such a historical role is an open question.[17]

Whatever the case may have been in the early modern period, the current estrangement between the humanities and law can be said to resemble something like unrequited love; the humanities may provide amusing distractions (an enriching or fresh perspective, perhaps) to the study of law, but the moments of engagement between law and humanistic disciplines are fleeting, episodic, and characterized by a use that is neither lasting nor productive. Richard Posner's allowances, by way of examples, that "revenge literature can supply insights into the nature and origins of law by depicting the system of justice that precedes an organized legal system," or that "the well-educated lawyer should have some acquaintance with current controversies in literary theory" (an acquaintance made necessary, he explains, because some scholars have criticized his view that literary theory is not relevant to statutory or constitutional theory and a learned practitioner needs to know the criticism) illustrate the capacity of law to judge its relationship to other disciplines only by the utility provided in the exchange.[18] Indeed, some in the legal academy have even claimed that the humanities stand to benefit more from law than law stands to gain from the humanities. In a 1906 *Michigan Law Review* article entitled "Law as Cultural Study," Edson Sutherland complained about curricular rules that excluded university students in the humanistic and scientific disciplines from taking courses in the law school. Such restrictions, he argued, kept undergraduate students from an essential part of their education. Law, he claimed, "is broader and more

---

51:84–102; For similar issues in the early American republic, see Robert A. Ferguson, *Law and Letters in American Culture* (Cambridge, MA: Harvard University Press, 1984).

[15] Walter Ullmann, "Reflections on Medieval Torture," *The Juridical Review* 56:123–37 (1944). Edward Peters finds Ullmann's view to "echo a number of other historians" ("Juristic Theology?" 37).

[16] The phrase is Johann Huizinga's, *The Waning of the Middle Ages*, Hopman, trans. (New York: Anchor Books, 1999) 25. Huizinga does not locate the decline in humanistic education as a cause of judicial cruelty as directly as Walter Ullmann did.

[17] More recent accounts of the emergence of humanitarian sensibilities and their role in the demise of institutions like slavery, judicial torture, or public executions have tended to look not at humanistic education but at emergence of capitalism and modern modes of discipline. See, e.g., Thomas L. Haskell, "Capitalism and the Origins of the Humanitarian Sensibility," *American Historical Review* 90 (1985): 339–61 (part 1), 547–66 (part 2); Haskell, *Objectivity is not Neutrality: Explanatory Schemes in History* (Johns Hopkins University Press, 2000).

[18] Richard A. Posner, *Law and Literature: A Misunderstood Relation* (Cambridge, MA: Harvard University Press, 1988) 354–5. It should be stressed that many of Posner's critics on the question of the relationship between law and literature disagree with him only in their assessment of the profitability of such an encounter, but share his underlying presumption that such a relationship can be judged by its efficacy in achieving some desired result, either for the lawyer or the nonlawyer scholar.

fundamental" than either humanistic study or science, and therefore should hold a central place in higher education. "To exclude, therefore, law from the hierarchy of the humanities is to take the keystone from the arch."[19] Legal education promised, in Sutherland's view, to provide young students with a more profound "fitness for this world" and a deeper understanding of justice and equity than the traditional liberal arts (from which law was lamentably "an exile").[20] If it was the case in 1906, as Sutherland suggested, that law yearned to end its exile from the humanities, the situation today is reversed. When the *Harvard Law Review* dedicated its 2002 symposium issue to the future of legal scholarship, scholars in humanistic disciplines were left to observe that the symposium failed to say a word about the substantial legal scholarship produced by scholars in the humanities and liberal arts.[21]

It may be helpful at this point to complicate things even further by noting that the word "Humanities" is a neologism, one that does not even merit entry in the Oxford English Dictionary.[22] Without hazarding a guess about the moment of its coinage, I merely point out that the word "Humanities" appears to have come into regular English usage at the end of nineteenth century. Although catalogues of what the Humanities entailed varied, a fairly standard definition included "philology, poetry, rhetoric, grammar, and archaeology, as well as the Greek and Latin classics."[23] The term Humanities, it seems, was derived from the Latin expression *literae humaniores* (humane letters). "Humane letters," then, designated the course of education that was proper to one who aspired to cultivate his *humanitas*, a task that in antiquity was meant to distinguish *Romanitas* from barbarism. During the Renaissance and early modern period, humane letters and humanism were understood as a project in opposition to the strictures of medieval scholastic theology.[24] In more recent history, the Humanities have defined themselves in opposition to the empirical social sciences and the physical sciences and asserted their particular role in inculcating virtue, judgment, humanitarianism, and democratic values (articulated with varying degrees of intelligibility), whereas other modes of inquiry

---

[19] Edson Sutherland, "Law as Culture Study," *Michigan Law Review* (1906) 4:179–88, 182.

[20] Ibid., 188 and 182.

[21] "Symposium: Law, Knowledge, and the Academy," *Harvard Law Review* 115 (2002): 1101; Austin Sarat, "Situating Legal Scholarship in the Liberal Arts," in *Law in the Liberal Arts* Austin Sarat, ed. (Ithaca, Cornell University Press, 2004) p. 1.

[22] Fowler allows it, though. *Modern English Usage* (1926), 240, equating it with *literae humaniores*.

[23] For example, Henry S. Carhart, "The Humanistic Element in Science," *Science* (new series) vol. 4, no. 83 (July 31, 1896) 124–30, at 124. Although Carhart's list excludes Philosophy, there is reason to believe it was conventional to include it. Note that Oxford University's humane letters curriculum includes Philosophy. History, originally a subdivision of grammar within the medieval Trivium, was sometimes included in the humanities by nineteenth-century writers as well.

[24] Crucial here is Martin Heidegger's "Letter on Humanism," in *Basic Writings*, David Ferrel Krell, ed., Frank A. Capuzzi with J. Glenn Gray, trans. (San Francisco: Harper Collins, 1977, 1993) 217–65; based on the German text published as "Brief über den Humanismus," in *Wegmarken* (Frankfurt am Main: Vittorio Klostermann Verlag, 1967) 145–94.

Punishment 523

are characterized as utilitarian, practical, or even mercenary.[25] Whatever its origin, it is worth noting that the disciplinary endeavors we now group under the rubric "Humanities" have generally been defined negatively, *in opposition* to some other mode of inquiry – as not barbarous, not scholastic, not technical. On this last point – the not-technical character of the humanities – we might add that the humanities, unlike the social sciences, were not, at least historically, justified by the effectiveness with which they solve problems in the world. Indeed, any account of the humanities grounded in the supposed effectiveness of the humanities for producing some result in this world would be an account that measured the humanities by the yardstick of the social sciences. In other words, it may be, for example, that the decline of humanistic education among lawyers caused an increase in judicial cruelty and senseless brutality in early modern punishments; this felicitous consequence cannot justify the humanities or give them any special claim on discussion of punishment in our own world. Insofar as the worth of the humanities is justified by some result obtained in the world, the humanities are debased, no longer freeing mankind for thinking but instead binding mankind to some necessity.

By way of a positive statement, and by direct reference to the historical relation of the term humanities to *humanitas* and Renaissance humanism, we might say that the humanities are concerned with humankind's freeing of itself for its own humanity and finding worth in such a freeing.[26] Such an account of what the humanities strive to do, of course, presupposes what it means to be human.[27] If one were constructing a catalogue of accounts of the essence of man in the Western intellectual tradition, it might include man as the animal that has language (Plato); man as the political animal (Aristotle); man as created in the image of God (Christianity); man as the social animal (Marx); man as the "animal with the right to make promises"[28] (Nietzsche); man as the being to whom it is given to think (Heidegger). This crude list should make immediately clear that whatever is at stake in thinking about the essence of man, no particular academic discipline or professional pursuit can claim priority over it.

[25] See, for example, Chas. E. Bessy, "Science and Culture," *Science* (new series), vol. 4, no. 83 (July 31, 1896) 121–4, where science education is defended from the claim that it has no "culture-value." One of the more well-known accounts of the "chasm" between the humanities and sciences is C. P. Snow, *The Two Cultures* and the Scientific Revollution (Cambridge: Cambridge University Press, 1963).

[26] This is a generic definition of humanism, similar to the one that prompted Heidegger to write the "Letter on Humanism" in response to Jean Beaufret. As Heidegger notes, and Sartre had noted as well, cast this way, even Christianity would count as a humanism. I avoid here any definition of "Humanities" that relies merely on the arbitrary and occasionally contradictory divisions imposed for administrative reasons on university departments and curricula.

[27] Heidegger, "Letter on Humanism," 225.

[28] Friedrich Nietzsche, *On the Genealogy of Morals*, Walter Kaufmann and R. J. Hollingdale, trans. (New York: Vintage Books, 1989) 57.

Returning to our question, namely the humanities and punishment, we might assert the following: The humanities provide a realm for thinking about man as a being who punishes, and to think about this essential quality of man in a manner that is not bound by any necessary result (e.g., the demand for more effective crime policies, more or less democratic punishments, etc). Rather, within the humanities, the possibility is given to think about punishment without regard for the consequences of such thinking and without the constraint of fashioning policy to meet any particular social need – to think about punishment in utterly *useless* ways, which nonetheless grant us deeper (if utterly impracticable) understandings of ourselves, insofar as we are historical beings who punish.

Nietzsche remarks in the *Genealogy of Morals* that "today it is impossible to say for certain *why* people are really punished."[29] The impossibility is due, he tells us, to punishment's historical character. Because punishment (like humanity itself) has a history, it is impossible to distill from any historical ritual of punishment a single meaning. Rather, he says, punishment is "overladen" with meanings, any one of which from time to time "comes to the fore and dominates at the expense of the others." One element may appear to overcome the others (he suggests that deterrence may be the predominate meaning of punishment in the modern world), but the possibility of "shifts in value" and "rearrangement" of punishment's meanings always lurks.[30] By considering "a few chance instances," Nietzsche then offered an impressive list of punishment's possible meanings through history:

> Punishment as a means of rendering harmless, preventing further harm. Punishment as recompense to the injured party for the harm done, rendered in any form. . . . Punishment as the isolation of a disturbance of equilibrium, so as to guard against the further spread of the disturbance. Punishment as a means of inspiring fear of those who determine and execute the punishment. Punishment as a kind of repayment for the advantages the criminal has enjoyed hitherto. . . . Punishment as the expulsion of a degenerate element. Punishment as a festival, namely as the rape and mockery of a finally defeated enemy. Punishment as the making of a memory, whether for him who suffers the punishment – so-called improvement – or for those who witness its execution. . . . Punishment as a compromise with revenge in its natural state. . . . Punishment as a declaration of war. . . .[31]

The list could provide an index to a library full of histories of punishment as it has appeared in the ancient, medieval, and modern societies. The claim that it is

[29] Ibid., 80.
[30] Ibid., 80–1.
[31] Ibid.

Punishment   525

impossible to assert any single meaning or purpose to punishment, however, is
not a claim that punishment itself is senseless or can never have meaning. Rather
the catalogue presents us with a challenge to thinking, a challenge for a renewed
engagement with our own shared past. The best humanities scholarship seeks to do
just this, and in so doing opens up questions that escape the doctrinal strictures of
law as a discipline, as well as the metrics of the empirical social sciences.

Perhaps the most famous account of punishment to appear in the last half of the
twentieth century is Michel Foucault's *Discipline and Punish*.[32] The basic features
of his account are well known.[33] The Enlightenment critique of the harsh, public
punishments of old regime Europe (primarily France) was not, as the received wisdom had it, the result of any emergent desire to bring humanitarian sensibilities
to bear on punishment. Rather, the decline in enthusiasm for corporal and capital punishment that emerged at the end of the eighteenth century in Europe and
the New World, and that led to the rapid growth of penitentiaries with explicitly
rehabilitative goals, represented a more refined and invasive form of sociopolitical
domination that sought not to destroy bodies through punishment but to reshape
individuals through disciplinary regimes that extended punishment through time
(incarceration) and made criminals into objects of a technology of power (the rise
of the professionalized social sciences). Foucault's account, which owed much to
Nietzsche and Max Weber, has come to predominate accounts of modern punishment and the prison and has spawned a thriving literature that interrogates more
deeply modern punishment's character as a technology of control.[34]

Discipline and Punish of course also prompted critical reactions, particularly from
historians, who have offered competing accounts of why and how judicial torture
and public executions declined in the eighteenth century and thereafter. Some
have found the abolition of judicial torture in evidentiary reforms that rendered
the old regime proof-taking methods (which were heavily reliant on confessions)
obsolete.[35] Others resist Foucault's account of Enlightenment reformers as less
interested in humanity and more interested inserting "the power to punish more

---

[32] *Discipline and Punish: The Birth of the Prison*, Alan Sheridan, trans. (New York: Pantheon Books,
1977).

[33] Stanley Cohen, *Visions of Social Control: Crime, Punishment, and Classification* (Cambridge: Polity
Press, 1985) 10 remarks that "to write today about punishment... without Foucault is like talking about
the unconscious without Freud."

[34] Among the leading accounts in this tradition are Tom Dumm, *Democracy and Punishment: Disci-
plinary Origins of the United States* (Madison: University of Wisconsin Press, 1987); David Garland,
Punishment and Welfare: A History of Penal Strategies (Aldershot, 1985) and his *Punishment and Mod-
ern Society; A Study in Social Theory* (Chicago: University of Chicago Press, 1990); Jonathan Simon,
Poor Discipline: Parole and the Social Control of the Underclass, 1890–1990 (Chicago: University of
Chicago Press, 1997).

[35] John Langbein, *Torture and the Law of Proof* (Chicago: University of Chicago Press, 1976).

deeply into the social body."[36] Foucault's chief critic, perhaps, among historians is Pieter Spierenberg, who argues that there is no necessary contradiction between the humanitarian language of the Enlightenment reformers and their desire for penal policies that offered greater social control and that the self-described humane impulses of the reformers need to be taken seriously.[37]

Although historians continue to argue over the origins and purposes of the modern penitentiary, scholars of literature and art have found the prison and its corresponding array of rehabilitative ideals and programs to be a fruitful field of inquiry. John Bender's now classic *Imagining the Penitentiary* examined the prehistory of eighteenth-century English penitentiary reforms and found an intellectual preparation of the prison already present in the art and literary production of eighteenth-century England. Rather than reflecting its age, Georgian literature and art, in Bender's account, helped produce the conditions for penal reform that ushered in the prison. Since Bender, there have been a number of rich accounts of the relationship among novels, art and penal discipline.[38]

Although incarceration came to replace public executions in the modern period, the persistence of capital punishment in certain corners of the Western world, particularly in the United States, has generated a large body of scholarship seeking to explain and understand the punishment of crime by death. Some of this work has been historical,[39] and some of it cultural,[40] exploring the anxieties and tensions harbored within a legal system that stakes its legitimacy to capital punishment. Recent scholarship has also taken up the question of how to explain the retention of capital punishment in the United States (or, rather, in thirty-eight states within the United States) in light of its abandonment in Western Europe and many other countries around the world. Some have offered the view that there is something exceptional about the United States, either in its history of racialized slavery, historical lack of aristocratic power structures, tradition of lay participation in trials, or tendency to elect judicial officials and prosecutors through democratic process, that sets it

---

[36] Foucault, *Discipline and Punish*, 82.

[37] *The Spectacle of Suffering: Executions and the Evolution of Repression* (Cambridge, 1984). See also, Michael Ignatieff, *A Just Measure of Pain: The Penitentiary and the Industrial Revolution* (London, 1978); David Rothamn, *Conscience and Convenience: The Asylum and its Alternatives in Progressive America* (Boston, 1980).

[38] Hal Gladfelder, *Criminality and Narrative in Eighteenth-Century England: Beyond the Law* (Baltimore: Johns Hopkins University Press, 2001); Jonathan Grossman, *The Art of Alibi: English Law Courts and the Novel* (Baltimore: Johns Hopkins University Press, 2002); Anna Kaladiouk, "Pattern Penitence: Penitential Narrative and Moral Reform Discourse in Nineteenth-Century Britain," in *Punishment, Politics, and Culture, Studies in Law, Politics, and Culture* 30:3–31 (2004).

[39] Stuart Banner, *The Death Penalty: An American History* (Cambridge, MA: Harvard University Press, 2003).

[40] See especially, *When the State Kills: Capital Punishment and the American Condition* (Princeton University Press, 2001); *The Killing State: Capital Punishment in Law, Politics, and Culture*, Austin Sarat, ed. (New York: Oxford University Press, 1999).

Punishment

apart from other legal systems.[41] This has given rise to a recent debate over whether there is such a thing as "American exceptionalism" in punishment and whether it tells us anything about the persistence of modes of punishment such as the death penalty.[42]

Concern with capital punishment has also led scholars to examine the legal and cultural practices that surround the avoidance of punishment in clemency and pardons. As scholars have noted, the powerful pull that wrongdoing and its responses exert upon our legal and cultural imagination open also the realm in which punishment is replaced with forbearance, forgiveness, and mercy. Hannah Arendt identified the power to forgive as one of our most crucial social faculties, allowing us to participate in a world with other human beings.[43] Thus, to discussions of punishment belong also discussions of the propriety and place of mercy, the most profound of which challenge the conceptual opposition that would set mercy as something other than, or apart from, justice.[44]

The astute reader will have noticed that the "humanities" scholarship discussed here comes from scholars working not only in fields traditionally designated as the humanities, but also in professional law schools and social science departments. The domain of thinking is not determined by institutional or disciplinary boundaries. Thoughtfulness, like thoughtlessness, concerning punishment can appear anywhere.

In a letter he apparently wrote to a Berlin newspaper in 1807, Hegel posed the question: "Who thinks abstractly?"[45] Common opinion, he noted, already knows that the most educated are precisely those who are most capable of thinking abstractly and moreover that abstraction is an "exalted" mode of thought – "something special," something higher and nobler than the ordinary and everyday. Hegel did not say it directly, but he fairly intimated that common opinion might easily presume that the professional academic is the most abstract of thinkers.

We soon learn, however, that Hegel is having a joke on the reader. Far from noble, abstraction is base. It is simplistic, crude, and unseemly. To think abstractly, Hegel explained, is not to think at all. To illustrate, he then described a series of scenes of punishment. In the first: "A murderer is led to the place of execution. For the common populace he is nothing but a murderer." It may happen, however, that some

---

[41] James Q. Whitman, *Harsh Justice: Criminal Punishment and the Widening Divide between America and Europe* (Oxford: Oxford University Press, 2003); Frank Zimring, *The Contradictions of American Capital Punishment* (Oxford: Oxford University Press, 2003).

[42] See, David Garland, "Capital Punishment and American Culture," in *Punishment and Society* 7 (2005).

[43] *The Human Condition* (Chicago: University of Chicago Press, 1958) 237.

[44] See *Forgiveness, Mercy, and Clemency*, Austin Sarat and Nasser Hussain, eds. (Stanford: Stanford University Press, 2007) and, in particular, Linda Ross Meyer, "The Merciful State," 64–116.

[45] Walter Kaufmann, *Hegel: Texts and Commentary* (Garden City: Anchor Books, 1966) 113–18. Kaufmann's notes provide information about the original German text.

"ladies remark that he is a strong, handsome, interesting man." Overhearing, the common people find this remark outrageous. "What? A murderer handsome? How can one think so wickedly and call a murderer handsome; no doubt, you yourselves are something not much better!" The common crowd (and Hegel included here the learned priest) believes the remark to be a sure indication of the slackening morality of the day.

The reduction of the strong, handsome, interesting man into nothing other than a murderer, explained Hegel, is an abstraction. The condemned man's various qualities and attributes, his being, was taken away (*ab* + *tractare*) and replaced with one glaring act that blotted out everything about him and came to stand for him. Abstraction is not a kind of thinking, it is a flight from thinking.

Such abstractions, Hegel continued, might run in various directions. As a second example, he described the sentimentality of the Leipzig Rosicrucians who decorated the wheel, and the condemned bodies broken upon it, with violets and poppies. This, said Hegel, was nothing more than an ill-mannered abstraction working in the opposite direction of the crowd who saw nothing other than a murderer – the reduction of the condemned to an object of impotent, if theatrical, pity.

As a third example, Hegel described an old woman who looked upon a severed head, put on display at the scaffold. "The sun was shining" and she noticed "how beautifully... the sun of God's grace shines on his head." As Hegel explained:

> This woman saw that the murderer's head was struck by the sunshine and thus was still worthy of it. She raised it from the punishment of the scaffold into the sunny grace of God, and instead of accomplishing the reconciliation with violets and sentimental vanity, saw him accepted in grace in the higher sun.

The old woman, Hegel continued, "killed the abstraction of the murderer and brought him to life for honor."[46]

Hegel's example makes clear that thinking proper, that is, the ability not to abstract a being into some one-sided caricature, is not the special domain of the professional academic, nor is it a necessary product of formal education. The old woman's thinking is not the sort of activity that one could capture in formal doctrines of law, nor could one measure its occurrence by way of some empirical social sciences; nor could one examine it as a historical event. Indeed, the disciplines we designate under the rubric humanities have no special claim here, other than the simple claim

---

[46] The old woman in Hegel's story provides a glimpse into the account of punishment Hegel gave later in paragraph 97 of the *Grundlinien der Philosophie der Rechts* (volume 7 of Hegel's *Werke*, 20 vols, Frankfurt am Main: Suhrkamp Verlag, 1971); in English, Hegel's *Philosophy of Right*, T. M. Knox, trans. (New York: Oxford University Press, 1967) par. 97, p. 70. Essential here is Philippe Nonet, "Sanction," *Cumberland Law Review* 25:489–532 (1995).

Punishment

to provide a realm in which such thinking is not made impossible. Yet, when we open ourselves to the light cast by the "higher sun" we, like Hegel's old woman, can perhaps, on occasion, rise above our own thoughtlessness. If punishment may perhaps be anything other than a perpetual descent into senseless brutality, and if thinking is to avoid enslavement to necessity, we must.

Index

Aboriginals Ordinance of 1918 (Australia), 408
Abrams, Kathryn, 21–23
Abrams, M. H., 509–510
Ade Ajayi, A. F., 450
Agamben, Giorgio, 151, 409
Akyeampong, Emmanuel, 439
Allen, Christopher, 481–482
Amar, Akhil, 442
Anderson, Benedict, 419
Antaki, Mark, 497
Antigone, 143–144, 145–151, 157–158
Aquinas, Thomas, 144–145, 344
Architecture, postmodernism in,
      190–195
Arendt, Hannah, 430, 476–477
Aristotle, 63, 147, 161, 343
Art, imagining law in, 292–312
   art of law, 295–297
   copyright law, 300–305
   creativity and innovation, 300–305
   cultural internationalism, 299–300
   cultural nationalism, 299–300
   cultural property law, 299–300
   defining art, 307–310
   depiction of law in art, 297–298
   generally, 292–295
   intellectual property law, 300–305
   protection of culture, 298–300
   tension between law and art,
      305–307
Asad, Talal, 398
Auden, W. H., 390
Austen, Jane, 224, 225
Austen, Ralph, 439
Austin, J. L., 328–329, 383–384
Australia, aboriginals in, 409–410

Badiou, Alain, 336
Bakhtin, Mikhail, 214–215, 487
Balkin, Jack, 53, 57, 58–59, 325, 353–355, 505
Ball, Milner S., 466
Banville, John, 493
Barbie, Klaus, 426
Barkan, Elazar, 436, 448
Barmash, Pamela, 127
Barnett, Randy, 369
Barsky, Robert, 90
Bauman, Zygmunt, 193
Baumann, Gerlinde, 130
Beal, Timothy, 137
Beattie, John, 481
Beccaria, Cesare, 519
Beckett, Samuel, 500
Behn, Aphra, 217
Bell, Ian, 489
Bender, John, 215, 230, 488, 526
Benjamin, Walter, 328, 398, 509
Bentham, Jeremy, 483
Berger, Raoul, 351
Berkowitz, Roger, 497, 501–505, 507–510, 513, 514,
      515
Berk-Seligman, Susan, 324
Berlin, Ira, 422, 437
Berman, Nathaniel, 191, 295
Berry, Mary Frances, 445
Best, Stephen, 449
Biblical justice, 125–140
   abjection, 136–138
   anger of God, 130–131
   betrayal of God, 129–130, 138–139
   compassion, 126–127
   emotions of God, 133–134
   impurity and cleansing, 134–138

531

Biblical justice (*cont.*)
reflexive retribution, 139–140
retribution, 125–126, 128
sin and punishment, 128–129, 131–134
vengeance, 127–128
Billy Budd
continuity in, 92–97
heterogeneity in, 84–86
movement in, 75–80
overview, 73, 74–75
Bilsky, Leora, 429–430
Binder, Guyora, 430–431
Biondi, Martha, 445
Bittker, Boris, 447–448
Bix, Brian, 326, 347–348
Bleak House, 231–234, 489–490, 491–492
Blight, David, 422, 437
Bloody Code (UK), 457–458
Bourdieu, Pierre, 317–318, 337
Braidotti, Rosi, 56
Brandeis, Louis, 401
Brandwein, Pamela, 442
Brantlinger, Patrick, 487
Brewer, David, 365
Breyer, Stephen, 371
Brooks, Peter, 385–386, 478–479, 481, 484–485
Brooks, Roy L., 449
Brophy, Al, 445
Brown, Henry Billings, 388–389, 390, 391, 392, 396
Brown, Wendy, 335
Brown, William Wells, 392–393
Budd, Mike, 277–278
Burnett, Cathleen, 298
Burns, Robert P., 468
Bush, George W., 59, 103
Butler, Judith, 143, 335, 384–385

Calabresi, Guido, 10–11
Caldwell, John, 272–273
Camus, Jean-Yves, 450
Capital punishment, 107–108, 526–527
Carey, Peter, 493
Carlin, John, 302
Castle, Terry, 486
Character-driven story (CDS) form of justice, 163–164, 169–171, 174–175
Charles V (Spain), 65
Chirac, Jacques, 438
Chivallon, Christine, 438
Cicero, 63–64, 147, 343, 344
"Cinematic jurisprudence," 260–265
Cleland, John, 237
Collins, Wilkie, 234–235, 489

Community, centrality of, 120–121
Confessions, 483–485
Constable, Marianne, 99–100, 108, 324–325, 326, 327, 378–379, 385–387, 497
Contingency, 102–103, 117
Continuity, 92–97
Billy Budd, in, 92–97
Death and the Maiden, in, 92–94, 95–97
Cops, 283–290
Copyright law, 300–305
Corbin, Arthur, 362, 363–364
Cornell, Drucilla, 206, 325, 327, 328
Cornett, Judy, 486
Corrective justice, 171–176
Coughlin, Anne, 119
Cover, Robert, 93, 244, 261–262, 321, 322, 327–328, 332–333, 338, 381–382
Craig, Steve, 277–278
Crash, 410–413
Crenshaw, James, 125
Crenshaw, Kimberlè, 384
Criminal Evidence Act of 1898 (UK), 483
Critical legal studies, 203, 204–206, 380
Critical openness, 116–117
Critical Race Theory, 206, 384–385, 425
Criticisms of law and humanities, 113–115
"CSI effect," 269, 291
Cultural internationalism, 299–300
Cultural nationalism, 299–300
Cultural property law, 299–300
Culture, centrality of, 120–121
Cumberland, Richard, 155–156
Curtin, Philip, 439
Curtis, Dennis, 298
Cvetkovich, Ann, 235

Dante Alighieri, 165, 180
Dart, Gregory, 484–485
Death and the Maiden
continuity in, 92–94, 95–97
heterogeneity in, 87–89
movement in, 75–76, 80–84
overview, 73–75
Declaration of the Rights of Man and Citizen (France), 67
Deconstruction in law, 202–205, 208–209, 505–507
Defining humanities, 49–51
Defoe, Daniel, 217, 220–221, 236–238, 487
Deger, Jennifer, 260
Deleuze, Gilles, 205
Delgado, Richard, 384
de Man, Paul, 391, 397
Democracy and equality, 109–113

Index

533

de Quincey, Thomas, 485
Derrida, Jacques, 159–160, 202–205, 206, 208, 325, 328, 337, 399, 402–404, 405, 412, 413–414, 496–497, 498–501, 503, 505–506, 512, 514
de Tocqueville, Alexis, 468
Diamantides, Marinos, 336–337
Dickens, Charles, 231–234, 489–490, 491–492
diCorcia, Philip-Lorca, 292
Digital representation, 260–265
Dimock, Wai Chee, 382
Distributive justice, 176–181
Dr. Jekyll and Mr. Hyde, 387–388, 393–395, 396–397
Dodds, John, 62–63
Donohue, John J., 107–108
Dorff, Elliot, 126
Douglas, Lawrence, 84–85, 429, 469
Douzinas, Costas, 19–20, 202–203, 298, 306–307
Doyle, Aaron, 283, 284, 287
Dubois. W. E. B., 392
Durkheim, Emile, 54–55, 519–520
du Toit, André, 432
Dworkin, Ronald, 109, 141–142, 347, 348, 356–358, 369

Eades, Diana, 335–336
Economics, reductionism in, 104–107
Eichmann trial, 429, 430
Eisenhower, Dwight, 247
Eliot, George, 491
Elsen, Albert, 294
Elshtain, Jean Bethke, 432
Ely, John Hart, 369
Equality and democracy, 109–113
Erin Brockovich, 246
Eskridge, William, 367–368
European Convention on Human Rights, 494–495
Evans, David, 296–297
Evidence Act of 1843 (UK), 483
Ewick, Patricia, 317–318

Farley, Christine Haight, 32–34
Farmer, Lindsay, 41–43
Feagin, Joe R., 447
Felman, Shoshana, 387, 475, 494
Ferguson, Robert A., 297, 468, 474–475
Fiction. *See* Literature, imagining law in
Fielding, Henry, 217, 481, 486–487, 488–489
Fifteenth Amendment (US), 442–444
Films, imagining law in, 241–268. *See also specific film*
    "cinematic jurisprudence," 260–265

digital representation, 260–265
generally, 241–248
law and film studies, 265–268
law as film, 242–243, 254–260
law in film, 241–242, 248–253
Finnis, John, 145, 152, 157, 344–345
First Amendment (US), 384
Fish, Stanley, 90, 362–363, 379–380
Fishman, Jessica, 283, 284
Fiss, Owen M., 9–11
Fitzgerald, Robert, 401
Flanagan, Richard, 493
Force of Law, 498–501
The Fortunes and Misfortunes of the Famous Moll Flanders, 220–222, 487
Foucault, Michel, 230–231, 237, 458, 494, 525–526
Fourteenth Amendment (US), 351, 388, 442–444
Fourth Amendment (US), 279, 401
France, slavery in, 449–451
Frankfurter, Felix, 151–152
Fretheim, Terrence, 129
Freud, Sigmund, 144, 157, 159, 464
Frickey, Philip, 367–368
Frohmann, Lisa, 334
Fuller, Lon, 141–142, 500, 503
"Fundamentalism" of reason, 102–104

Gadamer, Hans-Georg, 356, 359, 373
Galanter, Marc, 424
Gammie, John, 133, 138
Garver, Gene, 99–100
Gaskell, Elizabeth, 491
Gates, Henry Louis, 328
Geller, Paul Edward, 302
Genesis of law and humanities, 2–11
Genocide, 181–182
Genocide Convention, 407
George, Robert, 157
Gerstenblith, Patty, 300
Gerwitz, Paul, 479
The Gift of Science, 501–505
Gillman, Derek, 300
Giraud, Michel, 450–451
Godwin, William, 485
Goodman, Nan, 382–383
Goodrich, Peter, 27–28, 220, 317–318, 323, 329–331, 336, 481
Gordon, Robert, 424–425
Gourevitch, Philip, 181–182, 185
Graber, Mark, 442
Greene, Graham, 237
Greenspan, Alan, 104–105
Grisez, Germain, 152, 157

534 Index

Gross, Ariela, 40–41
Grossman, Jonathan H., 228
Grotius, Hugo, 153–154
Gutmann, Amy, 433–434

Habermas, Jürgen, 328–329, 373–374, 421
Haggis, Paul, 410
Halberstam, Chaya, 23–24
Halbwachs, Maurice, 418
Haldar, Piyel, 297
Hamilton, Annette, 260
Hand, Learned, 59
Hart, H. L. A., 141–142, 346–348, 499, 500
Hartman, Saidiya, 439–440, 449
Hate speech, 384–385
Hausner, Gideon, 429, 430
Havemann, Paul, 409
Hayner, Priscilla B., 432–433
Haywood, Eliza, 217
Hegel, G. W. F., 54–55, 143, 148–149, 510, 527–529
Heidegger, Martin, 111, 355–356, 496–497, 501,
  503, 504, 506
Heinzelman, Susan Sage, 29–30
Hermeneutics
  interpretation and, 355–360
  suspicion, of, 116–117
Heterogeneity, 84–92
  Billy Budd, in, 84–86
  Death and the Maiden, in, 87–89
Historicism in postmodernism, 194
History of law and humanities, 61–70
Hobbes, Thomas, 54–55, 154–155, 195–202, 322
Hoffman, Lord, 59–60
Holmes, O. W., 58, 59, 308, 363
Hom, Sharon, 425
Homeland security, 287–289
Homer, 61–62, 401
Homestead Act (US), 447
Homicide, 280
Honoré, Tony, 172
Houck, Max, 269
Human rights, law and humanities and, 70–72
Humility, 121
Hurd, Heidi, 345
Husserl, Edmund, 317–318, 337

Ideas of justice
  Biblical justice (*See* Biblical justice)
  character-driven story (CDS) form, 163–164,
    169–171, 174–175
  corrective justice, 171–176
  distributive justice, 176–181
  generally, 161–164

narrative and justice, 164–166
natural law (*See* Natural law)
overview, 23–28
postmodern justice (*See* Postmodern justice)
retributive justice, 166–171
transitional justice, 181–187
utopian form, 163–164, 179–181, 186–187
Imagining law
  art, in (*See* Art, imagining law in)
  films, in (*See* Films, imagining law in)
  literature, in (*See* Literature, imagining law in)
  overview, 28–34
  television, in (*See* Television, imagining law in)
Indian Evidence Act of 1872 (UK), 494–495
Institutional processes in law
  judgment (*See* Judgment)
  overview, 41–46
  punishment (*See* Punishment)
  testimony (*See* Testimony)
  trials (*See* Trials)
Intellectual property law, 300–305
Intentionalism, 349–351
Interpretation and law, 339–376
  Constitutional law, in, 369–372
  contract law, in, 341–342, 360–363
  generally, 339–342
  hermeneutics and, 355–360
  intentionalism, 349–351
  legal positivism and, 346–348
  natural law and, 344–345
  originalism, 349
  parol evidence rule, 341–342, 360–363
  statutory law, in, 363–368
  textualism, 352–355
  theoretical approaches to, 343

Jackson, Michael, 455
Jameson, Frederic, 180–181
Jay, Martin, 298
Jencks, Charles, 191
"Jim Crow" laws, 440–441
John, Juliet, 492
Johnson, Barbara, 506
Johnson, James Weldon, 392–393
Johnston, Adrian, 151
Jordan, Emma Coleman, 447
Judgment, 496–516
  deconstruction and, 505–507
  generally, 496–498
  justice and, 512–515
  legal positivism, critiques of, 498–505
  literature, in, 510–511
  transcendentalism and, 507–510

Index

Kafka, Franz, 190–191
Kahn, Paul, 16–18, 383
Kainz, Howard, 142, 152
Kaminsky, Joel, 131
Kamir, Orit, 96
Kant, Immanuel, 54–55, 156–157, 159, 166–167
Kapczynski, Amy, 444–445
Karns, Alexander, 436
Katznelson, Ira, 447, 448
Kearns, Paul, 306
Kearns, Thomas, 377
Keenan, Thomas, 414
Kellogg, Catherine, 24–25
Kennedy, Duncan, 203, 380
Kingsley, Ben, 83
Klawans, Jonathan, 134–136, 138, 139
Koch, Klaus, 126, 131–134, 138, 139
Kozinski, Alex, 362–363
Kristeva, Julia, 136–138
Kucich, John, 494
Kuhns, Richard, 64
Kundera, Milan, 511
Kwall, Roberta Rosenthal, 301

Lacan, Jacques, 143–144, 149–151, 157–158, 328
LaCapra, Dominick, 419, 421, 423
LaFree, Gary, 334
Lane, Philip, 280
Lang, Fritz, 180
Langbein, John, 482
Langille, Brian, 500–501
Language and law, 315–338
  culture and, 336–337
  generally, 317–318
  instrumental and phenomenological
    relationship, 323–326
  pedagogy and, 331–333
  philosophical and theoretical relationship,
    326–331
  supplementary models of humanist theory,
    319
  theory *versus* practice, 333–336
Larsen, Nella, 392–393
las Cases, Bartholomé de, 65–66
Law and Order, 274–283
Law of Evidence Amendment Act of 1851 (UK),
  483
Lawrence, Charles R., 384
Lawrence, D. H., 237, 511
"Law with humanities," 51–57
"Law without humanities," 57–61
Learning from Las Vegas, 191–193
le Corbusier, Henri, 191

Lee, Susanna, 31–32
Lefort, Claude, 152
Legal positivism
  critiques of, 498–505
  interpretation and, 346–348
Legal writing, 331–333
Legendre, Pierre, 199, 336
Leibniz, Gottfried, 502
Leviathan, 195–202
Lévinas, Emmanuel, 203–204, 328, 506
Levinson, Sanford, 53, 57, 58, 59, 335
Lieber, Francis, 349–351, 355
Linguistic processes in law
  interpretation (*See* Interpretation and law)
  language (*See* Language and law)
  memory (*See* Memory and law)
  overview, 34–41
  rhetoric (*See* Rhetoric and law)
  translation (*See* Translation and law)
Literature, imagining law in, 213–240. *See also*
    specific novel or play
  generally, 213–216
  judgment in, 510–511
  misrepresentations in, 236
  obscenity, 236
  realism in, 216–222
  reformation in, 228–236
  romance in, 222–228
  "sensation novels," 234–235
  testimony in, 485–493
Lolita, 236–239
Luhmann, Niklas, 328
Lumet, Sidney, 248
Lyotard, Jean-François, 193–194, 399, 404–407,
    413–414

MacKinnon, Catharine, 326
Macpherson, Sandra, 225
Maier, Charles, 420–421, 434
Maine, Henry, 223
Manderson, Desmond, 44–45
Manley, Delarivier, 217
Marcus, George, 335–336
Marmor, Andrei, 348, 355
Marshall, Thurgood, 442, 443
Marx, Karl, 54–55, 186–187, 189
Matoesian, Gregory M., 334
Matsuda, Mari, 384
M'Bala M'Bala, Dieudonné, 450
McClean, Daniel, 302–303, 306
McKeon, Michael, 486
McLeod, Kembrew, 304
McNeil, William, 291

Melish, Joanne Pope, 437
Melville, Herman, 73
Memory and law, 416–452
  collective memory, 417–418
  debate regarding, 420–421
  generally, 416–417
  history, relationship with, 421–423
  invented traditions, 419
  Jewish history, in, 419–420
  limits of trials in shaping memory, 425–428
  psychoanalysis and, 419
  reforming past, use of law for, 423–425
  slavery and, 436–451
  truth and reconciliation commissions, role of, 431–436
  use of trials in shaping memory, 428–431
The Merchant of Venice, 402–404
Merleau-Ponty, Maurice, 102–103, 115, 117–118
Merryman, John Henry, 294, 299–300
Mertz, Elizabeth, 333, 334, 336
Metropolis, 180
Mezey, Naomi, 78
Michelman, Frank, 91
Mill, John Stuart, 161
Miller, D. A., 230, 233, 235
Miller, Henry, 237
Miller, Patrick, 128–129
Milosevic, Slobodan, 455
Milpururu, 309
Minow, Martha, 98–99, 431–432, 436
Miranda v. Arizona, 385–387
Misrepresentations in literature, 236
Mootz, Jay, 35–37
More, Thomas, 164, 165, 180, 186–187
Morris, Erroll, 246
Movement
  Billy Budd, in, 75–80
  Death and the Maiden, in, 75–76, 80–84
Movies. *See* Films, imagining law in
Mulcahy, Linda, 296–297
Murav, Harriet, 38–40

Nabokov, Vladimir, 236–237, 239
The Naked City, 170–171, 180
Narrative
  importance of, 381–383
  justice and, 164–166
Natural law, 141–160
  Antigone, in, 143–144, 145–151, 157–158
  evolution of, 152–159
  generally, 141–145
  interpretation and, 344–345
  new natural law theory, 151–152, 157, 344–345

Nerhot, Patrick, 343, 358–359
Neville, Alisoun, 407, 408
Nietzsche, Friedrich, 144, 374, 524, 525
Nonet, Philippe, 497, 503, 504
Nora, Pierre, 416, 417, 418, 450
Novak, Maximillian E., 229
Novels. *See* Literature, imagining law in
Nozick, Robert, 162, 177–178
Nuremberg Trials, 183, 426
Nussbaum, Martha, 53–54, 55–57

Obscenity, 236
The Odyssey, 401
Oedipus myth, 143, 145–147, 158–159
Ogletree, Charles, Jr., 446
Originalism, 349
Osiel, Mark, 426, 428
Overview, 18–46

Papon, Maurice, 426
Parol evidence rule, 341–342, 360–363
Peirce, Charles, 325
Pendas, Devin, 430
Perlman, Elliot, 493
Perspectives on scholarship in law and humanities, 19–23
Peters, Julie Stone, 435–436
Pether, Penny, 34–35
Philadelphoff-Puren, Nina, 337
Picasso, Pablo, 295
Plato, 54–55, 61–62, 164–165, 180, 186–187
Plessy v. Ferguson, 387–397
Polanski, Roman, 73–74, 83, 88
Popkin, William, 364
Posner, Richard A., 105–106, 521
Post, Robert, 109–113, 334–335
Postmodern justice, 188–209
  architectural analogy, 190–195
  critical legal studies and, 203, 204–206
  deconstruction in law, 202–205, 208–209
  defining, 188–189
  generally, 188–189
  historicism in postmodernism, 194
  "rendering" justice, 206–208
  roots of postmodernism, 189–190
Pound, Roscoe, 51–53, 56–57, 58–59, 365
Pride and Prejudice, 224–228
Primus, Richard, 442, 443–444
Prisoners' Counsel Act of 1836 (UK), 459–460, 482, 490
Psychoanalysis, 144, 159, 419
Pufendorf, Samuel, 155–156
Pugliese, Joseph, 337

Index

Punishment, 517–529
  abstract thought and, 527–529
  capital punishment, 107–108, 526–527
  connection with humanities, 517–518
  estrangement of law from humanities and,
    520–523
  historical development of, 518–520
  purposes of, 524–527
  thinking about in humanities framework,
    523–524

Radin, Margaret Jane, 91, 98
Rawls, John, 161, 165, 176–177, 179–180, 186–187,
  200–202
Raz, Joseph, 372–373
Reade, Charles, 489
Realism in literature, 216–222
Reconstruction, 442–445
Reconstructive trial, 457–466
Reed, Douglas, 247
Reformation in literature, 228–236
Reichman, Ravit, 37–38
"Rendering" justice, 206–208
Resistance to law and humanities, 11–18
Resnik, Judith, 298
Restatement (First) of Contracts, 361
Restatement (Second) of Contracts, 361
Retributive justice, 166–171
Revels, Hiram, 443–444
Rhetoric and law, 377–397
  generally, 377–381
  narrative, importance of, 381–383
  race and, 387–397
  speech and, 383–387
Richardson, Samuel, 217, 486, 493
Ricouer, Paul, 116–117
Robinson, Randall, 446
Rodensky, Lisa, 230–231, 233
Rodowick, D. N., 243, 262
Rollenhagen, Gabriel, 195
Romance in literature, 222–228
Ronell, Avital, 279
Rose, Gillian, 505–506
Rosenbloom, Jonathan, 297
Rosett, Arthur, 126
Rotberg, Robert, 433
Roth, Michael, 421, 422–423
Rousseau, Jean-Jacques, 179–180, 186–187, 484
Rousso, Henri, 427
Rozin, Paul, 139

Sanders, Mark, 414–415, 435
Santner, Eric, 144

Sarat, Austin, 246, 322, 377, 380–381
Sarony, Napoleon, 309
Savigny, Friedrich Carl von, 505
Scafidi, Susan, 302, 306
Scalia, Antonin, 352, 365–367, 370–371
Scarry, Elaine, 322
Schauer, Frederick, 326, 335
Scheppele, Kim Lane, 334
Schlag, Pierre, 90–91, 296
Schmitt, Carl, 497
Schoelcher, Victor, 450
Scholem, Gershom, 245
Schramm, Jan-Melissa, 43–44
Schütz, Anton, 336
Scipio, 63–64
Searle, John, 328–329, 506
Second Amendment (US), 369–372
Selden, John, 191
Sennett, Richard, 490
"Sensation novels," 234–235
Separate Car Act (Louisiana), 388, 391
Sepinwall, Alyssa, 437–438
Sepulveda, Ginés de, 65, 66
Shapiro, Barbara, 480–481, 486
Sherwin, Richard, 30–31, 87, 91, 269–270, 278,
  473, 476
Shoemaker, Karl, 45–46
Silbey, Susan S., 317–318
Simpson, O. J., 455
Slavery
  France, in, 449–451
  "Jim Crow" laws compared, 440–441
  memory of, 436–440
  Reconstruction and, 442–445
  reparations for, 445–449
  shaping law, role of memory in, 440–441
Smith, Matthew, 25–27
Sobchack, Vivian, 260–261, 262
Social and cultural functions of trials, 474–476
Solan, Lawrence, 323
Solomon, Robert, 127–128
Solove, Daniel, 90
Sophocles, 143, 145–147
South Africa, Truth and Reconciliation
  Commission, 413–415, 432, 435
Spaulding, Norman, 442–443
Spence, Michael, 305
Spiegel, Gabrielle, 423
Spierenberg, Peter, 526
Starr, Paul, 448–449
Steiner, George, 148
Steinman, Clay, 277–278
Sterne, Laurence, 487

Stevens, John Paul, 366, 371
Stevens, Wallace, 255
Stevenson, Robert Louis, 387–388, 393–395,
 396–397
Subjectivity, 114–115, 117–120
Sumser, John, 278, 279–280
Sutherland, Edson, 521–522

Tapper, Colin, 494–495
Taylor, Charles, 100–101
Taylor, Katharine F., 297, 466
Teitel, Ruti, 182, 434–435, 436
Television, imagining law in, 269–291. *See also*
 specific program
 "CSI effect," 269, 291
 generally, 269–274
 homeland security and, 287–289
 recording and, 272–273
 spectator participation, 270–272
 style and, 273
Testimony, 478–495
 confessions, 483–485
 Continental tradition, 483–485
 English common law, under, 479–483
 generally, 478–479
 humanities, current status in, 493–494
 law, current status in, 494–495
 literature, in, 485–493
Teubner, Guenther, 328–329
Textualism, 352–355
Thackeray, William, 489
Theater, trial as, 466–470
The Thin Blue Line, 246
Thirteenth Amendment (US), 388, 442–444
Thomas, Brook, 392
Thomas, Ronald, 490
Thompson, Dennis, 433–434
Thompson, Janna, 425
Tiersma, Peter M., 323
Todorov, Tzvetan, 66
Tourgée, Albion, 388, 391, 393
Touvier, Paul, 426, 427–428
Transcendentalism in law, 507–510
Transitional justice, 181–187
Translation and law, 398–415
 Australian Aboriginals, problems regarding,
  409–410
 biometrical data, 409–410
 fidelity to self and, 400–404
 generally, 398–400
 nonverbal forms of communication,
  407–410
 others, words of, 404–407

police and suspects, problems regarding,
  410–413
 South Africa Truth and Reconciliation
  Commission, problems regarding, 413–415
Trials, 455–477
 fascination with, 476–477
 reconstructive trial, 457–466
 significance of, 455–457
 social and cultural functions of, 474–476
 theater, trial as, 466–470
 "Trial of the Century," 455–457
 truth and communication in, 470–474
Trollope, Anthony, 489, 491
Trotsky, Leon, 182–183
Truth and communication in trials, 470–474
Truth and reconciliation commissions
 memory, role in shaping, 431–436
 translation, problems with, 413–415
12 *Angry Men*, 248–253

Ullman, B. L., 49–50
Ullman, Walter, 523
Umphrey, Martha, 85–86, 96, 473
Uniform Commercial Code, 361
United Kingdom, testimony in, 479–483
Utopian form of justice, 163–164, 179–181, 186–187

van Wolde, Ellen, 130–131
Venturi, Robert, 191–195
von Rad, Gerhard, 127

Wallace, Elizabeth Kowaleski, 438
Ward, Humphrey, 493
Warner, William, 220–221
Warrington, Ronnie, 202–203
Watson, Irene, 409
Watt, Ian, 216–219, 488
Weaver, Sigourney, 83
Weber, Max, 54–55, 525
Weil, Simone, 320
Weill, Stephen, 293
Weinreb, Lloyd, 345
Weisberg, Richard, 319, 320–322, 494, 497
Welsh, Alexander, 229, 488, 492–493
West, Robin, 4–8, 85, 322–323
Westley, Robert, 446
Wexler, Leila Sadat, 427–428
White, James Boyd, 2–7, 8, 10–11, 98, 99, 100, 113,
  118–119, 295, 319–320, 332, 378, 395, 399,
  400–402, 404–406, 409, 410, 412, 413–414, 415
Whittington, Keith, 352–353, 354–355
Wiesel, Elie, 494
Williams, Patricia, 206

Index

Wilson, Stuart, 83
Winter, Steven, 20–21, 91
Wither, George, 195–197
Witnesses. *See* Testimony
Wolf, Dick, 283
Wolf, Erik, 151
Wolfe, Christopher, 151–152
Wolfers, Justin, 107–108
Wolff, Tobias, 514–515
Wolterstorff, Nicholas, 125
The Woman in White, 234–235, 489

Wood, Nancy, 427
Wordsworth, William, 485

The Yale Journal of Law and the Humanities, 8–11
Yamamoto, Eric, 425
Yerushalmi, Yosef, 419–420
Yonge, Charlotte, 491

Zerubavel, Yael, 419, 421
Zizek, Salvoj, 66, 151
Zupancic, Alenka, 150–151, 157, 158

For EU product safety concerns, contact us at Calle de José Abascal, 56–1°, 28003 Madrid, Spain or eugpsr@cambridge.org.

www.ingramcontent.com/pod-product-compliance
Ingram Content Group UK Ltd.
Pitfield, Milton Keynes, MK11 3LW, UK
UKHW020451090825
461507UK00007B/178